CULTURAL RESISTANCE
READER

CULTURAL RESISTANCE READER

◆

STEPHEN DUNCOMBE

VERSO

London · New York

First published by Verso 2002
© Stephen Duncombe 2002
Individual contributions © the authors
All rights reserved

1 3 5 7 9 10 8 6 4 2

Verso
UK: 6 Meard Street, London W1F 0EG
US: 180 Varick Street, New York, NY 10014-4606
www.versobooks.com

Verso is the imprint of New Left Books

ISBN 1-85984-659-9
ISBN 1-85984-379-4 (pbk)

British Library Cataloguing in Publication Data
A catalogue record for this book is available from the British Library

Library of Congress Cataloging-in-Publication Data
A catalog record for this book is available from the Library of Congress

Typeset by The Running Head Limited, Cambridge, UK
www.therunninghead.com
Printed and bound in the USA by R. R. Donnelley & Sons Co.

To my comrades in the Lower East Side Collective and
Reclaim the Streets/New York City
who have taught me volumes
about cultural resistance

CONTENTS

ACKNOWLEDGMENTS

First and foremost I'd like to thank all the authors (some posthumously) whose words make up this book. To say I couldn't have done this without them is, for once perhaps, not merely a cliché. Almost as essential was Kerstin Mikalbrown, my research assistant on this project. Kerstin's scholarly mind and activist's instincts were invaluable in the process of selecting readings and shaping the narratives that link these readings together. A number of others also generously shared their insights and suggestions, these include: Agent mT aka Azoteas aka Geoff Kupferman, Paul Bartlett, Amanda Bird, Doug Cordell, Mark Dery, L.A. Kauffman, Jason King, Andrew Mattson, Christian Parenti, Hanna Radschinski, Mark Read, Ben Shepard, Bill Talen, Leila Walker, Jon Weiss and Gilda Zwerman. Thanks also to Colin Robinson of Verso who was enthusiastic about this anthology from the get go, Peter Bell and Richard Stack of SUNY Purchase who got me going along this path so long ago, and Stuart and Liz Ewen who have been there the whole way. Two institutions sustained this book: The Gallatin School of New York University, my home base for most of the work done on this project, and the Blue Mountain Center, who put me up for a beautiful and productive month in the Adirondacks to finish the job. I'm grateful to the administration, staff, and my colleagues and fellow residents at both these places for all their help. *Cultural Resistance* arose out of a course I taught at NYU called "Media Activism and Cultural Resistance" in the spring of 2000. All the students in that remarkable class helped create this book, but I'd like to single out my teaching assistant (and fellow RTSer) Eve Bradford for special appreciation. And finally, this book could only have been written with the support of my wife, frequent editor, and current contributor, Jean Railla. Jean continues to expand my definitions of politics and love.

ONE

INTRODUCTION

When I hear the word culture I reach for my revolver.

attributed to Joseph Goebbels

NEW YORK CITY, OCTOBER 4, 1998

It's a damp afternoon in early October. The clouds are heavy and low and periodically a light mist rolls down. For the past twenty minutes groups of young people, three here, five there, have been walking up to "The Cube," a large steel sculpture on a traffic island marking the entrance to Manhattan's East Village. Carrying portable radios and dressed in the young hipster uniform of oversized shirt and super-wide pants, they look like they're either coming home from or launching out on an all-night rave. Some look more anxious than others, and the most anxious of the lot scurry around talking too loudly into cell phones or more quietly in little huddles. Radios are tuned to the frequency of a pirate radio station and techno music flows out from fifty boomboxes. Thwump, thwump, thwump. Heads start to nod and feet shuffle. The crowd is visibly excited. Something is going to happen.

Meanwhile, a block south, an old bread truck is parked by the curb, invisibly emanating the pirate signal. Jammed inside its rusting body is a portable radio transmitter, a sound engineer, a couple of DJs, and enough pot smoke to levitate the vehicle. A block west a small crew of people, studiously feigning nonchalance, waits next to a bundle of three, thirty-foot-long steel poles, laid horizontally along the ground and linked at one end. Further down and around the corner stands another small group surrounding what looks like a garden wagon covered in a tarpaulin.

At a little after 3 pm, as the crowd had grown to more than a hundred, someone gives a signal. Led by a man holding aloft a large orange traffic sign with outlines of a man and woman dancing, the crowd moves tentatively off the curb of the traffic island and on to the street. "Move, move," the anxious ones yell and the crowd breaks into a run down Astor Place. It's one short block and a left turn onto Broadway – the major thoroughfare running the length of Manhattan. In the middle of the street the metal pipes are being pushed into the air to form a tripod. Once the tripod is up and stable a young man scrambles up and seats himself on top. The garden cart is wheeled out, its tarp ripped off, and – after many frustrating tries – a small generator fires up, powering a compact receiver and amplifier. Heavy beats pump from the sound system, echoed by the boomboxes now turned to full volume: THWUMP, THWUMP, THWUMP, Thwumpada Thwumpada Thwumpada. Curious crowds come off the sidewalk, people start to dance, and soon 300 people have turned Broadway on a Sunday afternoon into a street party.

The New York Police Department shows up, at first slowly and then in force. Dressed in riot gear they stand by bewildered, confused by a protest that doesn't look like a protest, mystified by the young man perched precariously twenty-five feet above the pavement, and unsure how to confront a street full of ravers, some with painted faces, a few decked out in Marie Antoinette garb, and one fellow dancing particularly energetically in a bright blue bunny suit.

Propaganda has been handed out to the crowd, proclaiming this as an action of the newly formed New York City chapter of Reclaim the Streets, thrown to protest the Mayor's draconian "Quality of Life" policing campaign and the increased privatization of public space. But such assertions were redundant. The protest itself spoke more eloquently about reclaiming the streets for free and public expression than any photocopied sheet of indictments and demands.[1]

I think it was there, in the middle of that happy, frenetic crowd, holding one of the legs of the tripod steady, that I fully realized the political potential of culture.

I had been a political activist my entire adult life. I began in college, pressuring the State University of New York to pull their money out of businesses in South Africa. From there I constructed houses in Nicaragua, shut down the City University of New York over tuition increases, protested the Gulf War, got arrested with ACT UP, walked picket lines to support immigrant restaurant and greengrocery workers, formed a community activist organization in the Lower East Side, and would soon assemble direct action affinity groups for world trade demonstrations. For fifteen years I built organizations, planned actions, strategized campaigns, and attended far too many meetings.

I was committed to the struggle for radical change, but also more than a bit disappointed in it: too many defeats, too much defeatism. The "Left" I was part of often seemed stuck in its ways and those ways were not working. But that afternoon with Reclaim the Streets I glimpsed something that filled me with hope. Instead of the exhausted march, chant, and civil disobedience protest model that we (and the police, media, and public) were used to, we had created our own liberatory culture and — at least for a little while — had demonstrated it to the world. In place of the sour Lefty cry of "No! We're against it," we yelled out triumphantly: "Yes! This is what we're for." I went to the first planning meeting of this action as a loyal skeptic, by the end of the afternoon I was a committed believer in the power of cultural resistance.[2]

It wasn't a hard sell. It was culture, punk rock culture, that led me to politics in the first place. I grew up with a supportive family, I went to a good school, I lived in a nice suburb, but I knew something was wrong. Black kids I'd never met stared me down in rage. White kids in work boots were tracked out of my college-bound high-school classes. Boys who were not sufficiently macho were called faggots and girls existed only to fuck. And to top it off, I was bored. For explanation I turned to what culture I had at the time: television. Informed and entertained, I was reassured that these problems are too complex for easy answers, smart men were working on them, it's all being taken care of, it's normal, it might not even exist, you're one of the lucky ones, shut up. I thought I must be crazy.

Then, sometime in my mid-teens, I heard the Sex Pistols.

Right! NOW! ha ha ha ha ha
I am an anti-Christ
I am an anarchist
don't know what I want,
but I know how to get it
I wanna destroy the passer by
'cos I, I wanna be . . . anarchy.

Damned if I could figure out what Johnny Rotten was singing about, but I did know that he was angry, and I was angry, and I was not alone. I remember that feeling. That wonderful feeling. A joyous homecoming to a world I hadn't even known existed.

About the same time I was listening to the Sex Pistols I discovered the

Ramones. Since they were from the US, I could better understand what they were saying (even through lead singer Joey's affected Cockney accent). But what I got from the Ramones wasn't from their funhouse lyrics – it was their music: high energy, repetitive, rock 'n' roll: G–G–G–G–G–G–G–C—D—. Two bar chords, three positions: "Hey, ho, let's go!" It was simple, it was stupid, anyone could play it . . . and so could I. Within months of listening to the Ramones some friends and I learned to "play" our instruments and we formed a band. I crossed the line from consumer to creator.

And so it was punk rock that taught me my first, and probably most important, political lessons. I learned the importance of community. Alone, I owned my problems: *I* was alienated, *I* was bored, *I* was too sensitive to injustice. But as a punk I found others who also had these problems, and since we all seemed to share them, we reasoned that they must not just be ours, but society's problems. *My* personal problems became *a* social problem. Us punks then supported each other, helping each other face a society we didn't like and working together to create a micro-world that functioned according to different principles. In Lefty parlance, I learned the power of "solidarity." But before I could do anything, I first had to believe I could do it. Initially, I didn't. Like most people growing up in liberal democracies and consumer economies, I was used to politics, products, and entertainment being created and carried out by others *for* me, my own action limited to spending a dollar or casting a vote. Punk taught me to DIY: Do-it-yourself. The idea that I could create my own culture – *do-it-myself* – was for me revolutionary, as it carried within it the promise that I could also create my own politics and my own world.

Punk provided me with political ideas, then ingrained them through experience. The first time I heard the term anarchist used as anything other than an insult was in the Sex Pistols' "Anarchy in the UK." The lyrics of that song, and later ones from more overtly ideological bands like The Clash, Dead Kennedys, and Stiff Little Fingers, lent me new words to interpret and talk about the world. And critically this culture spoke not in the pious slogans of sectarians or the priests' Latin of academics but in a rough, emotional language that was my own. I didn't read about "counterhegemonic cultures," I was surrounded by one: fun, messy, mine. As I spent time immersed within punk culture I internalized a way of looking at and acting in the world that became as "natural" as any set of habits or values I had held before. Smashing the state topped getting a prom date on my things-to-do list for Senior year. And what I learned, I learned by doing. Punk didn't work unless it was performed, and by writing songs, dressing up and playing out I learned to perform my passions. That is, I learned how to transform ideas into action. When I found my way to political activism a few years later, it was an easy step because I was already halfway there.

But only halfway. For just as many aspects of punk pulled me toward political resistance, there were equal forces pushing me away. Punk was a great tool for articulating the problems of my world, and providing a supportive culture where I could develop that critique, but punk in itself did nothing to affect the root causes of the things – racism, sexism, and class inequality – I was so angry about. Punk had no strategic plan; it had no plan at all. In some ways punk rock was merely a release, an escape valve for my political dissatisfaction: "I wanna be anarchy!" OK, I've said that, now I feel better. The culture of resistance that my friends and I had built became a safe place to hide. Fortified by our righteous sense of superiority, stocked with a steady supply of punk rock band, club, and scene trivia to keep us busy, boundaries between "us" and "them" clearly demarcated by dyed hair and leather jackets, we closed off the world. Eventually, however, punk did escape the ghetto walls we had constructed. Following the success of the band Nirvana and the discovery of "grunge" in the early 1990s, the signs and signifiers of punk became a way to market commercial products to a potentially lucrative "Generation X." When I heard Iggy Pop's proto-punk anthem "Search and Destroy" used to sell Nike sneakers I felt sick, but I also learned another important lesson: the politics of culture is not predetermined. Culture is pliable; it's how it is used that matters.

The very word "culture" is elastic. You've probably already noticed that I've been stretching its meaning. Here I'm referring to culture as a thing, there as a set of norms, behaviors and ways to make sense of the world, and, in still other places, I'm describing culture as a process. This is because the word "culture," as Raymond Williams will later elaborate, means all these things.

The term "cultural resistance" is no firmer. In the following pages I use it to describe culture that is used, consciously or unconsciously, effectively or not, to resist and/or change the dominant political, economic and/or social structure. But cultural resistance, too, can mean many things and take on many forms, and before we go much farther it may help to clarify some of its parameters, developing schematically some of the ideas sketched out more casually above and introducing new ones.

Let's begin by considering how cultural resistance works to foster or retard radical political activity. First off, cultural resistance can provide a sort of "free space" for developing ideas and practices. Freed from the limits and constraints of the dominant culture, you can experiment with new ways of seeing and being and develop tools and resources for resistance. And as culture is usually something shared, it becomes a focal point around which to build a community.

Equipped with new ideas, skills, confidence, and comrades, the step into the unknown terrain of political resistance may seem less frightening. And because cultural resistance often speaks in a more familiar and less demanding voice than political dissent it makes this move even easier. In this way cultural resistance works as a sort of stepping stone into political activity.

Cultural resistance can also be thought of *as* political resistance. Some theorists argue that politics is essentially a cultural discourse, a shared set of symbols and meanings, that we all abide by. If this is true then the rewriting of that discourse – which is essentially what cultural resistance does – is a political act in itself.

Taking a more pessimistic view, cultural resistance can be seen as an escape from politics and a way to release discontent that might otherwise be expressed through political activity. From this vantage point, cultural resistance is the creation of a sort of safe sanctuary, a "haven in a heartless world."[3] Within this private utopia an ideal society is conjured up, problems are magically resolved, but outside nothing changes at all.

And finally, continuing the pessimistic slide, you can argue that cultural resistance does not and cannot exist. The dominant system is one of such complete ideological and material hegemony than any cultural expression, even if it appears rebellious, is, or will soon be repackaged and transformed into, a component of the status quo. From this perspective cultural resistance as a political practice is at best a waste of time and at worst a delusional detour from real political resistance.

Next let's look at how culture conveys its politics. A message can travel via the *content* of culture. Returning to the Sex Pistols' "Anarchy in the UK" for example, the band counsels resistance through explicit lyrics. Reading or hearing these words provides you with a political vocabulary, analysis, and even an action plan (although in the case of the Sex Pistols' "I wanna destroy the passer by," a pretty dubious one).

Politics can also be transmitted through the *form* culture takes. It is one thing to read lyrics on a page, quite another to hear them sung with emotion or laid over a danceable beat. Similarly, a different message is conveyed by the same song recorded on a DIY label versus a CD manufactured and distributed by a multi-national corporation. And that song changes yet again depending on whether you are listening to it performed or mixed live at an underground party, or sung in a stadium where you've paid $50 to watch the performer from afar on a wall-sized video screen. To crib from Marshall McLuhan: "the medium is the message."[4]

How culture is received and made sense of – its *interpretation* – determines its politics as well. Even though Malcolm McLaren started the Sex Pistols as an art prank cum rock 'n' roll swindle, it didn't stop a kid like me across the Atlantic from hearing a call to arms. In the same way, Sister Sledge's disco hit "We Are Family" took on new meaning when appropriated as an anthem of gay and lesbian pride and solidarity in the 1980s.[5] Content and medium may carry a message, but the meaning and potential impact of that message lie dormant until interpreted by an audience.

And finally, the very *activity* of producing culture has political meaning. In a society built around the principle that we should consume what others have produced for us, throwing an illegal warehouse rave or creating an underground music label – that is creating your own culture – takes on a rebellious resonance. The first act of politics is simply to act.

Now we can consider the spectrum of political engagement, or what I call scales of resistance. Political self-consciousness is the first one. On one side of the scale is culture that may serve the function of resistance, but was not created with that in mind, nor with the idea that its participants understand it as such. The other pole is occupied by culture consciously created for political resistance and used for that purpose. Somewhere in the middle is culture appropriated for ends for which it was not intended. This can cut both ways: culture that was not meant to be rebellious can be turned and used for those political ends and, conversely, culture that was self-consciously fashioned with rebellion in mind can be made to serve very non-rebellious purposes.

The next scale measures the social unit engaged in cultural resistance. To the left is the individual, creating and perhaps even living out a culture that may – theoretically – challenge the dominant system to its very core. But that person does this in their own head, within their own little world, sharing it with no one. In the middle lies the subculture, a group that has been cut off, or more likely has cut itself off, from the dominant society in order to create a shared, inclusive set of cultural values and practices. To the right is society. If an entire society is engaged in cultural resistance it means one of two things: that the dominant culture and the power it props up are bound to fall away at any moment, or that cultural resistance has been so thoroughly incorporated into a society of spectacle that its practice is one of political futility.

Which brings us to the final scale: the results of cultural resistance. The spectrum here ranges from survival to revolution. Survival is the point at which cultural resistance is merely a way to put up with the daily grind and injustices of life while holding on to a semblance of dignity. Rebellion is where cultural resistance contributes to political activity against the powers-that-be. Results of this resistance may range from suffering repression to forcing meaningful reform, yet all of this occurs within the framework of the dominant power. And revolution, well, revolution is the complete overthrow of the ruling system and a time when the culture of resistance becomes just culture.

The following may help clarify things:

Cultural resistance and political action
- cultural resistance creates a "free space":
   ideologically: space to create new language, meanings, and visions of the future
   materially: place to build community, networks, and organizational models
- cultural resistance is a stepping stone, providing a language, practice, and community to ease the way into political activity
- cultural resistance *is* political activity: writing or rewriting political discourse and thus political practice
- culture resistance is a "haven in a heartless world," an escape from the world of politics and problems
- cultural resistance does not exist. All culture is, or will immediately become, an expression of the dominant power

Means of cultural resistance
- *content:* the political message resides within the content of the culture
- *form:* the political message is expressed through the medium of transmission
- *interpretation:* the political message is determined by how the culture is received and interpreted
- *activity:* the action of producing culture, regardless of content or form or reception, is the political message

Scales of cultural resistance

• unconsciously political	appropriation	self-consciously political
• individual	subculture	society
• survival	rebellion	revolution

Culture, of course, is made and maintained by people, and people don't fit neatly into charts and typologies. To get a feel of what cultural resistance is, how it works, and what it can do, we need to turn to people and their theories, descriptions, and proclamations. I believe that the readings that follow are, to borrow a line from one of the authors, "the best which has been thought and said" about cultural resistance. I've drawn from literature and memoir, history, philosophy, and the social sciences, and, of course, from the writings of cultural activists themselves. The essays span from the mid-nineteenth century to the present, and explore cultures of resistance from the Middle Ages to the new Millennium. I've picked the essays with an eye to readability and have judiciously edited a good number in order to make them more immediately enjoyable. I've divided the essays among eight sections, each addressing a particular aspect of cultural resistance. I start each section and each essay with a few words to provide some history and context, and raise key issues and questions for the readings that follow. Scattered alongside these essays are smaller snippets: sidebars of songs or stories, eyewitness accounts, historical examples, and other primary documents that enrich each selection. Finally, I've arranged the essays, both within each section and as a whole, in order to tell a story about cultural resistance. Like any good story, this one is full of conflict. Cultural resistance is not some specimen, anesthetized, classified, and mounted on a pin, but constitutes a lively, ongoing, and sometimes cantankerous, debate.

We open with an archetype: Christopher Hill's account of Gerrard Winstanley and the Diggers' seizure of St George's Hill in 1649. Laid out in the Diggers' action and Winstanley's words are nearly all the possibilities and pitfalls of cultural resistance that will be played out for centuries to come – and explored in the readings that follow.

The next section begins with an historical definition of the word culture from Raymond Williams. With one definition in hand we look toward another, asking what is meant by "The Politics of Culture?" Addressing this question are five influential theorists. Karl Marx and Frederick Engels, in selections from *The German Ideology*, argue that culture is a reflection of the economic and social, that is material, conditions of a society. Therefore, they argue, the ruling culture of every age expresses the world-view of those who rule. Matthew Arnold asserts much the opposite: that culture – "sweetness and light" – is what allows us to transcend politics, guiding us out of the morass of the material world. The Italian communist Antonio Gramsci, writing from a Fascist prison, further complicates our picture. Culture, for Gramsci, is not something "out there" but intimate, internalized into our consciousness and directing – often without our knowledge – our activity. Full of contradictions, culture is shot through with both revolutionary and reactionary tendencies. The job of the revolutionary is to untangle this mess and extract a culture of resistance. We wind up this first section with the brilliant and tragic Walter Benjamin, the patron saint of DIY culture. In his essay "The Author as Producer," Benjamin argues that the content of culture means little, for today's cultural resistance is tomorrow's art object or commercial product. Instead it is the conditions of cultural production, how culture is produced, that holds the political key.

The next section explores the theme of "A Politics that Doesn't Look Like Politics." Mikhail Bakhtin's study of the carnival of the Middle Ages, and the acts of rebellion played out within a drama of buffoonery and laughter, sets the stage. We then jump 500 years and halfway around the world to the fields of Malaysia, where anthropologist James C. Scott finds in the grumblings and gossip of peasants a potent "everyday form of resistance" that he then traces back through history. Nearly halfway around the world again and we are in urban Los Angeles, where historian Robin D.G. Kelley recounts a personal tale of working – and not working – in a McDonald's as a teenager. Here too, Kelley finds an everyday form of cultural resistance that falls outside mainstream definitions of political action. Others, however, are not so sure that these "hidden transcripts" of resistance are resistance at all. The critic Adolph Reed Jr. interprets these acts as simple survival techniques on the part of their participants and political fantasy for those who study them. Cultural politics and their valorization, Reed argues, are a dangerous retreat from real politics. But other theorists hold that it is the retreat from politics itself which is a new form of politics, one better suited to new forms of social control. So asks the always provocative postmodernist Jean Baudrillard: what better way to resist a consumer capitalist, liberal democracy where you are constantly being asked for your vote or dollar than simply to do nothing? Hakim Bey then puts a twist on the politics of retreat, calling for what he names temporary autonomous zones, zones of cultural resistance created only to disappear when confronted by a hostile all-powerful state or, worse, a very receptive consumer economy looking for new lifestyles to market. Next, music journalist Simon Reynolds, taking Ecstasy and entering into the world of rave culture, leads us into a blissful temporary autonomous zone. Once here Reynolds explores the utopian politics of raves, but stays long enough to come down off the high and critique its shortcomings. And finally, because there is a disturbing propensity within the field of cultural resistance to applaud uncritically any popular cultural activity as one of admirable rebellion, we end this section with a grisly and hopefully sobering warning: a 1920s newspaper account of the lynching of an African-American man; an example of a popular, spontaneous, anti-governmental cultural celebration of racism.

From here we move to "Subcultures and Primitive Rebels" and the study of groups that have separated themselves from the mainstream of society, often distinguishing their distance through the medium of style. In the first selection the great social historian Eric Hobsbawm excavates the world of the social bandit. The nineteenth-century Robin Hoods he studies respond to inequities of wealth and power with "pre-political" strategies of cultural rebellion, creating for themselves the myth, if not always the practice, of the peasant rebel, righting wrongs by stealing from the rich to give to the poor. A second essay by Robin Kelley links Hobsbawm's "primitive rebels" to gangsta rappers of the late twentieth century. Gangsta rap and OG, that is "Original Gangster" style, are a response to economic and social degradation faced by young and poor African-American men, but are also, as Kelley points out, a creative map they use to navigate the terrain of capitalism and racism. The infamous zoot-suit riots of 1943, in which white servicemen beat up and stripped zoot-suit wearing Chicanos, are the topic of the next selection. Recounted by historian Stuart Cosgrove, the riots illustrate how style was employed as a visual rejection of minority invisibility and understood, by both the Mexican-American youth and their tormenters, as a weapon. Then we go to Birmingham, England, home of the famed Centre for Contemporary Cultural Studies, for two classic subcultural studies. In the first, Dick Hebdige describes how mods appropriate mass cultural items, reassigning their meanings so that they speak in a subcultural tongue. In the second, John Clarke analyses how skinheads use their subculture to "resolve magically" the real problems they face as young working-class men in a deindustrializing England. Continuing with music identified subcultures, the Riot Grrrls, a network of post-punk young women, contribute their manifesto "Riot Grrrl Is . . ." which uses their subculture to redefine, on their own terms, what it is to be a woman. This is followed by an excerpt from an interview with Kathleen Hanna, one of the founding mothers of Riot Grrrl, in which she reflects upon the difficulties of trying to create a new world while still living in the old one. The radical playwright Bertolt Brecht then moves us out of subcultures and into the mainstream, insisting that in order to talk to people about your politics you need to speak a cultural language they understand, even if what you plan to do with that language is show them the possibility of a different culture. The last selection in this section is from Stuart Hall, a past director of the CCCS in Birmingham. In "Notes on Deconstructing the Popular," Hall argues that what a culture is — mainstream or subcultural, commercial or traditional — makes little political difference as these boundaries inevitably shift. What matters politically, is the political use to which culture is put.

The political uses of culture in anti-colonial resistance is the subject of our next section, "Dismantling the Master's House." We start with the "ghost dances" of 1890 and Elaine Goodale Eastman's first-hand account of the magical hope of the decimated Sioux Indians as they danced to bring back their land and buffalo, and the tragic outcome as the US cavalry responded with their guns. Next, a more successful anti-colonial warrior, Mahatma Gandhi, proposes a strategy of Indian cultural resistance. Writing as a young man in the pamphlet *Hind Swaraj*, Gandhi reasons that if India is to free herself from Britain, she must also purge herself – entirely – of the British culture she has adopted. But C.L.R. James, the radical critic and West Indian nationalist, complicates any such call for a pristine national culture. For in his beloved game of cricket James locates both a symbol of British rule *and* a lightning rod for West Indian national pride. Cultural complications continue as the historian Lawrence Levine demonstrates how African-American slaves blended a hybrid culture to articulate their longings for freedom. Using the master's tools of language and religion and the covert cultural blueprints of West African tradition, slaves used song as a means to imagine dismantling the master's house. George Lipsitz concludes this section by bringing us up to date, studying music created by young Algerian, West Indian, and Indian immigrants in France and Britain. These musicians mix ingredients from the old world with those of their new home, then fold in the music of immigrants of other ethnicities who have done the same, ending up with a polyglot creation that makes a mockery of cultural purity and may just point out fruitful directions for inter-ethnic immigrant alliances.

By focusing on cultural resistance as a public activity – on the streets, at the clubs, or in the field – resistance in the private sphere is often over-looked. Perhaps not coincidentally, this private sphere has also traditionally been a woman's place. The next section, "A Woman's Place" explores women's cultural resistance. The great novelist Virginia Woolf, in a selection from *A Room of One's Own*, starts us off. Sketching the unhappy life of an imaginary sister of Shakespeare, Woolf suggests that it is a woman's private place in the home that is her problem. Limited horizons and constant domestic demands have left women's culture stunted. To create a viable culture, Woolf argues, women must force their way into the public world now monopolized by men. Arriving in the second wave of feminism in the early 1970s, the Radicalesbian collective issues a call for "The Woman-Identified Woman," arguing that a woman can only be free if she is free of men's definitions of herself. Through a woman-centered culture, they argue, women can construct a new and liberatory identity. Riding the third wave in an article in *Bust* magazine in 2001, Jean Railla makes a case for re-evaluating the domestic sphere. Within this traditional women's place, devalued by men and feminists alike, Railla discovers a rich culture created and cultivated by women for millennia. In the next selection, literature professor Janice Radway studies a women's literature often devalued: romance novels. By asking women readers what they like about their romances, she finds that far from reading them as tales of women's dependence upon and subservience to men, the readers extract stories of reassurance and empowerment. Following this theoretical line to its perhaps illogical conclusion, John Fiske identifies shopping malls as "women's places," places which cater to their desires and spaces where they daily exert their power by buying products. This leads Fiske to the provocative claim that shopping is a form of cultural resistance.

The commodification of culture is, of course, a critical chapter in the contemporary story of cultural resistance. The next section, "Commodities, Co-optation, and Culture Jamming," starts where Fiske leaves us, but moves rapidly in the opposite direction toward different conclusions. We begin with one of the pioneers of cultural studies, Richard Hoggart, writing in the 1950s and noting how marketers pitch products to the working classes of Britain by drawing upon traditional signs and symbols of class culture. But, when these cultural markers are employed for purely commercial purposes, their meanings subtly but decisively change. Theodor Adorno's classic essay "On the Fetish-Character in Music and the Regression of Listening" follows. Capitalism, the author argues, transforms nearly all culture into commodities. This alienates us from the very things upon which we bestow meaning, and reduces our cultural passions, and even cultural rebellions, to "pseudo activity" easily incorporated back into the system. Illustrating Adorno's thesis is an excerpt from poet and critic Malcolm Cowley's memoirs of Greenwich Village bohemian life. As early as the 1920s, Cowley writes, the ostensibly anti-bourgeois values of bohemia were inadvertently working to support the then new business ethic of consumer capitalism. Thomas Frank then brings Cowley to the present, arguing in his essay "Why Johnny Can't Dissent" that cultural rebellion, far from challenging the powers-that-be, has become *the* mainstream philosophy of a business world built around endless consumption. But the appropriators can always be appropriated. Pioneering a strategy now called "culture jamming," 1960s' Yippie activists Abbie Hoffman and Jerry Rubin close this section with advice on hijacking the methods and means of commercial culture to communicate radical messages.

The final section, "Mixing Pop and Politics," takes theory to the streets, demonstrating how activists employ cultural resistance as a tool for social change, told by the activists themselves. We start with "The Politics of Pre-figurative Community," Barbara Epstein's study of anti-nuclear direct action protests in the US. These protests, later to provide the model for those in Seattle and beyond, stress means as well as (and sometimes in place of) ends, creating a culture of activism within the protest that "prefigures" the type of community desired for the future. Following this, activist and artist John Jordan unfolds the history and philosophy of Reclaim the Streets, describing and explaining their carnavalesque practice of protest which transforms the protest itself into a living, dancing example of the politics they advocate. Telling the story of his own arrest in a Disney store, Jason Grote then introduces us to Reverend Billy, a cartoon-like character created by performance artist Bill Talen, who battles the equally cartoonish, yet also very real, Disney Corporation over public space and private memories. Andrew Boyd, an organizer who specializes in theatrical agitprop, writes about activist "memes": a new and growing form of activist "organization," with no leadership, office, fixed membership, or ideology. In place of the material organization is an organized cultural idea that spreads and multiplies, is acted upon, and then disappears. Our last reading is an interview with Ricardo Dominguez, co-founder of the Internet activist group Electronic Disturbance Theater, and co-creator of the electronic civil disobedience tool FloodNet. It is a good finale, for Dominguez not only points toward the future of activism on the Internet, but also reaches back to tell his life story as an activist weaving culture and politics into effective resistance.

So that's the story. No, that's not true. This is *my* story, a story of cultural resistance whose contours are shaped by my scholarly strengths and weaknesses, and my political passions and prejudices, all of which, no doubt, will become clear as you read on. I have tried to be inclusive in the essays I've selected. I've covered the major debates within the field, stretched to include topics often neglected, and even included writers whose ideas I don't personally agree with but are important nevertheless. But in the end there was much that I did not include. I've left out many worthy authors and essays for simple reasons of space. Others, like those addressing the politics of the fine arts or high culture, I've largely excluded because the subject is better dealt with elsewhere. What follows is a selection, my selection, and it is not the final word on cultural resistance.

What I do hope I've included are words to inspire. To inspire you to think, and think hard, about the relationship between culture and politics, pushing ideas in new directions. But I also hope these words will inspire you to act: to create and cultivate cultures of resistance, imagining, and building a world turned upside down. And then to take it one step further, transforming resistance in the realm of culture to political action on terra firma. For if cultural resistance is to take its own rebellious claims seriously, this must be the goal. As those quixotic rebels who dug up St George's Hill so many centuries ago sung out in the last line of their song, "Glory *here*, Diggers all."

ONE

CULTURAL RESISTANCE

CHRISTOPHER HILL,
"LEVELLERS AND TRUE LEVELLERS," FROM
THE WORLD TURNED UPSIDE DOWN

In 1649 a group of landless commoners, radicalized by the English Civil War and disappointed by its less than radical outcome, occupied a hill outside London, planting crops and issuing manifestos calling for the "earth to be a common treasury." The crops didn't grow and the commoners were soon forcibly evicted, but the acts of the True Levellers, or Diggers, as they called themselves, and the words of their leader, Gerrard Winstanley, have reverberated ever since. Their action was a cultural one, through and through. The symbolism of taking back as common land what had been enclosed (i.e. privatized) overshadowed the negligible material value of planting corn in barren soil. But what these outcasts of the Cromwell's New Model Army did hold dear was the community they created in their act of resistance; it was a scale model of the universal brotherhood they demanded of the future. Rejecting the culture of class and property, the Diggers conjured up a new universe and, through Winstanley's masterful reworking of The Bible, a familiar text was made to speak the words of the commoner's rebellion. Alas, the Diggers' lack of political organization and disinterest in long-term strategy made their revolt a simple one to crush, but the same amorphous quality of their rebellion made the ideal of a "world turned upside down" exceedingly hard to contain. The seizure of St. George's Hill is a fitting place for this anthology to begin, for their struggle is archetypal, exhibiting many of the characteristics — pre-figurative symbolic protests, ideological appropriation of a master text, lack of strategy and organizational structure, spread of idea and ideal — that mark cultural resistance today. What follows is Christopher Hill's classic account of the Diggers' taking of St. George's Hill from his book *The World Turned Upside Down*.

All men have stood for freedom ... and those of the richer sort of you that see it are ashamed and afraid to own it, because it comes clothed in a clownish garment ... Freedom is the man that will turn the world upside down, therefore no wonder he hath enemies ... True freedom lies in the community in spirit and community in the earthly treasury, and this is Christ the true man-child spread abroad in the creation, restoring all things unto himself.

A Watch-Word to the City of London, Gerrard Winstanley (1649)[1]

St George's Hill

The years from 1620 to 1650 were bad; the 1640s were much the worst decade of the period. On top of the disruption caused by the civil war came a series of disastrous harvests. Between 1647 and 1650 food prices rose steeply above the pre-war level; money wages lagged badly behind, and the cost of living rose significantly.[2] Taxation was unprecedentedly heavy, and Pym's new tax, the excise, fell especially severely on articles of popular consumption like beer and tobacco. These were the years when sales of church, crown and royalists' lands were breaking traditional land-lord/tenant relations, whilst disbanded soldiers were trying to pick up a living again. The city of York's special fund for the assistance of lame sol-diers was doubled in 1649 because of increased calls upon it.[3] 'The poor', Wildman tells us in January 1648, 'did gather in troops of ten, twenty, thirty, in the roads and seized upon corn as it was carrying to market, and divided it among themselves before the owners' faces, telling them they could not starve.' 'Necessity dissolves all laws and government, and hunger will break through stone walls', *The Mournfull Cries of Many Thousand Poore Tradesmen* warned Parliament and the Army in the same month.[4] 'The common vote of the giddy multitude', a pamphleteer admitted in October 1648, would be for the King if it were allowed to express itself freely.[5] Rents had risen so much, cavalry troopers in Northumberland complained in December 1648, that copyholders had to hire themselves out as wage-labourers or shepherds.[6]

The economic and political situation in the early months of 1649 was particularly explosive. Levellers and Army radicals felt that they had been fooled in the negotiations which led up to the trial and execution of the King in January; and that the Independent Grandees had taken over repub-lican reforms from their programme without making any real concessions to their democratic content. The abysmal harvest of 1648 led to widespread hunger and unemployment, especially among disbanded soldiers. In March 1649 the poor of London were being supplied with free corn and coal. On

3 April Peter Chamberlen announced that many were starving for want of bread: he feared they would proceed to direct action unless something was done for them.[7] Clubmen reappeared in the Severn valley, seizing corn. Whilst food prices reached famine levels, the Levellers demanded re-election of Agitators and recall of the General Council of the Army. 'We were before ruled by King, Lords and Commons, now by a General, a Court Martial and House of Commons; and we pray you what is the difference?'[8] At the end of March Lilburne, Overton, Walwyn and Prince were arrested. A Leveller pamphlet, *More Light Shining in Buckinghamshire*, appealed to the soldiers 'to stand everyone in his place, to oppose all tyranny whatsoever', particularly that of lawyers, enclosing lords of manors and the Army Grandees who have rejected social reform and have done nothing for the poor.[9]

Next month mutinies broke out in the Army when men who refused to volunteer for service in Ireland were demobilized without payment of arrears – exactly what had driven the Army to revolt two years earlier, though then with the acquiescence of the generals. In May more serious revolts broke out among troops in Oxfordshire, Wiltshire and Buckinghamshire, and there were rumours of civilian support from the Southwest, the old Clubman area. Cromwell and Fairfax, acting with great vigour and determination, overwhelmingly defeated the mutinous regiments at Burford on 14 May. The period of crisis for the military régime was over. Frightened conservatives rallied to its support, as the lesser evil. Oxford University and the City of London hastened to honour Fairfax and Cromwell. The sermon preached on the latter occasion appropriately denounced those who aspired to remove their neighbour's landmark.[10] Leveller conspiracies continued, soon to be joined by Fifth Monarchist plots: but none of them offered a serious threat to the régime so long as the repeatedly purged Army remained securely under the control of its generals.

Nevertheless, the early months of 1649 had been a terrifying time for the men of property. It was for some time not so obvious to contemporaries as it is to us that the defeat at Burford had been final and decisive. As late as November 1649 Ralph Josselin tells us that men feared to travel because of danger from robbers, and the rich even felt insecure in their own houses. Poor people, he added the following month, 'were never more regardless of God than nowadays'.[11] This was the background against which not only the Levellers but also Peter Chamberlen, John Cook, Hugh Peter and very many others called for drastic social reform on behalf of the poor. It was also the background to the activities of the Ranter Abiezer Coppe, and to the Digger or True Leveller movement.

One Sunday in March or April 1649 the congregation of the parish church of Walton-on-Thames was startled to see the church invaded by a group of six soldiers after Master Faucet had preached his sermon. The soldiers, in a series of symbolical gestures and amid scenes of some excitement, announced that the Sabbath, tithes, ministers, magistrates and the Bible were all abolished.[12] On Sunday 1 April — quite possibly the same Sunday — a group of poor men (described as labourers in a legal action three months later)[13] collected on St George's Hill in the same parish and began to dig the waste land there. It was a symbolic assumption of ownership of the common lands. It was a further symbolic rejection of conventional pieties, which may link up with the soldiers' demonstration in the parish church, that the digging began on a Sunday.[14] One of the Diggers followed up the soldiers' demonstration in Walton Church by 'getting up a great burden of thorn and briars . . . into the pulpit of the church at Walton to stop out the parson'.[15] The numbers of the Diggers soon rose to twenty or thirty. 'They invite all to come in and help them', an observer noted, 'and promise them meat, drink and clothes . . . They give out, they will be four or five thousand within ten days . . . It is feared they have some design in hand.'[16]

Consider for a moment the area affected. St George's Hill was just outside London, within easy reach of any poor man there who might be interested in the colony. It lay on the edge of Windsor Great Forest, where in 1641 'scores and hundreds set upon the King's deer'.[17] It was unpromising agricultural land, the improver Walter Blith sniffed ('thousands of places more capable of improvement than this'. Winstanley agreed that it was 'in view of flesh . . . very barren'.[18]) Kingston, the nearest town, to which the Diggers were taken for trial by the local landlords, was a great corn market. It had a long standing radical tradition. In 1858 it had been the seat of Martin Marprelate's secret printing press.[19] The town lecturer at that time was the Puritan John Udall, sentenced to death in 1590. He clearly had a strong following. An artisan from Kingston told Bishop Bancroft that the prayer 'Thy kingdom come' was a petition 'that we might have pastors, doctors, elders and deacons in every parish, and so be governed by such eldership as Christ's holy discipline doth require' — the full Presbyterian system, in fact. Another burgess of Kingston hoped to pull the non-preaching clergy 'out of the church by the ears'.[20]

This radical tradition continued. In 1628 it was in Kingston that Buckingham's assassin, Felton, was welcomed by an old woman with the words 'God bless thee, little David!'[21] Seven years later Archbishop Laud's visitor found Kingston a 'very factious town'.[22] It had a Puritan vicar, and from

1642 a Puritan lecturer as well. Kingston, covering the southern approaches to London, with its bridge across the Thames, was a strategically significant centre. Charles sent troops to guard the Surrey magazine there at the time of his attempted arrest of the Five Members. Kingston was the scene of many civil war skirmishes, and after the Parliamentarians took over the area it was the seat of the county committee. When the Army advanced on London in July 1647 Fairfax sent Rainborough over the Thames at Kingston to link up with Army supporters in radical Southwark. The whole region was an Army centre from that time onwards. The Army council met at Kingston on 18 August 1647 to draw up a Declaration supporting the Agitators' demand for a purge of Parliament.[23]

The area continued to be radical after the ejection of the Diggers. In 1653 it was a Kingston jury which found Lord Chandos guilty of manslaughter (in a duel), notwithstanding his claim to privilege of peerage: he was sentenced to be burnt in the hand.[24] Next year James Nayler told Fox there was a constant Quaker meeting there.[25] In 1657 the Quaker Edward Burrough occupied his leisure time in Kingston gaol by computing the sum total paid in tithes in England and Ireland at £1½ million a year.[26] George Fox frequently resided at Kingston in later life.

This was the area to which Gerrard Winstanley came, not later than 1643. The son (probably) of a Wigan mercer with Puritan sympathies, Gerrard Winstanley came to London as a clothing apprentice in 1630, and set up for himself in 1637. But it was the worst possible time; by 1643 Winstanley had been 'beaten out of both estate and trade'. In 1649 he was described as of Walton-on-Thames. Here he herded cows, apparently as a hired labourer, and wrote religious pamphlets, until he had a vision in a trance telling him to publish it abroad that 'the earth should be made a common treasury of livelihood to whole mankind, without respect of persons'.[27]

Landowners in the area round St George's Hill were more disturbed by the digging than the Council of State or General Fairfax, who had a series of amicable conversations with Winstanley – despite the latter's refusal to remove his hat to a 'fellow-creature'. Nor does Oliver Cromwell seem to have been unduly alarmed when 'a northern prophetess' warned him, à propos the Diggers, that 'if provision be not made for them poor commoners, England will have new troubles'.[28] But Parson Platt and other lords of manors in Surrey organized raids on the colony and an economic boycott: they harassed the Diggers with legal actions. 'If the Digger's cause was good', an officer of the Kingston court said, 'he would pick out such a jury as should overthrow him'. One of the cases charging the Diggers with riot

led to a technical argument about their commitment which got into the law-books. Serjeant Wilde, who always seems to have done his best for radicals, argued that they should have been discharged because the Sheriff was not present at the finding of the riot. The court bailed but did not discharge them.[29] Even after the Diggers moved to Cobham Heath a few miles away the raids continued, and by April 1650 the colony had been forcibly dispersed, huts and furniture burnt, the Diggers chased away from the area. It was a brief episode in English history, involving perhaps a few score men and their families: we know the names of seventy-three of them.
. . .

Forests and Commons

Thus if we see the New Model Army as a short-lived school of political democracy, commons, wastes and forests were longer-lasting though less intensive schools in economic democracy. Winstanley thought that from a half to two-thirds of England was not properly cultivated. One-third of England was barren waste, which lords of manors would not permit the poor to cultivate.[30] 'If the waste land of England were manured by her children, it would become in a few years the richest, the strongest and [most] flourishing land in the world'; the price of corn would fall to 1s. a bushel or less (it was then more like 6s. or 7s.).[31] An increase in the cultivated area, the digger poet Robert Coster added, would bring down the price of land and therewith the cost of living.[32] The custom by which lords of manors claimed property rights in the commons, and so could prevent their cultivation to the advantage of the poor, argued Winstanley, should have been abolished by the overthrow of kingly power.[33] Communal cultivation could allow for capital investment in improvements without sacrificing the interest of commoners. There was land enough to maintain ten times the present population, abolish begging and crime, and make England 'first of the nations'.[34]

This was the programme which Winstanley conceived in the cruel winter of 1648–9. It seemed to him so novel and so important that he attributed it to a divine command. The vision which he had in a trance told him to declare abroad the message: 'Work together; eat bread together.' 'He that works for another, either for wages or to pay him rent, works unrighteously . . . but they that are resolved to work and eat together, making the earth a common treasury, doth join hands with Christ to lift up the creation from bondage, and restores all things from the curse.' After declaring this message both verbally and in print, Winstanley decided he must 'go forth and declare it in my action' by organizing 'us that are called common people to manure and work upon the common lands'.[35]

Winstanley's conclusion, that communal cultivation of the commons was the crucial question, the starting-point from which common people all over England could build up an equal community, was absolutely right. 'The whole Digger movement,' Mr Thomas has written, 'can be plausibly regarded as the culmination of a century of unauthorized encroachment upon the forests and wastes by squatters and local commoners, pushed on by land shortage and pressure of population' – and, Mrs Thirsk adds, by lack of employment for casual labour in the depression of 1648–9.[36] Winstanley had arrived at the one possible democratic solution which was not merely backward-looking, as all other radical proposals during the revolutionary decades – an agrarian law, partible inheritance, stable copyholds – tended to be. The economic arguments against those who merely defended commoners' traditional rights in the waste were overwhelming. England's growing population could be fed only by more intensive cultivation, by bringing marginal land under the plough. Enclosure by men with capital, brutally disregarding the rights of commoners, did at least do the job; in the long run, its advocates rightly claimed, it created more employment. But in the short run it disrupted a way of life, causing intense misery and the employment which it did ultimately create was not of a sort to attract free commoners.

Collective cultivation of the waste by the poor could have had the advantages of large-scale cultivation, planned development, use of fertilizers, etc. It could have fed the expanding English population without disrupting the traditional way of life to anything like the extent that in fact happened. The Diggers sowed their land with carrots, parsnips and beans – crops of the sort which were to transform English agriculture in the seventeenth century by making it possible to keep cattle alive throughout the winter in order to fertilize the land.[37] 'Manuring' is the crucial word in Winstanley's programme. ('True religion and undefiled is to let every one quietly have earth to manure.') Winstanley had got a solution to his own paradox: 'the bondage the poor complain of, that they are kept poor by their brethren in a land where there is so much plenty for everyone, if covetousness and pride did not rule as king in one brother over another'.[38]

The gentry and parsons around St George's Hill appreciated that the Diggers were doing something different in kind from the traditional squatting of cottagers. Even communal cultivation of the earth, Parson Platt assured Winstanley, was less intolerable than cutting timber that grew on the common. Squatting and cultivating the earth could be deemed to be done by courtesy of the lord of the soil; but cutting wood against his wishes was a direct assertion of a property right which could not be overlooked. And indeed it was intended by the Diggers 'to be a stock for ourselves and our poor brethren through the land of England, . . . to provide us bread to eat till the fruit of our labours in the earth bring forth increase'. The Diggers had ordered the lords of the manor to stop cutting down 'our common woods and trees . . . for your private use'. It was intended, as all the Diggers' actions were, to be a symbolic challenge as well as an economically necessary step.[39]

By 1650 the Diggers had added a demand for confiscated church, crown and royalists' land to be turned over to the poor. In *The Law of Freedom* Winstanley further suggested that the land sales authorized by Parliament should be repudiated, and that all lands confiscated at the dissolution of the monasteries a century earlier should be added to the Commonwealth land fund.[40] These last two proposals would bite deep into existing property relations. The danger from the Diggers was that they called on the poor to organize themselves for practical action. A series of collective communities, if they had lasted, would have overcome the dispersion of forces which bedevilled the Levellers: they would have been for the True Levellers what the New Model Army might have been for the Levellers; and they could have extended all over the country.

Collective manuring of the common lands was a religious act for the Diggers; for Parson Lee 'a hedge in the field is as necessary in its kind as government in the church or commonwealth'. Religion, liberty, property and government were closely linked for both sides in the dispute. 'The very name of reformation' [of the church], Lee added, 'is as much exploded by the vulgar as enclosure; those sacred ordinances of magistracy and ministry . . . are now become offensive to the leveling multitude.'[41]

True Commonwealth's Freedom

For Winstanley Jesus Christ was the Head Leveller.[42] Winstanley's thought incorporates many Leveller ideas: it goes beyond them, beyond the vision of the small proprietor, in its hostility to private property as such.

> In the beginning of time the great creator, Reason, made the earth to be a common treasury, to preserve beast, birds, fishes and man, the lord that was to govern this creation . . . Not one word was spoken in the beginning that one branch of mankind should rule over another . . . But . . . selfish imaginations . . . did set up one man to teach and rule over another. And thereby . . . man was

brought into bondage, and became a greater slave to such of his own kind than the beasts of the field were to him. And hereupon the earth . . . was hedged into enclosures by the teachers and rulers, and the others were made . . . slaves. And that earth that is within this creation made a common storehouse for all, is bought and sold and kept in the hands of a few, whereby the great Creator is mightily dishonoured, as if he were a respecter of persons, delighting in the comfortable livelihood of some and rejoicing in the miserable poverty and straits of others. From the beginning it was not so . . .

Winstanley told lords of manors that:

the power of enclosing land and owning property was brought into the creation by your ancestors by the sword; which first did murder their fellow creatures, men, and after plunder or steal away their land, and left this land successively to you, their children. And therefore, though you did not kill or thieve, yet you hold that cursed thing in your hand by the power of the sword; and so you justify the wicked deeds of your fathers, and that sin of your fathers shall be visited upon the head of you and your children to the third and fourth genera-tion, and longer too, till your bloody and thieving power be rooted out of the land.[43]

Winstanley extended the Leveller justification of political democracy to economic democracy:

The poorest man hath as true a title and just right to the land as the richest man . . . True freedom lies in the free enjoyment of the earth . . . If the common people have no more freedom in England but only to live among their elder brothers and work for them for hire, what freedom then have they in England more than we can have in Turkey or France?[44]

Winstanley transcended the Leveller theory of the Norman Yoke, that all we need is to get back the laws of the free Anglo-Saxons. 'The best laws that England hath', he declared, 'are yokes and manacles, tying one sort of people to another.' 'All laws that are not grounded upon equity and reason, not giving a universal freedom to all but respecting person, ought . . . to be cut off with the King's head.'[45] But England's rulers had not completed the Revolution:

While this kingly power reigned in one man called Charles, all sorts of people complained of oppression . . . Thereupon you that were the gentry, when you were assembled in Parliament, you called upon the poor common people to come and help you . . . That top bough is lopped off the tree of tyranny, and the kingly power in that one particular is cast out. But alas, oppression is a great tree still, and keeps off the sun of freedom from the poor commons still.

Kingly power, clergy, lawyers, and buying and selling were all linked: 'if one truly fall, all must fall'.[46]

Winstanley must have been expressing the opinions of many disappointed radicals when he wrote in 1652:

> Therefore, you Army of England's Commonwealth, look to it! The enemy could not beat you in the field, but they may be too hard for you by policy in counsel if you do not stick close to see common freedom established. For if so be that kingly authority be set up in your laws again, King Charles hath conquered you and your posterity by policy, and won the field of you, though you seemingly have cut off his head.[47]

The Diggers' aim, he had told Fairfax in 1649, was 'not to remove the Norman Yoke only' and restore Saxon laws. 'No, that is not it'; but to restore 'the pure law of righteousness before the Fall.'[48]

In 1652, two years after the collapse of the Digger colony at Cobham, Winstanley published *The Law of Freedom in a Platform*, a draft constitution for a communist commonwealth. 'All men have stood for freedom', he had written earlier; 'and now the common enemy is gone you are all like men in a mist, seeking for freedom and know not where nor what it is.' Winstanley could tell them. 'True freedom lies where a man receives his nourishment and preservation, that is in the use of the earth . . . A man had better have no body than to have no food for it.' True human dignity would be possible only when communal ownership was established, and buying and selling of land and labour ceased.[49] It is impossible to summarize *The Law of Freedom*: the reader must look at it for himself. Its significance lies not only in the general conception, remarkable enough at that date, but also in the detail with which it is worked out. *The Law of Freedom* seems to have been intended as a 'possibilist' document, dedicated to Oliver Cromwell in the hope that he would implement it. How else in 1652 could it have been realized? This may account for some apparent compromises, but on the while it is a straightforward statement of Winstanley's ideals as modified by his experience at St George's Hill.

Mr Dell pertinently pointed out some years ago that Winstanley gives two pictures of communist society.[50] The first can be deduced from his critical opposition to the evils of his own times. He depicted by contrast an anarchist society. Magistrates and lawyers would be superfluous when there was no buying or selling, just as a professional clergy would become unnecessary in a society where any mechanic is free to preach.[51] Winstanley then expected the state, in Marxist phrase, to wither away immediately. 'What need have we of imprisonment, whipping or hanging laws to bring one another into bondage?' Only covetousness made theft a sin. Execution even for murder would itself be murder: only God who gives life may take it away.[52] But after the collapse of the Digger colony, when Winstanley came to draft a constitution for his new society, he included laws because he realized that 'offences may arise from the spirit of unreasonable ignorance'. But prisons were abolished, and he insisted that all law must be corrective, not punitive.[53] He emphasized now that an army would be needed to 'restrict and destroy all who endeavour to keep up or bring in kingly bondage again', to protect the community against 'the rudeness of the people', and to enforce the laws; but this army was to be a popular militia, which would not obey any Parliament not representative of the people. Liberty is secured by a right of popular resistance.[54]

Winstanley's experience with 'rude freeholders' at St George's Hill, and perhaps with Ranters among his own ranks, had taught him that some compromises might be required. He now foresaw that a longer process of education and adaptation would be necessary than he had originally envisaged. He proposed to have magistrates, elected annually and responsible to 'their masters, the people, who chose them'. These officials should include planners ('Overseers'). During a transitional period such officers might receive pay and maintenance allowances, in order to ensure that poor men served. The laws for the preservation of the commonwealth were enforced by penalties, including deprivation of civil rights and forced labour. They extended even to the death penalty for murder, buying and selling, rape, or following the trade of lawyer or parson.[55] In 1649 Winstanley had written that 'all punishments that are to be inflicted . . . are only such as to make the offender . . . to live in the community of the righteous law of love one with another'. He had then postulated forced labour as a punishment for idleness, an offence which he associated with the gentry rather than with the poor.[56] In his ideal commonwealth there would be no lawyers, and prisons would be abolished; accused persons would appear on parole (the breaking of which was another offence punishable by death).

Since Winstanley envisaged no forcible expropriation, there was bound to be a time-lag during which persuasion was used against 'the spirit of unreasonable ignorance', 'the spirit of rudeness'.[57] No doubt for this reason the franchise was extended to all males except supporters of Charles I and those who had been too hasty to buy and sell commonwealth lands – which they were to restore. Officials need not be church members, i.e. universal toleration was instituted. Marriage was to be a civil ceremony, for love not money. Parliament, chosen annually, would be the highest court of equity in the land, overseeing all other courts and officials.[58]

Winstanley, like Harrington, attached great political importance to property in land. Although communal cultivation seemed to him the principal remedy for England's ills, he by no means ignored other aspects of economic life. His list of industries in *The Law of Freedom* illustrates the extent to which in seventeenth-century England virtually all industry was a matter of collecting and processing natural products. Winstanley criticized the way in which tolls in market towns pillaged the country people who used them.[59] This would end when buying and selling were abolished. Winstanley had thought out his problem sufficiently to appreciate that there would have to be a state monopoly for foreign trade, one of the first things the Soviet government established after taking over power in 1917.[60] Abolition of wage labour had as a necessary corollary the preservation of apprenticeship. In general Winstanley thought the system of government in London companies 'very rational and well ordered', provided officials were elected annually.[61]

Education naturally seemed to Winstanley of the greatest importance. It was to continue until a man was 'acquainted with all arts and languages'. Quite exceptionally for the seventeenth century, it was to be universal (for both sexes) and equal: there were to be no specialized scholars living 'merely upon the labours of other men', whose 'show of knowledge rests in reading or contemplating or hearing others speak'. Children should be trained 'in trades and some bodily employment, as well as in learning languages or history'.[62] Girls would learn music and to read, sew, knit, and spin. Experiment and invention were to be encouraged and rewarded. Hitherto 'fear of want and care to pay rent to taskmasters hath hindered many rare inventions'. 'Kingly power hath crushed the spirit of knowledge, and would not suffer it to rise up in its beauty and fullness.'[63] Inventions were to be publicized through the two Postmasters who were to be elected in each parish – officers unique to Winstanley, so far as I know. They would collect and report statistical information about the health and welfare of their communities, and would publicize important information from other parts of the country reported to them from regional centres. The idea may owe something to Hartlib's Office of Addresses, but its statistical approach links it with that political arithmetic which William Petty was to make so influential in England in the later seventeenth century. The Postmasters would thus at once make known any new invention or discovery. This was one of the many ways in which Winstanley's communist organization of society would break down internal barriers to national unity. Trade secrets would be abolished. So the commonwealth would be assisted to flourish in peace and plenty, and others would be stirred up 'to employ their reason and industry' in emulation, not merely in order to increase production, as a modern economist would insist, but 'to the beauty of our commonwealth', as Winstanley put it, in words of which William Blake or Herbert Marcuse might have approved.[64]

Winstanley spoke for 'the poor despised ones of the earth',[65] and it was these who formed his colony at St George's Hill. But he thought in terms of society as a whole, of humanity as a whole. 'Alas! You poor blind earth moles', he cried to 'lords of manors and Norman gentry', 'You strive to take away my livelihood, and the liberty of this poor weak frame my body of flesh, which is my house I dwell in for a time; but I strive to cast down your kingdom of darkness, and to open hell gates, and to break the devil's bonds asunder wherewith you are tied, that you my enemies may live in peace; and that is all the harm I would have you to have.'[66] The Ranter Abiezer Coppe thought there was 'a most glorious design' in the overthrow of property: 'equality, community and universal love shall be in request, to utter confounding of abominable pride, murder, hypocrisy, tyranny and oppression'.[67] Similarly Winstanley believed that

> wheresoever there is a people . . . united by common community of livelihood into oneness, it will become the strongest land in the world; for then they will be as one man to defend their inheritance . . . Whereas on the other side, pleading for property and single interest divides the people of a land and the whole world into parties, and is the cause of all wars and bloodshed and contention everywhere . . . But when once the earth becomes a common treasury again, as it must . . . then this enmity of all lands will cease, and none shall dare to seek dominion over others, neither shall any dare to kill another, nor desire more of the earth than another.[68]
>
> . . .

New Myths for Old

One of the most astonishing of the many astonishing things about Winstanley is his mythological use of Biblical material. There are of course precedents: the Family of Love was accused of turning the Bible into allegories, especially the story of the Fall.[69] So did many Ranters. Joseph Salmon taught that the true Christian was not he who believed the historical truth of the Bible, 'but he that by the power of the spirit believes all this history to be verified in the mystery; . . . the history is Christ for us, the mystery is Christ in us'.[70] Abiezer Coppe in an early pamphlet employed the imagery of the Song of Songs to depict an erotic union between Christ the male and man the female.[71] Hagar and Ishmael, Sarah and Isaac, were allegories, Erbery insisted, 'though such person were'.[72] The Quakers were accused of turning 'all things into allegories, or a Christ within them'.[73] They mythologized, for example, the story of the resurrection to such an extent that they were often believed to have claimed to raise from the dead when they only meant that they had effected a conversion.[74]

The mental habit was medieval. Calvin too taught that God spoke to the capacity of his audience. But it was one thing for the clergy to allegorize a Latin text whose sacredness was accepted on all sides; it was quite another for mechanic laymen to put their own allegorical constructions on a vernacular text available for all to read, and to do this against the background of a critical Protestant Biblical scholarship, in conditions of free and unfettered discussion which allowed popular attitudes free rein, and in an atmosphere charged with millennarian expectations.

In some ways Winstanley looks forward not only to Milton but also to Vico and Blake. His critical attitude towards the text of the Scripture is very clear. He noted the contradictions which Walwyn and Clarkson also saw: the Bible suggested the existence of men before Adam, for instance. But Winstanley used this not merely negatively, to discredit the Biblical narrative; but to insist that the story of Adam and Eve must be taken metaphorically, not literally.[75] By implication Winstanley denied the inspiration of the Bible, as Ranters, Clement Writer and the Quaker Samuel Fisher did. Winstanley was in fact not really interested in the historical truth or otherwise of the Bible: 'Whether there were such outward things or no, it matters not much.' 'The whole Scriptures are but a report of spiritual mysteries, held forth to the eye of flesh in words, but to be seen in the substantial matter of them by the eye of the spirit.' The Bible should be used to illustrate truths of which one was already convinced: Winstanley was prepared to use Acts 4.32 to justify community of property.[76]

The Virgin Birth was an allegory;[77] so was the resurrection. 'Christ lying in the grave, like a corn of wheat buried under the clods of earth for a time, and Christ rising up from the powers of your flesh, above that corruption and above those clouds, treading the curse under his feet, is to be seen within'; Winstanley appears to reject any other resurrection or ascension.[78] The resurrection of the dead occurs during our lives on earth: the day of judgement has already begun and some are already living in the kingdom of heaven.[79] The casting out of covetousness and the establishment of a classless society will be 'a new heaven and a new earth'. Even more remarkably, all the prophecies of the Old and New Testaments regarding the calling of the Jews and the restoration of Israel refer to 'this work of making the earth a common treasury'.[80] Salvation is liberty and peace. The second coming is 'the rising up of Christ in sons and daughters'; the worship of any other Christ but the Christ within man must then cease.[81]

The story of the Garden of Eden Winstanley treated as an idle tale unless taken allegorically. 'The public preachers have cheated the whole world by telling us of a single man called Adam that killed us all by eating a single fruit, called an apple': in fact 'you are the man and woman that hath eaten the forbidden fruit'; Adam symbolizes the power of covetousness in every man.[82] 'The apple that the first man eats is . . . the objects of the creation.' 'We may see Adam every day before our eyes walking up and down the street.' The symbolism of the garden has almost as great a significance for Winstanley as for Marvell or Milton. Eden is mankind.[83] In Eden is fought out the conflict between Reason on the one hand and covetous imagination on the other. 'This innocency or plain-heartedness in man was not an estate 6,000 years ago only but every branch of mankind passes through it . . . This is the field or heaven wherein Michael and the Dragon fights the great battle of God Almighty.' And this conflict still goes on. 'There is no man or woman needs go to Rome nor to hell below ground, as some talk, to find the Pope, Devil, Beast or power of darkness; neither to go up into heaven above the skies to find Christ the word of life. For both these powers are to be felt within a man, fighting against each other.'[84]

This poetic concern with spiritual meaning rather than with historical truth enabled Winstanley to blend the myth of the Fall with the myth of the Norman Conquest: 'the last enslaving conquest which the enemy got over Israel was the Norman over England'.[85] Equally allegorical is Winstanley's use of the stories of Cain and Abel, of Esau and Jacob: the younger brother being the 'poor oppressed'; the elder brother the rich freeholders.[86] 'Cain is still alive in all the great landlords', said one of the Digger pamphlets which Winstanley probably did not write.[87] But 'the earth is my birthright', says Winstanley's younger brother: God is no respecter of persons. To this the elder brother replies, like many seventeenth-century clerics, by quoting Scripture. But 'though this Jacob be very low, yet his time is now come'; he will supplant Esau, and 'takes both birthright and blessing from him'.[88] Use of the myth of the two brothers deserves further study. 'Esau is the ending of the old world', said a pamphlet which circulated in Norfolk in February 1649. 'The reign of Jacob, of the saints . . . begins the new world'.[89] The Ranter Abiezer Coppe linked 'the blood of the righteous Abel' with the 'blood of the last Levellers that were shot to death'.[90] George Fox used the myth in 1659.[91] 'Cain's brood', wrote Bunyan, were 'lords and rulers', while 'Abel and his generation have their necks under oppression.'[92]

"The Diggers' Song," attributed to Gerrard Winstanley

You noble Diggers all, stand up now,
   stand up now,
You noble Diggers all, stand up now,
The wast land to maintain, seeing
   Cavaleers by name
Your digging does maintain, and
   persons all defame
Stand up now, stand up now.

Your houses they pull down, stand up
   now, stand up now,
Your houses they pull down, stand up
   now.
Your houses they pull down to fright
   your men in town
But the gentrye must come down,
   and the poor shall wear the crown.
Stand up now, Diggers all.

With spades and hoes and plowes,
   stand up now, stand up now
With spades and hoes and plowes
   stand up now,
Your freedom to uphold, seeing
   Cavaliers are bold
To kill you if they could, and rights
   from you to hold.
Stand up now, Diggers all.

Theire self-will is theire law, stand up
   now, stand up now,
Theire self-will is theire law, stand up
   now.
Since tyranny came in they count it
   now no sin
To make a gaol a gin, to starve poor
   men therein.
Stand up now, Diggers all.

The gentrye are all round, stand up
   now, stand up now,
The gentrye are all round, stand up
   now.

Dr Thirsk has shown how actual were the problems of younger brothers in seventeenth-century England.[93] Opposition to primogeniture was perhaps more widespread and more significant than historians have appreciated. It was shared by the Levellers, Hugh Peter, James Harrington, William Sheppard, Champianus Northtonus (1655), Robert Wiseman (1656), William Covell, William Sprigge and the anonymous author of *Chaos* (1659). Abolition of primogeniture, in order to destroy 'the monopolies of elder brethren', was one of the objectives of Venner's Fifth Monarchist revolt in 1661.[94] Quaker converts from landed families after 1662 were mostly younger sons and daughters[95] – those most opposed to paternal authority to whom the rough egalitarianism of northern yeomen would most appeal. But the radicals gave the legend deeper mythological overtones. For men of property, however small their share, a birthright signified inheritance from ancestors; property was equivalent to freeborn status. Some, like John Bunyan, might be tempted to sell their birthright.[96] Inheritance was the backbone of seventeenth-century society. It was the basis of Ireton's defence of property, of the Levellers' demand for the rights of freeborn Englishmen. The doctrine of original sin assumes transmission of guilt from Adam to all men living, just as the notion of an original contract assumed that men in the state of nature could bind their posterity for all time.[97]

Winstanley took over and transformed other popular beliefs. The myth of the Everlasting Gospel goes back at least to Joachim of Fiore in the twelfth century. This divided human history into three ages: that of the Father, from the Fall to the death of Christ, the age of the Law; followed by that of the Son, the age of the Gospel; the third age, the age of the Spirit, was always the present age, in which the Holy Spirit was coming into the hearts of all men to free them from existing forms and ordinances. It was a heretical doctrine, for it not only rejected the authority of the institutionalized church, but it put the spirit within man above the letter of Scripture. This doctrine had been taken over by the Familists and Jacob Boehme; it was widespread in the England of the 1640s.[98]

Winstanley, by a remarkable imaginative feat, transmuted this apocalyptic vision into a theory of rationalism and democracy. The key lies in his equation of God with Reason, and Reason with the law of the universe. In the third age, now beginning, 'the Lord himself, who is the Eternal Gospel, doth manifest himself to rule in the flesh of sons and daughters'. Their hearts will be returned to the Reason which pervades the cosmos, to 'that spiritual power that guides all men's reasoning in right order to a right end'. Every man subject to Reason's law becomes a Son or God. He no longer 'looks upon a God and a ruler without him, as the beast of the field does'; his ruler is within, whether it be called conscience or love or Reason. This is Christ's second coming, after which 'the ministration of Christ in one single person is to be silent and draw back' before the righteousness and wisdom in every person.[99]

A similar transvaluation took place with the myth of Antichrist. Orthodox divines saw the Pope as Antichrist. More radical Puritans came to regard bishops and indeed the whole Church of England as antichristian, and the civil war as a crusade for Christ again Antichrist. Winstanley again pushed this farther still, seeing property itself as antichristian, embodied in covetousness or self-love.[100] 'The antichristian captivity is expiring', he thought; but the civil war had not completed Antichrist's overthrow. There was still a conflict of 'Beast against Beast, covetousness and pride against covetousness and pride'.[101] 'That government that gives liberty to the gentry to have all the earth, and shuts out the poor commoners from enjoying any part, . . . is the government of imaginary, self-seeking Antichrist', and must be rooted out. Winstanley hoped that England would be the first country to fall off from 'that Beast, kingly property'.[102]

Since the external world is the manifestation of

The gentrye are all round, on each
  side they are found,
Theire wisdom's so profound, to
  cheat us of our ground
Stand up now, stand up now.

The lawyers they conjoyne, stand up
  now, stand up now,
The lawyers they conjoyne, stand up
  now,
To arrest you they advise, such fury
  they devise,
The devill in them lies, and hath
  blinded both their eyes.
Stand up now, stand up now.

The clergy they come in, stand up
  now, stand up now,
The clergy they come in, stand up
  now.
The clergy they come in, and say it is
  a sin
That we should now begin, our
  freedom for to win.
Stand up now, Diggers all.

The tithes they yet will have, stand
  up now, stand up now,
The tithes they yet will have, stand
  up now.
The tithes they yet will have, and
  lawyers their fees crave,
And this they say is brave, to make
  the poor their slave.
Stand up now, Diggers all.

'Gainst lawyers and 'gainst Priests,
  stand up now, stand up now,
'Gainst lawyers and 'gainst Priests
  stand up now.
For tyrants they are both even flatt
  againnst their oath,
To grant us they are loath free meat
  and drink and cloth.
Stand up now, Diggers all.

The club is all their law, stand up
  now, stand up now,
The club is all their law, stand up
  now.
The club is all their law to keep men
  in awe,
But they no vision saw to maintain
  such a law.
Stand up now, Diggers all.

The Cavaleers are foes, stand up
  now, stand up now,
The Cavaleers are foes, stand up
  now;
The Cavaleers are foes, themselves
  they do disclose
By verses not in prose to please the
  singing boyes.
Stand up now, Diggers all.

To conquer them by love, come in
  now, come in now
To conquer them by love, come in
  now;
To conquer them by love, as it does
  you behove,
For hee is King above, noe power is
  like to love,
Glory here, Diggers all.

Winstanley's God, our senses are to be valued because by them we know this world. Man must live in himself, not out of himself; in his five senses, not in empty imaginations, books or hearsay doctrines. Then God walks and delights himself in his garden, mankind.[103] We know God by the senses, 'in the clear-sighted experience of one single creature, man, by seeing, hearing, tasting, smelling, feeling'.[104] When the five senses act in their own light, this is 'the state of simple plainheartedness or innocency'. When man places his good in outward objects, imagination 'corrupts the five senses' and this leads to a Hobbist state of nature, a state of competition bordering on war. Man finds no happiness here: only when 'the selfish, imaginary, covetous, murdering power' has been cast out does God become 'all in all, the alone king in that living soul or earth, or the five living senses'.[105] Winstanley passionately asserted the earthly nature of this Paradise of the senses: 'Oh ye hearsay preachers, deceive not the people any longer by telling them that this glory shall not be known and seen till the body is laid in the dust. I tell you, this great mystery is begun to appear, and it must be seen by the material eyes of the flesh: and those five senses that is in man shall partake of this glory'. 'All outward glory that is at a distance from the five senses . . . is of a transient nature; and so is the heaven that your preachers tell you of.' Heaven is here in this world. Winstanley made the point with his accustomed epigrammatic vigour by calling on 'proud priests' to 'leave off their trade' and '*stoop* unto our God'.[106] He was literally trying to bring them down to earth, to God in man. The last line of the Diggers' song called for: 'Glory *here*, Diggers all!'[107] But if God is everywhere, if matter is God, then there can be no difference between the sacred and the secular: pantheism leads to secularism.

Christopher Hill, *The World Turned Upside Down*, Harmondsworth: Peregrine/Penguin, 1972, pp. 107–13, 128–50.

TWO
THE POLITICS OF CULTURE

When I tell people I study the politics of culture they sometimes respond, often with a mild and vaguely condescending sigh: but it's *just* culture. I get this from politicos who consider culture a distraction from the "real" struggle and I get it from artists who think of culture as reflecting only their own personal struggles. But culture is deeply political. Culture, artistic creation, is an expression of culture: tradition and lived experience (cf. Williams). Both the culture we enjoy and the culture in which we live provide us with ideas of how things are and how they should be, frameworks through which to interpret reality and possibility. They help us account for the past, make sense of the present and dream of the future. Culture can be, and is, used as a means of social control. More effective than any army is a shared conception that the way things are is the way things should be. The powers-that-be don't remain in power by convincing us that they are the answer, but rather that there is no other solution. But culture can be, and is, used as a means of resistance, a place to formulate other solutions. In order to strive for change, you have first to imagine it, and culture is the repository of imagination.

RAYMOND WILLIAMS,
"CULTURE," FROM *KEYWORDS*

What does "culture" mean? Any number of things, as Raymond Williams points out in this selection from *Keywords*. As a young man at college, the author found to his surprise — and interest — that "culture" meant one thing to his working-class Welsh family, another to the elite Cambridge crowd of his university, and still something else to his socialist and artist friends. Even these meanings, he found, changed over the short course of history, the span of the Second World

War. This idea of culture as something created and debated via politics and history became the subject of Williams's seminal work of cultural studies, *Culture and Society* (1956), of which *Keywords* was planned as an appendix (it was jettisoned at his editor's insistence). Appearing in its own right two decades later, *Keywords* is a short list of problematic words: problematic in the sense that their meanings are contested terrain. Culture is just such a word. As Williams points out, culture has at least three distinct if not discrete meanings. Culture is first a process of cultivation and growth – this carries through today in its biological usage. Culture is also a pattern of living and a way of understanding. Anthropologists are comfortable with this definition. And finally (if one can use that word with such a slippery term) culture is a thing, a product, an art work. These meanings, of course, overlap: art, for example, is the product of a process which has its roots in a way of living. You will not leave Williams's essay with a definitive definition of culture, but the fact you won't explains a great deal about the broad range of how cultural resistance will be defined in the pages to come.

Culture is one of the two or three most complicated words in the English language. This is so partly because of its intricate historical development, in several European languages, but mainly because it has now come to be used for important concepts in several distinct intellectual disciplines and in several distinct and incompatible systems of thought.

The [forerunner of the word] is *cultura*, L [Latin], from [the root] *colere*, L. *Colere* had a range of meanings: inhabit, cultivate, protect, honour with worship. Some of these meanings eventually separated, though still with occasional overlapping, in the derived nouns. Thus 'inhabit' developed through *colonus*, L to *colony*. 'Honour with worship' developed through *cultus*, L to *cult*. *Cultura* took on the main meaning of cultivation or tendings, including, as in Cicero, *cultura animi*, though with subsidiary medieval meanings of honour and worship (cf. In English **culture** as 'worship' in Caxton (1483)). The French forms of *cultura* were *couture*, [Old French], which has since developed its own specialized meaning, and later *culture*, which by [early] eC15 [15th century] had passed into English. The primary meaning was then in husbandry, the tending of natural growth.

Culture in all its early uses was a noun of process: the tending *of* something, basically crops or animals. The subsidiary *coulter* – ploughshare, had travelled by a different linguistic route, from *culter*, L – ploughshare, *culter* [Old English], to the variant English spellings *culter, colter, coulter* and as late as eC17 **culture**. (Webster, *Duchess of Malfi*, III, ii: 'hot burning cultures'). This provided a further basis for the important next stage of meaning, by metaphor. From eC16 the tending of natural growth was extended to a process of human development, and this, alongside the original meaning in husbandry, was the main sense until [late] lC18 and eC19. Thus More: 'to the culture and profit of their minds'; Bacon: 'the culture and manurance of minds' (1605); Hobbes: 'a culture of their minds' (1651); Johnson: 'she neglected the culture of her understanding' (1759). At various points in this development two crucial changes occurred: first, a degree of habituation to the metaphor, which made the sense of human tending direct; second, an extension of particular processes to a general process, which the word could abstractly carry. It is of course from the latter development that the independent noun **culture** began its complicated modern history, but the process of change is so intricate, and the latencies of meaning are at times so close, that it is not possible to give any definite date. **Culture** as an independent noun, an abstract process or the product of such a process, is not important before lC18 and is not common before [mid] mC19. But the early stages of this development were not sudden. There is an interesting use in Milton, in the second (revised) edition of *The Readie and Easie Way to Establish a Free Commonwealth* (1660): 'spread much more Knowledg and Civility, yea, Religion, through all parts of the Land, by communicating the natural heat of Government and Culture more distributively to all extreme parts, which now lie num and neglected'. Here the metaphorical sense ('natural heat') still appears to be present, and *civility* is still written where in C19 we would normally expect **culture**. Yet we can also read 'government and culture' in a quite modern sense. Milton, from the tenor of his whole argument, is writing about a general social process, and this is a definite stage of development. In C18 England this general process acquired definite class associations though **cultivation** and **cultivated** were more commonly used for this. But there is a letter of 1730 (Bishop of Killala, to Mrs Clayton; cit Plumb, *England in the Eighteenth Century*) which has this clear sense: 'it has not been customary for persons of either birth of culture to breed up their children to the Church'. Akenside (*Pleasures of Imagination*, 1744) wrote: 'nor purple state nor culture can bestow'. Wordsworth wrote 'where grace of culture hath been utterly unknown' (1805), and Jane Austen (*Emma*, 1816) 'every advantage of discipline and culture'.

It is thus clear that **culture** was developing in English towards some of its modern senses before the decisive effects of a new social and intellectual movement. But to follow the development through this movement, in lC18 and eC19, we have to look also at developments in other languages and especially in German.

In French, until C18, **culture** was always accompanied by a grammatical form indicating the matter being cultivated, as in the English usage already noted. Its occasional use as an independent noun dates from mC18, rather later than similar occasional uses in English. The independent noun *civilization* also emerged in mC18; its relationship to **culture** has since been very complicated . . . There was at this point an important development in German: the word was borrowed from French, spelled first (lC18) *Cultur* and from C19 *Kultur*. Its main use was still as a synonym for *civilization*: first in the abstract sense of a general process of becoming 'civilized' or 'cultivated'; second, in the sense which had already been established for *civilization* by the historians of the Enlightenment, in the popular C18 form of the universal histories, as a description of the secular process of human development. There was then a decisive change of use in Herder. In his unfinished *Ideas on the Philosophy of the History of Mankind* (1784–91) he wrote of *Cultur*: 'nothing is more indeterminate than this word, and nothing more deceptive than its application to all nations and periods'. He attacked the assumption of the universal histories that 'civilization' or 'culture' – the historical self-development of humanity – was what we would now call a unilinear process, leading to the high and dominant point of C18 European culture. Indeed he attacked what he called European subjugation and domination of the four quarters of the globe, and wrote:

> Men of all the quarters of the globe, who have perished over the ages, you have not lived solely to manure the earth with your ashes, so that at the end of time your posterity should be made happy by European culture. The very thought of a superior European culture is a blatant insult to the majesty of Nature.

It is then necessary, he argued, in a decisive innovation, to speak of 'cultures' in the plural: the specific and variable cultures of different nations and periods, but also the specific and variable cultures of social and economic groups within a nation. This sense was widely developed, in the Romantic movement, as an alternative to the orthodox and dominant '*civilization*'. It was first used to emphasize national and traditional cultures, including the new concept of **folk-culture**. It was later used to attack what was seen as the '*mechanical*' character of the new civilization then emerging: both for its abstract rationalism and for the 'inhumanity' of current industrial development. It was used to distinguish between 'human' and 'material' development. Politically, as so often in this period, it veered between radicalism and reaction and very often, in the confusion of major social change, fused elements of both. (It should also be noted, though it adds to the real complication, that the same kind of distinction, especially between 'material' and 'spiritual' development, was made by von Humboldt and others, until as late as 1900, with the reversal of the terms, **culture** being material and *civilization* spiritual. In general, however, the opposite distinction was dominant.)

On the other hand, from the 1840s in Germany, *Kultur* was being used in very much the sense in which *civilization* had been used in C18 universal histories. The decisive innovation is G.F. Klemm's *Allgemeine Kulturgeschichte der Menschheit – General Cultural History of Mankind* (1843–52) – which traced human development from savagery through domestication to freedom. Although the American anthropologist Morgan, tracing comparable stages, used 'Ancient *Society*', with a culmination in *Civilization*, Klemm's sense was sustained, and was directly followed in English by Tylor in *Primitive Culture* (1870). It is along this line of reference that the dominant sense in modern social sciences has to be traced.

The complexity of the modern development of the word, and of its modern usage, can then be appreciated. We can easily distinguish the sense which depends on a literal continuity of physical process as now in 'sugar-beet culture' or, in the specialized physical application in bacteriology since the 1880s, 'germ culture'. But once we go beyond the physical reference, we have to recognize three broad active categories of usage. The sources of two of these we have already discussed: (i) the independent and abstract noun which describes a general process of intellectual, spiritual, and aesthetic development, from C18; (ii) the independent noun, whether used generally or specifically, which indicates a particular way of life, whether of a people, a period, a group, or humanity in general, from Herder and Klemm. But we have also to recognize (iii) the independent and abstract noun which describes the works and practices of intellectual and especially artistic activity. This seems often now the most widespread use: **culture** is music, literature, painting and sculpture, theatre and film. **A Ministry of Culture** refers to these specific activities, sometimes with the addition of philosophy, scholarship, history. This use, (iii), is in fact relatively late. It is difficult to date precisely because it is in origin an applied form of sense (i): the idea of a general process of intellectual, spiritual and aesthetic development was applied and effectively transferred to the works and practices which represent and sustain it. But it also developed from the earlier sense of process; cf. 'progressive culture of fine arts', Millar, *Historical View of the English Government*, IV, p. 314 (1812). In English (i) and (iii) are still close; at times, for internal reasons, they are indistinguishable as in Arnold, *Culture and Anarchy* (1867); while sense (ii) was decisively introduced into English by Tylor, *Primitive Culture* (1870), following Klemm. The decisive development of sense (iii) in English was in lC19 and eC20.

Faced by this complex and still active history of the word, it is easy to react by selecting one 'true' or 'proper' or 'scientific' sense and dismissing other senses as loose or confused. There is evidence of this reaction even in the excellent study by Kroeber and Kluckhohn, *Culture: A Critical Review of Concepts and Definitions*, where usage in North American anthropology is in effect taken as a norm. It is clear that, within a discipline, conceptual usage has to be clarified. But in general it is the range and overlap of meanings that is significant. The complex of senses indicates a complex argument about the relations between general human development and a particular way of life, and between both and the works and practices of art and intelligence. It is especially interesting that in archaeology and in *cultural anthropology* the reference to **culture** or **a culture** is primarily to *material* production, while in history and *cultural studies* the reference is primarily to *signifying* or *symbolic* systems. This often confuses but even more often conceals the central question of the relations between 'material' and 'symbolic' production, which in some recent argument – cf. my own *Culture* – have always to be related rather than contrasted. Within this complex argument there are fundamentally opposed as well as effectively overlapping positions; there are also, understandably, many unresolved questions and confused answers. But these arguments and questions cannot be resolved by reducing the complexity of actual usage. This point is relevant also to uses of forms of the word in languages other than English, where there is considerable variation. The anthropological use is common in the German, Scandinavian and Slavonic language groups, but it is distinctly subordinate to the senses of art and learning, or of a general process of human development, in Italian and French. Between languages as within a language, the range and complexity of sense and reference indicate both difference of intellectual position and some blurring or overlapping. These variations, of whatever kind, necessarily involve alternative views of the activities, relationships, and processes which this complex word indicates. The complexity, that is to say, is not finally in the word but in the problems which its variations of use significantly indicate.

It is necessary to look also at some associated and derived words. **Cultivation** and **cultivated** went through the same metaphorical extension from a physical to a social or education sense in C17, and were especially significant words in C18. Coleridge, making a classical eC19 distinction between civilization and culture, wrote (1830): 'the permanent distinction, and occasional contrast, between cultivation and civilization'. The noun in this sense has effectively disappeared but the adjective is still quite common, especially in relation to manners and tastes. The important adjective **cultural** appears to date from the 1870s; it became common by the 1890s. The word is only available, in its modern sense, when the independent noun, in the artistic and intellectual or anthropological sense, has become familiar. Hostility to the word **culture** in English appears to date from the controversy around Arnold's views. It gathered force in lC19 and eC20, in association with comparable hostility to *aesthete* and *aesthetic*. Its association with class distinction produced the mime-word *culchah*. There was also an area of hostility associated with anti-German feeling, during and after the 1914–18 War, in relation to propaganda about *Kultur.* The central area of hostility has lasted, and one element of it has been emphasized by the recent American phrase **culture-vulture.** It is significant that virtually all the hostility (with the sole exception of the temporary anti-German association) has been connected with uses involving claims to superior knowledge, refinement (*culchah)* and distinctions between 'high' art (**culture**) and popular art and entertainment. It thus records a real social history and a very difficult and confused phase of social and cultural development. It is interesting that the steadily extending social and anthropological use of **culture** and **cultural** and such formations as **sub–culture** (the culture of a distinguishable small group) has, except in certain areas (notably popular entertainment), either bypassed or effectively diminished the hostility and its associated unease and embarrassment. The recent use of *culturalism,* to indicate a methodological contrast with *structuralism* in social analysis, retains many of the earlier difficulties, and does not always bypass the hostility.

Raymond Williams, *Keywords: A Vocabulary of Culture and Society*, revised edition, New York: Oxford University Press, 1976/1985, pp. 87–93.

KARL MARX AND FREDERICK ENGELS, FROM *THE GERMAN IDEOLOGY*

Written in 1845–6 by Karl Marx and Frederick Engels, *The German Ideology* was, in Marx's words, "left to the gnawing criticism of the mice" and not published until 1932, long after their death. Written mainly for purposes of self-clarification (and self-amusement), it is indeed the clearest explication of Marx and Engels's materialist philosophy. In this selection they address a simple question: where do ideas – consciousness and culture – come from? Marx and Engels begin with "first premises," establishing that the first act of humans is to produce, and produce in interaction with the natural and social world. It is out of this activity that we arrive at our ideas. However, the world in which we act and think is not some primitive state of nature, but a complex and thoroughly political society. Therefore it stands to reason that those with power to shape society also have power to shape our consciousness, to wit: "the ideas of the ruling class are in every epoch the ruling ideas." Because these ideas are integrated into our everyday activity they become normalized and naturalized, invisible. They become, simply, our culture. It follows from Marx and Engels's materialism that in order to change this culture you must change the social and material base that produced it, and this is only accomplished, they believed, through revolutionary activity.

The Illusions of German Ideology

As we hear from German ideologists, Germany has in the last few years gone through an unparalleled revolution. The decomposition of the Hegelian philosophy, which began with Strauss, has developed into a universal ferment into which all the 'powers of the past' are swept. In the general chaos mighty empires have arisen only to meet with immediate doom, heroes have emerged momentarily only to be hurled back into obscurity by bolder and stronger rivals. It was a revolution beside which the French Revolution was child's play, a world struggle beside which the struggles of the Diadochi [successors of Alexander the Great] appear insignificant. Principles ousted one another, heroes of the mind overthrew each other with unheard-of rapidity, and in the three years 1842–5 more of the past was swept away in Germany than at other times in three centuries.

All this is supposed to have taken place in the realm of pure thought.

Certainly it is an interesting event we are dealing with: the putrescence of the absolute spirit. When the last spark of its life had failed, the various components of this *caput mortuum* began to decompose, entered into new combinations and formed new substances. The industrialists of philosophy, who till then had lived on the exploitation of the absolute spirit, now seized upon the new combinations. Each with all possible zeal set about retailing his apportioned share. This naturally gave rise to competition, which, to start with, was carried on in moderately staid bourgeois fashion. Later when the German market was glutted, and the commodity in spite of all efforts found no response in the world market, the business was spoiled in the usual German manner by fabricated and fictitious production, deterioration in quality, adulteration of the raw materials, falsification of labels, fictitious purchases, bill-jobbing, and a credit system devoid of any real basis. The competition turned into a bitter struggle, which is now being extolled and interpreted to us as a revolution of world significance, the begetter of the most prodigious results and achievements.

If we wish to rate at its true value this philosophic charlatanry, which awakens even in the breast of the honest German citizen a glow of national pride, if we wish to bring out clearly the pettiness, the parochial narrowness of this whole Young Hegelian movement and in particular the tragicomic contrast between the illusions of these heroes about their achievements and the actual achievements themselves, we must look at the whole spectacle from a standpoint beyond the frontiers of Germany.

German criticism has, right up to its latest efforts, never quitted the realm of philosophy. Far from examining its general philosophic premises, the whole body of its inquiries has actually sprung from the soil of a definite philosophical system, that of Hegel. Not only in their answers but in their very questions there was a mystification. This dependence on Hegel is the reason why not one of these modern critics has even attempted a comprehensive criticism of the Hegelian system, however much each professes to have advanced beyond Hegel. Their polemics against Hegel and against one another are confined to this – each extracts one side of the Hegelian system and turns this against the whole system as well as against the sides extracted by the others. To begin with they extracted pure unfalsified Hegelian categories such as 'substance' and 'self-consciousness', later they desecrated these categories with more secular names such as 'species', 'the Unique', 'Man', etc.

The entire body of German philosophical criticism from Strauss to Stirner is confined to criticism of *religious* conceptions. The critics started from real religion and actual theology. What religious consciousness and a religious conception really meant was determined variously as they went along. Their advance consisted in subsuming the allegedly dominant metaphysical, political, juridical, moral and other conceptions under the class of religious or theological conceptions; and similarly in pronouncing political, juridical, moral consciousness as religious or theological, and the political, juridical, moral man – '*man*' in the last resort – as religious. The dominance of religion was taken for granted. Gradually every dominant relationship was pronounced a religious relationship and transformed into a cult, a cult of law, a cult of the State, etc. On all sides it was only a question of dogmas and belief in dogmas. The world sanctified to an ever-increasing extent till at last our venerable Saint Max was able to canonize it *en bloc* and thus dispose of it once and for all.

The Old Hegelians had *comprehended* everything as soon as it was reduced to an Hegelian logical category. The Young Hegelians *criticized* everything by attributing to it religious conceptions or by pronouncing it a theological matter. The Young Hegelians are in agreement with the Old Hegelians in their belief in the rule of religion, of concepts, of a universal principle in the existing world. Only, the one party attacks this dominion as usurption, while the other extols it as legitimate.

Since the Young Hegelians consider conceptions, thoughts, ideas, in fact all the products of consciousness, to which they attribute an independent existence, as the real chains of men (just as the Old Hegelians declared them the true bonds of human society) it is evident that the Young Hegelians have to fight only against these illusions of consciousness. Since, according to their fantasy, the relationships of men, all their doings, their chains and their limitations are products of their consciousness, the Young Hegelians logically put to men the moral postulate of exchanging their present consciousness for human, critical, or egoistic consciousness, and thus of removing their limitations. This demand to change consciousness amounts to a demand to interpret reality in another way, i.e. to recognize it by means of another interpretation. The Young Hegelian ideologists, in spite of their allegedly 'world-shattering' statements, are the staunchest conservatives. The most recent of them have found the correct expression for their activity when they declare they are only fighting against *phrases.* They forget, however, that to these phrases they themselves are only opposing other phrases, and that they are in no way combating the real existing world when they are merely combating the phrases of this world. The only results which this philosophic criticism could achieve were a few (and at that thoroughly one-sided) elucidations of Christianity from the point of view of religious history; all the rest of their assertions are only further embellishments of their claim to have furnished, in these unimportant elucidations, discoveries of universal importance.

It has not occurred to any one of these philosophers to inquire into the connection of German philosophy with German reality, the relation of their criticism to their own material surroundings.

. . .

History: Fundamental Conditions

Since we are dealing with the Germans, who are devoid of premises, we must begin by stating the first premise of all human existence and, therefore, of all history, the premise, namely, that men must be in a position to live in order to be able to 'make history'. But life involves before everything else eating and drinking, a habitation, clothing and many other things. The first historical act is thus the production of the means to satisfy these needs, the production of material life itself. And indeed this is an historical act, a fundamental condition of all history, which today, as thousands of years ago, must daily and hourly be fulfilled merely in order to sustain human life. Even when the sensuous world is reduced to a minimum, to a stick as with Saint Bruno [Baur], it presupposes the action of producing the stick. There-fore in any interpretation of history one has first of all to observe this fundamental fact in all its significance and all its implications and to accord it its due importance. It is well know that the Germans have never done this, and they have never, therefore, had an *earthly* basis for history and con-sequently never an historian. The French and the English, even if they have conceived the relation of this fact with so-called history only in an extremely one-sided fashion, particularly as long as they remained in the toils of political ideology, have nevertheless made the first attempts to give the writing of history a materialistic basis by being the first to write histo-ries of civil society, of commerce and industry.

The second point is that the satisfaction of the first need (the action of satisfying, and the instrument of satisfaction which has been acquired) leads to new needs; and this production of new needs is the first historical act. Here we recognize immediately the spiritual ancestry of the great historical wisdom of the Germans who, when they run out of positive material and when they can serve up neither theological nor political nor literary rubbish, assert that this is not history at all, but the 'prehistoric era'. They do not, however, enlighten us as to how we proceed from this nonsensical 'pre-history' to history proper; although, on the other hand, in their historical speculation they seize upon this 'prehistory' with especial eagerness because they imagine themselves safe there from interference on the part of 'crude facts', and, at the same time, because there they can give full rein to their speculative impulse and set up and knock down hypotheses by the thousand.

The third circumstance which, from the very outset, enters into histori-cal development, is that men, who daily remake their own life, begin to make other men, to propagate their kind: the relation between man and woman, parents and children, the *family*. The family, which to begin with is the only social relationship, becomes later, when increased needs create new social relations and the increased population new needs, a subordinate one (except in Germany), and must then be treated and analysed according to the existing empirical data, not according to 'the concept of the family', as is the custom in Germany.[1] These three aspects of social activity are not of course to be taken as three different stages, but just as three aspects or, to make it clear to the Germans, three 'moments', which have existed simultaneously since the dawn of history and the first men, and which still assert themselves in history today.

The production of life, both of one's own in labour and of fresh life in procreation, now appears as a double relationship: on the one hand as a natural, on the other as a social relationship. By social we understand the co-operation of several individuals, no matter under what conditions, in what manner and to what end. It follows from this that a certain mode of production, or industrial stage, is always combined with a certain mode of co-operation, or social stage, and this mode of co-operation is itself a 'productive force'. Further, that the multitude of productive forces accessible to men determines the nature of society, hence, that the 'history of humanity' must always be studied and treated in relation to the history of industry and exchange. But it is also clear how in Germany it is impossible to write this sort of history, because the Germans lack not only the necessary power of comprehension and the material but also the 'evidence of their senses', for across the Rhine you cannot have any experience of these things since history has stopped happening. Thus it is quite obvious from the start that there exists a materialistic connection of men with one another, which is determined by their needs and their mode of production, and which is as old as men themselves. This connection is ever taking on new forms, and thus presents a 'history' independently of the existence of any political or religious nonsense which in addition may hold men together.

Only now, after having considered four moments, four aspects of the primary historical relationships, do we find that man also possesses 'consciousness', but, even so, not inherent, not 'pure' consciousness. From the start the 'spirit' is afflicted with the curse of being 'burdened' with matter, which here makes its appearance in the form of agitated layers of air, sounds, in short, of language. Language is as old as consciousness, language *is* practical consciousness that exists also for other men, and for that reason alone it really exists for me personally as well; language, like consciousness, only arises from the need, the necessity, of intercourse with other men. Where there exists a relationship, it exists for me: the animal does not enter into "relations" with anything, it does not enter into any relation at all. For the animal, its relation to others does not exist as a relation. Consciousness is, therefore, from the very beginning a social product, and remains so as long as men exist at all. Consciousness is at first, of course, merely consciousness concerning the *immediate* sensuous environment and consciousness of the limited connection with other persons and things outside the individual who is growing self-conscious. At the same time it is consciousness of nature, which first appears to men as a completely alien, all-powerful and unassailable force, with which men's relations are purely animal and by which they are overawed like beasts; it is thus a purely animal consciousness of nature (natural religion) just because nature is as yet hardly modified historically. (We see here immediately: this natural religion or this particular relation of men to nature is determined by the form of society and vice versa. Here, as everywhere, the identity of nature and man appears in such a way that the restricted relation of men to nature determines their restricted relation to one another, and their restricted relation to one another determines men's restricted relation to nature.) On the other hand, man's consciousness of the necessity of associating with the individuals around him is the beginning of the consciousness that he is living in society at all. This beginning is as animal as social life itself at this stage. It is mere herd-consciousness, and at this point man is only distinguished from sheep by the fact that with him consciousness takes the place of instinct or that his instinct is a conscious one. This sheep-like or tribal consciousness receives its further development and extension through increased productivity, the increase of needs, and, what is fundamental to both of these, the increase of population. With these there develops the division of labour, which was originally nothing but the division of labour in the sexual act, then that division of labour which develops spontaneously or 'naturally' by virtue of natural predisposition (e.g. physical strength), needs, accidents, etc., etc. Division of labour only becomes truly such from the moment when a division of material and mental labour appears. (The first form of ideologists, *priests*, is concurrent.) From this moment onwards consciousness *can* really flatter itself that it is something other than consciousness of existing practice, that it *really* represents something without representing something real; from now on consciousness is in a position to emancipate itself from the world and to proceed to the formation of 'pure' theory, theology, philosophy, ethics, etc. But even if this theory, theology, philosophy, ethics, etc. comes into contradiction with the existing relations, this can only occur because existing social relations have come into contradiction with existing forces of production; this, moreover, can also occur in a particular national sphere of relations through the appearance of the contradiction, not within the national orbit, but between this national consciousness and the practice of other nations, i.e. between the national and the general consciousness of a nation (as we see it now in Germany).

Moreover, it is quite immaterial what consciousness starts to do on its own: out of all such muck we get only the one inference that these three moments, the forces of production, the state of society, and consciousness, can and must come into contradiction with one another, because the *division of labour* implied the possibility, nay the fact that intellectual and material activity — enjoyment and labour, production and consumption — devolve on different individuals, and that the only possibility of their not coming into contradiction lies in the negation in its turn of the division of labour. It is self-evident, moreover, that 'spectres', 'bonds', 'the higher being', 'concept', 'scruple', are merely the idealistic, spiritual expression, the conception apparently of the isolated individual, the image of very empirical fetters and limitations, within which the mode of production of life and the form of intercourse coupled with it move.

. . .

Ruling Class and Ruling Ideas

The ideas of the ruling class are in every epoch the ruling ideas, i.e. the class which is the ruling *material* force of society, is at the same time its ruling *intellectual* force. The class which has the means of material production at its disposal, has control at the same time over the means of mental production, so that thereby, generally speaking, the ideas of those who lack the means of mental production are subject to it. The ruling ideas are nothing more than the ideal expression of the dominant material relationships, the dominant material relationships grasped as ideas; hence of the relationships which make the one class the ruling one, therefore, the ideas of its dominance. The individuals composing the ruling class possess among other things consciousness, and therefore think. Insofar, therefore, as they rule as a class and determine the extent and compass of an epoch, it is self-evident that they do this in its whole range, hence among other things rule also as thinkers, as producers of ideas, and regulate the production and distribution of the ideas of their age: thus their ideas are the ruling ideas of the epoch. For instance, in an age and in a country where royal power, aristocracy, and bourgeoisie are contending for mastery and where, therefore, mastery is shared, the doctrine of the separation of powers proves to be the dominant idea and is expressed as an 'eternal law'.

The division of labour, which we already saw . . . as one of the chief forces of history up till now, manifests itself also in the ruling class as the division of mental and material labour, so that inside this class one part appears as the thinkers of the class (its active, conceptive ideologists, who make the perfecting of the illusion of the class about itself their chief source of livelihood), while the other's attitude to these ideas and illusions is more passive and receptive, because they are in reality the active members of this class and have less time to make up illusions and ideas about themselves.

Within this class this cleavage can even develop into a certain opposition and hostility between the two parts, which, however, in the case of a practical collision, in which the class itself is endangered, automatically comes to nothing, in which case there also vanishes the semblance that the ruling ideas were not the ideas of the ruling class and had a power distinct from the power of this class. The existence of revolutionary ideas in a particular period presupposes the existence of a revolutionary class . . .

If now in considering the course of history we detach the ideas of the ruling class from the ruling class itself and attribute to them an independent existence, if we confine ourselves to saying that these or those ideas were dominant at a given time, without bothering ourselves about the conditions of production and the producers of these ideas, if we thus ignore the individuals and world conditions which are the source of the ideas, we can say, for instance, that during the time that the aristocracy was dominant, the concepts honour, loyalty, etc. were dominant, during the dominance of the bourgeoisie the concepts freedom, equality, etc. The ruling class itself on the whole imagines this to be so. This conception of history, which is common to all historians, particularly since the eighteenth century, will necessarily come up against the phenomenon that increasingly abstract ideas hold sway, i.e. ideas which increasingly take on the form of universality. For each new class which puts itself in the place of one ruling before it, is compelled, merely in order to carry through its aim, to represent its interest as the common interest of all the members of society, that is, expressed in ideal form: it has to give its ideas the form of universality, and represent them as the only rational, universally valid ones.

. . .

Whilst in ordinary life every shopkeeper is very well able to distinguish between what somebody professes to be and what he really is, our historians have not yet won even this trivial insight. They take every epoch at its word and believe that everything it says and imagines about itself is true.

Karl Marx and Frederick Engels, *The German Ideology*, C.J. Arthur (ed.), New York: International Publishers, 1970, pp. 39–41, 48–52, 64–7.

MATTHEW ARNOLD,
FROM *CULTURE AND ANARCHY*

You can read Matthew Arnold's *Culture and Anarchy* as Marx and Engels turned upside down. If culture for the latter arises out of the interchange of daily life, for

Arnold it promises transcendence, something that rises above the storm and stress of the everyday world. In philosophical terms, Arnold provides the idealist counterpart to Marx and Engels's materialism. True, both parties understand culture as political. But for Arnold there's a twist: the value of culture is in its anti-politics. Culture provides the means with which to resist the rancorous political, economic, and social divisions of the industrialist, imperialist, class-torn England of Arnold's time. Unlike the "anarchy" of politics, culture: "the best which has been thought and said in the world," provides a common ideal that can unite us all in the pursuit of perfection. Arnold is often dismissed – and sometimes championed – as a conservative elitist. As a professor at Oxford and national Inspector of Schools he was certainly a member of the cultural elite, but his conservatism is complex. Culture, for Arnold, is not meant to be the property of the few but what binds us *all*, and its purpose is to turn "a stream of fresh and free thought upon our stock notions and habits." Hardly the musings of an orthodox conservative. But still the thorny question remains: how will "real thought and real beauty; real sweetness and real light," that is real culture, be determined, and by whom?

The whole scope of the essay is to recommend culture as the great help out of our present difficulties; culture being a pursuit of our total perfection by means of getting to know, on all the matters which most concern us, the best which has been thought and said in the world, and, through this knowledge, turning a stream of fresh and free thought upon our stock notions and habits, which we now follow staunchly but mechanically, vainly imagining that there is a virtue in following them staunchly which makes up for the mischief of following them mechanically.

. . .

The disparagers of culture make its motive curiosity; sometimes, indeed, they make its motive mere exclusiveness and vanity. The culture which is supposed to plume itself on a smattering of Greek and Latin is a culture which is begotten by nothing so intellectual as curiosity; it is valued either out of sheer vanity and ignorance, or else as an engine of social and class distinction, separating its holder, like a badge or title, from other people who have not got it. No serious man would call this *culture*, or attach any value to it, as culture, at all. To find the real ground for the very differing estimate which serious people will set upon culture, we must find some motive for culture in the terms of which may lie a real ambiguity; and such a motive the word *curiosity* gives us. I have before now pointed out that in English we do not, like the foreigners, use this word in a good sense as well as in a bad sense; with us the word is always used in a somewhat disapproving sense; a liberal and intelligent eagerness about the things of the mind may be meant by a foreigner when he speaks of curiosity, but with us the word always conveys a certain notion of frivolous and unedifying activity. In the *Quarterly Review*, some little time ago, was an estimate of the celebrated French critic, Monsieur Sainte-Beuve, and a very inadequate estimate it, in my judgement, was. And its inadequacy consisted chiefly in this: that in our English way it left out of sight the double sense really involved in the word *curiosity*, thinking enough was said to stamp Monsieur Sainte-Beuve with blame if it was said that he was impelled in his operations as a critic by curiosity, and omitting either to perceive that Monsieur Sainte-Beuve himself, and many other people with him, would consider that this was praiseworthy and not blameworthy, or to point out why it ought really to be accounted worthy of blame and not of praise. For as there is a curiosity about intellectual matters which is futile, and merely a disease, so there is certainly a curiosity – a desire after the things of the mind simply for their own sakes and for the pleasure of seeing them as they are – which is, in an intelligent being, natural and laudable. Nay, and the very desire to see things as they are implies a balance and regulation of mind which is not often attained without fruitful effort, and which is the very opposite of the blind and diseased impulse of mind which is what we mean to blame when we blame curiosity. Montesquieu says: 'The first motive which ought to impel us to study is the desire to augment the excellence of our nature, and to render an intelligent being yet more intelligent'. This is the true ground to assign for the genuine scientific passion, however manifested, and for culture, viewed simply as a fruit of this passion; and it is a worthy ground, even though we let the term *curiosity* stand to describe it.

But there is of culture another view, in which not solely the scientific passion, the sheer desire to see things as they are, natural and proper in an intelligent being, appears as the ground of it. There is a view in which all the love of our neighbour, the impulses towards action, help, and beneficence, the desire for stopping human error, clearing human confusion, and dimin-ishing the sum of human misery, the noble aspiration to leave the world better and happier than we found it – motives eminently such as are called social – come in as part of the grounds of culture, and the main and pre-eminent part. Culture is then properly described not as having its origin in curiosity, but as having its origin in the love of perfection; it is *a study of per-fection*. It moves by the force, not merely or primarily of the scientific passion for pure knowledge, but also of the moral and social passion for doing good. As, in the first view of it, we took for its worthy motto Mon-tesquieu's words: 'To render an intelligent being yet more intelligent!' so, in the second view of it, there is no better motto which it can have than these words of Bishop Wilson: 'To make reason and the will of God prevail!' Only, whereas the passion for doing good is apt to be overhasty in determining what reason and the will of God say, because its turn is for acting rather than thinking, and it wants to be beginning to act; and whereas it is apt to take its own conceptions, which proceed from its own state of development and share in all the imperfections and immaturities of this, for a basis of action; what distinguishes culture is, that it is possessed by the scientific passion, as well as by the passion of doing good; that it has worthy notions of reason and the will of God, and does not readily suffer its own crude conceptions to substitute themselves for them; and that, knowing that no action or institution can be salutary and stable which are not based on reason and the will of God, it is not so bent on acting and instituting, even with the great aim of diminishing human error and misery ever before its thoughts, but that it can remember that acting and instituting are of little use, unless we know how and what we ought to act and to institute.

This culture is more interesting and more far-reaching than that other, which is founded solely on the scientific passion for knowing. But it needs times of faith and ardour, times when the intellectual horizon is opening and widening all round us, to flourish in. And is not the close and bounded intellectual horizon within which we have long lived and moved now lifting up, and are not new lights finding free passage to shine in upon us? For a long time there was no passage for them to make their way in upon us, and then it was of no use to think of adapting the world's action to them. Where was the hope of making reason and the will of God prevail among people who had a routine which they had christened reason and the will of God, in which they were inextricably bound, and beyond which they had no power of looking? But now the iron force of adhesion to the old routine – social, political, religious – has wonderfully yielded; the iron force of exclusion of all which is new has wonderfully yielded; the danger now is, not that people should obstinately refuse to allow anything but their old routine to pass for reason and the will of God, but either that they should allow some novelty or other to pass for these too easily, or else that they should underrate the importance of them altogether, and think it enough to follow action for its own sake, without troubling themselves to make reason and the will of God prevail therein. Now, then, is the moment for culture to be of service, culture which believes in making reason and the will of God prevail, believes in perfection, is the study and pursuit of perfection, and is no longer debarred, by a rigid invincible exclusion of whatever is new, from getting acceptance for its ideas, simply because they are new.

The moment this view of culture is seized, the moment it is regarded not solely as the endeavour to see things as they are, to draw towards a knowledge of the universal order which seems to be intended and aimed at in the world, and which it is a man's happiness to go along with or his misery to go counter to – to learn, in short, the will of God – the moment, I say, culture is considered not merely as the endeavour to *see* and *learn* this, but as the endeavour, also, to make it *prevail*, the moral, social, and benefi-cent character of culture becomes manifest. The mere endeavour to see and learn it for our own personal satisfaction is indeed a commencement for making it prevail, a preparing the way for this, which always serves this, and is wrongly, therefore, stamped with blame absolutely in itself, and not only in its caricature and degeneration. But perhaps it has got stamped with blame, and disparaged with the dubious title of curiosity, because in com-parison with this wider endeavour of such great and plain utility it looks selfish, petty, and unprofitable.

And religion, the greatest and most important of the efforts by which the human race has manifested its impulse to perfect itself – religion, that voice of the deepest human experience – does not only enjoin and sanc-tion the aim which is the great aim of culture, the aim of setting ourselves to ascertain what perfection is and to make it prevail; but also, in determin-ing generally in what human perfection consists, religion comes to a conclusion identical with that which culture – seeking the determination of this question through all the voices of human experience which have been heard upon it, art, science, poetry, philosophy, history, as well as reli-gion, in order to give a greater fullness and certainty to its solution – likewise reaches. Religion says: *The kingdom of God is within you*; and culture, in like manner, places human perfection in an *internal* condition, in the growth and predominance of our humanity proper, as distinguished from our animality, in the ever-increasing efficaciousness and in the general harmonious expansion of those gifts of thought and feeling which make the peculiar dignity, wealth, and happiness of human nature. As I have said on a former occasion: 'It is in making endless additions to itself, in the endless expansion of its powers, in endless growth in wisdom and beauty, that the spirit of the human race finds its ideal. To reach this ideal, culture is an indispensable aid, and that is the true value of culture.' Not a having and a resting, but a growing and a becoming, is the character of perfection as culture conceives it; and here, too, it coincides with religion. And because men are all members of one great whole, and the sympathy which is in human nature will not allow one member to be indifferent to the rest, or to have a perfect welfare independent of the rest, the expansion of our humanity, to suit the idea of perfection which culture forms, must be a *general* expansion. Perfection, as culture conceives it, is not possible while the individual remains isolated: the individual is obliged, under pain of being stunted and enfeebled in his own development if he disobeys, to carry others along with him in his march towards perfection, to be continually doing all he can to enlarge and increase the volume of the human stream sweeping thitherward; and here, once more, it lays on us the same obligation as religion, which says, as Bishop Wilson has admirably put it, that 'to promote the kingdom of God is to increase and hasten one's own happiness'. Finally, perfection — as culture, from a thorough disinterested study of human nature and human experience, learns to conceive it — is an harmonious expansion of *all* the powers which make the beauty and worth of human nature, and is not consistent with the over-development of any one power at the expense of the rest. Here it goes beyond religion, as religion is generally conceived by us.

If culture, then, is a study of perfection, and of harmonious perfection, general perfection, and perfection which consists in becoming something rather than in having something, in an inwards condition of the mind and spirit, not in an outward set of circumstances — it is clear that culture, instead of being the frivolous and useless thing which Mr Bright, and Mr Frederic Harrison, and many other liberals are apt to call it, has a very important function to fulfil for mankind. And this function is particularly important in our modern world, of which the whole civilization is, to a much greater degree than the civilization of Greece and Rome, mechanical and external, and tends constantly to become more so. But above all in our own country has culture a weighty part to perform, because here that mechanical character, which civilization tends to take everywhere, is shown in the most eminent degree. Indeed nearly all the characters of perfection, as culture teaches us to fix them, meet in this country with some powerful tendency which thwarts them and sets them at defiance. The idea of perfection as an *inward* condition of the mind and spirit is at variance with the mechanical and material civilization in esteem with us, and nowhere, as I have said, so much in esteem as with us. The idea of perfection as a *general* expansion of the human family is at variance with our strong individualism, our hatred of all limits to the unrestrained swing of the individual's personality, our maxim of 'every man for himself'. The idea of perfection as an *harmonious* expansion of human nature is at variance with our want of flexibility, with our inaptitude for seeing more than one side of a thing, with our intense energetic absorption in the particular pursuit we happen to be following. So culture has a rough task to achieve in this country, and its preachers have, and are likely long to have, a hard time of it, and they will much oftener be regarded, for a great while to come, as elegant or spurious Jeremiahs, than as friends and benefactors. That, however, will not prevent their doing in the end good service if they persevere; and meanwhile, the mode of action they have to pursue, and the sort of habits they must fight against, should be made quite clear to every one who may be willing to look at the matter attentively and dispassionately.

Faith in machinery is, I said, our besetting danger; often in machinery most absurdly disproportioned to the end which this machinery, if it is to do any good at all, is to serve; but always in machinery, as if it had a value in and for itself. What is freedom but machinery? What is population but machinery? What is coal but machinery? What are railroads but machinery? What is wealth but machinery? What are religious organizations but machinery? Now almost every voice in England is accustomed to speak of these things as if they were precious ends in themselves, and therefore had some of the characters of perfection indisputably joined to them. I have once before noticed Mr Roebuck's stock argument for proving the greatness and happiness of England as she is, and for quite stopping the mouths of all gainsayers. Mr Roebuck is never weary of reiterating this argument of his, so I do not know why I should be weary of noticing it. 'May not every man in England say what he likes?' Mr Roebuck perpetually asks; and that, he thinks, is quite sufficient, and when every man may say what he likes, our aspirations ought to be satisfied. But the aspirations of culture, which is the study of perfection, are not satisfied, unless what men say, when they may say what they like, is worth saying – has good in it, and more good than bad. In the same way *The Times*, replying to some foreign strictures on the dress, looks, and behaviour of the English abroad, urges that the English ideal is that every one should be free to do and to look just as he likes. But culture indefatigably tries, not to make what each raw person may like, the rule by which he fashions himself; but to draw ever nearer to a sense of what is indeed beautiful, graceful, and becoming, and to get the raw person to like that. And in the same way with respect to railroads and coal. Every one must have observed the strange language current during the late discussions as to the possible failure of our supplies of coal. Our coal, thousands of people were saying, is the real basis of our national greatness; if our coal runs short, there is an end of the greatness of England. But what *is* greatness? – culture makes us ask. Greatness is a spiritual condition worthy to excite love, interest and admiration; and the outward proof of possessing greatness is that we excite love, interest and admiration. If England were swallowed up by the sea to-morrow, which of the two, a hundred years hence, would most excite the love, interest, and admiration of mankind – would most, therefore, show the evidences of having possessed greatness – the England of the last twenty years, or the England of Elizabeth, of a time of splendid spiritual effort, but when our coal, and our industrial operations depending on coal, were very little developed? Well then, what an unsound habit of mind it must be which makes us talk of things like coal or iron as constituting the greatness of England, and how salutary a friend is culture, bent on seeing things as they are, and thus dissipating delusions of this kind and fixing standards of perfection that are real!

. . .

The pursuit of perfection, then, is the pursuit of sweetness and light. He who works for sweetness works in the end for light also; he who works for light works in the end for sweetness also. But he who works for sweetness and light united, works to make reason and the will of God prevail. He who works for machinery, he who works for hatred, works only for confusion. Culture looks beyond machinery, culture hates hatred; culture has but one great passion, the passion for sweetness and light. Yes, it has one yet greater! – the passion for making them *prevail*. It is not satisfied till we *all* come to a perfect man; it knows that the sweetness and light of the few must be imperfect until the raw and unkindled masses of humanity are touched with sweetness and light. If I have not shrunk from saying that we must work for sweetness and light, so neither have I shrunk from saying that we must have a broad basis, must have sweetness and light for as many as possible. Again and again I have insisted how those are the happy moments of humanity, how those are the marking epochs of a people's life, how those are the flowering times for literature and art and all the creative power of genius, when there is a *national* glow of life and thought, when the whole of society is in the fullest measure permeated by thought, sensible to beauty, intelligent and alive. Only it must be *real* thought and *real* beauty; *real* sweetness and *real* light. Plenty of people will try to give the masses, as they call them, an intellectual food prepared and adapted in the way they think proper for the actual condition of the masses. The ordinary popular literature is an example of this way of working on the masses. Plenty of people will try to indoctrinate the masses with the set of ideas and judgements constituting the creed of their own profession or party. Our religious and political organizations give an example of this way of working on the masses. I condemn neither way; but culture works differently. It does not try to teach down to the level of inferior classes; it does not try to win them for this or that sect of its own, with ready-made judgements and watchwords. It seeks to do away with classes; to make all live in an atmosphere of sweetness and light, and use ideas, as it uses them itself, freely – to be nourished and not bound by them.

This is the *social idea*; and the men of culture are the true apostles of equality. The great men of culture are those who have had a passion for diffusing, for making prevail, for carrying from one end of society to the other, the best knowledge, the best ideas of their time; who have laboured to divest knowledge of all that was harsh, uncouth, difficult, abstract, professional, exclusive; to humanize it, to make it efficient outside the clique of the cultivated and learned, yet still remaining the *best* knowledge and thought of the time, and a true source, therefore, of sweetness and light.

. . .

I conclude, therefore – what, indeed, few of those who do me the honour to read this disquisition are likely to dispute – that we can as little find in the working-class as in the aristocratic or in the middle-class our much-wanted source of authority, as culture suggests it to us.

Well, then, what if we tried to rise above the idea of class to the idea of the whole community, *the State*, and to find our centre of light and authority there? Every one of us has the idea of country, as a sentiment; hardly any one of us has the idea of *the State*, as a working power. And why? Because we habitually live in our ordinary selves, which do not carry us beyond the ideas and wishes of the class to which we happen to belong. And we are all afraid of giving to the State too much power, because we only conceive of the State as something equivalent to the class in occupation of the executive government, and are afraid of that class abusing power to its own purposes. If we strengthen the State with the aristocratic class in occupation of the executive government, we imagine we are delivering ourselves up captive to the ideas and wishes of Sir Thomas Bateson; if with the middle-class in occupation of the executive government, to those of the Rev. W. Cattle; if with the working-class, to those of Mr Bradlaugh. And with much justice; owing to the exaggerated notion which we English, as I have said, entertain of the right and blessedness of the mere doing as one likes, of the affirming oneself, and oneself just as it is. People of the aristocratic class want to affirm their ordinary selves, their likings and dislikings; people of the middle-class the same, people of the working-class the same. By our everyday selves, however, we are separate, personal, at war; we are only safe from one another's tyranny when no one has any power; and this safety, in its turn, cannot save us from anarchy. And when, therefore, anarchy presents itself as a danger to us, we know not where to turn.

But by our *best self* we are united, impersonal, at harmony. We are in no peril from giving authority to this, because it is the truest friend we all of us can have; and when anarchy is a danger to us, to this authority we may turn with sure trust. Well, and this is the very self which culture, or the study of perfection, seeks to develop in us; at the expense of our old untransformed self, taking pleasure only in doing what it likes or is used to do, and exposing us to the risk of clashing with every one else who is doing the same! So that our poor culture, which is flouted as so unpractical, leads us to the very ideas capable of meeting the great want of our present embarrassed times! We want an authority, and we find nothing but jealous classes, checks, and a dead-lock; culture suggests the idea of *the State*. We find no basis for a firm State-power in our ordinary selves; culture suggests one to us in our *best self.*

Matthew Arnold, *Culture and Anarchy: An Essay in Political and Social Criticism*, London: Smith, Elder and Co., 1869, pp. viii, 5-19, 47-9, 87-9.

ANTONIO GRAMSCI,
FROM *THE PRISON NOTEBOOKS*

"We must stop this brain from working for twenty years!" the Fascist prosecutor demanded at his trial in 1928. Antonio Gramsci, the young head of the Italian Communist Party, died in less than ten. But his brain never stopped working. The following is a small selection from the nearly 3,000 handwritten pages of notes smuggled out of prison. Gramsci, a theatre critic and theoretician as well as a political activist, had a keen interest in popular culture and consciousness. Everyone, he argues, is a philosopher; each of us carries with us ways of making sense of the world. These nascent philosophies, however, are imbedded so deeply that we often cannot recognize them. A great deal of these ideas reflect the ruling ideas of the ruling class (cf. Marx and Engels), but not all of them, not entirely. Growing up within a traditional peasant culture, working in a modern factory, these lived experiences give rise to their own, and sometimes conflicting, ways of seeing. One may even act out one philosophy while believing wholeheartedly in another. Human consciousness is exceedingly complex, "an infinity of traces, without leaving an inventory." Gramsci, however, was not a psychologist, but a revolutionary. The successes of the Catholic Church and the Fascist state taught him that political power rests upon cultural hegemony. Hearts and minds are as important as bodies and buildings. Thus part of any revolutionary project is creating a counterhegemonic culture. If this culture is to have real power, and communist integrity, it cannot – contra Arnold – be imposed from above, but must come out of the experiences and consciousness of people. Thus, the job of the revolutionary is to discover the progressive potentialities that reside within popular consciousness and from this material fashion a culture of resistance. However, it is important to remember that counterhegemonic culture is not an end in itself for Gramsci. It is merely a weapon, albeit an important one, for political, economic, and yes, cultural revolution.

The Study of Philosophy

It is essential to destroy the widespread prejudice that philosophy is a strange and difficult thing just because it is the specific intellectual activity of a particular category of specialists or of professional and systematic philosophers. It must first be shown that all men are 'philosophers', by defining the limits and characteristics of the 'spontaneous philosophy' which is proper to everybody. This philosophy is contained in: 1. language itself, which is a totality of determined notions and concepts and not just of words grammatically devoid of content; 2. 'common sense' and 'good sense'; 3. popular religion and, therefore, also in the entire system of beliefs, superstitions, opinions, ways of seeing things and of acting, which are collectively bundled together under the name of 'folklore'.

Having first shown that everyone is a philosopher, though in his own way and unconsciously, since even in the slightest manifestation of any intellectual activity whatever, in 'language', there is contained a specific conception of the world, one then moves on to the second level, which is that of awareness and criticism. That is to say, one proceeds to the question – is it better to 'think', without having a critical awareness, in a disjointed and episodic way? In other words, is it better to take part in a conception of the world mechanically imposed by the external environment, i.e. by one of the many social groups in which everyone is automatically involved from the moment of his entry into the conscious world (and this can be one's village or province; it can have its origins in the parish and the 'intellectual activity' of the local priest or aging patriarch whose wisdom is law, or in the little old woman who has inherited the lore of the witches or the minor intellectual soured by his own stupidity and inability to act)? Or, on the other hand, is it better to work out consciously and critically one's own conception of the world and thus, in connection with the labours of one's own brain, choose one's sphere of activity, take an active part in the creation of the history of the world, be one's own guide, refusing to accept passively and supinely from outside the moulding of one's personality?

Note I. In acquiring one's conception of the world one always belongs to a particular grouping which is that of all the social elements which share the same mode of thinking and acting. We are all conformists of some conformism or other, always man-in-the-mass or collective man. The question is this: of what historical type is the conformism, the mass humanity to which one belongs? When one's conception of the world is not critical and coherent but disjointed and episodic, one belongs simultaneously to a multiplicity of mass human groups. The personality is strangely composite: it contains Stone Age elements and principles of a more advanced science, prejudices from all past phases of history at the local level and intuitions of a future philosophy which will be that of a human race united the world over. To criticize one's own conception of the world means therefore to make it a coherent unity and to raise it to the level reached by the most advanced thought in the world. It therefore also means criticism of all previous philosophy, in so far as this has left stratified deposits in popular philosophy. The starting-point of critical elaboration is the consciousness of what one really is, and is 'knowing thyself' as a product of the historical process to date which has deposited in you an infinity of traces, without leaving an inventory.

Note II. Philosophy cannot be separated from the history of philosophy, nor can culture from the history of culture. In the most immediate and relevant sense, one cannot be a philosopher, by which I mean have a critical and coherent conception of the world, without having a consciousness of its historicity, of the phase of development which it represents and of the fact that it contradicts other conceptions or elements of other conceptions. One's conception of the world is a response to certain specific problems posed by reality, which are quite specific and 'original' in their immediate relevance. How is it possible to consider the present, and quite specific present, with a mode of thought elaborated for a past which is often remote and superseded? When someone does this, it means that he is a walking anachronism, a fossil, and not living in the modem world, or at the least that he is strangely composite. And it is in fact the case that social groups which in some ways express the most developed modernity, lag behind in other respects, given their social position, and are therefore incapable of complete historical autonomy.

Note III. If it is true that every language contains the elements of a conception of the world and of a culture, it could also be true that from anyone's language one can assess the greater or lesser complexity of his conception of the world. Someone who only speaks dialect, or understands the standard language incompletely, necessarily has an intuition of the world which is more or less limited and provincial, which is fossilized and anachronistic in relation to the major currents of thought which dominate world history. His interests will be limited, more or less corporate or econ-omistic, not universal. While it is not always possible to learn a number of foreign languages in order to put oneself in contact with other cultural lives, it is at the least necessary to learn the national language properly. A great culture can be translated into the language of another great culture, that is to say a great national language with historic richness and complex-ity, and it can translate any other great culture and can be a world-wide means of expression. But a dialect cannot do this.

Note IV. Creating a new culture does not only mean one's own individ-ual 'original' discoveries. It also, and most particularly, means the diffusion in a critical form of truths already discovered, their 'socialization' as it were, and even making them the basis of vital action, an element of co-ordination and intellectual and moral order. For a mass of people to be led to think coherently and in the same coherent fashion about the real present world, is a 'philosophical' event far more important and 'original' than the discovery by some philosophical 'genius' of a truth which remains the property of small groups of intellectuals.

Connection between 'Common Sense', Religion and Philosophy

Philosophy is intellectual order, which neither religion nor common sense can be. It is to be observed that religion and common sense do not coincide either, but that religion is an element of fragmented common sense. Moreover common sense is a collective noun, like religion: there is not just one common sense, for that too is a product of history and a part of the historical process. Philosophy is criticism and the superseding of reli-gion and 'common sense'. In this sense it coincides with 'good' as opposed to 'common' sense.

Relation between Science, Religion and Common Sense

Religion and common sense cannot constitute an intellectual order, because they cannot be reduced to unity and coherence even within an individual consciousness, let alone collective consciousness. Or rather they cannot be so reduced 'freely' – for this may be done by 'authoritarian' means, and indeed within limits this has been done in the past.

Note the problem of religion taken not in the confessional sense but in the secular sense of a unity of faith between a conception of the world and a corresponding norm of conduct. But why call this unity of faith 'religion' and not 'ideology', or even frankly 'politics'?

Philosophy in general does not in fact exist. Various philosophies or conceptions of the world exist, and one always makes a choice between them. How is this choice made? Is it merely an intellectual event, or is it something more complex? And is it not frequently the case that there is a contradiction between one's intellectual choice and one's mode of conduct? Which therefore would be the real conception of the world: that logically affirmed as an intellectual choice? or that which emerges from the real activity of each man, which is implicit in his mode of action? And since all action is political, can one not say that the real philosophy of each man is contained in its entirety in his political action?

This contrast between thought and action, i.e. the co-existence of two conceptions of the world, one affirmed in words and the other displayed in effective action, is not simply a product of self-deception [*malafede*]. Self-deception can be an adequate explanation for a few individuals taken separately, or even for groups of a certain size, but it is not adequate when the contrast occurs in the life of great masses. In these cases the contrast between thought and action cannot but be the expression of profounder contrasts of a social historical order. It signifies that the social group in question may indeed have its own conception of the world, even if only embryonic; a conception which manifests itself in action, but occasionally and in flashes – when, that is, the group is acting as an organic totality. But this same group has, for reasons of submission and intellectual subordination, adopted a conception which is not its own but is borrowed from another group; and it affirms this conception verbally and believes itself to be following it, because this is the conception which it follows in 'normal times' – that is when its conduct is not independent and autonomous, but submissive and subordinate. Hence the reason why philosophy cannot be divorced from politics. And one can show furthermore that the choice and the criticism of a conception of the world is also a political matter.

What must next be explained is how it happens that in all periods there co-exist many systems and currents of philosophical thought, how these currents are born, how they are diffused, and why in the process of diffusion they fracture along certain lines and in certain directions. The fact of this process goes to show how necessary it is to order in a systematic, coherent and critical fashion one's own intuitions of life and the world, and to determine exactly what is to be understood by the word 'systematic', so that it is not taken in the pedantic and academic sense. But this elaboration must be, and can only be, performed in the context of the history of philosophy, for it is this history which shows how thought has been elaborated over the centuries and what a collective effort has gone into the creation of our present method of thought which has subsumed and absorbed all this past history, including all its follies and mistakes. Nor should these mistakes themselves be neglected, for, although made in the past and since corrected, one cannot be sure that they will not be reproduced in the present and once again require correcting.

What is the popular image of philosophy? It can be reconstructed by looking at expressions in common usage. One of the most usual is 'being philosophical about it', which, if you consider it, is not to be entirely rejected as a phrase. It is true that it contains an implicit invitation to resignation and patience, but it seems to me that the most important point is rather the invitation to people to reflect and to realize fully that whatever happens is basically rational and must be confronted as such, and that one should apply one's power of rational concentration and not let oneself be carried away by instinctive and violent impulses. These popular turns of phrase could be compared with similar expressions used by writers of a popular stamp – examples being drawn from a large dictionary – which contain the terms 'philosophy' or 'philosophically'. One can see from these examples that the terms have a quite precise meaning: that of overcoming bestial and elemental passions through a conception of necessity which gives a conscious direction to one's activity. This is the healthy nucleus that exists in 'common sense', the part of it which can be called 'good sense' and which deserves to be made more unitary and coherent. So it appears that here again it is not possible to separate what is known as 'scientific' philosophy from the common and popular philosophy which is only a fragmentary collection of ideas and opinions.

But at this point we reach the fundamental problem facing any conception of the world, any philosophy which has become a cultural movement, a 'religion', a 'faith', any that has produced a form of practical activity or will in which the philosophy is contained as an implicit theoretical 'premise'. One might say 'ideology' here, but on condition that the word is used in its highest sense of a conception of the world that is implicitly manifest in art, in law, in economic activity and in all manifestations of individual and collective life. This problem is that of preserving the ideological unity of the entire social bloc which that ideology serves to cement and to unify. The strength of religions, and of the Catholic church in particular, has lain, and still lies, in the fact that they feel very strongly the need for the doctrinal unity of the whole mass of the faithful and strive to ensure that the higher intellectual stratum does not get separated from the lower.

The Roman church has always been the most vigorous in the struggle to prevent the 'official' formation of two religions, one for the 'intellectuals' and the other for the 'simple souls'. This struggle has not been without serious disadvantages for the Church itself, but these disadvantages are connected with the historical process which is transforming the whole of civil society and which contains overall a corrosive critique of all religion, and they only serve to emphasize the organizational capacity of the clergy in the cultural sphere and the abstractly rational and just relationship which the Church has been able to establish in its own sphere between the intellectuals and the simple. The Jesuits have undoubtedly been the major architects of this equilibrium, and in order to preserve it they have given the Church a progressive forward movement which has tended to allow the demands of science and philosophy to be to a certain extent satisfied. But the rhythm of the movement has been so slow and methodical that the changes have passed unobserved by the mass of the simple, although they appear 'revolutionary' and demagogic to the 'integralists'.

One of the greatest weaknesses of immanentist philosophies in general consists precisely in the fact that they have not been able to create an ideological unity between the bottom and the top, between the 'simple' and the intellectuals. In the history of Western civilization the fact is exemplified on a European scale, with the rapid collapse of the Renaissance and to a certain extent also the Reformation faced with the Roman church. Their weakness is demonstrated in the educational field, in that the immanentist philosophies have not even attempted to construct a conception which could take the place of religion in the education of children. Hence the pseudo-historicist sophism whereby non-religious, non-confessional, and in reality atheist, educationalists justify allowing the teaching of religion on the grounds that religion is the philosophy of the infancy of mankind renewed in every non-metaphorical infancy. Idealism has also shown itself opposed to cultural movements which 'go out to the people', as happened with the so-called 'Popular Universities' and similar institutions. Nor was the objection solely to the worst aspects of the institutions, because in that case they could simply have tried to improve them. And yet these movements were worthy of attention, and deserved study. They enjoyed a certain success, in the sense that they demonstrated on the part of the 'simple' a genuine enthusiasm and a strong determination to attain a higher cultural level and a higher conception of the world. What was lacking, however, was any organic quality either of philosophical thought or of organizational stability and central cultural direction. One got the impression that it was all rather like the first contacts of English merchants and the negroes of Africa:

trashy baubles were handed out in exchange for nuggets of gold. In any case one could only have had cultural stability and an organic quality of thought if there had existed the same unity between the intellectuals and the simple as there should be between theory and practice. That is, if the intellectuals had been organically the intellectuals of those masses, and if they had worked out and made coherent the principles and the problems raised by the masses in their practical activity, thus constituting a cultural and social bloc. The question posed here was the one we have already referred to, namely this: is a philosophical movement properly so called when it is devoted to creating a specialized culture among restricted intellectual groups, or rather when, and only when, in the process of elaborating a form of thought superior to 'common sense' and coherent on a scientific plane, it never forgets to remain in contact with the 'simple' and indeed finds in this contact the source of the problems it sets out to study and to resolve? Only by this contact does a philosophy become 'historical', purify itself of intellectualistic elements of an individual character and become 'life'.[1]

A philosophy of praxis cannot but present itself at the outset in a polemical and critical guise, as superseding the existing mode of thinking and existing concrete thought (the existing cultural world). First of all, therefore, it must be a criticism of 'common sense', basing itself initially, however, on common sense in order to demonstrate that 'everyone' is a philosopher and that it is not a question of introducing from scratch a scientific form of thought into everyone's individual life, but of renovating and making 'critical' an already existing activity. It must then be a criticism of the philosophy of the intellectuals out of which the history of philosophy developed and which, in so far as it is a phenomenon of individuals (in fact it develops essentially in the activity of single particularly gifted individuals) can be considered as marking the 'high points' of the progress made by common sense, or at least the common sense of the more educated strata of society but through them also of the people. Thus an introduction to the study of philosophy must expound in synthetic form the problems that have grown up in the process of the development of culture as a whole and which are only partially reflected in the history of philosophy. (Nevertheless it is the history of philosophy which, in the absence of a history of common sense, impossible to reconstruct for lack of documentary material, must remain the main source of reference.) The purpose of the synthesis must be to criticize the problems, to demonstrate their real value, if any, and the significance they have had as superseded links of an intellectual chain, and to determine what the new contemporary problems are and how the old problems should now be analysed.

The relation between common sense and the upper level of philosophy is assured by 'politics', just as it is politics that assures the relationship between the Catholicism of the intellectuals and that of the simple. There are, however, fundamental differences between the two cases. That the Church has to face up to a problem of the 'simple' means precisely that there has been a split in the community of the faithful. This split cannot be healed by raising the simple to the level of the intellectuals (the Church does not even envisage such a task, which is both ideologically and economically beyond its present capacities), but only by imposing an iron discipline on the intellectuals so that they do not exceed certain limits of differentiation and so render the split catastrophic and irreparable. In the past such divisions in the community of the faithful were healed by strong mass movements which led to, or were absorbed in, the creation of new religious orders centred on strong personalities (St Dominic, St Francis).[2]

But the Counter-Reformation has rendered sterile this upsurge of popular forces. The Society of Jesus is the last of the great religious orders. Its origins were reactionary and authoritarian, and its character repressive and 'diplomatic'. Its birth marked the hardening of the Catholic organism. New orders which have grown up since then have very little religious significance but a great 'disciplinary' significance for the mass of the faithful. They are, or have become, ramifications and tentacles of the Society of Jesus, instruments of 'resistance' to preserve political positions that have been gained, not forces of renovation and development. Catholicism has become 'Jesuitism'. Modernism has not created 'religious orders', but a political party – Christian Democracy.[3]

The position of the philosophy of praxis [i.e. Marxism] is the antithesis of the Catholic. The philosophy of praxis does not tend to leave the 'simple' in their primitive philosophy of common sense, but rather to lead them to a higher conception of life. If it affirms the need for contact between intellectuals and simple it is not in order to restrict scientific activity and preserve unity at the low level of the masses, but precisely in order to construct an intellectual-moral bloc which can make politically possible the intellectual progress of the mass and not only of small intellectual groups.

The active man-in-the-mass has a practical activity, but has no clear theoretical consciousness of his practical activity, which nonetheless involves understanding the world in so far as it transforms it. His theoretical consciousness can indeed be historically in opposition to his activity. One might almost say that he has two theoretical consciousnesses (or one contradictory consciousness): one which is implicit in his activity and which in reality unites him with all his fellow-workers in the practical transformation of the real world; and one, superficially explicit or verbal, which he has inherited from the past and uncritically absorbed. But this verbal conception is not without consequences. It holds together a specific social group, it influences moral conduct and the direction of will, with varying efficacity but often powerfully enough to produce a situation in which the contradictory state of consciousness does not permit of any action, any decision or any choice, and produces a condition of moral and political passivity. Critical understanding of self takes place therefore through a struggle of political 'hegemonies' and of opposing directions, first in the ethical field and then in that of politics proper, in order to arrive at the working out at a higher level of one's own conception of reality. Consciousness of being part of a particular hegemonic force (that is to say, political consciousness) is the first stage towards a further progressive self-consciousness in which theory and practice will finally be one. Thus the unity of theory and practice is not just a matter of mechanical fact, but a part of the historical process, whose elementary and primitive phase is to be found in the sense of being 'different' and 'apart', in an instinctive feeling of independence, and which progresses to the level of real possession of a single and coherent conception of the world. This is why it must be stressed that the political development of the concept of hegemony represents a great philosophical advance as well as a politico-practical one. For it necessarily supposes an intellectual unity and an ethic in conformity with a conception of reality that has gone beyond common sense and has become, if only within narrow limits, a critical conception.

Antonio Gramsci, *Selections from the Prison Notebooks*, Quintin Hoare and Geoffrey Nowell Smith (translators and eds.), New York: International Publishers, 1971, pp. 323–34.

WALTER BENJAMIN,
"THE AUTHOR AS PRODUCER"

In 1934, the brilliant and tragic critic Walter Benjamin asked a simple question: what is radical culture? In his essay "The Author as Producer,"[1] presented in its entirety below, he offers up a novel answer: it is not the content of the culture that makes it radical, instead it is the conditions of its production. In his day Benjamin observed that the most radical of content could be assimilated and thus neutralized if presented within the context of high art or commercial entertainment (cf. Cowley and Frank). This, however, does not mean that radical culture cannot exist. The problem, he insisted, was that the wrong question was being posed. Instead of asking what politics a piece of art is representing, we should be asking about the politics of how it is produced. Truly radical culture, Benjamin argued, was that which can "transcend the specialization in the process of production" of capitalism. In other words, radical culture erodes the line between artist and spectator, producer and consumer, challenging the hierarchical division of labor and encouraging everyone to create. With this, Benjamin changes the terms of debate regarding cultural resistance, shifting focus from product to production. Although, like Gramsci, Benjamin was to die young and tragically, committing suicide while fleeing the Nazis, he lives on as the patron saint of Do-it-Yourself culture.

> The task is to win over the intellectuals to the working class by making them aware of the identity of their spiritual enterprises and of their conditions as producers.
>
> Ramon Fernandez

You will remember how Plato, in his model state, deals with poets. He banishes them from it in the public interest. He had a high conception of the power of poetry. But he believed it harmful, superfluous — in a *perfect* community, of course. The question of the poet's right to exist has not often, since then, been posed with the same emphasis; but today it poses itself. Probably it is only seldom posed in this *form*. But it is more or less familiar to you all as the question of the autonomy of the poet: of his freedom to write whatever he pleases. You are not disposed to grant him this autonomy. You believe that the present social situation compels him to decide in whose service he is to place his activity. The bourgeois writer of entertainment literature does not acknowledge this choice. You prove to him that, without admitting it, he is working in the service of certain class interests. A more advanced type of writer does recognize this choice. His decision, taken on the basis of a class struggle, is to side with the proletariat. That puts an end to his autonomy. His activity is now decided by what is useful to the proletariat in the class struggle. Such writing is commonly called *tendentious*.

There you have the catchword around which has long circled a debate familiar to you. Its familiarity tells you how unfruitful it has been. For it has not advanced beyond the monotonous reiteration of arguments for and against: *on one hand*, the correct political line is demanded of the poet; *on the other*, it is justifiable to expect his work to have quality. Such a formulation is of course unsatisfactory as long as the connection between the two factors, political line and quality, has not been *perceived*. Of course, the connection can be asserted dogmatically. You can declare: a work that shows the correct political tendency need show no other quality. You can also declare: a work that exhibits the correct tendency must of necessity have every other quality.

This second formulation is not uninteresting, and further: it is correct. I make it my own. But in doing so I abstain from asserting it dogmatically. It must be *proved*. And it is in order to attempt to prove it that I now claim your attention. – This is, you will perhaps object, a very specialized, out-of-the-way theme. And how do I intend to promote the study of fascism with such a proof? – That is indeed my intention. For I hope to be able to show you that the concept of political tendency, in the summary form in which it usually occurs in the debate just mentioned, is a perfectly useless instrument of political literary criticism. I should like to show you that the tendency of a literary work can only be politically correct if it is also literarily correct. That is to say that the politically correct tendency includes a literary tendency. And I would add straight away: this literary tendency, which is implicitly or explicitly contained in every *correct* political tendency, alone constitutes the quality of the work. The correct political tendency of a work includes its literary quality *because* it includes its literary *tendency*.

This assertion – I hope I can promise you – will soon become clearer. For the moment, I should like to interject that I might have chosen a different starting point for my reflections. I started from the unfruitful debate on the relationship between tendency and quality in literature. I could have started from an even older and no less unfruitful debate: what is the relationship between form and content, particularly in political poetry? This kind of question has a bad name: rightly so. It is the textbook case of the attempt to explain literary connections with undialectical clichés. Very well. But what, then, is the dialectical approach to the same question?

The dialectical approach to this question – and here I come to my central point – has absolutely no use for such rigid, isolated things as: work, novel, book. It has to insert them into the living social context. You rightly declare that this has been done time and again among our friends. Certainly. Only it has often been done by launching at once into large, and therefore necessarily often vague, questions. Social conditions are, as we know, determined by conditions of production. And when materialist criticism approached a work, it was accustomed to ask how this work stood in relation to the social relations of production of its time. This is an important question. But also a very difficult one. Its answer is not always unambiguous.

And I should like now to propose to you a more immediate question. A question that is somewhat more modest, somewhat less far-reaching, but which has, it seems to me, more chance of receiving an answer. Instead of asking: what is the attitude of a work to the relations of production of its time? Does it accept them? Is it reactionary – or does it aim at overthrowing them? Is it revolutionary? Instead of this question, or at any rate before this question, I should like to propose another. Rather than asking: what is the *attitude* of a work to the relations of production of its time? I should like to ask: what is its *position* in them? This question directly concerns the function the work has within the literary relations of production of its time. It is concerned, in other words, directly with the literary *technique* of works.

In the concept of technique, I have named that concept which makes literary products directly accessible to a social and therefore a materialist analysis. At the same time, the concept of technique provides the dialectical starting point from which the unfruitful antithesis of form and content can be surpassed. And furthermore, this concept of technique contains an indication of the correct determination of the relation between tendency and quality, the question raised at the outset. If, therefore, we stated earlier that the correct political tendency of a work includes its literary quality, because it includes its literary tendency, we can now formulate this more precisely by saying that this literary tendency can consist either of progress or of regression in literary technique.

You will certainly approve if I now pass on, with only an appearance of arbitrariness, to very concrete literary conditions. Russian conditions. I should like to direct your attention to Sergei Tretiakov and to the type, defined and embodied by him, of the "operating" writer. This operating writer provides the most tangible example of the functional interdependency which always and under all conditions exists between the correct political tendency and progressive literary technique. I admit only one example: I hold others in reserve. Tretiakov distinguishes the operating from the informing writer. His mission is not to report but to struggle; not to play the spectator but to intervene actively. He defines this mission by the account he gives of his own activity. When, in 1928, at the time of the total collectivization of agriculture, the slogan "Writers to the kolkhoz!" was proclaimed, Tretiakov went to the commune "Communist Lighthouse" and there, during two lengthy stays, set about the following tasks: calling mass meetings; collecting funds to pay for tractors; persuading independent peasants to enter the *kolkhoz* [collective farm]; inspecting the reading rooms; creating wall newspapers and editing the *kolkhoz* newspaper; reporting for Moscow newspapers; introducing radio and mobile cinemas, etc. It is not surprising that the book *Commanders of the Field*, which Tretiakov wrote following these stays, is said to have had considerable influence on the further development of collective agriculture.

You may have a high regard for Tretiakov, and yet still be of the opinion that his example does not prove a great deal in this context. The tasks he performed, you will perhaps object, are those of a journalist or a propagandist; all this has little to do with literature. However, I did intentionally quote the example of Tretiakov in order to point out to you how comprehensive is the horizon within which we have to rethink our conceptions of literary forms or *genres* in view of the technical factors affecting our present situation, if we are to identify the forms of expression that channel the literary energies of the present. There were not always novels in the past, and there will not always have to be; not always tragedies, not always great epics; not always were the forms of commentary, translation, indeed, even so-called plagiarism, playthings in the margins of literature; they had a place not only in the philosophical but also in the literary writings of Arabia and China. Rhetoric has not always been a minor form, but set its stamp in antiquity on large provinces of literature. All this is to accustom you to the thought that we are in the midst of a mighty recasting of literary forms, a melting-down in which many of the opposites in which we have been accustomed to think may lose their force. Let me give an example of the unfruitfulness of such opposites and of the process of their dialectical transcendence. And we shall remain with Tretiakov. For this example is the newspaper. "In our writing," a left-wing author writes,[2]

opposites which in happier periods fertilized one another, have become insoluble antinomies. Thus science and *belles lettres*, criticism and production, education and politics, fall apart in disorder. The theatre of this literary confusion is the newspaper, its content 'subject matter,' which denies itself any other form of organization than that imposed on it by the readers' impatience. And this impatience is not only that of the politician expecting information or of the speculator on the lookout for a tip; behind it smoulders that of the man on the sidelines who believes he has the right to see his own interests expressed. The fact that nothing binds the reader more tightly to his paper than this impatient longing for daily nourishment, the publishers have long exploited by constantly opening new columns to his questions, opinions, protests. Hand in hand, therefore, with the indiscriminate assimilation of facts goes the equally indiscriminate assimilation of readers who are instantly elevated to collaborators. In this, however, a dialectic moment is concealed: the decline of writing in the bourgeois press proves to be the formula for its revival in that of Soviet Russia. For as writing gains in breadth what it loses in depth, the conventional distinction

between author and public, which is upheld by the bourgeois press, begins in
the Soviet press to disappear. For the reader is at all times ready to become a
writer, that is, a describer, but also a prescriber. As an expert – even if not on a
subject but only on the post he occupies – he gains access to authorship. Work
itself has its turn to speak. And the account it gives of itself is a part of the competence needed to perform it. Literary qualification is no longer founded on
specialized but rather on polytechnic education, and is thus public property. It
is, in a word, the literarization of the conditions of living that masters the otherwise insoluble antinomies, and it is in the theatre of the unbridled debasement
of the word – the newspaper – that its salvation is being prepared."

I hope to have shown by this quotation that the description of the
author as a producer must extend as far as the press. For by the press, at any
rate by the Soviet Russian press, one recognizes that the mighty process of
recasting which I spoke of earlier not only affects the conventional distinction between *genres*, between writer and poet, between scholar and
popularizer, but also revises even the distinction between author and
reader. Of this process the press is the decisive example, and therefore any
consideration of the author as producer must include it.

It cannot, however, stop at this point. For the newspaper in Western
Europe does not constitute a serviceable instrument of production in the
hands of the writer. It still belongs to capital. Since on one hand the newspaper, technically speaking, represents the most important literary position,
but on the other, this position is in the hands of the opposition, it is no
wonder that the insight of the writer into his social conditionality, his technical means and his political task, has to grapple with the most immense
difficulties. It has been one of the decisive processes of the last ten years in
Germany that a considerable proportion of its productive minds, under the
pressure of economic conditions, have passed through a revolutionary
development in their attitudes, without being able simultaneously to
rethink their own work, their relation to the means of production, their
technique, in a really revolutionary way. I am speaking, as you see, of the so-
called left-wing intellectuals, and will limit myself to the bourgeois Left. In
Germany, the leading politico-literary movements of the last decade have
emanated from this left-wing intelligentsia. I shall mention two of them,
Activism and New Matter-of-Factness, to show by these examples that a
political tendency, however revolutionary it may seem, has a counterrevolutionary function as long as the writer feels his solidarity with the
proletariat only in his attitudes, but not as a producer.

The catchword in which the demands of Activism are summed up is
"logocracy," in plain language, rule of the mind. This is apt to be translated

as rule of the intellectuals. In fact, the concept of the intellectual, with its attendant spiritual values, has established itself in the camp of the left-wing intelligentsia, and dominates its political manifestos from Heinrich Mann to Döblin. It can readily be seen that this concept has been coined without any regard for the position of the intellectuals in the process of production. Hiller, the theoretician of Activism, himself means intellectuals to be understood not as "members of certain professions" but as "representatives of a certain characterological type." This characterological type naturally stands as such between the classes. It encompasses any number of private individuals without offering the slightest basis for organizing them. When Hiller formulates his denunciation of the party leaders, he concedes them a good deal; they may be "in important matters better informed . . . have more popular appeal . . . fight more courageously" than he, but of one thing he is sure: that they "think more defectively." Probably so, but what does that matter, since politically it is not private thinking but, as Brecht once expressed it, the art of thinking in other people's heads, that is decisive. Activism attempted to replace materialistic dialectics by the notion – in class terms unquantifiable – of common sense.[3] Its intellectuals represent at best a social group. In other words: the principle itself on which this collective is formed is reactionary; no wonder that its effect could never be revolutionary.

However, this pernicious principle of collectivization continues to operate. This could be seen three years ago when Döblin's *Wissen und Verändern [Know and Change]* came out. As is known, this pamphlet was written in reply to a young man – Döblin calls him Herr Hocke – who had put to the famous author the question "What is to be done?" Döblin invites him to join the cause of socialism, but with reservations. Socialism, according to Döblin is: "freedom, a spontaneous union of men, the rejection of all compulsion, indignation at injustice and coercion, humanity, tolerance, a peaceful disposition." However this may be, on the basis of this socialism, he sets his face against the theory and practice of the radical workers' movement. "Nothing," Döblin declares, "can come out of anything that was not already in it – and from a murderously exacerbated class war justice can come, but not socialism." "You, my dear sir," thus Döblin formulates the recommendation which, for these and other reasons, he gives Herr Hocke, "cannot put into effect your agreement in principle with the struggle (of the proletariat) by joining the proletarian front. You must be content with an agitated and bitter approval of this struggle, but you also know that if you do more, an immensely important post will remain unmanned . . . the original communistic position of human individual freedom, of the spontaneous solidarity and union of men . . . It is this position, my dear sir, that alone falls to you." Here it is quite palpable where the conception of the "intellectual," as a type defined by his opinions, attitudes or dispositions, but not by his position in the process of production, leads. He must, as Döblin puts it, find his place *beside* the proletariat. But what kind of place is that? That of a benefactor, of an ideological patron. An impossible place. And so we return to the thesis stated at the outset: the place of the intellectual in the class struggle can be identified, or better, chosen, only on the basis of his position in the process of production.

For the transformation of the forms and instruments of production in the way desired by a progressive intelligentsia – that is, one interested in freeing the means of production and serving the class struggle – Brecht coined the term *Umfunktionierung* [functional transformation]. He was the first to make of intellectuals the far-reaching demand: not to supply the apparatus of production without, to the utmost extent possible, changing it in accordance with socialism. "The publication of the *Versuche*," the author writes in introducing the series of writings bearing this title, "occurred at a time when certain works ought no longer to be individual experiences (have the character of works), but should rather concern the use (transformation) of certain institutes and institutions." It is not spiritual renewal, as fascists proclaim, that is desirable: technical innovations are suggested. I shall come back to these innovations. I should like to content myself here with a reference to the decisive difference between the mere supplying of a productive apparatus and its transformation. And I should like to preface my discussion of the "New Matter-of-Factness" with the proposition that to supply a productive apparatus without – to the utmost extent possible – changing it would still be a highly censurable course even if the material with which it is supplied seemed to be of a revolutionary nature. For we are faced by the fact – of which the past decade in Germany has furnished an abundance of examples – that the bourgeois apparatus of production and publication can assimilate astonishing quantities of revolutionary themes, indeed, can propagate them without calling its own existence, and the existence of the class which owns it, seriously into question. This remains true at least as long as it is supplied by hack writers, even though they be revolutionary hacks. I define the hack writer as the man who abstains in principle from alienating the productive apparatus from the ruling class by improving it in ways serving the interests of socialism. And I further maintain that a considerable proportion of so-called left-wing literature possessed no other social function than to wring from the political situation a continuous stream of novel effects for the entertainment of the public. This brings me to the New Matter-of-Factness. Its stock-in-trade was reportage. Let us ask ourselves to whom this technique was useful.

For the sake of clarity I shall place its photographic form in the foreground. What is true of this can be applied to the literary form. Both owe the extraordinary increase in their popularity to the technology of publication: the radio and the illustrated press. Let us think back to Dadaism. The revolutionary strength of Dadaism consisted in testing art for its authenticity. Still lifes put together from tickets, spools of thread, cigarette butts, were linked with artistic elements. They put the whole thing in a frame. And they thereby show the public: look, your picture frame ruptures the age; the tiniest authentic fragment of daily life says more than paintings. Just as the bloody finger print of a murderer on a page of a book says more than the text. Much of this revolutionary content has sought survival in photomontage. You need only think of the work of John Heartfield, whose technique made the book cover into a political instrument. But now follow the path of photography further. What do you see? It becomes ever more *nuancé*, ever more modern, and the result is that it can no longer photograph a tenement block or a refuse heap without transfiguring it. It goes without saying that it is unable to say anything of a power station or a cable factory other than this: what a beautiful world! "A Beautiful World" that is a title of the well-known picture anthology by Renger-Patsch, in which we see New Matter-of-Fact photography at its peak. For it has succeeded in making even abject poverty, by recording it in a fashionably perfected manner, into an object of enjoyment. For if it is an economic function of photography to restore to mass consumption, by fashionable adaptation, subjects that had earlier withdrawn themselves from it – springtime, famous people, foreign countries – it is one of its political functions to renew from within – in other words: fashionably – the world as it is.

Here we have a flagrant example of what it means to supply a productive apparatus without changing it. To change it would have meant to overthrow another of the barriers, to transcend another of the antitheses, which fetter the production of intellectuals. In this case, the barrier between writing and image. What we require of the photographer is the ability to give his picture that caption which wrenches it from modish commerce and gives it revolutionary use-value. But we shall make this demand most emphatically when we – the writers – take up photography. Here, too, therefore, technical progress is for the author as producer the foundation of his political progress. In other words: only by transcending the specialization in the process of production which, in the bourgeois view, constitutes its order, is this production made politically valuable; and the limits imposed by specialization must be breached jointly by both the productive forces that they were set up to divide. The author as producer discovers – in discovering his solidarity with the proletariat – that simultaneity with certain other producers who earlier seemed scarcely to concern him. I have spoken of the photographer; I shall very briefly insert a word on the musician that we have from Eisler:

> In the development of music, too, both in production and in reproduction, we must learn to perceive an ever-increasing process of rationalization . . . The gramophone record, the sound film, jukeboxes can purvey top quality music . . . canned as a commodity. The consequence of this process of rationalization is that musical reproduction is consigned to ever diminishing, but also ever more highly qualified, groups of specialists. The crisis of the commercial concert is the crisis of an antiquated form of production made obsolete by new technical inventions.

The task therefore consisted of an *Umfunktionierung* of the form of the concert that had to fulfill two conditions: to eliminate the antithesis first between performers and listeners and second between technique and content. On this Eisler makes the following illuminating observation: "One must beware of overestimating orchestral music and considering it the only high art. Music without words gained its great importance and its full extent only under capitalism." This means that the task of changing the concert is impossible without the collaboration of the word. It alone can effect the transformation, as Eisler formulates it, of a concert into a political meeting. But that such a transformation does indeed represent a peak of musical and literary technique, Brecht and Eisler prove with the didactic play *The Measures Taken*.

If you look back from this vantage point on the recasting of literary forms that I spoke of earlier, you can see how photography and music, and whatever else occurs to you, are entering the growing molten mass from which the new forms are cast. You find it confirmed that only the literarization of all the conditions of life provides a correct understanding of the extent of this melting-down process, just as the state of the class struggle determines the temperature at which – more or less perfectly – it is accomplished.

I spoke of the procedure of a certain modish photography whereby poverty is made an object of consumption. In turning to New Matter-of-Factness as a literary movement, I must take a step further and say that it has made the *struggle against poverty* an object of consumption. The political importance of the movement was indeed exhausted in many cases by the conversion of revolutionary reflexes, insofar as they occurred in the bourgeoisie, into objects of amusement which found their way without difficulty into the big-city cabaret business. The transformation of the political struggle from a compulsion to decide into an object of contemplative enjoyment, from a means of production into a consumer article, is the defining characteristic of this literature. A perceptive critic has explained this, using the example of Erich Kästner, as follows:

> With the workers' movement this left-wing radical intelligentsia has nothing in common. It is rather, as a phenomenon of bourgeois decomposition, a counterpart of the feudalistic disguise which the Second Empire admired in the reserve officer. The radical-left publicists of the stamp of Kästner, Mehring or Tucholsky are the proletarian camouflage of decayed bourgeois strata. Their function is to produce, from the political standpoint, not parties but cliques; from the literary standpoint, not schools but fashions; from the economic standpoint, not producers but agents. Agents or hacks who make a great display of their poverty, and a banquet of yawning emptiness. One could not be more totally accommodated in an uncozy situation.

This school, I said, made a great display of its poverty. It thereby shirked the most urgent task of the present-day writer: to recognize how poor he is and how poor he has to be in order to begin again from the beginning. For that is what is involved. The Soviet state will not, it is true, banish the poet like Plato, but it will – and this is why I recalled the Platonic state at the outset – assign him tasks which do not permit him to display in new masterpieces the long-since counterfeit wealth of creative personality. To expect a renewal in terms of such personalities and such works is a privilege of fascism, which gives rise to such scatterbrained formulations as that with which Günter Gründel in his *Mission of the Young Generation* rounds off the section on literature: "We cannot better conclude this . . . survey and prognosis than with the observation that the *Wilhelm Meister* and the *Green Henry* of our generation have not yet been written." Nothing will be farther from the author who has reflected deeply on the conditions of present-day production than to expect, or desire, such works. His work will never be merely work on products but always, at the same time, on the means of production. In other words: his products must have, over and above their character as works, an organizing function, and in no way must their organizational usefulness be confined to their value as propaganda. Their political tendency alone is not enough. The excellent Lichtenberg has said: "A man's opinions are not what matters, but the kind of man these opinions make of him." Now it is true that opinions matter greatly, but the best are of no use if they make nothing useful out of those who have them. The best political tendency is wrong if it does not demonstrate the attitude with which it is to be followed. And this attitude the writer can only demonstrate in his particular activity: that is in writing. A political tendency is the necessary, never the sufficient condition of the organizing function of a work. This further requires a directing, instructing stance on the part of the writer. And today this is to be demanded more than ever before. *An author who teaches writers nothing, teaches no one.* What matters therefore is the exemplary character of production, which is able first to induce other producers to produce, and second to put an improved apparatus at their disposal. And this apparatus is better the more consumers it is able to turn into producers, that is, readers or spectators into collaborators. We already possess such an example, to which, however, I can only allude here. It is the epic theater of Brecht.

Tragedies and operas are constantly being written that apparently have a well-tried theatrical apparatus at their disposal, while in reality they do nothing but supply one that is derelict. "The lack of clarity about their situation that prevails among musicians, writers and critics," says Brecht, "has immense consequences that are far too little considered. For, thinking that they are in possession of an apparatus which in reality possesses them, they defend an apparatus over which they no longer have any control and which is no longer, as they still believe, a means for the producers, but has become a means against the producers." This theater, with its complicated machinery, its gigantic supporting staff, its sophisticated effects, has become a means against the producers not least in seeking to enlist the producers in the hopeless competitive struggle in which film and radio have enmeshed it. This theater – whether in its educating or its entertaining role; both are complementary – is that of a sated class for which everything it touches becomes a stimulant. Its position is lost. Not so that of a theater which, instead of competing with newer instruments of publication, seeks to use and learn from them, in short, to enter into debate with them. This debate the epic theater has made its own affair. It is, measured by the present state of development of film and radio, the contemporary form.

For the sake of this debate Brecht fell back on the most primitive elements of the theater. He contented himself, broadly, with a podium. He dispensed with wide-ranging plots. He thus succeeded in changing the functional connection between stage and public, text and performance, director and actor. Epic theater, he declared, had to portray situations rather than to develop plots. It obtains such situations, as we shall see presently, by interrupting the plot. I remind you here of the songs, which have their chief function in interrupting the action. Here – in the principle of interruption – epic theater, as you see, takes up a procedure that has become familiar to you in recent years from film and radio, press and photography. I am speaking of the procedure of montage: the superimposed element disrupts the context in which it is inserted. But that this procedure has here a special, perhaps indeed a perfect right, allow me briefly to indicate. The interruption of action, on account of which Brecht described his theater as *epic*, constantly counteracts an illusion in the audience. For such illusion is a hindrance to a theater that proposes to make use of elements of reality in experimental rearrangements. But it is at the end, not the beginning, of the experiment that the situation appears. A situation which, in this or that form, is always ours. It is not brought home to the spectator but distanced from him. He recognizes it as the real situation, not with satisfaction, as in the theater of naturalism, but with astonishment. Epic theater, therefore, does not reproduce situations, rather it discovers them. This discovery is accomplished by means of the interruption of sequences. Only interruption does not have here the character of a stimulant but of an organizing function. It arrests the action in its course, and thereby compels the listener to adopt an attitude vis-à-vis the process, the actor vis-à-vis his role. I should like to show you by an example how Brecht's discovery and use of the *gestus* is nothing other than the restoration of the method of montage decisive in radio and film, from an often merely modish procedure to a human event. Imagine a family scene: the wife is just about to grab a bronze sculpture to throw it at her daughter; the father is opening the window to call for help. At this moment a stranger enters. The process is interrupted; what appears in its place is the situation on which the stranger's eyes now fall: agitated faces, open window, disordered furniture. There are eyes, however, before which the more usual scenes of present-day existence do not look very different. The eyes of the epic dramatist.

To the dramatic total art work he opposes the dramatic laboratory. He makes use in a new way of the great ancient opportunity of the theater – to expose what is present. At the center of his experiment is man. Present-day man; a reduced man, therefore, chilled in a chilly environment. Since, however, this is the only one we have, it is in our interest to know him. He is subjected to tests, examinations. What emerges is this: events are alterable not at their climaxes, not by virtue and resolution, but only in their strictly habitual course, by reason and practice. To construct from the smallest elements of behavior what in Aristotelian dramaturgy is called "action," is the purpose of epic theater. Its means are therefore more modest than those of traditional theater; its aims likewise. It is less concerned with filling the public with feelings, even seditious ones, than with alienating it in an enduring manner, through thinking, from the conditions in which it lives. It may be noted by the way that there is no better start for thinking than laughter. And, in particular, convulsion of the diaphragm usually provides better opportunities for thought than that of the soul. Epic theater is lavish only in occasions for laughter.

It has perhaps struck you that the train of thought that is about to be concluded presents to the writer only one demand, the demand *to think*, to reflect on his position in the process of production. We may depend on it: this reflection leads, sooner or later, for the writers *who matter*, that is, for the best technicians in their subject, to observations which provide the most factual foundation for their solidarity with the proletariat. I should like to conclude by adducing a topical illustration in the form of a small extract from a journal published here, *Commune*. *Commune* circulated a questionnaire: "For whom do you write?" I quote from the reply of René Maublanc and from the comment added by Aragon. "Unquestionably," says Maublanc,

> I write almost exclusively for a bourgeois public. First, because I am obliged to [here Maublanc refers to his professional duties as a grammar school teacher] and second, because I have bourgeois origins and a bourgeois education and come from a bourgeois *milieu*, and so am naturally inclined to address myself to the class to which I belong, that I know and understand best. This does not mean, however, that I write in order to please or support it. On one hand I am convinced that the proletarian revolution is necessary and desirable, on the other that it will be the more rapid, easy, successful, and the less bloody, the weaker the opposition of the bourgeoisie . . . the proletariat today needs allies from the camp of the bourgeoisie, exactly as in the eighteenth century the bourgeoisie needed allies from the feudal camp. I wish to be among those allies.

On this Aragon comments:

> Our comrade here touches on a state of affairs that affects a large number of present-day writers. Not all have the courage to look it in the face . . . those who see their own situation as clearly as René Maublanc are few. But precisely from them more must be required . . . it is not enough to weaken the bourgeoisie from within, it is necessary to fight them *with* the proletariat . . . René Maublanc and many of our friends among the writers who are still hesitating are faced by the example of the Soviet Russian writers who came from the Russian bourgeoisie and nevertheless became pioneers of the building of socialism.

Thus Aragon. But how did they become pioneers? Certainly not without very bitter struggles, extremely difficult debates. The considerations I have put before you are an attempt to draw some conclusions from these struggles. They are based on the concept to which the debate on the attitude of the Russian intellectuals owes its decisive clarification: the concept of the specialist. The solidarity of the specialist with the proletariat – herein lies the beginning of this clarification – can only be a mediated one. The Activists and the representatives of New Matter-of-Factness could gesticulate as they pleased: they could not do away with the fact that even the proletarianization of an intellectual hardly ever makes a proletarian. Why? Because the bourgeois class gave him, in the form of education, a means of production which, owing to educational privilege, makes him feel solidarity with it, and still more it with him. It was thereby entirely correct when Aragon, in another connection, declared: "The revolutionary intellectual appears first and foremost as the betrayer of his class of origin." This betrayal consists, in the case of the writer, in conduct which turns him, from a supplier of the productive apparatus, into an engineer who sees it as his task to adapt this apparatus to the purposes of the proletarian revolution. This is a mediating activity, yet it frees the intellectual from that purely destructive task to which Maublanc and many of his comrades believe it necessary to confine him. Does he succeed in promoting the socialization of the intellectual means of production? Does he see ways of himself organizing the intellectual workers in the production process? Has he proposals for the *Umfunktionierung* of the novel, the drama, the poem? The more completely he can orient his activity towards this task, the more correct will be the political tendency, and necessarily also the higher the technical quality, of his work. And on the other hand: the more exactly he is thus informed on his position in the process of production, the less it will occur to him to lay claim to "spiritual" qualities. The spirit that holds forth in the name of fascism *must* disappear. The spirit which, in opposing it, trusts in its own miraculous powers, *will* disappear. For the revolutionary struggle is not between capitalism and spirit but between capitalism and the proletariat.

Walter Benjamin, "The Author as Producer," *Reflections*, Peter Demetz (ed.), New York: Schocken Books, 1986, pp. 220–38.

THREE

A POLITICS THAT DOESN'T LOOK LIKE POLITICS

Is laughter revolutionary? Does throwing a party constitute a political act? Can doing nothing be considered doing something? According to a respected source like the *Oxford English Dictionary*, the answer is clear: no. Politics, the OED defines, is a matter of states and governments, organization and administration.[1] This is a valid, but also very limited, definition. Defined this way "politics" leaves out most people and most of life, yet these populations and their activities are exactly what compose states and legitimize governments, and makes organization and administration either possible or impossible. Thus our definition of politics needs to be expanded. Countless times throughout the day each of us thinks and acts through a culture which reflects and reinforces a dominant way of seeing and being in the world, or we think and act in ways which challenge and undermine this culture (or, as Gramsci might argue, we often do both). While these everyday events frequently take place in the margins of what is commonly understood as politics, these cultural practices are, indeed, political. What follows is a group of essays which explore, champion and call into question this politics that doesn't look like politics.

MIKHAIL BAKHTIN,
FROM *RABELAIS AND HIS WORLD*

François Rabelais, the great French humorist of the sixteenth century, was a comic of the belly and the fart, the grotesque and the scatological. In his book Gargantua (c. 1534) he devotes a chapter to evaluating ways to wipe one's ass ("a good downy gosling" wins the prize). To understand Rabelais, argues the Russian literary critic Mikhail Bakhtin, you must understand the folk humor and frequent festivals of his time. Central to Bakhtin's analysis is the carnival. Far from the commercial entertainment that it has become in our time, the carnival of the Middle Ages and Renaissance was a popular production of subversion. In the carnival the fool was made king and the king a fool, the sacred ceremonies and rigid strictures of Church and State were defiled and ridiculed (see sidebar). It was, in Bakhtin's words, a "world inside out." Not merely just imagined, but bodily experienced, this "second world" of flattened hierarchies, utopian plenty and bodily pleasure provided a stage for the population to act out a play of resistance – a drama performed in flesh and steel in France and across Europe in the great revolutions of centuries to come. By resurrecting Rabelais, Bakhtin implies that he has something to say to our age as well. His championing of the laughter of the common people and the subversive qualities that lie therein is perhaps as much a critical commentary on the "people's state" of the Soviet Union in which Bakhtin lived and wrote, as it is on Europe of years past. In even more recent times, Bakhtin's celebration of the carnival has inspired direct action groups like Reclaim the Streets (cf. Jordan), and encouraged scholars to look for politics in places, among people, and in activities that at first glance might not seem so political.

Laughter and its forms represent . . . the least scrutinized sphere of the people's creation. The narrow concept of popular character and of folklore was born in the pre-Romantic period and was basically completed by von Herder and the Romantics. There was no room in this concept for the peculiar culture of the marketplace and of folk laughter with all its wealth of manifestations. Nor did the generations that succeeded each other in that marketplace become the object of historic, literary, or folkloristic scrutiny as the study of early cultures continued. The element of laughter was accorded the least place of all in the vast literature devoted to myth, to folk lyrics, and to epics. Even more unfortunate was the fact that the peculiar nature of the people's laughter was completely distorted; entirely alien notions and concepts of humor, formed within the framework of bourgeois modern culture and aesthetics, were applied to this interpretation. We may therefore say without exaggeration that the profound originality expressed by the culture of folk humor in the past has remained unexplored until now.

And yet, the scope and the importance of this culture were immense in the Renaissance and the Middle Ages. A boundless world of humorous forms and manifestations opposed the official and serious tone of medieval ecclesiastical and feudal culture. In spite of their variety, folk festivities of the carnival type, the comic rites and cults, the clowns and fools, giants, dwarfs, and jugglers, the vast and manifold literature of parody – all these

"Kings are nothing but dumb calves . . .," François Rabelais

I want to tell you how Panurge treated his prisoner [the king] Anarche . . . [O]ne day he dressed up his said king in a fine little linen doublet, all slashed like an Albian's cap, and nice sailor's breeches, without shoes (for, he said, they would spoil his vision), and a little blue cap with one big capon's feather – I'm wrong, I think he had two – and a handsome blue and green belt, saying that this livery served him well, seeing that he had been perverse [a pun on the French words for blue and green]. In this state he brought him before Pantagruel and said to him:

"Do you recognize this clown?"

"No, indeed," said Pantagruel.

"It's Milord the pluperfect king; I want to make a good man of him. These devils the kings are nothing but dumb calves; they know nothing and they're good for nothing, except to do harm to their poor subjects, and trouble the whole world by making war, for their wicked and detestable pleasure. I want to set him to a trade, and make him a hawker of green sauce [made of onions]. So now start shouting: 'Don't you need some green sauce?'"

And the poor devil shouted.

"That's too soft," said Panurge; and he took him by the ear and said: "Sing louder, in the key of G. So, you poor devil! You have a strong throat, you've never been so lucky as not to be king any more."

from "Pantagruel," c. 1532, *The Complete Works of François Rabelais*, Donald M. Frame (trans.), Berkeley: University of California Press, 1991, Chapter 31, p. 237 (paras 3–6)

forms have one style in common: they belong to one culture of folk carnival humor.

. . .

Carnival festivities and the comic spectacles and ritual connected with them had an important place in the life of medieval man. Besides carnivals proper, with their long, and complex pageants and processions, there was the "feast of fools" (*festa stultorum*) and the "feast of the ass"; there was a special free "Easter laughter" (*risus paschalis*) consecrated by tradition. Moreover, nearly every Church feast had its comic folk aspect, which was also traditionally recognized. Such, for instance, were the parish feasts, usually marked by fairs and varied open-air amusements, with the participation of giants, dwarfs, monsters, and trained animals. A carnival atmosphere reigned on days when mysteries and *soties* were produced. This atmosphere also pervaded such agricultural feasts as the harvesting of grapes (*vendange*) which was celebrated also in the city. Civil and social ceremonies and rituals took on a comic aspect as clowns and fools, constant participants in these festivals, mimicked serious rituals such as the tribute rendered to the victors at tournaments, the transfer of feudal rights, or the initiation of a knight. Minor occasions were also marked by comic protocol, as for instance the election of a king and queen to preside at a banquet "for laughter's sake" (*roi pour rire*).

All these forms of protocol and ritual based on laughter and consecrated by tradition existed in all the countries of medieval Europe; they were sharply distinct from the serious official, ecclesiastical, feudal, and political cult forms and ceremonials. They offered a completely different, nonofficial, extraecclesiastical and extrapolitical aspect of the world, of man, and of human relations; they built a second world and a second life outside officialdom, a world in which all medieval people participated more or less, in which they lived during a given time of the year. If we fail to take into consideration this two-world condition, neither medieval cultural consciousness nor the culture of the

Renaissance can be understood. To ignore or to underestimate the laughing people of the Middle Ages also distorts the picture of European culture's historic development.

This double aspect of the world and of human life existed even at the earliest stages of cultural development. In the folklore of primitive peoples, coupled with the cults which were serious in tone and organization were other, comic cults which laughed and scoffed at the deity ("ritual laughter"); coupled with serious myths were comic and abusive ones; coupled with heroes were their parodies and doublets. These comic rituals and myths have attracted the attention of folklorists.[1]

But at the early stages of preclass and prepolitical social order it seems that the serious and the comic aspects of the world and of the deity were equally sacred, equally "official." This similarity was preserved in rituals of a later period of history. For instance, in the early period of the Roman state the ceremonial of the triumphal procession included on almost equal terms the glorifying and the deriding of the victor. The funeral ritual was also composed of lamenting (glorifying) and deriding the deceased. But in the definitely consolidated state and class structure such an equality of the two aspects became impossible. All the comic forms were transferred, some earlier and others later, to a nonofficial level. There they acquired a new meaning, were deepened and rendered more complex, until they became the expression of folk consciousness, of folk culture. Such were the carnival festivities of the ancient world, especially the Roman Saturnalias, and such were medieval carnivals. They were, of course, far removed from the primitive community's ritual laughter.

What are the peculiar traits of the comic rituals and spectacles of the Middle Ages? Of course, these are not religious rituals like, for instance, the Christian liturgy to which they are linked by distant genetic ties. The basis of laughter which gives form to carnival rituals frees them completely from all religious and ecclesiastic dogmatism, from all mysticism and piety. They are also completely deprived of the character of magic and prayer; they do not command nor do they ask for anything. Even more, certain carnival forms parody the Church's cult. All these forms are systematically placed outside the Church and religiosity. They belong to an entirely different sphere.

Because of their obvious sensuous character and their strong element of play, carnival images closely resemble certain artistic forms, namely the spectacle. In turn, medieval spectacles often tended toward carnival folk culture, the culture of the marketplace, and to a certain extent became one of its components. But the basic carnival nucleus of this culture is by no means a purely artistic form nor a spectacle and does not, generally speaking, belong to the sphere of art. It belongs to the borderline between art and life. In reality, it is life itself, but shaped according to a certain pattern of play.

In fact, carnival does not know footlights, in the sense that it does not acknowledge any distinction between actors and spectators. Footlights would destroy a carnival, as the absence of footlights would destroy a theatrical performance. Carnival is not a spectacle seen by the people; they live in it, and everyone participates because its very idea embraces all the people. While carnival lasts, there is no other life outside it. During carnival time life is subject only to its laws, that is, the laws of its own freedom. It has a universal spirit; it is a special condition of the entire world, of the world's revival and renewal, in which all take part. Such is the essence of carnival, vividly felt by all its participants. It was most clearly expressed and experienced in the Roman Saturnalias, perceived as a true and full, though temporary, return of Saturn's golden age upon earth. The tradition of the Saturnalias remained unbroken and alive in the medieval carnival, which expressed this universal renewal and was vividly felt as an escape from the usual official way of life.

Clowns and fools, which often figure in Rabelais' novel, are characteristic of the medieval culture of humor. They were the constant, accredited representatives of the carnival spirit in everyday life out of carnival season. Like Triboulet[2] at the time of Francis I, they were not actors playing their parts on a stage, as did the comic actors of a later period, impersonating Harlequin, Hanswurst, etc., but remained fools and clowns always and wherever they made their appearance. As such they represented a certain form of life, which was real and ideal at the same time. They stood on the borderline between life and art, in a peculiar midzone as it were; they were neither eccentrics nor dolts, neither were they comic actors.

Thus carnival is the people's second life, organized on the basis of laughter. It is a festive life. Festivity is a peculiar quality of all comic rituals and spectacles of the Middle Ages.

All these forms of carnival were also linked externally to the feasts of the Church. (One carnival did not coincide with any commemoration of sacred history or of a saint but marked the last days before Lent, and for this reason was called *Mardi gras* or *carême-prenant* in France and *Fastnacht* in Germany.) Even more significant is the genetic link of these carnivals with ancient pagan festivities, agrarian in nature, which included the comic element in their rituals.

The feast (every feast) is an important primary form of human culture. It cannot be explained merely by the practical conditions of the community's work, and it would be even more superficial to attribute it to the physiological demand for periodic rest. The feast had always an essential, meaningful philosophical content. No rest period or breathing spell can be rendered festive per se; something must be added from the spiritual and ideological dimension. They must be sanctioned not by the world of practical conditions but by the highest aims of human existence, that is, by the world of ideals. Without this sanction there can be no festivity.

The feast is always essentially related to time, either to the recurrence of an event in the natural (cosmic) cycle, or to biological or historic timeliness. Moreover, through all the stages of historic development feasts were linked to moments of crisis, of breaking points in the cycle of nature or in the life of society and man. Moments of death and revival, of change and renewal always led to a festive perception of the world. These moments, expressed in concrete form, created the peculiar character of the feasts.

In the framework of class and feudal political structure this specific character could be realized without distortion only in the carnival and in similar marketplace festivals. They were the second life of the people, who for a time entered the utopian realm of community, freedom, equality, and abundance.

On the other hand, the official feasts of the Middle Ages, whether ecclesiastic, feudal, or sponsored by the state, did not lead the people out of the existing world order and created no second life. On the contrary, they sanctioned the existing pattern of things and reinforced it. The link with time became formal; changes and moments of crisis were relegated to the past. Actually, the official feast looked back at the past and used the past to consecrate the present. Unlike the earlier and purer feast, the official feast asserted all that was stable, unchanging, perennial: the existing hierarchy, the existing religious, political, and moral values, norms, and prohibitions. It was the triumph of a truth already established, the predominant truth that was put forward as eternal and indisputable. This is why the tone of the official feast was monolithically serious and why the element of laughter was alien to it. The true nature of human festivity was betrayed and distorted. But this true festive character was indestructible; it had to be tolerated and even legalized outside the official sphere and had to be turned over to the popular sphere of the marketplace.

As opposed to the official feast, one might say that carnival celebrated temporary liberation from the prevailing truth and from the established order; it marked the suspension of all hierarchical rank, privileges, norms, and prohibitions. Carnival was the true feast of time, the feast of becoming, change, and renewal. It was hostile to all that was immortalized and completed.

The suspension of all hierarchical precedence during carnival time was of particular significance. Rank was especially evident during official feasts; everyone was expected to appear in the full regalia of his calling, rank, and merits and to take the place corresponding to his position. It was a consecration of inequality. On the contrary, all were considered equal during carnival. Here, in the town square, a special form of free and familiar contact reigned among people who were usually divided by the barriers of caste, property, profession, and age. The hierarchical background and the extreme corporative and caste divisions of the medieval social order were exceptionally strong. Therefore such free, familiar contacts were deeply felt and formed an essential element of the carnival spirit. People were, so to speak, reborn for new, purely human relations. These truly human relations were not only a fruit of imagination or abstract thought; they were experienced. The utopian ideal and the realistic merged in this carnival experience, unique of its kind.

This temporary suspension, both ideal and real, of hierarchical rank created during carnival time a special type of communication impossible in everyday life. This led to the creation of special forms of marketplace speech and gesture, frank and free, permitting no distance between those who came in contact with each other and liberating from norms of etiquette and decency imposed at other times. A special carnivalesque, marketplace style of expression was formed which we find abundantly represented in Rabelais' novel.

During the century-long development of the medieval carnival, prepared by thousands of years of ancient comic ritual, including the primitive Saturnalias, a special idiom of forms and symbols was evolved – an extremely rich idiom that expressed the unique yet complex carnival experience of the people. This experience, opposed to all that was ready-made and completed, to all pretense at immutability, sought a dynamic expression; it demanded ever changing, playful, undefined forms. All the symbols of the carnival idiom are filled with this pathos of change and renewal, with the sense of the gay relativity of prevailing truths and authorities. We find here a characteristic logic, the peculiar logic of the "inside out" (*à l'envers*), of the "turnabout," of a continual shifting from top to bottom, from front to rear, of numerous parodies and travesties, humiliations, profanations, comic crownings and uncrownings. A second life, a second world of folk culture is thus constructed; it is to a certain extent a parody of the extracarnival life, a "world inside out."

Mikhail Bakhtin, *Rabelais and His World*, Helene Iswolsky (trans.), Bloomington: Indiana University Press, 1965/1988, pp. 4–11.

JAMES C. SCOTT,
FROM *WEAPONS OF THE WEAK*

The anthropologist James C. Scott is one of the most eloquent defenders of a politics that doesn't look like politics. Studying peasants in Malaysia, Scott realized that a form of politics was being performed each day between the Malay peasants and landowners. These were not the open and episodic politics of land seizures or violent revolutions, but continuous activities more subtle and nuanced – grumbling and gossip, laughter and laziness, stupidity and sabotage – a culture of resistance by which peasants rebel against the psychic and material superiority of their "betters." Scott calls these acts "everyday forms of resistance." That these acts occur every day and often out of sight of authorities ("hidden transcripts" of "infrapolitics" Scott calls them in his later work *Domination and the Arts of Resistance* (1990)), lends them their strength. Such practices slowly and silently wear down the power of the powerful, and perhaps even serve as an off-stage rehearsal for open assault. What follows is a passage from *Weapons of the Weak,* Scott's original study of resistance among Malay peasants, in which he reveals traces of these everyday forms of resistance throughout history.

The fact is that, for all their importance when they do occur, peasant rebellions, let alone peasant "revolutions," are few and far between. Not only are the circumstances that favor large-scale peasant uprisings comparatively rare, but when they do appear the revolts that develop are nearly always crushed unceremoniously. To be sure, even a failed revolt may achieve something: a few concessions from the state or landlords, a brief respite from new and painful relations of production[1] and, not least, a memory of resistance and courage that may lie in wait for the future. Such gains, however, are uncertain, while the carnage, the repression, and the demoralization of defeat are all too certain and real. It is worth recalling as well that even at those extraordinary historical moments when a peasant-backed revolution actually succeeds in taking power, the results are, at very best, a mixed blessing for the peasantry. Whatever else the revolution may achieve, it almost always creates a more coercive and hegemonic state apparatus – one that is often able to batten itself on the rural population like no other before it. All too frequently the peasantry finds itself in the ironic position of having helped to power a ruling group whose plans for industrialization, taxation, and collectivization are very much at odds with the goals for which peasants had imagined they were fighting.[2]

For all these reasons it occurred to me that the emphasis on peasant rebellion was misplaced. Instead, it seemed far more important to under-stand what we might call *everyday* forms of peasant resistance – the prosaic but constant struggle between the peasantry and those who seek to extract labor, food, taxes, rents, and interest from them. Most of the forms this struggle takes stop well short of collective outright defiance. Here I have in mind the ordinary weapons of relatively powerless groups: foot dragging, dissimulation, false compliance, pilfering, feigned ignorance, slander, arson, sabotage, and so forth. These Brechtian forms of class struggle have certain features in common. They require little or no coordination or planning; they often represent a form of individual self-help; and they typically avoid any direct symbolic confrontation with authority or with elite norms. To understand these commonplace forms of resistance is to understand what much of the peasantry does "between revolts" to defend its interests as best it can.

It would be a grave mistake, as it is with peasant rebellions, to overly romanticize the "weapons of the weak." They are unlikely to do more than marginally affect the various forms of exploitation that peasants confront. Furthermore, the peasantry has no monopoly on these weapons, as anyone can easily attest who has observed officials and landlords resisting and dis-rupting state policies that are to their disadvantage.

On the other hand, such Brechtian modes of resistance are not trivial. Desertion and evasion of conscription and of corvée labor have undoubt-edly limited the imperial aspirations of many a monarch in Southeast Asia[3] or, for that matter, in Europe. The process and its potential impact are nowhere better captured than in R.C. Cobb's account of draft resistance and desertion in postrevolutionary France and under the early Empire:

> From the year V to the year VII, there are increasingly frequent reports, from a variety of Departments . . . of every conscript from a given canton having returned home and living there unmolested. Better still, many of them did not return home; they had never left it in the first place . . . In the year VII too the severed fingers of right hands – the commonest form of self-mutilation – begin to witness statistically to the strength of what might be described as a vast movement of collective complicity, involving the family, the parish, the local authorities, whole cantons.
>
> Even the Empire, with a vastly more numerous and reliable rural police, did not succeed in more than temporarily slowing down the speed of the hemor-rhage which . . . from 1812, once more reached catastrophic proportions. There could have been no more eloquent referendum on the universal unpopularity of an oppressive regime; and there is no more encouraging spectacle for a histo-rian than a people that has decided it will no longer fight and that, without fuss,

returns home . . . the common people, at least, in this respect, had their fair share in bringing down France's most appalling regime.[4]

The collapse of the Confederate army and economy in the course of the Civil War in the United States is a further example of the decisive role of silent and unde-clared defections. Nearly 250,000 eligible whites are estimated to have deserted or to have avoided con-scription altogether.[5] The reasons appear to have been both moral and material, as one might expect. Poor whites, especially those from the nonslaveholding hill country, were deeply resentful of fighting for an insti-tution whose principal beneficiaries were often excluded from service by law.[6] Military reverses and what was called the "subsistence crisis of 1862" prompted many to desert and return to their hard-pressed families. On the plantations themselves, the shortage of white overseers and the slaves' natural affin-ity with the North's objective, gave rise to shirking and flight on a massive scale. As in France, one could claim here too that the Confederacy was undone by a social avalanche of petty acts of insubordination carried out by an unlikely coalition of slaves and yeomen – a coali-tion with no name, no organization, no leadership, and certainly no Leninist conspiracy behind it.

In a similar fashion, flight and evasion of taxes have classically curbed the ambition and reach of Third World states – whether precolonial, colonial, or inde-pendent.

. . .

The persistent efforts of the colonial government in Malaya to discourage the peasantry from growing and selling rubber that would compete with the plantation sector for land and markets is a case in point.[7] Various restriction schemes and land use laws were tried from 1922 until 1928 and again in the 1930s with only mod-est results because of massive peasant resistance. The efforts of peasants in self-styled socialist states to prevent and then to mitigate or even undo unpopular forms of

***Shooting an Elephant,*
*George Orwell***

I glanced round at the crowd that had followed me. It was an immense crowd, two thousand at the least and growing every minute. It blocked the road for a long distance on either side. I looked at the sea of yellow faces above the garish clothes – faces all happy and excited over this bit of fun, all certain that the ele-phant was going to be shot. They were watching me as they would watch a conjurer about to perform a trick. They did not like me, but with the magical rifle in my hands I was momentarily worth watching. And suddenly I realized that I should have to shoot the elephant after all. The people expected it of me and I had got to do it; I could feel their two thousand wills pressing me forward, irresistibly. And it was at this moment, as I stood there with the rifle in my hands, that I first grasped the hollowness, the futility of the white man's dominion in the East. Here was I, the white man with his gun, standing in front of the unarmed native crowd – seemingly the leading actor of the piece; but in reality I was only an absurd puppet pushed to and fro by the will of those yellow faces behind. I perceived in this moment that when the white man turns tyrant it is his own freedom that he destroys. He becomes a sort of hollow, posing dummy, the con-ventionalized figure of a sahib. For it is the condition of his rule that he shall spend his life in trying to impress the 'natives', and so in every crisis he has got to do what the 'natives' expect of him. He wears a mask, and his face grows to fit it. I had got to shoot the elephant. I had committed myself to doing it when I sent for the rifle. A sahib has got to act like a sahib; he has got to appear resolute, to know his own mind and do definite things. To come all that way, rifle in hand, with two thousand people marching at my heels, and then to trail feebly away, having done nothing – no, that was impossible. The crowd would laugh at me. And my whole life, every white man's life in the East, was one long struggle not to be laughed at.

From *Shooting an Elephant and Other Essays*, New York: Harcourt Brace & World, 1950, pp. 7–8

collective agriculture represent a striking example of defensive techniques available to a beleaguered peasantry. Again the struggle is marked less by massive and defiant confrontations than by a quiet evasion that is equally massive and often far more effective.[8]

The style of resistance in question is perhaps best described by contrasting paired forms of resistance, each aimed more or less at the same objective. The first of each pair is "everyday" resistance, in our meaning of the term; the second represents the open defiance that dominates the study of peasant and working-class politics. In one sphere, for example, lies the quiet, piecemeal process by which peasant squatters have often encroached on plantation and state forest lands; in the other a public invasion of land that openly challenges property relations. In terms of actual occupation and use, the encroachments by squatting may accomplish more than openly defiant land invasion, though the de jure distribution of property rights is never publicly challenged. Turning to another example, in one sphere lies a rash of military desertions that incapacitates an army and, in the other, an open mutiny aiming at eliminating or replacing officers. Desertions may, as we have noted, achieve something where mutiny may fail, precisely because it aims at self-help and withdrawal rather than institutional confrontation. And yet, the massive withdrawal of compliance is in a sense more radical in its implications for the army as an institution than the replacement of officers. As a final example, in one sphere lies the pilfering of public or private grain stores; in the other an open attack on markets or granaries aiming at an open redistribution of the food supply.

What everyday forms of reuistance share with the more dramatic public confrontations is of course that they are intended to mitigate or deny claims made by superordinate classes or to advance claims vis-à-vis those superordinate classes. Such claims have ordinarily to do with the material nexus of class struggle – the appropriation of land, labor, taxes, rents, and so forth.

Where everyday resistance most strikingly departs from other forms of resistance is in its implicit disavowal of public and symbolic goals. Where institutionalized politics is formal, overt, concerned with systematic, de jure change, everyday resistance is informal, often covert, and concerned largely with immediate, de facto gains.[9]

It is reasonably clear that the success of de facto resistance is often directly proportional to the symbolic conformity with which it is masked. Open insubordination in almost any context will provoke a more rapid and ferocious response than an insubordination that may be as pervasive but never ventures to contest the formal definitions of hierarchy and power. For most subordinate classes, which, as a matter of sheer history, have had little prospect of improving their status, this form of resistance has been the only option. What may be accomplished *within* this symbolic straitjacket is nonetheless something of a testament to human persistence and inventiveness, as this account of lower-caste resistance in India illustrates:

> Lifelong indentured servants most characteristically expressed discontent about their relationship with their master by performing their work carelessly and inefficiently. They could intentionally or unconsciously feign illness, ignorance, or incompetence, driving their master to distraction. Even though the master could retaliate by refusing to give his servant the extra fringe benefits, he was still obliged to maintain him at a subsistence level if he did not want to lose his investment completely. *This method of passive resistance, provided it was not expressed as open defiance, was nearly unbeatable*, it reinforced the Haviks' stereotype concerning the character of low caste persons, but gave them little recourse to action.[10]

Such forms of stubborn resistance are especially well documented in the vast literature on American slavery, where open defiance was normally foolhardy. The history of resistance to slavery in the antebellum US South is largely a history of foot dragging, false compliance, flight, feigned ignorance, sabotage, theft, and, not least, cultural resistance. These practices, which rarely if ever called into question the system of slavery *as such*, nevertheless achieved far more in their unannounced, limited, and truculent way than the few heroic and brief armed uprisings about which so much has been written. The slaves themselves appear to have realized that in most circumstances their resistance could succeed only to the extent that it hid behind the mask of public compliance. One imagines parents giving their children advice not unlike advice contemporary wage laborers on plantations in Indonesia apparently hear from their own parents:

> I tell them [the youngsters] remember, you're selling your labor and the one who buys it wants to *see* that he gets something for it, so work when he's around, then you can relax when he goes away, but make sure you always *look like* you're working when the inspectors are there.[11]

Two specific observations emerge from this perspective. First the nature of resistance is greatly influenced by the existing forms of labor control and by beliefs about the probability and severity of retaliation. Where the consequences of an open strike are likely to be catastrophic in terms of permanent dismissal or jail, the work force may rest to a slowdown or to shoddy work on the job. The often undeclared and anonymous nature of such action makes it particularly difficult for the antagonist to assess blame or apply sanctions. In industry, the slowdown has come to be called an "Italian" strike; it is used particularly when repression is feared, as in Poland under martial law in 1983.[12] Piece-work has of course often been used as a means of circumventing forms of resistance open to workers who are paid by the hour or day. Where piece-work prevails, as it did in silk and cotton weaving in nineteenth-century Germany, resistance is likely to find expression not in slowdowns, which are self-defeating, but in such forms as the "shortweighting of finished cloth, defective workmanship, and the purloining of materials."[13] Each form of labor control or payment is thus likely, other things equal, to generate its own distinctive forms of quiet resistance and "counterappropriation."

The second observation is that resistance is not necessarily directed at the immediate source of appropriation. Inasmuch as the objective of the resisters is typically to meet such pressing needs as physical safety, food, land, or income, and to do so in relative safety, they may simply follow the line of least resistance. Prussian peasants and proletarians in the 1830s, beleaguered by dwarf holdings and wages below subsistence, responded by emigration or by poaching wood, fodder, and game on a large scale. The pace of "forest crime" rose as wages declined, as provisions became more expensive, and where emigration was more difficult; in 1836 there were 207,000 prosecutions in Prussia, 150,000 of which were for forest offenses.[14] They were supported by a mood of popular complicity that originated in earlier traditions of free access to forest, but the poachers cared little whether the rabbits or firewood they took came from the land or their particular employer or landlord. Thus, the reaction to an appropriation in one sphere may lead its victims to exploit small openings available elsewhere that are perhaps more accessible and less dangerous.[15]

Such techniques of resistance are well adapted to the particular characteristics of the peasantry. Being a diverse class of "low classness," scattered across the countryside, often lacking the discipline and leadership that would encourage opposition of a more organized sort, the peasantry is best suited to extended guerrilla-style campaigns of attrition that require little or no coordination. Their individual acts of foot dragging and evasion are often reinforced by a venerable popular culture of resistance. Seen in the light of a supportive subculture and the knowledge that the risk to any single resister is generally reduced to the extent that the whole community is involved, it becomes plausible to speak of a social movement. Curiously, however, this is a social movement with no formal organization, no formal leaders, no manifestos, no dues, no name and no banner. By virtue of their institutional invisibility, activities on anything less than a massive scale are, if they are noticed at all, rarely accorded any social significance.

Multiplied many thousandfold, such petty acts of resistance by peasants may in the end make an utter shambles of the policies framed up by their would-be superiors in the capital. The state may respond in a variety of ways. Policies may be recast in line with more realistic expectations. They may be retained but reinforced with positive incentives aimed at encouraging voluntary compliance. And, of course, the state may simply choose to employ more coercion. Whatever the response, we must not miss the fact that the action of the peasantry has changed or narrowed the policy options available to the state. It is in this fashion, and not through revolts, let alone legal political pressure, that the peasantry has classically made its political presence felt. Thus any history or theory of peasant politics that attempts to do justice to the peasantry as a historical actor must necessarily come to grips with what I have chosen to call *everyday forms of resistance*. For this reason alone it is important to both document and bring some conceptual order to this seeming welter of human activity.

Everyday forms of resistance make no headlines.[16] Just as millions of anthozoan polyps create, willy-nilly, a coral reef, so do thousands upon thousands of individual acts of insubordination and evasion create a political or economic barrier reef of their own. There is rarely any dramatic confrontation, any moment that is particularly newsworthy. And whenever, to pursue the simile, the ship of state runs aground on such a reef, attention is typically directed to the shipwreck itself and not to the vast aggregation of petty acts that made it possible. It is only rarely that the perpetrators of these petty acts seek to call attention to themselves. Their safety lies in their anonymity. It is also extremely rare that officials of the state wish to publicize the insubordination. To do so would be to admit that their policy is unpopular, and, above all, to expose the tenuousness of their authority in the countryside – neither of which the sovereign state finds in its interest.[17]

The nature of the acts themselves and the self-interested muteness of the antagonists thus conspire to create a kind of complicitous silence that all but expunges everyday forms of resistance from the historical record.

James C. Scott, *Weapons of the Weak: Everyday Forms of Peasant Resistance*, New Haven: Yale University Press, 1985, pp. 29–36.

ROBIN D.G. KELLEY,
FROM *RACE REBELS*

As the following personal narrative by historian and cultural theorist Robin D.G. Kelley makes clear, the everyday forms of resistance that Scott identifies are not limited to the fields of Malaysia or to past history. Resistance can also be found among black and Chicano youth working, and clowning, in a Los Angeles McDonald's. While not hostile to political organizations – his first book, *Hammer and the Hoe* (1990), was a study of the Communist Party in Alabama – Kelley ends this essay with a call for rethinking and redefining what we understand to be authentically political, looking past (or perhaps in front of) mainstream institutions like unions and political organizations, and toward activities that have often been considered on the margins of the "real struggle." Important skirmishes can take place in arenas like corporate fast food restaurants, by teenagers, over issues like whose definition of culture will prevail.

"McDonald's is a happy place!" I really believed that slogan when I began working there in 1978. For many of us employed at the central Pasadena franchise, Mickey D's actually meant food, folks, and fun, though our main objective was *funds*. Don't get me wrong; the work was tiring and the polyester uniforms unbearable. The swing managers, who made slightly more than the rank-and-file, were constantly on our ass to move fast and smile more frequently. The customers treated us as if we were stupid, probably because 90 percent of the employees at our franchise were African-Americans or Chicanos from poor families. But we found inventive ways to compensate. Like virtually all my fellow workers, I liberated McDonaldland cookies by the boxful, volunteered to clean "lots and lobbies" in order to talk to my friends, and accidentally cooked too many Quarter Pounders and apple pies near closing time, knowing full well that we could take home whatever was left over. Sometimes we (mis)used the available technology to our advantage. Back in the day, the shakes did not come ready mixed. We had to pour the frozen shake mix from the shake machine into a paper cup, add flavored syrup, and place it on an electric blender for a couple of minutes. If it was not attached correctly, the mixer blade would cut the sides of the cup and cause a disaster. While these mishaps slowed us down and created a mess to clean up, anyone with an extra cup handy got a little shake out of it. Because we were underpaid and overworked, we accepted consumption as just compensation – though in hindsight eating Big Macs and Fries to make up for low wages and mistreatment was probably closer to self-flagellation.

That we were part of the "working class" engaged in workplace struggles never crossed our minds, in part because the battles that were dear to most of us and the strategies we adopted fell outside the parameters of what most people think of as traditional "labor disputes." I've never known anyone at our McDonald's to argue about wages; rather, some of us occasionally asked our friends to punch our time cards before we arrived, especially if we were running late. And no one to my knowledge demanded that management extend our break; we simply operated on "CP" (colored people's) time, turning fifteen minutes into twenty-five. What we fought over were more important things like what radio station to play. The owner and some of the managers felt bound to easy listening; we turned to stations like K-DAY on AM or KJLH and K-ACE on the FM dial so we could rock to the funky sounds of Rick James, Parliament, Heat wave, the Ohio Players, and – yes – Michael Jackson. Hair was perhaps the most contested battle ground. Those of us without closely cropped cuts were expected to wear hairnets, and we were simply not having it. Of course, the kids who identified with the black and Chicano gangs of the late seventies had no problem with this rule since they wore hairnets all the time. But to net one's gheri curl, a lingering Afro, a freshly permed doo was outrageous. We fought those battles with amazing tenacity – and won most of the time. We even attempted to alter our ugly uniforms by opening buttons, wearing our hats tilted to the side, rolling up our sleeves a certain way, or adding a variety of different accessories.

Nothing was sacred, not even the labor process. We undoubtedly had our share of slowdowns and deliberate acts of carelessness, but what I remember the most was the way many of us stylized our work. We ignored the films and manuals and turned work into performance. Women on the cash register maneuvered effortlessly with long, carefully manicured nails and four finger rings. Tossing trash became an opportunity to try out our best Dr. J moves. The brothers who worked the grill (it was only *brothers* from what I recall) were far more concerned with looking cool than ensuring an equal distribution of reconstituted onions on each all-beef patty. Just imagine a young black male "gangsta limpin'" between the toaster and the grill, brandishing a spatula like a walking stick or a microphone. And while all of this was going on, folks were signifying on one another, talking loudly about each other's mommas, daddys, boyfriends, girlfriends, automobiles (or lack thereof), breath, skin color, uniforms; on occasion describing in hilarious detail the peculiarities of customers standing on the other side of the counter. Such chatter often drew in the customers, who found themselves entertained or offended – or both – by our verbal circus and collective dialogues.[1]

The employees at the central Pasadena McDonald's were constantly inventing new ways to rebel, ways rooted in our own peculiar circumstances. And we never knew where the struggle would end; indeed, I doubt any of us thought we were part of a movement that even had an end other than punching out a time card (though I do think the "Taylorizing" of McDonald's, the introduction of new technology to make service simpler and more efficient, has a lot to do with management's struggle to minimize these acts of resistance and reaction).[2] But *what* we fought for *is* a crucial part of the overall story; the terrain was often cultural, centering on identity, dignity, and fun. We tried to turn work into pleasure, to turn our bodies into instruments of pleasure. Generational and cultural specificity had a good deal to do with our unique forms of resistance, but a lot of our actions were linked directly to the labor process, gender conventions, and our class status.

Like most working people throughout the world, my fellow employees at Mickey D's were neither total victims of routinization, exploitation, sexism, and racism, nor were they "rational" economic beings driven by the most base utilitarian concerns. Their lives and struggles were so much more complicated. If we are to make meaning of these kinds of actions rather than dismiss them as manifestations of immaturity, false consciousness, or primitive rebellion, we must begin to dig beneath the surface of trade union pronouncements, political institutions, and organized social movements, deep into the daily lives, cultures, and communities which make the working classes so much more than people who work. We have to step into the complicated maze of experience that renders "ordinary" folks so extraordinarily multifaceted, diverse, and complicated. Most importantly, we need to break away from traditional notions of politics. We must not only redefine what is "political" but question a lot of common ideas about what are "authentic" movements and strategies of resistance. By "authentic" I mean the assumption that only certain organizations and ideologies can truly represent particular group interests (e.g., workers' struggles must be located within labor organizations, or African-American concerns are most clearly articulated in so-called "mainstream" civil rights organizations such as the NAACP or the Urban League). Such an approach not only disregards diversity and conflict within groups, but it presumes that the only struggles that count take place through institutions.

If we are going to write a history of black working-class resistance, where do we place the vast majority of people who did not belong to either "working-class" organizations or black political movements? A lot of black working people struggled and survived without direct links to the kinds of organizations that dominate historical accounts of African-American or US working-class resistance. The so-called margins of struggle, whether it is the unorganized, often spontaneous battles with authority or social movements thought to be inauthentic or unrepresentative of the "community's interests," are really a fundamental part of the larger story waiting to be told.

Robin D.G. Kelley, *Race Rebels: Culture, Politics, and the Black Working Class*, New York: Free Press, 1994, pp. 1–4.

ADOLPH REED JR.,
"WHY IS THERE NO BLACK POLITICAL MOVEMENT?"

Others are less convinced than Scott and Kelley in the political efficacy of "everyday forms of resistance." In this short selection from his essay "Why Is There No Black Political Movement?" Adolph Reed Jr., an academic political scientist and popular journalist, vehemently rejects the notion that such practices lead to social justice. Sure, he argues, people resist every day, but "that and a buck fifty will get you on the subway." Reed identifies this so-called culture of resistance as merely normal forms of survival for the powerless. At best, it is a way to mitigate the everyday degradation and humiliation of subservience; at worst, it's an escape valve for political passions that, acted out in other ways, might change the system. What we need instead, he argues at a later point, is old-fashioned, self-consciously political, broad-based social organizations.

Sure there's infrapolitics – there always is, and there always will be; whenever there's oppression, there's resistance. That's one of the oldest slogans on the left. But it's also a simple fact of life. People don't like being oppressed or exploited, and they respond in ways that reflect that fact. That and a buck fifty will get you on the subway. "Daily confrontations" are to political movements as carbon, water, and oxygen are to life on this planet. They are the raw material for the movements of political change, and expressions of dissatisfaction that reflect the need for change, but their presence says nothing more about the potential for such a movement to exist, much less its actuality.

At best, those who romanticize "everyday resistance" or "cultural politics" read the evolution of political movements teleologically; they presume that those conditions necessarily, or even typically, lead to political action. They don't. Not any more than the presence of carbon and water necessarily leads to the evolution of Homo sapiens. Think about it: infrapolitics is ubiquitous, developed political movements are rare.

At worst, and more commonly, defenders of infrapolitics treat it as politically consequential in its own right. This idealism may stem from a romantic confusion, but it's also an evasive acknowledgement that there is no real popular political movement. Further, it's a way of pretending that the missing movement is not a problem – that everyday, apolitical social practices are a new, maybe even more "authentic," form of politics.

. . .

The only possible successful strategy is one based on genuinely popular, deliberative processes and concrete, interest-based organizing that connects with people's daily lives.

Adolph Reed Jr., *Class Notes: Posing as Politics and Other Thoughts on the American Scene*, New York: The New Press, 2000, pp. 3–4, 9.

JEAN BAUDRILLARD, "THE MASSES: THE IMPLOSION OF THE SOCIAL IN THE MEDIA"

For critics like Reed, promoting a politics that doesn't always look like politics signals a disastrous retreat from the political stage. But for the always provocative post-modernist Jean Baudrillard, the disappearance of political struggle – as it's commonly perceived – is something to applaud. In the following essay, printed here in its entirety, Baudrillard argues that strategies of resistance change to reflect strategies of control. Against a system that excludes or represses the individual, the natural demand is one of inclusion: to become a citizen, a subject of history. This, however, is not the world we live in. In the capitalist democracies people are bombarded with appeals to their representation and participation: "This Bud's for you," "Vote!," "Speak your Mind," yet still we realize that our choice, vote or voice matters little. Against such a system which justifies its existence by the consent (or consumer purchases) of those it governs, Baudrillard's solution is simple: withdraw your consent. Cultivate disengagement, apathy, ironic detachment, and silence: "the strategic resistance is the refusal of meaning and the refusal of speech." Or, as the faux religion/conspiracy cabal, the SubGenius Foundation (see sidebar), puts it: celebrate slack.

Up to now there have been two great versions of the analysis of the media (as indeed that of the masses), one optimistic and one pessimistic. The optimistic one has assumed two major tonalities, very different from one another. There is the technological optimism of Marshall McLuhan: for him the electronic media inaugurate a generalized planetary communication and should conduct us, by the mental effect alone of new technologies, beyond the atomizing rationality of the Gutenberg galaxy to the global village, to the new electronic tribalism – an achieved transparency of information and communication. The other version, more traditional, is that of dialectical optimism inspired by progressivist and Marxist thought: the media constitute a new, gigantic productive force and obey the dialectic of productive forces. Momentarily alienated and submitted to the law of capitalism, their intensive development can only eventually explode this monopoly. "For the first time in history," writes Hans Enzensberger, "the media make possible a mass participation in a productive process at once social and socialized, a participation whose practical means are in the hands of the masses themselves."[1] These two positions more or less, the one technological, the other ideological, inspire the whole analysis and the present practice of the media.[2]

It is more particularly to the optimism of Enzensberger that I formerly opposed a resolutely pessimist vision in "Requiem for the Media." In that I described the mass media as a "speech without response." What characterizes the mass media is that they are opposed to mediation, intransitive, that they fabricate noncommunication – if one accepts the definition of communication as an exchange, as the reciprocal space of speech and response, and thus of *responsibility*. In other words, if one defines it as anything other than the simple emission/reception of information. Now the whole present architecture of the media is founded on this last definition: they are what finally forbids response, what renders impossible any process of exchange (except in the shape of a simulation of a response, which is itself integrated

into the process of emission, and this changes nothing
in the unilaterality of communication). That is their
true abstraction. And it is in this abstraction that is
founded the system of social control and power. To
understand properly the term *response*, one must appreciate it in a meaning at once strong, symbolic, and
primitive: power belongs to him who gives and to
whom no return can be made. To give, and to do it in
such a way that no return can be made, is to break
exchange to one's own profit and to institute a
monopoly: the social process is out of balance. To make
a return, on the contrary, is to break this power relationship and to restore on the basis of an antagonistic
reciprocity the circuit of symbolic exchange. The same
applies in the sphere of the media: there speech occurs
in such a way that there is no possibility of a return.
The restitution of this possibility of response entails
upsetting the whole present structure; even better (as
started to occur in 1968 and the 70s), it entails an "anti-
media" struggle.

In reality, even if I did not share the technological
optimism of McLuhan, I always recognized and considered as a gain the true revolution which he brought
about in media analysis (this has been mostly ignored
in France). On the other hand, though I also did not
share the dialectical hopes of Enzensberger, I was not
truly pessimistic, since I believed in a possible subversion of the code of the media and in the possibility
of an alternate speech and a radical reciprocity of symbolic exchange.

Today all that has changed. I would no longer interpret in the same way the forced silence of the masses in
the mass media. I would no longer see in it a sign of
passivity and of alienation, but to the contrary an original strategy, an original response in the form of a
challenge; and on the basis of this reversal I suggest to
you a vision of things which is no longer optimistic or
pessimistic, but ironic and antagonistic.

I will take the example of opinion polls, which are
themselves a mass medium. It is said that opinion polls

constitute a manipulation of democracy. This is certainly no more the case than that publicity is a manipulation of need and of consumption. It too produces demand (or so it claims) and invokes needs just as opinion polls produce answers – and induce future behavior. All this would be serious if there were an objective truth of needs, an objective truth of public opinion. It is obvious that here we need to exercise extreme care. The influence of publicity, of opinion polls, of all the media, and of information in general would be dramatic if we were certain that there exists in opposition to it an authentic human nature, an authentic essence of the social, with its needs, its own will, its own values, its finalities. For this would set up the problem of its radical alienation. And indeed it is in this form that traditional critiques are expressed.

Now the matter is at once less serious and more serious than this. The uncertainty which surrounds the social and political effect of opinion polls (do they or do they not manipulate opinion?), like that which surrounds the real economic efficacy of publicity, will never be completely relieved – and it is just as well! This results from the fact that there is a compound, a mixture of two heterogeneous systems whose data cannot be transferred from one to the other. An operational system which is statistical, information-based, and simulational is projected onto a traditional values system, onto a system of representation, will, and opinion. This collage, this collusion between the two, gives rise to an indefinite and useless polemic. We should agree neither with those who praise the beneficial use of the media, nor with those who scream about manipulation, for the simple reason that there is no relationship between a system of meaning and a system of simulation. Publicity and opinion polls would be incapable, even if they wished and claimed to do so, of alienating the will or the opinion of anybody at all, for the reason that they do not act in the time-space of will and of representation where judgment is formed. For the same reason, though reversed, it is quite impossible for them to throw any light at all on public opinion or individual will, since they do not act in a public space, on the stage of a public space. They are strangers to it, and indeed they wish to dismantle it. Publicity and opinion polls and the media in general can only be imagined; they only exist on the basis of a disappearance, the disappearance from the public space, from the scene of politics, of public opinion in a form at once theatrical and representative as it was enacted in earlier epochs. Thus we can be reassured: they cannot destroy it. But we should not have any illusions: they cannot restore it either.

It is this lack of relationship between the two systems which today plunges us into a state of stupor. That is what I said: stupor. To be more objective one would have to say: a radical uncertainty as to our own desire, our own choice, our own opinion, our own will. This is the clearest result of the whole media environment, of the information which makes demands on us from all sides and which is as good as blackmail.

We will never know if an advertisement or opinion poll has had a real influence on individual or collective wills, but we will never know either what would have happened if there had been no opinion poll or advertisement.

The situation no longer permits us to isolate reality or human nature as a fundamental variable. The result is therefore not to provide any additional information or to shed any light on reality, but on the contrary, because we will never in future be able to separate reality from its statistical, simulative projection in the media, a state of suspense and of definitive uncertainty about reality. And I repeat: it is a question here of a completely new species of uncertainty, which results not from the *lack* of information but from information itself and even from an *excess* of information. It is information itself which produces uncertainty, and so this uncertainty, unlike the traditional uncertainty which could always be resolved, is irreparable.

This is our destiny: subject to opinion polls, information, publicity, statistics; constantly confronted with the anticipated statistical verification of our behavior, and absorbed by this permanent refraction of our least movements, we are no longer confronted with our own will. We are no longer even alienated, because for that it is necessary for the subject to be divided in itself, confronted with the other, to be contradictory. Now, where there is no other, the scene of the other, like that of politics and of society, has disappeared. Each individual is forced despite himself or herself into the undivided coherency of statistics. There is in this a positive absorption into the transparency of computers, which is something worse than alienation.

There is an obscenity in the functioning and the omnipresence of opinion polls as in that of publicity. Not because they might betray the secret of an opinion, the intimacy of a will, or because they might violate some unwritten law of the private being, but because they exhibit this redundancy of the social, this sort of continual voyeurism of the group in relation to itself: it must at all times know what it wants, know what it thinks, be told about its least needs, its least quivers, *see* itself continually on the videoscreen of statistics, constantly watch its own temperature chart, in a sort of hypochondriacal madness. The social becomes obsessed with itself; through this autoinformation, this permanent autointoxication, it becomes its own vice, its own perversion. This is the real obscenity. Through this feedback, this incessant anticipated accounting, the social loses its own scene. It no longer enacts itself; it has no more time to enact itself; it no longer occupies a particular space, public or political; it becomes confused with its own control screen. Overinformed, it develops ingrowing obesity. For everything which loses its scene (like the obese body) becomes for that very reason *ob-scene*.

The silence of the masses is also in a sense obscene. For the masses are also made of this useless hyperinformation which claims to enlighten them, when all it does is clutter up the space of the representable and annul itself in a silent equivalence. And we cannot do much against this obscene circularity of the masses and of information. The two phenomena fit one another: the masses have no opinion and information does not inform them. Both of them, lacking a scene where the meaning of the social can be enacted, continue to feed one another monstrously – as the speed with which information revolves increases continually the weight of the masses as such, and not their self-awareness.

So if one takes opinion polls, and the uncertainty which they induce about the principle of social reality, and the type of obscenity, of statistical pornography to which they attract us – if we take all that seriously, if we confront all that with the claimed finalities of information and of the social itself, then it all seems very dramatic. But there is another way of taking things. It does not shed much more credit on opinion polls, but it restores a sort of status to them, in terms of derision and of play. In effect we can consider the indecisiveness of their results, the uncertainty of their effects, and their unconscious humor, which is rather similar to that of meteorology (for example, the possibility of verifying at the same time contradictory facts or tendencies); or again the casual way in which everybody uses them, disagreeing with them privately and especially if they verify exactly one's own behavior (no one accepts a perfect statistical evaluation of his chances). That is the real problem of the credibility accorded to them.

Statistics, as an objective computation of probabilities, obviously eliminate any elective chance and any personal destiny. That is why, deep down, none of us believes in them, any more than the gambler believes in chance, but only in Luck (with a capital, the equivalent of Grace, not with lower case, which is the equivalent of probability). An amusing example of this obstinate denial of statistical chance is given by this news item: "If this will reassure you, we have calculated that, of every 50 people who catch the metro twice a day for 60 years, only one is in danger of being attacked. Now there is no reason why it should be *you!*" The beauty of statistics is never in their objectivity but in their involuntary humor.

So if one takes opinion polls in this way, one can conceive that they could work for the masses themselves as a game, as a spectacle, as a means of deriding both the social and the political. The fact that opinion polls do their best to destroy the political as will and representation, the political as meaning, precisely through the effect of simulation and uncertainty – this fact can only give pleasure to the ironic unconscious of the masses (and to our individual political unconscious, if I may use this expression), whose deepest drive remains the symbolic murder of the political class, the symbolic murder of political *reality*, and this murder is produced by opinion polls in their own way. That is why I wrote in *Silent Majorities* that the masses, which have always provided an alibi for political representation, take their revenge by allowing themselves the theatrical representation of the political scene.[3] The people have become *public*. They even allow themselves the luxury of enjoying day by day, as in a home cinema, the fluctuations of their own opinion in the daily reading of the opinion polls.

It is only to this extent that they believe in them, that we all believe in them, as we believe in a game of malicious foretelling, a double or quits on the green baize of the political scene. It is, paradoxically, as a game that the opinion polls recover a sort of legitimacy. A game of the undecidable; a game of chance; a game of the undecidability of the political scene, of the equifinality of all tendencies; a game of truth effects in the circularity of questions and answers. Perhaps we can see here the apparition of one of these collective forms of game which Caillois called *aléa*[4] – an irruption into the polls themselves of a ludic, aleatory process, an ironic mirror for the use of the masses (and we all belong to the masses) of a political scene which is caught in its own trap (for the politicians are the only ones to believe in the polls, along with the pollsters obviously, as the only ones to believe in publicity are the publicity agents).

In this regard, one may restore to them a sort of positive meaning: they would be part of a contemporary cultural mutation, part of the era of simulation.

In view of this type of consequence, we are forced to congratulate ourselves on the very failure of polls, and on the distortions which make them undecidable and chancy. Far from regretting this, we must consider that there is a sort of fate or evil genius (the evil genius of the social itself?) which throws this too beautiful machine out of gear and prevents it from achieving the objectives which it claims. We must also ask if these distortions, far from being the consequence of a bad angle of refraction of information onto an inert and opaque matter, are not rather the consequence of a resistance of the social itself to its investigation, the shape taken by an occult duel between the pollsters and the object polled, between information and the people who receive it?

This is fundamental: people are always supposed to be willing partners in the game of truth, in the game of information. It is agreed that the object can always be persuaded of its truth; it is inconceivable that the object of the investigation, the object of the poll, should not adopt, generally speaking, the strategy of the subject of the analysis, of the pollster. There may certainly be some difficulties (for instance, the object does not understand the question; it's not its business; it's undecided; it replies in terms of the interviewer and not of the question, and so on), but it is admitted that the poll analyst is capable of rectifying what is basically only a lack of adaptation to the analytic apparatus. The hypothesis is never suggested that all this, far from being a marginal, archaic residue, is the effect of an offensive (not defensive) counterstrategy by the object; that, all in all, there exists somewhere an original, positive, possibly victorious strategy of the object opposed to the strategy of the subject (in this case, the pollster or any other producer of messages).

This is what one could call the evil genius of the object, the evil genius of the masses, the evil genius of the social itself, constantly producing failure in the truth of the social and in its analysis, and for that reason unacceptable, and even unimaginable, to the tenants of this analysis.

To reflect the other's desire, to reflect its demand like a mirror, even to anticipate it: it is hard to imagine what powers of deception, of absorption, of deviation – in a word, of subtle revenge – there is in this type of response. This is the way the masses escape as reality, in this very mirror, in those simulative devices which are designed to capture them. Or again, the way in which events themselves disappear behind the television screen, or the more general screen of information (for it is true that events have no probable existence except on this deflective screen, which is no longer a mirror). While the mirror and screen of alienation was a mode of production (the imaginary subject), this new screen is simply its mode of disappearance. But disappearance is a very complex mode: the object, the individual, is not only condemned to disappearance, but *disappearance is also its strategy*; it is its way of response to this device for capture, for networking, and for forced identification. To this *cathodic* surface of recording, the individual or the mass reply by a *parodic* behavior of disappearance. What are they; what do they do, what do they become behind this screen? They turn themselves into an impenetrable and meaningless surface, which is a method of disappearing. They eclipse themselves; they melt into the superficial screen in such a way that their reality and that of their movement, just like that of particles of matter, may be radically questioned without making any fundamental change to the probabilistic analysis of their behavior. In fact, behind this "objective" fortification of networks and models which believe they can capture them, and where the whole population of analysts and expert observers believe that they capture them, there passes a wave of derision, of reversal, and of parody which is the active exploitation, the parodic enactment by the object itself of its mode of disappearance.

There is and there always will be major difficulties in analyzing the media and the whole sphere of information through the traditional categories of the philosophy of the subject: will, representation, choice, liberty, deliberation, knowledge, and desire. For it is quite obvious that they are absolutely contradicted by the media; that the subject is absolutely alienated in its sovereignty. There is a distortion of principle between the sphere of information, and the moral law which still dominates us and whose decree is: you shall know yourself, you shall know what is your will and your desire. In this respect the media and even technics and science teach us nothing at all; they have rather restricted the limits of will and representation; they have muddled the cards and deprived any subject of the disposal of his or her own body, desire, choice, and liberty.

But this idea of alienation has probably never been anything but a philosopher's ideal perspective for the use of hypothetical masses. It has probably never expressed anything but the alienation of the philosopher himself; in other words, the one who *thinks himself or herself other*. On this subject Hegel is very clear in his judgment of the *Aufklärer*, of the *philosophe* of the Enlightenment, the one who denounces the "empire of error" and despises it.

Reason wants to enlighten the superstitious mass by revealing trickery. It seeks to make it understand that it is *itself*, the mass, which enables the despot to live and not the despot which makes it live, as it believes when it obeys him. For the demystifier, credulous consciousness is mistaken *about itself*.

> The Enlightenment speaks as if juggling priests had, by sleight of hand, spirited away the being of consciousness for which they substituted something absolutely *foreign* and *other*; and, at the same time, the Enlightenment says that this foreign thing is a being of consciousness, which believes in consciousness, which trusts it, which seeks to please it.[5]

There is obviously a contradiction, says Hegel: one cannot confide oneself to another than oneself and be mistaken about oneself, since when one confides in another, one demonstrates the certainty that one is safe with the other; in consequence, consciousness, which is said to be mystified, knows very well where it is safe and where it is not. Thus there is no need to correct a mistake which only exists in the *Aufklärer* himself. It is not *consciousness*, concludes Hegel, which takes itself for another, but it is the *Aufklärer* who takes himself for another, another than this common man whom he endeavors to make aware of his own stupidity. "When the question is asked if it is allowable to deceive a people, one must reply that the question is worthless, because it is impossible to deceive a people about itself."[6]

So it is enough to reverse the idea of a mass alienated by the media to evaluate how much the whole universe of the media, and perhaps the whole technical universe, is the result of a secret strategy of this mass which is claimed to be alienated, *of a secret form of the refusal of will*, of an in-voluntary challenge to everything which was demanded of the subject by philosophy – that is to say, to all rationality of choice and to all exercise of will, of knowledge, and of liberty.

In one way it would be no longer a question of revolution but of massive *devolution*, of a massive delegation of the power of desire, of choice, of responsibility, a delegation to apparatuses either political or intellectual, either technical or operational, to whom has devolved the duty of taking care of all of these things. A massive de-volution, a massive desisting from will, but not through alienation or voluntary servitude (whose mystery, which is the modern enigma of politics, is unchanged since La Boétie because the problem is put in terms of the consent of the subject to his own slavery, which fact no philosophy will ever be able to explain). We might argue that there exists another philosophy of lack of will, a sort of radical antimetaphysics whose secret is that the masses are deeply aware that they do not have to make a decision about themselves and the world; that they do not have to wish; that they do not have to know; that they do not have to desire.

The deepest desire is perhaps to give the responsibility for one's desire to someone else. A strategy of ironic investment in the other, in the others; a strategy toward others not of appropriation but, on the contrary, of expulsion, of philosophers and people in power, an expulsion of the obligation of being responsible, of enduring philosophical, moral, and political categories. Clerks are there for that, so are professionals, the representative holders of concept and desire. Publicity, information, technics, the whole intellectual and political class are there to tell us what we want, to tell the masses what they want – and basically we thoroughly enjoy this massive transfer of responsibility because perhaps, very simply, it is not easy to want what we want; because perhaps, very simply, it is not very interesting to know what we want to decide, to desire. Who has imposed all this on us, even the need to desire, unless it be the philosophers?

Choice is a strange imperative. Any philosophy which assigns man to the exercise of his will can only plunge him in despair. For if nothing is more flattering to consciousness than to know what it wants, on the contrary nothing is more seductive to the other consciousness (the unconscious?) – the obscure and vital one which makes happiness depend on the despair of will – than not to know what it wants, to be relieved of choice and diverted from its own objective will. It is much better to rely on some insignificant or powerful instance than to be dependent on one's own will or the necessity of choice. Beau Brummel had a servant for that purpose. Before a splendid landscape dotted with beautiful lakes, he turns toward his valet to ask him: "Which lake do I prefer?"

Even publicity would find an advantage in discarding the weak hypothesis of personal will and desire. Not only do people certainly not want to be *told* what they wish, but they certainly do not want to *know* it, and it is not even sure that they want to *wish* at all. Faced with such inducements, it is their evil genius who tells them not to want anything and to rely finally on the apparatus of publicity or of information to "persuade" them, to construct a choice for them (or to rely on the political class to order things) – just as Brummel did with his servant.

Whom does this trap close on? The mass knows that it knows nothing, and it does not want to know. The mass knows that it can do nothing, and it does not want to achieve anything. It is violently reproached with this mark of stupidity and passivity. But not at all: the mass is very snobbish; it acts as Brummel did and delegates in a sovereign manner the faculty of choice to someone else by a sort of game of irresponsibility, of ironic challenge, of sovereign lack of will, of secret ruse. All the mediators (people of the media, politicians, intellectuals, all the heirs of the *philosophes* of the Enlightenment in contempt for the masses) are really only adapted to this purpose: to manage by delegation, by procuration, this tedious matter of power and of will, to unburden the masses of this transcendence for their greater pleasure and to turn it into a show for their benefit. *Vicarious*: this would be, to repeat Thorstein Veblen's concept, the status of these so-called privileged classes, whose will would be, in a way, diverted against themselves, toward the secret ends of the very masses whom they despise.

We live all that, subjectively, in the most paradoxical mode, since in us, in everyone, this mass coexists with the intelligent and voluntary being who condemns it and despises it. Nobody knows what is truly opposed to consciousness, unless it may be the repressive unconscious which psychoanalysis has imposed on us. But our true unconscious is perhaps in this ironic power of nonparticipation, of nondesire, of nonknowledge, of silence, of absorption of all powers, of *expulsion* of all powers of all wills, of all knowledge, of all meaning onto representatives surrounded by a halo of derision. Our unconscious would not then consist of drives, of *pulsions*, whose destiny is sad repression; it would not be repressed at all; it would be made of this joyful *expulsion* of all the encumbering superstructures of being and of will.

We have always had a sad vision of the masses (alienated), a sad vision of the unconscious (repressed). On all our philosophy weighs this sad correlation. Even if only for a change, it would be interesting to conceive the mass, the object-mass, as the repository of a finally delusive, illusive, and allusive strategy, the correlative of an ironic, joyful, and seductive unconscious.

About the media you can sustain two opposing hypotheses: they are the strategy of power, which finds in them the means of mystifying the masses and of imposing its own truth. Or else they are the strategic territory of the ruse of the masses, who exercise in them their concrete power of the refusal of truth, of the denial of reality. Now the media are nothing else than a marvelous instrument for destabilizing the real and the true, all historical or political truth (there is thus no possible political strategy of the media: it is a contradiction in terms). And the addiction that we have for the media, the impossibility of doing without them, is a deep result of this phenomenon: it is not a result of a desire for culture, communication, and information, but of this perversion of truth and falsehood, of this destruction of meaning in the operation of the medium. The desire for a show, the desire for simulation, which is at the same time a desire for dissimulation. This is a vital reaction. It is a spontaneous, total resistance to the ultimatum of historical and political reason.

It is essential today to evaluate this double challenge: the challenge to meaning by the masses and their silence (which is not at all a passive resistance), and the challenge to meaning which comes from the media and their fascination. All the marginal alternative endeavors to resuscitate meaning are secondary to this.

Obviously there is a paradox in the inextricable entanglement of the masses and the media: is it the media that neutralize meaning and that produce the "formless" (or informed) mass; or is it the mass which victoriously resists the media by diverting or by absorbing without reply all the messages which they produce? Are the mass media on the side of power in the manipulation of the masses, or are they on the side of the masses in the liquidation of meaning, in the violence done to meaning? Is it the media that fascinate the masses, or is it the masses who divert the media into showmanship? The media toss around sense and nonsense; they manipulate in every sense at once. No one can control this process: the media are the vehicle for the simulation which belongs to the system and for the simulation which destroys the system, according to a circular logic, exactly like a Möbius strip – and it is just as well. There is no alternative to this, no logical resolution. Only a logical *exacerbation* and a catastrophic resolution. That is to say, this process has no return.

In conclusion, however, I must make one reservation. Our relationship to this system is an insoluble "double blind" – exactly that of children in their relationship to the demands of the adult world. They are at the same time told to constitute themselves as autonomous subjects, responsible, free, and conscious, and to constitute themselves as submissive objects, inert, obedient, and conformist. The child resists on all levels, and to these contradictory demands he or she replies by a double strategy. When we ask the child to be object, he or she opposes all the practices of disobedience, of revolt, of emancipation; in short, the strategy of a subject. When we ask the child to be subject, he or she opposes just as obstinately and successfully a resistance as object; that is to say, exactly the opposite: infantilism, hyperconformity, total dependence, passivity, idiocy. Neither of the two strategies has more objective value than the other. Subject resistance is today given a unilateral value and considered to be positive – in the same way as in the political sphere only the practices of liberation, of emancipation, of expression, of self-constitution as a political subject are considered worthwhile and subversive. This is take no account of the equal and probably superior impact of all the practices of the object, the renunciation of the position of subject and of meaning – exactly the practices of the mass – which we bury with the disdainful terms *alienation* and *passivity*. The liberating practices correspond to *one* of the aspects of the system, to the constant ultimatum we are given to constitute ourselves as pure objects; but they do not correspond at all to the other demand to constitute ourselves as subjects, to liberate, to express ourselves at any price, to vote, to produce, to decide, to speak, to participate, to play the game: blackmail and ultimatum are just as serious as the other, probably more serious today. To a system whose argument is oppression and repression, the strategic resistance is to demand the liberating rights of the subject. But this seems rather to reflect an earlier phase of the system; and even if we are still confronted with it, it is no longer a strategic territory: the present argument of the system is to maximize speech, to maximize the production of meaning, of participation. And so the strategic resistance is that of the refusal of meaning and the refusal of speech; or of the hyperconformist simulation of the very mechanisms of the system, which is another form of refusal by overacceptance. It is the actual strategy of the masses. This strategy does not exclude the other, but it is the winning one today, because it is the most adapted to the present phase of the system.

Jean Baudrillard, "The Masses: The Implosion of the Social in the Media," Marie Maclean (trans.), *New Literary History*, vol. 16, no. 3 (Spring 1985), pp. 577–89.

HAKIM BEY,
FROM *TAZ: THE TEMPORARY AUTONOMOUS ZONE*

The politics of disappearance are taken a step further by Hakim Bey in his influential essay *TAZ*. TAZ stands for Temporary Autonomous Zone, an area – not unlike medieval carnivals or contemporary Reclaim the Streets protests – wherein transitory "pirate utopias" can be hastily assembled as fly-by-night sites of cultural resistance (cf. Bakhtin, Jordan). These utopias are not built to last. Haunted by specters of revolutions leading to police states and acutely aware of the ease in which consumer capitalism can turn the most rebellious idea into consumer product, Bey counsels permanent temporality: "As soon as the TAZ is named (represented, mediated), it must vanish, it will vanish . . . once again invisible because undefinable in terms of the Spectacle." Given the propensity for rebellions to end at the guillotine or in a shopping mall this strategy of impermanence makes sense, but is, as Bey admits, a "counsel of despair." It is always a fleeting uprising, never a permanent revolution.

> . . . this time however I come as the victorious Dionysus, who will turn the world into a holiday . . . Not that I have much time.
>
> Nietzsche (from his last "insane" letter to Cosima Wagner)

Pirate Utopias

The Sea-rovers and Corsairs of the 18th century created an "information network" that spanned the globe: primitive and devoted primarily to grim business, the net nevertheless functioned admirably. Scattered throughout the net were islands, remote hideouts where ships could be watered and provisioned, booty traded for luxuries and necessities. Some of these islands supported "intentional communities," whole mini-societies living consciously outside the law and determined to keep it up, even if only for a short but merry life.

Some years ago I looked through a lot of secondary material on piracy hoping to find a study of these enclaves – but it appeared as if no historian has yet found them worthy of analysis. (William Burroughs has mentioned the subject, as did the late British anarchist Larry Law – but no systematic research has been carried out.) I retreated to primary sources and constructed my own theory, some aspects of which will be discussed in this essay. I called the settlements "Pirate Utopias."

Recently Bruce Sterling, one of the leading exponents of Cyberpunk science fiction, published a near-future romance based on the assumption that the decay of political systems will lead to a decentralized proliferation of experiments in living: giant worker-owned corporations, independent enclaves devoted to "data piracy," Green-Social-Democrat enclaves, Zerowork enclaves, anarchist liberated zones, etc. The information economy which supports this diversity is called the Net; the enclaves (and the book's title) are *Islands in the Net*.

The medieval Assassins founded a "State" which consisted of a network of remote mountain valleys and castles, separated by thousands of miles, strategically invulnerable to invasion, connected by the information flow of secret agents, at war with all government, and devoted only to knowledge. Modern technology, culminating in the spy satellite, makes this kind of *autonomy* a romantic dream. No more pirate islands! In the future the same technology – freed from all political control – could make possible an entire world of *autonomous zones*. But for now the concept remains precisely science fiction – pure speculation.

Are we who live in the present doomed never to experience autonomy, never to stand for one moment on a bit of land ruled only by freedom? Are we reduced either to nostalgia for the past or nostalgia for the future? Must we wait until the entire world is freed of political control before even one of us can claim to know freedom? Logic and emotion untie to condemn such a supposition. Reason demands that one cannot struggle for what one does not know; and the heart revolts at a universe so cruel as to visit such injustices on *our* generation alone of humankind.

To say that "I will not be free till all humans (or all sentient creatures) are free" is simply to cave in to a kind of nirvana-stupor, to abdicate our humanity, to define ourselves as losers.

I believe that by extrapolating from the past and future stories about "islands in the net" we may collect evidence to suggest that a certain kind of "free enclave" is not only possible in our time but also existent. All my research and speculation has crystallized around the concept of the TEMPORARY AUTONOMOUS ZONE (hereafter abbreviated TAZ). Despite its synthesizing force for my own thinking, however, I don't intend the TAZ to be taken as more than an *essay* ("attempt"), a suggestion, almost a poetic fancy. Despite the occasional Ranterish enthusiasm of my language I am not trying to construct political dogma. In fact I have deliberately refrained from defining the TAZ — I circle around the subject, firing off exploratory beams. In the end the TAZ is almost self-explanatory. If the phrase became current it would be understood without difficulty . . . understood in action.

Waiting for the Revolution

How is it that "the world turned upside-down" always manages to *Right* itself? Why does reaction always follow revolution, like seasons in Hell?

Uprising, or the Latin form *insurrection*, are words used by historians to label *failed* revolutions — movements which do not match the expected curve, the consensus-approved trajectory: revolution, reaction, betrayal, the founding of a stronger and even more oppressive State — the turning of the wheel, the return of history again and again to its highest form: jackboot on the face of humanity forever.

By failing to follow this curve, the *up-rising* suggests the possibility of a movement outside and beyond the Hegelian spiral of that "progress" which is secretly nothing more than a vicious circle. *Surgo* — rise up, surge. *Insurgo* — rise up, raise oneself up. A bootstrap operation. A goodbye to that wretched parody of the karmic round, historical revolutionary futility. The slogan "Revolution!" has mutated from tocsin to toxin, a malign pseudo-Gnostic fate-trap, a nightmare where no matter how we struggle we never escape that evil Aeon, that incubus the State, one State after another, every "heaven" ruled by yet one more evil angel.

If History IS "Time," as it claims to be, then the uprising is a moment that springs up and out of Time, violates the "law" of History. If the State IS History, as it claims to be, then the insurrection is the forbidden moment, an unforgivable denial of the dialectic — shimmying up the pole and out of the smokehole, a shaman's maneuver carried out at an "impossible angle" to the universe.

History says the Revolution attains "permanence," or at least duration, while the uprising is "temporary." In this sense an uprising is like a "peak experience" as opposed to the standard of "ordinary" consciousness and

"Train Parties",
Sheena Bizarre

We were told to meet at the Christopher Street station. "Be there on point, at said time. Wear red! It's the red line, bring red treats! It's Valentine's Day! If you see confused people wearing red, encourage them to come with you!"

I did the NYC beat minute, running out of time, so typical for this seconds-skimming town. I ran. Half the fun was getting there. People decked in red were pouring into the subway station, holding red balloons, lollipops. Then the train rolled in. We stepped in to find that the train was already decorated. The harsh white lights that show your every pore and smile lines were covered with red gels, bathing the subway car in an eerie dream-state like light.

There was a brass band on one side, and a boy with a boom box pumping techno on the other. We immediately started to dance around. I was given cups full of red wine. We smoked pot, and smiled at one another. The City that has trained us to avoid eye contact and clutch our personals was now hosting the exact opposite. A blessing. There was candy offered and you weren't afraid to accept it.

And then the first stop, ushering in New Yorkers who had no idea there could be a party on the MTA. There are two kinds of New Yorkers: Those who love and those who hate. The first passenger was a man in his fifties. He turned to me and said, "This is why I love New York. I've been in LA for a few years now, and this is why I came back! I love NY." I could only imagine this

experience. Like festivals, uprisings cannot happen every day – otherwise they would not be "nonordinary." But such moments of intensity give shape and meaning to the entirety of a life. The shaman returns – you can't stay up on the roof forever – but things have changed, shifts and integrations have occurred – a *difference* is made.

You will argue that this is a counsel of despair. What of the anarchist dream, the Stateless state, the Commune, the autonomous zone with *duration*, a free society, a free *culture?* Are we to abandon that hope in return for some existentialist *acte gratuit?* The point is not to change consciousness but to change the world.

I accept this as a fair criticism. I'd make two rejoinders nevertheless; first, *revolution* has never yet resulted in achieving this dream. The vision comes to life in the moment of uprising – but as soon as "the Revolution" triumphs and the State returns, the dream and the ideal are *already* betrayed. I have not given up hope or even expectation of change – but I distrust the word *Revolution*. Second, even if we replace the revolutionary approach with a concept of *insurrection blossoming spontaneously into anarchist culture*, our own particular historical situation is not propitious for such a vast undertaking. Absolutely nothing but a futile martyrdom could possibly result now from a head-on collision with the terminal State, the megacorporate information State, the empire of Spectacle and Simulation. Its guns are all pointed at us, while our meager weaponry finds nothing to aim at but a hysteresis, a rigid vacuity, a Spook capable of smothering every spark in an ectoplasm of information, a society of capitulation ruled by the image of the Cop and the absorbent eye of the TV screen.

In short, we're not touting the TAZ as an exclusive end in itself, replacing all other forms of organization, tactics, and goals. We recommend it because it can provide the quality of enhancement associated with the uprising without necessarily leading to violence and martyrdom. The TAZ is like an uprising which does not engage directly with the State, a guerilla operation which liberates an area (of land, of time, of imagination) and then dissolves itself to reform elsewhere/elsewhen, *before* the State can crush it. Because the State is concerned primarily with Simulation rather than substance, the TAZ can "occupy" these areas clandestinely and carry on its festal purposes for quite a while in relative peace. Perhaps certain small TAZs have lasted whole lifetimes because they went unnoticed, like hill-billy enclaves – because they never intersected with the Spectacle, never appeared outside that real life which is invisible to the agents of Simulation.

Babylon takes its abstractions for realities; precisely *within* this margin of error the TAZ can come into existence. Getting the TAZ started may involve tactics of violence and defense, but its greatest strength lies in its invisibility – the State cannot recognize it because History has no definition of it. As soon as the TAZ is named (represented, mediated), it must vanish, it *will* vanish, leaving behind it an empty husk, only to spring up again somewhere else, once again invisible because undefinable in terms of the Spectacle. The TAZ is thus a perfect tactic for an era in which the State is omnipresent and all-powerful and yet simultaneously riddled with cracks and vacancies. And because the TAZ is a microcosm of that "anarchist dream" of a free culture, I can think of no better tactic by which to work toward that goal while at the same time experiencing some of its benefits here and now.

In sum, realism demands not only that we give up *waiting* for "the Revolution" but also that we give up *wanting* it. "Uprising," yes – as often as possible and even at the risk of violence. The *spasming* of the Simulated State will be "spectacular," but in most cases the best and most radical tactic will be to refuse to engage in spectacular violence, to *withdraw* from the area of simulation, to disappear.

The TAZ is an encampment of guerilla ontologists: strike and run away. Keep moving the entire tribe, even if it's only data in the Web. The TAZ must be

being a tourism commercial for the city. In my ideal world, it would be! I played MC with a drunk transient type. We sang aloud, the train car in unison singing, "THE ROOF/ THE ROOF/ THE ROOF IS ON FIRE/ WE DON'T NEED NO WATER, LET IT BURN, LET IT BURN!" He opened his bag to reveal wine bottles and passed them around. He stated, "This is the best day of my life!" We were lead off the train, and had a mini-parade in the underground. Brass band followed by happy kids in red, skipping, laughing, and wondering where we would end up.

from "Train Parties" by Azoteas, unpublished manuscript, 2001 capable of defense; but both the "strike" and the "defense" should, if possible, evade the violence of the State, which is no longer a *meaningful* violence. The strike is made at structures of control, essentially at ideas; the defense is "invisibility," a *martial art*, and "invulnerability" – an "occult" art within the martial arts. The "nomadic war machine" conquers without being noticed and moves on before the map can be adjusted. As to the future – Only the autonomous can *plan* autonomy, organize for it, create it. It's a bootstrap operation. The first step is somewhat akin to *satori* – the realization that the TAZ begins with a simple act of realization.

Hakim Bey, *TAZ: The Temporary Autonomous Zone: Ontological Anarchy, Poetic Terrorism*, New York: Autonomedia, 1985, pp. 97–102.

SIMON REYNOLDS,
FROM *GENERATION ECSTASY*

It's hard to pinpoint exactly when and where raves began. The electronic beat-heavy dance music arose out of German art rock of the late 1970s, remixed and reinterpreted in the black suburbs of Detroit in the early 1980s. The all-night warehouse parties came from the depressed industrial towns of Northern England like Manchester (aka Madchester) in the late 1980s and 1990s, then spread across the world. What's easier to assert is what a rave is: an all encompassing party, a temporary autonomous zone (cf. Bey), a place where just maybe you can loose yourself in a state of – mental, physical, chemical – ecstasy. Author and former senior editor at *Spin* magazine Simon Reynolds begins the selection below with a literary trip on Ecstasy. His second part is a bit more sobering. Simon explores the utopian politics of rave culture – and its limitations: when you come down off the high the world looks pretty much the same as before you left.

The Ecstasy trip divides into three distinct phases. Depending on the emptiness of your stomach, it take approximately an hour to "come up": the senses light up, you start "rushing," and for a short while the experience can be overwhelming, with dizziness and mild nausea. Then there's the plateau stage, which lasts about four hours, followed by a long, gentle comedown and an afterglow phase that can last well into the next day. What you experience during the plateau phase is highly dependent on "set and setting" (the early LSD evangelists' term for the mind-set of the drug taker and the context in which the drug is taken). In a one-on-one session (lovers, close friends, analyst and analyzed) the emphasis is on the breaking down of emotional defenses, the free flow of verbal and tactile affection. The first time I took Ecstasy was in a romantic, private context. The experience was so intense, so special, that I felt it would be sacrilegious to repeat it lest it become routinized, and it was over two years before I did it again.

At a rave the emotional outpouring and huggy demonstrativeness is still a major part of the MDMA experience (which is why ravers use the term "lovedup"), but the intimacy is dispersed into a generalized bonhomie: you bond with the gang you came with, but also with people you've never met. Anyone who's been to a rave knows the electric thrill of catching a stranger's eye, making contact through the shared glee of knowing that you're both buzzing off the same drug/music synergy. Part of what makes the classic rave experience so rewarding and so addictive are the "superficial" but literally touching rituals of sharing water, shaking hands, having someone a tad worse for wear lean on you as if you were bosom buddies.

The blitz of noise and lights at a rave tilts the MDMA experience toward the drug's purely sensuous and sensational effects. With its mildly trippy, prehallucinogenic feel, Ecstasy makes colors, sounds, smells, tastes, and tactile sensations more vivid (a classic indication that you've "come up" is that chewing gum suddenly tastes horribly artificial). The experience combines crisp clarity with a limpid radiance. Ecstasy also has a particular physical sensation that's hard to describe: an oozy yearn, a bliss-ache, a trembly effervescence that makes you feel like you've got champagne for blood.

All music sounds better on E – crisper and more distinct, but also engulfing in its immediacy. House and techno sound especially fabulous. The music's emphasis on texture and timbre enhances the drug's mildly synesthetic effects so that sounds seem to caress the listener's skin. You feel like you're dancing inside the music; sound becomes a fluid medium in which you're immersed. Ecstasy has been celebrated as the *flow drug* for the way it melts bodily and psychological rigidities, enabling the dancer to move with greater fluency and "lock" into the groove. Rave music's hypnotic beats and sequenced loops also make it perfectly suited to interact with another attribute of Ecstasy: recent research suggests that the drug stimulates the brain's 1b receptor, which encourages repetitive behavior. Organized around the absence of crescendo or narrative progression, rave music instills a pleasurable tension, a rapt suspension that fits perfectly with the sustained preorgasmic plateau of the MDMA high.

These Ecstasy-enhancing aspects latent in house and techno were unintended by their original creators and were discovered accidentally by the first people who mixed the music and the drug. But over the years, rave music has gradually evolved into a self-conscious science of intensifying MDMA's sensations. House and techno producers have developed a drug-determined repertoire of effects, textures, and riffs that are expressly designed to trigger the tingly rushes that traverse the Ecstatic body. Processes like EQ-ing, phasing, panning, and filtering are used to tweak the frequencies, harmonics, and stereo imaging of different sounds, making them leap out of the mix with an eerie three-dimensionality or glisten with a hallucinatory vividness. Today's house track is a forever-fluctuating, fractal mosaic of glow-pulses and flicker-riffs, a teasing tapestry whose different strands take turns to move in and out of the sonic spotlight. Experienced under the influence of MDMA, the effect is synesthetic – like tremulous fingertips tantalizing the back of your neck, or the simultaneously aural/tactile equivalent of a shimmer. In a sense, Ecstasy turns the entire body surface into an ear, an ultrasensitized membrane that responds to certain frequencies. Which is why the more functionalist, drug determined forms of rave music arguably are really "understood" (in a physical, nonintellectual sense) only by the drugged and really "audible" only on a big club sound system that realizes the sensurround, immersive potential of the tracks.

Beyond its musical applications, Ecstasy is above all a *social* drug. It's rarely used by a solitary individual, because the feelings it unleashes would have nowhere to go. (A friend of mine, bored, once took some leftover E at home and spent the night kissing the walls and hugging himself.) In the rave context, Ecstasy's urge to merge can spill over into an oceanic mysticism. Rave theorists talk of tribal consciousness, "morphic resonance," an empathy that shades into the telepathic. Writing about his memories of London's most hedonistic gay club, Trade, Richard Smith came up with the brilliant phrase "a . . . communism of the emotions." The closest I've had to a mystical experience occurred, funnily enough, at Trade. Borne aloft in the cradling rush of sound, swirled up and away into a cloud of unknowing, for the first time I truly *grasped* what it was to be "lost in music." There's a whole hour for which I can't account.

. . .

Rave as Counterculture and Spiritual Revolution

By the mid-nineties, the British media had woken up to the fact that the nation contained two societies: the traditional leisure culture of alcohol and entertainment (spectator sports, TV) versus the more participatory, effusive culture of all-night dancing and Ecstasy. The clash between old Britain and young Britain was dramatized to hilarious effect in an episode of *Inspector Morse* entitled "Cherubim and Seraphics." The plot concerns a series of mysterious teenage deaths that appear to be connected to a new drug called Seraphic. Despite its overt "just say no" slant, the episode mostly works as an exhilarating advert for Ecstasy culture. (*Literally*, insofar as Morse's remark to his detective partner – "it's a rave, Lewis!" – was sampled and used by a pirate station.)

This collision of old and new Englands reaches its peak when the detective duo arrive at the stately home where a rave called Cherub is taking place. Morse drones on about the noble history of the building; inside, the kids have transformed it into a future wonderland. Sure, the crooked lab researcher responsible for the Seraphic drug gets his comeuppance. But the episode ends by allowing the sixteen-year-old girlfriend of one Seraphic casualty to utter a paean to Ecstasy: "You love everyone in the world, you want to touch everyone." And it transpires that the teenagers didn't kill themselves because the drug unbalanced their minds; rather, having glimpsed heaven on earth, they decided that returning to reality would be a comedown. Who wouldn't want to give E a try after that? And who would possibly side with decrepit Morse, with his booze and classical music CDs, against the shiny happy people of Generation E?

This episode of *Inspector Morse* signaled a dawning awareness in the media that recreational drug culture had become firmly installed in Britain during the early nineties and was now omnipresent almost to the point of banality. Every weekend, anywhere from half a million to two million people under the age of thirty-five were using psychedelics and stimulants. This geographically dispersed but spiritually connected network of Love-Ins, Freak-Outs, and All Night Raves constituted a weekly Woodstock (or rather Woodstock and Altamont rolled into one, given that Ecstasy's dark side was starting to reveal itself). The question, then, is this: has rave proved itself a form of mass bohemia, or is it merely a futuristic update of traditional youth leisure, where the fun-crazed weekend redeems the drudgery of the working week? What are the politics of Ecstasy culture?

Among Ecstasy's social effects, the most obvious is the way it has utterly transformed youth leisure in Britain and Europe. Because alcohol muddies the MDMA high, rave culture rapidly developed an antialcohol taboo. It could be argued that Ecstasy's net effect has actually been to save lives, by reducing the number of alcohol-fueled fights and drunk–driving fatalities.

Like alcohol, Ecstasy removes inhibitions. But because it also diminishes aggression (including sexual aggression), E has had the salutary effect of transforming the nightclub from a "cattle market" and combat zone into a place where women come into their own and men are too busy dancing and bonding with their mates to get into fights. These benign side effects spilled outside clubland: with football fans turning onto E and house, by 1991–2 soccer hooliganism in Britain was at its lowest level in five years.

Generally speaking, Ecstasy seems to promote tolerance. One of the delights of the rave scene at its height was the way it allowed for mingling across lines of class, race, and sexual preference. MDMA rid club culture of its cliqueishness and stylistic sectarianism; hence drug culture researcher Sheila Henderson's phrase "luvdup and de-elited". Rave's explosive impact in the UK, compared to its slower dissemination in America, may have something to do with the fact that Britain remains one of the most rigidly class-stratified counties in the Western world. Perhaps the drug simply wasn't as *needed* in America as it was in the UK. For in many ways, MDMA is an antidote to the English disease: reserve, inhibition, emotional constipation, class consciousness.

Yet for all the rhetoric of spiritual revolution and counterculture, it remains a moot point whether Ecstasy's effects have spilled outside the domain of leisure. From early on, commentators noted that the controlled hedonism of the MDMA experience is much more compatible with a basically normal, conformist lifestyle than other drugs. Norman Zinberg called it "the yuppie psychedelic"; others have compared it to a "mini-vacation," an intense burst of "quality time." In his essay "The Ecstasy of Disappearance," Antonio Melechi uses the historical origins of rave in Ibiza as the foundation for a theory of rave as a form of *internal tourism*: a holiday from everyday life and from your everyday self. At the big one-shot raves, some kids spend – on drinks, drugs, souvenir merchandise, travel – as much as they would on a short vacation. Rejecting the idea that this is simply escapism, a safety valve for the tensions generated by capitalist work patterns, Melechi argues that rave supersedes the old model of subcultural activity as resistance through rituals. Where earlier style-terrorist subcultures like mod and punk were exhibitionist, a kick in the eye of straight society, rave is a form of collective disappearance, an investment in pleasure that shouldn't be written off as mere retreat or disengagement.

Melechi's theory of rave – as neither subversive nor conformist but more than both – appeals to the believer in me. From a more dispassionate perspective, though, rave appears more like a new twist on a very old idea. There is actually a striking continuity in the work hard/play hard structure of working-class leisure, from the mods' sixty-hour weekends and Northern Soul's speed-freak stylists, to disco's Saturday-night fever dreams and jazzfunk's All-Dayers and Soul Weekends. When I listen to the Easybeats'

1967 Aussie-mod anthem "Friday on My Mind," I'm stunned by the way the lyrics – a thrilling anatomy of the working-class weekender lifecycle of drudgery, anticipation, and explosive release – still resonate. Thirty years on, we're no nearer to overhauling the work/leisure structures of industrial society. Instead, all that rage and frustration is vented through going mental on the weekend ("Tonight, I'll spend my bread / Tonight, I'll lose my head"), helped along by a capsule or three of instant euphoria.

From the Summer of Love rhetoric of the early UK acid house evangelists to San Francisco's cyberdelic community, from the neopaganism of Spiral Tribe to the transcendentalism of the Megatripolis/Goa Trance scene, rave has also been home to another "politics of Ecstasy," one much closer to the original intent behind Timothy Leary's phrase. Ecstasy has been embraced as one element of a bourgeois-bohemian version of rave, in which the music-drugs-technology nexus is fused with spirituality and vague hippy-punk-anarcho politics to form a nineties would-be counterculture.

The fact that the same drug can be at the core of two different "politics of ecstasy" – raving as safety valve versus raving as opting out – can be traced back to the double nature of MDMA as a *psychedelic amphetamine*. The psychedelic component of the experience lends itself to utopianism and an at least implicit critique of the way things are. Amphetamine, though, does not have a reputation as a consciousness-raising chemical. While they popped as many pills as other strata of society, the hippies regarded amphetamine as a straight person's drug: after all, it was still legal and being prescribed in vast amounts to tired housewives, overworked businessmen, dieters, and students cramming for exams. Amphetamine's ego-boosting and productivity-raising effects ran totally counter to the psychedelic creed of selfless surrender, indolence, and Zen passivity. So when the spread of methamphetamine poisoned Haight-Ashbury's love-and-peace vibe, the counterculture responded with the "speed kills" campaign. The hippies' hostility toward amphetamine is one reason the punks embraced the chemical.

In their 1975 classic *The Speed Culture: Amphetamine Use and Abuse in America*, Lester Grinspoon and Peter Hedblom draw an invidious comparison between marijuana and amphetamine, arguing that pot smoking instills values that run counter to capitalist norms, while amphetamine amplifies all the competitive, aggressive, and solipsistic tendencies of Western industrial life. Terence McKenna, an evangelist for Gaia-given plant psychedelics like magic mushrooms, classes amphetamine as one of the "dominator drugs," alongside cocaine and caffeine.

Chemically programmed into MDMA is a sort of less-is-more effect: what starts out as an empathy enhancer degenerates, with repeated use, into little more than amphetamine, at least in terms of its effects. When MDMA's warm glow cools through overuse, ravers often turn to the cheaper, more reliable amphetamine. Both these syndromes – excessive intake of E, the use of amphetamine as a substitute – explain the tendency of rave subcultures to mutate into speed-freak scenes after a couple of years.

From all this we might conclude that when the amphetamine component of the MDMA experience comes to the fore, rave culture loses much of its "progressive" edge. At one end of the class spectrum are the working-class weekender scenes, where MDMA is used in tandem with amphetamine and the subcultural raison d'être is limited and ultimately conformist: stimulants are used to provide energy and delay the need for sleep, to intensify and maximize leisure time. At the other, more bohemian end of rave culture, MDMA is used in tandem with LSD and other consciousness-raising hallucinogens, as part of a subcultural project of turning on, tuning in, and dropping out.

But the picture is a bit more complicated than this. LSD is widely used in working-class rave scenes, although arguably in ways that break with the Timothy Leary/Terence McKenna model of enlightenment through altered states. Hallucinogens appeal as another form of teenage kicks, a way of making the world into a cartoon or video game. (Hence brands of acid blotter like Super Mario and Power Rangers.) And amphetamine, in high doses or with prolonged use, can have its own hallucinatory and delusory effects. Like MDMA, speed makes perceptions more vivid; its effect of hyperacousia can escalate into fullblown auditory hallucinations. The sensory flood can seem visionary, pregnant with portent. Serious speed freaks often have a sense of clairvoyance and gnosis, feel plugged into occult power sources, believe they alone can perceive secret patterns and conspiracies.

Nonetheless, there is a tension in rave culture between consciousness raising and consciousness razing, between middle-class technopagans for whom MDMA is just one chemical in the pharmacopoeia of a spiritual revolution and weekenders for whom E is just another tool for "obliviating" the boredom of workaday life. This class-based divide has quite a history. Witness the snobbish dismay of highbrow hallucinogen fiends like R. Gordon Wasson, who wrote about his psilocybin visions for *Life* magazine in 1957, only to be appalled when thrill-seeking "riff-raff" promptly descended on the magic mushroom fields of Mexico, or worse, turned to its synthetic equivalent, LSD. Wasson refused to use the pop culture term "psychedelic," preferring the more ungainly and overtly transcendentalist "entheogen" (a substance that puts you in touch with the divine). Such linguistic games and terminological niceties often seem like the only way that intellectuals can distinguish their "discriminating" use of drugs from the heedless hedonism of the masses.

Wasson's writings are one of the sources for John Moore's brilliant 1988 monograph *Anarchy and Ecstasy: Visions of Halcyon Days*. Using shreds of historical evidence, Moore imaginatively reconstructs prehistoric pagan rites dedicated to Gaia worship; he argues for the contemporary revival of these "Eversion Mysteries," insisting that a ritualized, mystical encounter with Chaos (what he calls "bewilderness") is an essential component of any truly vital anarchistic politics.

Anarchy and Ecstasy, written in the mid-eighties, reads like a prophecy and program for rave culture. Crucial preparations for the Mystery rites include fasting and sleep deprivation, in order to break down "inner resistances" and facilitate possession by the "sacred wilderness." The rites themselves consist of mass chanting, dancing ("enraptured abandonment to a syncopated musical beat" that "flings aside rigidities, be they postural, behavioral or characterological"), and the administering of hallucinogenic drugs in order that "each of the senses and faculties [be] sensitized to fever pitch prior to derangement into a liberatingly integrative synaesthesia." The worshippers are led into murky, mazelike caverns, whose darkness is illuminated only by "mandalas and visual images."

All this sounds very like any number of clubs with their multiple levels and corridors decorated with psychotropic imagery. As for the "hierophants" with their intoxicating poisons, this could be the dealers touting "Es and trips." Moore's description of the peak of Mystery rites also sounds very like the effect of MDMA: "The initiate becomes androgynous, unconcerned with the artificial distinctions of gender . . . Encountering total saturation, individuals transcend their ego boundaries and their mortality in successive waves of ecstasy."

Hardly surprising, then, that organized religion has noticed the way rave culture provides "the youth of today" with an experience of collective communion and transcendence. Just as the early Church co-opted heathen rituals, there have been attempts to *rejuvenate* Christianity by incorporating elements of the rave experience: dancing, lights, mass fervor, demonstrative and emotional behavior. Most (in)famous of these was the Nine O'clock Service in Sheffield, the brainchild of "rave vicar" Chris Brain, whose innovations were greeted with keen interest and approval on the part of the Anglican hierarchy until it was discovered that the reverend was loving some of his female parishioners a little too much. Despite this embarrassment, rave-style worship has spread to other cities in the UK, such as Gloucester and Bradford (where the Cathedral holds services called Eternity). There have also been a number of attempts to lure lost and confused youth into the Christian fold via drug-and-alcohol-free rave nights: Club X in Bath (organized by Billy Graham's Youth for Christ) and Bliss (a Bournemouth night started by the Pioneer Network).

None of these quasi-rave clubs administer Ecstasy as a holy sacrament. But perhaps they should, for if any drug induces a state of soul that approximates the Christian ideal – overflowing with trust and goodwill to all men – then surely it's MDMA. While rave behavior is a little outré for the staid Church of England, it chimes in nicely with the more ecstatic and gesturally demonstrative strains of Christianity. Indeed, Moby, techno's most visible and outspoken Christian, claims that "the first rave was when the Ark of Covenant was brought into Jerusalem, and King David went out and danced like crazy and tore off all his clothes."

But the rave experience probably has more in common with the goals and techniques of Zen Buddhism: the emptying out of meaning via mantric repetition; nirvana as the paradox of the full void. Nicholas Saunders's *E Is For Ecstasy* quotes a Rinzai Zen monk who approves of raving as a form of active meditation, of being "truly in the moment and not in your head." Later in Saunders's book, there's an extract from an Ecstasy memoir in which the anonymous author describes the peculiar, depthless quality of the MDMA experience: "There's no inside"; "I was empty. I seemed to have become pure presence." At its most intense, the Ecstasy rush resembles the kundalini energy that yoga seeks to awaken: "liquid fire" that infuses the nervous system and leaves the consciousness "aglow with light."

What makes rave culture so ripe for religiosity is the "spirituality" of the Ecstasy experience: its sense of access to a wonderful secret that can be understood only by direct, unmediated experience, and the way it releases an outflow of all-embracing but peculiarly asexual love. Clearly the most interesting and "subversive" attributes of the MDMA experience, these aspects are also what makes rave fraught with a latent nihilism.

If one word crystallizes this ambivalence at the heart of the rave experience, it's "intransitive" – insofar as the music and the culture lack an objective or object. Rave culture has no goal beyond its own propagation; it is about the celebration of celebration, about an intensity without pretext or context. Hence the urgent "nonsense" of MCs at raves and on pirate radio. Witness the following Index FM phone-in session on Christmas Eve

1992, with its strange combination of semantic impoverishment and extreme affective charge.

MC 1:   Sounds of the Dominator, Index FM. And it's getting busy tonight, London. Rrrrrrush!!! 'Ello mate?

Caller 1:   (giggly, very out-of-it) Elio, London, I'd like to give a big shout out to the Car Park posse, yeah? There's my friend, my brother, Eli, and there's my friend over there called Anthony, and he's, like, smasher, he's hard –

MC 1:   Like you, mate!

Caller 1:   Innit, of course!

MC 1:   You sound wrecked.

Caller 1:   Yeah, I'm totally wrecked, mate.

[UPROAR, chants of "Oi, oi! Oi, oi!"]

Caller 1:   My bruvva my bruvva my bruvva my bruvva my bruvva.

MC 1:   Make some noise!

Caller 1:   Believe you me, mate, 'ardkore you know the score!

MC 1:   Respect, mate! 'Ardkore noise!

Caller 1:   Oi, can you gimme gimme gimme "Confusion," mate? 2 Bad Mice.

MC 1:   (getting emotional, close to tears) Yeah, we'll sort that one out for you. Last caller, we're gonna have to go. Respect going out to you, mate! Hold it down, last caller, *rude boy* FOR YEEEEAAARS! Believe me, send this one out to you, last caller! From the Dominator! Send this one out to you, mate. You're a bad boy, BELIEF!!! 90–3, the Index, comin' on strong, belief!!!

MC 2:   Don't forget, people – New Year's Eve, Index FM are going to be throwing a free rave in conjunction with UAC Promotions. *Rrrrrave, rrrrrave!!!!* Three mental floors of mayhem, lasers, lights, all the works – you know the score.

MC 1:   (gasping feyly) *Oh goshhhh!!!* Keep the pagers *rushing!* Come and go. *OOOOOOH goshhhh!!* We're comin' on, we're comin on strong, *believe* . . . Deeper! Deeper into the groove . . . Yeah, London Town, we've got another caller, wants to go live!

Caller 2:   (sounding rehearsed) Hi, I wanna give a big shout to all Gathall Crew, all Brockley crew, Pascal, Bassline, Smasher . . . We're in the house and we're rocking, you be shocking, for '92, mate!!

MC 1:   Believe it, mate!

Caller 2:   'ARD-KORE, you *know* the score!!!

MC 1:   Where you coming from, mate?

Caller 2:   South London, mate.

MC 1:   Wicked. Shout to the South London crew. Respect! Index! Yeah, London, you're in tune to the live line, Index FM, *runnin' tings in London right 'bout now.* The one and only.

Rapt then and now by phone-in sessions like this one, by the listeners' fervent salutations and the MC's invocations, I'm struck by the crusading zeal and intransitive nature of the utterances: "Rushing! . . . Buzzin' hard!," "Get busy!," "Come alive, London!," "Let's go!," "Time to get hyper, helter-skelter! . . . Hardcore's firing!," and, especially prominent in the Index-at-Xmas session, the near-gnostic exhortation "Belief!"

Gnosis is the esoteric knowledge of spiritual truth that various pre-Christian and early Christian cults believed could be apprehended directly only by the initiate, a truth that cannot be mediated or explained in words. In rave, catchphrases like "hardcore, you know the score" or "you know the key" are code for the secret knowledge to which only "the headstrong people" are privy. And this is drug *knowledge*, the physically felt intensities induced by Ecstasy, amphetamine, and the rest of the pharmacopoeia. The MC's role, as master of the sacra-mental ceremonies, is ceaselessly to reiterate that secret without ever translating it. The MC is an encryptor; a potent inclusion/exclusion device – for if you're not down with the program, you'll never know what that idiot is raving about.

The transcript of the Index-at-Xmas exchange can't convey the electricity of everyone in the studio coming up on their Es at the same time, of the NRG currents pulsing across the cellular-phone ether from kids buzzing at home. Listening to pirate phone-in sessions like this, I felt there was a feedback loop of ever-escalating exultation switching back and forth between the station and the raving "massive" at home. The whole subculture resembled a giant mechanism designed to generate fervor without aim.

The rave and the pirate radio show (the "rave on the air") are exemplary real-world manifestations of two influential theoretical models, Hakim Bey's "temporary autonomous zone" (TAZ) and Gilles Deleuze and Felix Guattari's "desiring machine." The feedback loop of the phone-in sessions makes me think of Hakim Bey's vision of the TAZ as a temporary "power surge" against normality, as opposed to a doomed attempt at permanent revolution. A power surge is what it feels like – like being plugged into the national electrical grid. The audience is galvanized, shocked out of the living death of normality: "Come alive, London!" The combination of the DJ's interminable metamusic flow and the MC's variations on a small set of themes has the effect of abolishing narrative in favor of a thousand plateaus of crescendo. Again and again, the DJ and the MC affirm "we're here, we're now, this is the place to be, you and I are *we*." This radical immediacy fits Hakim Bey's anarcho-mystical creed of "immediatism," so named to indicate its antagonism to all forms of mediated, passivity-inducing leisure and culture.

The rave also corresponds to Deleuze and Guattari's model of the "desiring machine": a decentered, nonhierarchical assemblage of people and technology characterized by flow-without-goal and expression-without-meaning. The rave works as an intensification machine, generating a series of heightened here-and-nows – sonically, by the music's repetitive loops, and visually, by lights, lasers, and above all the strobe (whose freeze-frame effect creates a concatenated sequence of ultravivid tableaux).

Just as a rave can't function without ravers, similarly the "desiring machine" depends on its human components – what Deleuze and Guattari call the "body-without-organs." The opposite of the organism – which is oriented around survival and reproduction – the body-without-organs is composed out of all the potentials in the human nervous system for pleasure and sensation without purpose: the sterile bliss of perverse sexuality, drug experiences, play, dancing, and so forth. In the rave context, the desiring machine and the body-without-organs are fueled by the same energy source: MDMA. Plugged into the sound system, charged up on E, the raver's body-without-organs simply buzzes, bloated with unemployable energy: a feeling of "arrested orgasm" captured in pirate MC ejaculations like "oooooh gosh!"

Described by Deleuze and Guattari as "a continuous, self-vibrating region of intensities whose development avoids any orientation toward a culmination point or external end," the body-without-organs is an update of Freud's notion of polymorphous perversity: a diffuse eroticism that's connected to the nongenital, nonorgasmic sensuality of the pre-Oedipal infant. The body-without-organs also echoes age-old mystical goals: Zen's Uncarved Block, a blissful, inchoate flux preceding individuation and gender; the "translucent" or "subtle body," angelic and androgynous, whose resurrection was sought by the gnostics and alchemists.

In *Omens of Millennium* – a book about the contemporary resurgence of gnostic preoccupations with angels and near-death experiences – Harold Bloom argues: "To be drugged by the embrace of nature into what we call most natural in us, our sleepiness and our sexual desires, is at once a pleasant and an unhappy fate, since what remains immortal in us is both androgynous and sleepless." MDMA, an "unnatural" designer drug whose effects are antiaphrodisiac and insomniac, might be a synthetic shortcut to recovering our angelhood. I remember one time on E enjoying a radical sensation of being without gender, a feeling of docility and angelic gentleness so novel and exquisite I could only express it clumsily: "I feel really *effeminate*." The subliminal hormonal "hum" of masculinity was suddenly silenced.

Such sensations of sexual indifference have everything to do with MDMA's removal of aggression, especially sexual aggression. E's reputation as the "love drug" has more to do with cuddles than copulation, sentimentality than secretions. E is notorious for making erection difficult and male orgasm virtually impossible; women fare rather better, although one female therapist suggests that on Ecstasy "the particular organization and particular focusing of the body and the psychic energy necessary to achieve orgasm [are] . . . very difficult" Despite this, MDMA still has a reputation as an aphrodisiac – partly because it enhances touch, and partly because affection, intimacy, and physical tenderness are, for many people, inextricably entangled and conflated with sexual desire.

Unaware of Ecstasy's effects, many early commentators were quick to ascribe the curiously chaste vibe at raves to a post-AIDS retreat from adult sexuality. But one of the most radically novel and arguably subversive aspects of rave culture is precisely that it's the first youth subculture that's *not* based on the notion that sex is transgressive. Rejecting all that tired sixties rhetoric of sexual liberation, and recoiling from our sex-saturated pop culture, rave locates bliss in prepubescent childhood. Hence the garish colors and baggy clothing, the backpacks and satchels, the lollipops and pacifiers and teddy bears – even the fairground sideshows. It's intriguing that a drug originally designed as an appetite suppressant should have this effect. Anorexia has long been diagnosed as a refusal of adult sexual maturity and all its accompanying hassles. Ecstasy doesn't negate the body, it intensifies the pleasure of physical expression while completely emptying out the sexual content of dance. For men, the drug/music interface acts to de-phallicize the body and open it up to enraptured, abandoned, "effeminate" gestures. But removing the heterosexist impulse can mean that women are rendered dispensable. As with that earlier speed-freak scene, the mods (who dressed sharp and posed to impress their mates, not to lure a mate), there's a homosocial aura to many rave and club scenes. Hence the autoerotic/autistic quality to rave dance. Recent converts to raving often express the sentiment "it's better than sex."

The samples that feature in much rave music – orgasmic whimpers and sighs, soul diva beseechings – induce a feverish state of *intransitive amorousness*. The ecstatic female vocals don't signify a desirable/desirous woman, but (as in gay disco) a hypergasmic rapture that the male identifies with and aspires toward. The "you" or "it" in vocal samples refers not to a person but a sensation. With E, the full-on raver lifestyle means literally falling in love every weekend, then (with the inevitable midweek crash) having your heart broken. Millions of kids across the globe are riding this emotional roller coaster. Always looking ahead to their next tryst with E, addicted to love, in love with . . . nothing?

In her memoir *Nobody Nowhere*, the autistic Donna Williams describes how as a child she would withdraw from a threatening reality into a private preverbal dream-space of ultravivid color and rhythmic pulsations; she could be transfixed for hours by iridescent motes in the air that only she could perceive. With its dazzling psychotropic lights, its sonic pulses, rave culture is arguably a form of *collective autism*. The rave is utopia in its original etymological sense: a nowhere/nowhen wonderland.

So perhaps the best classification for Ecstasy is "utopiate," R. Blum's term for LSD. The Ecstasy experience can be like heaven on Earth. Because it's not a hallucinogen but a sensation intensifier, MDMA actually makes the world seem *realer*; the drug also feels like it's bringing out the "real you," freed from all the neurosis instilled by a sick society. But "utopiate" contains the word "opiate," as in "religion is the opium of the people." A sacrament in that secular religion called "rave," Ecstasy can just as easily be a counterrevolutionary force as it can fuel a hunger for change. For it's too tempting to take the easy option: simply repeating the experience, installing yourself permanently in rave's virtual reality pleasuredome.

Simon Reynolds, *Generation Ecstasy: Into the World of Techno and Rave Culture*, New York: Routledge, 1999, pp. 83–6, 237–48.

"HUGE MOB TORTURES NEGRO . . .,"
LYNCHING ACCOUNT FROM *100 YEARS OF LYNCHING*,
RALPH GINZBURG, ED.

There is a temptation to consider any and all popular and unofficial celebrations as "cultures of resistance" worth celebrating. This following selection will, I hope, temper that enthusiasm and warn us to be careful about how we define cultural resistance. It is an account of a lynching of a black man by a white mob in the state of Georgia on June 21, 1920. Put together out of local and largely sympathetic press reports of the time by amateur historian and civil rights advocate

Ralph Ginzburg, this is a fairly typical account of that period. Lynchings were festive occasions. Thousands of people showed up to watch the brutal displays, dancing and singing and eating out of the picnic baskets they had brought. The victim's toes and fingers and more private extremities were cut off as souvenirs, and local photographers would often memorialize the event and later sell the images on postcards. Lynchings were not state sanctioned affairs. Sometimes local Sheriffs and the Home Guard would look the other way, but other times they used tear gas to disperse crowds or were shot trying to defend the lynching victim. Lynchings like the one recorded below were genuine rebellious expressions of the popular culture of white racism.

Huge Mob Tortures Negro to Avenge Brutal Slaying

June 21, 1920   Within a few hours after he had been captured near Stilson in Bulloch county yesterday Philip Gathers, the negro who brutally murdered Miss Anza Jaudon near Rincon ten days ago, was lynched on the spot where the body of the young woman was found.

The murder of the beautiful young woman was avenged in a manner that ought to strike terror to those who might be tempted to commit a similar crime. After his body had been mutilated, while he was alive, the negro was saturated with gasoline and burned, and while he was burning his body was literally riddled with bullets and buckshot.

The mob numbered several thousand, and was composed of men and women from Effingham, Bulloch, Chatham and Screven counties. The crime was committed in Effingham about three miles from Rincon. And it was there that the black brute paid the supreme penalty for the crime.

The execution of the negro was witnessed by hundreds of persons, and many thousand who were in the crowd literally fought to get close enough to see the actual details. Almost every person who had a firearm, and it seemed that every one carried a gun or a pistol, emptied the weapon into the man's prostrate body. He was not shot until he had been mutilated and saturated with gasolene and a match touched. The infuriated mob could hold itself in check no longer. One shot was fired from a revolver and it was the signal for a thousand shots which made mince meat of the body.

Four young women from the crowd pushed their way through the outer rim of the circle and emptied rifles into the negro. They stood by while other men cut off fingers, toes and other parts of the body and passed them around as souvenirs.

After all of the ammunition had been used more wood was piled on the remains and gasolene poured on the pile. Later the charred remains were tied to the limb of a tree and left dangling over the road. The lower part of the body hung so low there was hardly room for automobiles to clear it.

The first news of the capture was received in Savannah by the *Morning News*. It was telegraphed from Stilson by J.S. Kenan, the *Morning News* correspondent at Statesboro, who had been with the Bulloch posse almost constantly since Saturday morning when Gathers was first discovered in Bulloch.

The news spread rapidly. Chief Harley of the county police sent around the corner to the Grantham Motor Company and borrowed a new Apperson car, driven by George Waters. In this he and County Policeman O'Neal and a *Morning News* reporter, made a quick trip to the scene of the murder.

Mr. Kenan telegraphed that Gathers had been captured a mile and a half from Stilson and that he would be taken to the home of Miss Jaudon's mother, three miles from Rincon. This automobile went to Rincon and was directed via McCall's road to the Jaudon home. None of the captors had arrived so the party drove into the narrow road through the swamp to the scene of the murder. There they found the exact spot where the body of Miss Jaudon was found. Two other machines were already there.

Shortly afterward cars began arriving from every direction. Within an hour there were nearly 500 machines in the swamp and the crowd was rapidly swelling. An hour and ten minutes after the first car arrived on this lonely road where Miss Jaudon was murdered, the posse from Bulloch arrived with the negro.

His arrival was heralded with a shout, but there was really no disorder at that time. Older heads commanded the hot-bloods to be careful and not shoot.

Among those waiting were a brother and sister of the victim. The crowd was forced back and they were allowed to talk to Gathers.

The sister begged the negro to tell her what her sister's last words were, but he refused to admit that he committed the crime. The brother had said he hoped a confession would be obtained before the lynchers did their work, but he said afterwards that he was absolutely certain the right man had been punished.

A pile of wood had been placed on the spot where the body was discovered a week ago yesterday. As Gathers was being dragged, pushed and shoved along men reached over the shoulders of comrades and struck the negro on the head with the butts of their guns. Others slashed him with knives. One man stabbed him several times. While he was being chained to a small tree over the wood pile he was treated to further surgical punishment below the belt. Through it all he never murmured.

A match was applied after he had been chained around the chest and legs to the sapling. The wood was wet and soggy and burned so slowly the mob became impatient and somebody called for gasolene. Up to this time not a shot had been fired and the crowd was remarkably quiet under the circumstances.

Two quarts of gasolene were drawn from an automobile. It was poured over the negro. The blaze enveloped the body and caused the crowd to fall back. With a yell the negro lunged forward and broke the chains that held him to the tree. The force with which he tore himself free carried him ten feet away. As he fell a shot was fired, and then it sounded like a hundred machine guns had cut loose.

There was scrambling for cover, and it was remarkable that many were not shot, as men standing in a complete circle about the body were firing as fast as they could pull the trigger and reload. After all of the shooting was over it was discovered that H.J. Haterick of Oliver had been hit by a stray bullet. He was hit in the left leg about half way between the knee and ankle. Dr. Usher examined and bandaged the wound and said the bullet had glanced off the bone and come out without doing serious injury.

The original program of the searchers was to take the negro by the home so Mrs. Jaudon could see him, but this was not done as she was almost prostrated. The captors left Stilson about 9 o'clock and made the trip around by Oliver, and Springfield. No effort was made to interfere with them.

The lynching took place at 12.15 o'clock.

Just before the prisoner was delivered to the scene of the lynching it was reported that the Savannah Home Guard had been called out. This did not cause the crowd a great deal of concern as they expected to finish their task before the military could arrive. And they did.

The first of the Guard reached Montieth in time to meet the crowds returning from the lynching.

100 Years of Lynching, Ralph Ginzburg (ed.), Baltimore: Black Classic Press, 1962, pp. 132–5.

FOUR

SUBCULTURES AND
PRIMITIVE REBELS

Ravers, rastas, mods and skins. Punks, hippies, beats and b-boys. Zoot-suiters, hotrodders, lowriders, drag queens and drag kings. Headbangers and deadheads, riot grrrls and rude-boys, Bowery b'hoys and Bowery g'hals, fops and flappers, gangsters and gangstas. Bohemians. For as long as there has been a "mainstream" culture there have been those who have staked their position outside. There they fashion their own identities and communities, customs and styles, often, but not always, coming together around "Culture" like music or clothing or even cars, and through these artifacts construct a "culture" of their own. Through this cultural lens they view the world, dividing it into good and bad, in the process creating a system of values and norms distinct from, and often in opposition to, those of greater society. These are subcultures; micro-worlds created by those who feel they don't belong in the world at large: the young, the passed over, the outcast. This cultural space offers great political potential, for subcultures provide a place to test out new identities, ideas and activities that deviate from the status quo. And, because they are self-constructed, subcultures grant their constituents the power of creation and then a sense of ownership over what they have created. These are key ingredients of any political formation. But subcultures can also become an escape from politics; a safe space to dream up magical cultural solutions to real-world problems and a place to lock yourself away from those who don't see the world the same as you. Subcultures are cultural resistance. The question is where does this resistance lead?

E.J. HOBSBAWM,
SELECTIONS FROM *PRIMITIVE REBELS*

Nearly everyone knows of Robin Hood, the hero of Sherwood Forest who stole from the rich to give to the poor. The story perseveres because it speaks to enduring conditions of inequality and injustice, and equally enduring fantasies of righteous rebellion. This myth of the social bandit is part of our cultural heritage (cf. Kelley). In this next section the historian Eric Hobsbawm, better known for his grand sweeping narratives of revolution and industrial empire, examines the lives and politics of obscure social bandits. These "primitive rebels" protest the wrongs of the world by conjuring up and acting out a culture of resistance, removing themselves from society and living according to their own code. In the bandit Hobsbawm locates a "pre-political" figure, a "people who have not yet found, or only begun to find, a specific language in which to express their aspirations about the world." He argues, however, that these aspirations often remain just that: aspirations. While their causes are commonly just, the rebel's responses, politically speaking, are usually fantastic and frequently futile. Nonetheless, in these pre-political responses lay the seeds, perhaps, of later and more mature, political fruit.

The history of social movements is generally treated in two separate divisions. We know something about the ancient and medieval ones: slave revolts, social heresies and sects, peasant risings, and the like. To say that we possess a 'history' of them is perhaps misleading, for in the past they have been treated largely as a series of episodes, punctuating the general story of humanity, though historians have disagreed on their importance in the historical process and still debate their precise relationship to it. So far as modern times are concerned such agitations have been regarded by all, except anthropologists who are obliged to deal with pre-capitalist or imperfectly capitalist societies, simply as 'forerunners' or odd survivals. On the other hand 'modern' social movements, that is to say those of Western Europe from the later 18th century, and those of increasingly large sectors of the world in subsequent periods, have normally been treated according to a long-established and reasonably sound scheme. For obvious reasons the historians have concentrated on labour and socialist movements, and such other movements as have been fitted into the socialist framework. These are commonly regarded as having their 'primitive' stages – journeymen's societies and Luddism, Radicalism, Jacobinism and Utopian Socialisms – and eventually as developing towards a modern pattern which varies from one country to the next but has considerable general application. Thus labour movements develop certain forms of trade union and co-operative organization, certain types of political organization such as mass parties, and certain types of programme and ideology, such as secularist Socialism.

The subjects of this book fit into neither category. At first sight they belong to the first division. At any rate nobody would be surprised to encounter Vardarelli and bodies such as *Mafia*, or millennarian movements, in the European Middle Ages. But the point about them is that they do *not* occur in the Middle Ages, but in the 19th and 20th centuries, and indeed the past 150 years have produced them in abnormally large numbers, for reasons discussed in the text. Nor can they be simply written off as marginal or unimportant phenomena, though older historians have often tended to do so, partly out of rationalist and 'modernist' bias, partly because, as I hope to show, the political allegiance and character of such movements is often undetermined, ambiguous or even ostensibly 'conservative,' partly because historians, being mainly educated and townsmen, have until recently simply not made sufficient effort to understand people who are unlike themselves. For, with the exception of the ritual brotherhoods of the Carbonaro type, all the phenomena studied in this book belong to the world of people who neither write nor read many books – often because they are illiterate –, who are rarely known by name to anybody except their friends, and then often only by nickname, who are normally inarticulate, and rarely understood even when they express themselves. Moreover, they are *pre-political* people who have not yet found, or only begun to find, a specific language in which to express their aspirations about the world. Though their movements are thus in many respects blind and groping, by the standards of modern ones, they are neither unimportant nor marginal. Men and women such as those with whom this book deals form the large majority in many, perhaps in most, countries even today, and their acquisition of political consciousness has made our century the most revolutionary in history. For this reason the study of their movements is not merely curious, or interesting, or moving for anyone who cares about the fate of men, but also of practical importance.

. . .

The Social Bandit

Bandits and highwaymen preoccupy the police, but they ought also to preoccupy the social historian. For in one sense banditry is a rather primitive form of organized social protest, perhaps the most primitive we know. At any rate in many societies it is regarded as such by the poor, who consequently protect the bandit, regard him as their champion, idealize him, and turn him into a myth: *Robin Hood* in England, *Janošik* in Poland and Slovakia, *Diego Corrientes* in Andalusia, who are probably all real figures thus transmuted. In return, the bandit himself tries to live up to his role even when he is not himself a conscious social rebel. Naturally Robin Hood, the archetype of the social rebel 'who took from the rich to give to the poor and never killed but in self-defence or just revenge', is not the only man of his kind. The tough man, who is unwilling to bear the traditional burdens of the common man in a class society, poverty and meekness, may escape from them by joining or serving the oppressors as well as by revolting against them. In any peasant society there are 'landlords' bandits' as well as 'peasant bandits' not to mention the State's bandits, though only the peasant bandits receive the tribute of ballads and anecdotes. Retainers, policemen, mercenary soldiers are thus often recruited from the same material as social bandits. Moreover, as the experience of Southern Spain between 1850 and 1875 shows, one sort of bandit can easily turn into another – the 'noble' robber and smuggler into the *bandolero*, protected by the local rural boss or *cacique*. Individual rebelliousness is itself a socially neutral phenomenon, and consequently mirrors the divisions and struggles within society . . .

However, something like an ideal type of social banditry exists, and this is what I propose to discuss, even though few bandits of recorded history, as distinct from legend, correspond completely to it. Still, some – like Angelo Duca (Angiolillo) – do even that.

To describe the 'ideal' bandit is by no means unrealistic. For the most startling characteristic of social banditry is its remarkable uniformity and standardization. The material used in this chapter comes almost wholly from Europe in the 18th to 20th centuries, and indeed mainly from Southern Italy.[1] But the cases one looks at are so similar, though drawn from periods as widely separated as the mid-18th and the mid-20th centuries and places as independent of one another as Sicily and Carpatho-Ukraine, that one generalizes with very great confidence. This uniformity applies both to the bandit myths – that is, to the part for which the bandit is cast by the people – and to his actual behaviour.

A few examples of such parallelism may illustrate the point. The population hardly ever helps the authorities to catch the 'peasants' bandit,' but on the contrary protects him. This is so in the Sicilian villages of the 1940s as in the Muscovite ones of the 17th century.[2] Thus his standard end – for if he makes too much of a nuisance of himself almost every individual bandit will be defeated, though banditry may remain endemic – is by betrayal. Oleksa Dovbush, the Carpathian bandit of the 18th century, was betrayed by his mistress; Nikola Shuhaj, who is supposed to have flourished *c.* 1918–20, by his friends.[3] Angelo Duca (Angiolillo), *c.* 1760–84, perhaps the purest example of social banditry, of whose career Benedetto Croce has given a masterly analysis,[4] suffered the same fate. So, in 1950, did Salvatore

Giuliano of Montelepre, Sicily, the most notorious of recent bandits, whose career has lately been described in a moving book.[5] So, if it comes to that, did Robin Hood himself. But the law, in order to hide its impotence, claims credit for the bandit's capture or death: the policemen shoot bullets into Nikola Shuhaj's dead body to claim the kill, as they did, if Gavin Maxwell is to be believed, into Giuliano's. The practice is so common that there is even a Corsican proverb to describe it: 'Killed after death, like a bandit by the police.'[6] And the peasants in turn add invulnerability to the bandit's many other legendary and heroic qualities. Angiolillo was supposed to possess a magic ring which turned away bullets. Shuhaj was invulnerable because – theories diverged – he had a green twig with which he waved aside bullets, or because a witch had made him drink a brew that made him resist them; that is why he had to be killed with an axe. Oleksa Dovbush, the legendary 18th-century Carpathian bandit-hero, could only be killed with a silver bullet that had been kept one year in a dish of spring wheat, blessed by a priest on the day of the twelve great saints and over which twelve priests had read twelve masses. I have no doubt that similar myths are part of the folklore of many other great bandits. Obviously none of these practices or beliefs are derived from one another. They arise in different places and periods, because the societies and situations in which social banditry arises are very similar.

It may be convenient to sketch the standardized picture of the social bandit's career. A man becomes a bandit because he does something which is not regarded as criminal by his local conventions, but is so regarded by the State or the local rulers. Thus Angiolillo took to the hills after a quarrel over cattle-straying with a field-guard of the Duke of Martina. The best-known of the current bandits in the Aspromonte area of Calabria, Vicenzo Romeo of Bova (which is, incidentally, the last Italian village speaking ancient Greek), became an outlaw after abducting a girl he subsequently married, while Angelo Macri of Delianova killed a policeman who had shot his brother.[7] Both blood-feud (the *faida*) and marriage by abduction are common in this part of Calabria.[8] Indeed, of the 160-odd outlaws reported at large in the province of Reggio Calabria in 1955, most of the forty who took to the hills for 'homicide' are locally regarded as 'honourable' homicides. The State mixes in 'legitimate' private quarrels and a man becomes a 'criminal' in its eyes. The State shows an interest in a peasant because of some minor infraction of the law, and the man takes to the hills because how does he know what a system which does not know or understand peasants, and which peasants do not understand, will do to him? Mariani Dionigi, a Sardinian bandit of the 1890s, went because he was about to be arrested for complicity in a 'just' homicide. Goddi Moni Giovanni, another, went for the same reason. Campesi (nicknamed Piscimpala) was admonished by the police in 1896, arrested a little later for 'contravention of the admonition' and sentenced to ten days and a year under surveillance; also to a fine of 12.50 lire for letting his sheep pasture on the grounds of a certain Salis Giovanni Antonio. He preferred to take to the hills, attempted to shoot the judge and killed his creditor.[9] Giuliano is supposed to have shot a policeman who wanted to beat him up for black-marketing a couple of bags of wheat while letting off another smuggler who had enough money to bribe him; an act which would certainly be regarded as 'honourable'. In fact, what has been observed of Sardinia almost certainly applies more generally:

> The 'career' of a bandit almost always begins with some incident, which is not in itself grave, but drives him into outlawry: a police charge for some offence brought against the man rather than for the crime; false testimony; judicial error or intrigue; an unjust sentence to forced residence (*confino*), or one felt to be unjust.[10]

It is important that the incipient social bandit should be regarded as 'honourable' or non-criminal by the population, for if he was regarded as a criminal against local convention, he could not enjoy the local protection on which he must rely completely. Admittedly almost anyone who joins issue with the oppressors and the State is likely to be regarded as a victim, a hero or both. Once a man is on the run, therefore, he is naturally protected by the peasants and by the weight of local conventions which stands for 'our' law – custom, blood-feud or whatever it might be – against 'theirs', and 'our' justice against that of the rich. In Sicily he will, unless very troublesome, enjoy the goodwill of *Mafia*, in Southern Calabria of the so-called *Onorata Società*,[11] everywhere of public opinion. Indeed, he may – and perhaps mostly will – live near or in his village, whence he is supplied. Romeo, for instance, normally lives in Bova with his wife and children and has built a house there. Giuliano did the same in his town of Montelepre. Indeed, the extent to which the ordinary bandit is tied to his territory – generally that of his birth and 'his' people – is very impressive. Giuliano lived and died in Montelepre territory, as his predecessors among Sicilian bandits, Valvo, Lo Cicero and Di Pasquale had lived and died in Montemaggiore or Capraro in Sciacca.[12] The worst thing that can happen to a bandit is to be cut off from his local sources of supply, for then he is genuinely forced to rob and steal, that is to steal from his people, and may therefore become a criminal who may be denounced. The phrase of the

Corsican official who regularly left wheat and wine for bandits in his country cottage, expresses one side of this situation: 'Better to feed them in this way than to oblige them to steal what they need.'[13] The behaviour of the brigands in the Basilicata illustrates the other side. In this area brigandage died out during the winter, some brigands even emigrating to work, because of the difficulty of getting food for outlaws. In spring, as food became available again, the brigandage season began.[14] These Lucanian cut-throats knew why they did not force the poor peasants to feed them, as they would certainly have done had they been an occupying force. The Spanish government in the 1950s ended Republican guerilla activity in the Andalusian mountains by moving against Republican sympathizers and suppliers in the villages, thus obliging the outlaws to steal food and alienate the non-political shepherds, who therefore became willing to inform against them.[15]

A few remarks may complete our sketch of the mechanics of the bandit's life. Normally he will be young and single or unattached, if only because it is much harder for a man to revolt against the apparatus of power once he has family responsibilities: two-thirds of the bandits in the Basilicata and Capitanata in the 1860s were under 25 years old.[16] The outlaw may of course remain alone – indeed, in cases where a man commits a traditional 'crime' which may, by custom, allow an eventual return to full legality (as in vendetta or abduction) this may be the usual case. Of the 160 or so existing South Calabrian outlaws most are said to be lone wolves of this sort; that is, individuals living on the margin of their villages, attached to them by threads of kin or support, kept from them by enmities and the police. If he joins or forms a band, and is thus economically committed to a certain amount of robbery, it will rarely be very large, partly for economic reasons, partly for organizational ones; for the band is held together only by the personal prestige of its leader. Some very small bands are known – e.g. the three men who were caught in the Maremma in 1897 (I need hardly say, by treachery).[17] Extremely large bands of up to sixty are reported among the Andalusian *bandoleros* of the 19th century, but they enjoyed the support of local lords (*caciques*) who used them as retainers; for this reason perhaps they do not belong in this chapter at all.[18] In periods of revolution, when bands become virtual guerilla units, even larger groups of some hundreds occurred, but in Southern Italy these also enjoyed financial and other support from the Bourbon authorities. The normal picture of even brigand-guerilla bands is one of a multiplicity of much smaller units, combining for operations. In the Capitanata under Joachim Murat there were something like seventy bands, in the Basilicata of

the early sixties thirty-nine, in Apulia some thirty. Their average membership in the Basilicata is given as 'from twenty to thirty', but can be
computed from the statistics as fifteen to sixteen. On may guess that a band
of thirty, such as Giuseppe de Furia led for many years in Napoleonic and
Restoration times, represents about the limit which can be dominated by
an average leader without organization and discipline such as few brigand
chieftains were capable of maintaining, larger units leading to secessions. (It
may be observed that this is also something like the figure in tiny fissi-
parous Protestant sects, such as the West Country Bible Christians, who
averaged thirty-three members per chapel in the 1870s.)[19]

How long a band lasted we do not know exactly. It would depend, one
imagines, on how much of a nuisance it made of itself, or how tense the
social situation, or how complex the international situation was – in the
period from 1799 to 1815 Bourbon and British help to local bandits might
make it easy to survive for many years –, and how much protection it had.
Giuliano (with heavy protection) lasted six years, but at a guess a Robin
Hood of some ambition would be lucky to survive for more than two to
four years: Janošik, the prototype bandit of the Carpathians in the early
18th century, and Shuhaj lasted for two years, Sergeant Romano in Apulia
after 1860 for thirty months, and five years broke the back of the most
tenacious Bourbon brigands in the South. However, an isolated small band
without great pretensions, such as that of Domenico Tiburzi on the confines of Latium, could carry on for twenty years (c. 1870–90). If the State let
him, the bandit might well survive and retire into ordinary peasant life, for
the ex-bandit was easily integrated into society, since it was only the State
and the gentry who considered his activities criminal.[20]

It does not greatly matter whether a man began his career for quasi-
political reasons like Giuliano, who had a grudge against the police and
government, or whether he simply robs because it is a natural thing for an
outlaw to do. He will almost certainly try to conform to the Robin Hood
stereotype in some respects; that is, he will try to be 'a man who took from
the rich to give to the poor and never killed but in self-defence or just
revenge'. He is virtually obliged to, for there is more to take from the rich
than from the poor, and if he takes from the poor or becomes an 'illegiti-
mate' killer, he forfeits his most powerful asset, public aid and sympathy. If
he is free-handed with his gains, it may only be because a man in his position in a society of pre-capitalist values shows his power and status by
largesse. And if he himself does not regard his actions as a social protest, the
public will, so that even a purely professional criminal may come to
pander to its view. Schinderhannes, the most famous, though not the most

remarkable of the gang-leaders who infested the Rhineland in the late 1790s,[21] was in no sense a social bandit. (As his name shows, he came from a low-caste trade traditionally associated with the underworld.) Yet he found it advantageous for his public relations to advertise the fact that he robbed only Jews, that is, dealers and moneylenders, and in return the anecdotes and chap-books which multiplied around him, gave him many of the attributes of the idealized Robin Hood hero: the open-handedness, the righting of wrongs, the courtesy, sense of humour, cunning and valour, the ubiquity amounting to invisibility – all bandits in anecdotes go about the countryside in impenetrable disguises –, and so on. In his case the tributes are totally undeserved, and one's sympathies are entirely with Jeanbon St André, the old member of the Committee of Public Safety, who laid these gangsters low. Nevertheless, he may well have felt himself at least part of the time as a 'protector of the poor'. Criminals come from the poor and are sentimental about some things. So characteristic a professional crook as Mr Billy Hill, whose autobiography (1955) deserves more sociological study than it has received, lapses into the usual maudlin self pity when he explains his continued career as a thief and gangster by the need to distribute money to 'his' people, that is to various families of Irish unskilled workers in Camden Town. Robin Hoodism, whether they believe in it or not, is useful to bandits.

However, many do not need to have the role thrust upon them. They take to it spontaneously, as did Pasquale Tanteddu of Sardinia whose views (somewhat influenced by communism) are more fully set out [elsewhere]. Again, I am told that a leading Calabrian bandit of pre-1914 vintage gave regular donations to the Socialist Party. Systematic Robin Hoods are known. Gaetano Vardarelli of Apulia, who was pardoned by the King and then betrayed and killed by him in 1818, was always distributing part of his booty to the poor, distributing salt free, ordering bailiffs to give bread to estate workers on pain of massacre, and commanding the local landed bourgeoisie to allow the poor to glean their fields. Angiolillo was exceptional in his systematic pursuit of a more general justice than could be achieved by casual gifts and individual interventions. 'When he arrived in any village' it is reported 'he had a tribunal set up, heard the litigants, pronounced sentence and fulfilled all the offices of a magistrate.' He is even supposed to have prosecuted common-law offenders. He ordered grain-prices to be lowered, confiscated the grain-stores held by the rich and distributed them to the poor. In other words, he acted as a parallel government in the peasants' interest. It is hardly surprising that as late as 1884 his village wanted to name the main street after him.

In their more primitive way the Southern brigands of the 1860s, like those of 1799–1815, saw themselves as the people's champions against the gentry and the 'foreigners'. Perhaps Southern Italy in these periods provides the nearest thing to a mass revolution and war of liberation led by social bandits. (Not for nothing has 'bandit' become a habitual term foreign governments use to describe revolutionary guerillas.) Thanks to a large scholarly literature the nature of these epochs of brigandage is now well understood, and few students now share the incomprehension of middle-class Liberals who saw in them nothing but 'mass delinquency', and barbarism if not Southern racial inferiority, an incomprehension which is still found in Norman Douglas' *Old Calabria*.[22] And Carlo Levi, among others, has reminded us in *Christ Stopped at Eboli* how profound the memory of the bandit heroes is among the Southern peasants, for whom the 'years of the brigands' are among the few parts of history which are alive and real, because, unlike the kings and wars, they belong to them. In their way the brigands, dressed in torn peasant costume with Bourbon rosettes, or in more gorgeous apparel, were avengers and champions of the people. If their way was a blind alley, let us not deny them the longing for liberty and justice which moved them.

Consequently also the characteristic victims of the bandit are the quintessential enemies of the poor. As recorded in tradition, they are always those groups which are particularly hated by them: lawyers (Robin Hood and Dick Turpin), prelates and idle monks (Robin Hood and Angiolillo), money-lenders and dealers (Angiolillo and Schinderhannes), foreigners and others who upset the traditional life of the peasant. In pre-industrial and prepolitical societies they rarely if ever include the sovereign, who is remote and stands for justice. Indeed, the legend frequently shows the sovereign pursuing the bandit, failing to suppress him, and then asking him to court and making his peace with him, thus recognizing that in a profound sense his and the sovereign's interest, justice, is the same. Thus with Robin Hood and Oleksa Dovbush.[23]

The fact that the bandit, especially when he was not himself filled with a strong sense of mission, lived well and showed off his wealth did not normally put the public off. Giuliano's solitaire ring, the bunches of chains and decorations with which the anti-French bandits of the 1790s festooned themselves in Southern Italy, would be regarded by the peasants as symbols of triumph over the rich and powerful, as well as, perhaps, evidences of the bandit's power to protect them. For one of the chief attractions of the bandit was, and is, that he is the poor boy who has made good, a surrogate for the failure of the mass to lift itself out of its own poverty, helplessness and meekness.[24] Paradoxically therefore the conspicuous expenditure of the bandit, like the gold-plated Cadillacs and diamond-inlaid teeth of the slum-boy who has become world boxing champion, serves to link him to his admirers and not to separate him from them; providing always that he does not step too far outside the heroic role into which the people have cast him.

The fundamental pattern of banditry, as I have tried to sketch it here, is almost universally found in certain conditions. It is rural, not urban. The peasant societies in which it occurs know rich and poor, powerful and weak, rulers and ruled, but remain profoundly and tenaciously traditional, and pre-capitalist in structure. An agricultural society such as that of 19th-century East Anglia or Normandy or Denmark is not the place to look for social banditry. (This is no doubt the reason why England, which has given the world Robin Hood, the archetype of the social bandit, has produced no notable example of the species since the 16th century. Such idealization of criminals as has become part of popular tradition, has seized upon urban figures like Dick Turpin and MacHeath, while the miserable village labourers have risen to little more than the modest admiration for exceptionally daring poachers.) Moreover, even in backward and traditional bandit societies, the social brigand appears only before the poor have reached political consciousness or acquired more effective methods of social agitation. The bandit is a pre-political phenomenon, and his strength is in inverse proportion to that of organized agrarian revolutionism and Socialism or Communism. Brigandage in the Calabrian Sila went out before the First World War, when Socialism and peasant leagues came in. It survived in the Aspromonte, the home of the great Musolino and numerous other popular heroes for whom the women prayed movingly.[25] But there peasant organization is less developed. Montelepre, Giuliano's town, is one of the few places in Palermo province which lacked any peasant league of importance even during the national peasant rising of 1893[26] and where even today people vote much less than elsewhere for the developed political parties and much more for lunatic fringe groups like monarchists or Sicilian separatists.

In such societies banditry is endemic. But it seems that Robin Hoodism is most likely to become a major phenomenon when their traditional equilibrium is upset: during and after periods of abnormal hardship, such as famines and wars, or at the moments when the jaws of the dynamic modern world seize the static communities in order to destroy and transform them. Since these moments occurred, in the history of most peasant societies, in the 19th or 20th centuries, our age is in some respects the classical age of the social bandit. We observe his upsurge — at least in the minds of the people – in Southern Italy and the Rhineland during the Revolutionary transformations and wars at the end of the 18th century; in Southern Italy after Unification, fanned by the introduction of capitalist law and economic policy.[27] In Calabria and Sardinia the major epoch of brigandage began in the 1890s, when the modern economy (and agricultural depression and emigration) made their impact. In the remote Carpathian mountains banditry flared up in the aftermath of the First World War, for social reasons which Olbracht has, as usual, described both accurately and sensibly.

But this very fact expressed the tragedy of the social bandit. The peasant society creates him and calls upon him, when it feels the need for a champion and protector – but precisely then he is incapable of helping it. For social banditry, though a protest, is a modest and unrevolutionary protest. It protests not against the fact that peasants are poor and oppressed, but against the fact that they are sometimes excessively poor and oppressed. Bandit-heroes are not expected to make a world of equality. They can only right wrongs and prove that sometimes oppression can be turned upside down. Still less can they understand what is happening to Sardinian villages that makes some men have plenty of cattle and others, who used to have a few, have none at all; that drives Calabrian villagers into American coalmines, or fills the Carpathian mountains with armies, guns and debt. The bandit's practical function is at best to impose certain limits to traditional oppression in a traditional society, on pain of lawlessness, murder and extortion. He does not even fulfill that very well, as a walk through Montelepre will convince the observer. Beyond that, he is merely a dream of how wonderful it would be if times were always good. 'For seven years he fought in our country,' the Carpathian peasants say about Dovbush, 'and while he lived things went well with the people'. It is a powerful dream, and that is why myths form about the great bandits which lend them superhuman power and the sort of immortality enjoyed by the great just kings of the past who have not really died, but are asleep and will return again. Just so Oleksa Dovbush sleeps while his buried axe moves every year nearer to the earth's surface by the breadth of a poppyseed, and when it emerges another hero will arise, a friend to the people, a terror to the lords, a fighter for justice, an avenger of injustice. Just so, even in the USA of yesterday in which small and independent men fought – if necessary by terror like the IWW – against the victory of big men and corporations, there were some who believed that the bandit Jesse James had not been killed but had gone to California. For what would happen to people if their champions were irrevocably dead?[28]

Thus the bandit is helpless before the forces of the new society which he cannot understand. At most he can fight it and seek to destroy it

> to avenge injustice, to hammer the lords, to take from them the wealth they have robbed and with fire and sword to destroy all that cannot serve the common good: for joy, for vengeance, as a warning for future ages – and perhaps for fear of them.[29]

That is why the bandit is often destructive and savage beyond the range of his myth, which insists mainly on his justice and moderation in killing. Vengeance, which in revolutionary periods ceases to be a private matter and becomes a class matter, requires blood, and the sight of iniquity in ruins can make men drunk.[30] And destruction, as Olbracht has correctly seen, is not simply a nihilistic release, but a futile attempt to eliminate all that would prevent the construction of a simple, stable, peasant community: the products of luxury, the great enemy of justice and fair dealing. For destruction is never indiscriminate. What is useful for poor men is spared.[31] And thus the Southern brigands who conquered Lucanian towns in the 1860s, swept through them, opening jails, burning archives, sacking the houses of the rich and distributing what they did not want to the people: harsh, savage, heroic and helpless.

For banditry as a social movement in such situations was and is inefficient in every way. First, because it is incapable even of effective guerilla organization. Bandits certainly succeeded in launching a Bourbon rising against the Northern conquest – that is, genuine bandits, not simply political partisans so called by their opponents. But when a Spanish Bourbon soldier, Borjes, attempted to form them into an effective guerilla movement, they resisted and threw him out:[32] the very structure of the spontaneous band precluded more ambitious operations, and though the thirty-nine Lucanian bands could continue to make the country unsafe for some years to come, they were doomed. Second, because their ideology debarred them from making revolt effective. Not because bandits were generally traditionalists in politics – for their first loyalty was to the peasants – but because the traditional forces whose side they took were either doomed, or because old and new oppression coalesced, leaving them isolated and helpless. The Bourbons might promise to distribute the land of the gentry to the peasants, but they never did; at most they gave a few ex-bandits commissions in the army. More likely than not they betrayed and killed them when they had done with them. Giuliano became the plaything of political forces he did not understand, when he allowed himself to become the military leader of the (*Mafia*-dominated) Sicilian Separatists.

The one obvious fact about the men who used him and threw him away is that their conception of an independent Sicily was very different from his, which was certainly closer to that of the organized peasants whose May Day meeting he massacred at the Portella della Ginestra in 1947.

To be effective champions of their people, bandits had to stop being bandits; that is the paradox of the modern Robin Hoods. They could indeed assist peasant risings, for in these mass movements it is generally the smallish band, rather than the vast crowd, which prepares the ground for effective action outside the actual village,[33] and what better nucleus for such shocktroops than the existing bands of the brigands? Thus in 1905 the peasant activities of the Ukrainian village of Bykhvostova were largely initiated by the cossack Vassili Potapenko (the 'tsar' of his band), the peasant Pyotr Cheremok (his 'minister') and their band, two men who had been formerly expelled from the village community for crimes – we do not know whether voluntarily or under pressure – and later re-admitted. As in other villages, these bands who represented poor and landless peasants, and the sense of the community against the individualists and enclosers, were later killed by a village counter-revolution of the *kulaks*.[34] However, the band could not be a lasting form of organization for revolutionary peasants. It could at best be a temporary auxiliary for otherwise unorganized ones.

Thus the romantic poets who idealized the bandit, like Schiller in *The Robbers*, were mistaken in believing them to be the real 'rebels'. The Bakuninist anarchists, who idealized them more systematically because of their very destructiveness, and who believed that they could harness them to their cause, were wasting their and the peasants' time.[35] They might succeed from time to time. There is at least one case in which a primitive peasant movement in which anarchist doctrine was combined with 'a strong bandit streak' became a major if temporary regional revolutionary force. But who really believes that, with all its chief's genius for irregular warfare, the 'Makhnovshchina' of the Southern Ukraine 1918–21 would have faced anything but defeat, whoever won ultimate power in the Russian lands?[36]

The future lay with political organization. Bandits who do not take to the new ways of fighting for the peasants' cause, as many of them do as individuals, generally converted in jails or conscript armies, cease to be champions of the poor and become mere criminals or retainers of landlords' and merchants' parties. There is no future for them. Only the ideals for which they fought, and for which men and women made up songs about them, survive, and round the fireside these still maintain the vision of the just society, whose champions are brave and noble as eagles, fleet as stags, the sons of the mountains and the deep forests.

E.J. Hobsbawm, *Primitive Rebels: Studies in Archaic Forms of Social Movement in the 19th and 20th Centuries*, New York: W.W. Norton, 1959/1965, pp. 1–3, 13–28.

ROBIN D.G. KELLEY,
"OGS IN POSTINDUSTRIAL LOS ANGELES: EVOLUTION OF A STYLE"

The glorification of the "gangsta" has deep roots in many cultures, African-American culture being no exception (cf. Hobsbawm). In the following selection, historian Robin D.G. Kelley explores the meaning of the OG, the original gangsta, in contemporary rap music. Like social banditry, gangsta rap is a magical response to political, economic, and social degradation: a fantasy of gun-blazing, dick-swinging omnipotence. But it is also, Kelley argues, an indigenous cultural medium with which rappers and their listeners navigate and critique capitalism and racism (see sidebar). The culture of social banditry, however, takes a new twist at the end of the twentieth century when the message of poor, urban black rage is bought and sold by multi-national corporations and eagerly consumed by, among others, white, middle-class, suburban teenagers. Given gangsta rap's popular and commercial appeal, Kelley touches upon an important question: is this culture of resistance reporting and reflecting upon the rough injustice of the ghetto or merely perpetuating and profiting by it?

LA might be the self-proclaimed home of the gangsta rap, but black Angelenos didn't put the gangsta into hip hop. Gangsta lyrics and style were part of the whole hip hop scene from its origins in the South Bronx during the mid-1970s. In Charlie Ahearn's classic 1982 film *Wild Style* about the early hip hop scene in New York, the rap duo Double Trouble stepped on stage decked out in white "pimp-style" suits, matching hats, and guns galore. Others in the film are "strapped" (armed) as well, waving real guns as part of the act. The scene seems so contemporary, and yet it was shot over a decade before the media paid attention to such rap songs as Onyx's "Throw Ya Guns in the Air."[1]

But to find the roots of gangsta rap's violent images, explicit language, and outright irreverence, we need to go back even further. Back before Lightin' Rod (aka Jalal Uridin of the Last Poets) performed toasts (narrative

"Squeeze the Trigger,"
Ice-T

Squeeze the trigger

Rampage on stage, my crews in a
rage
Searched my posse, found the Uzi
but missed the 12 gauge
Maniac, I'm a rhyme brainiac, livin' on
the edge of a razor
Remember that
Cold rollin' thick as a shake, I'm
rockin' hard as a quake
I can't live on bread and water or
lobster and steak
My mino's a riot gun, there ain't
none bigger
About to unload the ammo, "E"
squeeze the trigger

They say I'm violent, they should
watch their TV
They say I'm brutal, they should
check their PD
You made me, now your kids rave
me
I rap about the life that the city
streets gave me

Murder, intrigue, somebody must
bleed
Miami Vice is small time, LA's the big
league
From the rollin' 60s to the nickerson
"G"
Pueblos, grape street, this is what I
see
The jungle, the 30s, the VNG
Life in LA ain't no cup of tea

Squeeze the trigger
. . .
Cops hate kids, kids hate cops, cops
kill kids with warnin' shots
What is crime and what is not?
What is justice? I think I forgot

poetry from the black oral tradition) over live music on a popular album called *Hustlers' Convention* in 1973; before Lloyd Price recorded the classic black baaadman narrative, "Stagger Lee", in 1958; even before Screamin' Jay Hawkins recorded his explicitly sexual comedy "rap" "Alligator Wine." Indeed, in 1938 folklorist Alan Lomax recorded Jelly Roll Morton performing a number of profane and violent songs out of the black vernacular, including "The Murder Ballad" and "Make Me a Pallet on the Floor." Morton's lyrics rival the worst of today's gangsta rappers: "Come here you sweet bitch, give me that pussy, let me get in your drawers / I'm gonna make you think you fuckin' with Santa Claus." In other words, we need to go back to the blues, to the baaadman tales of the late nineteenth century, and to the age-old tradition of "signifying" if we want to discover the roots of the "gangsta" aesthetic in hip hop. Irreverence has been a central, component of black expressive vernacular culture, which is why violence and sex have been as important to toasting and signifying as playfulness with language. Many of these narratives are about power. Both the baaadman and the trickster embody a challenge to virtually *all* authority (which makes sense to people for whom justice is a rare thing), creates an imaginary upside-down world where the oppressed are the powerful, and it reveals to listeners the pleasures and price of reckless abandon. And in a world where male public powerlessness is often turned inward on women and children, misogyny and stories of sexual conflict are very old examples of the "price" of being baaad.[2]

Nevertheless, while gangsta rap's roots are very old, it does have an identifiable style of its own, and in some respects it is a particular product of the mid-1980s. The inspiration for the specific style we now call gangsta rap seems to have come from Philadelphia's Schooly D, who made *Smoke Some Kill*, and the Bronx-based rapper KRS 1 and Scott La Rock of Boogie Down Productions, who released *Criminal Minded*. Although both albums appeared in 1987, these rappers had been developing an East Coast gangsta style for some time. Ice-T who started out with the technopop wave associated with Radio and Uncle Jam's Army (recording his first single, "The Coldest Rap", in 1981), moved gangsta rap to the West Coast when he recorded "6 in the Mornin'" in 1986. Less than a year later, he released his debut album, *Rhyme Pays*.[3]

Ice-T was not only the first West Coast gangsta-style rapper on wax, but he was himself an experienced OG whose narratives were occasionally semi-autobiographical or drawn from things he had witnessed or heard on the street. A native of New Jersey who moved to Los Angeles as a child, "T" (Tracy Marrow) joined a gang while at Crenshaw High School and began a very short career as a criminal. He eventually graduated from Crenshaw, attended a junior college, and, with practically no job prospects, turned to the armed services. After four years in the service, he pursued his high school dream to become a rapper and starred in a documentary film called *Breaking and Entering*, which captured the West Coast break dance scene. When Hollywood made a fictionalized version of the film called *Breakin'*, Ice-T also made an appearance. Although Ice-T's early lyrics ranged from humorous boasts and tales of crime and violence to outright misogyny, they were clearly as much fact as fiction. In "Squeeze the Trigger" he leads off with a brief autobiographical, composite sketch of his gangsta background, insisting all along that he is merely a product of a callous, brutal society.[4]

Even before *Rhyme Pays* hit the record stores (though banned on the radio because of its explicit lyrics), an underground hip hop community was forming in Compton, a predominantly black and Latino city south of Los Angeles, that would play a pivotal role in the early history of gangsta rap. Among the participants was Eric Wright – better known as Eazy E – who subsequently launched an independent label known as Ruthless Records. He eventually teamed up with Dr. Dre and Yella, both of whom had left the rap group

We buy weapons to keep us strong
Reagan sends guns where they don't belong
The controversy is thick and the drag is strong
But no matter the lies we all know who's wrong
Homeless sleep on the city streets
Waitin' to die with nothin' to eat
While rich politicians soak their feet
In the pools at their ten million buck retreats
People hate people for color of face
No one had a choice in the race we were placed
A brother in Queens was beaten and chased
Murdered cold in the streets, a godamn disgrace
Just because of his race, his life went to waste
And no one went to jail when the court heard the case
Justice or corruption?
It's all interlaced
How can you swallow this?
I can't stand the taste

Squeeze the trigger.

From "Squeeze the Trigger," *Rhyme Pays*, Sire Records, 1987

World Class Wreckin Cru, and Ice Cube, who was formerly a member of a group called The CIA. Together they formed Niggas With Attitude and moved gangsta rap to another level. Between 1987 and 1988, Ruthless produced a string of records, beginning with their twelve-inch *NWA and the Posse*, Eazy E's solo album, *Eazy Duz It*, and the album which put NWA on the map, *Straight Outta Compton*.[5] Dr. Dre's brilliance as a producer – his introduction of hard, menacing beats, sparse drum tracks, and heavy bass with slower tempos – and Ice Cube's genius as a lyricist, made NWA one of the most compelling groups on the hip hop scene in years.

A distinctive West Coast style of gangsta rap, known for its rich descriptive storytelling laid over heavy funk samples[6] from the likes of George Clinton and the whole Parliament-Funkadelic family, Sly Stone, Rick James, Ohio Players, Average White Band, Cameo, Zapp and, of course, the Godfather himself – James Brown – evolved and proliferated rapidly soon after the appearance of Ice-T and NWA. The frequent use of Parliament-Funkadelic samples led one critic to dub the music "G-Funk (gangsta attitude over P-Funk beats)."[7] Within three years, dozens of Los Angeles-based groups came onto the scene, many produced by either Eazy E's Ruthless Records, Ice-T and Afrika Islam's Rhyme Syndicate Productions, Ice Cube's post-NWA project, Street Knowledge Productions, or Dr. Dre's Deathrow Records. The list of West Coast gangsta rappers includes Above the Law, Mob Style, Compton's Most Wanted, King Tee, The Rhyme Syndicate, Snoop Doggy Dogg, (Lady of) Rage, Poison Clan, Capital Punishment Organization (CPO), the predominantly Samoan Boo-Yaa Tribe, the DOC, DJ Quick, AMG, Hi-C, Low Profile, Nu Niggaz on the Block, South Central Cartel, Compton Cartel, 2nd II None, WC and the MAAD (Minority Alliance of Anti-Discrimination) Circle, Cypress Hill, and Chicano rappers like Kid Frost and Proper Dos.

Although they shared much with the larger hip hop community, gangsta rappers drew both praise and ire from their colleagues. Indeed, gangsta rap has generated more debate both within and without the hip hop world than any other genre.[8] Unfortunately, much of this debate, especially in the media, has only disseminated misinformation. Thus, it is important to clarify what gangsta rap is *not*. First, gangsta rappers have never merely celebrated gang violence, nor have they taken a partisan position in favor of one gang over another. Gang bangin' (gang participation) itself has never even been a central theme in the music. Many of the violent lyrics are not intended to be literal. Rather, they are boasting raps in which the imagery of gang bangin' is used metaphorically to challenge competitors on the microphone – an element common to all hard-core hip hop. The mic becomes a Tech–9 or AK–47, imagined drive-bys occur from the stage, flowing lyrics become hollow-point shells. Classic examples are Ice Cube's "Jackin' for Beats," a humorous song that describes sampling other artists and producers as outright armed robbery, and Ice-T's "Pulse of the Rhyme" or "Grand Larceny" (which brags about stealing a show), Capital Punishment Organization's aptly titled warning to other perpetrating rappers, "Homicide," NWA's "Real Niggaz", Dr. Dre's "Lyrical Gangbang," Ice Cube's, "Now I Gotta Wet'cha," Compton's Most Wanted's "Wanted" and "Straight Check N 'Em." Sometimes, as in the case of Ice-T's "I'm Your Pusher," an antidrug song that boasts of pushing "dope beats and lyrics/no beepers needed," gangsta rap lyrics have been misinterpreted by journalists and talk show hosts as advocating criminality and violence.[9]

This is not to say that all descriptions of violence are simply metaphors. Exaggerated and invented boasts of criminal acts should sometimes be regarded as part of a larger set of signifying practices. Performances like The Rhyme Syndicate's "My Word Is Bond" or J.D.'s storytelling between songs on Ice Cube's *AmeriKKKa's Most Wanted* are supposed to be humorous and, to a certain extent, unbelievable. Growing out of a much older set of cultural practices, these masculinist narratives are essentially verbal duels over who is the "baddest motherfucker around." They are not meant as literal descriptions of violence and aggression, but connote the playful use of language itself. So when J.D. boasts about how he used to "jack them motherfuckers for them Nissan trucks," the story is less about stealing per se than about the way in which he describes his bodaciousness.[10]

When gangsta rappers do write lyrics intended to convey a sense of social realism, their work loosely resembles a sort of street ethnography of racist institutions and social practices, but told more often than not in the first person. Whether gangsta rappers step into the character of a gang banger, hustler, or ordinary working person – that is, products and residents of the "hood" – the important thing to remember is that they are stepping into character; it is for descriptive purposes rather than advocacy. In some ways, these descriptive narratives, under the guise of objective "street journalism," are no less polemical (hence political) than nineteenth-century slave narratives in defense of abolition. When Ice Cube was still with NWA he explained, "We call ourselves underground street reporters. We just tell it how we see it, nothing more, nothing less."[11]

It would be naive to claim that descriptive lyrics, as an echo of the city, do not, in turn, magnify what they describe – but to say so is a far cry from claiming that the purpose of rap is to advocate violence. And, of course, rappers' reality is hardly "objective" in the sense of being detached; their standpoint is that of the ghetto dweller, the criminal, the victim of police repression, the teenage father, the crack slinger, the gang banger, and the female dominator. Much like the old "baaadman" narratives that have played an important role in black vernacular folklore, the characters they create, at first glance, appear to be apolitical individuals only out for themselves; and like the protagonist in Melvin Van Peebles's cinematic classic, *Sweet Sweetback's Baaadass Song*, they are reluctant to trust anyone. It is hard not to miss the influences of urban toasts and "pimp narratives," which became popular during the late 1960s and early 1970s. In many instances the characters are almost identical, and on occasion rap artists pay tribute to black vernacular oral poetry by lyrically "sampling" these early pimp narratives.[12]

For other consumers of gangsta rap, such as middle-class white males, the genre unintentionally serves the same role as blaxploitation films of the 1970s or, for that matter, gangster films of any generation. It attracts listeners for whom the "ghetto" is a place of adventure, unbridled violence, erotic fantasy, and/or an imaginary alternative to suburban boredom. White music critic John Leland once praised NWA because they "dealt in evil as fantasy: killing cops, smoking hos, filling quiet nights with a flurry of senseless buckshot." This kind of voyeurism partly explains NWA's huge white following and why their album, *Efil4zaggin*, shot to the top of the charts as soon as it was released. As one critic put it, "in reality, NWA have more in common with a Charles Bronson movie than a PBS documentary on the plight of the inner-cities." And why should it be otherwise? After all, NWA members have even admitted that some of their recent songs were not representations of reality "in the hood" but inspired by popular films like *Innocent Man* starring Tom Selleck and *Tango and Cash* starring Sylvester Stallone and Kurt Russell.[13]

While I'm fully aware that some rappers are merely "studio gangstas," and that the *primary* purpose of this music is to produce "funky dope rhymes" for our listening pleasure, we cannot ignore the fact that West Coast gangsta rap originated in, and continues to maintain ties to, the streets of LA's black working-class communities. The generation that came of age in the 1980s was the product of devastating structural changes in the urban economy that date back at least to the late 1960s. While the city as a whole experienced unprecedented growth, the communities of Watts and Compton faced increased economic displacement, factory closures, and an unprecedented deepening of poverty. The uneven development of LA's postindustrial economy meant an expansion of high-tech firms like Aerospace and Lockheed, and the disappearance of rubber and steel manufacturing firms, many of which were located in or near Compton and

Watts. Deindustrialization, in other words, led to the establishment of high-tech firms in less populated regions like Silicon Valley and Orange County. Developers and local governments helped the suburbanization process while simultaneously cutting back expenditures for parks, recreation, and affordable housing in inner-city communities. Thus since 1980 economic conditions in Watts deteriorated on a greater scale than in any other LA community, and by some estimates Watts is in worse shape now than in 1965. A 1982 report from the California Legislature revealed that South Central neighborhoods experienced a 50 percent rise in unemployment while purchasing power dropped by one-third. The median income for South Central LA's residents was a paltry $5,900–$2,500 below the median income for the black population a few years earlier.

Youth were the hardest hit. For all of Los Angeles County, the unemployment rate of black youth remained at about 45 percent, but in areas with concentrated poverty the rate was even higher. As the composition of LA's urban poor becomes increasingly younger, programs for inner-city youth are being wiped out at an alarming rate. Both the Neighborhood Youth Corps and the Comprehensive Employment and Training Act (CETA) have been dismantled, and the Jobs Corps and Los Angeles Summer Job Program have been cut back substantially.[14]

Thus, on the eve of crack cocaine's arrival on the urban landscape, the decline in employment opportunities and growing immiseration of black youth in LA led to a substantial rise in property crimes committed by juveniles and young adults. Even NWA recalls the precrack illicit economy in a song titled "The Dayz of Wayback," in which Dr. Dre and M.C. Ren wax nostalgic about the early to mid-1980s, when criminal activity consisted primarily of small-time muggings and robberies.[15] Because of its unusually high crime rate, LA had by that time gained the dubious distinction of having the largest urban prison population in the country. When the crack economy made its presence felt in inner-city black communities, violence intensified as various gangs and groups of peddlers battled for control over markets. In spite of the violence and financial vulnerability that went along with peddling crack, for many black youngsters it was the most viable economic option.[16]

While the rise in crime and the ascendance of the crack economy might have put money into some people's pockets, for the majority it meant greater police repression. Watts, Compton, Northwest Pasadena, Carson, North Long Beach, and several other black working-class communities were turned into war zones during the mid- to late 1980s. Police helicopters, complex electronic surveillance, even small tanks armed with battering rams became part of this increasingly militarized urban landscape. During this same period, housing projects, such as Imperial Courts, were renovated along the lines of minimum security prisons and equipped with fortified fencing and an LAPD substation. Imperial Court residents were now required to carry identity cards and visitors were routinely searched. As popular media coverage of the inner city associated drugs and violence with black youth, young African-Americans by virtue of being residents in South Central LA and Compton were subject to police harassment and, in some cases, feared by older residents.[17]

All of these problems generated penetrating critiques by gangsta rappers. M.C. Ren, for example, blamed "the people who are holding the dollars in the city" for the expansion of gang violence and crime, arguing that if black youth had decent jobs, they would not need to participate in the illicit economy. "It's their fault simply because they refused to employ black people. How would you feel if you went for job after job and each time, for no good reason, you're turned down?"[18] Ice-T blames capitalism entirely, which he defines as much more than alienating wage labor; the market-place itself as well as a variety of social institutions are intended to exercise social control over African-Americans. "Capitalism says you must have an upper class, a middle class, and a lower class . . . Now the only way to guarantee a lower class, is to keep y'all uneducated and as high as possible."[19] According to Ice-T the ghetto is, at worst, the product of deliberately oppressive policies, at best, the result of racist neglect. Nowhere is this clearer than in his song "Escape from the Killing Fields," which uses the title of a recent film about the conflict in Cambodia as a metaphor for the warlike conditions in today's ghettos.[20]

Gangsta rappers construct a variety of first-person narratives to illustrate how social and economic realities in late capitalist LA affect young black men. Although the use of first-person narratives is rooted in a long tradition of black aesthetic practices,[21] the use of "I" to signify both personal and collective experiences also enables gangsta rappers to navigate a complicated course between what social scientists call "structure" and "agency." In gangsta rap there is almost always a relationship between the conditions in which these characters live and the decisions they make. Some gangsta rappers – Ice Cube in particular – are especially brilliant at showing how, if I may paraphrase Marx, young urban black men make their own history but not under circumstances of their own choosing.

Robin D.G. Kelley, *Race Rebels: Culture, Politics, and the Black Working Class*, New York: Free Press, 1994, pp. 187–94.

STUART COSGROVE,
"THE ZOOT-SUIT AND STYLE WARFARE"

Style is the most intimate of media. The clothes you wear, how you speak, and even the way you walk telegraph your individual identity and group allegiance. In sixteenth-century England sumptuary laws restricted what each class could and could not wear, keeping the visual lines of power clearly demarcated. "Silke of purple color are forbidden in garments, save those of Earls and above that rank and Knights of the Garter in their purple mantles" one such proclamation of 1597 read.[1] Working class Irish-American youth, known as Bowery B'hoys and G'hals, signified their presence in early nineteenth-century New York with garish costume. The B'hoy wore his front locks grown long and greased into a roll, topped with a shiny black broad-brimmed hat pushed far back. Below the neck he wore an open collared shirt, colorful satin vest and a black frock coat extending low to the knee. The G'hal dressed "high" according to one observer at the time, wearing dress and shawl that contrasted "bright yellow with a brighter red, and a green with a dashing purple."[2] In more recent times, during the Second World War, young Chicanos in Los Angeles defied war-time sobriety and their second-class invisibility by dressing in elaborate "Zoot-suits," an outlandish sartorial style of "a killer-diller coat with a drapeshape, reat-pleats and shoulders padded like a lunatic's cell." Implicitly understanding that such dress symbolized a status challenge, white serviceman on leave in LA went on a rampage, beating up and stripping Zoot-suiters. In the following section the historian Stuart Cosgrove describes these "zoot-suit riots" and analyzes this open skirmish of a larger cultural war.

The Silent Noise of
Sinister Clowns

What about those fellows waiting still and silent there on the platform, so still and silent they clash with the crowd in their very immobility, standing noisy in their very silence; harsh as a cry of terror in their quietness? What about these three boys, coming now along the platform, tall and slender, walking with swinging shoulders in their well-pressed, too-hot-for-summer suits, their collars high and tight about their necks, their identical hats of black cheap felt set upon the crowns of their heads with a severe formality above their conked hair? It was as though I'd never seen their like before: walking slowly, their shoulders swaying, their legs swinging from their hips in trousers that ballooned upward from cuffs fitting snug about their ankles; their coats long and hip-tight with shoulders far too broad to be those of natural western men. These fellows whose bodies seemed – what had one of my teachers said of me? – "You're like one of those African sculptures, distorted in the interest of design." Well, what design and whose?[3]

Ralph Ellison, *Invisible Man*

The zoot-suit is more than an exaggerated costume, more than a sartorial statement, it is the bearer of a complex and contradictory history. When the nameless narrator of Ellison's *Invisible Man* confronted the subversive sight of three young and extravagantly dressed blacks, his reaction was one of fascination not of fear. These youths were not simply grotesque dandies parading the city's secret underworld, they were 'the stewards of something uncomfortable',[4] a spectacular reminder that the social order had failed to contain their energy and difference. The zoot-suit was more than the drape-shape of 1940s fashion, more than a colourful stage-prop hanging from the shoulders of Cab Calloway, it was, in the most direct and obvious ways, an emblem of ethnicity and a way of negotiating an identity. The zoot-suit was a refusal: a subcultural gesture that refused to concede to the manners of subservience. By the late 1930s, the term 'zoot' was in common circulation within urban jazz culture. Zoot meant something worn or performed in an extravagant style, and since many young blacks wore suits with outrageously padded shoulders and trousers that were fiercely tapered at the ankles, the term zoot-suit passed into everyday usage. In the subcultural world of Harlem's nightlife, the language of rhyming slang succinctly described the zoot-suit's unmistakable style: 'a killer-diller coat with a drapeshape, reat-pleats and shoulders padded like a lunatic's cell'.

The study of the relationship between fashion and social action is notoriously underdeveloped, but there is every indication that the zoot-suit riots that erupted in the United States in the summer of 1943 had a profound effect on a whole generation of socially disadvantaged youths. It was during his period as a young zoot-suiter that the Chicano union activist Cesar Chavez first came into contact with community politics, and it was through the experiences of participating in zoot-suit riots in Harlem that the young pimp 'Detroit Red' began a political education that transformed him into the Black radical leader Malcolm X. Although the zoot-suit occupies an almost mythical place within the history of jazz music, its social and political importance has been virtually ignored. There can be no certainty about when, where or why the zoot-suit came into existence, but what is certain is that during the summer months of 1943 'the killer-diller coat' was the uniform of young rioters and the symbol of a moral panic about juvenile delinquency that was to intensify in the post-war period.

At the height of the Los Angeles riots of June 1943, the *New York Times* carried a front page article which claimed without reservation that the first zoot-suit had been purchased by a black bus worker, Clyde Duncan, from a tailor's shop in Gainesville, Georgia.[5] Allegedly, Duncan had been inspired by the film *Gone with the Wind* and had set out to look like Rhett Butler. This explanation clearly found favour throughout the USA. The national press forwarded countless others. Some reports claimed that the zoot-suit was an invention of Harlem night life, others suggested it grew out of jazz culture and the exhibitionist stage costumes of the band leaders, and some argued that the zoot-suit was derived from military uniforms and imported from Britain. The alternative and independent press, particularly *Crisis* and *Negro Quarterly*, more convincingly argued that the zoot-suit was the product of a particular social context.[6] They emphasized the importance of Mexican-American youths, or *pachucos*, in the emergence of zoot-suit style and, in tentative ways, tried to relate their appearance on the streets to the concept of *pachuquismo*.

In his pioneering book, *The Labyrinth of Solitude*, the Mexican poet and social commentator Octavio Paz throws imaginative light on *pachuco* style and indirectly establishes a framework within which the zoot-suit can be understood. Paz's study of the Mexican national consciousness examines the changes brought about by the movement of labor, particularly the generations of Mexicans who migrated northwards to the USA. This movement, and the new economic and social patterns it implies, has, according to Paz, forced young Mexican-Americans into an ambivalent experience between two cultures.

> What distinguishes them, I think, is their furtive, restless air: they act like persons who are wearing disguises, who are afraid of a stranger's look because it could strip them and leave them stark naked . . . This spiritual condition or lack of a spirit, has given birth to a type known as the *pachuco*. The *pachucos* are youths, for the most part of Mexican origin, who form gangs in southern cities; they can be identified by their language and behavior as well as by the clothing they affect. They are instinctive rebels, and North American racism has vented its wrath on them more than once. But the *pachucos* do not attempt to vindicate their race or the nationality of their forebears. Their attitude reveals an obstinate, almost fanatical will-to-be, but this will affirms nothing specific except their determination . . . not to be like those around them.[7]

Pachuco youth embodied all the characteristics of second generation working-class immigrants. In the most obvious ways they had been stripped of their customs, beliefs and language. The *pachucos* were a disinherited generation within a disadvantaged sector of North American society; and

predictably their experiences in education, welfare and employment alienated them from the aspirations of their parents and the dominant
assumptions of the society in which they lived. The *pachuco* subculture was
defined not only by ostentatious fashion, but by petty crime, delinquency
and drug-taking. Rather than disguise their alienation or efface their hostility to the dominant society, the *pachucos* adopted an arrogant posture. They
flaunted their difference, and the zoot-suit became the means by which that
difference was announced. Those 'impassive and sinister clowns' whose
purpose was 'to cause terror instead of laughter',[8] invited the kind of attention that led to both prestige and persecution. For Octavio Paz the *pachuco's*
appropriation of the zoot-suit was an admission of the ambivalent place he
occupied. 'It is the only way he can establish a more vital relationship with
the society he is antagonizing. As a victim he can occupy a place in the
world that previously ignored him; as a delinquent, he can become one of
its wicked heroes.'[9] The zoot-suit riots of 1943 encapsulated this paradox.
They emerged out of the dialectics of delinquency and persecution, during
a period in which American society was undergoing profound structural
change.

The major social change brought about by the United States' involvement in the war was the recruitment to the armed forces of over four
million civilians and the entrance of over five million women into the wartime labour force. The rapid increase in military recruitment and the radical
shift in the composition of the labour force led in turn to changes in family
life, particularly the erosion of parental control and authority. The large
scale and prolonged separation of millions of families precipitated an
unprecedented increase in the rate of juvenile crime and delinquency. By
the summer of 1943 it was commonplace for teenagers to be left to their
own initiatives whilst their parents were either on active military service or
involved in war work. The increase in night work compounded the
problem. With their parents or guardians working unsocial hours, it became
possible for many more young people to gather late into the night at major
urban centres or simply on the street corners.

The rate of social mobility intensified during the period of the zoot-suit
riots. With over 15 million civilians and 12 million military personnel on
the move throughout the country, there was a corresponding increase in
vagrancy. Petty crimes became more difficult to detect and control; itiner-
ants became increasingly common, and social transience put unforeseen
pressure on housing and welfare. The new patterns of social mobility also
led to congestion in military and industrial areas. Significantly, it was the
overcrowded military towns along the Pacific coast and the industrial

towns of Detroit, Pittsburgh and Los Angeles that witnessed the most violent outbreaks of zoot-suit rioting.[10]

'Delinquency' emerged from the dictionary of new sociology to become an everyday term, as wartime statistics revealed these new patterns of adolescent behaviour. The *pachucos* of the Los Angeles area were particularly vulnerable to the effects of war. Being neither Mexican nor American, the *pachucos*, like the black youths with whom they shared the zoot-suit style, simply did not fit. In their own terms they were '24-hour orphans', having rejected the ideologies of their migrant parents. As the war furthered the dislocation of family relationships, the *pachucos* gravitated away from the home to the only place where their status was visible, the streets and bars of the towns and cities. But if the *pachucos* laid themselves open to a life of delinquency and detention, they also asserted their distinct identity, with their own style of dress, their own way of life and a shared set of experiences.

The Zoot-Suit Riots: Liberty, Disorder and the Forbidden

The zoot-suit riots sharply revealed a polarization between two youth groups within wartime society: the gangs of predominantly black and Mexican youths who were at the forefront of the zoot-suit subculture, and the predominantly white American servicemen stationed along the Pacific coast. The riots invariably had racial and social resonances but the primary issue seems to have been patriotism and attitudes to the war. With the entry of the United States into the war in December 1941, the nation had to come to terms with the restrictions of rationing and the prospects of conscription. In March 1942, the War Production Board's first rationing act had a direct effect on the manufacture of suits and all clothing containing wool. In an attempt to institute a 26 percent cut-back in the use of fabrics, the War Production Board drew up regulations for the wartime manufacture of what *Esquire* magazine called, 'streamlined suits by Uncle Sam'.[11] The regulations effectively forbade the manufacture of zoot-suits and most legitimate tailoring companies ceased to manufacture or advertise any suits that fell outside the War Production Board's guidelines. However, the demand for zoot-suits did not decline and a network of bootleg tailors based in Los Angeles and New York continued to manufacture the garments. Thus the polarization between servicemen and *pachucos* was immediately visible: the chino shirt and battledress were evidently uniforms of patriotism, whereas wearing a zoot-suit was a deliberate and public way of flouting the regulations of rationing. The zoot-suit was a moral and social scandal in the eyes of the authorities, not simply because it was associated with petty crime and violence, but because it openly snubbed the laws of rationing. In the fragile harmony of wartime society, the zoot-suiters were, according to Octavio Paz, 'a symbol of love and joy or of horror and loathing, an embodiment of liberty, of disorder, of the forbidden'.[12]

The zoot-suit riots, which were initially confined to Los Angeles, began in the first few days of June 1943. During the first weekend of the month, over 60 zoot-suiters were arrested and charged at Los Angeles county jail, after violent and well publicized fights between servicemen on shore leave and gangs of Mexican-American youths. In order to prevent further outbreaks of fighting, the police patrolled the eastern sections of the city, as rumours spread from the military bases that servicemen were intending to form vigilante groups. The *Washington Post*'s report of the incidents, on the morning of Wednesday 9 June 1943, clearly saw the events from the point of view of the servicemen.

> Disgusted with being robbed and beaten with tire irons, weighted ropes, belts and fists employed by overwhelming numbers of the youthful hoodlums, the uniformed men passed the word quietly among themselves and opened their campaign in force on Friday night.
>
> At central jail, where spectators jammed the sidewalks and police made no efforts to halt auto loads of servicemen openly cruising in search of zoot-suiters, the youths streamed gladly into the sanctity of the cells after being snatched from bar rooms, pool halls and theaters and stripped of their attire.[13]

During the ensuing weeks of rioting, the ritualistic stripping of zoot-suiters became the major means by which the servicemen re-established their status over the *pachucos*. It became commonplace for gangs of Marines to ambush zoot-suiters, strip them down to their underwear and leave them helpless in the streets. In one particularly vicious incident, a gang of drunken sailors rampaged through a cinema after discovering two zoot-suiters. They dragged the *pachucos* onto the stage as the film was being screened, stripped them in front of the audience and as a final insult, urinated on the suits.

The press coverage of these incidents ranged from the careful and cautionary liberalism of the *Los Angeles Times* to the more hysterical hate-mongering of William Randolph Hearst's west coast papers. Although the practice of stripping and publicly humiliating the zoot-suiters was not prompted by the press, several reports did little to discourage the attacks:

. . . zoot-suits smoldered in the ashes of street bonfires where they had been tossed by grimly methodical tank forces of service men . . . The zooters, who earlier in the day had spread boasts that they were organized to 'kill every cop' they could find, showed no inclination to try to make good their boasts . . . Searching parties of soldiers, sailors and Marines hunted them out and drove them out into the open like bird dogs flushing quail. Procedure was standard: grab a zooter. Take off his pants and frock coat and tear them up or burn them. Trim the 'Argentine Ducktail' haircut that goes with the screwy costume.[14]

The second week of June witnessed the worst incidents of rioting and public disorder. A sailor was slashed and disfigured by a *pachuco* gang; a policeman was run down when he tried to question a car load of zoot-suiters; a young Mexican was stabbed at a party by drunken Marines; a trainload of sailors were stoned by *pachucos* as their train approached Long Beach; streetfights broke out daily in San Bernardino; over 400 vigilantes toured the streets of San Diego looking for zoot-suiters, and many individuals from both factions were arrested.

. . .

As the zoot-suit riots spread throughout California to cities in Texas and Arizona, a new dimension began to influence press coverage of the riots in Los Angeles. On a day when 125 zoot-suited youths clashed with Marines in Watts and armed police had to quell riots in Boyle Heights, the Los Angeles press concentrated on a razor attack on a local mother, Betty Morgan. What distinguished this incident from hundreds of comparable attacks was that the assailants were girls. The press related the incident to the arrest of Amelia Venegas, a woman zoot-suiter who was charged with carrying, and threatening to use, a brass knuckleduster. The revelation that girls were active within *pachuco* subculture led to consistent press coverage of the activities of two female gangs: the Slick Chicks and the Black Widows.[15] The latter gang took its name from the members' distinctive dress, black zoot-suit jackets, short black skirts and black fish-net stockings . . . The Black Widows clearly existed outside the orthodoxies of war-time society: playing no part in the industrial war effort, and openly challenging conventionl notions of feminine beauty and sexuality.

Towards the end of the second week of June, the riots in Los Angeles were dying out. Sporadic incidents broke out in other cities, particularly Detroit, New York and Philadelphia, where two members of Gene Krupa's dance band were beaten up in a station for wearing the band's zoot-suit costumes; but these, like the residual events in Los Angeles, were not taken seriously. The authorities failed to read the inarticulate warning signs proffered in two separate incidents in California: in one a zoot-suiter was arrested for throwing gasoline flares at a theatre; and in the second another was arrested for carrying a silver tomahawk. The zoot-suit riots had become a public and spectacular enactment of social disaffection. The authorities in Detroit chose to dismiss a zoot-suit riot at the city's Cooley High School as an adolescent imitation of the Los Angeles disturbances.[16] Within three weeks Detroit was in the midst of the worst race riot in its history.[17] The United States was still involved in the war abroad when violent events on the home front signalled the beginnings of a new era in racial politics.

. . .

The Mystery of the Signifying Monkey

The *pachuco* is the prey of society, but instead of hiding he adorns himself to attract the hunter's attention. Persecution redeems him and breaks his solitude: his salvation depends on him becoming part of the very society he appears to deny.[18]

The zoot-suit was associated with a multiplicity of different traits and conditions. It was simultaneously the garb of the victim and the attacker, the persecutor and the persecuted, the 'sinister clown' and the grotesque dandy. But the central opposition was between the style of the delinquent and that of the disinherited. To wear a zoot-suit was to risk the repressive intolerance of wartime society and to invite the attention of the police, the parent generation and the uniformed members of the armed forces. For many *pachucos* the zoot-suit riots were simply high times in Los Angeles when momentarily they had control of the streets; for others it was a realization that they were outcasts in a society that was not of their making. For the black radical writer, Chester Himes, the riots in his neighbourhood were unambiguous: 'Zoot Riots are Race Riots.'[19] For other contemporary commentators the wearing of the zoot-suit could be anything from unconscious dandyism to a conscious 'political' engagement. The zoot-suit riots were not political riots in the strictest sense, but for many participants they were an entry into the language of politics, an inarticulate rejection of the 'straight world' and its organization.

It is remarkable how many post-war activists were inspired by the zoot-suit disturbances. Luis Valdez of the radical theatre company, El Teatro Campesino, allegedly learned the 'chicano' from his cousin the zoot-suiter Billy Miranda.[20] The novelists Ralph Ellison and Richard Wright both conveyed a literary and political fascination with the power and potential of the zoot-suit. One of Ellison's editorials for the journal *Negro Quarterly* expressed his own sense of frustration at the enigmatic attraction of zoot-suit style.

> A third major problem, and one that is indispensable to the centralization and direction of power is that of learning the meaning of myths and symbols which abound among the Negro masses. For without this knowledge, leadership, no matter how correct its program, will fail. Much in Negro life remains a mystery; perhaps the zoot-suit conceals profound political meaning; perhaps the symmetrical frenzy of the Lindy-hop conceals clues to great potential powers, if only leaders could solve this riddle.[21]

Although Ellison's remarks are undoubtedly compromised by their own mysterious idealism, he touches on the zoot-suit's major source of interest. It is in everyday rituals that resistance can find natural and unconscious expression. In retrospect, the zoot-suit's history can be seen as a point of intersection, between the related potential of ethnicity and politics on the one hand, and the pleasures of identity and difference on the other. It is the zoot-suit's political and ethnic associations that have made it such a rich reference point for subsequent generations. From the music of Thelonious Monk and Kid Creole to the jazz-poetry of Larry Neal, the zoot-suit has inherited new meanings and new mysteries. In his book *Hoodoo Hollerin' Bebop Ghosts*, Neal uses the image of the zoot-suit as the symbol of Black America's cultural resistance. For Neal, the zoot-suit ceased to be a costume and became a tapestry of meaning, where music, politics and social action merged. The zoot-suit became a symbol for the enigmas of Black culture and the mystery of the signifying monkey:

> But there is rhythm here
> Its own special substance:
> I hear Billie sing, no Good Man, and dig Prez, wearing the Zoot suit of life, the Porkpie hat tilted at the correct angle; through the Harlem smoke of beer and whisky, I understand the mystery of the Signifying Monkey.[22]

Stuart Cosgrove, "The Zoot-suit and Style Warfare," *History Workshop Journal*, 18, Autumn 1984, pp. 77–85, 89–90.

DICK HEBDIGE, "THE MEANING OF MOD," AND JOHN CLARKE, "THE SKINHEADS AND THE MAGICAL RECOVERY OF COMMUNITY," FROM *RITUALS OF RESISTANCE*

Begun by Richard Hoggart and later directed by Stuart Hall, the Centre for Contemporary Cultural Studies at the University of Birmingham made its name with studies of subcultures in the 1970s (cf. Hoggart and Hall). Subcultures had been investigated before, the classic studies of street gangs by University of Chicago sociologists in the 1930s come to mind, but the scholars of the CCCS pioneered an approach which examined subcultures not as a problem to be solved, but as a culture of resistance to be respected. What follows are two classic studies drawn from a collection of the working papers of the CCCS, each developing a key concept of subcultural analysis. Dick Hebdige explores how mods reassign meanings of common commodities in a type of semiotic jujitsu. Thus within mod style, short hair, a fine suit, and a motor scooter are transformed from markers of respectability into symbols of subversion. Likewise insults hurled at the mods from the straight world: laziness, arrogance, and vanity, are reappropriated as badges of honor. Looking at skinheads, John Clarke observes how they utilize their subculture as a "magical resolution" of real world problems. As such, the skinhead's exaggerated – and violent – territorial machismo is a fantastic attempt to resurrect the dignity, privileges, and community of their white working-class fathers in the face of immigration and deindustrialization.

The Meaning of Mod

Its appearance

Like most primitive vocabularies, each word of Wolverine,[1] the universal Pop Newspeak, is a prime symbol and serves a dozen or a hundred functions of communication. Thus 'mod' came to refer to several distinct styles, being essentially an umbrella-term used to cover everything which contributed to the recently launched myth of 'swinging London'.

Thus groups of art-college students following in Mary Quant's footsteps and developing a taste for the outrageous in clothing were technically 'mods'[2] and Lord Snowdon earned the epithet when he appeared in a polo-necked sweater and was hastily grouped with the 'new breed' of 'important people' like Bailey and Terence Stamp who showed a 'swinging' disregard for certain dying conventions. But for our purposes, we must limit the definition of the mods to working class teenagers who lived mainly in London and the new towns of the South and who could be readily identified by characteristic hairstyles, clothing etc. According to Melly,[3] the progenitors of this style appear to have been a group of working-class dandies, possibly descended from the devotees of the Italianate style known throughout the trad world as mods who were dedicated to clothes and lives in London. Only gradually and with popularization did this group accumulate other distinctive identity symbols (the scooter, the pills, the music). By 1963, the all night R and B clubs held this group firmly in Soho and central London, whilst around the ring roads the Ton up boys thundered on unperturbed, nostalgically clinging on to rock and roll and the tougher working-class values.

Whether the mod/rocker dichotomy was ever really essential to the self-definition of either group remains doubtful. The evidence suggests that the totally disparate goals and life styles of the two groups left very little room for interaction of any kind. After the disturbances of Whitsun 1964, at Clacton, in which hostilities between mods and rockers played no important part (the main targets for aggression being the pathetically inadequate entertainment facilities and small shopkeepers), the media accentuated and rigidified the opposition between the two groups, setting the stage for the conflicts which occurred at Margate and Brighton during the Easter weekend and at Hastings during the August bank holiday.[4] The fact that the mod clashed before the camera with the rocker is, I suspect, more indicative of the mod's vanity than of any really deeply felt antagonism between the two groups. The mods rejected the rocker's crude conception of masculinity, the transparency of his motivations, his clumsiness, and embraced a less obvious style, which in turn was less easily ridiculed or dismissed by the parent culture. What distinguished the bank holidays of 1964 from all the previous bank holidays was not the violence (this was a fairly regular feature) but the public debut of this style at the coastal resorts. The very visible presence at Margate, Brighton, and Hastings of thousand of disturbingly ordinary, even smart teenagers from London and its environs somehow seemed to constitute a threat to the old order (the retired colonels, the tourist-oriented tradesmen who dominated the councils of the South coast resorts). The mods, according to Laing, 'looked alright but there was something in the way they moved which adults couldn't make out'.[5] They seemed to consciously invert the values associated with smart dress, to deliberately challenge the assumptions, to falsify the expectations derived from such sources. As Stan Cohen puts it, they were all the more disturbing by the impression they gave of 'actors who are not quite in their places'.[6]

I shall go on now to analyse the origins of this style in the experience of the mods themselves by attempting to penetrate and decipher the

mythology of the mods. Finally, I should like to offer an explanation of why
an overtly inoffensive style could manage to project menace so effectively.

Halfway to Paradise on the Piccadilly Line

The mod's adoption of a sharp but neat and visually understated style can
be explained only partly by his reaction to the rocker's grandiloquence. It is
partly explained by his desire to do justice to the mysterious complexity of
the metropolis in his personal demeanour, to draw himself closer to the
Negro whose very metabolism seemed to have grown into, and kept pace
with that of the city. It is partly explained by his unique and subversive attitude toward the commodities he habitually consumed (more of this second
point later).

The life style to which the mod ideally aspired revolved around night
clubs and city centres which demanded a certain exquisiteness of dress. In
order to cope with the unavoidable minute by minute harassments, the
minutiae of highspeed interactions incumbent upon an active night-life in
the city, the mod had to be on the ball at all times, functioning at an emotional and intellectual frequency high enough to pick up the slightest insult
or joke or challenge or opportunity to make the most of the precious
night. Thus speed[7] was needed to keep mind and body synchronized perfectly. His ideal model-mentor for this ideal style would be the Italian
Mafiosi-type so frequently depicted in crime films shot in New York (one
step above London in the mod hierarchy). The Brooklyn sharp kid had
been emulated by the wartime black marketer, the 'wide boy' and the post
war 'spiv' and the style was familiar, readily accessible and could be easily
worked up. Alternatively, an equally acceptable, perhaps even more desirable image was projected by the Jamaican hustler (or later 'rudie') whom
the mod could see with increasing regularity as the decade wore on operating with an enviable *savoir-faire* from every available street-corner. Thus the
pork-pie hat and dark glasses were at one time essential mod accessories. If
the grey people (who oppressed and constricted both mod and Negro)
held a monopoly on daytime business, the blacks held more shares in the
action of the night hours.[8]

Another and perhaps more pervasive influence can be traced to that of
the indigenous British gangster style, the evolution of which coincides
almost exactly with that of the mods.[9] With the introduction of the
Gaming Laws in 1963, London had become a kind of European Las Vegas
and offered rich rewards and a previously unattainable status to Britain's
more enterprising criminals. The famous protection gangs of the Krays and
the Richardsons (from East and South London respectively; both major

breeding grounds of mod) began converging on the West End, and many working-class teenagers followed their elders into the previously inviolable citadels of Soho and Westminster to see what fruits were offered. The city centre, transfigured and updated by the new nightlife, offered more opportunities for adventure and excitement to the more affluent working-class youth; and the clandestine, intergang warfare, the ubiquitous, brooding menace, provided a more suitable background of the mod's ideal life-style. As the gangsters stuck faithfully to their classic Hollywood scripts, dressing in sober suits, adopting classic Capone poses, using sawn off shotguns on each other, petrol bombing each other's premises, being seen in whispered consultation with bespectacled 'consiglieres', Soho became the perfect soil on which thriller fiction fantasies and subterranean intrigue could thrive; and this was the stuff for which the mod lived and in which his culture was steeped.[10] It was as if the whole submerged criminal underworld had surfaced, in 1965, in the middle of London, and had brought with it its own submarine world of popular fiction, sex and violence fantasy. As it acquired power it explored the possibilities for realizing those fantasies – the results were often bizarre and frequently terrifying. The unprecedented marriage between East and South London criminal cultures and West End high life and the Chelsea jet sets bore some strange and exotic fruit, and one of its most exquisite creatures was the Soho mod.

A Mugshot of the Ideal Mod

In a *Sunday Times* magazine of April 1964, Denzil, the seventeen-year-old mod interviewee fulfils the ideal mod role, 'looking excruciatingly sharp in all the photographs and describing an average week in the life of the ideal London mod'.

> Monday night meant dancing at the Mecca, the Hammersmith Palais, the Purley Orchard, or the Streatham Locarno.
>
> Tuesday meant Soho and the Scene club.
>
> Wednesday was Marquee night.
>
> Thursday was reserved for the ritual washing of the hair.
>
> Friday meant the Scene again.
>
> Saturday afternoon usually meant shopping for clothes and records, Saturday night was spent dancing and rarely finished before 9.00 or 10.00 Sunday morning.
>
> Sunday evening meant the Flamingo or, perhaps, if one showed signs of weakening, could be spent sleeping.

Even allowing for exaggeration the number of mods who managed to even approximate this kind of life could not exceed a few hundred, perhaps at most a few thousand. In fact probably no one possesses the super-human stamina (even with a ready supply of pills), let alone the hard cash which would be required to get a mod through this kind of schedule but the fact remains that Denzil did not let the side down. He has pushed the group-fantasy, projected the image of the impossible good life that everybody needed, right down and onto the indelible printed page. And meanwhile, every mod was preparing himself psychologically so that if the opportunity should arise, if the money was there, if Welwyn Garden City should be metamorphosed into Piccadilly Circus, he would be ready. Every mod was existing in a ghost world of gangsterism, luxurious clubs and beautiful women even if reality only amounted to a draughty Parker anorak, a beaten-up Vespa and fish and chips out of a greasy bag.

Snapshot of the Standard Mod

The reality of mod life was somewhat less glamorous. The average mod, according to the survey of the 43 Margate offenders interviewed by Barker and Little[11] earned about 11 pounds a week, was either a semi-skilled or more typically an office worker who had left secondary-modern school at fifteen. Another large section of mods were employed as department store clerks, messengers, and occupied menial positions in the various service industries of the West End. The mods are often described as exploring the upward option, but it seems probable that this has been deduced incorrectly from the mod's fanatical devotion to appearance, and the tendency to boast when in a blocked or amphetamine-induced state. As Denzil says: 'There's a lot of lying when you're blocked about the number of girls you go out with in the week, how much your suit costs, etc.' The archetypal mod, would, I think, be more likely to be the eighteen-year-old interviewed in the Barker-Little sample whose only articulated ambition – to become the owner of a Mayfair drinking-club – towered so high above his present occupation as a meat porter that he no longer seriously entertained it; but had realistically if resentfully accepted society's appraisal of his worth ('more or less manual – that's all I am'), and existed purely for and through his leisure-time. The bell-boy hero in Pete Townshend's new rock opera about the mod experience – *Quadrophrenia* – is, apparently, similarly resigned to an insignificant and servile role during the day, but is all the more determined to make up for it at night. Like the fifteen-year-old office boy in Wolfe's essay 'The Noonday Underground'[12] whose clothes are more exquisitely tailored than the bosses', the mod was determined to compensate for his relatively low position in the daytime status-stakes over which he had no control, by exercising complete dominion over his private estate – his appearance and choice of leisure pursuits.

The wide gap between the inner world where all was under control, contained and lit by self-love, and the outer world, where all was hostile, daunting, and loaded in 'their' favour, was bridged by amphetamines.[13] Through the alchemy of 'speed', the mod achieved a magical omnipotence, whereby the dynamics of his movements were magnified, the possibilities of action multiplied, their purposes illuminated. Amphetamine made life tolerable, 'blocked' one's sensory channels so that action and risk and excitement were possible, kept one going on the endless round of consumption, and confined one's attention to the search, the ideal, the goal, rather than the attainment of the goal – relief rather than release. The Who's song 'The Searcher' stresses the importance of the search-as-end-in-itself: 'I ain't gonna get what I'm after / Till the day I die'.

Speed suspended the disappointment when the search failed, inevitably, to turn up anything substantial and gave one the energy to pick up and start again. It also tended to retard mental and emotional development (by producing dependency, by working against communication, stimulating incessant vocal at the expense of aural activity) whilst accelerating physical deterioration. The mod lived now and certainly paid later. As the mod was swept along the glossy surface of the 60s hopelessly attempting to extend himself through an endless succession of objects, he would realize at some point that his youth (perhaps the unstated and impossible goal) was by no means everlasting. Tommy, the pinball wizard, would eventually, and with great reluctance, face up to the fact that the game was limited by time and that there were never any replays. Hence the mid-60s obsession with the process of ageing apparent in the songs of The Who and the Rolling Stones (both mod heroes).

From The Who's *My Generation*, the theme song of the battlefields of 1964:

Things they do look awful cold / Hope I die 'fore I get old.

From the Rolling Stones record *Mother's Little Helper*, which deals with middle-aged amphetamine-addiction, an understandably predictable mod nightmare.

What a drag it is getting old.

And thus, finally we come to the elaborate consumer rituals of the mods, their apparently insatiable appetite for the products of the capitalist society in which they lived, their fundamental and inescapable confinement within that society.

Whilst not suggesting that the mod style had stumbled across any serious flaw in the monolith of capitalism, I shall now attempt to indicate how it did handle the commodities it took to itself in a unique and subversive manner. If it found no flaws it did at least come across a few hairline cracks. It did at least beat against the bars of its prison.

Conspicious Consumption and the Transformed Commodity

The mods are often charged by the self-styled commentators of pop with a debilitating tendency to multiple addiction. The argument goes something like this – being typically alienated consumers, the mods eagerly swallowed the latest brand of pills in order to borrow enough energy to enable them to spend the maximum amount of time consuming the maximum amount of commodities, which, in turn, could only be enjoyed under the influence of speed. However, despite his overwhelming need to consume, the mod was never a passive consumer, as his hedonistic middle-class descendant often was.[14] The importance of style can never be overstressed – mod was pure, unadulterated STYLE, the essence of style. In order to project style it became necessary first to appropriate the commodity, then to redefine its use and value and finally to relocate its meaning within a totally different context. This pattern, which amounted to the semantic rearrangement of those components of the objective world which the mod style required, was repeated at every level of the mod experience and served to preserve a part at least of the mod's private dimension against the passive consumer role it seemed in its later phases ready to adopt.

Thus the scooter, a formerly ultra-respectable means of transport, was appropriated and converted into a weapon and a symbol of solidarity. Thus pills, medically diagnosed for the treatment of neuroses, were appropriated and used as an end-in-themselves, and the negative evaluations of their capabilities imposed by school and work were substituted by a positive assessment of their personal credentials in the world of play (i.e. the same qualities which were assessed negatively by their daytime controllers – e.g. laziness, arrogance, vanity etc. – were positively defined by themselves and their peers in leisure time).

Thus, the mods learned to make their criticisms obliquely, having learned by experience (at school and work) to avoid direct confrontations where age, experience, economic and civil power would inevitably have told against them. The style they created, therefore, constituted a parody of the consumer society in which they were situated. The mod dealt his blows by inverting and distorting the images (of neatness, of short hair) so cherished by his employers and parents, to create a style, which while being overtly close to the straight world was nonetheless incomprehensible to it.

The mod triumphed with symbolic victories and was the master of the theatrical but ultimately enigmatic gesture. The bank holiday incidents, and the 5th November 1966 scooter-charge on Buckingham Palace (a scarcely remembered and largely unreported event of major importance to the mods involved) whilst holding a certain retrospective fascination for the social historian and calling forth an Agincourt-like pride in those who took part, fail to impress us as permanently significant events, and yet an eighteen-year-old mod could say at the time about Margate: 'Yes, I was there . . . It was like we were taking over the country'.[15]

The basis of style is the appropriation and reorganization by the subject of elements in the objective world which would otherwise determine and constrict him. The mod's cry of triumph, quoted above, was for a romantic victory, a victory of the imagination; ultimately for an imagined victory. The mod combined previously disparate elements to create himself into a metaphor, the appropriateness of which was apparent only to himself. But the mods underestimated the ability of the dominant culture to absorb the subversive image and sustain the impact of the anarchic imagination. The magical transformations of commodities had been mysterious and were often invisible to the neutral observer and no amount of stylistic incantation could possibly affect the oppressive economic mode by which they had been produced. The state continued to function perfectly no matter how many of Her Majesty's colours were defiled and draped around the shoulders of skinny pill-heads in the form of sharply cut jackets.

Autopsy Report on One White Negro
Now Deceased

I have already emphasized the positive values of the mod's relative exclusiveness, his creation of a whole supportive universe which provided him not only with a distinctive dress, music, etc. but also with a complete set of meanings. I should like to conclude by suggesting that it was this same esotericism, this same retreatism which led to the eventual and inevitable decline of mod as a movement. For the mod was the first all-British White Negro of Mailer's essay,[16] living on the pulse of the present, resurrected after work only by fierce devotion to leisure, and creating through the dynamics of his personality (or more accurately through the dynamics of the collective personality of the group), a total style armed, albeit inadequately, against a patronizing adult culture, and which need look no further than itself for its justifications and ethics. Ultimately it was this very self-sufficiency which led to the mod's self-betrayal. Being determined to cling to the womb of Noonday Afternoon, the smokefilled clubs and the good life without ever facing the implications of its own alienation and to look merely to its own created and increasingly commercialized (and therefore artificial and stylized) image, mesmerized by music, stultified by speed, mod was bound eventually to succumb; to be cheated and exploited at every level. The consumer rituals were refined and multiplied ad infinitum and came to involve the use of commodities directed specifically at a mod market by a rapidly expanding pop industry. Dress was no longer innovative – nobody 'discovered' items like Levi jeans or Hush Puppies any more. Style was manufactured from above instead of being spontaneously created from within. When a mod magazine could declare authoritatively that there was a 'NEW MOD WALK: feet out, head forward, hands in jacket pockets', then one had to acknowledge, reluctantly, that this particular white negro had, somewhere along the line, keeled over and died.

Dick Hebdige, "The Meaning of Mod," *Resistance through Rituals: Youth Subcultures in Post-war Britain*, Stuart Hall and Tony Jefferson (eds.), London: Routledge, 1993, pp. 87–94. First published in 1975 as *Working Papers in Cultural Studies*, no. 7/8, Centre for Contemporary Cultural Studies, University of Birmingham.

The Skinheads and the Magical Recovery of Community

Our basic thesis about the skinheads centres around the notion of community. We would argue that the skinhead style represents an attempt to re-create through the 'mob' the traditional working-class community, as a substitution for the *real* decline of the latter. The underlying social dynamic for the style, in this light, is the relative worsening of the situation of the working class, through the second half of the 60s, and especially the more rapidly worsening situation of the lower working class (and of the young within that). This, allied to the young's sense of exclusion from the existing 'youth subculture' (dominated in the public arena by the music and styles derived from the 'underground') produced a return to an intensified 'Us–Them' consciousness among the lower working-class young, a sense of being excluded and under attack from a variety of points. The resources to deal with this sense of exclusion were not to be found within either the emergent or incorporated elements of youth subcultures, but only in those images and behaviours which stressed a more traditional form of collective solidarity. Material from *The Paint House* illustrates this sense of oppression:

> Everywhere there are fucking bosses, they're always trying to tell you what to do . . . don't matter what you do, where you go, they're always there. People in authority, the people who tell you what to do and make sure you do it. It's the system we live in, it's the governer system.
>
> Schools, you 'ave to go, doncha? The teachers and the headmaster, they're the authority, ain't they? They're telling you what to do and you're glad to get out and leave and that, aren't ya? They think because you're young and they pay you and that, that they can treat you how they like and say what they want. Then there's the 'old bill' and courts . . . they're all part of authority. Official and all kinds of people in uniforms. Anyone with a badge on, traffic wardens and council and all that . . . yeah, even the caretaker at the flats, they even 'as goes at you. Then when you finish at work or at school, you go to the clubs and the youth leaders are all just a part of it.[1]

But the skinheads felt oppressed by more than just the obvious authority structure; they resented those who tried to get on and 'give themselves false airs', people from within the neighbourhood who had pretensions to social superiority; they resented the 'people on our backs':

> All these dummoes at school, who always do what they're told . . . they're the ones who end up being coppers and that.
>
> I hate them do-gooders who come to 'elp the poor in them slums . . . they're all nice and sweet and kind, they pretend to be on your side and by talking nicely find out about you but social workers and people like that, they ain't on your side. They think they know how you should live. They're really authority pretending to be your friends. They try to get you to do things and if you don't do them, they've got the law on their side. With all this lot against us, we've still got the yids, Pakis, wogs, 'ippies on our backs.[2]

The sense of being 'in the middle' of this variety of oppressive and exploitative forces produces a need for group solidarity, which though essentially defensive, in the skinheads was coupled with an aggressive content, the expression of frustration and discontent through the attacking of scapegoated outsiders. The content of this solidarity, as we shall see in our consideration of the elements of the skinhead style, derived from the traditional content of the working-class community – the example, *par excellence*, of the defensively organized collective.

However, the skinhead style does not revive the community in a real sense; the post-war decline of the bases of that community had removed it as a real source of solidarity; the skinheads had to use an *image* of what that community was as the basis of their style. They were the 'dispossessed inheritors'; they received a tradition which had been deprived of its real social bases. The themes and imagery still persisted, but the reality was in a state of decline and disappearance. We would suggest that this dislocated relation to the traditional community accounts for the exaggerated and intensified form which the values and concerns of that community received in the form of the skinhead style. Daniel and McGuire claim that:

> Rather than a community spirit, the Collinwood gang tends to have an affinity with an image of the East Enders, as being tough, humorous and a subculture of their own . . . The gang sees itself as a natural continuation of the working class tradition of the area, with the same attitudes and behaviour as their parents and grandparents before them. They believe that they have the same stereotyped prejudices against immigrants and aliens as they believe their parents have and had, *but they play these roles outsides of the context of the community experienced by their parents.*[3]

These observations are reinforced by comments from the skinheads themselves about the gang and its relation to the locality:

> When people kept saying skinheads, when they're talking about the story of us coming up from the East End, this has happened for generations before, past . . . I mean where does skinhead come into it?
> It's a community, a gang, isn't it, it's only another word for community, kids, thugs, whatever.[4]

The kids inherit the oral tradition of the area from the parent culture, especially that part which refers to the community's self-image, its collective solidarity, its conception of masculinity, its orientation to 'outsiders' and so on. It is perhaps not surprising that the areas with which the skinheads are most associated should be the East End, which from a sociological standpoint has been seen as the archetypal working-class community. Its internal self-image has always been a particularly strong one, and has been strengthened by its public reputation as a 'hard' area, a reputation which in the mid 60s was further intensified by the glamorous careers of the Krays.

Finally, we would like to exemplify this relation between the skinheads and the image of the community through some of the central elements of the skinhead style. One of the most crucial aspects is the emphasis on territorial connections for the skinheads – the 'mobs' were organized on a territorial basis, identifying themselves with and through a particular locality (e.g. the Smethwick Mob, etc.). This involved the mobs in the demarcation and defence of their particular 'patch', marking boundaries with painted slogans ('Quinton Mob rules here', etc.) and maintaining those boundaries against infractions by other groups. This territoriality, like the community, has its own focal points around which interaction articulates – the street corner meeting place, the pub, and the football ground. Although the football ground did not necessarily coincide with the mob's patches, its own local identification and the already existent activities of the East Enders provided a particular focal point for the mobs to organize around.

Football, and especially the violence articulated around it, also provided one arena for the expression of the skinheads' concern with a particular, collective, masculine self-conception, involving an identification of masculinity with physical toughness, and unwillingness to back down in the face of 'trouble'.[5] The violence also involved the mobs' stress on collective solidarity and mutual support in times of 'need'. This concern with toughness was also involved in the two other most publicized skinhead activities – 'Paki-bashing' and 'Queer-bashing'. Paki-bashing involved the ritual and aggressive defence of the social and cultural homogeneity of the community against its most obviously scapegoated outsiders – partly because of their particular visibility within the neighbourhood (in terms of shop ownership patterns, etc.) by comparison with West Indians, and also because of their different cultural patterns (especially in terms of their unwillingness to defend themselves and so on) – again by comparison with West Indian youth.

'Queer-bashing' may be read as a reaction against the erosion of traditionally available stereotypes of masculinity, especially by the hippies. The skinhead operational definition of 'queer' seems to have extended to all those males who by their standards looked 'odd', as this statement from a Smethwick skinhead may indicate:

> Usually it'd be just a bunch of us who'd find somebody they thought looked odd – like this one night we were up by Warley Woods and we saw this bloke who looked odd – he'd got long hair and frills on his trousers.

We may see these three interrelated elements of territoriality, collective solidarity and 'masculinity' as being the way in which the skinheads attempted to recreate the inherited imagery of the community in a period in which the experiences of increasing oppression demanded forms of mutual organization and defence. And we might finally see the intensive violence connected with the style as evidence of the 'recreation of the community' being indeed a 'magical' or 'imaginary' one, in that it was created without the material and organizational basis of that community and consequently was less subject to the informal mechanisms of social control characteristic of such communities. In the skinhead style we can see both the elements of community (in terms of the style's content), and discontinuity (in terms of its form), between parent culture and youth subculture.

John Clarke, "The Skinheads and the Magical Recovery of Community", *Resistance through Rituals: Youth Subcultures in Post-war Britain*, Stuart Hall and Tony Jefferson (eds.), London: Routledge, 1993, pp. 99–102. Originally published in 1975 as *Working Papers in Cultural Studies*, no. 7/8, Centre for Contemporary Cultural Studies, University of Birmingham.

RIOT GRRRL,
"RIOT GRRRL IS . . ."

Riot Grrrl arose out of the punk and alternative rock subculture in the US in the early 1990s. Bound together through fanzines and music shows, it was a loose network of women, who, in the words of one zine editorial, were "tired of being written out – out of history, out of the 'scene,' out of our bodies" (see sidebar). What follows is the oft reprinted Riot Grrrl manifesto, "Riot Grrrl Is . . ." The manifesto demonstrates an important aspect of subcultures: using culture to create a communal identity, often in opposition to the identities offered up by the outside world. Creating this identity is considered a political act, "a revolutionary soul force that can, and will, change the world for real" as the closing line of the manifesto reads (cf. Radicalesbians). However, in defining oneself against the world, Riot Grrrl, like all subcultures, faces the danger of self-ghettoization, becoming more concerned with tending – and policing – subcultural identity than reaching out to engage, and change, the outside world. In an interview in the zine *Punk Planet*, Kathleen Hanna, lead singer for the band Bikini Kill and founding mother of Riot Grrrl, raises this issue, addressing the contradictions of creating a new community while living in an old world.

BECAUSE us girls crave records and books and fanzines that speak to US, that WE feel included in and can understand in our own ways.

BECAUSE we wanna make it easier for girls to see/hear each other's work so that we can share strategies and criticize-applaud each other.

BECAUSE we must take over the means of production in order to create our own meanings.

BECAUSE viewing our work as being connected to our girlfriends–politics–real lives is essential if we are gonna figure out how what we are making impacts, reflects, perpetuates, or DISRUPTS the status quo.

BECAUSE we recognize fantasies of Instant Macho Gun Revolution as impractical lies meant to keep us simply dreaming instead of becoming our dreams AND THUS seek to create revolution in our own lives every single day by envisioning and creating alternatives to the bullshit christian capitalist way of doing things.

BECAUSE we want and need to encourage and be encouraged, in the face of all our own insecurities, in the face of beergutboyrock that tells us we can't play our instruments, in the face of The Man who says our bands and zines are "the worst" things he's seen and claims the only reason we even exist is to profit from girlzine bandwagon hype.

BECAUSE we don't wanna assimilate to someone else's (Boy) standards of what is or isn't "good" music or punk rock or "good" writing AND THUS need to create forums where we can recreate, destroy and define our own visions.

BECAUSE we are unwilling to falter under claims that we are reactionary "reverse sexists" and not the true-punkrocksoulcrusaders that WE KNOW we really are.

BECAUSE we know that life is much more than physical survival and are patently aware that the punk rock "you can do anything" idea is crucial to the coming angry grrrl rock revolution which seeks to save the psychic and cultural lives of girls and women everywhere, according to their own terms, not ours.

BECAUSE we are interested in creating non hierarchical ways of being AND making music, friends, and scenes based on communication + understanding, instead of competition + good/bad categorizations.

BECAUSE doing/reading/seeing/hearing cool things that validate and challenge us can help us gain the

"Letter from the Editors,"
Riot Grrrl #3

The Start: we are not quite sure what we're about – in a lot of ways we are a work in progress. But we do know that we're women and quite proud of it. We also know that we're tired of being written out – out of history, out of the "scene," out of our bodies . . . for this reason we have created our zine and scene. The following pages are an essential means of expression for us and this zine is about us. Please think hard as you read, be proud of being a grrrl and be proud of the grrrls you know. This is for you!!!

Jen Devosby and Suzanne, Allie, Jenna, Sara, Margaret, Jessica, Colette and Jong, from *Riot Grrrl #3*, May 1992, Amherst, MA strength and sense of community that we need in order to figure out how bullshit like racism, able-bodyism, ageism, speciesism, classism, thinism, sexism, anti-semitism and heterosexism figures in our own lives.

BECAUSE we see fostering and supporting girl scenes and girl artists of all kinds as integral to this process.

BECAUSE we hate capitalism in all its forms and see our main goal as sharing information and staying alive, instead of making profits or being cool according to traditional standards.

BECAUSE we are angry at a society that tells us Girl = Dumb, Girl = Bad, Girl = Weak.

BECAUSE we are unwilling to let our real and valid anger be diffused and/or turned against us via the internalization of sexism as witnessed in girl/girl jealousies and self-defeating girltype behaviors.

BECAUSE self defeating behaviors (like fucking boys without condoms, drinking to excess, ignoring truesoul girlfriends, belittling ourselves and other girls, etc.) would not be so easy if we lived in communities where we felt loved and wanted and valued.

BECAUSE i believe with my holeheartmindbody that girls constitute a revolutionary soul force that can, and will, change the world for real.

"Riot Grrrl Is . . .," *Riot Grrrl #6½*, December 1991, Arlington VA.

KATHLEEN HANNA, FROM AN INTERVIEW IN *PUNK PLANET*

Daniel Sinker: Let's talk about capitalism in relation to Bikini Kill and Riot Grrrl for a second. Both of those phenomena caught an incredible amount of media attention. At a certain point, it seemed like all of you lost control of your own representation. It became larger than any of you and mutated into something really different . . . What do you think went wrong there? Do you ever wish that things could have played themselves out differently?

Kathleen Hanna: I don't wish anything was different. If anything was different I wouldn't be where I am and I wouldn't have the friends I have. I wish certain people hadn't died, but other than that, I don't have any big regrets. As far as the mainstream media goes, when it first started happening of course it felt really fucked up. It's scary to see something that at one point in time was really important to you turned into a sound bite. But I still get a lot of really cool mail from girls all over the world and that's definitely a result of the media attention. When I was growing up, I didn't have access to fanzines. I didn't know about punk. Growing up in DC, it seemed like most of the people who were into punk were private school people. The public school kids had no fucking idea – we feathered our hair and listened to Molly Hatchet. I can't change the fact that I didn't have access to it, so I don't want to be an asshole by saying "You heard about it through *Rolling Stone*, so you're not really blah blah."

But it's gross when things like Riot Grrrl or feminism become a product. It's like "Let's get it in as many magazines as possible so then everyone will know about it." I don't necessarily think that's the way to go about things because that's still reproducing a market economy. That's still saying, "Here are the managers that know the product that's best for you and you're just stupid consumers that are supposed to consume it." Whether that product is feminism or that product is Colgate, as long as you're using those marketing concepts, you're still treating people like they're idiots and you're still reinforcing capitalism. I have a lot of mixed feelings about it.

Do you remember the show *Night Flight*?

Daniel Sinker: Yeah, they showed *Another State of Mind* like every three weeks.

Kathleen Hanna: Yeah! That's how I learned about punk. That was one of my main influences when I was younger. I didn't do anything about it for years, but I knew it was there and just knowing it was there made my life a little easier.

Daniel Sinker: It's a never-ending argument about access to information. I'm stuck in the middle of that argument right now because of the barcode on the cover of *Punk Planet*.

Kathleen Hanna: I've had a similar problem. I was in this video. I was fucking broke and I thought it would be fun because I wanted to see how major rock stars made rock videos. Anyway, I got 200 bucks, which helped pay my rent. People were really pissed off at me about it and said I was a big sellout. I figured out who most of the people were who were pissed off and they were people who live at home with their parents and don't pay their own rent! I care what kids think, but it's a different thing when you're out in the world and you have to pay your bills. I'm not saying that I'm going to sellout to Sony. I'm just saying cut some people some slack. If you're putting something nourishing out in the world, you have to nourish yourself, too. Who gives a shit? Why is a barcode such a big fucking deal? I don't see what the big deal is! What if you work really hard to put out your fanzine and you spend a lot of time on the writing and you can't afford to give it away for free? If you spend all your money on printing a zine, you can't really afford to not get paid. Meanwhile, the kid who has the dad whose secretary xeroxed them all can go to a show and give them away for free. That could make you feel really fucked up if you can't afford that. All I'm saying is that certain people can afford to be more generous than other people and it's important to look at that. In second-wave feminism, there was a similar problem. There's a lot of really good stuff in this book *Daring to Be Bad*. There's this concept about how if you're successful, you're being "male" and I've always equated it with a punk thing or if you're trying to earn a living, you're being "capitalist." I think the basis that both of these arguments stem from is the idea that power is always corrupt and that it's not possible for anyone to have any kind of power without being an asshole with it. That's a really pessimistic idea. It allows the oppressors to define what success is. I think there are a thousand variations on what success is. Why can't we take over the word success and have different forms of success that are about doing things that make us really happy without sacrificing ourselves? Why is sacrificing yourself the highest order of the day in Western society? It's sick! I'm not saying that everybody should start businesses and become capitalists and fuck people over. It doesn't have to be like that. We can try to create alternative models for economic systems. It scares me because I don't want to be reformist. I don't believe in reformism. I don't just want my piece of the pie. I believe in revolutionary action. I don't believe in trying to change the system as it is because the whole system has to change. In a way, I'm contradicting myself because I'm saying we need to earn a living, but the ultimate goal is that we change the entire system. But unless we build models – even small Lego ones in our houses – we're not going to figure out how that's going to go about.

Kathleen Hanna, *Punk Planet*, #27 (1998), interviewed by Daniel Sinker. Also included in *We Owe You Nothing, Punk Planet: The Collected Interviews*, Daniel Sinker (ed.), New York: Akashic Books, 2001.

BERTOLT BRECHT,
"EMPHASIS ON SPORT"

Stepping away from subcultures and into the mainstream, the radical playwright Bertolt Brecht makes a case for embracing – and using – popular culture. Speaking to his artistic contemporaries who complain of a German public that would rather watch soccer games than attend the theatre, Brecht argues that radical artists need to leave their (subcultural) garrets and walk the street, learning from mass entertainment how to create a culture which is lively and fun . . . and popular. This, however, does not mean making art that does not challenge the public or contest the way things are. To borrow Brecht's metaphor: once you have the prevailing wind in your sails, you can tack right, or jibe left; you can use your art to say what you like. But without any wind you are at a standstill, speaking to no one but yourself and the other miserable souls becalmed around you.

We pin our hopes to the sporting public.

Make no bones about it, we have our eye on those huge concrete pans, filled with 15,000 men and women of every variety of class and physiognomy, the fairest and shrewdest audience in the world. There you will find 15,000 persons paying high prices, and working things out on the basis of a sensible weighing of supply and demand. You cannot expect to get fair conduct on a sinking ship. The demoralization of our theatre audiences springs from the fact that neither theatre nor audience has any idea what is supposed to go on there. When people in sporting establishments buy their tickets they know exactly what is going to take place; and that is exactly what does take place once they are in their seats: viz. highly trained persons developing their peculiar powers in the way most suited to them, with the greatest sense of responsibility yet in such a way as to make one feel that they are doing it primarily for their own fun. *Against that the traditional theatre is nowadays quite lacking in character.*

There seems to be nothing to stop the theatre having its own form of 'sport'. If only someone could take those buildings designed for theatrical purposes which are now standing eating their heads off in interest, and treat them as more or less empty spaces for the successful pursuit of 'sport', then they would be used in a way that might mean something to a contemporary public that earns real contemporary money and eats real contemporary beef.

It may be objected that there is also a section of the public that wants to see something other than 'sport' in the theatre. But we have never seen a single piece of evidence to prove that the public at present filling the theatres *wants* anything at all. The public's well-padded resistance to any attempt to make it give up those two old stalls which it inherited from grandpa should not be misinterpreted as a brand-new assertion of its will.

People are always telling us that we mustn't simply produce what the public demands. But I believe that an artist, even if he sits in strictest seclusion in the traditional garret working for future generations, is unlikely to produce anything without some wind in his sails. And this wind has to be the wind prevailing in his own period, and not some future wind. There is nothing to say that this wind must be used for travel in any particular direction (once one has a wind one can naturally sail against it; the only impossibility is to sail with no wind at all or with tomorrow's wind), and no doubt an artist will fall far short of achieving his maximum effectiveness today if he sails with today's wind. It would be quite wrong to judge a play's relevance or lack of relevance by its current effectiveness. Theatres don't work that way.

A theatre which makes no contact with the public is a nonsense. Our theatre is accordingly a nonsense. The reason why the theatre has at present no contact with the public is that it has no idea what is wanted of it. It can no longer do what it once could, and if it could do it it would no longer wish to. But it stubbornly goes on doing what it no longer can do and what is no longer wanted. All those establishments with their excellent heating systems, their pretty lighting, their appetite for large sums of money, their imposing exteriors, together with the entire business that goes on inside them: all this doesn't contain five pennyworth of *fun*. There is no theatre today that could invite one or two of those persons who are alleged to find fun in writing plays to one of its performances and expect them to feel an urge to write a play for it. They can see at a glance that there is no possible way of getting any *fun* out of this. No wind will go into anyone's sails here. There is no 'sport'.

Take the actors, for instance. I wouldn't like to say that we are worse off for talent than other periods seem to have been, but I doubt if there has ever been such an overworked, misused, panic-driven, artificially whipped-up band of actors as ours. *And nobody who fails to get fun out of his activities can expect them to be fun for anybody else.*

The people at the top naturally blame the people at the bottom, and the favourite scapegoat is the harmless garret. The people's wrath is directed against the garret; the plays are no good. To that it must be said that so long as they have been fun to write they are bound to be better than the theatre that puts them on and the public that goes to see them. A play is simply unrecognizable once it has passed through this sausage-machine. If we come along and say that both we and the public had imagined things differently – that we are in favour, for instance, of elegance, lightness, dryness, objectivity – then the theatre replies innocently: those passions which you have singled out, my dear sir, do not beat beneath any dinner-jacket's manly chest. As if even a play like *Vatermord* could not be performed in a simple, elegant and, as it were, classically rounded way!

Behind a feigned intensity you are offered a naked struggle in lieu of real competence. They no longer know how to stage anything remarkable, and therefore worth seeing. In his obscure anxiety not to let the audience get away the actor is immediately so steamed up that he makes it seem the most natural thing in the world to insult one's father. At the same time it can be seen that acting takes a tremendous lot out of him. *And a man who strains himself on the stage is bound, if he is any good, to strain all the people sitting in the stalls.*

I cannot agree with those who complain of no longer being in a position to prevent the imminent decline of the west. I believe that there is such a wealth of subjects worth seeing, characters worth admiring and lessons worth learning that once a good sporting spirit sets in one would have to build theatres if they did not already exist. The most hopeful element, however, in the present-day theatre is the people who pour out of both ends of the building after the performance. They are dissatisfied.

Bertolt Brecht, "Mehr guten Sport," from *Berliner Borsen-Courier*, February 6, 1926; reprinted in *Brecht on Theatre*, John Willett (ed. and trans.), New York: Hill and Wang, 1964, pp. 6–8.

STUART HALL,
"NOTES ON DECONSTRUCTING 'THE POPULAR'"

Stuart Hall, famed director of the CCCS, makes another case for popular culture – with qualifications. Yes, he concedes to the critics, contemporary popular culture is commercial, produced as a means to the ends of profit. But it also reflects genuine popular dreams and aspirations, struggles, and discontent, and in fact must if it is to open the public's purse. In addition, cultures are forever in transition. Yesterday's rebellious subculture is today's commercial pap and today's pap can become the basis for tomorrow's culture of resistance (cf. Cowley, Frank, and Hebdige). Within this shifting terrain what matters most, Hall argues, is what you do with culture, that is: the political uses to which culture, all culture, is employed. "That," he concludes this essay, "is why 'popular culture' matters. Otherwise, to tell you the truth, I don't give a damn about it."

I want to say something about 'popular'. The term can have a number of different meanings: not all of them useful. Take the most common-sense meaning: the things which are said to be 'popular' because masses of people listen to them, buy them, read them, consume them, and seem to enjoy them to the full. This is the 'market' or commercial definition of the term: the one which brings socialists out in spots. It is quite rightly associated with the manipulation and debasement of the culture of the people. In one sense, it is the direct opposite of the way I have been using the word earlier. I have, though, two reservations about entirely dispensing with this meaning, unsatisfactory as it is.

First, if it is true that, in the twentieth century, vast numbers of people *do* consume and even indeed enjoy the cultural products of our modern cultural industry, then it follows that very substantial numbers of working people must be included within the audiences for such products. Now, if the forms and relationships, on which participation in this sort of commercially provided 'culture' depend, are purely manipulative and debased, then the people who consume and enjoy them must either be themselves debased by these activities or else living in a permanent state of 'false consciousness'. They must be 'cultural dopes' who can't tell that what they are being fed is an up-dated form of the opium of the people. That judgement may make us feel right, decent and self-satisfied about our denunciations of the agents of mass manipulation and deception – the capitalist cultural industries: but I don't know that it is a view which can survive for long as an adequate account of cultural relationships: and even less as a socialist perspective on the culture and nature of the working class. Ultimately, the notion of the people as a purely *passive*, outline force is a deeply unsocialist perspective.

Second, then: can we get around this problem without dropping the inevitable and necessary attention to the manipulative aspect of a great deal of commercial popular culture? There are a number of strategies for doing so, adopted by radical critics and theorists of popular culture, which, I think, are highly dubious. One is to counterpose to it another, whole, 'alternative' culture – the authentic 'popular culture'; and to suggest that the 'real' working class (whatever that is) isn't taken in by the commercial substitutes. This is a heroic alternative; but not a very convincing one. Basically what is wrong with it is that it neglects the absolutely essential relations of cultural power – of domination and subordination – which is an intrinsic feature of cultural relations. I want to assert on the contrary that there is *no* whole, authentic, autonomous 'popular culture' which lies outside the field of force of the relations of cultural power and domination. Second, it greatly underestimates the power of cultural implantation. This is a tricky point to make, for as soon as it *is* made, one opens oneself to the charge that one is subscribing to the thesis of cultural incorporation. The study of popular culture keeps shifting between these two, quite unacceptable, poles: pure 'autonomy' or total incapsulation.

Actually, I don't think it is necessary or right to subscribe to either. Since ordinary people are not cultural dopes, they are perfectly capable of recognizing the way the realities of working-class life are reorganized, reconstructed and reshaped by the way they are represented (i.e. re-presented) in, say, *Coronation Street*. The cultural industries do have the power constantly to rework and reshape what they represent; and, by repetition and selection, to impose and implant such definitions of ourselves as fit more easily the descriptions of the dominant or preferred culture. That is what the concentration of cultural power – the means of culture-making in the heads of the few – actually means. These definitions don't have the power to occupy our minds; they don't function on us as if we are blank screens. But they do occupy and rework the interior contradictions of feeling and perception in the dominated classes; they *do* find or clear a space of recognition in those who respond to them. Cultural domination has real effects – even if these are neither all-powerful nor all-inclusive. If we were to argue that these imposed forms have no influence, it would be tantamount to arguing that the culture of the people can exist as a separate enclave, outside the distribution of cultural power and the relations of cultural force. I do not believe that. Rather, I think there is a continuous and necessarily uneven and unequal struggle, by the dominant culture, constantly to disorganize and reorganize popular culture; to enclose and confine its definitions and forms within a more inclusive range of dominant forms. There are points of resistance; there are also moments of supersession. This is the dialectic of cultural struggle. In our times, it goes on continuously, in the complex lines of resistance and acceptance, refusal and capitulation, which make the field of culture a sort of constant battlefield. A battlefield where no once-for-all victories are obtained but where there are always strategic positions to be won and lost.

The first definition, then, is not a useful one for our purposes; but it might force us to think more deeply about the complexity of cultural relations, about the reality of cultural power and about the nature of cultural implantation. If the forms of provided commercial popular culture are not purely manipulative, then it is because, alongside the false appeals, the foreshortenings, the trivialization and shortcircuits, there are also elements of recognition and identification, something approaching a recreation of recognizable experiences and attitudes, to which people are responding. The danger arises because we tend to think of cultural forms as whole and coherent: either wholly corrupt or wholly authentic. Whereas, they are deeply contradictory; they play on contradictions, especially when they function in the domain of the 'popular'. The language of the *Daily Mirror* is neither a pure construction of Fleet Street 'newspeak' nor is it the language which its working-class readers actually speak. It is a highly complex species of linguistic *ventriloquism* in which the debased brutalism of popular journalism is skilfully combined and intricated with some elements of the directness and vivid particularity of working-class language. It cannot get by without preserving some element of its roots in a real vernacular – in 'the popular'. It wouldn't get very far unless it were capable of reshaping popular elements into a species of canned and neutralized demotic populism.

The second definition of 'popular' is easier to live with. This is the descriptive one. Popular culture is all those things that 'the people' do or have done. This is close to an 'anthropological' definition of the term: the culture, mores, customs and folkways of 'the people'. What defines their 'distinctive way of life'. I have two difficulties with this definition, too.

First, I am suspicious of it precisely because it is too descriptive. This is putting it mildly. Actually, it is based on an infinitely expanding inventory. Virtually *anything* which 'the people' have ever done can fall into the list. Pigeon-fancying and stamp-collecting, flying ducks on the wall and garden gnomes. The problem is how to distinguish this infinite list, in any but a descriptive way, from what popular culture is *not*.

But the second difficulty is more important – and relates to a point made earlier. We can't simply collect into one category all the things which 'the people' do, without observing that the real analytic distinction arises, not from the list itself – an inert category of things and activities – but from the key opposition: the people/not of the people. That is to say, the structuring principle of 'the popular' in this sense is the tensions and oppositions between what belongs to the central domain of elite or dominant culture, and the culture of the 'periphery'. It is this opposition which constantly structures the domain of culture into the 'popular' and the 'non-popular'. But you cannot construct these oppositions in a purely descriptive way. For, from period to period, the *contents* of each category changes. Popular forms become enhanced in cultural value, go up the cultural escalator –

find themselves on the opposite side. Others thing cease to have high cultural value, and are appropriated into the popular, becoming transformed in the process. The structuring principle does not consist of the contents of each category – which, I insist, will alter from one period to another. Rather it consists of the forces and relations which sustain the distinction, the difference: roughly, between what, at any time, counts as an elite cultural activity or form, and what does not. These categories remain, though the inventories change. What is more, a whole set of institutions and institutional processes are required to sustain each – and to continually mark the difference between them. The school and the education system is one such institution – distinguishing the valued part of the culture, the cultural heritage, the history to be transmitted, from the 'valueless' part. The literary and scholarly apparatus is another – marking-off certain kinds of valued knowledge from others. The important fact, then, is not a mere descriptive inventory – which may have the negative effect of freezing popular culture into some timeless descriptive mould – but the relations of power which are constantly punctuating and dividing the domain of culture into its preferred and its residual categories.

So I settle for a third definition of 'popular', though it is a rather uneasy one. This looks, in any particular period, at those forms and activities which have their roots in the social and material conditions of particular classes; which have been embodied in popular traditions and practices. In this sense, it retains what is valuable in the descriptive definition. But it goes on to insist that what is essential to the definition of popular culture is the relations which define 'popular culture' in a continuing tension (relationship, influence and antagonism) to the dominant culture. It is a conception of culture which is polarized around this cultural dialectic. It treats the domain of cultural forms and activities as a constantly changing field. Then it looks at the relations which constantly structure this field into dominant and subordinate formations. It looks at the *process* by which these relations of dominance and subordination are articulated. It treats them as a process: the process by means of which some things are actively preferred so that others can be dethroned. It has at its centre the changing and uneven relations of force which define the field of culture – that is, the question of cultural struggle and its many forms. Its main focus of attention is the relation between culture and questions of hegemony.

What we have to be concerned with, in this definition, is not the question of the 'authenticity' or organic wholeness of popular culture. Actually, it recognizes that almost *all* cultural forms will be contradictory in this sense, composed of antagonistic and unstable elements. The meaning of a cultural form and its place or position in the cultural field is *not* inscribed inside its form. Nor is its position fixed once and forever. This year's radical symbol or slogan will be neutralized into next year's fashion; the year after, it will be the object of a profound cultural nostalgia. Today's rebel folksinger ends up, tomorrow, on the cover of *The Observer* colour magazine. The meaning of a cultural symbol is given in part by the social field into which it is incorporated, and practices with which it articulates and is made to resonate. What matters is *not* the intrinsic or historically fixed objects of culture, but the state of play in cultural relations: to put it bluntly and in an over-simplified form – what counts is the class struggle in and over culture.

Almost every fixed inventory will betray us. Is the novel a 'bourgeois' form? The answer can only be historically provisional: When? Which novels? For whom? Under what conditions?

. . .

This provides us with a warning against those self-enclosed approaches to popular culture which, valuing 'tradition' for its own sake, and treating it in an a-historical manner, analyse popular cultural forms as if they contained within themselves, from their moment of origin, some fixed and unchanging meaning or value. The relationship between historical position and aesthetic value is an important and difficult question in popular culture. But the attempt to develop some universal popular aesthetic, founded on the moment of origin of cultural forms and practices, is almost certainly profoundly mistaken. What could be more eclectic and random than that assemblage of dead symbols and bric-à-brac, ransacked from yesterday's dressing-up box, in which, just now, many young people have chosen to adorn themselves? These symbols and bits and pieces are profoundly ambiguous. A thousand lost cultural causes could be summoned up through them. Every now and then, amongst the other trinkets, we find that sign which, above all other signs, ought to be fixed – solidified – in its cultural meaning and connotation forever: the swastika. And yet there it dangles, partly – but not entirely – cut loose from its profound cultural reference in twentieth-century history. What does it mean? What is it signifying? Its signification is rich, and richly ambiguous: certainly unstable. This terrifying sign may delimit a range of meanings but it carries no guarantee of a single meaning within itself. The streets are full of kids who are not 'fascist' because they may wear a swastika on a chain. On the other hand, perhaps they *could* be . . . What this sign means will ultimately depend, in the politics of youth culture, less on the intrinsic cultural symbolism of the thing in itself, and more on the balance of forces between, say the National Front and the Anti-Nazi League, between White Rock and the Two Tone Sound.

Not only is there no intrinsic guarantee within the cultural sign or form itself. There is no guarantee that, because at one time it was linked with a pertinent struggle, it will always be the living expression of a class: so that every time you give it an airing it will 'speak the language of socialism'. If cultural expressions register for socialism, it is because they have been linked as the practices, the forms and organization of a living struggle, which have succeeded in appropriating those symbols and giving them a socialist connotation. Culture is not already permanently inscribed with the conditions of a class before that struggle begins. The struggle consists in the success or failure to give 'the cultural' a socialist accent.

The term 'popular' has very complex relations to the term 'class'. We know this, but are often at pains to forget it. We speak of particular forms of working-class culture; but we use the more inclusive term, 'popular culture' to refer to the general field of enquiry. It's perfectly clear that what I've been saying would make little sense without reference to a class perspective and to class struggle. But it is also clear that there is no one-to-one relationship between a class and a particular cultural form or practice. The terms 'class' and 'popular' are deeply related but they are not absolutely interchangeable. The reason for that is obvious. There are no wholly separate 'cultures' paradigmatically attached, in a relation of historical fixity, to specific 'whole' classes – although there are clearly distinct and variable class-cultural formations. Class cultures tend to intersect and overlap in the same field of struggle. The term 'popular' indicates this somewhat displaced relationship of culture to classes. More accurately, it refers to that alliance of classes and forces which constitute the 'popular classes'. The culture of the oppressed, the excluded classes: this is the area to which the term 'popular' refers us. And the opposite side to that – the side with the cultural power to decide what belongs and what does not – is, by definition, not another 'whole' class, but that other alliance of classes, strata and social forces which constitute what is not 'the people' and not the 'popular classes': the culture of the power-bloc.

The people versus the power-bloc: this, rather than 'class-against-class', is the central line of contradiction around which the terrain of culture is polarized. Popular culture especially is organized around the contradiction: the popular forces versus the power-bloc. This gives to the terrain of cultural struggle its own kind of specificity. But the term 'popular', and even more, the collective subject to which it must refer – 'the people' – is highly problematic. It is made problematic by, say, the ability of Mrs Thatcher to pronounce a sentence like, 'We have to limit the power of the trade unions because that is what the people want.' That suggests to me that, just as there is no fixed content to the category of 'popular culture', so there is no fixed subject to attach to it – 'the people'. 'The people' are not always back there, where they have always been, their culture untouched, their liberties and their instincts intact, still struggling on against the Norman yoke or whatever: as if, if only we can 'discover' them and bring them back on stage, they will always stand up in the right, appointed place and be counted. The capacity to *constitute* classes and individuals as a popular force – that is the nature of political and cultural struggle: to *make* the divided classes and the separated peoples – divided and separated by culture as much as by other factors – *into* a popular-democratic cultural force.

We can be certain that *other* forces also have a stake in defining 'the people' as something else: 'the people' who need to be disciplined more, ruled better, more effectively policed, whose way of life needs to be protected from 'alien cultures', and so on. There is some part of both those alternatives inside each of us. Sometimes we can be constituted as a force against the power-bloc: that is the historical opening in which it is possible to construct a culture which is genuinely popular. But, in our society, if we are not constituted like that, we will be constituted into its opposite: an effective populist force, saying 'Yes' to power. Popular culture is one of the sites where this struggle for and against a culture of the powerful is engaged: it is also the stake to be won or lost *in* that struggle. It is the arena of consent and resistance. It is partly where hegemony arises, and where it is secured. It is not a sphere where socialism, a socialist culture – already fully formed – might be simply 'expressed'. But it is one of the places where socialism might be constituted. That is why 'popular culture' matters. Otherwise, to tell you the truth, I don't give a damn about it.

Stuart Hall, "Notes on Deconstructing 'The Popular'," *People's History and Socialist Theory*, Raphael Samuel (ed.), London: Kegan Paul–Routledge, 1981, pp. 231–5, 237–9.

FIVE

DISMANTLING THE MASTER'S HOUSE

Culture has been used as a weapon throughout history. In modern times, English was made the official language of India and other British colonies. American Indians were forced to abandon their religion and way of life, and Africans, upon arriving in the Americas, were deprived of their traditions as well as their freedom. Partly out of a chauvinism that believes one culture naturally superior, partly as part of a pragmatic strategy of social control, conquerors impress their culture upon those they conquer. Thus any struggle for liberation must also include a fight for cultural independence. But the campaign for an independent culture, uncontaminated by the oppressor, is exceedingly difficult, if not impossible. For, unlike armies or laws, culture is internalized. It isn't something you can shoot or tear up, instead it is part of the self – the very same self-demanding autonomy. As the anti-colonialist writer Albert Memmi points out: it is one thing to throw the colonizer out of your country, it is still another to expel the colonizer within yourself.[1] Given that the struggle for a purified culture often ends in failure (Gandhi's India is now a global center for high-tech computer development) or a bloodbath (the massacre of the Sioux at Wounded Knee, or Cambodia under the victorious Khmer Rouge) other strategies of cultural resistance have been developed. The most successful among these are hybrid cultures which use the tools of the master, carefully reshaped, to dismantle the master's own house.

ELAINE GOODALE EASTMAN,
"THE GHOST DANCE WAR"
FROM *SISTER TO THE SIOUX*

In 1888 a Paiute Indian named Wovoka had a vision: the Messiah was coming, bringing peace, resurrecting dead ancestors, and returning the American continent and her buffalo to the Indians. The Messiah, Wovoka revealed, could be hastened by communal dancing and singing – the "ghost dance." Offering hope to a population whose land had been taken away and whose ways of life were under assault by white settlers and the US government, the ghost dance spread rapidly through the Great Plains to a dozen reservations. The dance took a particularly strong hold among the Dakota Sioux who had been devastated by drought, disease, and reduced government rations. Interpreting the dances as preparation for war, the US government dispatched troops to the Pine Ridge reservation. The confrontation between Sioux and soldiers ended in the "Battle" of Wounded Knee in 1890 when the 7th Cavalry Division massacred 146 (400 by Sioux estimates) men, women, and children. It was the end of the ghost dance and the last military battle against the Indians in the US. What follows is an eyewitness account of the ghost dances, and the official reaction to them, by Elaine Goodale Eastman, a white teacher and Indian advocate then living on the Sioux reservation. "The Ghost Dance War" is a story of the power of cultural resistance, giving hope and strength to a decimated Plains Indian population and frightening the US government. But it's also a cautionary tale. For in the end songs and dances were no match for dollars and guns.

The Buffalo Are Coming!

The Pratt commission of 1888 had been followed in the next year by a more successful effort, directed by General Crook, to purchase nearly half of the vast wastelands formerly reserved to the Sioux. At about the same time the huge Territory of Dakota had been cut in two and two new states admitted to the Union. However, the rush to homestead claims fell far short of expectations, aroused to a high pitch by the tremendous boom in the more fertile and inviting "Cherokee Strip."

The Sioux had naturally hoped for immediate benefit from the reluctant sale of more than nine million acres to which they had clung from sentiment and tradition, although as a matter of fact it was of little use to them without the bison herds that had once covered it. They expected to receive cows, farm tools, and (most pressing at the moment) an increased beef ration. Instead, the issue of beef at the two western-most agencies was cut from one to two million pounds, causing real privation. The men whose consent to the act had been so lately courted with fair words were ignored and snubbed.

To make matters worse, that summer of 1890 was one of a cycle of dry years, so familiar today. A veritable "Dust Bowl" extended from the Missouri River almost to the Black Hills. In the persistent hot winds the pitiful little gardens of the Indians curled up and died. Even the native hay crop was a failure. I had never before seen so much sickness. The appearance of the people shocked me. Lean and wiry in health, with glowing skins and a look of mettle, many now displayed gaunt forms, lackluster faces, and sad, deep-sunken eyes.

Not until I came to Standing Rock, so far as I remember, did I hear again the fanciful story told one evening by Chasing Crane, twelve months earlier, on the road to the sand hills. We should not lay the Ghost Dance upheaval among the Dakotas solely to the wrongs suffered by them. The touching legend of a Messiah did not originate with them, but crept like a fire in the grass all the way from Mason Valley in Nevada. The story was wonderingly repeated in many tongues beside hundreds of distant camp-fires, even as far south as Oklahoma. It was more or less seriously accepted in several tribes, but it is true that nowhere except among the wilder bands of Sioux did credulity lead to disaster. The special conditions that existed at Rosebud, Pine Ridge, and Standing Rock – drought, unwise reduction of rations, and dissatisfaction with the results of the last agreement, which many had fought to the end – these made the Dakotas a ready prey to a dangerous illusion. They were the dry grass – tinder dry; the match was the thrilling promise of supernatural help, a Savior for the red man!

. . .

A party including Short Bull, Kicking Bear, Good Thunder, and one or two more from Rosebud and Pine Ridge had either volunteered or been commissioned to journey over the mountains to look into this strange rumor of a Messiah. They were away for several months and on their return in the spring of 1890 immediately began an active crusade, though discouraged by the agent at Pine Ridge to the point of putting one of their number in the guardhouse. Kicking Bear was summoned to Grand River, where Sitting Bull was living, sometime during the summer and about the time of my arrival had begun to instruct the people in the mysteries of the "Spirit Dance."

. . .

On the high plateau overlooking Oak Creek, two hundred tents of Christian Indians had been pitched in horseshoe form, almost surrounding the little mission of Saint Elizabeth. Since the chapel could seat only a tithe of the assembled worshipers, most services were held under a rude arbor of freshly cut green boughs. Each evening a ring was formed in the open, in native fashion, for the impressive sunset service, when several white and as many Sioux clergymen in their snowy robes, facing representatives of Bishop Hare's seventeen hundred communicants from all the Dakota agencies, filled the clear air of the high plains with sweetly ordered sounds of praise and prayer.

Meantime, a very different scene was being enacted on the Grand River, forty miles away. It seemed as if a rival religious ceremony had been inaugurated at a dramatic moment and by deliberate design. No Christian chapel, I believe, was ever disturbed by the Ghost Dancers, but they preferred to plant their "sacred tree" as near as possible to church or schoolhouse. They steadily maintained that they, too, worshiped the Christ in this his second appearing!

From Saint Elizabeth's I drove to the nearest day school and found half the children absent with their parents, celebrating the strange rites taught them by Kicking Bear. At the agency everyone was talking of the new craze, treating it as a folly soon to be forgotten. Agent McLaughlin, one of the steadiest and most experienced men in the service, sent his Indian police to forbid the dance and order Kicking Bear to leave the reservation. The prophet left, but the people were in a defiant mood and continued to dance. Merely as a passing novelty, with the added charm of the forbidden, this excitement might easily have served as an outlet for suppressed emotions in a season of gloom and depression.

. . .

At our last meal on the prairie before reaching Pine Ridge agency, I talked for a long time with Good Thunder, one of the messengers returned from Nevada. He was an old man of winning appearance, with hoary locks that hung nearly to his waist, and the soft voice and ingratiating manner characteristic of many old-time Sioux. I still have my penciled notes of the conversation, made on the spot. "With three others," said Good Thunder

> I traveled a long time to find the Christ. We crossed Indian reservations and passed through white men's towns. On a broad prairie covered with Indians I saw him at last. We could not tell whence he came. Suddenly he appeared before us — a man of surpassing beauty, with yellow hair, clad in a blue robe. He did not look at us or speak, but read our thoughts and answered without speech. I saw the prints of the nails on his hands and feet.
>
> He said that he had come upon the earth once before. Then he had appeared to the white people, who had scorned him and finally killed him. Now he came to red men only. He said their crying had sounded loud in his ears. They were dying of starvation and disease. The Messiah said that he had come to save them. He had thought to come in three days (explaining to me that meant three years) but their cries had so moved him to pity that he would come tomorrow (meaning next summer). He would gather together the souls of all Indians who had died and they would be with the living in Paradise, once more hunting the

buffalo, dressing in skins, and dwelling in skin tents as of old. The souls of thieves and murderers must wait for some time outside. The people offered him a pipe, tobacco pouch, and moccasins. He handed the two first to others standing by, but kept the moccasins. Three birds – an eagle, a hawk, and a dove – attended him.

The story is obviously in large part an invention, as we learned later that the original "dreamer" was an illiterate Paiute Indian, known as Wovoka or Jack Wilson – a man subject to trances, possibly a cataleptic. The yellow hair and blue robe, the nail prints, and hint of Purgatory are clearly reflected from Christian teaching. The birds and other accessories are typically Indian. All the stories, which were related with a convincing air of sincerity, stressed the return of the buffalo, so necessary to the primitive existence of the plains people. There was no hint of violence or of contemplated war, and no weapons were carried in the dance. Some declared that "a wave of earth" would roll over the cities, leaving the land once more in undisturbed possession of the first inhabitants.

The Ghost Dance War

The Sioux had been thoroughly "conquered" in the eighteen-seventies and I had never considered the possibility of another Indian war. Any resistance on their part, I knew, must be only a short-lived revolt led by a handful of hopeless and desperate men. Yet there was a growing sense of fear, suspicion, and anxiety on all sides. Futile attempts to forbid the dancing only fanned the flame. Those who did not dance became gradually infected with a contagious excitement. The inexperienced agent at Pine Ridge, a recent political appointee, losing all control, grew more and more nervous.

. . .

There was no secrecy about the dance which had caused such frantic alarm. It was held in the open, with neither fire nor light, after the participants had fasted for a day or two and passed through the purifying

Arapaho and Sioux ghost dance songs

My Father, have pity on me!
I have nothing to eat,
I am dying of thirst –
Everything is gone!

Arapaho

The whole world is coming
A nation is coming, a nation is
   coming,
The Eagle has brought the message
   to the tribe.
The father says so, the father says so.
Over the whole earth they are
   coming.
The buffalo are coming, the buffalo
   are coming,
The Crow has brought the message
   to the tribe,
The father says so, the father says so.

Sioux

From *The Ghost-Dance Religion and the Sioux Outbreak of 1890*, James Mooney, 14th Annual Report of the Bureau of Ethnology, 1892–3, Washington: GPO, 1896 ordeal of the sweat-lodge. Anyone might look on, and on a bright November night I joined a crowd of spectators near Porcupine Tail Butte – the only person who was not a Sioux.

Under the soft glow of the hunter's moon perhaps a hundred men, women, and children, with clasped hands and fingers interlocked, swung in a great circle about their "sacred tree," chanting together the monotonous Ghost Dance songs. The hypnotic repetition of the words: "Once more we shall hunt the buffalo – Our Father has said it!" alternated with short invocations by prophet or priest and occasional intervals of wailing by the women – that musical heart-piercing sound which, once heard, is never forgotten. No one with imagination could fail to see in the rite a genuine religious ceremony, a faith which, illusory as it was, deserved to be treated with respect.

"You have your churches; why can we not have ours?" was the natural reaction of the people.

In the course of an hour or two, one of the worshipers would break abruptly from the ring, rush wildly about, and fall in a trance or faint, lying for some time motionless. One old woman fell so near me that I could have touched her. Presently she stirred, got to her feet unaided, and addressed the gathering in a strong voice:

"My children, I have seen those dear ones we lost long ago!'

"Ah-h-h! He-ye-ye!" responded the people.

"They are living in a most beautiful country covered with buffalo!"

"He-ye-ye! Ate heye lo!" (Our Father has said it.)

"Their tipis are of skins. They are feasting and playing. They are perfectly happy!" (After each statement the people intone their deep-voiced response.)

"Here everything looks hateful to me – how can I bear it!"

The congregation responds with groans and cries. Then the priest repeats that the Messiah will appear "with the new grass" in spring and the vision will come true for all believers.

After listening to this strange litany for half the night, I lay down in my tent quite worn out with sympathetic excitement. The spell, or incantation, or rite continued with increasing fervor until dawn.

The prophets of the Messiah now began to instruct their converts that they should throw away everything brought by the white man, wear only native dress, and revive the old, obsolete customs. While there was a noticeable trend in this direction, it was impossible to conform strictly. Knives, kettles, cotton, cloth, blankets, and flour – to mention only a few items – had long since become indispensable. Some bows and arrows were made.

One woman, recovering from her trance, announced that she had been told of a garment that all must wear. It was a shirt for men, a robe for women, fashioned of coarse unbleached muslin, heavily fringed and painted in symbolic figures. It was supposed to be sewed with sinew for thread. This tawdry imitation of the departed skin clothing was typical of the whole pitiful delusion. After troops had come it was asserted that the "sacred shirts" were bullet-proof.

Moving on to Medicine Root, some fifty miles from the agency, I received a call from the wife of Little Wound, the local chief. Excitedly she defended the new cult, in which her husband had become a leader and which was opposed by a strong party of native Christians headed by the Reverend Amos Ross.

On this same evening Little Wound himself approached the day school teacher and indignantly demanded of him why soldiers were coming. The troops so insistently demanded by the agent had in fact reached Rushville (at least seventy miles from Medicine Root) that very evening. An all-night march brought them to the agency by daybreak the next morning. But neither of us had heard of this nor could we guess how Little Wound knew.

All employees in the outlying districts now received peremptory orders to report immediately at the agency. The teacher taught half a day for my benefit before setting out on horseback. That night there was dancing again and I slept quietly in my tent within a few rods of hundreds of excited worshipers. Thrilling cries and the dull beat of many moccasined feet mingled strangely with my dreams.

While we sat at breakfast in the open, a native policeman who had ridden all night brought me a polite note from the agent, requesting an immediate interview. I never learned why I had not been recalled at the same time as the others. Possibly Mr. Royer supposed that I would take fright and come in without being sent for. Perhaps he did not feel responsible for the safety of an independent government officer. Or he may have resented the casual way in which I mingled with the people.

I soon found that this time the whole population had been ordered in. There was a great commotion – ponies hurriedly caught, tents razed, goods packed, and the roads were soon black with long convoys moving in two different directions. There was nothing for me to do in a deserted camp. Reluctantly I gave the order and we covered the fifty miles before sunset.

Now that troops were actually quartered at the agency the unexpected order to "come in" had divided the Sioux. Many families were broken up and feeling was intense. Submission was easy for the "church party," but the Ghost Dancers who had defied police authority, fearing summary punishment, fled in terror to the Bad Lands. From that seventeenth day of November on, the thousands encamped close about the agency were known as the "friendlies." Those poor creatures who retreated in desperation to their natural fortress, subsisting miserably on such part of the government herd as they had been able to carry away, were dubbed "hostiles" – although they had committed no hostile act. The truth is that their flight was merely a stampede and there were no raids whatever outside the reservation.

It was a time of grim suspense. We seemed to be waiting – helplessly waiting – as if in some horrid nightmare, for the inevitable catastrophe. It seems to me today that I have already lived once through the European situation, where nations armed to the teeth confront one another in mutual dread and mutual menace. Something like it, on a far smaller scale, was that tragic Christmas season of 1890 among the Sioux.

Elaine Goodale Eastman, *Sister to the Sioux: The Memoirs of Elaine Goodale Eastman, 1885–91*, Kay Graber (ed.), Lincoln: University of Nebraska Press, 1978, pp. 136–41, 143–5, 148–52.

M.K. GANDHI,
FROM *HIND SWARAJ*

Written as a pamphlet in 1910, *Hind Swaraj* is a young Mahatma Gandhi's call for – and definition of – home rule for India. He argues that if the Indian people are to be free of English political and economic rule they must also free themselves from British, and modern European, culture. As Gandhi asks of his imaginary interlocutor, "Why do you forget that our adoption of their civilization makes their presence at all possible?" If the master's house is to be dismantled, it cannot be done with the master's tools. It is from this vantage point that he makes his famous appeal for India to weave its own cloth, Khaddar, to "establish in thousands of households the ancient and sacred handlooms," not only to break the classic economic dependency that binds the colony to colonizer, but more importantly, to free oneself mentally and spiritually from Western machines and materialism. Gandhi, however, also understands the difficulty of what he is asking, acknowledging in closing that it is a Western printing press that allows him to disseminate his ideas of doing away with printing presses.

How Can India Become Free?

Reader: I appreciate your views about civilization. I will have to think over them. I cannot take in all at once. What, then, holding the views you do, would you suggest for freeing India?

Editor: I do not expect my views to be accepted all of a sudden. My duty is to place them before readers like yourself. Time can be trusted to do the rest. We have already examined the conditions for freeing India, but we have done so indirectly; we will now do so directly. It is a world-known maxim that the removal of the cause of a disease results in the removal of the disease itself. Similarly, if the cause of India's slavery be removed, India can become free.

Reader: If Indian civilization is, as you say, the best of all, how do you account for India's slavery?

Editor: This civilization is unquestionably the best, but it is to be observed that all civilizations have been on their trail. That civilization that is permanent outlives it. Because the sons of India were found wanting, its civilization has been placed in jeopardy. But its strength is to be seen in its ability to survive the shock. Moreover, the whole of India is not touched. Those alone who have been affected by western civilization have become enslaved. We measure the universe by our own miserable foot-rule. When we are slaves, we think the whole universe is enslaved. Because we are in an abject condition, we think the whole of India is in that condition. As a matter of fact, it is not so, but it is as well to impute our slavery to the whole of India. But if we bear in mind the above fact, we can see that, if we become free, India is free. And in this thought you have a definition of Swaraj. It is Swaraj when we learn to rule ourselves. It is, therefore, in the palm of our hands. Do not consider this Swaraj to be like a dream. Hence there is no idea of sitting still. The Swaraj I wish to picture before you and me is such that, after we have once realized it, we will endeavour to the end of our lifetime to persuade others to do likewise. But such Swaraj has to be experienced by each one for himself. One drowning man will never save another. Slaves ourselves, it would be a mere pretension to think of freeing others. Now you will have seen that it is not necessary to have as our goal the expulsion of the English. If the English become Indianized, we can accommodate them. If they wish to remain in India along with their civilization, there is no room for them. It lies with us to bring such a state of things

Reader: It is impossible that Englishmen should ever become Indianized.

Editor: To say that is equivalent to saying that the English have no humanity in them. And it is really beside the point whether they become so or not. If we keep our own house in order, only those who are fit to live in it will remain, others will leave on their own accord. Such things occur within the experience of all of us.

Reader: But it has not occurred in history.

Editor: To believe that what has not occurred in history will not occur at all is to argue disbelief in the dignity of man. At any rate, it behoves us to try what appeals to our reason. All countries are not similarly conditioned. The condition of India is unique. Its strength is immeasurable. We need not, therefore, refer to the history of other countries. I have drawn attention to the fact that, when other civilizations have succumbed, the Indians have survived many a shock.

Reader: I cannot follow this. There seems little doubt that we shall have to expel the English by force of arms. So long as they are in the country, we cannot rest. One of our poets says that slaves cannot even dream of happiness. We are day by day becoming weakened owing to the presence of the English. Our greatness is gone, our people look like terrified men. The English are in the country like a blight which we must remove by every means.

Editor: In your excitement, you have forgotten all we have been considering. We brought the English, and we keep them. Why do you forget that our adoption of their civilization makes their presence in India at all possible? Your hatred against them should be transferred to their civilization.

. . .

Machinery

Reader: When you speak of driving out Western civilization, I suppose you will also say that we want no machinery.

Editor: By raising this question you have opened the wound I had received. When I read Mr Dutt's *Economic History of India*, I wept; and, as I think of it again, my heart sickens. It is machinery that has impoverished India. It is difficult to measure the harm that Manchester[1] has done to us. It is due to Manchester that Indian handicraft has all but disappeared.

But I make a mistake. How can Manchester be blamed? We wore Manchester cloth, and that is why Manchester wove it. I was delighted when I read about the bravery of Bengal. There are no cloth-mills in that Presidency. They were, therefore, able to restore the original hand-weaving occupation. It is true, Bengal encourages the mill industry of Bombay. If Bengal had proclaimed a boycott of *all* machine-made goods, it would have been much better.

Machinery has begun to desolate Europe. Ruination is now knocking at the English gates. Machinery is the chief symbol of modern civilization; it represents a great sin.

The workers in the mills of Bombay have become slaves. The condition of the women working in the mills is shocking. When there were no mills, these women were not starving. If the machinery craze grows in our country, it will become an unhappy land. It may be considered a heresy, but I am bound to say that it was better for us to send money to Manchester and use flimsy Manchester cloth, than to multiply mills in India. By using Manchester cloth we would only waste our money, but by reproducing Manchester in India, we shall keep our money at the price of our blood, because our very moral being will be sapped, and I call in support of my statement the very mill-hands as witnesses. And those who have amassed wealth out of factories are not likely to be better than other rich men. It would be folly to assume that an Indian Rockefeller would be better than the American Rockefeller. Impoverished India can be free, but it will be hard for an India made rich through immortality to regain its freedom. I fear that we will have to admit that moneyed men support British rule; their interest is bound up with their stability. Money renders a man helpless. The other thing is as harmful as sexual vice. Both are poison. A snake-bite is lesser poison than these two, because the former merely destroys the body, but the latter destroy body, mind and soul. We need not, therefore, be pleased with the prospect of growth of the mill industry.

Reader: Are the mills, then, to be closed down?

Editor: That is difficult. It is no easy task to do away with a thing that is established. We, therefore, say that the non-beginning of a thing is supreme wisdom. We cannot condemn mill-owners; we can but pity them. It would be too much to expect them to give up the mills, but we may implore them not to increase them. If they would be good, they would gradually contract their business. They can establish in thousands of households the ancient and sacred hand-looms, and they can buy out the cloth that may be thus woven. Whether the mill owners do this or not, people can cease to use machine-made goods.

Reader: You have so far spoken about machine-made cloth, but there are innumerable machine-made things. We have either to import them or to introduce machinery into our country.

Editor: Indeed, our gods even are made in Germany. What need then to speak of matches, pins and glassware? My answer can be only one. What did India do before these articles were introduced? Precisely the same should be done to-day. As long as we cannot make pins without machinery, so long will we do without them. The tinsel splendour of glassware we will have nothing to do with, and we will make wicks, as of old, with home-grown cotton, and use hand-made earthen saucers for lamps. So doing, we shall save our eyes and money, and will support Swadeshi, and so shall we attain Home Rule.

It is not to be conceived that all men will do all these things at one time, or that some men will give up all machine-made things at once. But, if the thought is sound, we will always find out what we can give up, and will gradually cease to use this. What a few may do, others will copy, and the movement will grow like the coconut of the mathematical problem. What the leaders do, the populace will gladly follow. The matter is neither complicated nor difficult. You and I shall not wait until we can carry others with us. Those will be the losers who will not do it; and those who will not do it, although they appreciate the truth, will deserve to be called cowards.

Reader: What, then, of the tram-cars and electricity?

Editor: This question is now too late. It signifies nothing. If we are to do without the railways, we shall have to do without the tram-cars. Machinery is like a snake-hole which may contain from one to a hundred snakes. Where there is machinery there are large cities; and where there are large cities, there are tram-cars and railways; and there only does one see electric light. English villages do not boast any of these things. Honest physicians will tell you that, where means of artificial locomotion have increased, the health of the people have suffered. I remember that, when in a European town there was a scarcity of money, the receipts of the tram-way company, of the lawyers and of the doctors, went down, and the people were less unhealthy. I cannot recall a single good point in connection with machinery. Books can be written to demonstrate its evils.

Reader: Is it a good point or bad one that all you are saying will be printed through machinery?

Editor: This is one of those instances which demonstrate that sometimes poison is used to kill poison. This, then, will not be a good point regarding machinery. As it expires, the machinery, as it were, says to us: 'Beware and avoid me. You will derive no benefit from me, and the benefit that may accrue from printing will avail only those who are infected with the machinery-craze.' Do not, therefore, forget the main thing. It is necessary to realize that machinery is bad. We shall then be able gradually to do away with it. Nature has not provided any way whereby we may reach a desired goal all of a sudden. If, instead of welcoming machinery as a boon, we would look upon it as an evil, it would ultimately go.

M.K. Gandhi, *Indian Home Rule*, Madras: Ganesh & Co. (Nationalist Press), 1919, pp. 71–5, 118–24.

C.L.R. JAMES, FROM *BEYOND A BOUNDARY*

This next selection further complicates the debate of cultures of resistance versus cultures of oppression. It is from a memoir of sorts by C.L.R. James, the renowned Marxist critic, radical historian, West Indian nationalist, and cricket fanatic. Growing up in Trinidad, at the time a British colony, James was educated at an English school, read English authors, and played English sports. All this: the education, the literature, the cricket, reinforced the English way of seeing the world; as James writes: "everything began from the basis that Britain was the source of all light and leading, and our business was to admire, wonder, imitate, learn." It was the culture of imperialism. But it was also James's – and Trinidad's – culture, something they identified with and held dear. And so when British racism determines the selection of the West Indies cricket team, the injustice becomes all the more evident for flying in the face of the cultural norms of sportsmanship and "fair play" that the English themselves have instilled. It is, ironically, through British culture itself that the early rumblings of anti-British West Indian nationalism expresses itself.

Against the Current

We know nothing, nothing at all, of the results of what we do to children. My father had given me a bat and ball, I had learnt to play and at eighteen was a good cricketer. What a fiction! In reality my life up to ten had laid the powder for a war that lasted without respite for eight years, and intermittently for some time afterwards – a war between English Puritanism, English literature and cricket, and the realism of West Indian life.

. . .

It is only now as I write that I fully realize what a catastrophe I was for all – and there were many – who were so interested in me. How were they to know that when I put my foot on the steps of the college building in January 1911 I carried within me the seeds of revolt against all it formally stood for and all that I was supposed to do in it? My scholastic career was one long nightmare to me, my teachers and my family. My scholastic shortcomings were accompanied by breaches of discipline which I blush to think of even today. But at the same time, almost entirely by my own effort, I mastered thoroughly the principles of cricket and of English literature, and attained a mastery over my own character which would have done credit to my mother and Aunt Judith if only they could have understood it. I could not explain it to their often tear-stained faces for I did not understand it myself. I look back at that little boy with amazement, and, as I have said, with a gratitude that grows every day. But for his unshakable defiance of the whole world around him, and his determination to stick to his own ideas, nothing could have saved me from winning a scholarship, becoming an Honourable Member of the Legislative Council and ruining my whole life.

The first temptation was cricket and I succumbed without a struggle. On the first day of the term you were invited, if you wanted to play, to write your name on a paper pinned to the school notice-board. I wrote down mine. The next day the names appeared divided up into five elevens. The college had its own ground in the rear of the building and with a little crowding there was room for five elevens. That afternoon the elevens met and elected their captains. Later, as I grew older and won my place in the cricket and soccer elevens, I took my part in the elections of the captains, the secretaries and the committees. A master presided, but that was all he did. We managed our own affairs from the fifth eleven to the first. When I became the secretary I kept a check on the implements used in all the elevens, wrote down what was wanted on a sheet of paper, had it signed by a master and went off to buy them myself for over two hundred boys. We chose our own teams, awarded colours ourselves, obeyed our captains implicitly. For me it was life and education.

I began to study Latin and French, then Greek, and much else. But particularly we learnt, I learnt and obeyed and taught a code, the English public-school code. Britain and her colonies and the colonial peoples. What do the British people know of what they have done there? Precious little. The colonial peoples, particularly West Indians, scarcely know themselves as yet. It has taken me a long time to begin to understand.

One afternoon in 1956, being at that time deep in this book, I sat in a hall in Manchester, listening to Mr Aneurin Bevan. Mr Bevan had been under much criticism for 'not playing with the team', and he answered his critics. He devastated them and brought his audience to a pitch of high receptivity and continuous laughter by turning inside out and ripping holes in such concepts as 'playing with the team', 'keeping a stiff upper lip', 'playing with a straight bat' and the rest of them. I too had had my fun with them on the public platform often enough, but by 1956 I was engaged in a more respectful re-examination and I believe I was the solitary person among those many hundreds who was not going all the way with Mr Bevan. Perhaps there was one other. When Mr Bevan had had enough of it he tossed the ball lightly to his fellow speaker, Mr Michael Foot. 'Michael is an old public-school boy and he knows more about these things than I.' Mr Foot smiled, but if I am not mistaken the smile was cryptic.

I smiled too, but not whole-heartedly. In the midst of his fireworks Mr Bevan had dropped a single sentence that tolled like a bell. 'I did not join the Labour Party, I was brought up in it.' And I had been brought up in the public-school code.

It came doctrinally from the masters, who for two generations, from the foundation of the school, had been Oxford and Cambridge men. The striking thing was that inside the classrooms the code had little success. Sneaking was taboo, but we lied and cheated without any sense of shame. I know I did. By common understanding the boys sitting for the valuable scholarships did not cheat. Otherwise we submitted, or did not submit, to moral discipline, according to upbringing and temperament.

But as soon as we stepped on to the cricket or football field, more particularly the cricket field, all was changed. We were a motley crew. The children of some white officials and white business men, middle-class blacks and mulattos, Chinese boys, some of whose parents still spoke broken English, Indian boys, some of whose parents could speak no English at all, and some poor black boys who had won exhibitions or whose parents had starved and toiled on plots of agricultural land and were spending their hard-earned money on giving the eldest boy an education. Yet rapidly we learned to obey the umpire's decision without question, however irrational it was. We learned to play with the team, which meant subordinating your personal inclinations, and even interest, to the good of the whole. We kept a stiff upper lip in that we did not complain about ill-fortune. We did not denounce failures, but 'Well tried' or 'Hard luck' came easily to our lips. We were generous to opponents and congratulated them on victories, even when we knew they did not deserve it. We lived in two worlds. Inside the classrooms the heterogeneous jumble of Trinidad was battered and jostled and shaken down into some sort of order. On the playing field we did what ought to be done. Every individual did not observe every rule. But the majority of the boys did. The best and most-respected boys were precisely the ones who always kept them. When a boy broke them he knew what he had done and, with the cruelty and intolerance of youth, from all sides our denunciations poured in on him. Eton or Harrow had nothing on us.

Another source of this fierce, self-imposed discipline were the magazines and books that passed among us from hand to hand. *The Boy's Own Paper*, a magazine called *The Captain*, annual of which I remember the name of only one: *Young England*, the Mike stories by P.G. Wodehouse and scores of similar books and magazines. These we understood, these we lived by, the principles they taught we absorbed through the pores and practised instinctively. The books we read in class meant little to most of us.

To all this I took as a young duck in water. The organizing of boys into elevens, the selection of teams, the keeping of scores, all that I had been doing at second-hand with Grace and Ranjitsinhji and Trumper I now practised in real life with real people. I read the boys' books and magazines, twice as many as any other boy. I knew what was done and what was not done. One day when I bowled three maiden overs in succession and a boy fresh from England said to me, 'James, you must take yourself off now, three maiden overs', I was disturbed. I had not heard that one before, this boy was from England and so he probably knew.

Before very long I acquired a discipline for which the only name is Puritan. I never cheated, I never appealed for a decision unless I thought the batsman was out, I never argued with the umpire, I never jeered at a defeated opponent, I never gave to a friend a vote or a place which by any stretch of imagination could be seen as belonging to an enemy or to a stranger. My defeats and disappointments I took as stoically as I could. If I caught myself complaining or making excuses, I pulled up. If afterwards I remembered doing it I took an inward decision to try not to do it again. From the eight years of school life this code became the moral framework of my existence. It has never left me. I learnt it as a boy, I have obeyed it as a man and now I can no longer laugh at it. I failed to live up to it at times, but when I did I knew and that is what matters. I had a clue and I cared, I couldn't care more. For many years I was a cricket correspondent in the West Indies, having to write about myself, my own club, my intimate friends, and people who hated me. Mistakes in judgment I made often enough, but I was as righteous as the Angel Gabriel, and no one ever challenged my integrity. Thus it was that I could not join whole-heartedly in the laughter at Mr Bevan's witticisms. Particularly so because in order to acquire this code I was driven to evasions, disobedience, open rebellious-ness, continuous lies, and even stealing.

My business at school was to do my lessons, win prizes and ultimately win the scholarship. Nobody every doubted that if I wanted to I could. The masters wrote regularly in my reports 'Bad' or 'Good', as the case might be, but usually added, 'Could do much better if he tried'.

I did not try. Without any difficulty I could keep up in school, but an exhibition winner was being paid for by Government money and had to maintain a certain standard. I fell below it. My distracted father lectured me, punished me, flogged me. I would make good resolutions, do well for one term and fall from grace again. Then came a resounding scandal. I was reported to the Board of Education and threatened with the loss of my exhibition. It appeared in the public Press and all the teaching fraternity, who always read the reports of the meetings of the Board, read it, and thus learned what was happening to the prospective scholarship winner and Honourable Member of the Legislative Council. There were family meet-ings, the whole family, to talk to me and make me see the error of my ways. I was not only ruining my own chances. My godfather was a teacher, Judith's husband was a teacher, my sister's godfather was a teacher. The James clan had a proud status in the teaching profession, my father was an acknowledged star in that firmament and here was I bringing public dis-grace upon him and all of them.

I was given orders to stop playing and get home by a certain train. I just couldn't do it. I would calculate that it would take me twenty-five minutes to catch the train. Then I would think I could do it in twenty, then just one last over and then it was too late to try anyway. I invented beforehand excuses which would allow me to stay and play and take the late train. When I got into the eleven there were matches on Saturdays. I devised Saturday duties which the masters had asked me to perform, I forged letters, I borrowed flannels, I borrowed money to pay my fare, I borrowed bicycles to ride to the matches and borrowed money to repair them when I smashed them. I was finally entangled in such a web of lies, forged letters, borrowed clothes, and borrowed money that it was no wonder that the family looked on me as a sort of trial from heaven sent to test them as Job was tested. There were periods when my father relented and I lived normally. But then bad reports would come, the prohibitions would be re-imposed and I would plan to evade them. I was not a vicious boy. All I wanted was to play cricket and soccer, not merely to play but to live the life, and nothing could stop me. When all my tricks and plans and evasion failed, I just went and played and said to hell with the consequences.

Two people lived in me: one, the rebel against all family and school discipline and order; the other, a Puritan who would have cut off a finger sooner than do anything contrary to the ethics of the game.

To complicate my troubled life with my distracted family the Queen's Royal College fed the other of my two obsessions, English literature. When I entered the school at ten I was already primed for it, and the opportunities it offered completed my ruin for what the school and my father considered to be my duty. I spent eight years in its classrooms. I studied Latin with Virgil, Caesar and Horace, and wrote Latin verse. I studied Greek with Euripides and Thucydides. I did elementary and applied mathematics, French and French literature, English and English literature, English history, ancient and modern European history. I took certain examinations which were useful for getting jobs. I was fortunate enough to go back to the same school for some years as a teacher and so saw the system from within. As schools go, it was a very good school, though it would have been more suitable to Portsmouth than to Port of Spain.

What did all this matter to me when I discovered in the college library that besides *Vanity Fair* Thackeray had written thirty-six other volumes, most of them with pictures by himself? I read them through straight, two volumes at a time, and read them for twenty years after. (I stopped only when I came to England in 1932 and read him only sporadically. Recently I have started again.) After Thackeray there was Dickens, George Eliot and the whole bunch of English novelists. Then followed the poets in Matthew Arnold's selections, Shelley, Keats and Byron; Milton and Spenser. But in the public library in town there was everything, Fielding, Byron, with all of *Don Juan*. I discovered criticism: Hazlitt, Lamb and Coleridge, Saintsbury and Gosse, *The Encyclopaedia Britannica*, *Chambers' Encyclopaedia*. Burke led me to the speeches: Canning, Lord Brougham, John Bright. I cannot possibly remember all that I read then, and every now and then I still look up an essay or a passage and find that I had read it before I was eighteen. And all the time I read the boys' books, *Eric, or Little by Little*, *St Winifred's or The World of School*, *The Hill* by H.A. Vachell, Kipling's *Stalky and Co.*, an incredible number of books by G.A. Henty – there is no need to go through them all – and at the same time I kept up with (and now supplemented) my mother's ever-expanding list. The literature of cricket was easier. There were not many around, so those I could put my hands on I had to read over and over again. *The Jubilee Book of Cricket* by Ranjitsinhji was large, with many words on the page – I treasured it.

But this school was in a colony ruled autocratically by Englishmen. What then about the National Question? It did not exist for me. Our principal, Mr W. Burslem, MA, formerly, if I remember rightly, of Clare College, Cambridge, part Pickwick, part Dr Johnson, part Samuel Smiles, was an Englishman of the nineteenth century, and if it were not outside the scope of what I am doing I could spend many pages recalling his quirks. But no more devoted, conscientious, and self-sacrificing official ever worked in the colonies. He was immensely kind to me and often after telling me at the end of a term that he hoped he would never see my face again (implying that he would report me a second time to the Board of Education – which meant the guillotine) he would write mitigating words in my report, call me to do some personal task for him (a way of showing favour) and in the course of it try to show me the error of my ways. He did it constantly with me and other waywards. He was a man with a belief in the rod which he combined with a choleric and autocratic disposition. But he was beloved by generations of boys and was held in respectful admiration throughout the colony. To such a degree that when he died a journalist who had never been one of his pupils was moved to a piece of obituary prose which had all the old boys reading to one another for days. How not to look up to the England of Shakespeare and Milton, of Thackeray and Dickens, of Hobbs and Rhodes, in the daily presence of such an Englishman and in the absence of any nationalist agitation outside? In the nationalist temper of today Mr Burslem would be an anachronism, his bristling Britishness a perpetual reminder not of what he was doing but of what he represented. I write of him as he was, and today, forty years after, despite all that I have learnt between, what I think of him now is not very different from what I thought then.

It was only long years after that I understood the limitation on spirit, vision, and self-respect which was imposed on us by the fact that our masters, our curriculum, our code of morals, *everything* began from the basis that Britain was the source of all light and leading, and our business was to admire, wonder, imitate, learn; our criterion of success was to have succeeded in approaching that distant ideal – to attain it was, of course, impossible. Both masters and boys accepted it as in the very nature of things. The masters could not be offensive about it because they thought it was their function to do this, if they thought about it at all; and as for me, it was the beacon that beckoned me on.

The race question did not have to be agitated. It was there. But in our little Eden it never troubled us.

. . .

Patient Merit

I haven't the slightest doubt that the clash of race, caste, and class did not retard but stimulated West Indian cricket. I am equally certain that in those years social and political passions, denied normal outlets, expressed themselves so fiercely in cricket (and other games) precisely because they were games. Here began my personal calvary. The British tradition soaked deep into me was that when you entered the sporting arena you left behind you the sordid compromises of everyday existence. Yet for us to do that we would have had to divest ourselves of our skins. From the moment I had to decide which club I would join the contrast between the ideal and the real fascinated me and tore at my insides. Nor could the local population see it otherwise. The class and racial rivalries were too intense. They could be fought out without violence or much loss except pride and honour. Thus the cricket field was a stage on which selected individuals played representative roles which were charged with social significance. I propose now to place on record some of the characters and as much as I can reproduce (I remember everything) of the social conflict. I have been warned that some of these characters are unknown and therefore unlikely to interest non-West Indian readers. I cannot think so. Theirs is the history of cricket and of the West Indies, a history so far unrecorded as so much village cricket in England and of cricketers unknown to headlines have been recorded, and read with delight even in the West Indies.

George John, the great fast bowler, indeed knight-errant of fast bowling . . . had a squire. This squire was not short and fat and jovial. He was some six foot four inches tall and his name was Piggott. Where he came from, what he did in the week, I do not know and never asked. He came every Saturday to play and was a man of some idiosyncrasy: Piggott never or rarely wore a white shirt, but played usually in a shirt with coloured stripes without any collar attached. He did it purposely, for all his colleagues wore white shirts. His place in history is that he was John's wicketkeeper, and never was fast bowler better served. Piggott was one of the world's great wicketkeepers of the period between the wars. He always stood up to John, his hand one inch behind the stumps, and if you edged or drew your toe over the line you were through.

I wish some of our modern batsmen had had the experience of playing Lindwall or Miller with a wicketkeeper's hands an inch behind the wicket. Something startled where you thought you were safest. Your concentration on John was diluted. Everton Weekes says he pays no attention to short-legs. He plays as usual, keeping the ball down as usual, placing it as usual.

Long may his method flourish! But, with Piggott so close behind, ordinary mortals felt as if they were being attacked from front and rear at the same time.

He had a peculiar trick that was characteristic of him. On the rare occasions that John bowled on the leg-side, Piggott jumped sideways with both feet and pushed his legs at the ball, hoping to bounce it on to the wicket and catch the batsman out of his crease. (He was also credited with being able to flick a bail if the ball was passing very close to the wicket and might miss. But I never saw him do it and never heard of any authentic instance. The legend, however, illustrates his uncanny skill.) He may not have been quite so good at slow bowling, but I am inclined to believe that it was the constant miracles he performed standing up to John which put his other keeping in the shade. He was no Evans. He didn't fall five feet to the right or hurl himself like a goalkeeper to the left and scoop up a leg-glance with tip of his fingers. He had less need to, standing where he did. In his own way and in his own style he was unique. In addition Piggott was one of the few comic characters I have known in West Indies cricket. He walked with shoulders very much bent forward and with a kind of hop. When he was excited he gabbled rather than spoke. He was apt to get upset when things went wrong – usually a catch or sometimes two in an over missed in the slips off John. At the end of the over John would stamp off to his place in the slips glaring at the offender, while Piggott ambled up the pitch peering from side to side over his bent shoulders, gesticulating and muttering to himself.

He was without the slightest doubt the finest wicketkeeper we had ever seen, and to this day I have not seen or heard of any West Indian wicketkeeper who surpassed him. No one ever dared to say otherwise. The sight of him standing up to John and Francis in England in 1923 would have been one of the never-to-be-forgotten sights of modern cricket. Yet, to the astonishment of all Trinidadians, when the 1923 team was selected he was left out and Dewhurst taken instead. The only excuse current at the time was the following: 'You can't depend on a man like that. Who knows, when you are looking for him for some important match you will find him somewhere boozing.'

It was untrue. It was also stupid.

The real reason could be seen in a glance at the Trinidad contribution to the 1923 side. John and Small (Stingo), Constantine and Pascall (Shannon). Piggott would have meant three Stingo and two Shannon. All would have been absolutely black. Not only whites but the Queen's Park Club would have been left out altogether. Dewhurst was a fine wicketkeeper, and he was recognized as such and praised in England. But it was a guilty conscience that made so many people say to me: 'And, by the way, everywhere the team goes they comment on our stumper – they say he is very good.' I knew that as well as anybody else. I read more English papers than they.

Poor Piggott was a nobody. I felt the injustice deeply. So did others. He was a man you couldn't miss in a crowd and one day at the Queen's Park Oval during a big match I stood and talked with him. Dewhurst, now firmly established as the island and West Indian 'keeper', was doing his job excellently as he always did. But as the ordinary people came and went an astonishing number of them came up to tell Piggott, 'You should be out there, Piggie.' 'If you had his skin, Piggie, you would be behind today.' Most of them didn't know him except by sight. Piggott was very good-natured about it. What is most curious is that to this day I don't know whether this superb cricketer was a tailor, a casual labourer or a messenger. Socially he did not register.

. . .

The Proof of the Pudding

The populace in the West Indies are not fools. They knew what was going on and, if not altogether sure of all the implications, they were quite sure that these, whatever they might be, were directed against them. I was told of an expatriate who arrived in Trinidad to take up an important post which the people thought should be filled by a local candidate. Such a storm arose that the expatriate had to be sent away. In 1959 British Guiana was thrown into turmoil and strikes over a similar issue and the Governor had to retreat. In cricket these sentiments are at their most acute because everyone can see and can judge.

What do they know of cricket who only cricket know? West Indians crowding to Tests bring with them the whole past history and future hopes of the islands. English people, for example, have a conception of themselves breathed from birth – Drake and Nelson, Shakespeare, Waterloo, the Charge of the Light Brigade, the few who did so much for so many, the success of parliamentary democracy, those and such as those constitute a national tradition. Underdeveloped countries have to go back centuries to rebuild one. We of the West Indies have none at all, none that we know of. To such people the three Ws, Ram and Val wrecking English batting, help to fill a huge gap in their consciousness and in their needs. In one of the sheds on the Port of Spain wharf is a painted sign: 365 Garfield Sobers. If the old Maple-Shannon-Queen's Park type of rivalry was now insignificant, a nationalist jealousy had taken its place.

All this was as clear to me as day. I tried to warn the authorities that there was danger in the air. Many of them, I am sure of this, were unable even to understand what I was saying.

C.L.R. James, *Beyond a Boundary*, New York: Pantheon, 1963/1983, pp. 30–39, 72–4, 224–5.

LAWRENCE LEVINE,
"SLAVE SONGS AND SLAVE CONSCIOUSNESS"

Stripped of their culture as well as their freedom when they arrived in the US, Africans devised ways to hang on to both. In the following selection, historian Lawrence Levine argues that African-American slaves used song to link themselves back to their African heritage, position themselves in the present, and project themselves forward to a world of freedom. Through their songs, and the communal performance of these songs, slaves created a space free from the master's control; constructing a cultural landscape to compensate for an impoverished physical one. With characters lifted from The Bible and words sung in English, slave songs were not so much a rejection of the master's culture – something impossible given the circumstances – than a reworking of it, an incorporation and adaptation that put it to radically different uses.

Negroes in the United States, both during and after slavery, were anything but inarticulate. They sang songs, told stories, played verbal games, listened and responded to sermons, and expressed their aspirations, fears and values through the medium of an oral tradition that had characterized the West African cultures from which their ancestors had come. By largely ignoring this tradition, much of which has been preserved, historians have rendered an articulate people historically inarticulate, and have allowed the record of their consciousness to go unexplored.

. . .

For all of its horrors, slavery was never so complete a system of psychic assault that it prevented the slaves from carving out independent cultural forms. It never pervaded all of the interstices of their minds and their culture, and in those gaps they were able to create an independent art form and a distinctive voice. If North American slavery eroded the African's linguistic and institutional life, if it prevented him from preserving and developing his rich heritage of graphic and plastic art, it nevertheless allowed him to continue and develop the patterns of verbal art which were so central to his past culture. Historians have not yet come to terms with what the continuance of the oral tradition meant to blacks in slavery.

In Africa, songs, tales, proverbs, and verbal games served the dual function of not only preserving communal values and solidarity, but also providing occasions for the individuals to transcend, at least symbolically, the inevitable restrictions of his environment and his society by permitting him to express deeply held feelings which he ordinarily was not allowed to verbalize. Among the Ashanti and the Dahomeans, for example, periods were set aside when the inhabitants were encouraged to gather together, and through the medium of song, dance, and tales, to openly express their feelings about each other. The psychological release this afforded seems to have been well understood. "You know that everyone has a *sunsum* (soul) that may get hurt or knocked about or become sick, and so make the body ill," an Ashanti high priest explained to the English anthropologist R.S. Rattray:

> Very often . . . ill health is caused by the evil and hate another has in his head against you. Again, you too may have hatred in your head, against another, because of something that person has done to you, and that, too, causes your *sunsum* to fret and become sick. Our forebears knew this to be the case, and so they ordained a time, once every year, every man and woman, free man and slave, should have freedom to speak out just what was in their head, to tell their neighbors just what they thought of them, and of their actions, and not only of their neighbors, but also the king or chief. When a man has spoken freely thus, he will feel his *sunsum* cool and quieted, and the *sunsum* of the other person against whom he has now openly spoken will be quieted also.

Utilization of verbal art for this purpose was widespread throughout Africa, and was not confined to those ceremonial occasions when one could directly state one's feelings. Through innuendo, metaphor, and circumlocution, African's could utilize their songs as outlets for individual release without disturbing communal solidarity.[1]

There is abundant internal evidence that the verbal art of the slaves in the United States served many of these traditional functions. Just as the process by which the spirituals were created allowed for simultaneous individual and communal creativity, so their very structure provided simultaneous outlets for individual and communal expression. The overriding antiphonal structure of the spirituals – the call and response pattern which Negroes brought with them from Africa and which was reinforced by the similar white practice of "lining out" hymns – placed the individual in continual dialogue with his community, allowing him at once to preserve his voice as a distinct entity and to blend it with those of his fellows. Here again slave music confronts us with evidence that however seriously the slave system may have diminished the sense of community that had bound Africans together, it never totally destroyed it or left the individual atomized and emotionally and physically defenseless before his white masters. In fact, the form and structure of slave music presented the slave with a potential outlet for his individual feelings even while it continually drew him back into the communal presence and permitted him the comfort of basking in the warmth of the shared assumptions of those around him.

Those "shared assumptions" can be further examined by an analysis of the content of slave songs. Our preoccupation in recent years with the degree to which the slaves actually resembled the "Sambo" image held by their white masters has obscured the fact that slaves developed images of their own which must be consulted and studied before any discussion of slave personality can be meaningful. The image of the trickster, who through cunning and unscrupulousness prevails over his more powerful antagonists, pervades slave tales. The trickster figure is rarely encountered in slave songs, though its presence is sometimes felt in the slave's many allusions to his narrow escapes from the Devil.

> The Devil's mad and I'm glad
> He lost the soul he thought he had.[2]
>
> Ole Satan toss a ball at me.
> O me no weary yet . . .
>
> Him think de ball would hit my soul.
> O me no weary yet . . .
>
> De ball for hell and I for heaven.
> O me no weary yet.[3]
>
> Ole Satan thought he had a mighty aim;
> He missed my soul and caught my sins,
> Cry Amen, cry Amen, cry Amen to God!
>
> He took my sins upon his back;
> Went muttering and grumbling down to hell.
> Cry Amen, cry Amen, cry Amen to God.[4]

The single most persistent image the slave songs contain, however, is that of the chosen people. The vast majority of the spirituals identify the singers as "de people dat is born of God," "We are the people of God," "we are de people of de Lord," "I really do believe I am a child of God," "I'm a child ob God wid my soul so free," "I'm born of God, I know I am." Nor is there ever any doubt that "To the promised land I'm bound to go," "I walk de heavenly road," "Heav'n shall-a be my home," "I gwine to meet my Savior," "I seek my Lord and I find Him," "I'll hear the trumpet sound / In that morning."[5]

The force of this image cannot be diminished by the observation that similar images were present in the religious singing of white evangelical churches during the first half of the nineteenth century. White Americans could be expected to sing of triumph and salvation, given their long-standing heritage of the idea of a chosen people which was reinforced by the belief in inevitable progress and manifest destiny, the spread-eagle oratory, the bombastic folklore, and, paradoxically, the deep insecurities concomitant with the tasks of taming a continent and developing an identity. But for this same message to be expressed by Negro slaves who were told endlessly that they were members of the lowliest of races *is* significant. It offers an insight into the kinds of barriers the slaves had available to them against the internalization of the stereotyped images their masters held and attempted consciously and unconsciously to foist upon them.

The question of the chosen people image leads directly into the larger problem of what role religion played in the songs of the slave. Writing in 1862, James McKim noted that the songs of the Sea Island freedman "are all religious, barcaroles and all. I speak without exception. So far as I heard or was told of their singing, it was all religious." Others who worked with recently emancipated slaves recorded the same experience, and Colonel Higginson reported that he rarely heard his troops sing a profane or vulgar song. With a few exceptions, "all had a religious motive."[6] In spite of this testimony, there can be little doubt that the slaves sang nonreligious songs. In 1774, an English visitor to the United States, after his first encounter with slave music, wrote in his journal: "In their songs they usually relate the usage they have received from their Masters or Mistresses in a very satirical stile and manner."[7] Songs fitting this description can be found in the nineteenth-century narratives of fugitive slaves. Harriet Jacobs recorded that during the Christmas season the slaves would ridicule stingy white by singing:

> Poor Massa, so de say;
> Down in de heel, so dey say;
> Got no money, so de say;
> God A'mighty bress you, so dey say.[8]

"Once in a while among a mass of nonsense and wild frolic," Frederick Douglass noted, "a sharp hit was given to the meanness of slaveholders."

We rise de wheat,
Dey gib us de corn;
We bake de bread,
Dey gib us the crust;
We sif de meal,
Dey gib us de huss;
We peal de meat,
Dey gib us de skin;
And dat's de way
Dey take us in;
We skim de pot,
Dey gib us de liquor,
And say dat's good enough for nigger.[9]

Both of these songs are in the African tradition of utilizing song to bypass both internal and external censors and give vent to feelings which could be expressed in no other form. Nonreligious songs were not limited to the slave's relations with his masters, however, as these rowing songs, collected by contemporary white observers, indicate:

We are going down to Georgia, boys,
Aye, aye.
To see the pretty girls, boys,
Yoe, yoe.
We'll give 'em a pint of brandy, boys,
Aye, aye.
And a hearty kiss, besides, boys,
Yoe, yoe.[10]

Jenny shake her toe at me,
Jenny gone away;
Jenny shake her toe at me,
Jenny gone away.
Hurrah, Miss Susy, oh!
Jenny gone away;
Hurrah! Miss Susy, oh!
Jenny gone away.[11]

The variety of nonreligious songs in the slave's repertory was wide. There were songs of in-group and out-group satire, songs of nostalgia, nonsense songs, songs of play and work and love. Nevertheless, the total stock of these songs is very small. It is possible to add to these by incorporating such post-bellum secular songs which have an authentic slavery ring to them as

"De Blue-Tail Fly," with its ill-concealed satisfaction at the death of a master, or the ubiquitous

> My ole Mistress promise me,
> W'en she died, she'd set me free,
> She lived so long dat 'er head got bal'
> An' she give out'n de notion a dyin' at all.[12]

The number can be further expanded by following Constance Rourke's suggestion that we attempt to disentangle elements of Negro origin from those of white creation in the "Ethiopian melodies" of white minstrel shows, many of which were similar to the songs I have just quoted.[13] Either of these possibilities, however, forces the historian to work with sources far more potentially spurious than those with which he normally is comfortable.

Spirituals, on the other hand, for all the problems associated with their being filtered through white hands before they were published, and despite the many errors in transcription that inevitably occurred, constitute a much more satisfactory source. They were collected by the hundred directly from slaves and freedmen during the Civil War and the decades immediately following, and although they came from widely different geographical areas they share a common structure and content, which seems to have been characteristic of Negro music wherever slavery existed in the United States. It is possible that we have a greater number of religious and nonreligious songs because slaves were more willing to sing these ostensibly innocent songs to white collectors who in turn were more anxious to record them, since they fit easily with their positive and negative images of the Negro. But I would argue that the vast preponderance of spiritual over any other sort of slave music, rather then being the result of accident or error, is instead an accurate reflection of slave culture during the antebellum period. Whatever songs the slaves may have sung before their wholesale conversion to Christianity in the late eighteenth and early nineteenth centuries, by the latter century spirituals were quantitatively and qualitatively their most significant musical creation. In this form of expression slaves found a medium which resembled in many important ways the worldviews they had brought with them from Africa, and afforded them the possibility of both adapting to and transcending their situation.

It is significant that the most common form of slave music we know of is sacred song. I use the term "sacred" not in its present usage as something antithetical to the secular world; neither the slaves nor their African forbearers ever drew modernity's clear line between the sacred and the secular. The usage to which spirituals were put is an unmistakable indication of this. They were not sung solely or even primarily in churches or praise houses, but were used as rowing songs, field songs, work songs, and social songs. On the Sea Islands during the Civil War, Lucy McKim heard the spiritual *Poor Rosy* sung in a wide variety of context and tempos.

> On the waters, the oars dip "Poor Rosy" to an even andante; a stout boy and girl at the hominy-hill will make the same "Poor Rosy" fly, to keep up with the whirling stone; and in the evening, after the day's work is done, "Heab'n shall-a be my home" [the final line of each stanza] peals up slowly and mournfully from the distant quarters.[14]

For the slaves, then, songs of God and the mythic heroes of their religion were not confined to any specific time or place, but were appropriate to almost every situation. It is in this sense that I use the concept sacred – not to signify a rejection of the present world but to describe the process of incorporating in this world all the elements of the divine. The religious historian Mircea Eliade, whose definition of sacred has shaped my own, has maintained that for men in traditional societies religion is a means of extending the world spatially upward so that communication with the other world becomes ritually possible, and extending it temporarily backward so that the paradigmatic acts of the gods and mythical ancestors can be continually reenacted and indefinitely recoverable. By creating sacred time and place, man can perpetually live in the presence of his gods, can hold on to the certainty that within one's own lifetime "rebirth" is continually possible, and can impose order on the chaos of the universe. "Life," as Eliade puts it, "is lived on a twofold plane; it takes its course as human existence and, at the same time, shares in a transhuman life, that of the cosmos or the god."[15]

This notion of sacredness gets at the essence of the spirituals, and through them at the essence of the slave's worldview. Denied the possibility of achieving an adjustment to the external world of the antebellum South which involved meaningful forms of personal integration, attainment of status, and feelings of individual worth that all human beings crave and need, the slaves created a new world by transcending the narrow confines of one in which they were forced to live. They extended the boundaries of their restrictive universe backward until it fused with the world of the Old Testament, and upward until it became one with the world beyond. The spirituals are the record of a people who found the status, the harmony, the values, and the order they needed to survive by internally creating an expanded universe, by literally willing themselves reborn. In this respect I agree with the anthropologist Paul Radin that

> The antebellum Negro was not converted to God. He converted God to himself. In the Christian God he found a fixed point and he needed a fixed point, for both within and outside of himself, he could see only vacillation and endlessly shifting . . . There was no other safety for people faced on all sides by doubt and the threat of personal disintegration, by the thwarting of instincts and the annihilation of values.[16]

The confinement of much of the slave's new world to dreams and fantasies does not free us from the historical obligation of examining the contours, weighing its implications for the development of the slave's psychic and emotional structure, and eschewing the kind of facile reasoning that leads Professor Elkins to imply that, since the slaves had no alternatives open to them, their fantasy life was "limited to catfish and watermelons."[17] Their spirituals indicate clearly that there *were* alternatives open to them – alternatives which they themselves fashioned out of the fusion of their African heritage and their new religion – and that their fantasy life was so rich and so important to them that it demands understanding if we are even to begin to comprehend their inner world.

The God the slaves sang of was neither remote nor abstract, but as intimate, personal, and immediate as the gods of Africa had been. "O when I talk I talk wid God," "Mass Jesus is my bosom friend," "I'm goin to walk with [talk with, live with, see] King Jesus by myself," were refrains that echoed through the spirituals.[18]

> In de mornin' when I rise
> Tell my Jesus huddy [howdy] oh,
> I wash my hands in de mornin' glory,
> Tell my Jesus huddy oh.[19]

> Gwine to argue wid de Father and chatter wid de son;
> The last trumpet shall sound, I'll be there.
> Gwine talk 'bout de bright world dey des' come from
> The last trumpet shall sound, I'll be there.[20]

> Gwine to write to Massa Jesus,
> To send some Valiant solider
> To turn back Pharaoh's army, Hallelu![21]

The heroes of the Scriptures – "Sister Mary," "Brudder Jonah," "Brudder Moses," "Brudder Daniel" – were greeted with similar intimacy and immediacy. In the world of the spirituals, it was not the masters and mistresses but God and Jesus and the entire pantheon of Old Testament figures who set the standard, established the precedents, and defined the values; who, in short constituted the "significant others." The world described by the slave songs was a black world in which no reference was made to any white contemporaries. The slave's positive reference group was composed entirely of his own peers, his mother, father, brother, sister, uncles, aunts, preacher, fellow "sinners" and "mourners" of whom he sang endlessly, to whom he sent messages via the dying, and with whom he was reunited joyfully in the next world.

The same sense of sacred time and place which shaped the slave's portraits of his gods and heroes also made his vision of the past and future immediate and compelling. Depictions of the Crucifixion communicate a sense of the actual presence of the singers:

> Dey pierced Him in the side . . . Dey nail Him to de cross . . . Dey rivet His feet . . . Dey hanged Him high . . . Dey stretch Him wide.

> Oh sometimes it causes me to tremble, tremble, tremble,
> Were you there when they crucified my Lord?[22]

The slaves' "shout" – that counterclockwise, shuffling dance which frequently occurred after the religious service and lasted long into the night – often became a medium through which the ecstatic dancers were formed into actual participants in historic nations: Joshua's army marching around the walls of Jericho, the children of Israel following Moses out of Egypt.[23]

The thin line between time dimensions is nowhere better illustrated than in the slave's visions of the future, which were, of course, a direct negation of his present. Among the most striking spirituals are those which pile detail upon detail in describing the Day of Judgment:

> You'll see de world on fire . . . see de element a meltin' . . . see the stars a fallin' . . . see the moon a bleedin' . . . see the forked lightning . . . Hear the rumblin' thunder . . . see the righteous marching . . . see my Jesus coming

and the world to come where

> Dere's no sun to burn you . . . no hard trials . . . no whips a crackin' . . . no stormy weather . . . no tribulation . . . no evil-doers . . . All is gladness in the Kingdom.[24]

This vividness was matched by the slave's certainty that he would partake in the triumph of judgments and the joys of the new world: "Dere's room enough, room enough, room enough in de heaven, my Lord / Room enough, room enough, I can't stay behind."[25]

Continually, the slaves sang of reaching out beyond the world that confined them, of seeing Jesus "in de wilderness," of praying "in de lone-some valley," of breathing in the freedom of the mountain peaks: "Did yo' ever / Stan' on mountun, / Wash yo' han's / In a cloud?"[26]

Continually they held out the possibility of imminent rebirth: "I look at de worl' and de worl' look new . . . I look at my hands an' they look so too . . . I looked at my feet, my feet was too."[27]

These possibilities, these certainties were not surprising. The religious revivals that swept large number of the slaves into the Christian fold in the late eighteenth and early nineteenth centuries were based upon a *practical* (not necessarily theological) Armianism: God would save all who believe in Him; Salvation was there for all to take hold of if they would. The effects of this message upon the slaves who were exposed to and converted by it have been passed over too easily by historians. Those effects are illustrated graphically in the spirituals which were the products of these revivals and which continued to spread the evangelic word long after the revivals had passed into history.

The religious music of the slaves is almost devoid of feelings of depravity or unworthiness, but it is rather, as I have tried to show, pervaded by a sense of change, transcendence, ultimate justice, and personal worth. The spiritu-als have been referred to as "sorrow songs," and in some respects they were. The slave sang of "rollin' thro' an unfriendly world," of being "a-trouble in de mind," of living in a world which was a "howling wilderness," "a hell to me," of feeling like "a motherless child," "a po' little orphan chile in de worl'," "a homeless child," of fearing that "Trouble will bury me down."[28]

But these feelings were rarely pervasive or permanent; almost always they were overshadowed by a triumphant note of affirmation. Even so despairing a wail as "Nobody Knows the Trouble I've Had" could suddenly have its mood transformed by lines like: "One morning I was a-walking down . . . Saw some berries a-hanging down . . . I pick de berry and I suck de juice . . . Just as sweet as de honey in de comb."[29] Similarly, amid the deep sorrow of "Sometimes I feel like a motherless chile," sudden release would come with the lines: "Sometimes I feel like / A eagle in de air . . . Spread my wings an' / Fly, fly, fly."[30] Slaves spent little time singing of the horrors of hell or damnation. Their songs of the Devil, quoted earlier, pic-tured a harsh but almost semicomic figure (often, one suspects, a surrogate for the white man), over whom they triumphed with reassuring regularity. For all of their inevitable sadness, slave songs were characterized by more of a feeling of confidence than of despair. There was confidence that contem-porary power relations were not immutable: "Did not old Pharaoh get lost, get lost, get lost . . . get lost in the Red Sea?"; confidence in the possibilities of instantaneous change: "Jesus make de dumb to speak . . . Jesus make de cripple walk . . . Jesus give de blind his sight . . . Jesus do most anything"; confidence in the rewards of persistence: "Keep a' inchining along like a poor inchworm, / Jesus will come bye 'nd bye"; confidence that nothing could stand in the way of the justice that they would receive: "You kin hender me here, but you can't do it dah," "O no man, no man, no man can hinder me"; confidence in the prospects of the future: "We'll walk de golden streets / Of de New Jerusalem." Religion, the slaves sang, "is good for anything . . . Religion make you happy . . . Religion gib me patience . . . O member, get Religion . . . Religion is so sweet."[31]

The slaves often pursued the "sweetness" of their religion in the face of many obstacles. Becky Illsey, who was 16 when she was emancipated, recalled many years later:

> 'Fo' de war when we'd have a meetin' at night, wuz mos' always 'way in de woods or de bushes some whar so de white folks couldn't hear, an' when dey'd sing a spiritual an' de spirit 'gin to shout some de elders would go 'mongst de folks an' put dey han' over dey mouf an' sometimes put a clof in dey mouf an' say: "Spirit don' talk so loud or de patterol break us up." You know dey had white patterols what went 'roun' at night to see de niggers didn't cut up no devilment, an' den de meetin' would break up an' some would go to one house a' some to er nudder an' dey would groan er w'ile, den go home.[32]

Elizabeth Ross Hite testified that although she and her fellow slaves on a Louisiana plantation were Catholics, "lots didn't like that 'ligion."

> We use to hide behind some old bricks and hold church ourselves. You see, the Catholic preachers from France would not let us shout, and the Lawd done said you gotta shout if you want to be saved. That's in the Bible.
>
> Sometimes we held church all night long, 'til way in the mornin'. We burned some grease in a can for the preacher to see the Bible by . . .
>
> See, our master didn't like us to have much 'ligion, said it made us lag in our work. He just wanted us to be Catholic on Sundays and go to mass and not study 'bout nothin' like that on week days. He didn't want us shoutin' and moanin' all day-long, but you gotta shout and gotta moan if you wants to be saved.[33]

The slaves clearly craved the affirmation and the promise of their religion. It would be a mistake, however, to see this urge as exclusively otherworldly. When Thomas Wentworth Higginson observed that the spirituals exhibited "nothing but patience for this life, nothing but triumph in the next," he, and later observers who elaborated upon this judgment, were indulging in hyperbole. Although Jesus was ubiquitous in the spirituals, it was not invariably the Jesus of the New Testament of whom the slaves sang, but frequently Jesus transformed into an Old Testament warrior: "Mass' Jesus" who engaged in personal combat with the Devil; "King Jesus" seated on a milk white horse with sword and shield in hand. "Ride on, King Jesus," "Ride on, conquering King," "The God I serve is a man of war," the slaves sang.[34] This transformation of Jesus is symptomatic of the slaves' selectivity in choosing those parts of the Bible which were to serve as the basis of their religious consciousness. Howard Thurman, a Negro minister who as a boy had the duty of reading the Bible to his grandmother, was perplexed by her refusal to allow him to read from the Epistles of Paul.

> When at length I asked the reason, she told me that during the days of slavery, the minister (white) on the plantation was always preaching from the Pauline letters – "Slaves, be obedient to your masters," etc. "I vowed to myself," she said, "that if freedom ever came and I learned to read, I would never read that part of the Bible!"[35]

Nor, apparently, did this part of the Scriptures ever constitute a vital element in slave songs or sermons. The emphasis of the spirituals, as Higginson himself noted, was upon the Old Testament and the exploits of the Hebrew children.[36] It is important that Daniel and David and Joshua and Jonah and Moses and Noah, all of whom fill the lines of the spirituals, were delivered in *this* world and delivered in ways which struck the imagination of the slaves. Over and over their songs dealt with the spectacle of the Red Sea opening to allow the Hebrew slaves past before inundating the mighty armies of the Pharaohs. They lingered delightedly upon the image of little David humbling the great Goliath with a stone – a pretechnological victory that postbellum Negroes were to expand upon in their own songs of John Henry. They retold in endless variation the stories of the blind and humbled Samson bringing down the mansions of his conquerors; of the ridiculed Noah patiently building the ark which would deliver him from the doom of a mocking world; of the timid Jonah attaining freedom from his confinement through faith. The similarity of these tales to the situation of the slaves was too clear for him not to see it; too clear for us to believe the songs had no worldly content for the black man in bondage. "O my lord delivered Daniel," the slaves observed, and responded logically; "O why not deliver me too?"

> He delivered Daniel from de lion's den,
> Jonah from de belly ob de whale,
> And de Hebrew children from de fiery furnace,
> And why not every man?[37]

These lines state as clearly as anything can the manner in which the sacred world of the slaves was able to fuse precedents of the past, the conditions of the present, and the promise of the future into one connected reality. In this respect there was always a latent and symbolic element of protest in the slave's religious songs which frequently became overt and explicit. Frederick Douglass asserted that for him and many of his fellow slaves the song, "O Canaan, sweet Canaan, / I am bound for the land of Canaan," symbolized "something more than reaching heaven. We meant to reach the *North*, and the North was our Canaan," and he wrote that the lines of another spiritual, "Run to Jesus, shun the danger, / I don't expect to stay much longer here," had a double meaning which first suggested to him the thought of escaping from slavery.[38] Similarly, when the black troops in Higginson's regiment sang: "We'll soon be free, [three times] / When de Lord will call us *home*" a young drummer boy explained to him, "Dey think *de Lord* mean for say *de Yankees*."[39] Nor is there any reason to doubt that slaves could have used their songs as a means of secret communication. An ex-slave told Lydia Parrish that when he and his fellow slaves "suspicioned" that one of their number was telling tales to the driver, they would sing lines like the following while working in the field:

> O Judyas he was a 'ceitful man
> He went an' betray a mos' innocen' man.
> Fo' thirty pieces of silver dat it wuz done
> He went in de woods an' e' self he hung.[40]

And it is possible, as many writers have argued, that such spirituals as the commonly heard "Steal away, steal away, steal away to Jesus!" were used as explicit calls to secret meetings.

But it is not necessary to invest the spirituals with a secular function only at the price of divesting them of their religious content, as Miles Mark Fisher has done.[41] While we may make such clear-cut distinctions, I have tried to show that the slaves did not. For them religion never constituted a simple escape from this world, because their conception of the world was more expansive than modern man's. Nowhere is this better illustrated than during the Civil War itself. While the war gave rise to such new spirituals as "Before I'd be a slave / I'd be buried in my grave / And go home to my Lord and be saved!" or the popular "Many thousand go," with its jubilant rejection of all the facts of slave life – "No more peck o' corn for me . . . no more driver's lash for me . . . no more pint o' salt for me . . . No more hundred lashes for me . . . No more mistress call for me"[42] – the important thing was not that large numbers of slaves now could create new songs which openly expressed their views of slavery; that was to be expected. More significant was the ease with which their old songs fit their new situation. With so much of their inspiration drawn from the events of the Old Testament and the Book of Revelation, the slaves had long sung of war, of battles, of the Army of the Lord, of Soldiers of the Cross, of trumpets summoning the faithful, of vanquishing the hosts of evil. These songs especially were, as Higginson put it, "available for camp purposes with very little strain upon their symbolism." "We'll cross de mighty river," his troops sang while marching or rowing,

> We'll cross de danger water . . .
> O Pharaoh's army drowned!
> My army cross over.

"O blow your trumpet, Gabriel," they sang,

> Blow your trumpet louder;
> And I want dat trumpet to blow me home
> To my new Jerusalem.

But they also found their less overtly militant songs quite as appropriate to warfare. Their most popular and effective marching song was:

> Jesus call you, Go in de wilderness,
> Go in de wilderness, go in de wilderness,
> Jesus call you, Go in de wilderness
> To wait upon de Lord.[43]

Black Union soldiers found it no more incongruous to accompany their fight for freedom with the sacred songs of their bondage than they had found it inappropriate as slaves to sing their spirituals while they were picking cotton or shucking corn. Their religious songs, like their religion itself, was of this world as well as the next.

Slave songs by themselves, of course, do not present us with a definitive key to the life and mind of the slave. They have to be seen within the context of the slave's situation and examined alongside such other cultural materials as folk tales. But slave songs do indicate a need to rethink a number of assumptions that have shaped recent interpretations of slavery, such as the assumption that because slavery eroded the linguistic and institutional side of African life it wiped out almost all the more fundamental aspects of African culture. Culture, certainly, is more than merely the sum total of institutions and language. It is also expressed by something less tangible, which the anthropologist Robert Redfield has called "style of life."

People as different as the Lapp and the Bedouin, Redfield has argued, with diverse languages, religions, customs and institutions, may still share an emphasis on certain virtues and ideals, certain manners of independence and hospitality, general ways of looking upon the world, which give them a similar lifestyle.[44] This argument applies to the West African cultures from which the slaves came. Though they varied widely in language, institutions, gods and familial patterns, they shared a fundamental outlook toward the past, present, and future and common means of cultural expression which could well have constituted the basis of a sense of community and identity capable of surviving the impact of slavery.

Slave songs present us with abundant evidence that in the structure of their music and dance, in the uses to which music was put, in the survival of the oral tradition, in the retention of such practices as spirit possession which often accompanied the creation of spirituals, and in the ways in which slaves expressed their new religion, important elements of their shared African heritage remained alive not just as quaint cultural vestiges but as vitally creative elements of slave culture. This could never have happened if slavery was, as Professor Elkins maintains, a system which so completely closed in around the slave, so totally penetrated his personality structure as to infantilize him and reduce him to a kind of *tabula rasa* upon which the white man could write what he chose.[45]

Slave songs provide us with the beginnings of a very different kind of hypothesis: that the preliterate, premodern Africans, with their sacred world view, were so imperfectly acculturated into the secular American society into which they were thrust, were so completely denied access to the ideology and dreams which formed the core of the consciousness of other Americans, that they were forced to fall back upon the only cultural frames of reference that made any sense to them and gave them any feeling of security. I use the word "forced" advisedly. Even if the slaves had had the opportunity to enter fully into the life of the larger society, they might still have chosen to retain and perpetuate certain elements of their African heritage. But the point is that they really had no choice. True acculturation was denied to most slaves. The alternatives were to either remain in a state of cultural limbo, divested of the old cultural patterns but not allowed to adopt those of their new homeland – which in the long run is no alternative at all – or to cling to as many as possible of the old ways of thinking and acting. The slaves' oral tradition, their music, and their religious outlook served this latter function and constituted a cultural refuge at least potentially capable of protecting their personalities from some of the worst ravages of the slave system.

The argument of Professors Tannenbaum and Elkins that the Protestant churches of the United States did not act as a buffer between the slave and his master is persuasive enough, but it betrays a modern preoccupation with institutional arrangements.[46] Religion is more than an institution, and because Protestant churches failed to protect the slave's inner being from the incursions of the slave system, it does not follow the spiritual message of Protestantism failed as well. Slave songs are a testament to the ways in which Christianity provided slaves with the precedents, heroes and future promise that allowed them to transcend the purely temporal bonds of the Peculiar Institution.

Historians have frequently failed to perceive the full importance of this because they have not taken the slave's religiosity seriously enough. A people cannot create a music as forceful and striking as slave music out of a mere uninternalized anodyne. Those who have argued that Negroes did not oppose slavery in any meaningful way are writing from a modern, political context. What they really mean is that the slaves found no *political* means to oppose slavery. But slaves, to borrow Professor Hobsbawm's term, were prepolitical beings in a prepolitical situation.[47] Within their frame of reference there were other – and from the point of view of personality development, not necessarily less effective – means of escape and opposition. If mid-twentieth-century historians have difficulty perceiving the sacred universe created by slaves as a serious alternative to the social system created by southern slaveholders, the problem may be the historians' and not the slaves'.

Above all, the study of slave songs forces the historian to move out of his own culture, in which music plays a peripheral role, and offers him the opportunity to understand the ways in which black slaves were able to perpetuate much of the centrality and functional importance that music had for their African ancestors. In the concluding lines of his perceptive study of primitive song, C.M. Bowra has written:

> Primitive song is indispensable to those who practice it . . . they cannot do without song, which both formulates and answers their nagging questions, enables them to pursue action with zest and confidence, brings them into touch with gods and spirits, and makes them feel less strange in the natural world . . . it gives to them a solid center in what otherwise would be almost chaos, and a continuity in their being, which would too easily dissolve before the calls of the implacable present . . . through its words men, who might otherwise give in to the malice of circumstances, find their old powers revived or new powers stirring in them, and through these life itself is sustained and renewed and fulfilled.[48]

This, I think, sums up concisely the function of song for the slave. Without a general understanding of that function, without a specific understanding of the content and meaning of slave song, there can be no full comprehension of the effects of slavery upon the slave or the meaning of the society from which slaves emerged at emancipation.

Lawrence Levine, *The Unpredictable Past*, New York: Oxford, 1993, pp. 37, 43–58.

GEORGE LIPSITZ,
"IMMIGRATION AND ASSIMILATION:
RAI, REGGAE, AND BHANGRAMUFFIN"

"Apache Indian" makes bhangramuffin music, a mix of Jamaican ragamuffin, African-American rap, and Indian bhangra music. His name is an invocation of his Punjabi ancestry and a tribute to a Jamaican musician who goes by "the wild Apache," a name itself likely influenced by the image of "wild Apaches" in Hollywood westerns. Apache Indian lives in urban England. As the cross-cultural scholar George Lipsitz makes crystal clear, there is nothing clear about cultural identity. Looking at music popular among young immigrants in France and England, Lipsitz describes how music can demarcate and solidify a hybrid ethnic identity, such as French-Algerian or British-Jamaican. Or, in the case of bhangramuffin music, map out and perhaps lead the way to inter-ethnic political alliances that so far have been elusive.

During the 1980s, popular-music listeners and enthusiasts throughout Europe began to notice new musical forms that captured their fancy. In London, the band Alaap blended bhangra music from the Indian state of Punjab with Greek, Middle Eastern, Spanish, and Anglo-American pop styles. At the same time, Joi Bangla, made up of immigrants from Bangla Desh, mixed African-American funk sounds with traditional Bengali folk songs.[1] For their part, listeners in Paris expressed enthusiasm for a techno-pop album displaying "a faintly Moorish" sound underneath English, French, and Arabic lyrics by a Mauritanian singer recording under the name Tahra.[2]

Soaring to popularity at the same time that immigrant populations in London and Paris faced increasing hostility and even attacks from anti-foreign thugs, these recordings demonstrate the complicated connections and contradictions that characterize the links between popular music and social life. Audiences and artists in these cities carried the cultural collisions of everyday life into music, at one and the same time calling attention to ethnic differences and demonstrating how they might be transcended. Sophisticated fusions of seemingly incompatible cultures in music made sense to artists and audiences in part because these fusions reflected their lived experiences in an inter-cultural society.

Of course, inter-cultural communication and creativity does not preclude political or even physical confrontations between members of groups fighting for a share of increasingly scarce resources. But the very existence of music demonstrating the interconnectedness between the culture of immigrants and the culture of their host country helps us understand how the actual lived experiences of immigrants are much more dynamic and complex than most existing models of immigration and assimilation admit.

. . .

Clearly the most important and most complicated expression of musical multiculturalism in France comes from the popularity of Algerian "rai" music. During the 1980s, political and cultural mobilizations by young people of North African origin competed with intense anti-Arab and anti-foreign organizing by French right wingers for the power to define "French" culture and citizenship.[3] Rai music took on extra-musical importance as a visible weapon in that struggle.

Referenced by many artists,. . . rai music blends Arabic lyrics and instruments with synthesizers, disco arrangements, blues chord progressions, and Jamaican reggae and Moroccan gnawa rhythms. Rai originated as women's music in the Algerian port city of Oran where *meddahas* sang to other women at weddings and other private occasions and by *chiekhas* who sang for men in taverns and brothels. In a city where French, Spanish, and Arabic are all spoken, the music known as "Oran Modern" emerged from interactions among Spanish, French, and North African musicians.[4] Now sung by both female Chebas and male Chebs, the term "rai" comes from the Arabic phrase "Ya Rai" ("It's my opinion").[5] Reed flutes and terracotta drums provided the original instrumentation for rai, but over the years musicians added violin, accordion, saxophone, and trumpet. Bellemou Messaoud played a particularly important role in the emergence of modern rai when he added guitars, trumpets, and synthesizers to rai ensembles.[6] Disco-influenced arrangements and blues chord progressions came later to bring rai closer to the Anglo-American international style.

A product of cultural collision between Europe and North Africa, rai music has its defenders and its detractors in both places. Some factions in Algeria see rai as too French, too Western, too modern, too obscene. At the same time, there are those in France who dismiss rai as too foreign, too primitive, too exotic, too strange. It is not easy to tell if a North African immigrant to France is being assimilationist or separatist by listening to rai music. Cheb Khaled spends more time in Marseilles than in Algiers, and uses rai music to comment on "racism in France, about what's happening in Algeria, and of course, I always sing about love."[7] Cheba Fadela created a sensation as a mini-skirted seventeen-year-old on French television in the late 1970s and helped start modern "pop rai" with her 1983 song "N'sel fik" ("You Are Mine").[8] Cheb Sid Ahmed is openly homosexual and performs with a troupe of traditional female wedding singers.[9] At the other extreme, Cheba Zahouania performs mainly at women's events, does not allow herself to be photographed, and does not appear on television, reportedly because her husband threatened to take her children from her if she sang in public for men.[10]

Not surprisingly, rai has been embroiled in repeated political controversies. "The history of rai is like the history of rock and roll," explains Cheb Khaled, one of the genre's premier performers.

> Fundamentalists don't want our concerts to happen. They come and break things up. They say rai is street music and that it's debauched. But that's not true. I don't sing pornography. I sing about love and social life. We say what we think, just like singers all over the world.[11]

The Algerian government has sporadically looked with favor on rai as a source of revenue and as a cultural voice capable of competing with Islamic fundamentalism. Its popularity in France persuaded the authorities in Algiers to sponsor international youth festivals featuring rai performers in Algiers and Oran in 1985.[12] In France, racist attacks on Arabs led to the formation of SOS-Racisme, a massive anti-racist organization affiliated with the Socialist Party. It embraced rai as an expression of faith in France's inter-cultural future.[13] They helped persuade the French government to sponsor a rai festival in a Paris suburb in 1986, which seemed to mark the emergence of rai as a permanent force in French popular music.[14] In fact, rai may have become more secure in France than it is in Algeria. When anti-government rioters in Algiers adopted Cheb Khaled's "El Harba Wine?" ("Where to Flee?") as their unofficial anthem in what became known as the "rai rebellion," many rai artists hastened to disassociate themselves from the violence.[15]

Yet, the popularity of rai music among French and "world beat" audiences may mean little for children of immigrants facing massive unemployment and racist attacks. In Lyons, for example, seventy percent of the children of immigrants between the ages of 16 and 25 have no jobs and no vocational training. Even the success of an assimilationist group like France-Plus which has managed to elect close to 400 people of North African lineage to municipal offices throughout France may increase rather than decrease the pressures on those immigrants and their children who seem less assimilated.[16]

Traditional arguments about immigration, assimilation, and accultura-tion assume that immigrants choose between two equally accessible cultures that are clearly differentiated and distinct from one another. But what if immigrants leave a country that has been shaped by its colonizers and enter one that has been shaped by those it colonized? What if immi-grants leave a modernizing country that turns anti-modern and fundamentalist while they are gone? What happens if the host country becomes deeply divided between anti-foreign nativists and anti-racist plu-ralists? Which culture do the immigrants carry with them? Into which culture do they assimilate? Rai music might be defended as either Algerian or French music, but a more exact interpretation would establish it as a register for the changing dimensions and boundaries of Algerian, French, and Beur (a popular term for Arab mostly used in Paris) identities.

Afro-Caribbean and Southwest Asian immigrants to Britain experience many of the same dynamic changes facing North African immigrants to France. Here again, musical syncretisms disclose the dynamics of cultural syncretisms basic to the processes of immigration, assimilation, and accul-turation in contemporary societies. Immigrants leaving the Caribbean and Asia took on new identities in Britain. If nothing else, they became "West Indian" or "East Indian" in England instead of Jamaican or Bahamian, Bengali, or Hindi as they had been at home. But they also became "Black" in Britain, an identity that they generally do not have in their home coun-tries, but which becomes salient to them in England as a consequence of racism directed at them from outside their communities as well as from its utility to them as a device for building unity within and across aggrieved populations. Of course, the influx of immigrants changes England too. Once immigrants from the Indian subcontinent or the Caribbean arrive in the UK, they transform the nature of British society and culture in many ways, changing the nature of the "inside" into which newer immigrants are expected to assimilate.

Popular music in Britain plays an important role in building solidarity within and across immigrant communities, while at the same time serving as a site for negotiation and contestation between groups. Music is a powerful but easily recognizable marker of cultural identity. It can be created by many people at many different sites because of the strength of diverse grass-roots musical traditions and because it requires relatively little access to capital. Although popular music can never be a "pure" or "authentic" expression of an undifferentiated group identity, as a highly visible (and audible) commodity, it comes to stand for the specificity of social experience in identifiable communities when it captures the attention, engagement, and even allegiance of people from many different social locations.

. . .

Mass migration from the West Indies to Britain began shortly after World War II. The expanding English economy offered jobs to immigrants, but the nation's cultural institutions rarely acknowledged their presence. According to Anthony Marks, as late as 1963, when some 15,000 records from Jamaica entered England every month, the British Broadcasting Corporation studiously ignored West Indian music and record shops rarely carried products from the Caribbean.[17] Denied the dignity of representation in the mainstream media, Afro-Caribbeans in England created spaces for themselves with neighborhood sound systems and record collections that enabled them to express their own culture and share it with others. At the heart of these new spaces was music from Jamaica.

While immigration flows included residents of all Caribbean islands, Jamaicans accounted for more than sixty percent of England's Caribbean population by the 1960s. Because of the size of the Jamaican-British community and because of the ways in which the politically-charged doctrines of Rastafarianism helped all diasporic Blacks in Britain understand and endure their treatment, Jamaican culture became the crucial unifying component in the composite Caribbean culture created in England. Differences between island identities that might be deeply felt in the West Indies, and even in England, receded in importance because of the unifying force of Jamaican music, but even more because of the uniformity of British racism against *all* West Indians: "When you're in school you all get harassed together," explained one immigrant.[18] Another adds, "I think most of my friends feel Jamaican, the English helped us do it."[19]

Popular music affirms the positive qualities of the unity forged in part by negative experiences with British racism. Through shared experiences with music, carnival celebrations, and the political activism that sometimes grows out of them, primary groups dispersed over a broad territory find themselves united by elements of a Jamaican culture that many of them had never known first hand.[20] Jazzie B of the British group Soul II Soul remembers the prominence of Jamaican "sound systems" – record players and amplified speakers – in his neighborhood as he grew up, and what they meant to him as the British-born son of immigrants from Antigua. "By the time I was 15 or 16, there was a sound system on every single street in the community. I'd guess that eight out of every ten black kids would be involved in one way or another in a sound system."[21] These devices offered a focal point for social gatherings, allowed disc jockeys opportunities to display their skills, and provided a soundtrack to mark the experiences and aspirations of inner-city life. But they also served as one of those sites where people made new identities for themselves as West Indians and as Black Britons.

Just as Paris . . . functions as an African city offering opportunities found nowhere in Africa, London and other British cities became important centers of West Indian and Jamaican cultural forms found nowhere in the Caribbean. But these forms have important uses and implications for Southwest Asians in Britain as well. The pervasive practices of British racism and occasional self-defense strategies by immigrants lead West Indians and East Indians to a shared identity as "Black" in England. Interactions between Afro-Caribbeans and Southwest Asians have a long if not completely comfortable history in the Caribbean, especially in Trinidad, but in Britain the antagonisms can be even sharper. For members of both groups, the things that divide them often seem more salient than those bringing them together. One survey showed that more than eighty percent of West Indians and more than forty percent of East Indians felt they had more in common with British whites than with each other. Almost a third of Indians and Pakistanis stated that they had nothing in common with either white Britons or West Indian Blacks. Only eight percent of West Indians and twenty percent of Pakistanis and Indians felt that they had more in common with each other than they had in common with the English.[22] In a few extremely significant cases, Afro-Asians and Afro-Caribbeans have successfully repressed their differences to defend themselves and each other from white racist attacks or judicial frame-ups, but sustained political and cultural alliances have been elusive.[23]

Yet, alliances between Southwest Asians and other groups that might appear unlikely in political life already exist within popular culture. Bhangra musicians fuse folk songs from the Indian state of Punjab with disco, pop, hip hop, and house music for appreciative audiences made up of people from many different groups. Like Algerian rai, bhangra originated in a part of the world characterized by extensive intercultural communication, but remained largely a music played for private parties, weddings, and harvest festivals before its emergence as a syncretic popular form. Bhangra brings together Punjabis of many religions (Hindu, Sikh, Muslim, Jain, and Christian) and from many countries (India, Pakistan, and Bangla Desh), but in the past decade has started to speak powerfully to new audiences and interests.[24]

Like West Indians, East Indians came to England in the years after World War II, and like West Indians they found that their labor was more welcome than their culture in their new nation. As Sabita Banerji notes in an apt phrase, "South Asian communities in Britain have remained invisible, and their music inaudible, for a surprisingly long time."[25] In the early 1980s, South Asian youths following the Jamaican example set up sound systems to play reggae, soul, jazz, and funk records during "daytimer" discos in dance halls and community centers. At first the disc jockeys and sound systems took Caribbean-sounding names, but when they started to mix bhangra with the other musical styles they used Punjabi names like "Gidian de Shingar" and "Pa Giddha Pa."[26] Almost a decade after Jamaican reggae established itself as a popular form capable of attracting audiences from every ethnic background, bhangra broke on the British scene as a viable commercial force. Alaap's 1984 album, *Teri chunni di sitare*, drew an enthusiastic response from listeners for its blend of disco, pop, and Caribbean styles with bhangra. Holle Holle and Heera drew large crowds to mainstream venues including the Hammersmith Palais by adding digital sampling to the mix in their music, while bhangra groups in the Midlands blended bhangra with house music.[27] But the ultimate fusion awaited – the mixture of Jamaican "ragamuffin" and African-American hip hop with "bhangra" to create the "bhangramuffin" sound of Apache Indian.

Steve Kapub took the name Apache Indian as a reference to his Punjabi ancestry and as a tribute to the Jamaican ragamuffin star "Super Cat," sometimes known as "the wild Apache."[28] But he took his art from the cultural crossroads he negotiated every day. He told a reporter,

> As a young Asian in Britain, you constantly lead a double life. At home, everything is as it was – very traditional, very strict. But when you close the front door and move onto the streets everything changes. I've had so many relatives disown my family because of my love for reggae. Now after hearing my music, and hearing the Indian influences in it, it appeals to them. But my music is first and foremost street music.[29]

For Apache Indian, the "street" is a place where Afro-Caribbean and South Asian youths learn from each other. As a teenager he wore his hair in dreadlocks, danced to the blues, and spent hours shopping for reggae records.[30] His first recording, "Move Over India," paid tribute to the India that he had only visited once but knew well from the Indian films that his parents watched "every time I went home."[31] Apache Indian knew that his music was a success when his West Indian neighbors began saying hello to him in Punjabi. His song "Come Follow Me" offers a hip hop history and travelogue of India for the edification of a West Indian friend who closes the number by telling Apache Indian that his country sounds "lovely, and next time you go send a ticket for me."[32]

Standing at the crossroads of Punjabi and Jamaican cultures, Apache Indian shows that Afro-Asian and Afro-Caribbean Britons share more than a common designation as Black people, that they share a common history of using culture to strengthen their communities from the inside and to attract support from the outside. Punjabis and Jamaicans both come from regions that contain diverse cultures and beliefs, and they both belong to populations that transnational capital has dispersed all over the globe. From their historical experiences at home no less from what they have learned in order to survive abroad, Punjabis and Jamaicans draw upon longstanding and rich traditions when they create cultural coalitions that transcend ethnic and political differences.

The music made by Apache Indian uses performance to call into being a community composed of Punjabis and Jamaicans, South Asian and West Indians, reggae fans and bhangra enthusiasts. But it also demonstrates the potential for all of Britain to learn a lesson from the extraordinary adaptability and creativity of its immigrant cultures. Apache Indian reads "British" culture selectively, by venerating Mahatma Gandhi and Bob Marley rather than Winston Churchill or George Frederick Handel. He assimilates into the culture of the country where he was born by proudly displaying the diverse identities that he has learned in its schools and streets. He creates problems for nation states with their narratives of discrete, homogeneous, and autonomous culture, but he solves problems for people who want cultural expressions as complex as the lives they live every day.

. . .

Anti-immigrant and anti-foreign sentiment plagues de-industrialized nations in the West as well as de-Stalinized countries in the East. During times of economic decline and social disintegration, it is tempting for people to blame their problems on others, and to seek succor and certainty from racist and nationalist myths. But the desire to seek certainty and stability by depicting the world solely as one story told from one point of view is more dangerous than ever before. As technology and trade inevitably provide diverse populations with common (although not egalitarian) experiences, the ability to adapt, to switch codes, and to see things from more than one perspective becomes more valuable. In the last analysis, nation states may be best served by those who refuse to believe in their unified narratives, and who insist instead on cultural and political practices that delight in difference, diversity, and dialogue. These do not need to be conjured up by political theorists, or wished into existence by mystics and visionaries. They already exist (albeit in embryonic form) in the communities called into existence by rai, ragamuffin, bhangra, and many other unauthorized and unexpected forms that people have for understanding and changing the world in which they live.

George Lipsitz, *Dangerous Crossroads: Popular Music, Postmodernism and the Poetics of Place*, London and New York: Verso, 1994, pp. 119, 124–32.

SIX

A WOMAN'S PLACE

There's something odd about the place of women in classic studies of cultural resistance. They have none. There's a mention here and there, but often as an addendum, an afterthought: oh yes, and remember the ladies! Some of this absence can be explained by the institutional sexism that kept women from academic scholarship until relatively recently, but this doesn't account for all of it. The problem instead, I believe, stems from the paradigm of cultural resistance as it is commonly understood. The cultural resistance we have been looking at so far is public – it takes place on the street or in the fields, on the barricades or in the bars. And this public sphere, historically, has been the province of men. Therefore, if we look for examples of women's cultural resistance here we are bound to be disappointed. However, turn your attention to the realm women have traditionally inhabited: the home and hearth – that is the private – and a different story is revealed. These are the stories of resistance told below. Some cultural battles are fought to join the public sphere, while others are waged for recognition and valuation of the private, but through them all is the constant struggle of women to create their own definition of what a woman is and her place in the world.

VIRGINIA WOOLF, FROM *A ROOM OF ONE'S OWN*

How can you write, the great writer Virginia Woolf asks, if you are constantly interrupted by children, husbands, and the myriad tasks of the household, if doubting men peer over your shoulder, and your horizons don't extend past the home? Her answer: you can't. Denied their physical freedom and financial independence, women, Woolf argues, have created a stunted culture: myopic in world view, crippled by self-doubt, deformed by anger, and above all, reigned in by men. In the following section she tracks an imaginary sister of Shakespeare from creative flowering to early suicide. (Woolf committed suicide herself in 1941.) Shakespeare's sister is Everywoman, held back from the public by barriers constructed by men, and then by something far worse: the internalization of those barriers. Woolf asks for more than just a room of one's own (and fifty pounds a year), for this is just a precondition for creativity; what she demands is a culture not shackled by gender.

I thought of that old gentleman, who is dead now, but was a bishop, I think, who declared that it was impossible for any woman, past, present, or to come, to have the genius of Shakespeare. He wrote to the papers about it. He also told a lady who applied to him for information that cats do not as a matter of fact go to heaven, though they have, he added, souls of a sort. How much thinking those old gentlemen used to save one! How much the borders of ignorance shrank back at their approach! Cats do not go the heaven. Women cannot write the plays of Shakespeare.

Be that as it may, I could not help thinking, as I looked at the works of Shakespeare on the shelf, that the bishop was right at least in this; it would have been impossible, completely and entirely, for any woman to have written the plays of Shakespeare in the age of Shakespeare. Let me imagine, since facts are so hard to come by, what would have happened had Shakespeare had a wonderfully gifted sister, called Judith, let us say. Shakespeare himself went, very probably – his mother was an heiress – to the grammar school, where he may have learnt Latin – Ovid, Virgil, and Horace – and the elements of grammar and logic. He was, it is well known, a wild boy who poached rabbits, perhaps shot a deer, and had, rather sooner than he should have done, to marry a woman in the neighbourhood, who bore him a child rather quicker than was right. That escapade sent him to seek his fortune in London. He had, it seemed, a taste for the theatre; he began by holding horses at the stage door. Very soon he got work in the theatre, became a successful actor, and lived at the hub of the universe, meeting everybody, knowing everybody, practising his art on the boards, exercising his wits in the streets, and even getting access to the palace of the queen. Meanwhile his extraordinarily gifted sister, let us suppose, remained at home. She was as adventurous, as imaginative, as agog to see the world as he was. But she was not sent to school. She had no chance of learning grammar and logic, let alone of reading Horace and Virgil. She picked up a book now and then, one of her brother's perhaps, and read a few pages. But then her parents came in and told her to mend the stockings or mind the stew and not moon about with books and papers. They would have spoken sharply but kindly, for they were substantial people who knew the conditions of life for a woman and loved their daughter – indeed, more likely than not she was the apple of her father's eye. Perhaps she scribbled some pages up in an apple loft on the sly, but was careful to hide them or set fire to them. Soon, however, before she was out of her teens, she was to be betrothed to the son of a neighbouring wool-stapler. She cried out that marriage was hateful to her, and for that she was severely beaten by her father. Then he ceased to scold her. He begged her instead not to hurt him, not to shame him in this matter of her marriage. He would give her a chain of beads or a fine petticoat, he said; and there were tears in his eyes. How could she disobey him? How could she break his heart? The force of her own gift alone drove her to it. She made up a small parcel of her belongings, let herself down by a rope one summer's night and took the road to London. She was not seventeen. The birds that sang in the hedge were not more musical than she was. She had the quickest fancy, a gift like her brother's, for the tune of words. Like him, she had a taste for the theatre. She stood at the stage door; she wanted to act, she said. Men laughed in her face. The manager – a fat, loose-lipped man – guffawed. He bellowed something about poodles dancing and women acting – no woman, he said, could possibly be an actress. He hinted – you can imagine what. She could get no training in her craft. Could she even seek her dinner in a tavern or roam the streets at midnight? Yet her genius was for fiction and lusted to feed abundantly upon the lives of men and women and the study of their ways. At last – for she was very young, oddly like Shakespeare the poet in her face, with the same grey eyes and rounded brows – at last Nick Greene the actor-manager took pity on her; she found herself with child by that gentleman and so – who shall measure the heat and violence of the poet's heart when caught and tangled in a woman's body? – killed herself one winter's night and lies buried at some cross-roads where the omnibuses now stop outside the Elephant and Castle.

That, more or less, is how the story would run, I think, if a woman in Shakespeare's day had had Shakespeare's genius. But for my part, I agree with the deceased bishop, if such he was – it is unthinkable that any woman in Shakespeare's day should have had Shakespeare's genius. For genius like Shakespeare's is not born among labouring, uneducated, servile people. It was not born in England among the Saxons and the Britons. It is not born today among the working classes. How, then, could it have been born among women whose work began, according to Professor Trevelyan, almost before they were out of the nursery, who were forced to it by their parents and held to it by all the power of law and custom? Yet genius of a sort must have existed among women as it must have existed among the working classes. Now and again an Emily Brontë or a Robert Burns blazes out and proves its presence. But certainly it never got itself on to paper. When, however, one reads of a witch being ducked, of a woman possessed by devils, of a wise woman selling herbs, or even of a very remarkable man who had a mother, then I think we are on the track of a lost novelist, a suppressed poet, of some mute and inglorious Jane Austen, some Emily Brontë who dashed her brains out on the moor or mopped and mowed about the highways crazed with the torture that her gift had put her to. Indeed, I would venture to guess that Anon, who wrote so many poems without signing them, was often a woman. It was a woman, Edward Fitzgerald, I think, suggested who made the ballads and the folk-songs, crooning them to her children, beguiling her spinning with them, or the length of the winter's night.

This may be true or it may be false — who can say? — but what is true in it, so it seemed to me, reviewing the story of Shakespeare's sister as I had made it, is that any woman born with a great gift in the sixteenth century would certainly have gone crazed, shot herself, ended her days in some lonely cottage outside the village, half witch, half wizard, feared and mocked at. For it needs little skill in psychology to be sure that a highly gifted girl who had tried to use her gift for poetry would have been so thwarted and hindered by other people, so tortured and pulled asunder by her own contrary instincts, that she must have lost her health and sanity to a certainty. No girl could have walked to London and stood at a stage door and forced her way into the presence of actor-managers without doing herself a violence and suffering an anguish which may have been irrational — for chastity may be a fetish invented by certain societies for unknown reasons — but were none the less inevitable. Chastity had then, it has even now, a religious importance in a woman's life, and has so wrapped itself round with nerves and instincts that to cut it free and bring it to the light of day demands courage of the rarest. To have lived a free life in London in the sixteenth century would have meant for a woman who was poet and playwright a nervous stress and dilemma which might well have killed her. Had she survived, whatever she had written would have been twisted and deformed, issuing from a strained and morbid imagination. And undoubtedly, I thought, looking at the shelf where there are no plays by women, her work would have gone unsigned. That refuge she would have sought certainly. It was the relic of the sense of chastity that dictated anonymity to women even so late as the nineteenth century. Currer Bell, George Eliot,

George Sand, all the victims of inner strife as their writings prove, sought ineffectively to veil themselves by using the name of a man. Thus they did homage to the convention, which if not implanted by the other sex was liberally encouraged by them ('the chief glory of a woman is not to be talked of', said Pericles, himself a much-talked-of man), that publicity in women is detestable. Anonymity runs in their blood. The desire to be veiled still possesses them. They are not even now concerned about the health of their fame as men are, and, speaking generally, will pass a tombstone or a signpost without feeling an irresistible desire to cut their names on it, as Alf, Bert or Chas. must do in obedience to their instinct, which murmurs if it sees a fine woman go by, or even a dog, *Ce chien est à moi*. And, of course, it may not be a dog, I thought, remembering Parliament Square, the Sièges Allée and other avenues; it may be a piece of land or a man with curly black hair. It is one of the great advantages of being a woman that one can pass even a very fine negress without wishing to make an Englishwoman of her.

That woman, then, who was born with a gift of poetry in the sixteenth century, was an unhappy woman, a woman at strife against herself. All the conditions of her life, all her own instincts, were hostile to the state of mind which is needed to set free whatever is in the brain. But what is the state of mind that is most propitious to the act of creation, I asked. Can one come by any notion of the state that furthers and makes possible that strange activity? Here I opened the volume containing the Tragedies of Shakespeare. What was Shakespeare's state of mind, for instance, when he wrote *Lear* and *Antony and Cleopatra*? It was certainly the state of mind most favourable to poetry that there has ever existed. But Shakespeare himself said nothing about it. We only know casually and by chance that he 'never blotted a line'. Nothing indeed was ever said by the artist himself about his state of mind until the eighteenth century perhaps. Rousseau perhaps began it. At any rate, by the nineteenth century self-consciousness had developed so far that it was the habit for men of letters to describe their minds in confessions and autobiographies. Their lives also were written, and their letters printed after their deaths. Thus, though we do not know what Shakespeare went through when he wrote *Lear*, we do know what Carlyle went through when he wrote the *French Revolution*; what Flaubert went through when he wrote *Madame Bovary*; what Keats was going through when he tried to write poetry against the coming of death and the indifference of the world.

And one gathers from this enormous modern literature of confession and self-analysis that to write a work of genius is almost always a feat of prodigious difficulty. Everything is against the likelihood that it will come from the writer's mind whole and entire. Generally material circumstances are against it. Dogs will bark; people will interrupt; money must be made; health will break down. Further, accentuating all these difficulties and making them harder to bear is the world's notorious indifference. It does not ask people to write poems and novels and histories; it does not need them. It does not care whether Flaubert finds the right word or whether Carlyle scrupulously verifies this or that fact. Naturally, it will not pay for what it does not want. And so the writer, Keats, Flaubert, Carlyle, suffers, especially in the creative years of youth, every form of distraction and discouragement. A curse, a cry of agony, rises from those books of analysis and confession. 'Mighty poets in their misery dead' – that is the burden of their song. If anything comes through in spite of all of this, it is a miracle, and probably no book is born entire and uncrippled as it was conceived.

But for women, I thought, looking at the empty shelves, these difficulties were infinitely more formidable. In the first place, to have a room of her own, let alone a quiet room or a sound-proof room, was out of the question, unless her parents were exceptionally rich or very noble, even up to the beginning of the nineteenth century. Since her pin money, which depended on the good will of her father, was only enough to keep her clothed, she was debarred from such alleviations as came even to Keats or Tennyson or Carlyle, all poor men, from a walking tour, a little journey to France, from the separate lodging which, even if it were miserable enough, sheltered them from the claims and tyrannies of their families. Such material difficulties were formidable; but much worse were the immaterial. The indifference of the world which Keats and Flaubert and other men of genius have found so hard to bear was in her case not indifference but hostility. The world did not say to her as it said to them, Write if you choose; it makes no difference to me. The world said with a guffaw, Write? What's the good of your writing? Here the psychologists of Newnham and Girton might come to our help, I thought, looking again at the blank spaces on the shelves. For surely it is time that the effect of discouragement upon the mind of the artist should be measured, as I have seen a dairy company measure the effect of ordinary milk and Grade A milk upon the body of the rat. They set two rats in cages side by side, and of the two one was furtive, timid, and small, and the other was glossy, bold and big. Now what food do we feed women as artists upon? I asked, remembering, I suppose, that dinner of prunes and custard. To answer that question I had only to open the evening paper to read that Lord Birkenhead is of the opinion – but really I am not going to trouble to copy out Lord Birkenhead's opinion upon the writing of women. What Dean Inge says I will leave in peace. The

Harley Street specialist may be allowed to rouse the echoes of Harley Street with his vociferations without raising a hair on my head. I will quote, however, Mr Oscar Browning, because Mr Oscar Browning was a great figure in Cambridge at one time, and used to examine the students at Girton and Newnham. Mr Oscar Browning was wont to declare 'that the impression left on his mind, after looking over any set of examination papers, was that, irrespective of the marks he might give, the best woman was intellectually the inferior of the worst man'. After saying that Mr Browning went back to his rooms – and it is this sequel that endears him and makes him a human figure of bulk and majesty – he went back to his rooms and found a stable-boy lying on the sofa – 'a mere skeleton, his cheeks were cavernous and sallow, his teeth were black, and he did not appear to have the full use of his limbs . . . "That's Arthur" [said Mr Browning]. He's a dear boy really and most high-minded."' The two pictures always seem to me to complete each other. And happily in this age of biography the two pictures often do complete each other, so that we are able to interpret the opinions of great men not only by what they say, but by what they do.

But though this is possible now, such opinions coming from the lips of important people must have been formidable enough even fifty years ago. Let us suppose that a father from the highest motives did not wish his daughter to leave home and become writer, painter or scholar. 'See what Mr Oscar Browning says', he would say; and there was not only Mr Oscar Browning; there was the *Saturday Review*; there was Mr Greg – the 'essentials of a woman's being', said Mr Greg emphatically, 'are that *they are supported by, and they minister to, men*' – there was an enormous body of masculine opinion to the effect that nothing could be expected of women intellectually. Even if her father did not read out loud these opinions, any girl could read them for herself; and the reading, even in the nineteenth century, must have lowered her vitality, and told profoundly upon her work. There would always have been that assertion – you cannot do this, you are incapable of doing that – to protest against, to overcome. Probably for a novelist this germ is no longer of much effect; for there have been women novelists of merit. But for painters it must still have some sting in it; and for musicians, I imagine, is even now active and poisonous in the extreme. The woman composer stands where the actress stood in the time of Shakespeare. Nick Greene, I thought, remembering the story I had made about Shakespeare's sister, said that a woman acting put him in mind of a dog dancing. Johnson repeated the phrase two hundred years later of women preaching. And here, I said, opening a book about music, we have the very words used again in this year of grace, 1928, of women who try to write music. 'Of Mlle Germaine Tailleferre one can only repeat Dr Johnson's dictum concerning a woman preacher, transposed into terms of music:"Sir, a woman's composing is like a dog's walking on his hind legs. It is not done well, but you are surprised to find it done at all."'[1] So accurately does history repeat itself.

Thus, I concluded, shutting Mr Oscar Browning's life and pushing away the rest, it is fairly evident that even in the nineteenth century a woman was not encouraged to be an artist. On the contrary, she was snubbed, slapped, lectured and exhorted. Her mind must have been strained and her vitality lowered by the need of opposing this, of disproving that. For here again we come within range of that very interesting and obscure masculine complex which has had so much influence upon the woman's movement; that deep-seated desire, not so much that *she* shall be inferior as that *he* shall be superior, which plants him wherever one looks, not only in front of the arts, but barring the way to politics too, even when the risk to himself seems infinitesimal and the suppliant humble and devoted. Even Lady Bessborough, I remembered, with all her passion for politics, must humbly bow herself and write to Lord Granville Leveson-Gower: '. . . notwithstanding all my violence in politics and talking so much on that subject, I perfectly agree with you that no woman has any business to meddle with that or any other serious business, farther than giving her opinion (if she is ask'd)'. And so she goes on to spend her enthusiasm where it meets with no obstacle whatsoever upon that immensely important subject, Lord Granville's maiden speech in the House of Commons. The spectacle is certainly a strange one, I thought. The history of men's opposition to women's emancipation is more interesting perhaps than the story of that emancipation itself. An amusing book might be made of it if some young student at Girton or Newnham would collect examples and deduce a theory – but she would need thick gloves on her hands, and bars to protect her of solid gold.

But what is amusing now, I recollected, shutting Lady Bessborough, had to be taken in desperate earnest once. Opinions that one now pastes in a book labelled cock-a-doodle-dum and keeps for reading to select audiences on summer nights once drew tears, I can assure you. Among your grandmothers and great-grandmothers there were many that wept their eyes out. Florence Nightingale shrieked aloud in her agony.[2] Moreover, it is all very well for you, who have got yourselves to college and enjoy sitting-rooms – or is it only bed-sitting rooms? – of your own to say that genius should disregard such opinions; that genius should be above caring what is said of it. Unfortunately, it is precisely the men or women of genius who

mind most what is said of them. Remember Keats. Remember the words
he had cut on his tombstone. Think of Tennyson; think – but I need hardly
multiply instances of the undeniable, if very unfortunate, fact that it is the
nature of the artist to mind excessively what is said about him. Literature is
strewn with the wreckage of men who have minded beyond reason the
opinions of others.

And this susceptibility of theirs is doubly unfortunate, I thought, returning again to my original inquiry into what state of mind is most propitious
for creative work, because the mind of an artist, in order to achieve the
prodigious effort of freeing whole and entire the work that is in him, must
be incandescent, like Shakespeare's mind, I conjectured, looking at the
book which lay open at *Antony and Cleopatra*. There must be no obstacle in
it, no foreign matter unconsumed.

For though we say that we know nothing about Shakespeare's state of
mind, even as we say that, we are saying something about Shakespeare's
state of mind. The reason perhaps why we know so little of Shakespeare –
compared with Donne or Ben Jonson or Milton – is that his grudges and
spites and antipathies are hidden from us. We are not held up by some 'revelation' which reminds us of the writer. All desire to protest, to preach, to
proclaim an injury, to pay off a score, to make the world the witness of
some hardship or grievance was fired out of him and consumed. Therefore
his poetry flows from him free and unimpeded. If ever a human being got
his work expressed completely, it was Shakespeare. If ever a mind was
incandescent, unimpeded, I thought, turning again to the bookcase, it was
Shakespeare's mind.

Virginia Woolf, *A Room of One's Own*, New York: Harcourt Brace & Co,
1929/1990, pp. 46–57.

RADICALESBIANS,
"THE WOMAN-IDENTIFIED WOMAN"

To be a woman, Simone de Beauvoir once wrote, is to be defined by men.[1] Predictably, men define women in such a way as to ensure their own superiority.
In 1970, coming out of the second wave of feminism, was a response: "The
Woman-Identified Woman." The authors of this proclamation were lesbian
writers and activists calling themselves first Lavender Menace (a reference to
Betty Friedan's attributed remark that lesbians were a "lavender menace" to the
feminist movement), and then Radicalesbians. Lesbianism, the Radicalesbians

argue, is about self-definition, looking to other women for identity rather than turning to men. It is from this new identity that a new and powerful consciousness, culture and politics can come; in their own words: "with that real self, with that consciousness, we begin a revolution." "The Woman-Identified Woman," as well as other similar statements of the time (see sidebar), laid the groundwork of what would come to be known as "identity politics."

What is a lesbian? A lesbian is the rage of all women condensed to the point of explosion. She is the woman who, often beginning at an extremely early age, acts in accordance with her inner compulsion to be a more complete and freer human being than her society – perhaps then, but certainly later – cares to allow her. These needs and actions, over a period of years, bring her into painful conflict with people, situations, the accepted ways of thinking, feeling and behaving, until she is in a state of continual war with everything around her, and usually with her self. She may not be fully conscious of the political implications of what for her began as personal necessity, but on some level she has not been able to accept the limitations and oppression laid on her by the most basic role of her society – the female role. The turmoil she experiences tends to induce guilt proportional to the degree to which she feels she is not meeting social expectations, and/or eventually drives her to question and analyze what the rest of her society more or less accepts. She is forced to evolve her own life pattern, often living much of her life alone, learning usually much earlier than her "straight" (heterosexual) sisters about the essential aloneness of life (which the myth of marriage obscures) and about the reality of illusions. To the extent that she cannot expel the heavy socialization that goes with being female, she can never truly find peace with herself. For she is caught somewhere between accepting society's view of her – in which case she cannot accept herself – and coming to understand what this sexist society has done to her and why it is functional and necessary for it to do so. Those of us who work that through find ourselves on the other side of a tortuous journey through a night that may have been decades long. The perspective gained from that journey, the liberation of self, the inner peace, the real love of self and of all women, is something to be shared with all women – because we are all women.

It should first be understood that lesbianism, like male homosexuality, is a category of behavior possible only in a sexist society characterized by rigid sex roles and dominated by male supremacy. Those sex roles dehumanize women by defining us as a supportive/serving caste *in relation to* the master

"The Combahee River Collective Statement", The Combahee River Collective

What We Believe

Above all else, our politics initially sprang from the shared belief that Black women are inherently valuable, that our liberation is a necessity not as an adjunct to somebody else's but because of our need as human persons for autonomy. This may seem so obvious as to sound simplistic, but it is apparent that no other ostensibly progressive movement has ever considered our specific oppression as a priority or worked seriously for the ending of that oppression. Merely naming the pejorative stereotypes attributed to Black women (e.g., mammy, matriarch, Sapphire, whore, bulldagger), let alone cataloging the cruel, often murderous, treatment we receive, indicates how little value has been placed upon our lives during four centuries of bondage in the Western Hemisphere. We realize that the only people who care enough about us to work consistently for our liberation are us. Our politics evolve from a healthy love for ourselves, our sisters and our community, which allows us to continue our struggle and work.

This focusing upon our own oppression is embodied in the concept of identity politics. We believe that the most profound and potentially most radical politics come directly out of our own identity, as opposed to working to end somebody else's oppression. In the case of Black women this is a particularly repugnant, dangerous, threatening,

caste of men, and emotionally cripple men by demanding that they be alienated from their own bodies and emotions in order to perform their economic/political/military functions effectively. Homosexuality is a by-product of a particular way of setting up roles (or approved patterns of behavior) on the basis of sex; as such it is an inauthentic (not consonant with "reality") category. In a society in which men do not oppress women, and sexual expression is allowed to follow feelings, the categories of homosexuality and heterosexuality would disappear.

But lesbianism is also different from male homosexuality, and serves a different function in the society. "Dyke" is a different kind of put-down from "faggot," although both imply you are not playing your socially assigned sex role ... are not therefore a "real woman" or a "real man." The grudging admiration felt for the tomboy, and the queasiness felt around a sissy boy point to the same thing: the contempt in which women – or those who play a female role – are held. And the investment in keeping women in that contemptuous role is very great. Lesbian is a word, the label, the condition that holds women in line. When a woman hears this word tossed her way, she knows she is stepping out of line. She knows that she has crossed the terrible boundary of her sex role. She recoils, she protests, she reshapes her actions to gain approval. Lesbian is a label invented by the Man to throw at any woman who dares to be his equal, who dares to challenge his prerogatives (including that of all women as part of the exchange medium among men), who dares to assert the primacy of her own needs. To have the label applied to people active in women's liberation is just the most recent instance of a long history; older women will recall that not so long ago, any woman who was successful, independent, not orienting her whole life about a man, would hear this word. For in this sexist society, for a woman to be independent means she *can't be* a woman – she must be a dyke. That in itself should tell us where women are at. It says as clearly as can be said: woman and person are contradictory terms. For a lesbian is not considered a "real woman." And yet, in popular thinking, there is really only one essential difference between a lesbian and other women: that of sexual orientation – which is to say, when you strip off all the packaging, you must finally realize that the essence of being a "woman" is to get fucked by men.

"Lesbian" is one of the sexual categories by which men have divided up humanity. While all women are dehumanized as sex objects, as the objects of men they are given certain compensations: identification with his power, his ego, his status, his protection (from other males), feeling like a "real woman," finding social acceptance by adhering to her role, etc. Should a woman confront herself by confronting another woman, there are fewer rationalizations, fewer buffers by which to avoid the stark horror of her dehumanized condition. Herein we find the overriding fear of many women toward being used as a sexual object by a woman, which not only will bring her no male-connected compensations, but also will reveal the void which is woman's real situation. This dehumanization is expressed when a straight woman learns that a sister is a lesbian; she begins to relate to her lesbian sister as her potential sex object, laying a surrogate male role on the lesbian. This reveals her heterosexual conditioning to make herself into an object when sex is potentially involved in a relationship, and it denies the lesbian her full humanity. For women, especially those in the movement, to perceive their lesbian sisters through this male grid of role definitions is to accept this male cultural conditioning and to oppress their sisters much as they themselves have been oppressed by men. Are we going to continue the male classification system of defining all females in sexual relation to some other category of people? Affixing the label lesbian not only to a woman who aspires to be a person, but also to any situation of real love, real solidarity, real primacy among women, is a primary form of divisiveness among women: it is the condition which keeps women within

and therefore revolutionary concept because it is obvious from looking at all the political movements that have preceded us that anyone is more worthy of liberation than ourselves. We reject pedestals, queenhood, and walking ten paces behind. To be recognized as human, levelly human, is enough.

from *Home Girls: A Black Feminist Anthology*, Barbara Smith (ed.), Latham, New York: Kitchen Table/Women of Color Press, 1977/1983, p. 272

the confines of the feminine role, and it is the debunking/scare term that keeps women from forming any primary attachments, groups, or associations among ourselves.

Women in the movement have in most cases gone to great lengths to avoid discussion and confrontation with the issue of lesbianism. It puts people up-tight. They are hostile, evasive, or try to incorporate it into some "broader issue." They would rather not talk about it. If they have to, they try to dismiss it as a "lavender herring." But it is no side issue. It is absolutely essential to the success and fulfillment of the women's liberation movement that this issue be dealt with. As long as the label "dyke" can be used to frighten women into a less militant stand, keep her separate from her sisters, keep her from giving primacy to anything other than men and family, then to that extent she is controlled by the male culture. Until women see in each other the possibility of a primal commitment which includes sexual love, they will be denying themselves the love and value they readily accord to men, thus affirming their second-class status. As long as male acceptability is primary – both to individual women and to the movement as a whole – the term lesbian will be used effectively against women. Insofar as women want only more privileges within the system, they do not want to antagonize male power. They instead seek acceptability for women's liberation, and the most crucial aspect of the acceptability is to deny lesbianism – i.e., to deny any fundamental challenge to the basis of the female. It should also be said that some younger, more radical women have honestly begun to discuss lesbianism, but so far it has been primarily as a sexual "alternative" to men. This, however, is still giving primacy to men, both because the idea of relating more completely to women occurs as a negative reaction to men, and because the lesbian relationship is being characterized simply by sex, which is divisive and sexist. On one level, which is both personal and political, women may withdraw emotional and sexual energies from men, and work out various alternatives for those energies in their own lives. On a different political/psychological level, it must be understood that what is crucial is that women begin disengaging from male defined response patterns. In the privacy of our own psyches, we must cut those cords to the core. For irrespective of where our love and sexual energies flow, if we are male-identified in our heads, we cannot realize our autonomy as human beings.

But why is it that women have related to and through men? By virtue of having been brought up in a male society, we have internalized the male culture's definition of ourselves. That definition consigns us to sexual and family functions, and excludes us from defining and shaping the terms of our lives. In exchange for our psychic servicing and for performing society's non-profit-making functions, the man confers on us just one thing: the slave status which makes us legitimate in the eyes of the society in which we live. This is called "femininity" or "being a real woman" in our cultural lingo. We are authentic, legitimate, real to the extent that we are the property of some man whose name we bear. To be a woman who belongs to no man is to be invisible, pathetic, inauthentic, unreal. He confirms his image of us – of what we have to be in order to be acceptable by him – but not our real selves; he confirms our womanhood – as he defines it, in relation to him – but cannot confirm our personhood, our own selves as absolutes. As long as we are dependent on the male culture for this definition, for this approval, we cannot be free.

The consequence of internalizing this role is an enormous reservoir of self-hate. This is not to say the self-hate is recognized or accepted as such; indeed most women would deny it. It may be experienced as discomfort with her role, as feeling empty, as numbness, as restlessness, as a paralyzing anxiety at the center. Alternatively, it may be expressed in shrill defensiveness of the glory and destiny of her role. But it does exist, often beneath the edge of her consciousness, poisoning her existence, keeping her alienated from herself, her own needs, and rendering her a stranger to other women. They try to escape by identifying with the oppressor, living through him, gaining status and identity from his ego, his power, his accomplishments. And by not identifying with other "empty vessels" like themselves. Women resist relating on all levels to other women who will reflect their own oppression, their own secondary status, their own self-hate. For to confront another woman is finally to confront one's self – the self we have gone to such lengths to avoid. And in that mirror we know we cannot really respect and love that which we have been made to be.

As the source of self-hate and the lack of real self are rooted in our male-given identity, we must create a new sense of self. As long as we cling to the idea of "being a woman," we will sense some conflict with that incipient self, that sense of I, that sense of a whole person. It is very difficult to realize and accept that being "feminine" and being a whole person are irreconcilable. Only women can give to each other a new sense of self. That identity we have to develop with reference to ourselves, and not in relation to men. This consciousness is the revolutionary force from which all else will follow, for ours is an organic revolution. For this we must be available and supportive to one another, give our commitment and our love, give the emotional support necessary to sustain this movement. Our energies must flow toward our sisters, not backward toward our oppressors. As long as woman's liberation tries to free women without facing the basic heterosexual structure that binds us in one-to-one relationship with our oppressors, tremendous energies will continue to flow into trying to straighten up each particular relationship with a man, into finding how to get better sex, how to turn his head around – into trying to make the "new man" out of him in the delusion that this will allow us to be the "new woman." This obviously splits our energies and commitments, leaving us unable to be committed to the construction of the new patterns which will liberate us.

It is the primacy of women relating to women, of women creating a new consciousness of and with each other, which is at the heart of women's liberation, and the basis for the cultural revolution. Together we must find, reinforce, and validate our authentic selves. As we do this, we confirm in each other that struggling, incipient sense of pride and strength, the divisive barriers begin to melt, we feel this growing solidarity with our sisters. We see ourselves as prime, find our centers inside of ourselves. We find receding the sense of alienation, of being cut off, of being behind a locked window, of being unable to get out what we know is inside. We feel a real-ness, feel at last we are coinciding with ourselves. With that real self, with that consciousness, we begin a revolution to end the imposition of all coercive identifications, and to achieve maximum autonomy in human expression.

Radicalesbians, *The Woman-Identified Woman*, Gay Flames pamphlet, New York, 1970/1972.

JEAN RAILLA,
"A BROOM OF ONE'S OWN"

The home, feminists have long understood, is where men put women. Therefore it was only natural that both first- and second-wave feminists demanded to be free from domesticity, liberated from a culture of subservience. Writing in the third-wave feminist magazine *Bust*, Jean Railla takes a fresh and personal look at "women's work." She discovers that domesticity is complex, communal, and fulfilling – not at all what she thought, or had been taught. For women's work has not only been devalued for millennia by men, but more recently, and more disturbingly, by many "liberated" women. Patriarchy, she argues, has been internalized to such a degree that women have learned to distance themselves from womanhood. While acknowledging that the lack of alternatives open to women remains a real problem, Railla, following pre-feminist, feminist footsteps (see sidebar), asks us to re-evaluate the domestic world that women have built, reclaiming it as genuine women's culture.

In 1972, as America embraced polyester pantsuits and protested the Vietnam war while strains of Helen Reddy's "I Am Woman" rang endlessly from the FM radio, twenty-one students were embarking on a mission to put together a feminist art project. Eager to develop a "personal is political" aesthetic, the students created a collaborative work called, simply, *Womanhouse.* Set in an actual condemned house, *Womanhouse* was an installation piece that explored the ways that women are trapped by the home. There was the "Nurturant Kitchen," with egg-like nipples applied to the ceiling and the walls; the "Menstruation Bathroom" with bloodied tampons; and the "Bridal Staircase," featuring a new bride in her new home/prison. Sandy Orgel, one of the student artists of the project, wrote about her piece "Linen Closet" (a sculpture of a woman trapped between shelves): "This is exactly where women have always been – in between the sheets and on the shelf. It is time now to come out of the closet."

This house has haunted me. I was raised on Betty Friedan-style feminism – I had a subscription to *Ms.* at age 12, and published my first letter in the magazine at 13. Growing up, I wanted nothing to do with domesticity, motherhood, marriage, or anything else that reeked of traditional womanhood. My dream was to escape my family, my suburban Southern California home, and the sexism that surrounded me by hitting the city and becoming a famous bohemian like the writer Anaïs Nin or the feminist artist Miriam Schapiro.

My attitude remained unchallenged throughout my college years. I was a Women's Studies major at UCLA in the early '90s, and my professors, like the artists who directed *Womanhouse,* perceived the home and its accompanying activities as something that women needed to free themselves from. Housework, we were taught, is nothing but boring drudgery – work done by women who don't know better. Smart, enlightened women became artists, writers, thinkers; they became *important.* They didn't have time for silly things like cooking, sewing, knitting, or cleaning. Of course, there were a few exceptions to this rule, but for the most part, the logic of the day was: work/career is good; home/domesticity is bad.

And it all made sense to me. After college, bad-ass and ambitious, I hopped from job to job, working as a filmmaker, a video editor, and a Web producer. My entire focus was on becoming successful. As a result, I never learned how to save my money or create a nice home. In fact, I spent almost my entire twenties either at work or out partying.

Then, at age 28, I crashed. Sure, I had built a "career" for myself, but by that point I also had a huge debt, a crappy apartment with the requisite futon on the floor, bad eating habits, worse boyfriend choices, and no real clue as to how to be a grown-up. I was also plagued by ongoing health issues.

I began re-evaluating who I was, and what I wanted, including many of the things that I had always dismissed because I didn't want to be one of "those" women. After all, I reasoned, what did I have to fear from domestic entrapment? I was a single girl living alone in the East Village with a job and a growing posse of girlfriends. I didn't have a husband or even a real home. I just wanted someplace nice to come home to and something more going on in my life besides work, party, work, party.

Before I know it, I was purchasing books on macrobiotics and natural healing. I made tinctures, read about Witches, and started meditating to help with my stress. Library books full of home furnishing suggestions and Feng Shui manuals became my nightly reading as I plotted out the new décor scheme for my apartment. I took up knitting, crafts, and sewing. I wasted time at work searching the Internet for patterns and craft how-to's. I made soap. I bought over-priced glossies of "cool" mags like *Wallpaper* and *Nest*. And I got secret subscriptions to *Martha Stewart Living* and *Gourmet* magazine.

And you know what I learned? All the stuff that I had always dismissed as stupid housework was actually quite complicated and required skill. Cooking, for instance, is a lot more difficult than it looks, and if you don't believe me, try making something without a recipe. Even with recipes, you have to know the basic elements of flavors – you have to learn secrets like a little vinegar can make bitter greens less bitter and that dried cherries can make any savory dish delish.

And don't even get me started on the basics like laundry, ironing, and cleaning. There are systems and rules to doing all these well – and they are not obvious, nor are they being taught anywhere. Do you know the proper way to sew a button or iron a shirt or bleach your whites? 'Cause I sure as hell didn't – and none of my friends did, either. In fact, I had to buy myself an old Home Economics textbook at a thrift store just to learn stuff like how to care for a sick person, simple color theory, and that linen is lighter than cotton and should be ironed inside out or the surface will get shiny.

As I started experimenting with different domestic tasks, I discovered which ones I liked (cooking, woodwork, knitting) and which ones I hated (ironing, laundry, dusting). I put off impractical tasks like growing herbs and sewing for when I have more time and don't live in New York City. And I learned that my favorite thing to do in the whole world is to grocery shop – I love to be around food, to smell it, touch it, and think about all the delicious things I'm going to create. I also learned that I am a crafty voyeur; I love shows like *This Old House* and I adore all cooking shows (although my absolute favorite celebrity chef is Julia Child). The history of domesticity, cooking, and home furnishings interests me no end, and I can spend days behind a book, doing zero actual crafting. In fact, I have been known to read more recipes than actually cook meals, but I figure I can just chalk it up to research.

Yet, even with all this joyous creativity, I still feel conflicted. After all, our culture continues to thumb its nose at domesticity. When I make a beautiful meal for a couple of friends – something that I have researched, read, shopped for and prepared – we enjoy it, and then it's gone. It isn't important in the economic system – I don't make money from it and it doesn't have the cultural capital of, say, writing a book or being a broke artist. Over the years, as I continue to cook, my meals will get better, but that doesn't mean that I will be compensated in any other way than a thank you. I worry that I will cease to be interesting, that I will get passed over.

More problematic for me is that it isn't just our culture at large that dismisses domesticity, but feminism itself. When Betty Friedan searched for the cause of the "problem that has no name" affecting middle-class white suburban housewives in 1963, she found it in housecleaning and caring for a family. According to Friedan, all things domestic were actually the root of women's problems and depression. As I read through the book now, almost forty years later, I have a lot sympathy and admiration for Friedan, but I think her analysis is off. It isn't the activity of housework that is so stifling (although it may be to some), but rather it is the fact that few other alternatives were available to women, and, perhaps even more importantly, that women's work has always been devalued.

From cooking to cleaning to caring for children, our culture thinks of typical historical women's work as stupid, simple, suffocating – things that can easily be replaced by mechanization, crappy fast food, hiring

The American Woman's Home, Catherine Beecher

The authors of this volume, while they sympathize with every honest effort to relieve the disabilities and sufferings of their sex, are confident that the chief cause of those evils is the fact that the honor and duties of the family state are not duly appreciated, that women are not trained for these duties as men are trained for their trades and professions, and that, as the consequence, family labor is poorly done, poorly paid, and regarded as menial and disgraceful.

To be the nurse of young children, a cook, a housemaid, is regarded as the lowest and last resort of poverty, and one which no woman of culture and position can assume without loss of caste and respectability.

It is the aim of this volume to elevate both the honor and the remuneration of all the employments that sustain the many difficult and sacred duties of the family state, and thus to render each department of woman's true profession as much desired and respected as are the most honored professions of men.

From *The American Woman's Home; or Principles of Domestic Science*, Catherine Beecher, New York: J.B. Ford, 1869, introduction poor women, and neglect. Even feminists aren't free from this type of thinking; we have internalized patriarchal thinking to such a degree that often we try very hard to distance ourselves from women and womanhood. And although we may not even be aware of it, we have bought into the lie that women are inferior, so we set out to be like men: important, big, self-centered, and good at getting ours.

But what if, instead, we thought of domesticity as our history, and therefore an important part of who we are? Don't get me wrong – I'm not suggesting that all women quit their jobs, get married, and stay at home in the suburbs. I don't think that every woman should love domestic things. But I am suggesting that we give "women's work" its props as something viable, interesting, and important – like knowing how to play an instrument or speaking a foreign language. And what about the skill, love, and creativity that goes into raising children and running a proper home? It's not stupid, it's not simple; it's damn hard work that we as a feminist movement need to start respecting.

. . .

Six months ago, I did something that I never thought I would do in a million years: I got married. The plan was that after the ceremony, my husband and I would live in separate apartments, the way we always had. I just couldn't bring myself to cohabitate with a man; I was afraid of losing my identity and having to "look after" him. In the end, after many conversations, we decided to take the plunge anyway.

It's been difficult, but we seem to have established a pretty equitable system. I do most of the cooking and grocery shopping, he does all the ironing, mending of clothes, and dish washing, and we split all other tasks right down the middle. We fight over stuff like vacuuming and whether we should order in again. But we also have a blast together: we painted our apartment sky blue, avocado green, café con leche, and bright pink, built tons of shelves, and furnished it with the finest thrift store finds to create a look that can only be described as post-French-neo-colonialism.

So here I am at age 30. I co-run a household with a man I am married to, work part-time as a Web producer for public radio, run a Web zine (www.getcrafty.com), knit scarves, cook like a demon, have a community of friends, belong to an artist's support group, and take care of a grouchy but lovable dog. My life is much more domestic and varied and interesting and creative and pastiche-like than I ever imagined. I didn't become a feminist artist like Judy Chicago or a bohemian writer like Anaïs Nin. Instead, I practice my feminism in the way that I live my life, the clothes I wear, the home I live in, the food I eat, and the company I keep. It's not totally glamorous, but it's fulfilling. Ironically, my experience is the exact opposite of that of the women who built *Womanhouse* and those who Betty Friedan wrote about in *The Feminine Mystique*. For me, embracing domesticity and women's work has freed me from depression and a feeling that life is meaningless. Best of all, I now have simple ways to give myself and others the gift of living well.

Jean Railla, "A Broom of One's Own," *Bust*, Spring 2001, pp. 41–5.

JANICE A. RADWAY,
FROM *READING THE ROMANCE*

There are few genres of literature thought to be more demeaning to woman than romance fiction. In page after bodice-heaving page, women are told that without a man they are somehow incomplete (see sidebar). Yet these novels are incredibly popular with women; are they willfully participating in their own oppression? In her book Reading the Romance, feminist scholar Janice Radway answers this question by asking another simple, yet surprisingly neglected, question: What do the readers themselves think about the romances they read? She finds that from these tales of ostensible subjugation, women draw out stories of reassurance and empowerment. The Midwestern working class women from "Smithton" that Radway studies identify with the strengths of the heroine, particularly her ability to move the male object of her desire out of the masculine world of money and power and into their world of care and nurturance. Through this re-reading, Radway argues, readers find a way to appreciate their own lives and dreams, a recognition they often don't find from their husbands and the male-centered world outside. But Radway also raises an important question about acts of cultural resistance like re-reading: finding empowerment in the pages of fantasy fiction, do these romance readers act upon it in their everyday life?

On first discussing romances with the Smithton readers, I was struck by the fact that individual books were inevitably registered in their memories as the stories of particular *women*. When specific titles were volunteered to illustrate a point, they were always linked with a capsule plot summary beginning with a statement about the heroine and continuing with the principal events of what was, to the speaker, her tale. Because of her perceived centrality in the romance and because of the admitted tendency to project themselves into the heroine's being, the Smithton readers hold particularly exacting expectations about the qualities the heroine should have and the kinds of behavior she should exhibit.

So consistent are their feelings about heroines, in fact, that no discrepancy appears between their orally reported preferences and those acknowledged on the anonymous questionnaires. Dot's customers inevitably responded to my query about the characteristics of a good heroine with the statement that she must have three traits: intelligence, a sense of humor, and independence. On the questionnaire, nineteen (45 percent) of the women selected intelligence from a list of nine other possibilities as the characteristic they *most* liked to see in a heroine, while nine (21 percent) picked a sense of humor. The only other traits to score significantly were femininity and independence. When the group's rankings are totaled, intelligence joins independence and a sense of humor as the three traits that score significantly higher than all of the others. It seems especially important to note that three-fourths of the group selected intelligence (79 percent) and a sense of humor (74 percent) at least once, whereas independence was chosen by almost half (48 percent) of the Smithton women. Femininity, with its connotation of demure deference was, however, still a choice of fourteen of the Smithton readers.

It may seem curious to insist here on the importance of the heroine's intelligence and independence to the Smithton women when so many "objective" students of the genre have commented on her typical passivity and quivering helplessness.[1] This harsh analytical judgment, however, is often founded on an assessment of the heroine's ultimate success in solving a mystery, making her desires known, or in refusing to be cowed by the hero. The *results* of her actions, in short, are always measured on a scale whose highest value is accorded the autonomous woman capable of accomplishing productive work in a nondomestic sphere. While the romantic heroine understandably compares badly with this ideal woman, it is important to note that neither Dot nor her readers find such an ideal attractive nor do they scrutinize and evaluate the heroine's success in effecting change or getting others to do what she wants in order to assess her character. The heroine's personality is, instead, inevitably and securely established for them at the beginning of the tale through a series of simple observations about her abilities, talents, and career choice. Because the Smithton women accept those assertions at face value, they search no further for incidents that might comment on or revise her early portrayal. Not only do they believe in the heroine's honest desire to take care of herself, but they also believe in the mimetic accuracy of the extenuating circumstances that always intervene to thwart her intended actions. The Smithton women are, in sum, significantly more inclined than their feminist critics to recognize the inevitability and reality of male power and the force of social convention to circumscribe a woman's ability to act in her own interests. It must also be said that they are comfortable with the belief that a woman should be willing to sacrifice extreme self-interest for a long-term relationship where mutually agreed-upon goals take precedence over selfish desire.

The point I want to make here is that when analysis proceeds from within the belief system actually brought to bear upon a text by its readers, the analytical interpretation of the meaning of a character's behavior is more likely to coincide with that meaning as it is constructed and understood by the readers themselves. Thus the account offered to explain the desire to experience this particular fantasy is also more likely to approximate the motives that actually initiate the readers' decisions to pick up a romance. While the romantic heroine may appear foolish, dependent, and even pathetic to a woman who has already accepted as given the equality of male and female abilities, she appears courageous, and even valiant, to another still unsure that such equality is a fact or that she herself might want to assent to it.

The Smithton women seem to be struggling simultaneously with the promise and threat of the women's movement as well as with their culture's now doubled capacity to belittle the intelligence and activities of "the ordinary housewife." Therefore, while they are still very conservative and likely to admit the rightness of traditional relations between men and women, at the same time they are angered by men who continue to make light of "woman's work" as well as by "women's libbers" whom they accuse of dismissing mothers and housewives as ignorant, inactive, and unimportant. Their desire to believe that the romantic heroine is as intelligent and independent as she is asserted to be even though she is also shown to be vulnerable and most interested in being loved is born of their apparently unconscious desire to realize some of

A Day for Dreaming, Jean Ferris

They wandered down the beach, stopping when something caught their fancy – the cry of a gull, a crab sidling into the water, a high-breaking wave.

"I never saw a more heavenly place," Rosie told him.

"Yes," Raider answered. "This seems the perfect spot to convalesce, or plan a battle strategy or conduct a love affair. But a dull place to live forever. I'm afraid I need more action in my life."

Rosie tried to wrench her thoughts back to natural beauties, but it was Raider's firm, sun-gilt chest innocently exposed by his open shirt that her mind kept turning to. Why couldn't she have been rescued from the *Lightning* by a snaggle-toothed barbarian instead of this beautiful, complex, unattainable man?

from *Song of the Sea*, New York: American Dreams, 1996

the benefits of feminism within traditional institutions and relationships – hence, the high value attached to the simple *assertion* of the heroine's special abilities. With a few simple statements rather than with truly threatening action on the part of the heroine, the romance author demonstrates for the typical reader the compatibility of a changed sense of the female self and an unchanged social arrangement. In the utopia of romance fiction, "independence" and a secure individual "identity" are never compromised by the paternalistic care and protection of the male.

I would like to quote here from a lengthy and exuberant discussion carried on in one of the interviews when I asked Dot, her daughter, Kit, and Ann to describe the "ideal" romantic heroine. Rather than list a series of abstract traits as others generally did, these women launched into a fifteen-minute, communally produced plot summary of Elsie Lee's *The Diplomatic Lover* (1971). The delight with which they described the heroine and what they perceived to be her constant control of her situation is as good an example as any of the desire they share with feminists to believe in the female sex's strength and capabilities and in themselves as well. When I asked them why they liked the book so much after they told me they had xeroxed the text for their own use (the book is now out of print), the extended reply began in the following way:

Dot: It's just classic.
Ann: She *decides* that she wants to lose her virginity and picks *him*.
Kit: Well, he's really nice looking; he's a movie star and he's . . .
Dot: Well, the thing is, actually, because she is in a modern workaday world. She's in Washington, DC, in the diplomatic corps.
Kit: And *she* makes the decision, you know.
Dot: And she's the only one [in the diplomatic community] who's a virgin and her name is Nanny.
Ann: Yes.
Dot: And they call her Nanny-No-No because she's always saying no, no, no!
Ann: She knows, she's read all the textbooks; but she's just never found anyone that set her blood to boiling.
Dot: And she's known him for years.
Ann: But he walks into the room at this one party and all of a sudden . . .
Kit: She makes the decision! It's her birthday.
Ann: She mentally licks her chops.
Kit: She's twenty-three. She decides, "Well, this is it!"
Ann: Yes.

Dot: But you know it's not distasteful. There's nothing . . . it was unusual.
Kit: It was very intimate.
Dot: It's not bold.[2]

In the midst of recounting the rest of the tale, they proudly exclaimed that Nanny "spoke six languages," was "a really good artist," and "did not want to marry him even though she was pregnant" because she believed he was an "elegant tomcat" and would not be faithful to her. These untraditional skills and unconventional attitudes are obviously not seen as fulfilling or quite proper by Lee herself because they are legitimated and rendered acceptable at the novel's conclusion when the hero convinces Nanny of his love, refuses to live without her, and promises to take care of her in the future. Here is the group's recitation of this moment:

Dot: He starts stalking her and this is visually . . .
Kit: It's hysterical.
Dot: You can see it.
Kit: She's backin' off.
Dot: She's trying to get to the stairway to get to her room.
Kit: And make a mad dash.
Ann: She's what they call a "petite pocket Venus type."
Dot: Yes, and he's stalking her and she's backing away and saying, "No, I
    won't marry you!"
Ann: "I ain't going!"
Kit: "No, just forget that!"
Dot: "No, I don't need you!"
Ann: And he says "I'll camp on your doorstep; I'll picket; unfair to", you
    know . . .

As in all romances, female defiance is finally rendered ineffectual and child-like as well as unnecessary by Lee's conclusion. Nonetheless, if we are to understand the full meaning of the story for these women, it is essential to recognize that their temporary reveling in her intelligence, independence, self-sufficiency, and initiative is as important to their experiencing of the book as the fact of her final capture by a man who admits that he needs her. Indeed, after recounting the resolution of this tale, Dot, Kit, and Ann relived again her "seduction of him" by marveling over the moment "when she asks him, and he's drinking and he about chokes to death!"

In novels like *The Diplomatic Lover,* which the Smithton women like best, the happy ending restores the status quo in gender relations when the hero enfolds the heroine protectively in his arms. That ending, however, can also be interpreted as an occasion for the vicarious enjoyment of a woman's ultimate triumph. Dot's readers so interpret it because the heroine, they claim, maintains her integrity on her own terms by exacting a formal commitment from the hero and simultaneously provides for her own future in the only way acceptable to her culture.

The Smithton readers' interest in a strong but still traditional heroine is complemented by their desire to see that woman loved by a very special kind of hero. As noted earlier these women will read many romances they do not especially like, even when the hero mistreats the heroine, because the experience of the happy ending is more important to them than anything else and because it successfully explains away many individual incidents they do not condone. Nevertheless, they prefer to see the heroine desired, needed, and loved by a man who is strong and masculine, but equally capable of unusual tenderness, gentleness, and concern for her pleasure. In fact, when asked to rank ten male personality traits as to desirability, not one of the Smithton readers listed independence in first, second, or third place. Although this might be explained by suggesting that the women felt no need to single this characteristic out because they assumed that men are, by nature, independent, their interview comments suggest otherwise. Throughout their discussions of particular books, they repeatedly insisted that what they remembered and liked most about favorite novels was the skill with which the author described the hero's recognition of his own deep feelings for the heroine and his realization that he could not live without her. While the women want to feel that the heroine will be protected by the hero, they also seem to want to see her dependency balanced by its opposite, that is, by the hero's dependence on her. In this context, the Smithton women's constant emphasis on the importance of mutuality in love makes enormous sense.

I do not want to suggest here that male protectiveness and strength are not important elements in the romantic fantasy; they are. Remember, sixteen (38 percent) of the women indicated that they think a weak hero is one of the three most objectionable features in a romance. In addition, almost 25 percent of Dot's customers agreed that out of nine traits strength is the third most important in a hero. Still, neither strength nor protectiveness is considered as important as intelligence, gentleness, and an ability to laugh at life, all of which were placed significantly more often by the readers in one of the three top positions on the questionnaire.

However, because Dot and her customers rarely initiated discussion of the romantic hero and just as seldom volunteered opinions about specific male characters, it has been difficult to develop a complex picture of their ideal or of the motivation prompting its formation. Even when their responses are displayed in a graph, certain mysteries persist.

The principal difficulty involves the marked preference for an "intelligent" hero. Although it is hard to say why intelligence was ranked so high by the Smithton women, it is possible that the choice is both consistent with the high value they place on books, learning, and education and their own upward mobility as well as a way of reaffirming male excellence and agentivity without also automatically implying female inferiority. The word did appear in discussions of the ideal hero, but the women offered little that would explain its prominence in their questionnaire responses. A few oral comments seemed to hint at the existence of an expectation that an "intelligent" man would be more likely to appreciate and encourage the extraordinary abilities of the ideal heroine, but this link was not volunteered consistently enough to warrant its formulation as the motive behind the fantasy. Equally hard to explain is the emphasis on a sense of humor, although I suspect the interest in this trait masks a desire to see a hero who is up to a "verbal duel" with the heroine. Not only does this create the air of "lightness" so important to the Smithton women, but it also helps to show off the heroine's tart-tongued facility to advantage.

This vagueness about the actual content of the hero's personality persisted throughout many commentaries that tended to center instead on his ability to establish the proper relationship with the heroine. The Smithton women are less interested in the particularities of their heroes as individuals than in the roles the most desirable among them perform. Gentleness and tenderness figure often in their accounts of favorite novels not so much as character traits exhibited by particular men but as the distinguishing feature of the attention accorded the heroine by all good heroes in the outstanding novels. The focus never shifts for these readers away from the woman at the center of the romance. Moreover, men are rarely valued for their intrinsic characteristics but become remarkable by virtue of the special position they occupy vis-à-vis the heroine. The romantic fantasy is therefore not a fantasy about discovering a uniquely interesting life partner, but a ritual wish to be cared for, loved, and validated in a particular way.

In distinguishing the ideal romance from Rosemary Roger's "perversions," one of the five customers I interviewed at length wondered whether her editor had been male because, she reasoned, "it's a man's type book." When pressed to elaborate, she retorted, "because a man likes the sex in it, you know, Matt Helm and all that type." The distinction she sees here between sex and romance was continually employed by the Smithton women to differentiate pornography, which they associate with men, from their own interest in "insightful love," which they wish men could manage. As Joy said of the recent Harlequins, "all they worry about is sex – that's the first thing on their minds. They don't worry about anything else." She continued, "they don't need that; they need humor and love and caring." Similarly, in one of our final discussions, Dot also elaborated on the differences between pornography and romance and between men and women and, in doing so, identified in a wistful tone the particular characteristics she and her customers believe all men should possess:

> I've always thought that women are more insightful into men's psyches than men are into women's. Well, men just don't take the time. They just don't. And it's always been interesting to me that psychiatrists are probably . . . 85 to 90 percent of the psychiatrists in this country are men and I'm sure they know the book. I'm sure they know the textbook. But as far as insightful, I think that is one of the most rare commodities that there is . . . is an insightful man . . . I don't think men look deep. I think they take even a man at face value. Whatever they see – that's what the man is.

What the Smithton women are looking for in their search for the perfect romantic fantasy is a man who is capable of the same attentive observation and intuitive "understanding" that they believe women regularly accord to men . . . The fantasy generating the ideal romantic story thus fulfills two deeply felt needs that have been activated in women by early object-relations and cultural conditioning in patriarchal society. On the one hand, the story permits the reader to identify with the heroine at the moment of her greatest success, that is, when she secures the attention and recognition of her culture's most powerful and essential representative, a man. The happy ending is, at this level, a sign of a woman's attainment of legitimacy and personhood in a culture that locates both for her in the roles of lover, wife, and mother.

On the other hand, by emphasizing the intensity of the hero's uninterrupted gaze and the tenderness of his caress at the moment he encompasses his beloved in his still always "masculine" arms, the fantasy also evokes the memory of a period in the reader's life when she was the center of a profoundly nurturant individual's attention. Because this imaginative emotional regression is often denied women in ordinary existence because men have been prompted by the culture's asymmetrical conditioning to deny their own capacities for gentle nurturance, it becomes necessary to fulfill this never-ending need in other areas. Nancy Chodorow has suggested, in *The Reproduction of Mothering*, that one way for women to provide this essential sustenance for themselves is through the mothering of others. By taking care of a child in this intense emotional way and by identifying with her child, Chodorow reasons, a woman is able to nurture herself, albeit vicariously. However, Chodorow does not comment at any length about whether this vicarious care and attention prove a perfectly adequate substitute. The ideal romance, at least as it is conceived by the Smithton women, argues effectively that it is not. Its stress on the emotional bond between hero and heroine suggests that women still desire to be loved, cared for, and understood by an adult who is singularly capable of self-abnegating preoccupation with a loved one's needs . . .

By immersing themselves in the romantic fantasy, women vicariously fulfill their needs for nurturance by identifying with a heroine whose principal accomplishment, if it can even be called that, is her success at drawing the hero's attention to herself, at establishing herself as the object of his concern and the recipient of his care. Because the reader experiences that care vicariously, her need is assuaged only as long as she can displace it onto a fictional character. When that character's story is completed, when the book must be closed, the reader is forced to return to herself and to her real situation. Although she may feel temporarily revived, she has done nothing to alter her relations with others. More often than not, those relations remain unchanged and in returning to them a woman is once again expected and willing to employ her emotional resources for the care of others. If she is then not herself reconstituted by another, romance reading may suggest itself again as a reasonable compensatory solution. Therefore, the romance's short-lived therapeutic value, which is made both possible and necessary by a culture that creates needs in women that it cannot fulfill, is finally the cause of its repetitive consumption.

Janice A. Radway, *Reading the Romance: Women, Patriarchy, and Popular Literature*, Chapel Hill: University of North Carolina Press, 1984, pp. 77–85.

JOHN FISKE,
"SHOPPING FOR PLEASURE"

A woman's place is in the mall. There's a truth to this silly bumper-sticker aphorism. Unlike taverns or streets or meeting halls, stores are one of the few public spaces that have historically been open to unaccompanied women. And, as John Fiske argues in this selection from his popular volume *Reading the Popular*, it is in the store that women exert a sort of power, "the power of the consumer."

This power is used by women to carve out a space in which their pleasure, their desires, their knowledge, and their actions are deemed important, a status often denied in our patriarchal world. As such, Fiske deems shopping an act of cultural resistance. His analysis, however, neglects an important detail. Stores have traditionally provided a space for women, but they are not places created by women (cf. Railla). In shopping malls and department stores women's pleasure and desires are catered to, but only in so far as they serve the greater interest of the market. If shopping is a culture of women's resistance it is a strange one, one manufactured and managed by the – predominantly male – powers-that-be.

Malls, Power and Resistance

Shopping malls are cathedrals of consumption – a glib phrase that I regret the instant it slides off my pen. The metaphor of consumerism as a religion, in which commodities become the icons of worship and the rituals of exchanging money for goods become a secular equivalent of holy communion, is simply too glib to be helpful, and too attractive to those whose intentions, whether they be moral or political, are to expose the evils and limitations of bourgeois materialism. And yet the metaphor *is* both attractive and common precisely because it does convey and construct *a* knowledge of consumerism; it does point to one set of "truths," however carefully selected a set.

Truths compete in a political arena, and the truths that the consumerism-as-contemporary-religion strives to suppress are those that deny the difference between the tenor and vehicle of the metaphor. Metaphor always works within that tense area within which the forces of similarity and difference collide, and aligns itself with those of similarity. Metaphor constructs similarity out of difference, and when a metaphor becomes a cliché, as the shopping mall-cathedral one has, then a resisting reading must align itself with the differences rather than the similarities, for clichés become clichés only because of their centrality to common sense: the cliché helps to construct the commonality of common sense.

So, the differences: the religious congregation is powerless, led like sheep through the rituals and meanings, forced to "buy" the truth on offer, all the truth, not selective bits of it. Where the interests of the Authority on High differ from those of the Congregation down Low, the congregation has no power to negotiate, to discriminate: all accommodations are made by the powerless, subjugated to the great truth. In the US marketplace, 90 percent of new products fail to find sufficient buyers to survive,[1] despite advertising, promotions, and all the persuasive techniques of the priests of consumption. In Australia, Sinclair[2] puts the new product failure rate at 80 percent – such statistics are obviously best-guesstimates: what matters is that the failure rate is high. The power of consumer discrimination evidenced here has no equivalent in the congregation: no religion could tolerate a rejection rate of 80 or 90 percent of what it has to offer.

Religion may act as a helpful metaphor when our aim is to investigate the power of consumerism; when, however, our focus shifts to the power of the consumer, it is counter-productive. Shopping malls and the cultural practices, the variety of shoppings that take place within them, are key arenas of struggle, at both economic and ideological levels, between those with the power of ideological practice (Althusser), hegemony (Gramsci), or strategy (de Certeau) and those whose construction as subjects in ideology is never complete, whose resistances mean that hegemony can never finally relax in victory, and whose tactics inflict a running series of wounds upon the strategic power. Shopping is the crisis of consumerism: it is where the art and tricks of the weak can inflict most damage on, and exert most power over, the strategic interests of the powerful. The shopping mall that is seen as the terrain of guerrilla warfare looks quite different from the one constructed by the metaphor of religion.

. . .

Consuming Women

Bowlby[3] takes as a premise "Women shop." Within this condensed truism, she finds a number of problems to do with the socially produced definitions of both women and shopping and with the connections between the two. While pondering some of these problems, I was browsing through a shop (where else?) selling cards and gifts. Three items took my eye. One was a bumper sticker proclaiming "When the going gets tough, the tough go shopping"; the second was a birthday card that said, "Happy Birthday to a guy who's sensitive, intelligent, and fun to be with – if you liked to shop you'd be perfect"; the third was a card designed for no specific occasion whose front cover showed a stylish, modern young woman and the words "Work to Live, Live to Love, and Love to Shop so you see . . ." the dots led to the inside and the words "if I can buy enough things I'll never have to work at love again."

These slogans are all commodities to be bought, and while from one perspective they may be yet more evidence of the power of consumerism to invade and take over our most personal lives in that they are seducing us to abrogate our ability to make our own utterances to a commercially motivated producer – the ultimate incorporation – we must recognize that these are not only commodities in the financial economy but also texts in the cultural economy. The meanings that are exchanged are in no way determined by the exchange of money at the cash register. Culturally all three are operating, with different emphases, in two semantic areas – those of gender difference and work versus leisure – and are questioning the distribution of power and values within them.

Each slogan is a feminine utterance, and each utterance depends for its effect upon its foregrounded difference from patriarchal norms. The bumper sticker sets its user apart as different form the "normal" (i.e., masculine) user of the saying's normal form – "When the going gets tough, the tough get going" – so as to distance her from its competitive masculinity (it is used typically to motivate sportsmen, soldiers, and, by extension, businessmen). In so doing, it manages simultaneously to mock such masculine power and to transfer it to a female practice, so that success in shopping becomes as much a source of power as success in sport, war, or business. Shopping entails achievement against a powerful oppositional force (that of capital) and the successful shopper is properly "tough." The user of such a slogan would pronounce "Women shop" in a quite different tone of voice from that used by, for instance, a dismissive patriarch. Shopping is seen as an oppositional, competitive act, and as such as a source of achievement, self-esteem, and power.

The uses of the message's masculine original deny the difference between work and leisure: masculinity is appropriately and equally achieved in sport, war, and work, and conflates these into the single category of the public domain, which it colonizes for the masculine, implicitly leaving the domestic or private for the feminine. Its feminine appropriation, then, speaks against the confinement of femininity to the domains of nonwork, nonpublic, and the "meaning" of the household, the meaning of the domestic, as the place of leisure, relaxation, and privacy – all of which are patriarchal meanings in that they deny the social, economic, and political meanings of the unwaged labor of women in the house.

Opposite the card shop was one selling kitchen equipment; hanging prominently in the window was an apron (the sign of women's domestic slavery) bearing the slogan "Woman's place is in the mall." Of course, one reading of this positions women as mere consumers in patriarchal capitalism, but the slogan also opposes "mall" to "home," and offers up oppositional meanings – if "home" means for women domestic slavery and the site of subordination of women to the demands of patriarchal capitalism exerted through the structure of the nuclear family, then the mall becomes the site of all the opposite, liberational meanings. The mall is where women can be public, empowered, and free, and can occupy roles other than those demanded by the nuclear family . . .

But my attention has wandered from the greeting cards. Both of the cards described above link shopping and romantic love as practices in which women excel and men are deficient. Even the "sensitive, intelligent" (i.e., nonjock) male recipient of the birthday card is incapable of understanding shopping. And for the other card, shopping has become, defiantly, the way to solve the problems faced by women in both work and love in a culture that patriarchally attempts to organize both in the interests of men. The conclusion, "If I can buy enough things I'll never have to work at love again," is nonsensical; it deliberately uses the logic of patriarchal capitalism to come to a nonsensical conclusion, the pleasure of which lies in exposing the nonsense for women of the dominant (i.e., patriarchal, capitalist) sense sof commodities, work, and love.

The connection made by the two cards between shopping and romantic love may, at first sight, seem odd. But as capitalism developed throughout the nineteenth century it produced and naturalized first the nuclear family as the foundation social unit, and second a new and specific role for women within this unit and thus within the social formation at large. The woman became the domestic manager of both the economic and emotional resources of the family. The romance genre developed as a form of emotional training of women for their wifely role within the capitalist nuclear family. This development of the feminine as the sensitive, emotional, romantic gender was a direct product of the capitalist economy, so there are clear historical reasons for the interlinking of the romantic and the economic within the definition of the feminine that we have inherited from the nineteenth century.

The popular TV gameshow *The New Price Is Right* shares many characteristics with the slogans on the cards and bumper sticker. Most obviously it takes women's skills as household managers, their knowledge of commodity prices, and their ability to assess relative values, and gives to them the power and public visibility that patriarchy more normally reserves for the masculine. These skills and knowledges are taken out of the devalued feminine sphere of the domestic, and displayed, like masculine skills, in public, on a studio set before an enthusiastic studio audience and millions of TV viewers. In "normal" life, deploying these skills meets with little acclaim or self-esteem – the woman is expected to be a good household manager and all too frequently her role is noticed only when she is deemed to have failed in it. On *The New Price Is Right*, however, her skills and successes are not just acclaimed, but receive excessive applause and approbation from the excited studio audience. The excess provides a carnivalesque inversion of the more normal silence with which such skills are met in everyday life. Such silence is, of course, a means of subjugation, a form of discipline exerted by patriarchy over the feminine; their excessively noisy recognition is thus a moment of licensed liberation from the normal oppression, and women's pleasure in it derives from a recognition that such skills and knowledges can produce positive values despite their devaluation in the patriarchal everyday. *The New Price Is Right* and "When the going gets tough, the tough go shopping" are both cultural resources that can be used to speak and assert the feminine within and against a patriarchal "normality." Similarly, the inadequacy of the sensitive, intelligent birthday boy when it comes to shopping would debar him from success on *The New Price Is Right*.

Successful contestants on the show receive expensive commodities or cash as their prizes. In another carnivalesque and therefore political inversion, the woman's skills are rewarded not by spending less of the family money (i.e., that earned by the man), but by money or goods for *her*. Feminine skills do not just *husband* (*sic*) masculine earnings and thus benefit the family, but actually produce rewards for the women. Similarly, in the "live" versions of this and other games sometimes played in shopping malls, the entry "ticket" is typically a receipt from one of the shops in the mall. The proof of having spent opens up the chance of winning. The receipt as money is a carnivalesque inversion of economic subjugation.

The deep structure of values that underlies patriarchal capitalism now needs to be extended to include earning as typically masculine, and, therefore, spending as typically feminine. So it is not surprising that such a society addresses women as consumers and men as producers. We may summarize the value structure like this:

The Masculine	*The Feminine*
Public	Private (domestic and subjective)
Work	Leisure
Earning	Spending
Production	Consumption
Empowered	Disempowered
Freedom	Slavery

Bowlby makes some interesting points about how shopping enables women to cross the boundary between the public and the private. In her history of the Paris store Bon Marché and its origins at the end of the last century, Bowlby notes that the "diaries" the store gave to its customers as a form of promotion contained detailed information about how to reach the store by public transport:

> That this should have been practically available to the bourgeois lady marks a significant break with the past: department stores were in fact the first public places — other than churches or cathedrals — which were considered respectable for her to visit without a male companion. But this also signified, at another level, stepping out from domestic bounds.[4]

The value to women of a public space to which they had legitimate and safe access is not confined to the late nineteenth century. Ferrier[5] makes a similar point about contemporary malls:

> For women there may be a sense of empowerment from their competency in shopping operations, their familiarity with the terrain and with what they can get out of it. The space is designed to facilitate their shopping practices, and in our built environment there are few places designed for women. The shopping-town offers public conveniences, free buses, parking, toilets, entertainment, free samples, competitions. In the shoppingtown, women have access to public space without the stigma or threat of the street.[6]

She goes on to associate the freedom malls offer women to reject the gendered opposition of public versus domestic with the equal opportunities to reject the gendered opposition between work and leisure, and the economic one of for sale (i.e., public) versus bought (i.e., private):

> The shoppingtown, with its carnival atmosphere, seems set to collapse the distinction between work and leisure . . . The consumer is allowed to wander in and out of private space to look at, handle and try out products that she does not own. In a department store it is possible to wander through privately owned space, holding or wearing someone else's property as if it were your own, without asking to do so, often without even having to go through the usual social intercourse appropriate to being a guest in someone's place. Boundaries between public and private become ambiguous.[7]

Women can find sources of empowerment both in "their" side of the structured values that patriarchy has provided for them (see above) and in their ability to escape the structure itself. Similarly, Bowlby finds evidence that spending the "man's" money can be a resisting act within the politics of marriage. She quotes a typical piece of advice given to a congressman's wife by Elizabeth Cady Stanton in her lectures in the 1850s:

> Go out and buy a new stove! Buy what you need! Buy while he's in Washington! When he returns and flies into a rage, you sit in a corner and weep. That

will soften him! Then, when he tastes his food from the new stove, he will know you did the wise thing. When he sees you so much fresher, happier in your new kitchen, he will be delighted and the bills will be paid. I repeat – GO OUT AND BUY!

Bowlby comments:

> Significantly, the injunction to buy comes from woman to woman, not from a man, and involves first bypassing and then mollifying a male authority. To "go out" and buy invokes a relative emancipation in women's active role as consumers.[8]

This is an example of de Certeau's[9] dictum that subordinated people "make do with what they have," and if the only economic power accorded to women is that of spending, then being a woman in patriarchy necessarily will involve feminine "tricks" that turn the system back on itself, that enable the weak to use the resources provided by the strong in their own interests, and to oppose the interests of those who provided the resources in the first place.

In the same way that language need not be used to maintain the social relations that produced it, so too commodities need not be used solely to support the economic system of capitalism, nor need the resources provided by patriarchy go solely to the support of the system. The conditions of production of any cultural system are not the same as, and do not predetermine, the conditions of its use or consumption.

. . .

So the greeting cards discussed earlier in this chapter are not merely silly. In "Work to Live, Live to Love, and Love to Shop," the female speaker recognizes that working, loving and shopping are all ways of forming social relations; the utterance inside the card – "If I can buy enough things I'll never have to work at love again" – recognizes that patriarchy's grip on working and love is tighter than its grip on shopping. Thus it is that buying commodities offers a sense of freedom, however irrational, from the work involved in working and loving under patriarchy: working and loving are conflated as chores from which shopping offers an escape.

John Fiske, *Reading the Popular*, Boston: Unwin Hyman, 1989, pp. 13–14, 18–24, 42.

SEVEN

COMMODITIES, CO-OPTATION, AND CULTURE JAMMING

"A commodity appears at first sight an extremely obvious, trivial thing. But its analysis brings out that it is a very strange thing, abounding in metaphysical subtleties and theological niceties." So Karl Marx describes the fantastic transformation that happens to everyday objects within a capitalist economy. When a thing becomes a commodity its value is no longer solely measured in usefulness, nor is its identity based in who produced it, instead these things are determined by the market. The result is that the products of human hands and minds "appear as autonomous figures endowed with a life of our own." This Marx called commodity fetishism.[1] When Marx wrote these words in 1867 the consumer market had already begun its historical expansion, extending past the traditional elite and opening up to "the masses" across much of the globe. Food, clothes, art, entertainment, lifestyles – all became things to be bought and sold. Where profit was to be made, seemingly anything could be made profitable, culture included. As a result the nature of culture changed. To whatever shapes and meanings it had held before it added a new, powerful and frequently overwhelming identity: that of a commodity. This commodification of culture is the subject of the essays below. It is an important topic as it raises a serious question for us, for how can culture be used as a means of resistance against the dominant capitalist system now that it has been transformed into the very building block of consumer capitalism?

THEODOR W. ADORNO, "ON THE FETISH-CHARACTER IN MUSIC AND THE REGRESSION OF LISTENING"

Theodor Adorno is the court pessimist – or perhaps realist – of cultural resistance. In this dense essay, reprinted here in full, this best known member of the Frankfurt School (cf. Benjamin) warns of the effect of capitalism upon culture.

Adorno begins by reminding us that music was once considered rebellious: Plato banishes music from his totalitarian Republic for stirring up the masses, and popular music at one time challenged the elite's monopoly on cultural production. But today music, high and low, is a commodity: fragmented, simplified, popularized, wrapped in packages of respectability or rebellion, all the better to be bought and sold. Far from challenging the system, most music is part of the system. Blind to its degradation, however, we invest this culture with our passion and our politics, unaware that this "pseudo-activity" only compounds our alienation. Thus we have all become like Adorno's jazz fan who "pictures himself as the individualist who whistles at the world. But what he whistles is its melody." The only hope for cultural resistance, Adorno believes, lies within the avant-garde, specifically the patently unpopular a-tonal music he enjoyed and later composed. Adorno is notorious for his own vulgar and fragmentary understanding of popular culture. He is no doubt mistaken about some things, the one dimensionality of jazz for instance, but to dismiss his insights into what culture becomes within consumer capitalism is to ignore the fundamental conditions of cultural production today.

Complaints about the decline of musical taste begin only a little later than mankind's twofold discovery, on the threshold of historical time, that music represents at once the immediate manifestation of impulse and the locus of its taming. It stirs up the dance of the Maenads and sounds from Pan's bewitching flute, but it also rings out from the Orphic lyre, around which the visions of violence range themselves, pacified. Whenever their peace seems to be disturbed by bacchantic agitation, there is talk of the decline of taste. But if the disciplining function of music has been handed down since Greek philosophy as a major good, then certainly the pressure to be permitted to obey musically, as elsewhere, is today more general than ever. Just as the current musical consciousness of the masses can scarcely be called Dionysian, so its latest changes have nothing to do with taste. The concept of taste is itself outmoded. Responsible art adjusts itself to criteria which approximate judgments: the harmonious and the inharmonious, the correct and the incorrect. But otherwise, no more choices are made; the question is no longer put, and no one demands the subjective justification of the conventions. The very existence of the subject who could verify such taste has become as questionable as has, at the opposite pole, the right to a freedom of choice which empirically, in any case, no one any longer exercises. If one seeks to find out who "likes" a commercial piece, one cannot voice the suspicion that liking and disliking are inappropriate to the situation, even if the person questioned clothes his reaction in those words. The familiarity of the piece is a surrogate for the quality ascribed to it. To like it is almost the same thing as to recognize it. An approach in terms of value judgments has become a fiction for the person who finds himself hemmed in by standardized musical goods. He can neither escape impotence nor decide between the offerings where everything is so completely identical that preference in fact depends merely on biographical details or on the situation in which things are heard. The categories of autonomously oriented art have no applicability to the contemporary reception of music; not even for that of the serious music, domesticated under the barbarous name of classical so as to enable one to turn away from it again in comfort. If it is objected that specifically light music and everything intended for consumption have in any case never been experienced in terms of those categories, that must certainly be conceded. Nevertheless, such music is also affected by the change in that the entertainment, the pleasure, the enjoyment it promises, is given only to be simultaneously denied. In one of his essays, Aldous Huxley has raised the question of who, in a place of amusement, is really being amused. With the same justice, it can be asked whom music for entertainment still entertains. Rather, it seems to complement the reduction of people to silence, the dying out of speech as expression, the inability to communicate at all. It inhabits the pockets of silence that develop between people molded by anxiety, work, and undemanding docility. Everywhere it takes over, unnoticed, the deadly sad role that fell to it in the time and the specific situation of the silent films. It is perceived purely as background. If nobody can any longer speak, then certainly nobody can any longer listen. An American specialist in radio advertising, who indeed prefers to make use of the musical medium, has expressed skepticism as to the value of this advertising, because people have learned to deny their attention to what they are hearing even while listening to it. His observation is questionable with respect to the advertising value of music. But it tends to be right in terms of the reception of the music itself.

In the conventional complaints about declining taste, certain motifs constantly recur. There is no lack of pouting and sentimental comments assessing the current musical condition of the masses as one of "degeneration." The most tenacious of these motifs is that of sensuality, which allegedly enfeebles and incapacitates heroic behavior. This complaint can already be found in Book III of Plato's *Republic* in which he bans "the harmonies expressive of sorrow" as well as the "soft" harmonies "suitable for drinking," without its being clear to this day why the philosopher ascribes these characteristics to the mixed Lydian, Lydian, bass Lydian and Ionian modes. In the Platonic state, the majority of later Western music, which corresponds to the Ionian, would have been tabooed. The flute and the "panharmonic" stringed instruments also fall under the ban. The only modes to be left are "warlike, to sound the note or accent which a brave man utters in the hour of danger and stern resolve, or when he faces injury, defeat or death, or any other misfortune, with the same steadfast endurance." Plato's *Republic* is not the utopia it is called by the official history of philosophy. It disciplines its citizens in terms of its existence and will to exist even in music, where the distinction made between soft and strong modes was by Plato's time already little more than a residue of the mustiest superstition. The Platonic irony reveals itself mischievously in jeering at the flute-player Marsyas, flayed by the sober-sided Apollo. Plato's ethical-musical program bears the character of an Attic purge in Spartan style. Other perennial themes of musical sermonizing are on the same level. Among the most prominent of these are the charge of superficiality and that of a "cult of personality." What is attacked is chiefly progress: social, essentially the specifically esthetic. Intertwined with the forbidden allurements are sensual gaiety and differentiating consciousness. The predominance of the person over collective compulsion in music marks the moment of subjective freedom which breaks through in later phases, while the profanation which frees it from its magic circle appears as superficiality. Thus, the lamented moments have entered into the great music of the West: sensory stimulation as the gate of entry into the harmonic and eventually the coloristic dimensions; the unbridled person as the bearer of expression and of the humanization of music itself; "superficiality" as a critique of the mute objectivity of forms, in the sense of Haydn's choice of the "gallant" in preference to the learned. Haydn's choice indeed, and not the recklessness of a singer with a golden throat or an instrumentalist of lip-smacking euphony. For those moments entered into great music and were transformed in it; but great music did not dissolve into them. In the multiplicity of stimulus and expression, its greatness is shown as a force for synthesis. Not only does the musical synthesis preserve the unity of appearance and protect it from falling apart into diffuse cullinary moments, but in such unity, in the relation of particular moments to an evolving whole, there is also preserved the image of a social condition in which above those particular moments of happiness would be more than mere appearance. Until the end of prehistory, the musical balance between partial stimulus and totality, between expression and synthesis, between the surface and the underlying, remains as unstable as the moments of balance between supply and demand in the capitalist economy. *The Magic Flute*, in which the utopia of the Enlightenment and the pleasure of a light opera comic song precisely coincide, is a moment by itself. After *The Magic Flute* it was never again possible to force serious and light music together.

But what are emancipated from formal law are no longer the productive impulses which rebelled against conventions. Impulse, subjectivity and profanation, the old adversaries of materialistic alienation, now succumb to it. In capitalist times, the traditional anti-mythological ferments of music conspire against freedom, as whose allies they were once proscribed. The representatives of the opposition to the authoritarian schema become witness to the authority of commercial success. The delight in the moment and the gay façade becomes an excuse for absolving the listener from the thought of the whole, whose claim is comprised in proper listening. The listener is converted, along his line of least resistance, into the acquiescent purchaser. No longer do the partial moments serve as a critique of that whole; instead, they suspend the critique which the successful esthetic totality exerts against the flawed one of society. The unitary synthesis is sacrificed to them; they no longer produce their own in place of the reified one, but show themselves complaisant to it. The isolated moments of enjoyment prove incompatible with the immanent constitution of the work of art, and whatever in the work goes beyond them to an essential perception is sacrificed to them. They are not bad in themselves but in their diversionary function. In the service of success they renounce that insubordinate character which was theirs. They conspire to come to terms with everything which the isolated moment can offer to an isolated individual who long ago ceased to be one. In isolation, the charms become dulled and furnish models of the familiar. Whoever devotes himself to them is as malicious as the Greek thinkers once were toward oriental sensuality. The seductive power of the charm survives only where the forces of denial are strongest: in the dissonance which rejects belief in the illusion of the existing harmony. The concept of the ascetic is itself dialectical in music. If asceticism once struck down the claims of the esthetic in a reactionary way, it has today become the sign of advanced art: not, to be sure, by an archaicizing parsimony of means in which deficiency and poverty are manifested, but by the strict exclusion of all culinary delights which seek to be consumed immediately for their own sake, as if in art the sensory were not the bearer of something intellectual which only shows itself in the whole rather than in isolated topical moments. Art records negatively just that possibility of happiness which the only partially positive anticipation of happiness ruinously confronts today. All "light" and pleasant art has become illusory and mendacious. What makes its appearance esthetically in the pleasure categories can no longer give pleasure, and the promise of happiness, once the definition of art, can no longer be found except where the mask has been torn from the countenance of false happiness. Enjoyment still retains a place only in the immediate bodily presence. Where it requires an esthetic appearance, it is illusory by esthetic standards and likewise cheats the pleasure-seeker out of itself. Only where its appearance is lacking is the faith in its possibility maintained.

The new phase of the musical consciousness of the masses is defined by displeasure in pleasure. It resembles the reaction to sport or advertising. The words "enjoyment of art" sound funny. If in nothing else, Schönberg's music resembles popular songs in refusing to be enjoyed. Whoever still delights in the beautiful passages of a Schubert quartet or even in the provocatively healthy fare of a Handel concerto grosso, ranks as a would-be guardian of culture among the butterfly collectors. What condemns him as an epicure is not perhaps "new." The power of the street ballad, the catchy tune and all the swarming forms of the banal has made itself felt since the beginning of the bourgeois era. Formerly, it attacked the cultural privilege of the ruling class. But today, when that power of the banal extends over the entire society, its function has changed. This change of function affects all music, not only light music, in whose realm it could comfortably enough be made innocuous. The diverse spheres of music must be thought of together. Their static separation, which certain caretakers of culture have ardently sought – the totalitarian radio was assigned to the task, on the one hand, of providing good entertainment and diversion, and on the other, of fostering the so-called cultural goods, as if there could still be good entertainment and as if the cultural goods were not, by their administration, transformed into evils – the neat parceling out of music's social field of force is illusionary.

Just as the history of serious music since Mozart as a flight from the banal reflects in reverse the outlines of light music, so today, in its key representatives, it gives an account of the ominous experiences which appear even in the unsuspecting innocence of light music. It would be just as easy to go in the other direction and conceal the break between the two spheres, assuming a continuum which permits a progressive education leading safely from commercial jazz and hit songs to cultural commodities. Cynical barbarism is no better than cultural dishonesty. What it accomplishes by disillusion on the higher level, it balances by the ideologies of primitivism and return to nature, with which it glorifies the musical underworld: an underworld which has long since ceased to assist the opposition of those excluded from culture to find expression, and now only lives on what is handed down to it from above.

The illusion of a social preference for light music as against serious is based on that passivity of the masses which makes the consumption of light music contradict the objective interest of those who consume it. It is claimed that they actually like light music and listen to the higher type only for reasons of social prestige, when acquaintance with the text of a single hit song suffices to reveal the sole function this object of honest approbation can perform. The unity of the two spheres of music is thus that of an unresolved contradiction. They do not hang together in such a way that the lower could serve as a sort of popular introduction to the higher, or that the higher could renew its lost collective strength by borrowing from the lower. The whole can not be put together by adding the separated halves, but in both there appear, however distantly, the changes of the whole, which only moves in contradiction. If the flight from the banal becomes definitive, if the marketability of the serious product shrinks to nothing, in consequence of its objective demands, then on the lower level the effect of the standardization of successes means it is no longer possible to succeed in an old style, but only in imitation as such. Between incomprehensibility and inescapability, there is no third way; the situation has polarized itself into extremes which actually meet. There is no room between them for the "individual." The latter's claims, wherever they still occur, are illusory, being copied from the standards. The liquidation of the individual is the real signature of the new musical situation.

If the two spheres of music are stirred up in the unity of their contradiction, the demarcation line between them varies. The advanced product has renounced consumption. The rest of serious music is delivered over to consumption for the price of its wages. It succumbs to commodity listening. The differences in the reception of official "classical" music and light music no longer have any real significance. They are only still manipulated for reasons of marketability. The hit song enthusiast must be reassured that his idols are not too elevated for him, just as the visitor to philharmonic concerts is confirmed in his status. The more industriously the trade erects wire fences between the musical provinces, the greater the suspicion that without these, the inhabitants could all too easily come to an understanding. Toscanini, like a second-rate orchestra leader, is called Maestro, if half ironically, and a hit song, "Music, maestro, please," had its success immediately after Toscanini was promoted to Marshal of the Air with the aid of the radio.

The world of the musical life, the composition business which extends peacefully from Irving Berlin and Walter Donaldson – "the world's best composer" – by way of Gershwin, Sibelius and Tchaikovsky to Schubert's B Minor Symphony, labeled *The Unfinished*, is one of fetishes. The star principle has become totalitarian. The reactions of the listeners appear to have no relation to the playing of the music. They have reference, rather, to the cumulative success which, for its part, cannot be thought of unalienated by the past spontaneities of listeners, but instead dates back to the command of publishers, sound film magnates and rulers of radio. Famous people are not the only stars. Works begin to take on the same role. A pantheon of best-sellers builds up. The programs shrink, and the shrinking process not only removes the moderately good, but the accepted classics themselves undergo a selection that has nothing to do with quality. In America, Beethoven's Fourth Symphony is among the rarities. This selection reproduces itself in a fatal circle: the most familiar is the most successful and is therefore played again and again and made still more familiar. The choice of the standard works is itself in terms of their "effectiveness" for programmatic fascination, in terms of the categories of success as determined by light music or permitted by the star conductors. The climaxes of Beethoven's Seventh Symphony are placed on the same level as the unspeakable horn melody from the slow movement of Tchaikovsky's Fifth. Melody comes to mean eight-beat symmetrical treble melody. This is catalogued as the composer's "idea" which one thinks he can put in his pocket and take home, just as it is ascribed to the composer as his basic property. The concept of the idea is far from appropriate to established classical music. Its thematic material, mostly dissected triads, does not at all belong to the author in the same specific sense as in a romantic song. Beethoven's greatness shows itself in the complete subordination of the accidentally private melodic elements to the form as a whole. This does not prevent all music, even Bach, who borrowed one of the most important themes of *The Well-Tempered Clavier,* from being examined in terms of the category of ideas, with musical larceny being hunted down with all the zeal of the belief in property, so that finally one music commentator could pin his success to the title of tune detective.

At its most passionate, musical fetishism takes possession of the public valuation of singing voices. Their sensuous magic is traditional as is the close relation between success and the person endowed with "material." But today it is forgotten that it is material. For musical vulgar materialists, it is synonymous to have a voice and to be a singer. In earlier epochs, technical virtuosity, at least, was demanded of singing stars, the castrati and prima donnas. Today, the material as such, destitute of any function, is celebrated. One need not even ask about capacity for musical performance. Even mechanical control of the instrument is no longer really expected. To legit-imate the fame of its owner, a voice need only be especially voluminous or especially high. If one dares even in conversation to question the decisive importance of the voice and to assert that it is just as possible to make beautiful music with a moderately good voice as it is on a moderately good piano, one will immediately find oneself faced with a situation of hostility and aversion whose emotional roots go far deeper than the occasion. Voices are holy properties like a national trademark. As if the voices wanted to revenge themselves for this, they begin to lose the sensuous magic in whose name they are merchandised. Most of them sound like imitations of those who have made it, even when they themselves have made it. All this reaches a climax of absurdity in the cult of the master violins. One promptly goes into raptures at the well announced sound of a Stradivarius or Amati, which only the ear of a specialist can tell from that of a good modern violin, forgetting in the process to listen to the composition and the execution, from which there is still something to be had. The more the modern technique of the violin bow progresses, the more it seems that the old instruments are treasured. If the moments of sensual pleasure in the idea, the voice, the instrument are made into fetishes and torn away from any functions which could give them meaning, they meet a response equally isolated, equally far from the meaning of the whole, and equally determined by success in the blind and irrational emotions which form the relationship to music into which those with no relationship enter. But these are the same relations as exist between the consumers of hit songs and the hit songs. Their only relation is to the completely alien, and the alien, as if cut off from the consciousness of the masses by a dense screen, is what seeks to speak for the silent. Where they react at all, it no longer makes any difference whether it is to Beethoven's Seventh Symphony or to a bikini.

The concept of musical fetishism cannot be psychologically derived. That "values" are consumed and draw feelings to themselves, without their specific qualities being reached by the consciousness of the consumer, is a later expression of their commodity character. For all contemporary musical life is dominated by the commodity form; the last pre-capitalist residues have been eliminated. Music, with all the attributes of the ethereal and sublime which are generously accorded it, serves in America today as an advertisement for commodities which one must acquire in order to be able to hear music. If the advertising function is carefully dimmed in the case of serious music, it always breaks through in the case of light music. The whole jazz business, with its free distribution of scores to bands, has abandoned the idea that actual performance promotes the sale of piano scores and phonograph records. Countless hit song texts praise the hit songs themselves, repeating their title in capital letters. What makes its appearance, like an idol, out of such masses of type is the exchange-value in which the quantum of possible enjoyment has disappeared. Marx defines the fetish-character of the commodity as the veneration of the thing made by oneself which, as exchange-value, simultaneously alienates itself from producer to consumer – "human beings."

> A commodity is therefore a mysterious thing, simply because in it the social character of men's labor appears to them as an objective character stamped upon the product of the labor; because the relation of the producers to the sum total of their own labor is presented to them as a social relation, existing not between themselves, but between the products of their labor.

This is the real secret of success. It is the mere reflection of what one pays in the market for the product. The consumer is really worshipping the money that he himself has paid for the ticket to the Toscanini concert. He has literally "made" the success which he reifies and accepts as an objective criterion, without recognizing himself in it. But he has not "made" it by liking the concert, but rather by buying the ticket. To be sure, exchange-value exerts its power in a special way in the realm of cultural goods. For in the world of commodities this realm appears to by exempted from the power of exchange, to be in an immediate relationship with the goods, and it is this appearance in turn which alone gives cultural goods their exchange-value. But they nevertheless simultaneously fall completely into the world of commodities, are produced for the market, and are aimed at the market. The appearance of immediacy is as strong as the compulsion of exchange-value is inexorable. The social compact harmonizes the contradiction. The appearance of immediacy takes possession of the mediated, exchange-value itself. If the commodity in general combines exchange-value and use-value, then the pure use-value, whose illusion the cultural goods must preserve in completely capitalist society, must be replaced by pure exchange-value, which precisely in its capacity as exchange-value deceptively takes over the function of use-value. The specific fetish-character of music lies in this *quid pro quo*. The feelings which go to the exchange-value create the appearance of immediacy at the same time as the absence of a relation to the object belies it. It has its basis in the abstract character of exchange-value. Every "psychological" aspect, every *ersatz* satisfaction, depends on such social substitution.

The change in the function of music involves the basic conditions of the relation between art and society. The more inexorably the principle of exchange-value destroys use-value for human beings, the more deeply does exchange-value disguise itself as the object of enjoyment. It has been asked what the cement is which still holds the world of commodities together. The answer is that this transfer of the use-value of consumption goods to their exchange-value contributes to a general order in which eventually every pleasure which emancipates itself from exchange-value takes on subversive features. The appearance of exchange-value in commodities has taken on a specific cohesive function. The woman who has money with which to buy is intoxicated by the act of buying. In American conventional speech, having a good time means being present at the enjoyment of others, which in its turn has as its only content being present. The auto religion makes all men brothers in the sacramental moment with the words: "That is a Rolls Royce," and in moments of intimacy, women attach greater importance to the hairdressers and cosmeticians than to the situation for the sake of which hairdressers and cosmeticians are employed. The relation to the irrelevant dutifully manifests its social essence. The couple out driving who spend their time identifying every passing car and being happy if they recognize the trademarks speeding by, the girl whose satisfaction consists solely in the fact that she and her boyfriend "look good," the expertise of the jazz enthusiast who legitimizes himself by having knowledge about what is in any case inescapable: all this operates according to the same command. Before the theological caprices of commodities, the consumers become temple slaves. Those who sacrifice themselves nowhere else can do so here, and here they are fully betrayed.

In the commodity fetishists of the new model, in the "sadomasochistic character," in those receptive to today's mass art, the same thing shows itself in many ways. The masochistic mass culture is the necessary manifestation of almighty production itself. When the feelings seize on exchange-value it is no mystical transubstantiation. It corresponds to the behavior of the prisoner who loves his cell because he has been left nothing else to love. The sacrifice of individuality, which accommodates itself to the regularity of the successful, the doing of what everybody does, follows from the basic fact that in broad areas the same thing is offered to everybody by the standardized production of consumption goods. But the commercial necessity of concealing this identity leads to the manipulation of taste and the official culture's pretense of individualism, which necessarily increases in proportion to the liquidation of the individual. Even in the realm of the superstructure, the appearance is not merely the concealment of the essence, but proceeds of necessity from the essence itself. The identical character of the goods which everyone must buy hides itself behind the rigor of the universally compulsory style. The fiction of the relation between supply and demand survives in the fictitiously individual nuances.

If the value of taste in the present situation is questioned, it is necessary to understand what taste is composed of in this situation. Acquiescence is rationalized as modesty, opposition to caprice and anarchy; musical analysis has today decayed as fundamentally as musical charm, and has its parody in the stubborn counting of beats. The picture is completed by accidental differentiation within the strict confines of the prescribed. But if the liquidated individual really makes the complete superficiality of the conventions passionately his own, then the golden age of taste has dawned at the very moment in which taste no longer exists. The works which are the basis of the fetishization and become cultural goods experience constitutional changes as a result. They become vulgarized. Irrelevant consumption destroys them. Not merely do the few things played again and again wear out, like the Sistine Madonna in the bedroom, but reification affects their internal structure. They are transformed into a conglomeration of irruptions which are impressed on the listeners by climax and repetition, while the organization of the whole makes no impression whatsoever.

The memorability of disconnected parts, thanks to climaxes and repetitions, has a precursor in great music itself, in the technique of late romantic compositions, especially those of Wagner. The more reified the music, the more romantic it sounds to alienated ears. Just in this way it becomes "property." A Beethoven symphony as a whole, spontaneously experienced, can never be appropriated. The man who in the subway triumphantly whistles loudly the theme of the final of Brahms' First is already primarily involved with its debris. But since the disintegration of the fetishes puts these themselves in danger and virtually assimilates them to hit songs, it produces a counter tendency in order to preserve their fetish-character. If the romanticizing of particulars eats away the body of the whole, the endangered substance is galvanically copper-plated. The climax which emphasizes the reified parts takes on the character of a magical ritual, in which all the mysteries of personality, inwardness, inspiration and spontaneity of reproduction, which have been eliminated from the work itself, are conjured up. Just because the disintegrating work renounces the moment of its spontaneity, this, just as stereotyped as the bits and pieces, is injected into it from the outside. In spite of all talk of new objectivity, the essential function of conformist performances is no longer the performance of the "pure" work but the presentation of the vulgarized one with a gesture which emphatically but impotently tries to hold the vulgarization at a distance.

Vulgarization and enchantment, hostile sisters, dwell together in the arrangements which have colonized large areas of music. The practice of arrangement extends to the most diverse dimensions. Sometimes it seizes on the time. It blatantly snatches the reified bits and pieces out of their context and sets them up as a potpourri. It destroys the multilevel unity of the whole work and brings forward only isolated popular passages. The minuet from Mozart's E-flat Major Symphony, played without the other movement, loses its symphonic cohesion and is turned by the performance into an artisan-type genre piece that has more to do with the "Stephanie Gavotte" than with the sort of classicism it is supposed to advertise.

Then there is the arrangement in coloristic terms. They arrange whatever they can get hold of, as long as the ukase of a famous interpreter does not forbid it. If in the field of light music the arrangers are the only trained musicians, they feel called on to jump around all the more unrestrainedly with cultural goods. All sorts of reasons are offered by them for instrumental arrangements. In the case of great orchestral works, it will reduce the cost, or the composers are accused of lacking technique in instrumentation. These reasons are lamentable pretexts. The argument of cheapness, which esthetically condemns itself, is disposed of by reference to the superfluity of orchestral means at the disposal of precisely those who most eagerly carry on the practice of arrangement, and by the fact that very often, as in instrumental arrangements of piano pieces, the arrangements turn out substantially dearer than performance in the original form. And finally, the belief that older music needs a coloristic freshening up presupposes an accidental character in the relation between color and line, such as could be assumed only as a result of the crudest ignorance of Vienna classicism and the so-eagerly arranged Schubert. Even if the real discovery of the coloristic dimension first took place in the era of Berlioz and Wagner, the coloristic parsimony of Haydn or Beethoven is of a piece with the predominance of the principle of construction over the melodic particular springing in brilliant colors out of the dynamic unity. Precisely in the context of such parsimony do the bassoon thirds at the beginning of the third *Leonore* overture or the oboe cadenza in the reprise of the first movement of the Fifth achieve a power which would be irretrievably lost in a multicolored sonority.

One must therefore assume that the motives for the practice of arranging are *sui generis*. Above all, arranging seeks to make the great distant sound, which always has aspects of the public and unprivate, assimilable. The tired businessman can clap arranged classics on the shoulder and fondle the progeny of their muse. It is a compulsion similar to that which requires radio favorites to insinuate themselves into the families of their listeners as uncles and aunts and pretend to a human proximity. Radical reification produces its own pretense of immediacy and intimacy. Contrariwise, the intimate is inflated and colored by arrangements precisely for being too spare. Because they were originally defined only as moments of the whole, the instants of sensory pleasure which emerge out of the decomposing unities are too weak even to produce the sensory stimulus demanded of them in fulfillment of their advertised role. The dressing up and puffing up of the individual erases the lineaments of protest, sketched out in the limitation of the individual to himself over and against the institution, just as in the reduction of the large-scale to the intimate, sight is lost of the totality in which bad individual immediacy was kept within bounds in great music. Instead of this, there develops a spurious balance which at every step betrays its falsity by its contradiction of the material. Schubert's *Serenade*, in the blown-up sound of the combination of strings and piano, with the silly excessive clarity of the imitative intermediate measures, is as nonsensical as if it had orginated in a girls' school. But neither does the prize song from *Meistersinger* sound any more serious when played by a string orchestra alone. In monochrome, it objectively loses the articulation which makes it viable in Wagner's score. But at the same time, it becomes quite viable for the listener, who no longer has to put the body of the song together from different colors, but can confidently give himself over to the single and uninterrupted treble melody. Here one can put one's hands on the antagonism to the audience into which works regarded as classic fall today. But one may suspect that the darkest secret of arrangement is the compulsion not to leave anything as it is, but to lay hands on anything that crosses one's path, a compulsion that grows greater the less the fundamental characteristics of what exists lend themselves to being meddled with. The total social grasp confirms its power and mastery by the stamp which is impressed on anything that falls into its machinery. But this affirmation is likewise destructive. Contemporary listeners would always prefer to destroy what they hold in blind respect, and their pseudoactivity is already prepared and prescribed by the production.

The practice of arrangement comes from salon music. It is the practice of refined entertainment which borrows its pretensions from the *niveau* of cultural goods, but transforms these into entertainment material of the type of hit songs. Such entertainment, formerly reserved as an accompaniment to people's humming, today spreads over the whole of musical life, which is basically not taken seriously by anyone any more and in all discussions of culture retreats further and further into the background. One has the choice of either dutifully going along with the business, if only furtively in front of the loudspeaker on Saturday afternoon, or at once stubbornly and impenitently acknowledging the trash served up for the ostensible or real needs of the masses. The uncompelling and superficial nature of the objects of refined entertainment inevitably leads to the inattentiveness of the listeners. One preserves a good conscience in the matter since one is offering the listeners first-class goods. To the objection that these are already a drug on the market, one is ready with the reply that this is what they wanted, an argument which can be finally invalidated by a diagnosis of the situation of the listeners, but only through insight into the whole process which unites producers and consumers in a diabolical harmony.

But fetishism takes hold of even the ostensibly serious practice of music, which mobilizes the pathos of distance against refined entertainment. The purity of service to the cause, with which it presents the works, often turns out to be as inimical to them as vulgarization and arrangement. The official ideal of performance, which covers the earth as a result of Toscanini's extraordinary achievement, helps to sanction a condition which, in a phrase of Eduard Steuermann, may be called the barbarism of perfection. To be sure, the names of famous works are no longer made fetishes, although the lesser ones that break into the programs almost make the limitation to the smaller repertoire seem desirable. To be sure, passages are not here inflated or climaxes overstressed for the sake of fascination. There is iron discipline. But precisely iron. The new fetish is the flawlessly functioning, metallically brilliant apparatus as such, in which all the cogwheels mesh so perfectly that not the slightest hole remains open for the meaning of the whole. Perfect, immaculate performance in the latest style preserves the work at the price of its definitive reificaiton. It presents it as already complete from the very first note. The performance sounds like its own phonograph record. The dynamic is so predetermined that there are no longer any tensions at all. The contradictions of the musical material are so inexorably resolved in the moment of sound that it never arrives at the synthesis, the self-production of the work, which reveals the meaning of every Beethoven symphony. What is the point of the symphonic effort when the material on which that effort was to be tested has already been ground up? The protective fixation of the work leads to its destruction, for its unity is realized in precisely that spontaneity which is sacrificed to the fixation. This last fetishism, which seizes on the substance itself, smothers it; the absolute adjustment of the appearance to the work denies the latter and makes it disappear unnoticed behind the apparatus, just as certain swamp-drainings by labor detachments take place not for their own sake but for that of the work. Not for nothing does the rule of the established conductor remind one of that of the totalitarian Führer. Like the latter, he reduces aura and organization to a common denominator. He is the real modern type of the virtuoso, as bandleader as well as in the Philharmonic. He has got to the point where he no longer has to do anything himself; he is even sometimes relieved of reading the score by the staff musical advisors. At one stroke he provides norm and individualization: the norm is identified with his person, and the individual tricks which he perpetrates furnish general rules. The fetish-character of the conductor is the most obvious and the most hidden. The standard works could probably be performed by the virtuosi of contemporary orchestras just as well without the conductor, and the public which cheers the conductor would be unable to tell that, in the concealment of the orchestra, the musical advisor was taking the place of the hero laid low by a cold.

The consciousness of the mass of listeners is adequate to fetishized music. It listens according to formula, and indeed debasement itself would not be possible if resistance ensued, if the listeners still had the capacity to make demands beyond the limits of what was supplied. But if someone tried to "verify" the fetish-character of music by investigating the reactions of listeners with interviews and questionnaires, he might meet with unexpected puzzles. In music, as elsewhere, the discrepancy between essence and appearance has grown to a point where no appearance is any longer valid, without mediation, as verification of the essence. The unconscious reactions of the listeners are so heavily veiled and their conscious assessment is so exclusively oriented to the dominant fetish categories that every answer one receives conforms in advance to the surface of that music business which is attacked by the theory being "verified." As soon as one presents the listener with the primitive question about liking or disliking, there comes into play the whole machinery which one had thought could be made transparent and eliminated by the reduction to this question. But if one tries to replace the most elementary investigative procedures with others which take account of the real dependence of the listener on the mechanism, this complication of the investigative procedure not merely makes the interpretation of the result more difficult, but it touches off the resistance of the respondents and drives them all the deeper into the conformist behavior in which they think they can remain concealed from the danger of exposure. No causal nexus at all can properly be worked out between isolated "impressions" of the hit song and its psychological effects on the listener. If indeed individuals today no longer belong to themselves, then that also means that they can no longer be "influenced." The opposing points of production and consumption are at any given time closely coordinated, but not dependent on each other in isolation. Their mediation itself does not in any case escape theoretical conjecture. It suffices to remember how many sorrows he is spared who no longer thinks too many thoughts, how much more "in accordance with reality" a person behaves when he affirms that the real is right, how much more capacity to use the machinery falls to the person who integrates himself with it uncomplainingly, so that the correspondence between the listener's consciousness and the fetishized music would still remain comprehensible even if the former did not unequivocally reduce itself to the latter.

The counterpart to the fetishism of music is a regression of listening. This does not mean a relapse of the individual listener into an earlier phase of his own development, nor a decline in the collective general level, since the millions who are reached musically for the first time by today's mass communication cannot be compared with the audience of the past. Rather, it is contemporary listening which has regressed, arrested at the infantile stage. Not only do the listening subjects lose, along with freedom of choice and responsibility, the capacity for conscious perception of music, which was from time immemorial confined to a narrow group, but they stubbornly reject the possibility of such perception. They fluctuate between comprehensive forgetting and sudden dives into recognition. They listen atomistically and dissociate what they hear, but precisely in this dissociation they develop certain capacities which accord less with the concepts of traditional esthetics than with those of football and motoring. They are not childlike, as might be expected on the basis of an interpretation of the new type of listener in terms of the introduction to the musical life of groups previously unacquainted with music. But they are childish; their primitivism is not that of the undeveloped, but that of the forcibly retarded. Whenever they have a chance, they display the pinched hatred of those who really sense the other but exclude it in order to live in peace, and who therefore would like best to root out the nagging possibility. The regression is really from this existent possibility, or more concretely, from the possibility of a different and oppositional music. Regressive, too, is the role which contemporary mass music plays in the psychological household of its victims. They are not merely turned away from more important music, but they are confirmed in their neurotic stupidity, quite irrespective of how their musical capacities are related to the specific musical culture of earlier social phases. The assent to hit songs and debased cultural goods belongs to the same complex of symptoms as do those faces of which one no longer knows whether the film has alienated them from reality or reality has alienated them from the film, as they wrench open a great formless mouth with shining teeth in a voracious smile, while the tired eyes are wretched and lost above. Together with sport and film, mass music and the new listening help to make escape from the whole infantile milieu impossible. The sickness has a preservative function. Even the listening habits of the contemporary masses are certainly in no way new, and one may readily concede that the reception of the prewar hit song "Puppchen" was not so very different from that of a synthetic jazz children's song. But the context in which such a children's song appears, the masochistic mocking of one's own wish for lost happiness, or the compromising of the desire for happiness itself by the reversion to a childhood whose unattainability bears witness to the unattainability of joy – this is the specific product of the new listening, and nothing which strikes the ear remains exempt from this system of assimilation. There are indeed social differences, but the new listening extends so far that the stultification of the oppressed affects the oppressors themselves, and they become victims of the superior's power of self-propelled wheels who think they are determining their direction.

Regressive listening is tied to production by the machinery of distribution, and particularly by advertising. Regressive listening appears as soon as advertising turns into terror, as soon as nothing is left for the consciousness but to capitulate before the superior power of the advertised stuff and purchase spiritual peace by making the imposed goods literally its own thing. In regressive listening, advertising takes on a compulsory character. For a while, an English brewery used for propaganda purposes a billboard that bore a deceptive likeness to one of those whitewashed brick walls which are so numerous in the slums of London and the industrial cities of the North. Properly placed, the billboard was barely distinguishable from a real wall. On it, chalk-white, was a careful imitation of awkward writing. The words said: "What we want is Watney's." The brand of the beer was presented like a political slogan. Not only does this billboard give an insight into the nature of up-to-date propaganda, which sells its slogans as well as its wares, just as here the wares masquerade as a slogan; the type of relationship suggested by the billboard, in which masses make a commodity recommended to them the object of their own action, is in fact found again as the pattern for the reception of light music. They need and demand what has been palmed off on them. They overcome the feeling of impotence that creeps over them in the face of monopolistic production by identifying themselves with the inescapable product. They thereby put an end to the strangeness of the musical brands which are at once distant from them and threateningly near, and in addition, achieve the satisfaction of feeling themselves involved in Mr. Know-Nothing's enterprises, which confront them at every turn. This explains why individual expressions of preference – or, of course, dislike – converge in an area where object and subject alike make such reactions questionable. The fetish-character of music produces its own camouflage through the identification of the listener with the fetish. This identification initially gives the hit songs power over their victims. It fulfills itself in the subsequent forgetting and remembering. Just as every advertisement is composed of the inconspicuous familiar and the unfamiliar conspicuous, so the hit song remains salutarily forgotten in the half-dusk of its familiarity, suddenly to become painfully over-clear through recollection, as if in the beam of a spotlight. One can almost equate the moment of this recollection with that in which the title or the words of the initial verse of this hit song confront the victim. Perhaps he identifies himself with this because he identifies it and thereby merges with his possession. This compulsion may well drive him to recall the title of the hit song at this time. But the writing under the note, which makes the identification possible, is nothing else but the trademark of the hit song.

Deconcentration is the perceptual activity which prepares the way for the forgetting and sudden recognition of mass music. If the standardized products, hopelessly like one another except for conspicuous bits such as hit lines, do not permit concentrated listening without becoming unbearable to the listeners, the latter are in any case no longer capable of concentrated listening. They cannot stand the strain of concentrated listening and surrender themselves resignedly to what befalls them, with which they can come to terms only if they do not listen to it too closely. Benjamin's reference to the apperception of the cinema in a condition of distraction is just as valid for light music. The usual commercial jazz can only carry out its function because it is not attended to except during conversation and, above all, as an accompaniment to dancing. Again and again one encounters the judgment that it is fine for dancing but dreadful for listening. But if the film as a whole seems to be apprehended in a distracted manner, deconcentrated listening makes the perception of a whole impossible. All that is realized is what the spotlight falls on – striking melodic intervals, unsettling modulations, intentional or unintentional mistakes, or whatever condenses itself into a formula by an especially intimate merging of melody and text. Here, too, listeners and products fit together; they are not even offered the structure which they cannot follow. If atomized listening means progressive decomposition for the higher music, there is nothing more to decompose in the lower music. The forms of hit songs are so strictly standardized, down to the number of beats and the exact duration, that no specific form appears in any particular piece. The emancipation of the parts from their cohesion, and from all moments which extend beyond their immediate present, introduces the diversion of musical interest to the particular sensory pleasure. Typically, the listeners show a preference not merely for particular showpieces for instrumental acrobatics, but for the individual instrumental colors as such. This preference is promoted by the practice of American popular music whereby each variation, or "chorus," is played with emphasis on a special instrumental color, with the clarinet, the piano, or the trumpet as quasi-soloist. This often goes so far that the listener seems to care more about treatment and "style" than about the otherwise indifferent material, but with the treatment validating itself only in particular enticing effects. Along with the attraction to color as such, there is of course the veneration for the tool and the drive to imitate and join in the game; possibly also something of the great delight of children in bright colors, which returns under the pressure of contemporary musical experience.

The diversion of interest from the whole, perhaps indeed from the "melody," to the charm of color and to the individual trick, could be optimistically interpreted as a new rupture of the disciplining function. But this interpretation would be erroneous. Once the perceived charms remain unopposed in a rigid format, whoever yields to them will eventually rebel against it. But then they are themselves of the most limited kind. They all center on an impressionistically softened tonality. It cannot be said that interest in the isolated color or the isolated sonority awakens a taste for new colors and new sonorities. Rather, the atomistic listeners are the first to denounce such sonorities as "intellectual" or absolutely dissonant. The charms which they enjoy must be of an approved type. To be sure, dissonances occur in jazz practice, and even techniques of intentional misplaying have developed. But an appearance of harmlessness accompanies all these customs; every extravagant sonority must be so produced that the listener can recognize it as a substitute for a "normal" one. While he rejoices in the mistreatment the dissonance gives to the consonance whose place it takes, the virtual consonance simultaneously guarantees that one remains within the circle. In tests on the reception of hit songs, people have been found who ask how they should act if a passage simultaneously pleases and displeases them. One may well suspect that they report an experience which also occurs to those who give no account of it.

The reactions to isolated charms are ambivalent. A sensory pleasure turns into disgust as soon as it is seen how it only still serves to betray the consumer. The betrayal here consists in always offering the same thing.

Even the most insensitive hit song enthusiast cannot always escape the feeling that the child with a sweet tooth comes to know in the candy store. If the charms wear off and turn into their opposite – the short life of most hit songs belongs in the same range of experience – then the cultural ideology which clothes the upper-level musical business finishes things off by causing the lower to be heard with a bad conscience. Nobody believes so completely in prescribed pleasure. But the listening nevertheless remains regressive in assenting to this situation despite all distrust and all ambivalence. As a result of the displacement of feelings into exchange-value, no demands are really advanced in music anymore. Substitutes satisfy their purpose as well, because the demand to which they adjust themselves has itself already been substituted. But ears which are still only able to hear what one demands of them in what is offered, and which register the abstract charm instead of synthesizing the moments of charm, are bad ears. Even in the "isolated" phenomenon, key aspects will escape them; that is, those which transcend its own isolation. There is actually a neurotic mechanism of stupidity in listening, too; the arrogantly ignorant rejection of everything unfamiliar is its sure sign. Regressive listeners behave like children. Again and again and with stubborn malice, they demand the one dish they have once been served.

A sort of musical children's language is prepared for them; it differs from the real thing in that its vocabulary consists exclusively of fragments and distortions of the artistic language of music. In the piano scores of hit songs, there are strange diagrams. They relate to guitar, ukulele and banjo, as well as the accordion – infantile instruments in comparison with the piano – and are intended for players who cannot read the notes. They depict graphically the fingering for the chords of the plucking instruments. The rationally comprehensible notes are replaced by visual directives, to some extent by musical traffic signals. These signs, of course, confine themselves to the three tonic major chords and exclude any meaningful harmonic progression. The regulated musical traffic is worthy of them. It cannot be compared with that in the streets. It swarms with mistakes in phrasing and harmony. There are wrong pitches, incorrect doublings of thirds, fifth and octave progressions, and all sorts of illogical treatments of voices, sometimes in the bass. One would like to blame them on the amateurs with whom most of the hit songs originate, while the real musical work is first done by the arrangers. But just as a publisher does not let a misspelled word go out into the world, so it is inconceivable that, well-advised by their experts, they publish amateur versions without checking them. The mistakes are either consciously produced by the experts or intentionally permitted to stand – for the sake of the listeners. One could attribute to the publishers and experts the wish to ingratiate themselves with the listeners, composing as nonchalantly and informally as a dilettante drums out a hit song after hearing it. Such intrigues would be of the same stripe, even if considered psychologically different, as the incorrect spelling in many advertising slogans. But even if one wanted to exclude their acceptance as too far-fetched, the typographical errors could be understood. On the one hand, the infantile hearing demands sensually rich and full sonority, sometimes represented by the luxuriant thirds, and it is precisely this demand in which the infantile musical language is in most brutal contradiction with the children's song. On the other hand, the infantile hearing always demands the most comfortable and fluent resolutions. The consequences of the "rich" sonority, with correct treatment of voices, would be so far from the standardized harmonic relations that the listener would have to reject them as "unnatural." The mistakes would then be the bold strokes which reconcile the antagonisms of the infantile listener's consciousness.

No less characteristic of the regressive musical language is the quotation. Its use ranges from the conscious quotation of folk and children's songs, by way of ambiguous and half accidental allusions, to completely latent similarities and associations. The tendency triumphs in the adaptation of whole pieces from the classical stock or the operatic repertoire. The practice of quotation mirrors the ambivalence of the infantile listener's consciousness. The quotations are at once authoritarian and a parody. It is thus that a child imitates the teacher.

The ambivalence of the retarded listeners has its most extreme expression in the fact that individuals, not yet fully reified, want to extricate themselves from the mechanism of musical reification to which they have been handed over, but that their revolts against fetishism only entangle them more deeply in it. Whenever they attempt to break away from the passive status of compulsory consumers and "activate" themselves, they succumb to pseudoactivity. Types rise up from the mass of the retarded who differentiate themselves by pseudoactivity and nevertheless make the regression more strikingly visible. There are, first, the enthusiasts who write fan letters to radio stations and orchestras and, at well-managed jazz festivals, produce their own enthusiasm as an advertisement for the wares they consume. They call themselves jitterbugs, as if they simultaneously wanted to affirm and mock their loss of individuality, their transformation into beetles whirring around in fascination. Their only excuse is that the term jitterbugs, like all those in the unreal edifice of films and jazz, is hammered into them by the entrepreneurs to make them think that they are on the inside. Their ecstasy is without content. That it happens, that the music is listened to, this replaces the content itself. The ecstasy takes possession of its object by its own compulsive character. It is stylized like the ecstasies savages go into in beating the war drums. It has convulsive aspects reminiscent of St. Vitus' dance or the reflexes of mutilated animals. Passion itself seems to be produced by defects. But the ecstatic ritual betrays itself as pseudoactivity by the moment of mimicry. People do not dance or listen "from sensuality" and sensuality is certainly not satisfied by listening, but the gestures of the sensual are imitated. An analogue is the representation of particular emotions in the film where there are physiognomic patterns for anxiety, longing, the erotic look; for smiling; for the atomistic expressive of debased music. The imitative assimilation to commodity models is intertwined with folkloristic customs of imitation. In jazz, the relation of such mimicry to the imitating individual himself is quite loose. Its medium is caricature. Dance and music copy stages of sexual excitement only to make fun of them. It is as if desire's surrogate itself simultaneously turned against it; the "realistic" behavior of the oppressed triumphs over his dream of happiness while being itself incorporated into the latter. And as if to confirm the superficiality and treachery of every form of ecstasy, the feet are unable to fulfill what the ear pretends. The same jitterbugs who behave as if they were electrified by syncopation dance almost exclusively the good rhythmic parts. The weak flesh punishes the lies of the willing spirit; the gestural ecstasy of the infantile listener misfires in the face of the ecstatic gesture. The opposite type appears to be the eager person who leaves the factory and "occupies" himself with music in the quiet of his bedroom. He is shy and inhibited, perhaps has no luck with girls, and wants in any case to preserve his own special sphere. He seeks this as a radio ham. At twenty, he is still at the stage of a boy scout working on complicated knots just to please his parents. This type is held in high esteem in radio matters. He patiently builds sets whose most important parts he must buy ready-made, and scans the air for shortwave secrets, though there are none. As a reader of Indian stories and travel books, he once discovered unknown lands and cleared his path through the forest primeval. As radio ham he becomes the discoverer of just those industrial products which are interested in being discovered by him. He brings nothing home which would not be delivered to his house. The adventurers of pseudoactivity have already organized themselves on a large scale; the radio amateurs have printed verification cards sent them by the shortwave stations they have discovered, and hold contests in which the winner is the one who can produce the most such cards. All this is carefully fostered from above. Of all fetishistic listeners, the radio ham is perhaps the most complete. It is irrelevant to him what he hears or even how he hears; he is only interested in the fact that he hears and succeeds in inserting himself, with his private equipment, into the public mechanism, without exerting even the slightest influence on it. With the same attitude, countless radio listeners play with the feedback or the sound dial without themselves becoming hams. Others are more expert, or at least more aggressive. These smart chaps can be found everywhere and are able to do everything themselves: the advanced student who in every gathering is ready to play jazz with machinelike precision for dancing and entertainment; the gas station attendant who hums his syncopation ingenuously while filling up the tank; the listening expert who can identify every band and immerses himself in the history of jazz as if it were Holy Writ. He is nearest to the sportsman: if not to the football player himself, then to the swaggering fellow who dominates the stands. He shines by a capacity for rough improvisations, even if he must practice the piano for hours in secret in order to bring the refractory rhythms together. He pictures himself as the individualist who whistles at the world. But what he whistles is its melody, and his tricks are less inventions of the moment than stored-up experiences from acquaintance with sought-after technical things. His improvisations are always gestures of nimble subordination to what the instrument demands of him. The chauffeur is the model for the listening type of the clever fellow. His agreement with everything dominant goes so far that he no longer produces any resistance, but of his own accord always does what is asked of him for the sake of the responsible functionary. He lies to himself about the completeness of his subordination to the rule of the reified mechanism. Thus, the sovereign routine of the jazz amateur is nothing but the passive capacity for adaptation to models from which to avoid straying. He is the real jazz subject: his improvisations come from the pattern, and he navigates the pattern, cigarette in mouth, as nonchalantly as if he had invented it himself.

Regressive listeners have key points in common with the man who must kill time because he has nothing else on which to vent his aggression, and with the casual laborer. To make oneself a jazz expert or hang over the radio all day, one must have much free time and little freedom. The dexterity which comes to terms with the syncopation as well as with the basic rhythm is that of the auto mechanic who can also repair the loudspeaker and the electric light. The new listeners resemble the mechanics who are simultaneously specialized and capable of applying their special skills to unexpected places outside their skilled trades. But this despecialization only seems to help them out of the system. The more easily they meet the demands of the day, the more rigidly they are subordinated to that system.

The research finding, that among radio listeners the friends of light music reveal themselves to be depoliticized, is not accidental. The possibility of individual shelter and of a security which is, as always, questionable, obstructs the view of a change in the situation in which one seeks shelter. Superficial experience contradicts this. The "younger generation" – the concept itself is merely an ideological catch-all – seems to be in conflict with its elders and their plush culture precisely through the new way of listening. In America, it is just the so-called liberals and progressives whom one finds among the advocates of light popular music, most of whom want to classify their activity as democratic. But if regressive hearing is progressive as opposed to the "individualistic" sort, it is only in the dialectical sense that it is better fitted to the advancing brutality than the latter. All possible mold has been rubbed off the baseness, and it is legitimate to criticize the esthetic residue of an individuality that was long since wrested from individuals. But this criticism comes with little force from the sphere of popular music, since it is just this sphere that mummifies the vulgarized and decaying remnants of romantic individualism. Its innovations are inseparably coupled with these remnants.

Machochism in hearing is not only defined by self-surrender and pseudo-pleasure through identification with power. Underlying it is the knowledge that the security of shelter under the ruling conditions is a provisional one, that it is only a respite, and that eventually everything must collapse. Even in self-surrender one is not good in his own eyes; in his enjoyment one feels that he is simultaneously betraying the possible and being betrayed by the existent. Regressive listening is always ready to degenerate into rage. If one knows that he is basically marking time, the rage is directed primarily against everything which could disavow the modernity of being with-it and up-to-date and reveal how little has in fact changed. From photographs and movies, one knows the effect produced by the modern grown old, an effect originally used by the surrealists to shock and subsequently degraded to the cheap amusement of those whose fetishism fastens on the abstract present. For the regressive listener, this effect is fantastically foreshortened. They would like to ridicule and destroy what yesterday they were intoxicated with, as if in retrospect to revenge themselves for the fact that the ecstasy was not actually such. This effect has been given a name of its own and repeatedly been propagated in press and radio. But we should not think of the rhythmically simpler, light music of the pre-jazz era and its relics as corny; rather, the term applies to all those syncopated pieces which do not conform to the approved rhythmic formula of the present moment. A jazz expert can shake with laughter when he hears a piece which in good rhythm follows a sixteenth note with a punctuated eight, although this rhythm is more aggressive and in no way more provincial in character than the syncopated connection and renunciation of all counter-stress practiced later. The regressive listeners are in fact destructive. The old-timer's insult has its ironic justification; ironic, because the destructive tendencies of the regressive listeners are in truth directed against the same thing that the old-fashioned hate, against disobedience as such, unless it comes under the tolerated spontaneity of collective excesses. The seeming opposition of the generations is nowhere more transparent than in rage. The bigots who complain to the radio stations in pathetic-sadistic letters of the jazzing up of holy things and the youth who delight in such exhibitions are of one mind. It requires only the proper situation to bring them together in a united front.

This furnishes a criticism of the "new possibilities" in regressive listening. One might be tempted to rescue it if it were something in which the "auratic" characteristics of the work of art, its illusory elements, gave way to the playful ones. However it may be with films, today's mass music shows little of such progress in disenchantment. Nothing survives in it more steadfastly than the illusion, nothing is more illusory than its reality. The infantile play has scarcely more than the name in common with the productivity of children. Otherwise, bourgeois sport would not want to differentiate itself so strictly from play. Its bestial seriousness consists in the fact that instead of remaining faithful to the dream of freedom by getting away from purposiveness, the treatment of play as a duty puts it among useful purposes and thereby wipes out the trace of freedom in it. This is particularly valid for contemporary mass music. It is only play as a repetition of prescribed models, and the playful release from responsibility which is thereby achieved does not reduce at all the time devoted to duty except by transferring the responsibility to the models, the following of which one makes into a duty for himself. In this lies the inherent pretense of the dominant music sport. It is illusory to promote the technical-rational moments of contemporary mass music – or the special capacities of the regressive listeners which may correspond to these moments – at the expense of a decayed magic, which nevertheless prescribes the rules for the bare functioning itself. It would also be illusory because the technical innovations of mass music really don't exist. This goes without saying for harmonic and melodic construction. The real coloristic accomplishment of modern dance music, the approach of the different colors to one another to the extent that one instrument replaces another without a break or one instrument can disguise itself as another, is as familiar to Wagnerian and post-Wagnerian orchestral technique as the mute effects of the brasses. Even in the techniques of syncopation, there is nothing that was not present in rudimentary form in Brahms and outdone by Schönberg and Stravinsky. The practice of contemporary popular music has not so much developed these techniques as conformistically dulled them. The listeners who expertly view these techniques with astonishment are in no way technically educated thereby, but react with resistance and rejection as soon as the techniques are introduced to them in those contexts in which they have their meaning. Whether a technique can be considered progressive and "rational" depends on this meaning and on its place in the whole of society as well as in the organization of the particular work. Technical development as such can serve crude reaction as soon as it has established itself as a fetish and by its perfection represents the neglected social tasks as already accomplished. This is why all attempts to reform mass music and regressive listening on the basis of what exists are frustrated. Consumable art music must pay by the sacrifice of its consistency. Its faults are not "artistic"; every incorrectly composed or outmoded chord bespeaks the backwardness of those to whose demand accommodation is made. But technically consistent, harmonious mass music purified of all the elements of bad pretense would turn into art music and at once lose its mass basis. All attempts at reconciliation, whether by market-oriented artists or collectively-oriented art educators, are fruitless. They have accomplished nothing more than handicrafts or the sort of products with which directions for use or a social text must be given, so that one may be properly informed about their deeper background.

The positive aspect for which the new mass music and regressive listening are praised – vitality and technical progress, collective breadth and relation to an undefined practice, into whose concepts there has entered the supplicant self-denunciation of the intellectuals, who can thereby finally end their social alienation from the masses in order to coordinate themselves politically with contemporary mass consciousness – this positive is negative, the irruption into music of a catastrophic phase of society. The positive lies locked up solely in its negativity. Fetishized mass music threatens the fetishized cultural goods. The tension between the two spheres of music has so grown that it becomes difficult for the official sphere to hold its ground. However little it has to do with the technical standards of mass music, if one compares the special knowledge of a jazz expert with that of a Toscanini worshipper the former is far ahead of the latter. But regressive listening represents a growing and merciless enemy not only to museum cultural goods but to the age-old sacral function of music as the locus for the taming of impulses. Not without penalty, and therefore not without restraint, are the debased products of musical culture surrendered to disrespectful play and sadistic humor.

In the face of regressive listening, music as a whole begins to take on a comic aspect. One need only listen to the uninhibited sonority of a choral rehearsal from outside. This experience was caught with great force in a film by the Marx brothers, who demolish an opera set as if to clothe in allegory the insight of the philosophy of history on the decay of the operatic form, or in a most estimable piece of refined entertainment, break up a grand piano in order to take possession of its strings in their frame as the true harp of the future, on which to play a prelude. Music has become comic in the present phase primarily because something so completely useless is carried on with all the visible signs of the strain of serious work. By being alien to solid people, music reveals their alienation from one another, and the consciousness of alienation vents itself in laughter. In music – or similarly in lyric poetry – the society which judged them comic becomes comic. But involved in this laughter is the decay of the sacral spirit of reconciliation. All music today can very easily sound as *Parsifal* did to Nietzsche's ear. It recalls incomprehensible rites and surviving masks from an earlier time, and is provocative nonsense. The radio, which both wears out music and overexposes it, makes a major contribution to this. Perhaps a better hour may at some time strike even for the clever fellows: one in which they may demand, instead of prepared material ready to be switched on, the improvisatory displacement of things, as the sort of radical beginning that can only thrive under the protection of the unshaken real world. Even discipline can take over the expression of free solidarity if freedom becomes its content. As little as regressive listening is a symptom of progress in consciousness of freedom, it could suddenly turn around if art, in unity with the society, should ever leave the road of the always-identical.

Not popular music but artistic music has furnished a model for this possibility. It is not for nothing that Mahler is the scandal of all bourgeois musical esthetics. They call him uncreative because he suspends their concept of creation itself. Everything with which he occupies himself is already there. He accepts it in its vulgarized form; his themes are expropriated ones. Nevertheless, nothing sounds as it was wont to; all things are diverted as if by a magnet. What is worn out yields pliantly to the improvising hand; the used parts win a second life as variants. Just as the chauffeur's knowledge of his old secondhand car can enable him to drive it punctually and unrecognized to its intended destination, so can the expression of a beat-up melody, straining under the pressure of clarinets and oboes in the upper register, arrive at places which the approved musical language could never safely reach. Such music really crystallizes the whole, into which it has incorporated the vulgarized fragments, into something new, yet it takes its material from regressive listening. Indeed, one can almost think that in Mahler's music this experience was seismographically recorded forty years before it permeated society. But if Mahler stood athwart the concept of musical progress, neither can the new and radical music whose most advanced practitioners give allegiance to him in a seemingly paradoxical way any longer be subsumed exclusively under the concept of progress. It proposes to consciously resist the phenomenon of regressive listening. The terror which Schönberg and Webern spread, today as in the past, comes not from their incomprehensibility but from the fact that they are all too correctly understood. Their music gives form to that anxiety, that terror, that insight into the catastrophic situation which others merely evade by regressing. They are called individualists, and yet their work is nothing but a single dialogue with the powers which destroy individuality – powers whose "formless shadows" fall gigantically on their music. In music, too, collective powers are liquidating an individuality past saving, but against them only individuals are capable of consciously representing the aims of collectivity.

Theodor W. Adorno, "On the Fetish-Character in Music and the Regression of Listening," in *The Essential Frankfurt School Reader*, Andrew Arato and Eike Gebhardt (eds.), New York: Continuum, 1938/1990, pp. 270–79.

RICHARD HOGGART, ## FROM *THE USES OF LITERACY*

At first read this selection from Richard Hoggart's seminal work of cultural studies, *The Uses of Literacy*, seems another simple attack on popular values and taste. It is not. Hoggart, the first director of Birmingham's Centre for Contemporary Cultural Studies, is from the class of which he writes; he has great pride in traditional working-class values. What he objects to is the shape they are taking in postwar Britain. The culprit, he believes, is commercial culture – not because it replaces traditional culture, but because it appeals to it. In the years after the Second World War the "masses" became an increasingly important market for media and entertainment, and the golden rule of marketing then as now is that to sell to the people you must speak their language. As such, traditional working-class values like community and egalitarianism became familiar pitches and hooks to move new cultural products. But employed within a different context and created by people with other agendas, these values take on new meaning. Thus what begins as the ideals of democracy and solidarity become, through commercial media and entertainment, the values of self-satisfied and complacent prejudice that, in the end, serve to further disempower the very class to whom they appeal. This is the same principle of appropriation we've seen in previous examples of cultural resistance; this time, however, it is used by the opposing side.

Up to this point I have been chiefly concerned with the way in which some older elements persist in working-class life. And the most remarkable feature seems to me the extent to which, in view of all the appeals now made to working-class people from other areas, older attitudes do manage to survive, whether for good or ill. I need only recall once more the great success of Mr Wilfred Pickles. His manner is too 'blokeish', too evidently 'all pals together', 'rough diamonds but hearts of gold', for my taste. He seems to me to indulge the northern working-classes, by echoing their own view that no one can beat them at salty repartee and an unaffected four-square wisdom. But a large part of his success comes from the fact that his programme, 'Have a Go', provides a forum in which they can express and applaud the values they still admire. These have, again, a simple and limited range, but in spite of the pretentiousness which such a programme can tend to encourage, they are not meaningless to the people who applaud them. 'Straight-dealing', 'good neighbourliness', 'looking on the bright side', 'openness', 'lending a helping hand', 'not being stuck up or a getter-on', 'loyalty'; all these are a good deal more healthy than the commercial values – pride, ambition, outdoing your acquaintances, show for its own sake, conspicuous consumption – which working-class people are consistently invited to adopt nowadays. And their persistence is not merely formal and in the head.

I turn now to some features of contemporary life which seem to encourage working-class people to adopt different attitudes or to modify the old. To concentrate on the probable effects of certain developments in publications and entertainments is, of course, to isolate only one segment in a vastly complicated interplay of social, political and economic changes. All are helping to alter attitudes, and some of them undoubtedly for the better. I shall be especially concerned with regrettable aspects of change, since these seem the more evident and important in the field I am examining.

Yet throughout it will be necessary to remember, and I shall try to recall when relevant, the evidence of this first part. For what have been called the 'older' attitudes and those now to be discussed can be found at the same time in the same people. Changes in attitudes work their way very slowly through many aspects of social life. They are incorporated into existing attitudes and often seem, at first, to be only freshly presented forms of those 'older' attitudes. Individuals can therefore inhabit more than one 'mental climate' without conscious strain. Though the nature of the 'older' order may be more immediately evident in middle-aged people, the newer appeals obviously touch them also. Conversely, a young man who seems at first almost completely typical of the second half of this century will reveal attitudes which recall his great-grandfather. It follows that the success of the more powerful contemporary approaches is partly decided by the extent to which they can identify themselves with 'older' attitudes.

. . .

'Everybody's Doing It Now' or 'The Gang's All Here': The Group Sense and Democratic Egalitarianism

[T]he strong sense of the group among working-class people can express itself as a demand for conformity. The group is warm and friendly; it does a great deal to make life more pleasant and manageable. But it has sharp methods with those who, from within it, begin to deride its values.

I suggest that this sense of the importance and the predominant rightness of the group is being linked to, and increasingly made to subserve, a callow democratic egalitarianism, which is itself the necessary ground for the activities of the really popular publicists. There is, it is true, a powerful pressure, notably from advertising copy-writers, to sell to all classes the ramified forms of individualism by which their kind of commerce must live, in the stress on the virtue of 'going one better', 'getting on', 'being wide awake', outdoing all others. But I can see little evidence that there they have so far had any considerable success with working-class people. Sometimes an advertising copy-writer will get his lines crossed and produce copy designed to reach the body of the working-classes (rather than the minority who are much affected by these assumptions), though appealing to assumptions more characteristic of other classes. But on the whole the accuracy of the advertisers' aim is formidable. They have by now had plenty of practice and yearly gain in sureness.

To point to this phenomenon today is not to discover, as though it were something new in human nature, that we all sometimes, and some of us much of the time, like to feel that we are going the way the world is going, that our actions are supported by a general consent. Nor is it to forget the respectable ancestry of the idea of equality in Western Europe. But that common desire, reinforced by a galloping egalitarianism, has during the past sixty or seventy years been more and more played upon to move and persuade, in magazines and newspapers specifically designed to attract a literate working-class.

From then on has developed, with increasing elaboration, all the well-known cant of 'the common man'; a grotesque and dangerous flattery, since he is conceived as the most common or commonplace man. 'Rely on the people'; all are equal, all have a vote; all are 'as good as one another'; 'the voice of the people is the voice of God' (to recall an old-fashioned form); therefore in all things, says the publicist, your attitudes are as good as anyone else's: but since you share the opinions of the great majority, you are more right than the odd outsiders. The popular papers, always identifying themselves with 'the people', conduct polls on this matter and questionnaires on that matter among their readers, and so elevate the counting of heads into a substitute for judgement.

Behind all this an important radical principle is being appealed to, one always central to working-class people. One can hear behind 'Ah'm as good as you', the assertion of an independence of spirit which holds fast to this fundamental equality, which will not tolerate false professions of superiority, and which is strengthened today by a suspicion that at bottom, in spite of 'all the talk about democracy', 'ordinary people' do not matter, 'do not count'. But, from giving a proper sense of self-respect, 'Ah'm as good as you' can turn into the surly 'Yer no better than me', which is the harsh ass-cry of the philistine in his straw, who will tolerate no suggestion of a challenge or awkward example. It can become a cocksure refusal to recognize any sort of differentiation, whether of brains or of character. One of its forms is illustrated in the newer kinds of competition in some popular publications, where the process of arriving at a correct answer can only be one of pure luck. Any advantage gained by brains or effort has been precluded; and in the more advanced forms of competition everyone gets a prize of sorts. Everyone wins; the 'competitors' pay sufficient on their entry forms to cover the cost of the prize they are given, but no one feels bettered by anyone else.

Whatever is, is right – if the people believe it. 'The little man' is made to seem big because everything is scaled down to his measure; his responses, the limits of his vision, are the recognized limits. Thus, if a writer fails to appeal at once and on the usual first inadequate reading, then he is at fault, and never the reader. The idea of literature as direct communication is paramount; there is no intermediate link. The writer does not stand before his experience and try to recreate it in a form of words, with which –

rather than with the writer himself directly – the reader must seek an understanding according to its complexity. Complex – that is, searching or taxing – literature must therefore be discounted; good writing cannot be popular today, and popular writing cannot genuinely explore experience.

'It is you, the ordinary people, and not the members of the Cabinet, who decide this country's fate'; one can see the truth there, but constant inflation makes it equivalent to a lie. In strip-cartoons, in magazine short stories, in the intimate gossip-columns, the hero is the little man; 'Just Joe', as a song title has it. He is the little man who is not brave or beautiful or talented, yet who is loved, not in spite of but because of this. 'I love you . . .', says the girl in the final paragraph, revealing to the overwhelmed young man that all the time he had the sixty-four-dollar answer but did not know it, '. . . because you are ordinary.' I found three post-O. Henry quick-twist tales in two successively read women's magazines, each having the happy revelation in the last paragraph that he or she, far from being 'clever' or 'highbrow', was just a decent ordinary person after all. On Sundays, in particular, journalists with suitably democratic names make their columns ring with straight pride in speaking for the common sense of the ordinary man, which is better than all the subtlety of the intellectuals who 'have notions'. We are encouraging a sense, not of the dignity of each person but of a new aristocracy, the monstrous regiment of the most flat-faced.

Something of the success of the radio 'soap-operas', with working-class women as with others, is due to the consummateness of their attention to this kind of attitude, to their remarkably sustained presentation of the perfectly ordinary and unremarkable. In the strip-cartoons, watch the 'little man' worrying for days on end about his daughter's chances in the school cookery-competition. Here the initial criterion is the exact reverse of Keats's 'load every rift with ore'; to succeed, not to startle or puzzle or otherwise put off, the cartoonists must carry out a daily exercise in spinning out the unimportant and insignificant.

In cartoons the little man is no longer likely to deflate the boss's pretensions by pointing out something truly silly about him, or by scratching an ear and then quietly doing the job that has cost the big men so much trouble and fuss; that could be comic art, and so in the end serious. Now he beats the boss for silly reasons, or asserts that he is better simply because he is a little man. And his successes are always intolerably small successes; but he wins through in the end, as little men's values always do in this 'great big shaggy old world of ours'. Democratic egalitarianism, paradoxically, requires the continuance of the 'Them' and 'Us' idea in some of its poorer forms.

More and more the weekly magazines invite their readers to write their papers for them in the form of contributed snippets. It may be cheaper, and certainly the customers like it. The anecdotes have to be funny or odd – 'she woo'd and won him with Yorkshire pudding' – but still 'it might have happened to you'. They encourage at once both the pally feeling that we are all little men together, but that still 'we do see life'.

As is often pointed out, popular journalists describing some important figure shy away from suggesting differences between him and 'ordinary folk'. The impulse behind this is a good one. People want to feel that to those who are engaged in organizing their lives 'human things' do matter. This attitude is probably healthier than that which prefers major public figures to be remote and godlike. As usual the problem is one of degree, of how an attitude which can be valuable when it is in a working relationship with others which qualify it, becomes a weakness when it is emphasized in isolation. In America, a former President of Harvard says, the only innate differences of ability which will be recognized are in sport. In England, matters are not yet quite so far gone; though it is assumed that one should not make much of intellectual ability. Every rich girl is a poor little rich girl underneath, really wanting nothing more than a home like the rest of us. Every tycoon, general or major politician, of our Party, is at bottom ordinary and 'homely', fond of his pipe, of his chair at the fireside and of his visit to a football match, when he 'mingles with the rest of us'. In Dewey's words: 'We praise even our most successful men, not for their ruthless and self-centred energy in getting ahead, but because of their love of flowers, children, and dogs, or their kindness to aged relatives.'

For officially high-ranking, but anonymous or colourless figures, not even irrelevant grounds for praise need be sought. All senior civil servants are tea-drinking 'buzz-fuzzes', hidebound and lazy. We recall Auden's counter-balancing lines about those who work on: 'problems no smiling/ Can dismiss . . . / [unseen by] the weak, / The inattentive, seeking / Someone to blame'.

'Highbrow-hating', in anger bred by fear of an implied criticism, is not strong among working-class people. But much of the glorification of 'the common man' clearly provides good grounds for an extension into high-brow-hunting, and many of the popular journalists try to introduce that sport to their working-class customers. Whilst writing this section, I picked up the current copy of a popular paper and found a columnist describing a chance meeting with some 'bearded arty-arty boys'. My impression is that this kind of attack has not so far had much success. Working-class people are on the whole just not interested in artists or intellectuals; they know of their existence, but regard them as oddities rarely seen within their orbit, like snail-eating Frenchmen. Meanwhile, some journalists, those who have a dislike of whatever is intellectual or serious, continue to use their columns to discharge their dislike and fear. The publication of the British Council report is made a yearly excuse for a tirade on the waste of good public money on highbrow exercises by flabby young men. A case of homosexuality is used as the jumping-off ground for an attack on the debased world of Bohemia. Modern art will only be mentioned if someone has given an excuse for trouncing the odd. The Arts Council is a 'fiddle' by a lot of 'cissies' who despise the amusements of the plain Englishman; and the BBC is little better. Any University Extension lecturer is a stodgy 'do-gooder' and his students spotty-faced and thin-blooded. Anyone who in any way suggests that there may be some things to have doubts about in our present forms of recreation or our mass public assumptions is a spoil-sport and crank.

Hence the aggressive 'plain man', the embattled lowbrow tone of many columnists and leader-writers; the inverted snobbery of those film critics who insist that they are 'simple and ordinary men-in-the-street', who seek only to be amused and leave more intellectual pretensions to others; or the lowbrow snobbery of some of the more popular question-answerers in those numerous wireless programmes of the brains-trust type. In these pro-grammes the democratic lust for widespread and fragmentary opinion unites with a slight residual awe for knowledgeable people and also with a slight resentment of them. The latter has some satisfaction in hearing the experts fall out; at such times there arise from the programme what Mr Gilbert Harding has described as 'the elemental odours of the bull-ring and of the bear-pit'.

. . .

How inadequate for a political democracy is this kind of ostrich act. It undervalues enemies and induces a blindness to some of the dangerous realities of the search for power. In some countries, where other factors assist the growth of a leader-cult, this very reduction of the great has come in as a reinforcement. The man-of-power pursues his plans in realms unimagined by the ordinary man; the ordinary man meanwhile happily stares at picture postcards of the man-of-power smiling understandingly at an aged peasant-woman, or dandling a steel-worker's fat baby or laughing at a popular variety-turn.

On the other hand, this attitude encourages a disregard for whatever worthwhile qualities may have contributed to the arrival at a socially bene-ficial position. It depreciates the value of a fine application of intellectual gifts, the courage to take unsentimental and unpopular decisions, a disciplining of the self. The word 'discipline', for example, is almost unusable in popular writing, except in a derogatory sense; it suggests 'pushing people around', the Armed Services, 'being got at', and is rejected out-of-hand. The people who have trained themselves to exercise these qualities can be assumed not to feel the want of public admiration, and one does not regret the lack of that. One can regret the softening effect of this view on those who hold it.

These are peculiarly dangerous comforts of unreason, and peculiarly those of a democracy. As in so many things a working-man here seems to be in different situations in his private and in his public life. At work, in the world he really knows, he can still recognize the worth and the admirable qualities of 'a good boss', and does not usually mean by that an indulgent boss, but one who ''as 'is 'ead screwed on t'right way', and whose yea is yea and nay is nay. In his local area, he can still recognize and admire 'a good man', a reliable or devoted or independent spirit. Outside, the great sea of undifferentiated porridge awaits him, where all the crucial characteristics, the dangerous troughs as well as the guiding features, have been obliterated. All he needs to float across, it is suggested, is 'a heart in the right place', a sense of humour which prevents him from being a spoilsport and prompts a laugh at anything odd, and that sense of 'how far to go' which is indispensable to the decent and reasonable man. A song the Scouts are said to have sung has a specialist bias, but its tone is closely related to that of the popular columnists:

> He'll look without dread at the snags on ahead,
> Wine, Women and Highbrows too;
> He won't run aground but will work his way round;
> With a smile . . .

Oh, wonderful second line! – the stiff upper lip and a ready cheerfulness outstaring the aesthetic Gorgon.

By all these means the fact of being able to 'rejoice in concurring with the common opinion', being able to feel one of the main herd, is made the excuse for gross insensitivity; that insensitivity feeds on its own pride, the 'hubris' of the 'ordinary chap'. More, working-class people may be the readier to accept this kind of appeal precisely because, though they traditionally like to feel members of a group and are ready to assume the virtue of agreement with the group, there is much in the public world which puzzles them. When you are taking part in some mass-activity, no matter how mechanical the activity may be, there is something warming in the feeling that you are with everyone else. I have heard people give, as their reason for listening to a popular wireless programme, not the fact that it is amusing, but that it 'gives you something to talk about' with everyone else at work. The advertisers sense this when they ask, 'When they are all talking about the big match on TV, will you have to remain silent?' There is more than keeping up with the Joneses in that; there is being one of a group. Lonely people, listening to the wireless booming out the voices of a thousand workers on holiday singing 'If you were the only girl in the world', can derive some comfort from the fact that every wireless in the street is linking the neighbours in a sort of communion. There can be an added pleasure in the warm dark super-cinemas, from the fact that the 'you' who is cajoled, invited to laugh, flattered, is not simply the individual 'you', but a great composite 'you' of the unexceptional ordinary folk; minnows in a heated pool. The same kind of thing may sometimes be seen in an undiscriminating looking-in, night after night, at TV. Everything and almost anything is acceptable because, as important as the intrinsic interest of any programme itself, is the sense that you are one in the big group watching the world (the world of events and personages) unroll before you. These tendencies, I think, may assist the emergence of a cultural group almost as large as the sum of all other groups. But it would be a group only in the sense that its members shared a passivity. For the majority of them work would be dull and ambition out of place. But nightly, dead from the eyes downwards, they would be able to link on to the Great Mother. They might spend their days fixing a dozen screws on each of a hundred TV sets, but their nights could be passed sitting in front of one. The eyes would register but not connect to the nerves, the heart and the brain; they would connect to a sense of shared pleasure, of pleasure in simply sharing the unifying object, not in the object itself.

. . .

Writing in the latter part of the last century, William Morris regretted the lack of a popular art and looked forward to its revival: 'Popular art has no chance of a healthy life or, indeed, of a life at all, till we are on the way to fill up this terrible gap between riches and poverty.' If that gap were closed there might be an end, he continued, to: 'that fatal division of men into the cultivated and degraded classes which competitive commerce has bred and fosters'.

The gap between riches and poverty has not been closed to an extent or in a manner which would have satisfied Morris. But much has been done to narrow the gap; the activities of competitive commerce can do much less than formerly to keep it open. Has the gap between the 'cultivated' and the 'degraded' classes lessened? Are we even a little nearer a popular art of the kind William Morris would have recognized?

We are moving towards a mass-art; millions each week and each day see the same paper and see few other publications. To become a mass-art it has to grip and hold down the level of taste, and is doing so with great effectiveness. Competitive commerce has changed horses and rides now as the champion of those hitherto 'degraded' classes, because now those classes, if all their contributory sixpences are added together, are worth riding for. And the new champions of the working-classes must keep them together, united at the level of their more indulgent instincts. Inhibited now from ensuring the 'degradation' of the masses economically, the logical processes of competitive commerce, favoured from without by the whole climate of the time and from within assisted by the lack of direction, the doubts and uncertainty before their freedom of working-people themselves (and maintained as much by ex-working-class writers as by others), are ensuring that working-people are culturally robbed. Since these processes can never rest, the holding down, the constant pressure not to look outwards and upwards, becomes a positive thing, becomes a new and stronger form of subjection; this subjection promises to be stronger than the old because the chains of cultural subordination are both easier to wear and harder to strike away than those of economic subordination. 'We are betrayed by what is false within,' by our common weaknesses and by the ability of these popular journals to have things both ways, to express our habitual moral assumptions but in such a way that they weaken the moral code they evoke; to say the right things for the wrong reasons.

Richard Hoggart, *The Uses of Literacy: Aspects of Working-Class Life with Special Reference to Publications and Entertainments*, New York: Oxford University Press, 1957/1990, pp. 141–2, 148–53, 155–7, 200–201.

MALCOLM COWLEY,
FROM *EXILE'S RETURN*

One of the great ironies of bohemia is that it is embraced most passionately by the very culture it professes to despise. This odd relationship dates back to the first cultural bohemia of Paris in the mid-nineteenth century, chronicled by Henri Murger in *La Vie de Bohème*, transformed into the opera *La Bohème* by Puccini, and thereafter celebrated across Europe by the bourgeoisie. In this selection from his memoir of bohemian life in Greenwich Village in the 1920s, the poet and critic

Malcolm Cowley helps explain why bohemia is such a hit in the world it opposes. The answer lies in bohemia's love of the libertine. While such freedom may have once shocked a previous – real or imagined – uptight and stuffy middle class, times have changed. No longer does the economy rely upon sober values like discipline, thrift and savings, instead it depends on heedless consumption. Within the context of consumer capitalism the bohemian call to be freed from yesterday's conventions translates easily into freedom to buy tomorrow's products. As Cowley writes, "everything fitted into the business picture" (see sidebar).

Greenwich Village was not only a place, a mood, a way of life: like all bohemias, it was also a doctrine. Since the days of Gautier and Murger, this doctrine had remained the same in spirit, but it had changed in several details. By 1920, it had become a system of ideas that could roughly be summarized as follows:

1. *The idea of salvation by the child* Each of us at birth has special potentialities which are slowly crushed and destroyed by a standardized society and mechanical methods of teaching. If a new educational system can be introduced, one by which children are encouraged to develop their own personalities, to blossom freely like flowers, then the world will be saved by this new, free generation.
2. *The idea of self-expression* Each man's, each woman's, purpose in life is to express himself, to realize his full individuality through creative work and beautiful living in beautiful surroundings.
3. *The idea of paganism* The body is a temple in which there is nothing unclean, a shrine to be adorned for the ritual of love.
4. *The idea of living for the moment* It is stupid to pile up treasures that we can enjoy only in old age, when we have lost the capacity for enjoyment. Better to seize the moment as it comes, to dwell in it intensely, even at the cost of future suffering. Better

"To reach them you need an 'in'...," Janine Lopiano-Misdom and Joanne De Luca

Everything about the future and our tomorrow has been planted, molded and nurtured by what is happening in the present. There are no such things as "futurists"; there are no crystal balls or big secrets to unfold. To get there – to be ready for the big explosion of tomorrow – we just need to look at what is brewing today in the progressive micro-cultures of the streets – those thinkers and doers who move in individual mind-sets, not the masses. What we consider mainstream – the trends, the fads, the gadgets, the styles, the tastes that become popular – often comes from the visual, sensory emotional cues of those who are considered "the fringe" or "the underground."

To reach them, you need an "in," an entry into their circle. That's what we do at Sputnik. Armed with a video camera, our nationwide network of young correspondents find those progressive thinkers and doers – young street designers, club promoters, DJ's, web developers, filmmakers, electronic musicians – and communicate with them on their level, on their turf. We uncover their belief systems and translate how their thoughts and actions will eventually influence mainstream youth lifestyle.

Why is it important to listen to the progressive street cultures? Because these are the mind-sets – the collective thinkers and influencers – that are behind youth's latest infatuation with digital pets, beverages with floating objects, wash-in glitters and mascara hair colors, electronic music that can't be found on any contemporary radio station – and the list goes on.

Through "Mindtrends," our biannual trend report, we track the movements among these progressive mind-sets and interpret them into actionable opportunities for marketing, new product development, brand management and advertising. With more than twenty-eight years of experience in advertising and youth marketing between us, we recognized a need for businesses to get ahead of the so-called "trend curve" and to anticipate the shift or movement that becomes the next "trend."

The tracking of so-called "trends" and "what's cool" is a hot topic these days, mainly because mainstream businesses have been trying to crack the tastes, preferences and styles of the elusive and fickle youth culture. It's understandable why. With over thirty-six billion dollars of expendable income – and yes, they are spending those dollars – everybody wants a piece of the "cool" spenders. But in actuality it's not about what's cool; it's about seeking those with progressive interests, getting inside their heads and understanding the movements they will affect.

Whatever we choose to call them, subcultures or countercultures have entered the mainstream with an idea, a set of values and often, a challenge to what is. From James Dean in the fifties, flower power in the sixties, punk in the seventies, heavy metal and hip-hop in the eighties to grunge in the nineties, trends emanating from youth culture have had a reverberating effect on

to live extravagantly, gather June rosebuds, "burn my candle at both ends . . . It gives a lovely light."

5. *The idea of liberty* Every law, convention or rule of art that prevents self-expression or the full enjoyment of the moment should be shattered and abolished. Puritanism is the great enemy. The crusade against puritanism is the only crusade with which free individuals are justified in allying themselves.

6. *The idea of female equality* Women should be the economic and moral equals of men. They should have the same pay, the same working conditions, the same opportunity for drinking, smoking, taking or dismissing lovers.

7. *The idea of psychological adjustment* We are unhappy because we are maladjusted, and maladjusted because we are repressed. If our individual repressions can be removed – by confessing them to a Freudian psychologist – then we can adjust ourselves to any situation, and be happy in it. (But Freudianism is only one method of adjustment. What is wrong with us may be our glands, and by a slight operation, or merely by taking a daily dose of thyroid, we may alter our whole personalities. Again, we may adjust ourselves by some such psycho–physical discipline as was taught by Gurdjieff. The implication of all of these methods is the same – that the environment itself need not be altered. That explains why most radicals who became converted to psychoanalysis or glands or Gurdjieff[1] gradually abandoned their political radicalism.)

8. *The idea of changing place* "They do things better in Europe." England and Germany have the wisdom of old cultures; the Latin peoples have admirably preserved their pagan heritage. By expatriating himself, by living in Paris, Capri or the South of France, the artist can break the puritan shackles, drink, live freely and be wholly creative.

All these, from the standpoint of the business-Christian ethic then represented by the *Saturday Evening Post*, were corrupt ideas. This older ethic is familiar to most people, but one feature of it has not been sufficiently emphasized. Substantially, it was a *production* ethic. The great virtues it taught were industry, foresight, thrift and personal initiative. The workman should be industrious in order to produce more for his employer; he should look ahead to the future; he should save money in order to become a capitalist himself; then he should exercise personal initiative and found new factories where other workmen would toil industriously, and save, and become capitalists in their turn.

During the process many people would suffer privations: most workers would live meagerly and wrack their bodies with labor; even the employers would deny themselves luxuries that they could easily purchase, choosing instead to put back the money into their business; but after all, our bodies were not to be pampered; they were temporary dwelling places, and we should be rewarded in Heaven for our self-denial. On earth, our duty was to accumulate more wealth and produce more goods, the ultimate use of which was no subject for worry. They would somehow be absorbed, by new markets opened in the West, or overseas in new countries, or by the increased purchasing power of workmen who had saved and bettered their position.

That was the ethic of a young capitalism, and it worked admirably, so long as the territory and population of the country were expanding faster than its industrial plant. But after the war the situation changed. Our industries had grown enormously to satisfy a demand that suddenly ceased. To keep the factory wheels turning, a new domestic market had to be created. Industry and thrift were no longer adequate. There must be a new ethic that encouraged people to buy, a *consumption* ethic.

It happened that many of the Greenwich Village ideas proved useful in the altered situation. Thus, *self-expression* and *paganism* encouraged a demand for all sorts of products — modern furniture, beach pajamas, cosmetics, colored bathrooms with toilet paper to

our mainstream culture, creating "movements." These movements have influenced impressions that affect our tastes, lifestyles, fashion, music, and purchasing decisions.

Society, whether we admit it or not, is seeking that next youthquake – the next great movement to define the millennium. We are anxiously awaiting that rebellious and radical surge from youth culture to fuel our creative thoughts, ideas and products for tomorrow.

From *Street Trends: How Today's Alternative Youth Cultures Are Creating Tomorrow's Mainstream Markets*, New York: HarperBusiness, 1997, pp. xiii–xiv match. *Living for the moment* meant buying an automobile, radio or house, using it now and paying for it tomorrow. *Female equality* was capable of doubling the consumption of products – cigarettes, for example – that had formerly been used by men alone. Even *changing place* would help to stimulate business in the country from which the artist was being expatriated. The exiles of art were also trade missionaries: involuntarily they increased the foreign demand for fountain pens, silk stockings, grapefruit, and portable typewriters. They drew after them an invading army of tourists, thus swelling the profits of steamship lines and travel agencies. Everything fitted into the business picture.

. . .

On more than one occasion [the *Saturday Evening Post*] announced that the Village was dead and buried: "The sad truth is," it said in the Autumn of 1931, "that the Village was a flop." Perhaps it was true that the Village was moribund – of that we can't be sure, for creeds and ways of life among artists are hard to kill. If, however, the Village was really dying, it was dying of success. It was dying because it became so popular that too many people insisted on living there. It was dying because women smoked cigarettes on the streets of the Bronx, drank gin cocktails in Omaha and had perfectly swell parties in Seattle and Middletown – in other words, because American business and the whole of middle-class America had been going Greenwich Village.

Malcolm Cowley, *Exile's Return: A Literary Odyssey of the 1920s*, London: Penguin Books, 1934/1976, pp. 59–63, 65.

THOMAS FRANK,
"WHY JOHNNY CAN'T DISSENT"

In 1929 Edward Bernays convinced a number of young, "liberated" women to march in New York City's Easter parade while smoking cigarettes. Holding aloft these "torches of freedom," as Bernays called them, they boldly challenged the long-held prejudice against women smoking in public. The event caused a sensation. Stories and pictures ran in newspapers across the country; editorials were written and debates ensued over the rights of women to smoke. Bernays was pleased; he had been hired to increase the market for Lucky Strikes cigarettes.[1] Thomas Frank, editor of *The Baffler*, the journal in which this essay originally appeared, uncovers this practice of marketing liberation and packaging dissent as it continues – and expands – into the present day (see sidebar). In the course of exploring why commodifying dissent is so prevalent in recent times, Frank raises a critical question for readers of this anthology: if cultural rebellion serves as merely another marketing tool for transnational corporations, then just how effective a rebellion can cultural resistance be?

Capitalism is changing, obviously and drastically. From the moneyed pages of the *Wall Street Journal* to TV commercials for airlines and photocopiers we hear every day about the new order's globe-spanning, cyber-accumulating ways. But our notion about what's wrong with American life and how the figures responsible are to be confronted haven't changed much in thirty years. Call it, for convenience, the "countercultural idea." It holds that the paramount ailment of our society is conformity, a malady that has variously been described as over-organization, bureaucracy, homogeneity, hierarchy, logocentrism, technocracy, the Combine, the Apollonian. We all know what it is and what it does. It transforms humanity into "organization man," into "the man in the gray flannel suit." It is "Moloch whose mind is pure machinery," the "incomprehensible prison" that consumes "brains and imagination." It is artifice, starched shirts, tailfins, carefully mowed lawns, and always, always, the consciousness of impending nuclear destruction. It is a stiff, militaristic order that seeks to suppress instinct, to forbid sex and pleasure, to deny basic human impulses and individuality, to enforce through a rigid uniformity a meaningless plastic consumerism.

As this half of the countercultural idea originated during the 1950s, it is appropriate that the evils of conformity are most conveniently summarized with images of 1950s suburban correctness. You know, that land of sedate music, sexual repression, deference to authority, Red Scares, and smiling white people standing politely in line to go to church. Constantly appearing as a symbol of arch-backwardness in advertising and movies, it is an image we find easy to evoke.

The ways in which this system are to be resisted are equally well understood and agreed-upon. The Establishment demands homogeneity; we revolt by embracing diverse, individual lifestyles. It demands self-denial and rigid adherence to convention; we revolt through immediate gratification, instinct uninhibited, and liberation of the libido and the appetites. Few have put it more bluntly than Jerry Rubin did in 1970: "Amerika says: Don't! The yippies say: Do It!" The countercultural idea is hostile to any law and every establishment. "Whenever we see a rule, we must break it," Rubin continued. "Only by breaking rules do we discover who we are." Above all rebellion consists of a sort of Nietzschean antinomianism, an automatic questioning of the rules, a rejection of whatever social prescriptions we've happened to inherit. Just Do It is the whole of the law.

The patron saints of the countercultural idea are, of course, the Beats, whose frenzied style and merry alienation still maintain a powerful grip on the American imagination. Even forty years after the publication of *On the Road*, the works of Kerouac, Ginsberg, and Burroughs remain the *sine qua non* of dissidence, the model for aspiring poets, rock stars, or indeed anyone who feels vaguely artistic or alienated. That frenzied sensibility of pure experience, life on the edge, immediate gratification, and total freedom from moral restraint, which the Beats first propounded back in those heady days when suddenly everyone could have their own TV and powerful V-8, has stuck with us through all the intervening years and become something of a permanent American style. Go to any poetry reading and you can see a string of junior Kerouacs go through the routine, upsetting cultural hierarchies by pushing themselves to the limit, straining for that gorgeous moment of original vice when Allen Ginsberg first read "Howl" in 1955 and the patriarchs of our fantasies recoiled in shock. The Gap may have since claimed Ginsberg and *USA Today* may run feature stories about the brilliance of the beloved Kerouac, but the rebel race continues today regardless, with ever-heightening shit-references calculated to scare Jesse Helms, talk about sex and smack that is supposed to bring the electricity of real life, and ever-more determined defiance of the repressive rules and mores of the American 1950s – rules and mores that by now we know only from movies.

But one hardly has to go to a poetry reading to see the countercultural idea acted out. Its frenzied ecstasies have long since become an official aesthetic of consumer society, a monotheme of mass as well as adversarial culture. Turn on the TV and there it is instantly: the unending drama of consumer unbound and in search of an ever-heightened good time, the inescapable rock 'n' roll soundtrack, dreadlocks and ponytails bounding into Taco Bells, a drunken, swinging-camera epiphany of tennis shoes, outlaw soda pops, and mind-bending dandruff shampoos. Corporate America, it turns out, no longer speaks in the voice of oppressive order that it did when Ginsberg moaned in 1956 that *Time* magazine was: "always telling me about responsibility. Businessmen are serious. Movie producers are serious. Everybody's serious but me."

Nobody wants you to think they're serious today, least of all Time Warner. On the contrary: the Culture Trust is now our leader in the Ginsbergian search for kicks upon kicks. Corporate America is not an oppressor but a sponsor of fun, provider of lifestyle accoutrements, facilitator of carnival, our slang-speaking partner in the quest for that ever-more apocalyptic orgasm. The countercultural idea has become capitalist orthodoxy, its hunger for transgression upon transgression now perfectly suited to an economic-cultural regime that runs on ever-faster cyclings of the new; its taste for self-fulfillment and its intolerance for the confines of tradition now permitting vast latitude in consuming practices and lifestyle experimentation.

Consumerism is no longer about "conformity" but about "difference." Advertising teaches us not in the ways of puritanical self-denial (a bizarre notion on the face of it), but in orgiastic, never-ending self-fulfillment. It counsels not rigid adherence to the tastes of the herd but vigilant and constantly updated individualism. We consume not to fit in, but to prove, on the surface at least, that we are rock 'n' roll rebels, each one of us as rule-breaking and hierarchy-defying as our heroes of the 60s, who now pitch cars, shoes and beer. This imperative of endless difference is today the genius at the heart of American capitalism, an eternal fleeing from "sameness" that satiates our thirst for the New with such achievements of civilization as the infinite brands of identical cola, the myriad colors and irrepressible variety of the cigarette rack at 7-Eleven.

As existential rebellion has become a more or less official style of Information Age capitalism, so has the countercultural notion of a static, repressive Establishment grown hopelessly obsolete. However the basic impulses of the countercultural idea may have disturbed a nation lost in Cold War darkness, they are today in fundamental agreement with the basic tenets of Information Age business theory. So close are they, in fact, that it has become difficult to understand the countercultural idea as anything more than the self-justifying ideology of the new bourgeoisie that has arisen since the 1960s, the cultural means by which this group has proven itself ever so much better skilled than its slow-moving, security-minded forebears at adapting to the accelerated, always-changing consumerism of today. The anointed cultural opponents of capitalism are now capitalism's ideologues.

"Now, you too can be a rioting anarchist . . .," Associated Press

TACOMA, Wash. (AP) — Now, you too can be a rioting anarchist — and never leave the comfort of your living room.

A new video game based on the 1999 World Trade Organization riots and protests in Seattle allows players to earn points by busting a plate glass window, punching out a police officer in riot gear or attacking innocent bystanders.

The game, "State of Emergency," is billed as an "urban riot game set in the near future, where the oppressive American Trade Organization has declared a state of emergency. It is up to you to smash up everything and everyone in order to destabilize the ATO."

Rockstar Games revealed the game, due in October for Sony PlayStation 2, earlier this month at the Electronic Entertainment Expo in Los Angeles.

It is already drawing criticism.

"If you want your child to become a violent anarchist, this is a great training game," said State Rep. Mary Lou Dickerson.

Associated Press, May 29, 2001

The two come together in perfect synchronization in a figure like Camille Paglia, whose ravings are grounded in the absolutely noncontroversial ideas of the golden sixties. According to Paglia, American business is still exactly what it was believed to have been in that beloved decade, that is, "puritanical and desensualized." Its great opponents are, of course, liberated figures like "the beatniks," Bob Dylan, and the Beatles. Culture is, quite simply, a binary battle between the repressive Apollonian order of capitalism and the Dionysian impulses of the counterculture. Rebellion makes no sense without repression; we must remain forever convinced of capitalism's fundamental hostility to pleasure in order to consume capitalism's rebel products as avidly as we do. It comes as little surprise when, after criticizing the "Apollonian capitalist machine" (in her book, *Vamps and Tramps*), Paglia applauds American mass culture (in *Utne Reader*), the preeminent product of that "capitalist machine," as a "third great eruption" of a Dionysian "paganism." For her, as for most other designated dissidents, there is no contradiction between replaying the standard critique of capitalist conformity and repressiveness and then endorsing its rebel products – for Paglia the car culture and Madonna – as the obvious solution: the Culture Trust offers both Establishment and Resistance in one convenient package. The only question that remains is why Paglia has not yet landed an endorsement contract from a soda pop or automobile manufacturer.

Other legendary exponents of the countercultural idea have been more fortunate – William S. Burroughs, for example, who appears in a television spot for the Nike corporation. But so openly does the commercial flaunt the confluence of capital and counterculture that is has brought considerable criticism down on the head of the aging beat. Writing in the *Village Voice*, Leslie Savan marvels at the contradiction between Burroughs' writings and the faceless corporate entity for which he is now pushing product. "Now the realization that *nothing* threatens the system has freed advertising to exploit even the most marginal elements of society," Savan observes. "In fact, being hip is no longer quite enough – better the pitchman be 'underground.'" Meanwhile Burroughs' manager insists, as all future Cultural Studies treatments of the ad will no doubt also insist, that Burroughs' presence actually makes the commercial "deeply subversive" – "I hate to repeat the usual mantra, but you know, homosexual drug addict, manslaughter, accidental homicide." But Savan wonders whether, in fact, it is Burroughs who has been assimilated by corporate America. "The problem comes," she writes, "in how easily any idea, deed, or image can become part of the sponsored world."

The most startling revelation to emerge from the Burroughs/Nike partnership is not that corporate America has overwhelmed its cultural foes or that Burroughs can somehow remain "subversive" through it all, but the complete lack of dissonance between the two sides. Of course Burroughs is not "subversive," but neither has he "sold out": his ravings are no longer appreciably different from the official folklore of American capitalism. What's changed is not Burroughs, but business itself. As expertly as Burroughs once bayoneted American proprieties, as stridently as he once proclaimed himself beyond the laws of man and God, he is today a respected ideologue of the Information Age, occupying roughly the position in the pantheon of corporate-cultural thought once reserved strictly for Notre Dame football coaches and positive-thinking Methodist ministers. His inspirational writings are boardroom favorites, his dark nihilistic burpings the happy homilies of the new corporate faith.

For with the assumption of power by Drucker's and Reich's new class has come an entirely new ideology of business, a way of justifying and exercising power that has little to do with the "conformity" and the "establishment" so vilified by the countercultural idea. The management theorists and "leadership" charlatans of the Information Age don't waste time prattling about hierarchy and regulation, but about disorder, chaos, and the meaninglessness of convention. With its reorganization around information, capitalism has developed a new mythology, a sort of corporate antinomianism according to which the breaking of rules and the elimination of rigid corporate structure have become the central article of faith for millions of aspiring executives.

Dropping *Naked Lunch* and picking up *Thriving on Chaos*, the groundbreaking 1987 management text by Tom Peters, the most popular business writer of the past decade, one finds more philosophical similarities than one would expect from two manifestos of, respectively, dissident culture and business culture. If anything, Peters' celebration of disorder is, by virtue of its hard statistics, bleaker and more nightmarish than Burroughs'. For this popular lecturer on such once-blithe topics as competitiveness and pop psychology there is nothing, absolutely nothing, that is certain. His world is one in which the corporate wisdom of the past is meaningless, established customs are ridiculous, and "rules" are some sort of curse, a remnant of the foolish fifties that exist to be defied, not obeyed. We live in what Peters calls "A World Turned Upside Down," in which whirl is king and, in order to survive, business must eventually embrace Peters' universal solution: "Revolution!" "To meet the demands of the fast-changing competitive scene," he counsels, "we must simply learn to love change as much as we have hated it in the past." He advises businessmen to become Robespierres of routine, to demand of their underlings, "'What have you changed lately?' 'How fast are you changing?' and 'Are you pursuing bold enough change goals?'" "Revolution," of course, means for Peters the same thing it did to Burroughs and Ginsberg, Presley and the Stones in their heyday: breaking rules, pissing off the suits, shocking the bean-counters: "Actively and publicly hail defiance of the rules, many of which you doubtless labored mightily to construct in the first place." Peters even suggests that his readers implement this hostility to logocentrism in a carnivalesque celebration, drinking beer out in "the woods" and destroying "all the forms and rules and discontinued reports" and, "if you've got real nerve," a photocopier as well.

Today corporate antinomianism is the emphatic message of nearly every new business text, continually escalating the corporate insurrection begun by Peters. Capitalism, at least as it is envisioned by the best-selling management handbooks, is no longer about enforcing Order, but destroying it. "Revolution," once the totemic catchphrase of the counterculture, has become the totemic catchphrase of boomer-as-capitalist. The Information Age businessman holds inherited ideas and traditional practices not in reverence, but in high suspicion. Even reason itself is now found to be an enemy of true competitiveness, an out-of-date faculty to be scrupulously avoided by conscientious managers. A 1990 book by Charles Handy entitled the *Age of Unreason* agrees with Peters that we inhabit a time in which "there can be no certainty" and suggests that readers engage in full-fledged epistemological revolution: "Thinking Upside Down," using new ways of "learning which can . . . be seen as disrespectful if not downright rebellious," methods of approaching problems that have "never been popular with upholders of continuity and of the status quo." Three years later the authors of *Reengineering the Corporation* ("A Manifesto for Business Revolution," as its subtitle declares) are ready to push this doctrine even farther. Not only should we be suspicious of traditional practices, but we should cast out virtually everything learned over the past two centuries!

> Business reengineering means putting aside much of the received wisdom of two hundred years of industrial management. It means forgetting how work was done in the age of the mass market and deciding how it can best be done now. In business reengineering, old job titles and old organizational arrangements – departments, divisions, groups, and so on – cease to matter. They are artifacts of another age.

As countercultural rebellion becomes corporate ideology, even the beloved Buddhism of the Beats wins a place on the executive bookshelf. In *The Leader as Martial Artist* (1993), Arnold Mindell advises men of commerce in the ways of the Tao, mastery of which he likens, of course, to surfing. For Mindell's Zen businessman, as for the followers of Tom Peters, the world is a wildly chaotic place of opportunity, navigable only to an enlightened "leader" who can discern the "timespirits" at work behind the scenes. In terms Peters himself might use were he a more meditative sort of inspiration professional, Mindell explains that "the wise facilitator" doesn't seek to prevent the inevitable and random clashes between "conflicting field spirits," but to anticipate such bouts of disorder and profit thereby.

Contemporary corporate fantasy imagines a world of ceaseless, turbulent change, of centers that ecstatically fail to hold, of joyous extinction for the craven gray-flannel creature of the past. Businessmen today decorate the walls of their offices not with portraits of President Eisenhower and emblems of suburban order, but with images of extreme athletic daring, with sayings about "diversity" and "empowerment" and "thinking outside the box." They theorize their world not in the bar car of the commuter train, but in weepy corporate retreats at which they beat their tom-toms and envision themselves as part of the great avant-garde tradition of edge-livers, risk-takers, and ass-kickers. Their world is a place not of sublimation and conformity, but of "leadership" and bold talk about defying the herd. And there is nothing this new enlightened species of businessman despises more than "rules" and "reason." The prominent culture-warriors of the right may believe that the counterculture was capitalism's undoing, but the antinomian businessmen know better. "One of the T-shirt slogans of the sixties read, 'Question authority,'" the authors of *Reengineering the Corporation* write. "Process owners might buy their reengineering team members the nineties version: 'Question assumptions.'"

The new businessman quite naturally gravitates to the slogans and sensibility of the rebel sixties to express his understanding of the new Information World. He is led in what one magazine calls "the business revolution" by the office-park subversives it hails as "business activists," "change agents," and "corporate radicals." He speaks to his comrades through commercials like the one for "Warp," a type of IBM computer operating system, in which an electric guitar soundtrack and psychedelic video effects surround hip executives with earrings and hairdos who are visibly stunned by the product's gnarly 'tude (it's a "totally cool way to run your computer," reads the product's print ads). He understands the world through *Fast Company*, a successful new magazine whose editors take their inspiration from Hunter S. Thompson and whose stories describe such things as a "dis-organization" that inhabits an "anti-office" where "all vestiges of hierarchy have disappeared" or a computer scientist who is also a "rabble rouser, an agent provocateur, a product of the 1960s who never lost his activist fire or democratic values." He is what sociologists Paul Leinberger and Bruch Tucker have called "The New Individualist," the new and improved manager whose arty worldview and creative hip derive directly from his formative sixties days. The one things this new executive is definitely *not* is Organization Man, the hyper-rational counter of beans, attender of church, and wearer of stiff hats.

In television commercials, through which the new American business-man presents his visions and self-understanding to the pubic, perpetual revolution and the gospel of rule-breaking are the orthodoxy of the day. You only need to watch for a few minutes before you see one of these slogans and understand the grip of antinomianism over the corporate mind:

> Sometimes You Gotta Break the Rules – *Burger King*
> If You Don't Like the Rules, Change Them – *WXRT-FM*
> The Rules Have Changed – *Dodge*
> The Art of Changing – *Swatc*
> There's no one way to do it – *Levi's*
> This is different. Different is good – *Arby's*
> Just Different From the Rest – *Special Export Beer*
> The Line Has Been Crossed: The Revolutionary New Supra – *Toyota*
> Resist the Usual – the slogan of both *Clash Clear Malt* and *Young & Rubicam*
> Innovate Don't Imitate – *Hugo Boss*
> Chart Your Own Course – *Navigator Cologne*
> It separates you from the crowd – *Vision Cologne*

In most, the commercial message is driven home with the vanguard iconography of the rebel: screaming guitars, whirling cameras, and startled old timers who, we predict, will become an increasingly indispensable prop as consumers require ever-greater assurances that, Yes! You *are* a rebel! Just look at how offended they are!

Our businessmen imagine themselves rebels, and our rebels sound more and more like ideologists of business. Henry Rollins, for example, the maker of loutish, overbearing music and composer of high-school-grade-poetry, straddles both worlds unproblematically. Rollins' writing and lyrics strike all the standard alienated literary poses: He rails against over-civilization and yearns to "disconnect." He veers back and forth between vague threats toward "weak" people who "bring me down" and blustery declarations of his weightlifting ability and physical prowess. As a result he ruled for several years as the preeminent darling of *Details* magazine, a periodical handbook for the young executive on the rise, where rebellion has achieved a perfect synthesis with corporate ideology. In 1992, *Details* named Rollins a "rock 'n' roll samurai," an "emblem . . . of a new masculinity" whose "enlightened honesty" is "a way of being that seems to flesh out many of the ideas expressed in contemporary culture and fashion." In 1994, the magazine consummated its relationship with Rollins by naming him "Man of the Year," printing a fawning story about his muscular worldview and decorating its cover with a photo in which Rollins displays his tattoos and rubs his chin in a thoughtful manner.

Details found Rollins to be such an appropriate role model for the struggling young businessman not only because of his music-product, but because of his excellent "self-styled identity," which the magazine describes in terms normally reserved for the breast-beating and soul-searching variety of motivational seminars. Although he derives it from the quality-maximizing wisdom of the East rather than the unfashionable doctrines of Calvin, Rollins' rebel posture is identical to that fabled ethic of the small capitalist whose regimen of positive thinking and hard work will one day pay off. *Details* describes one of Rollins' songs, quite seriously, as "a self-motivational superforce, an anthem of empowerment," teaching lessons that any aspiring middle-manager must internalize. Elsewhere, Iggy Pop, that great chronicler of the ambitionless life, praises Rollins as a "high achiever" who "wants to go somewhere." Rollins himself even seems to invite such an interpretation. His recent spoken-word account of touring with Black Flag, delivered in an unrelenting two-hour drill-instructor staccato, begins with the timeless bourgeois story of opportunity taken, of young Henry leaving the security of a "straight job," enlisting with a group of visionaries who were "the hardest working people I have ever seen," and learning "what hard work is all about." In the liner notes he speaks proudly of his Deming-esque dedication to quality, of how his bandmates "Delivered under pressure at incredible odds." When describing his relationship with his parents for the readers of *Details*, Rollins quickly cuts to the critical matter, the results that such dedication has brought: "Mom, Dad, I outgross both of you put together," a happy observation he repeats in his interview with the *New York Times Magazine*.

Despite the extreme hostility of punk rockers with which Rollins had to contend all through the 1980s, it is he who has been chosen by the commercial media as the godfather of rock 'n' roll revolt. It is not difficult to see why. For Rollins the punk rock decade was but a lengthy seminar on leadership skills, thriving on chaos, and total quality management. Rollins' much celebrated anger is indistinguishable from the anger of the frustrated junior executive who finds obstacles on the way to the top. His discipline and determination are the automatic catechism of any small entrepreneur who's just finished brainwashing himself with the latest leadership and positive-thinking tracts; his poetry is the inspired verse of *21 Days to Unlimited Power* or *Let's Get Results, Not Excuses.* Henry Rollins is no more a threat to established power in America than was Dale Carnegie. And yet Rollins as king of the rebels – peerless and ultimate – is the message hammered home wherever photos of his growling visage appear. If you're unhappy with your lot, the Culture Trust tell us with each new tale of Rollins, if you feel you must rebel, take your cue from the most disgruntled guy of all: Lift weights! Work hard! Meditate in your back yard! Root out the weaknesses deep down inside yourself! But whatever you do, *don't* think about who controls power or how it is wielded.

The structure and thinking of American business have changed enormously in the years since our popular conceptions of its problems and abuses were formulated. In the meantime the mad frothings and jolly apolitical revolt of Beat, despite their vast popularity and insurgent air, have become powerless against a new regime that, one suspects, few of Beat's present-day admirers and practitioners feel any need to study or understand. Today that beautiful countercultural idea, endorsed now by everyone from the surviving Beats to shampoo manufacturers, is more the official doctrine of corporate America than it is a program of resistance. What we understand as "dissent" does not subvert, does not challenge, does not even question the cultural faiths of Western business. What David Rieff wrote of the revolutionary pretensions of multiculturalism is equally true of the countercultural idea: "The more one reads in academic multiculturalist journals and in business publications, and the more one contrasts the speeches of CEOs and the speeches of noted multiculturalist academics, the more one is struck by the similarities in the way they view the world." What's happened is not co-optation or appropriation, but a simple and direct confluence of interest.

The problem with cultural dissent in America isn't that it's been co-opted, absorbed or ripped-off. Of course it's been all of these things. But it has proven so hopelessly susceptible to such assaults for the same reason it has become so harmless in the first place, so toothless even before Mr. Geffen's boys discovered it angsting away at some bar in Lawrence, Kansas: It is no longer any different from the official culture it's supposed to be subverting. The basic impulses of the countercultural idea, as descended from the holy Beats, are about as threatening to the new breed of antinomian businessmen as Anthony Robbins selling success and how to achieve it on a late-night infomercial.

The people who staff the Combine aren't like Nurse Ratched. They aren't Frank Burns, they aren't the Church Lady, they aren't Dean Wormer from *Animal House*, they aren't those repressed old folks in the commercials who want to ban Tropicana Fruit Twisters. They're hipper than you can ever hope to be because *hip is their official ideology*, and they're always going to be there at the poetry reading to encourage your "rebellion" with a hearty "right on, man!" before you even know they're in the auditorium. You can't outrun them, or even stay ahead of them for very long: it's their racetrack, and that's them waiting at the finish line to congratulate you on how *outrageous* your new style is, on how you *shocked* those stuffy prudes out in the heartland.

Thomas Frank, "Why Johnny Can't Dissent," *Commodify Your Dissent: Salvos from The Baffler*, Thomas Frank and Matt Weiland (eds.), New York: Norton, 1997, pp. 31–45. Originally printed in *The Baffler #6*, 1995.

ABBIE HOFFMAN,
FROM *REVOLUTION FOR THE HELL OF IT*, AND
JERRY RUBIN,
FROM *DO IT!*

Abbie Hoffman and Jerry Rubin, two of the founders of the late 1960s Youth International Party, aka Yippie!, mastered the politics of the prank. They brought the New York Stock Exchange to a halt by throwing dollar bills from an observation balcony onto the trading floor, dressed in Revolutionary war costume to make a mockery of congressional hearings, and nominated a pig for president at the 1968 Democratic Convention. But behind their absurdist humor lies a serious strategy. Hoffman and Rubin understand that for better or worse mass media shapes mass consciousness. Therefore, they reason, instead of making your own culture out of whole cloth, it's more effective to hijack the dominant culture and make it mouth your message. Using advertising as a model for radical propaganda, and the TV news as a theater for revolution, they turn the power of commercial culture against itself. As Rubin writes, "Every guerrilla must know how to use the terrain of the culture he is trying to destroy." There's a retributive justice in this practice now known as "culture jamming." As commercial culture borrows signs and symbols from cultures of resistance, the latter now poaches from the former. But this brings up a question for both sides: when you hijack a vehicle do you carry along a bit of its meaning? That is: when commercial media is pirated for radical messages do these messages become mere entertainment or product? And conversely: When the image of hip rebellion sells a product, does it also sell the image that rebellion is hip?

Revolution for the Hell of It

Blank space as communication

It is a preview. Have you ever noticed how movie previews are done? They are done by the best minds in Hollywood. TV ads, as of lately, have the same effectiveness. They create a dynamism. The viewer becomes involved. Expectations are built up. Needs are addressed. They are totally absorbing with all the quick cuts, slogans, flashing images and exciting tempos. Movie previews and TV ads are written by our modern poets. They know how to create the blank space into which the viewer can place himself. Television is more like swimming than reading books.

All movie previews are rumors. They all exaggerate. "The greatest movie in twenty years!" Fireworks explode. Wow! "Don't miss this one." Zoom. "Bare-backed girl." Flash. "Exposed." Everything spins. Eight scenes compressed in five-second flashes.

TV ads are also rumors. They are not always hot as the image of the movie preview. Some are cool. Cool images promote security. They typify banks, insurance companies, airlines, government agencies. A typical one is the ad for the Dreyfus Fund. A lion walks unnoticed down Wall Street. Slump. Slump. Slump. Strong, determined, with a sense of the future. You are the lion amid the sterile world around you. Where are you going? The lion jumps onto the word "Dreyfus." "*Growl.*" He is satisfied. "INVEST IN DREYFUS." Few words are needed. Words confuse. Words are hot. A lion in a street of people is worth a thousand words. It is a wonderful ad, fantastically filmed. A lion walking in a crowded street is totally absorbing. There is an underlying tension of course, but overall coolness. No chaos. No anarchy. No risks. Just give us your dough. Maybe we should run a lion for President?

Projecting cool images is not our goal. We do not wish to project a calm secure future. We are disruption. We are hot. In our ad the lion cracks. Races through the streets. We are cannibals, cowboys, Indians, witches, warlocks. Weird-looking freaks that crawl out of the cracks in America's nightmare. Very visible and, as everyone knows, straight from the white middle-class suburban life. We are a pain in the ass to America because we cannot be explained. Blacks riot because they are oppressed. An Italian cabdriver told me, "If I was black, I'd be pissed, too." America understands the blacks.

We are alienated. What's that all about? Existential lovers in a plastic society. Our very existence is disruptive. Long hair and freaky clothes are total information. It is not necessary to say we are opposed to the ———. Everybody already knows. It is a mistake to tell people what they already know. We alienate people. We involve people. Attract-Repel. We play on the generation gap. Parents shit. They are baffled, confused. They want the cool lion. We tear through the streets. Kids love it. They understand it on an internal level. We are living TV ads, movies. Yippie! There is no program. Program would make our movement sterile. We are living contradictions. I cannot really explain it. I do not even understand it myself.

Blank space, the interrupted statement, the unsolved puzzle, they are all involving. There is a classic experiment in psychology. Subjects are given problems to solve. Some tasks they complete; others are interrupted. Six months later they are given a memory test. They consistently remember the problems that were interrupted. Let's postulate a third setting, in which the subject is shown how to solve the problem by an instructor. It would probably be the least remembered of the three. It is called "going to school" and is the least involving relationship.

When we opened the FREE STORE we circulated a leaflet with a beautiful work of art, and under it in Spanish was the line: *Everything is free at the store of the Diggers.* No address. No store hours. No list of items and services. It was tremendously effective. Puerto Ricans began asking questions. Puerto Ricans talked to hippies. Everybody searched for the FREE STORE together.

I stare at a button. Bright pink on purple background: Yippie! It pops right out. It's mispelled. Good. Misspelling can be a creative act. What does Yippie! mean? Energy – excitement – fun – fierceness – exclamation point! Last December three of us sat in a room discussing plans to bring people to Chicago to make a statement about the Democratic Convention. Hippies are dead. Youth International Party – Y.I.P. – YIP – YIPPIE! We're all jumping around the room, Paul Krassner, Jerry Rubin, and I. Playing Yippie! games. "Y." "Right." That's our symbol. That's our question. "Join the Y." "God, Nixon will attack us in three months for confusing the image of the YMCA." Within fifteen minutes we have created a myth. Head for the media. "Hello, my name is Paul Yippie, what's yours!" Within two weeks every underground paper has a Yippie! story. In a month *Newsweek* writes "the Yippies Are Coming." Lawrence Lipton, in the LA *Free Press*, analyzes Yippie! origins. *Y*s appear magically on walls around the country.

All the while, the excitement and energy are focused on Chicago and people get involved. A Yippie! button produces a question. The wearer must answer. He tells a little story. He mentions Chicago, a festival of music, violence (Americans love to go to accidents and fires), guerrilla theater, Democrats. Each story is told in a different way. There is mass participation in the Yippie! myth. Can we change an H to a Y? Can myths involve people to the extent that they will make the journey to far-off Chicago? Can magic media succeed where organizing has failed? Y not?

Blank space is the transmission of information whereby the viewer has an opportunity
to become involved as a participant.

In Saigon, the newspapers are censored. Various pages have sections of blank articles. There is more information in those blank articles than you might suspect. I go on television and make a point of swearing. I know the little fuckers don't get through, but the image of me blabbing away with the enthusiasm and excitement of a future world better than this while being sliced up by the puritanical, sterile culture of the Establishment is information worth conveying.

Abbie Hoffman (aka "Free"), *Revolution for the Hell of It*, New York: Pocket Books, 1968/1970, pp. 83–6.

Do It!

Every revolutionary needs a color TV

Walter Cronkite is SDS's best organizer. Uncle Walter brings out the map of the US with circles around the campuses that blew up today. The battle reports.

Every kid out there is thinking, "Wow! I wanna see *my* campus on that map!"

Television proves the domino theory: one campus falls and they all fall.

The first "student demonstration" flashed across the TV tubes of the nation as a myth in 1964. That year the first generation being raised from birth on TV was 9, 10 and 11 years old. "First chance I get," they thought, "I wanna do that too."

The first chance they got was when they got to junior high and high school five years later – 1969! And that was the year Amerika's junior high and high schools exploded! A government survey shows that three out of every five high schools in the country had "some form of active protest" in 1969.

TV is raising generations of kids who want to grow up and become demonstrators.

Have you ever seen a boring demonstration on TV? Just being on TV makes it exciting. Even picket lines look breathtaking. Television creates myths bigger than reality.

Demonstrations last hours, and most of that time nothing happens. After the demonstration we rush home for the six o'clock news. The drama review. TV packs all the action into two minutes – a commercial for the revolution.

The mere idea of a "story" is revolutionary because a "story" implies disruption of normal life. Every reporter is a dramatist, creating a theater out of life.

Crime in the streets is news; law and order is not. A revolution is news; the status quo ain't.

The media does not *report* "news," it *creates* it. An event *happens* when it goes on TV and becomes myth.

The media is not "neutral." The presence of a camera transforms a demonstration, turning us into heroes. We take more chances when the press is there because we know whatever happens will be known to the entire world within hours.

Television keeps us escalating our tactics; a tactic becomes ineffective when it stops generating gossip or interest – "news."

Politicians get air time just by issuing statements. Rockefeller doesn't have to carry a picket sign to make a point. But ordinary people must take to the streets to get on television. One person, doing the right thing at the right time, can create a myth. The disruption of Nixon's speech reduces Nixon to background.

TV time goes to those with the most guts and imagination.

I never understand the radical who comes on TV in a suit and tie. Turn off the sound and he could be the mayor!

The *words* may be radical, but television is a nonverbal instrument! The way to understand TV is to shut off the sound. No one remembers any words they hear; the mind is a technicolor movie of images, not words.

I've never seen "bad" coverage of a demonstration. It makes no difference what they *say* about us. The pictures are the story.

Our power lies in our ability to strike fear in the enemy's heart: so the more the media exaggerate, the better. When the media start saying nice things about us, we should get worried.

If the yippies controlled national TV, we could make the Viet Kong and the Black Panthers the heroes of swooning Amerikan middle-aged housewives everywhere within a week.

The movement is too puritanical about the use of the media. After all, Karl Marx never watched television!

You can't be a revolutionary today without a television set – it's as important as a gun!

Every guerrilla must know how to use the terrain of the culture that he is trying to destroy!

Jerry Rubin, *Do It!: Scenarios of the Revolution*, New York: Ballantine Books, 1970, pp. 106–8.

EIGHT

MIXING POP AND POLITICS

Culture has always had a place in political struggle, usually pushed to the side. Whether theatrical pageants to raise money, or murals to raise consciousness, culture has been cast in a supporting role to the "real" work of organizing (cf. Reed). No longer. A new generation of activists, like those writing below, consider culture a key component of their tactics, strategy, and campaigns. Why the shift? Look at changes in the larger world: culture, in the form of entertainment and information, is one the leading sectors of the economy. From the artistic directors and software coders to the person who works the counter at the video store, producing and handling culture is now part of our life. The same can be said for consuming. Our leisure time is spent watching TV, going to movies, and playing video games. The idea of a performed cultural world seems second nature to us. Add into this mix the Internet, the virtual world of signs and symbols where an increasing amount of our everyday life takes place, and it's no surprise that activism has embraced culture. Activists have become cultural guerillas because this is the terrain of the battles they fight.

BARBARA EPSTEIN,
"THE POLITICS OF PREFIGURATIVE COMMUNITY:
THE NON-VIOLENT DIRECT ACTION MOVEMENT"

In 1999 activists surprised the world, and themselves, by shutting down the meetings of the World Trade Organization in Seattle, Washington. The primary organization behind the protests was the Direct Action Network. But DAN isn't really an organization. There's no membership, headquarters, ideology, or chains of command; instead there is a loose network of activists sharing the same process of organization: affinity groups, spokescouncil meetings, consensus building, and a common concern with creating a supportive community for political action. This style of organizing precedes Seattle. Spokescouncil meetings bear more than a passing resemblance to the early Soviets of revolutionary Russia. Spanish anarchists in 1930s used affinity groups, and civil rights organizers in the Student Nonviolent Coordinating Committee in the 1960s stressed the creation of what they called the "beloved community" in their activism. All these ingredients came together in the direct action protests of the late 1970s and early 1980s against nuclear power. These protests were characterized by objectives that were as much cultural as they were material. The goal was to shut down nuclear power plants, but in the act of doing this demonstrators attempted to "prefigure" an ideal society (cf. Hill). This culture-infused politics of prefigurative community, its strengths as well as its weaknesses, is the subject of activist/scholar Barbara Epstein's essay excerpted below.

My introduction to the non-violent direct action movement came in June of 1983, when I found myself in jail with roughly a thousand other people who had blocked the road in front of the Lawrence Livermore Laboratory, the University of California's nuclear weapons research facility about fifty miles southeast of Oakland. The action had been organized by the Livermore Action Group (LAG), a Bay Area organization with affiliated groups throughout Northern California dedicated to closing down Livermore and challenging the arms race through non-violent direct action. Thirteen hundred people had been arrested at a previous LAG action the year before. During that action demonstrators had a choice of signing police citations and receiving a fine, or going to jail for a couple of nights without further prosecution.

At the 1983 action I intended to go to jail rather than "cite out," but I expected that the experience would be similar to that of the year before, and that I would be out in two days at the most. This time, however, the judge decided to try to break the movement by keeping us in jail as long as possible. For the first three days no-one was allowed to bail out except for medical reasons. We were then told that we could come for arraignment and receive sentences of two years' probation restraining our participation in further civil disobedience. Most of us opted to stay in jail, holding out for eleven days until we won an agreement that there would be no probation.

Mass jail experiences tend to be terrible or wonderful. Either people cannot get along with each other, cannot agree on how to behave in jail or on what demands should be made, and tensions escalate, or people are able to work together well in an atmosphere of militant community. Our 1983 jail stay showed the movement at its best, breeding a solidarity that sustained everyone through eleven days of uncertainty and uncomfortable conditions: terrible food, sleep disturbed by lights and constant talk of the guards, cold nights without enough blankets. Because the Santa Rita Prison was already full to overflowing, circus tents were set up for us in the prison grounds, the women's tents beside the freeway, the men's tents perhaps a quarter of a mile farther back. Because we had not yet been arraigned we had the right to access to telephones, which those already sentenced did not have. Two banks of pay telephones, one on the women's side, one on the men's, allowed us to arrive at common strategies and to communicate with the outside world.

We were organized by "affinity groups" of ten to fifteen people; affinity groups were combined in clusters, and every time a decision had to be made (often, several times a day) the clusters would meet to work out their views and arrive at consensus. Someone who disagreed passionately with a collective decision had the resort of blocking it, although it was understood that this power should not be used unless a fundamental moral issue was at stake. Each cluster sent a "spokes" to a "spokescouncil" which met simultaneously with the clusters; runners would go between clusters and spokescouncil, bringing questions to the clusters and conveying the decisions to the spokescouncil. Spokes were rotated daily, so as to discourage the emergence of a leading group. But even though there was no formal leadership, there was an informal group of people who were looked to for leadership, and who spent a good deal of time meeting among themselves, and with others, trying to find ways of avoiding problems and facilitating the operation of what we were coming to call the peace camp in the tents.

When we were not meeting in our clusters or affinity groups, there were workshops and seminars on everything from how to fold paper cranes to the history of the Cold War. Some people spent a good deal of their time sunbathing. In the evenings, there were talent shows: on Emma Goldman's birthday, we held a party: first there were presentations on Emma Goldman's life and the history of anarchism, and then we danced to drum music improvised from empty aluminum storage cans.

But the authorities did not leave us to our own devices for long. Twice a day the guards would round us up and herd us into one of the tents, where we would sit with our clusters in case quick decisions were needed. The sheriff would then announce through a bullhorn that the court was open and the judge was waiting for us to present ourselves to be arraigned. Each time several women would go to board the bus for the court; our spokeswoman would then present the refusal of the rest of us, pointing out that we had not yet been offered a satisfactory sentence. (The same scene was played out simultaneously on the men's side.)

The first time this happened, as the women who had decided to leave boarded the bus, the rest of us, relieved that they were so few, rose and sang "Solidarity Forever." In the brief general meeting that followed, one woman expressed her dismay: to sing "Solidarity Forever" while a few women were leaving was, she pointed out, to exclude them from that solidarity; it was an implicit criticism of their action. A committee was formed to try to find some way of affirming our solidarity without implying that those who left were breaking it. The next day, when we were again invited to go for arraignment, women in pairs began to form a bridge with their outstretched arms; the bridge lengthened to include everyone who was not leaving. As those who were leaving walked under this human bridge, the women who made up the bridge sang to them, "Listen, listen, listen, to our heart song, we will never forget you, we will never forsake you." Those who were part of the bridge were able to hug and kiss the departing women as they left. Only after the buses had departed did the rest of us sing "Solidarity Forever."

I had been part of the left for a long time before I ended up in Santa Rita. When I was in high school, in the late fifties and early sixties, I joined the peace movement; later I was a member of both the Communist Party and SDS. I joined the protests against the war in Vietnam and the early women's movement. Especially in the late sixties and early seventies, I became quite accustomed to being told by self-designated left and/or feminist authorities what was or was not correct behavior. Even in better times, I had never seen a movement that actually went out of its way to affirm its solidarity with those who had decided to leave an action or separate themselves in some other way from the main course the movement was taking. It made me want to learn more about the history and ethos of the movement. I was also struck by the fact that I had known very few of the women in the tents before being in jail with them. There were very few academics among them, and hardly anyone from the Bay Area intellectual/left/feminist circles I am familiar with, which tend to lay claim to the legacy of sixties activism.

The women in jail with me ranged in age from eighteen to eighty, though the majority were in their twenties and thirties. (One sixteen-year-old had disguised her age when she was arrested; she hid in one of the privies when the authorities tried to find her and release her.) Many of the women worked in health care, elementary and high-school teaching, social work or therapy of various kinds. The counter-culture was well represented, and a substantial number worked in health food stores or lived in rural communes. Lesbians, who tended to know their own community, estimated that they made up about a third of the camp. There were also many older women, some long-time peace activists, but also suburban housewives who had never been involved in protest activity but who found the issues of war and disarmament compelling.

Occasional tensions arose between the older, more conventional group and the younger women; many older women were disturbed at the sight of young women sunbathing naked in full view of male prison guards, but the dominant strain was the strong sense of family in the camp, of each generation needing the other. At one point, when prospects of a reasonable settlement with the judge seemed particularly discouraging and many people were tempted to give up, a general meeting was held at which older women talked about their years of political involvement and the importance of not giving up. This meeting probably prevented the collapse of the action. The older women were also aware that the action would not have happened without the younger, more culturally radical women, who had played a major role in planning it and whose energy was at its center.

Religious differences, like generational differences, were more complementary than divisive. There were a number of Christian affinity groups, some from Bay Area congregations. One, involving younger women, was from the radical Christian community outside the organized church. There was an affinity group of witches, and a broader grouping of women who considered themselves Pagans.[1] The many Jewish women tended to be secular and, in the context of a community which had strong and various religious overtones, relatively silent. Feminism, pacifism, and environmentalism were all part of the ethos of the camp; though there were many who would have called themselves socialists, anarchism provided the vocabulary for political discussion. If any one group brought all these tendencies together and set a common tone, it was the witches and the Pagans, whose rituals were open to anyone who cared to participate.

My discovery of the Livermore Action Group, and the sense that it represented something new and growing, led me back to the history of the anti-nuclear energy movement, in particular the Clamshell Alliance on the New England coast, and the Abalone Alliance, which focused on Pacific Gas and Electric's Diablo Canyon plant on the central California coast. It also prompted me to look at the radical religious community and the brand of feminism which some call "ecofeminism," both of which are strong subcurrents in the movement and have helped to shape its distinctive culture.

The Culture of Non-Violent Direct Action

Non-violent anarchism, spirituality, and the attempt to build a prefigurative community are the basic components of the culture which has gradually emerged in the direct action movement. Feminism is implied in all of these as well, but it has been not so much an active ingredient as a background assumption. Each of these components has played a part in drawing people into the movement, and in cementing it together. There have been tensions, and sometimes open debate, over how these themes are to be understood. In a number of instances the movement has had to confront the twin dangers that it could marginalize itself by too rigid an insistence on its ideals, and that by compromising its ideals it could lose its special identity.

The two issues most consistently debated within the movement have been how non-violence and the consensus process should be interpreted. While non-violence has always been accepted as a basic principle, questions have been raised whether non-violence includes attacks on property, or actions non-violent in themselves but which might incite violence from the police . . . At the LAG mass actions, for instance, some people were afraid that carrying objects of any kind, whether banners, models of missiles or crosses, would be interpreted by the police as aggressive and would incite them to violence. It was agreed that one area in front of the gate would be kept free of such objects.

The question of consensus, and the larger issue of how one creates a democratic, egalitarian organization which functions effectively, has been more difficult. The Clamshell Alliance never deviated from a total adherence to consensus process. Some of the contradictions of this method of decision-making became apparent when the anarchists used their power to block consensus to prevent the holding of a strictly non-violent occupation, and again when the old guard concluded that a decision had to be reached quickly and bypassed consensus process. This point was never reached in Abalone or LAG, but Abalone modified the consensus process so that a decision of the whole organization could be blocked only by an entire local group which had reached consensus to do so, not by one individual. This modification was also adopted by LAG, but it has not solved all the problems. The larger an organization becomes, the more unwieldy the consensus process is. Many people find it intolerably slow and lose interest in attending meetings.[2]

In spite of these problems, the direct action movement's attempt to put a philosophy of non-violent anarchism into practice, both in its actions and in its internal life, has contributed in major ways to the popular appeal of the movement. The movement's emphasis on small groups and autonomous action has encouraged creativity, especially in the period since affinity groups came into their prime, that is, in the latter part of Abalone's history and in LAG. LAG in particular contained affinity groups based on a wide variety of interests and political projects or approaches, including Salt and Pepper, an affinity group made up of older people, Revolutionary Garden Party, made up of gardeners, the Peace Navy, made up of skippers interested in conducting actions on the water, and many others.

One LAG affinity group, the Communist Dupes (who took their name when Reagan said that peace activists were either Soviet agents or Communist dupes), were regarded as exemplary in their ability to design events which could be carried out by a small group and which combined direct action with guerilla theatre, usually with a twist of ironic humor. Once, when the Alameda Board of Supervisors had reprimanded Berkeley City Council for failing to salute the flag at its meetings, the Dupes and their friends, dressed as solid citizens, attended a meeting of the Board of Supervisors and, when they rose to salute the flag, burst into "The Star Spangled Banner" and other similar songs. The Supervisors, at first pleased by the evident patriotism of the group, became increasingly uneasy as the concert showed no sign of ending, and finally had to escape to a back room to conduct their meeting. One Supervisor told the press that this was taking a good thing too far; it smacked of "patriotic coercion." The Dupes, also interviewed on their way out, said that they were patriotic citizens who had come to praise the flag, and that they did not know when they would be back. "We never know," said one "when the patriotic urge will hit."

Consensus, often called "feminist process," draws many people, especially women, into the movement; it assures those with little political experience or intellectual self-confidence that they will be heard. Charlotte Davis, who had been a medical technician in a hospital in San Francisco, contrasted working with Abalone with the job she had left, where her superior would call a meeting, announce the agenda, and talk at the technicians present. In Abalone, Charlotte said, there were no superiors, everyone's input was sought and valued.

> For me, the most important thing was that in almost every meeting I was in, we went around in a circle and everyone said what they had to say. As we went around and people said what they really thought and felt, it became clear to me that every person in the world thinks well, if you give them enough time and space. If one person came up with an objection that made sense, we all listened

to it. We were not forced to vote. That's how I think ideas should develop. That kind of feeling of all of us working together on a problem was real important to me. And bullies were exposed immediately, because they couldn't bear to sit and listen.

The Religious Community

The anarchism of the direct action movement is very much part of an American tradition of anti-authoritarianism and grassroots democracy.[3] But it speaks a language not easily assimilated into current political discourse and which sounds foreign to many outside the Left. In contrast, the religious or spiritual tone of the direct action movement, especially in its most recent phases, provides a more familiar basis for communication with mainstream Americans, especially women. The movement's emphasis on moral witness, on personal responsibility based on religious faith, allows more people to enter who would find no point of contact with an entirely secular and strategically-oriented movement.

Pat Daane, for instance, found her way into LAG through her church; joining the peace movement was for her an affirmation of faith and a conversion experience. Pat lives in Pidemont, an upper-middle-class section of Oakland generally regarded as quite conservative. She was educated in a Catholic girls' school, and spent three years in a convent. She married, had three children, and has been a member of the Junior League and of the Newman Center, an East Bay Catholic church. Sometime during the winter of 1982 a friend asked her to watch *The Last Epidemic*, a film which portrays the effects on San Francisco of a nuclear war. When Pat described the film to her family, her son, then six, asked, "Does that mean I'll never grow up?" "Not if I have anything to do with it," Pat answered. She put the issue out of her mind until, a few months later, she saw an announcement in the Newman Center newspaper of a Mother's Day action at the Livermore Lab.

Pat went with some other women from the Center. She was disturbed at the way some of the women were dressed, in costumes representing death, clown costumes and so forth, but other than that the morning passed uneventfully. As Pat and her companions were preparing to leave, they saw a number of women, sitting in the road in front of the main gate, being arrested. Pat was frightened, feeling that she might be drawn into this scene herself. She hid behind a police van and peered out from behind it.

One [of the women sitting in the road] had gray hair and was wearing a skirt – I could relate to skirts, right? And I thought, "That woman is laying down her life for my children." Then I knew that I would get arrested the next time there was an action; I would go to jail, and I knew I would fast the whole time. I didn't know why I knew that. We walked back to the car; I was in a sort of trance, I guess. I remember we prayed together, and I prayed out loud to have the courage to act on my responsibility. I knew at that moment that I would be getting arrested and I would be fasting. You don't turn back after that.

The Christians in the direct action movement take personal responsibility very seriously. It is they who tend to take the greatest risks, both in terms of physical safety and length of jail sentences.

In August 1982, the Spirit affinity group, with others, blockaded a Trident nuclear submarine which was entering the port of Seattle. The members of Spirit just spent five days in prayer with members of the Pacific Life Community, a Christian pacifist group based in the area. Then for two weeks, they went out in boats and waited for the submarine. When it approached, it was preceded by the Coast Guard, who directed water cannons at the protesters, boarded their ships and arrested them at gunpoint. One of the members of Spirit who participated in this action, Darla Rucker, is confined to a wheelchair. Charges against the protesters were eventually dropped because the Coast Guard had illegally assaulted them without warning, but if it had not been for this they could have received long sentences.

Terry Rucker told me that he and the members of Spirit believe they are called upon to risk more than others, and that it is the role of Christians to be at the cutting edge. At times others in the movement find the Christians' emphasis on self-sacrifice disconcerting. There have been many debates between the Christians and others about whether to accept or to fight long jail sentences. The radical Christians especially tend to be critical of people who, as Terry said, "want to negotiate light little sentences and waltz out of jail." The anarchists and the Pagans, on the other hand, often argue in favor of getting out of jail as quickly as possible, so as to be able to continue the protest. The Pagans reject the Christians' emphasis on suffering and bring a lighter tone to the movement. "The difference between Christians and Pagans is that Christians like to fast, Pagans like to feast," Starhawk, a member of the witches' affinity group, Matrix, told me.

. . .

Despite its influence, the language of Christian radicalism has not permeated the movement to nearly the same extent as has the language of Pagan/feminist anarchism. Large actions rarely draw their metaphors from organized religion; their symbolism and language are more likely to invoke

"Spirals: How to Conjure Justice," Starhawk

This is how it works: there are twelve of us and the rattlesnake makes thirteen. We are in the redwoods, next to the river we have been fighting to defend, among the trees that will be cut if the Timber Harvest Plan goes through. The snake is in a bucket: she appeared on the driveway as one of our friends was leaving to come to the ritual. We have with us a pile of letters that have been written, a petition that all the neighbors have signed. We know that the man who will take possession of this land, if the Timber Harvest Plan goes through, has lied, cheated, has destroyed ancient trees and has desecrated graves with bulldozers. The California Department of Forestry has no mechanism for integrating this information. There is nothing in its process that truly allows the voice of our concerns for the river, the land the community to be heard, as there is nothing in the deliberations of the World Bank or the International Monetary Fund or the World Trade Organization or the political processes that support them that truly opens an ear to concerns of justice. Within these institutions are good people who truly desire to protect the forests, to help the poor. Yet whatever efforts they make, and regardless of what is stated in press conferences or political campaigns, injustice is embedded in the very structure of these bodies, in the procedures that must be followed, in the questions that can and cannot be asked, in how the debate is framed. If we want justice, we have to conjure it up from another framework. We have to step outside the institutions, walk out into the streets, the forests,

what are called the "earth religions." This is true even of those actions which draw large numbers of older women, and include sponsorship from organizations outside the core of the direct action movement. At the 1987 Mother's Day action at the Nevada Test site, largely organized by the American Peace Test, a committee which originated in the Freeze, a number of speakers mentioned the need to reclaim a connection with the earth they associated with ancient matriarchies and Goddess-oriented religions. There was a guided meditation and the crowd was led in song; both were taken from the Pagan tradition.

It is the feminists, especially those with a Pagan/anarchist perspective, who have a sense of how to build an inclusive community, of how the movement can incorporate those outside its boundaries. Margot Adler, a witch and a reporter for National Public Radio, argues that Pagan/feminist anarchism is able to speak to many people in spite of its dissonance with the prevailing culture because it contains means of building community, of enabling people to acknowledge their bonds with other people and with nature, and that, in a culture which disparages these bonds and denies the need for them, this is something that many people crave.

To illustrate this point Margot tells a story. Several years ago she was invited to Harvard as a Neimann Fellow, to take part in a several-month program for established journalists. Even though it is public knowledge that she is a witch (she is the author of a well-regarded study of witchcraft in the US, written from an insider's perspective), Margot felt shy about discussing this with her mostly conventional fellow students. But as the program was drawing to a close, she felt she needed to acknowledge this side of herself, so she invited the other members of her class to a ritual in the garden of the Niemann Center. More than half the class came, including a number of straight middle-aged men. Margot conducted a ritual around the theme of protection from danger, because several members of the class were headed for crisis spots in various parts of the globe. She served her fellow students glasses of wine, had them stand in a circle holding hands, and taught them a few songs. It was her impression that many of them had never had an experience like that before, but they seemed to enjoy it and thanked her when they left. A few weeks later, a final banquet was held and after the dinner was over, to Margot's surprise, the class stood up, held hands and sang one of the songs she had taught them. Two of the men cried. One of them was one of the crustiest journalists in the class. Since that time members of the class have remained in better touch than any previous group of Niemann Fellows, and a number have told Margot that this is because of what she did, which allowed them to acknowledge the ties that they had developed among themselves.[4]

Prefigurative Community and Political Strategy

There is a good deal in the style of the non-violent direct action movement which makes people outside it uncomfortable: the emphasis on civil disobedience, the consensus process and the language that goes along with it and, even more, the focus on spirituality, especially the Pagans and the witches and the rituals they bring into the movement.

The social democratic and Marxist Left in particular object that the direct action movement is so foreign to mainstream American culture that it can only alienate people from the Left. It is however possible that the real issue is the discomfort many social democrats and Marxists feel with the movement's challenge to a secular, rationalist worldview. One of the sources of the direct action movement is the counter-culture of the sixties, and the key to understanding current tensions between the movement and other sections of the contemporary Left is the counter-culture/politico split of the sixties, now being replayed on different terrain. The difference is that the counter-cultural or spiritually-oriented side of this split is more politically

drawing impermanent spirals in the face of fear.

So we gather in the woods to claim this forest as sacred space, to charge our letters, our petition, our phone calls, with magic, that extra something that may shift the structures just a bit, create an opening for something new. We sing, we chant, we make offerings, we claim this land as sacred space. We dare to call upon the ancestors although we recognize ourselves as the inheritors of stolen lands. Out of these contradictions, out of our willingness to listen, to guard the soil and the trees and the rivers, to cherish each other and the love that arises from our history of everyday work and quarrels and our common song, we intend to conjure back the salmon, the ancient groves, the community of those indigenous to this place. We draw spirals in the dirt. We leave feathers, yarn, a shell: our altar. We release the snake from her bucket. She is beautiful, the scales on her back glistening in diamond shape, her tale crowned with many rattles. She leans her chin on the shell filled with waters of the world and listens as we sing to her. When we go, she will coil her body into a spiral and remain, a fitting guardian for this land.

This is how it works: someone has a vision that arises from a fierce and passionate love. To make it real, we must love every moment of what we do. Impermanent spirals embed themselves in asphalt, concrete, in dust. Slowly, slowly, they eat into the foundations of the structures of power. Deep transformations take time. Regeneration arises from decay. *Si se puede!* It can be done.

From "Spirals: How to Conjure Justice," www.starhawk.org (2001) focused and vital than before, while the Marxist/rationalist wing is in decline.

There is a sense in which Marxism has given up on the future: existing socialism no longer provides the basis for a compelling vision of the future, and few on the Left believe it likely that a socialist revolution will occur soon enough to halt the drift toward catastrophe. One of the reasons the Christian Left is now able to espouse Marxist precepts with an enthusiasm the secular Left lacks is that Christians find the powers in faith which secular Marxists once saw in historical class forces. Feminism and religion have an increasing influence in movements attempting to address questions of global violence: that the patriarchal organization of society may have a good deal to do with militarism also raises questions beyond the limits of Marxism, at least as conventionally understood. The common emphasis on values, on the attempt to define a humane future, and on the building of community allows feminist spirituality and Christian pacifism to coexist and in some cases to work together closely in spite of their historical tensions.

Both the religious and feminist sections of the movement valorize the creation of "community." What they usually mean is a sense of unity, of harmonious integration, based on entirely voluntary ties. This definition of community can cause problems for the movement, because it is static. It excludes internal struggle, and it tends to set community against forward political motion. One of the weaknesses of the direct action movement, and for that matter of most American social movements, is that they are largely voluntary; communities tend to be stronger if they include some degree of compulsion, if people are forced into contact with one another over time even if they do not always get along. When there is some degree of compulsion, or at least pressure to remain together, a community is less likely to be destroyed by internal conflicts. The civil rights movement was built on the Black community, in particular the Black churches; the CIO was built on the workplace in basic industry. The direct action movement draws people from already existing communities and institutions, in particular the counter-culture and the churches, but it is not itself tied to any of these; its base is moral conviction, ideological commitment. This rootless quality gives it both strengths and weaknesses. It frees the movement to address the largest questions, to develop a vision unconstrained by ties to existing social institutions. But it also means that the movement is fragile, that when there is internal conflict, or its momentum slows for other reasons, it is easy for people to leave.

. . .

The fact that the direct action movement takes community seriously is an enormous advance over the anti-war movement, and also over the current social democratic Left which has emerged from it. But because the direct action movement wants community and politics to be the same thing, it tends to overlook the contradictions between the two. All the most distinctive features of the direct action movement – the focus on civil disobedience, the consensus process, the non-hierarchical style of organization – are intended to contribute to the building of community. Each has also contributed to the fragility of the movement.

The focus on civil disobedience, which more than anything else gives the movement its definition, has produced a movement that rises and falls in brief cycles. Clamshell and Abalone at least started out with the intention of using a range of methods, but each was taken over by a singular focus on civil disobedience. In each case the actions were quite successful, but neither organization knew what to do once that action was over. Each action had mobilized around the issue in question a large proportion of those people willing to commit civil disobedience. To have gone on to more militant action would have been against the principles of many of the people involved. It would probably also have driven many people away. To repeat the same action would have been anti-climactic. The result was that both declined rapidly after those moments of greatest success.

Like the focus on civil disobedience, the consensus process is simultaneously a strength and a weakness of the direct action movement. Consensus process creates strong bonds within the movement and helps to keep it egalitarian; it ensures that everyone will participate and will be heard. It is an important factor in the level of solidarity the movement is capable of attaining. It works best in small groups of people who know and trust one another, or in action or jail situations where there is a sense of crisis. Consensus does not work as well in large organizations, especially if factions have developed which are more interested in having their views prevail than in coming to a mutual understanding. And it does not work very well when quick decisions are needed.

Another distinctive characteristic of the direct action movement, the attempt to build an entirely non-hierarchical, leaderless movement, has fewer advantages than the focus on civil disobedience or the use of the consensus process. In fact an informal leadership has emerged in each of the movement's main organizations; that it has gone unacknowledged has caused trouble in each case. This informal hierarchy has the potential to undermine democracy, because it means that the leadership has no particular accountability to the rest of the organization. What has been more of a problem is that its anti-leadership rhetoric encourages the expression of hostility toward anyone who assumes a leadership role; the people who take on most of the work are given lots of criticism and little support, and they tend to become bitter and burnt out. Again, because there is no recognition of the need for leadership, there is no regular way of replacing them. When the first leadership group retires, the organization is likely to fall apart.

This critique of the direct action movement is based on the assumption that it would be better if more continuous identity and political presence could be achieved. Many people in the movement would disagree, arguing that it is only when organizations rise and fall with the issues they represent that bureaucratic entrenchment is avoided. The problem is that when organizations fall apart, some local or affinity groups survive but others do not; the movement contracts. Lessons which might have been learned are not, because few people stay around to discuss what went wrong. Thus the same mistakes may be repeated in the next cycle of the movement. The direct action movement asks those who participate in it to make major changes in their lives, and, on occasion, to take genuine risks; if its organizations cannot be counted on to survive, many people will be more reluctant to do so.

The direct action movement is organizationally fragile and often lacking in political direction, and it cannot substitute for other sections of the movement: short of a moment of broadly perceived crisis, it is likely to remain predominantly white, middle-class and made up of people with flexible schedules who are willing to assume a degree of marginality, at least politically. But in spite of these weaknesses, it has been a source of political vitality and new ideas on the American Left. In the early sixties, Communists and social democrats criticized the emergent New Left for not being enough like the Old Left, rather than learning from it. Partly as a result of this, the Old Left quickly became politically irrelevant. It is to be hoped that this mistake will not be repeated by current veterans of the movements of the sixties.

Barbara Epstein, "The Politics of Prefigurative Community: The Non-violent Direct Action Movement," *Reshaping the US Left: Popular Struggles in the 1980s*, Mike Davis and Michael Sprinker (eds.), London and New York: Verso, 1988, pp. 63–8, 79–83, 85–90.

JOHN JORDAN,
"THE ART OF NECESSITY:
THE SUBVERSIVE IMAGINATION OF ANTI-ROAD
PROTEST AND RECLAIM THE STREETS"

"Should I play it safe and stay on the sidewalks, or should I go into the street?" One contemporary protest group has a decisive answer: Reclaim the Streets (see sidebar). Growing out of the anti-roads protests in England in the early 1990s, and energized by an influx of newly politicized partiers mid-decade, the London-born Reclaim the Streets pioneered a new, or rather resurrected a very old, style of protest: the street carnival (cf. Bakhtin). But RTS reclaimed more than a style of protest – they popularized a model of political action wherein the protest itself is a living, breathing and in this case, dancing, political message. By filling the streets with people freely expressing themselves, RTS not only protests what it is against, but also creates an experiential model of the culture it is for (cf. Bey, Epstein). More a cultural idea than a material organization, RTS has spread rapidly throughout the UK to Helsinki, Prague, Sydney, Tel Aviv, Berkeley, New York, and countless other cities across the globe. In the selection below RTS activist and artist John Jordan recounts the ideas and actions of the progenitor of this culture of resistance: Reclaim the Streets/London.

> The new artist protests, he no longer paints; he creates directly . . . life and art make One.
>
> Tristan Tzara, Dada manifesto (1919)

Since the beginning of this century, avant-garde agitational artists[1] have tried to demolish the divisions between art and life[2] and introduce creativity, imagination, play and pleasure into the revolutionary project. My argument is that the DIY protest movement has taken these 'utopian' demands and made them real, given them a 'place'. Inspired by and following in the footsteps of the protest movements and countercultures of the sixties, seventies and eighties, the DIY protest movement is finally breaking down the barriers between art and protest. It seems that at the close of this century new forms of creative and poetic resistance have finally found their time.

. . .

Separating art from politics and everyday life is a relatively recent historical phenomenon and one that has been very much located in societies that have taken on western cultural values – the same cultural values that are at the centre of the global ecological and social problems. American Earth

"Propaganda," Reclaim the Streets/London

For the city, the streets are the commons, but in the hands of industry and power brokers the streets have become mere conduits for commerce and consumption – the economic hero of which is, of course, the car. A symbol and a symptom of the social and ecological nightmare that state and capitalism create, the car which promises individual freedom ends up guaranteeing noise, destruction and pollution for all. For Reclaim the Streets, the car is a focus – the insanity of its system clearly visible – that leads to questioning both the myth of 'the market' and its corporate and institutional enforcers.

With a metal river on one side and endless windows of consumerism on the other, the street's true purpose, social interaction, becomes an uneconomic diversion. In its place the corporate-controlled one-way media of newspapers, radio and television become 'the community'. Their interpretation, our reality. In this sense the streets are the alternative and subversive form of the mass media. Where authentic communication, immediate and reciprocal, takes place.

. . .

The street is an extremely important symbol because your whole enculturation experience is geared around keeping you out of the street . . . The idea is to keep everyone indoors. So, when you come to challenge the powers that be, inevitably you find yourself on the curbstone of indifference, wondering 'should I play it safe and stay on the sidewalks, or should I go into the street?' And it

First! activist, film maker and medievalist Christopher Manes believes that

> the biological meltdown is most directly the result of values fundamental to what we have come to recognize as culture under the regime of technological society: economic growth, 'progress', property rights, consumerism, religious doctrines about humanity's dominion over nature, technocratic notions about achieving an optimum human existence at the expense of all other life-forms.[3]

If the problem is one of values – a cultural problem – it therefore requires a cultural response. It is not simply a question of science but also one of art, the process of value finding and aesthetics. Interestingly enough, the Latin root of the word aesthetics – *aesthesis* – means *noticing* the world. It's not difficult to notice the state of this world, yet so many artists immured in their enclosures of studio, gallery, theatre or museum seem blind to it. Those who attempt to push the boundaries of the revolutionary project are rapidly recuperated, neutralized, their political ideas forgotten, their work turned into commodities. Even those with the most revolutionary cultural agendas – the Dadaists, Surrealists and even the Situationists – have become impotent figures in an apolitical art history; all three movements' radical political dreams were destroyed because they still clung on, if half-heartedly, to the question of *art*: its arguments over definitions, its non-participatory relationship with audience and many of its traditional contexts.

Art has clearly failed historically as a means to bring imagination and creativity to movements of social change.[4] Present political conditions require a shift away from such a category; indeed a movement away from all categories, be they art, politics or science. What makes DIY protest powerful is that it 'clearly embodies a rejection of the specialized sphere of old politics, as well as of art and everyday life'.[5] Its insistence on creativity and yet the invisibility of art or artists in its midst, singles it out as a historical turning point in the current of creative resistance. By making the art completely invisible, DIY protest gives art back its original socially transformative power; as Dubuffet said: 'Art . . . loves to be incognito. Its best moments are when it forgets what it is called.'[6]

. . .

The MII Link Road will stretch from Wanstead to Hackney in east London. To build it the Department of Transport had to knock down 350 houses, displace several thousand people, cut through one of London's last ancient woodlands and devastate a community with a six-lane-wide stretch of tarmac — at a cost of £240 million, apparently to save six minutes on a car journey. It has now been officially admitted that when it opens it will already be full to capacity. Which suggests the need for another road.

For over thirty years the MII Link Road had been opposed by conventional political means — demonstrations, planning inquiries, lobbying and petitions. Despite the dedication of local residents the bulldozers arrived in the autumn of 1993. So it was time to develop new creative political methods, using direct action, performance art, sculpture and installation and armed with faxes, modems, computers and video cameras. A new breed of 'artist activist' emerged whose motto could well have been creativity, courage and cheek.[7] Their art was not to be about representation but presence; their politics was not about deferring social change to the future but about change now, about immediacy, intuition and imagination.

. . .

The mutation of Claremont Road into a phenomenally imaginative theatre of creative resistance[8] was a transformation of personal and social space.

Claremont Road was a street of thirty-five terraced houses, directly in the path of the link road. Resisting the bulldozers with the campaigners on this street was 92-year-old Dolly, who had lived there for her entire life. Leaving Claremont Road was inconceivable to Dolly. In defiance of the Department of Transport she remained there till the final minute.[9] In Claremont

is the ones who are taking the most risks that will ultimately effect the change in society.

From the Reclaim the Streets website, www.gn.apc.org/rts/

Road every house apart from Dolly's was taken over by the campaign. One of the first acts of resistance was to close the road off to traffic and open it up to the art of living. In a superb act of *détournement*,[10] the road – normally a space dominated by the motor car, a space for passing not living, a dead duct between *a* and *b* – was reclaimed and turned into a vibrant space in which to live, eat, talk and sleep.

Furniture was moved out of the houses into the road, laundry was hung up to dry, chess games were played on a giant painted chess board, snooker tables were installed, fires were lit, a stage was built and parties were held. The 'road' had been turned into a 'street', a street like none other, a street which provided a rare glimpse of utopia, a kind of temporary microcosm of a truly liberated, ecological culture.[11]

Some of the most aesthetic aspects of Claremont Road were the barricades, built to resist eviction by the Department of Transport. Sunk into the tarmac, large swirls of sculptural steel cabling were juxtaposed with the carcasses of transformed cars. One with 'RUST IN PEACE' meticulously painted on its side had grass growing all over it; another was turned into a zebra crossing by being painted black and white, cut in half, each half being placed on the kerbstone with a crossing painted between them. These were not just ephemeral monuments to the end of car culture but also beautiful and effective barricades.

Many of the barricades inside the houses echoed conceptual artists' installations of the past. Yet these creative constructions were not just site-specific sculptures which resonated with and reflected the architectural structures of the houses, they were creative social transformations, imagination rigorously applied to real situations, art embedded into everyday life. These houses were not only frames for art, they were homes, real places which could have been renovated and rehoused some of the thousands of homeless young people who end up on London's streets every year.

The 1970s saw artists like Gordon Matta Clarke cut a hole through the side of a house and Walter de la Maria fill a whole room with earth. More recently Turner Prize-winner Rachel Whiteread cast in concrete an abandoned terrace house, due for demolition in nearby Hackney. In Claremont Road a hole was cut in the connecting walls of the row of thirty-five houses to create a stunning tunnel that linked several homes: a strategy to evade the bailiffs, but also a metaphor for communal living; an intervention that cuts through the isolation of individual domestic units. In some houses rooms were filled with earth, often lit by the eerie brightness of a single hanging light bulb. These earth-filled rooms disguised entrances to bunkers which held activists during the eviction. Not knowing the whereabouts of the bunkers, the bailiffs when they arrived would be forced to search with shovels, instead of tearing through the houses with a bulldozer: a much more time-consuming activity, and, at £20,000 per hour for an eviction, expensive! Other houses were packed not with concrete but with rubbish, the detritus of urban decay: washing machines, old mattresses, broken furniture and, most symbolically, old tyres;[12] yet more ingenious engineerings of the imagination to slow down the eviction.

These barricades were accompanied by slogans hastily daubed in bright paint and colourful murals: horses galloping, a daisy chain across the front of every house, a large spoof billboard proclaiming 'WELCOME TO CLAREMONT ROAD – IDEAL HOMES.' Hanging from the defended trees were shop dummies, ribbons, old televisions – a fusion of found objects each hung purposefully as symbolic statement and obstacle for the tree surgeons. A whole house was turned into 'the art house' and more traditional 'artists' filled every nook and cranny with representative images that critiqued car culture.[13] Two cafés were opened up and in the middle of the terrace a stark banner asked passers-by to: 'IMAGINE THIS PLACE, AS A HOME, A WOOD OR THE M11 LINK ROAD.'

A final symbol of contempt for the DoT's plans to evict Claremont was the extraordinary 100-foot scaffolding tower[14] nicknamed Dolly, which broke through the roof of one of the houses. Made from hundreds of 'found' lengths of scaffolding, joined together in a complex and chaotic lattice-work and looking like a cross between Tatlin's monument to the Third International and a NASA launch pad, the tower could be seen from miles away. For its short life Dolly became a local landmark which competed with the Babylon blandness of Canary Wharf on the horizon. This insane piece of crazed, brightly painted and greased scaffolding not only provided the most effective defence against the bailiffs, but also became the most powerful image for the final showdown.

For four cold days in November 1994 Claremont Road and the quarter of a mile of sealed-off streets became the site for a final operatic battle. To the sounds of rave music[15] blasting from the top of the tower, 1300 riot policemen and bailiffs trooped in and out of the area as if in a fine choreographed routine. Activists were hanging in nets suspended across the road, locked into the tarmac and on to chimney pots, sitting on the roofs, buried in the bunkers and welded into a cage at the top of the tower. Enormous 'cherrypickers' completely surrounded by dozens of security guards moved their aerial platforms through the air like mechanical dinosaurs attempting to extract the wriggling activists from their stupendous backdrop. At night bright arc lights illuminated the enclave and an eerie silence fell. Suddenly the place felt like the film set of an apocalyptic movie. Every now and then a firework would shoot out of the tower, and a chorus of 'Power to the tower!' would ascend from the street below.

This was theatre like you'd never seen it; theatre on a scale that would not fit in any opera house. It was a spectacle that cost the government over £2 million to enact; a spectacle in which we were in control, for which we had set the stage, provided the actors and invited the state to be in our play; to play our game. Eighty-eight hours later the last person left was plucked off the tower; all that was left to do was destroy the street and with it not only a hundred years of local history but also an extraordinary site of creative resistance.

No sign, relic or trace of Claremont Road remains. We always knew that one day all this would be rubble, and this awareness of impermanence gave us immense strength – the impossibility of failure – the strength to move this Temporary Autonomous Zone on to somewhere else. Our festival of resistance could never be evicted. We would continue to transgress the distinction between art and everyday life. We would continue to make every political act a moment of poetry. If we could no longer reclaim Claremont Road, we would reclaim the streets of London.[16]

. . .

Claremont Road had provided us with a taste of a free society. Tasting such fruit is dangerous, because it leaves a craving to repeat the exhilarating experience. Within three months we re-formed the group Reclaim the Streets[17] and began planning the first street party.

The idea of the street party was to take over major roads in London and transform them into ephemeral festivals of resistance. The street party itself was a form 'reclaimed from the inanities of royal jubilees and state "celebrations"'.[18] Turning to proactive, instead of defensive, direct action enabled us to expand our remit into a wider cultural critique. Activist Paul Morozzo from Reclaim the Streets and the M11 campaign clarifies this expansion:

> We are basically about taking back public space from the enclosed private arena. At its simplest it is an attack on cars as a principal agent of enclosure. It's about reclaiming the streets as public inclusive space from the private exclusive use of the car. But we believe in this as a broader principle, taking back those things which have been enclosed within capitalist circulation and returning them to collective use as a commons.[19]

The M11 campaign had already placed the anti-road and ecological arguments of Twyford Down in an urban, social context. This merging of social and ecological principles into a wider cultural critique was to become key in Reclaim the Streets' later alliances with striking public transport and dock workers.[20] For Reclaim the Streets, just getting rid of cars from the streets was not enough. Activist Del Bailie explains:

> Won't the streets be better without cars? Not if all that replaces them are aisles of pedestrianized consumption or shopping 'villages' safely protected from the elements. To be against the car for its own sake is inane; claiming one piece as the whole jigsaw. The struggle for carfree space must not be separated from the struggle against global capitalism for in truth the former is encapsulated in the latter. The streets are as full of capitalism as of cars and the pollution of capitalism is much more insidious.[21]

The first stages of uprisings have often been theatrical and carnivalesque, 'a revelatory and sensuous explosion outside the "normal pattern of politics"'.[22] The street party would become a revolutionary carnival in the spirit of

> great moments of revolutionary history, the enormous popular festivals of the Bastille, the Paris Commune, Paris '68. From the middle ages onwards the carnival has offered glimpses of the world turned upside down, a topsy turvy universe free of toil, suffering and inequality. Carnival celebrates temporary liberation from the prevailing truth and the established order; it marks the suspension of all hierarchical rank, privileges, norms and prohibitions.[23]

Raoul Vaneigem wrote that 'revolutionary moments are carnivals in which the individual life celebrates its unification with a regenerated society'. But:

> the Street Party can be read as a situ-esque reversal of this assertion; as an attempt to make Carnival *the* revolutionary moment. Placing 'what could be' in the path of 'what is' and celebrating the 'here and now' in the road of the rush for 'there and later', it hopes to reenergize the possibility of radical change . . . It is an expansive desire; for freedom, for creativity; to truly live.[24]

Imagine a busy high street, Saturday afternoon. Shoppers mingle on the thin strip of pavement that separates the shops from the busy road. Suddenly two cars career into each other and block the road: the drivers get out and begin to argue. One of the drivers brandishes a hammer and starts to smash up the other driver's car. Passers-by are astonished; time stands still. Then people surge out of the anonymous shopping crowd and start to jump on top of the cars, multicoloured paint is thrown everywhere. An enormous banner is unfurled from the roofs of the two destroyed vehicles – 'RECLAIM THE STREETS – FREE THE CITY/KILL THE CAR,' it proclaims. Five hundred people are now surging out of the tube station and take over the street. As the Surrealists might have said, everyday life has been penetrated by the marvellous.

Thus began street party number 1, in Camden High Street in May 1995. All afternoon 500 people danced to the sound of the mobile bicycle-powered Rinky-Dink sound system. Free food was served up from long trestle-tables that stretched down the middle of the road and children played on a climbing frame placed in the middle of a now liberated cross-road junction. As evening fell and people drifted off, riot police moved in and tried to reassert their authority, having spent the entire day without it!

Once again we were introducing play into politics, challenging official culture's claims to authority, stability, sobriety, immutability and immortality by cheekily taking over a main traffic artery. The road became a stage for a participatory ritual theatre: ritual because it is efficacious, it produces real effects by means of symbolic causes; participatory because the street party has no division between performer and audience, it is created by and for everyone, it avoids all mediation, it is experienced in the immediate moment by all, in a spirit of face-to-face subversive comradeship. The street party when it is in full swing – when thousands of people have reclaimed a major road and declared it a 'street now open'; when music, laughter and song have replaced the roar of engines; when road rage becomes road rave, and tarmac grey is smothered by the living colour of a festival[25] – fulfils Lautréamont's desire that 'Poetry must be made by all. Not by one.'[26]

Two months later and the street party reappeared,[27] this time with 3,000 people dancing to two sound systems in the middle of Upper Street, Islington.

Imagine: it's a hot summer's day, four lanes of traffic move sluggishly through the grey stinking city haze, an airhorn pierces the drone of cars. Suddenly several groups of people appear running out from side streets carrying 20-foot-long scaffolding poles. In a perfectly choreographed acrobatic drill, the scaffolding poles are erected bang in the middle of the road in the form of tripods[28] and people climb to the top, balancing gracefully 20 feet above the tarmac. The road is now blocked to traffic but open to pedestrians. Then that spine-tingling peak experience occurs. Drifting across this extraordinary scene is Louis Armstrong's voice singing 'What a Wonderful World' – this wondrous sound is coming from an armoured personnel carrier which is now standing in the car-free street. Within minutes thousands of people have filled the road. Huge colourful banners are stretched from lampposts; some are in support of the striking London Underground workers, others just say 'BREATHE' or 'STREET NOW

OPEN'; one that simply says 'CAR FREE' is made of numerous strips which stretch down to the tarmac, like tendrils, creating a soft fabric curtain across the road. During the party these tendrils are tied together to create huge bouncing swings for people to play on. Soon the street is a riot of colour; a band turns a bus stop into a stage and plays folk music; people dance; a choir sings; and a ton of sand is poured on to the tarmac, turning it into an instant beach for children.[29]

Official festivals, displays and entertainments[30] are arranged in neat rectangles and straight lines: trooping the colour or a traditional march, for example. The street party, however, is vortexed, whirling; people dance on anything, climb lampposts, move in every direction: an uncontrollable state of creative chaos. The street party breaks a cultural obsession with linearity, order and tidiness, epitomized by roads and cars; as a flyer for the Upper Street party declared, 'CARS CANNOT DANCE: When they move they are violent and brutish, they lack sensitivity and rhythm. CARS CANNOT PLAY: When they diverge from the straight and narrow, they kill. CARS CANNOT SOCIALIZE: They privatize, separate, isolate and alienate.' Schechner writes that:

> to allow people to assemble in the streets is always to flirt with the possibility of improvisation – and the unexpected might happen . . . Official culture wants its festivals to be entertaining and ordered. When entertainment is really free, when it gets out of hand, when there is no fixed calendrical conclusion to the celebration, then the authorities get nervous. Such festivals reverberate through the population in unforeseen ways.[31]

Later that evening the authorities did get nervous. Riot police appeared on the scene, and this time they closed off both ends of the road, closed down the tube station and aggressively pushed people down side streets. When asked why they had sealed off all exits a policeman replied, 'Because we want people to disperse.'[32] And people did, but not in the way the state expected; by the time London Reclaim the Streets threw its third party in July 1996, nine more street parties had taken place across the country, each one different, each one rooted in its locality and transforming the traffic-filled space into pleasure-filled place. All over the country people were enjoying taking to the streets and celebrating life's fertile possibilities.

The street party had caught on, and the next one in London would be difficult to organize due to increased police surveillance. For the few days running up to the party, activists were constantly followed and the Reclaim the Streets office was closely monitored from a house opposite. When the day came on Saturday 13 July 1996, and we saw thousands of people arriving at the meeting point, we just prayed that the location had not been found out by the police. Ten west-bound Central Line tube trains filled with people sped off into the unknown, and we waited with bated breath.

Imagine: thousands of people emerge from Shepherd's Bush tube station, no-one knows where they are going – the mystery and excitement of it all is electrifying. Shepherd's Bush Green comes to a standstill as people pour on to it; up ahead a line of police has already sealed off the roundabout and blocked the way. A man takes off all his clothes and starts to dance on the roof of a stationary car. The crowd knows this is not the place: where is the sound system, the tripods? Then, as if by some miracle of collective telepathy, everyone turns back and disappears around the corner; a winding journey through backstreets, under railway bridges and then up over a barrier and suddenly they are on an enormous motorway and right *behind* the police lines. People run into the fast lane yelping with joy; up ahead they can see the sound system and tripods surrounded by police. The police line at the end of the motorway is completely confused; they turn around and start to chase after everyone. Their line, their order and control, has been broken. For a few interminable seconds it looks like the thin line between festival and riot is about to be transgressed – but thousands of people are now pouring on to the six lanes of baking hot tarmac, hundreds of white frisbees start to fly in the air. The police try to regroup but everyone is just breaking through their attempts at blocking the way. The ecstatic crowd gravitates towards the truck carrying the sound system which is parked on the hard shoulder. People start banging on the side of the police van guarding it. The truck is now swarming with people. The police van decides it has lost control of the situation and starts to drive off; as it does so the sides of the truck are lifted and the gut-shaking thump of techno blasts out of the sound system. The crowd roars – we've liberated a motorway through sheer numbers, through people power!

Until early the next morning the M41, Britain's shortest stretch of motorway, played host to the largest festival of resistance yet. Ten thousand people danced, chatted, ate, met friends and made new ones. The hard shoulder was taken over by stalls and a café, the central reservation became a picnic site and a stage for fire jugglers and performers, and the fast lane another children's sandpit. Stretching across the six lanes were huge, vivid banners: a giant yellow sun, a burst of Matisse-inspired 10-foot-high flowers, 'SUPPORT THE TUBE WORKERS', 'DESTROY POWER' and the Situationists' 'THE SOCIETY THAT ABOLISHES EVERY ADVENTURE MAKES ITS OWN ABOLITION THE ONLY POSSIBLE

ADVENTURE'. The unbounded creativity was so catching that even a scrap-metal yard that overlooked the motorway decided to hang up a wrecked van using its crane, a creative gesture to join in the carnivalesque spirit of fun, irony and subversion.

Some of the most striking images were the two huge carnival figures, 30 feet high with 10-feet-wide hooped skirts, with bagpipe players wearing Restoration wigs installed at the top of them. These seemingly innocent figures were wheeled up and down the motorway all day and night, but hidden under the skirts, away from the eyes of the police, and drowned out by the sound of techno, people were busy drilling into the tarmac with Kanga hammers and planting saplings rescued from the path of the M11 link road, which was still in the process of being built.[33] The next morning, finding tarmac pock-marked with freshly planted saplings, the Highways Agency was forced to close the motorway for several days and resurface it.

Schechner writes that 'the difference between temporary and permanent change distinguishes carnival from revolution,'[34] yet in this act of insurrectionary imagination carnival became revolution, real trees were planted, real transformations occurred. Real people, in a real space, in real time (that is, not framed by a calendrical festive date), underwent real change as they developed a new sense of confidence and an awareness of their individual and collective power; for a rare moment they had experienced the breath of the possible touching them – they had transformed the world. They had had experiences that would remain with them permanently.

This street party was the perfect propaganda of the possible – it was a day full of those priceless moments where everything slips away and immense cracks appear in the facades of authority and power. Ten thousand people had enjoyed collectively committing the offence of obstructing the public highway, held an illegal party in contravention of the Criminal Justice Act and caused substantial creative criminal damage. To quote Abbie Hoffman, 'Revolution is anything you can get away with.'

John Jordan, "The Art of Necessity: The Subversive Imagination of Anti-Road Protest and Reclaim the Streets," in *DIY Culture: Party & Protest in Nineties Britain*, George McKay (ed.), London and New York: Verso, 1998, pp. 129–32, 135–46.

JASON GROTE,
"THE GOD THAT PEOPLE WHO DO NOT BELIEVE
IN GOD BELIEVE IN: TAKING A BUST
WITH REVEREND BILLY"

Picture this: Times Square in New York City at the millennium. A consortium of political muscle and corporate money has pushed out the porn shops and the hot dog stands, the street hustlers and the street preachers, to make the neighborhood safe for chain stores and restaurants to do business. The major player in this drama is the Disney/ABC/Cap Cities corporation and their Disney flagship store occupies a prominent corner in Times Square. Across the street, or in front of their door, or sometimes in the store itself, there's one street preacher who hasn't gotten the message that his kind is no longer welcome. His name is Reverend Billy and he preaches the sin of shopping. In the following section, Jason Grote, playwright, political activist and disciple of the Church of Stop Shopping, narrates a personal account of a Billy-led protest and civil disobedience inside the Disney Store. (Full disclosure: your editor was arrested there too.) What the demonstration demanded from Disney – "stop shopping"? – was beside the point. The real goal of the action, and the mission of Reverend Billy, is to contrast publicly a culture of commercialism that has a hold on all of us – the Reverend is, after all, a sort of Disney cartoon – with a culture of resistance: the stories and struggles of real people (see sidebar). "We can," Reverend Billy insists, "begin to recall what desire was when it was not supervised."

In New York, about a month and a half before New Year's Eve, 1999, some friends of mine and I were arrested in the Times Square Disney Store. It was intentional; we were participating in a protest and media stunt. The idea was that a group of us would be marched out the front door of the store in handcuffs, and on that evening's news there would appear, ironically juxtaposed, cheery, primary-colored Disneyana and scary NYPD repression. Just to convey the full visual, our ringleader was dressed in a televangelist costume, complete with frosted hair, a white sport coat, and a clerical collar. Our march out the front door was a nice, Abbie Hoffmanish moment, a sort of perfect balance of truth-to-power nobility and public foolishness. When the police led us out, we were walked through a crowd of people with cameras, just like in the movies. As I walked past, hands bound, I grinned widely into a video camera and shouted, "Arrest Mickey!" Our arrest was later shown in a PBS program called *Egg*, wherein I was featured prominently with my ensemble of bad hair, mismatched clothes, and handcuffs. I was also interviewed about the protest on National Public Radio, an interview in which I mispronounced the word "hegemony" (they left it in).

What were we doing in the Disney store? There are short – and correct – answers, most of which would be familiar to anyone who has paid attention to Left activism in the 1990s: Disney's participation in the sweatshop economy; their role in the displacement of low-income residents and small businesses; their collusion with Mayor Giuliani in turning New York City into a highly-policed suburban-style mall. Then there is the long answer, which is the following story:

We're supposed to meet an hour or so before the action, in the basement of St. Clement's Church in Hell's Kitchen. My job is to show up with lyrics of a song parody I wrote entitled "Whistle While You Work for Fifteen Cents an Hour" (said amount being the average salary of Disney's subcontracted Indonesian sweatshop workers; its Chinese workers only make eleven cents, but that didn't scan), pass them out, and act as a sort of low-rent musical director to the assembled activists. Never having been on time for anything in my life, ever, I run into the basement forty-five minutes late, huffing and red-faced. We rush through a couple of off-key rounds of the song, talk through the day's game plan, and file out to meet the media at the Howard Johnson's on 46th Street and Broadway.

I have noticed that there is a collective upswell of emotion that seems to occur at demonstrations, or at least at the good ones. I think it would be dangerous if I were to feel it more often: a mix of inspiration, sentimentality, camaraderie, self-righteousness, righteous anger, abject fear, and what I think Che Guevara must have been talking about when he said that the true revolutionary was guided by great feelings of love: a deep, abiding compassion for everything and everyone. It is an enormously sexy feeling. I imagine that it's similar to the way workers in the 1930s used to feel when they sang the "Internationale," or to the feeling that allowed civil rights marchers to brave attack dogs and high-pressure hoses in the 1960s. Something in me suspects that it is also akin to the feeling of absolute certitude that genocidal maniacs or suicide bombers possess.

Today this weird euphoria is intensified and compounded by the queasy, blinding insanity of millennial Times Square. As we walk through and around the slow-moving, anesthetized crowd, the handfuls of extant street hustlers, and the ubiquitous construction scaffolding, I feel like a floating, disembodied head attached to a string. We reach the corner of 42nd and 7th. I stand on the curb and stare at the Disney Store, which is making my stomach churn even more than it ordinarily would. I hesitate for a minute, then take a deep breath and open the door.

The good cheer is blinding. The environment is controlled, immaculate, and intolerably bright. I don't know where to look. The bad karma is palpable: the frozen smiles on the anthropomorphic merchandise remind me of the stiff, clammy grins of guilty politicians in editorial cartoons. The world is thrown into a sharp, us-versus-them relief. There are nearly forty of us nervously milling around trying to look like we are, for some reason, shopping for souvenirs before noon on a weekday. None of us look even remotely like what one would expect a Times Square Disney Store patron to look like; we're the wrong ages, wearing the wrong clothes, saying the wrong things. Some of our party are actually carrying large pieces of camera equipment, while others have very visible piercings, tattoos, or creative facial hair. We are about as inconspicuous as turds in a punchbowl. The staff knows that something is up but they're not sure what. The rank-and-file workers look excited that something might actually break up the relentless cheery monotony, and the security personnel are running around the store dramatically and whispering urgently into their hand-held radios, as if they have just uncovered a plot to assassinate Goofy.

The action begins innocuously enough. Two of our number, Ron and Ben, grab armfuls of stuffed animals and get on line. Out of all of us, they look the least troublesome. Both of them wear dress shirts, ties, and eyeglasses. They are very personable. They make conversation with the middle-aged woman standing behind them on line, talking about buying toys for their nieces. I imagine that this woman thinks that they are a nice gay couple, and that she is talking herself into thinking that she is having a New York moment, secretly congratulating herself on her open-mindedness and cosmopolitanism. The banter continues as the young woman behind the counter starts to ring up the stuffed animals. Ron's temperament gradually goes from affable to agitated as he sees the prices of the unmarked toys. "Wait, that's *how* much?," he says to the surprised checkout woman. "That *can't* be that much." The woman behind the counter looks confused. "Come on," he is saying. "This is Times Square. Let's haggle. Didn't you used to be able to haggle in Times Square?" The people behind them on line are starting to do that impatient New York thing, sighing, rolling their eyes, conspicuously checking their watches, shifting their weight from foot to foot. Getting held up on line by a crazy person, I want to tell them: that's a New York moment. The checkout woman, managing to remain pleasant, totals the random selection of oversized plush toys. The total is absurdly high, over six hundred dollars. Ben and Ron feign shock at the high price; neither of them has that kind of money. The security personnel are starting to pay attention to them. This is my cue.

Subsequent to this event, I will learn some lessons about street performance. These lessons will include the fact that the visual matters much, much
more than the verbal, and that keeping matters simple is generally a good
idea. For some reason, I have it my head that it will be funny if I speak in
an exaggerated Southern accent. Also, the front page of that day's *New York
Times* states that China has just entered the World Trade Organization, and
it is very important to me that I connect this news to our protest. While
there is and always has been a very clear connection between the global
economy, sweatshops, and chain stores that pay minimum wage and despoil
neighborhoods, this is not a very easy idea to communicate, quickly and in
lay terms, to a store full of bewildered, anxious tourists, especially when
one is terrified of imminent arrest. I try anyway.

"I cay-unt believe this," I say, flailing. "They cay-unt even satisfah two
customers. Whah, ever-a-body knows that the American consumer is ay-ut
the tawp of the food chain. Whah else would they let China into the World
Trade Organization?" I am not making any converts. My scene partner
Steve steps in. In his normal voice, he says, "But China treats their workers
horribly." To which I say, "Whah, they don't hay-uve it so bay-ud. Whah, if
ah was their supah-visah, ah would just tell them to . . ."

With a flourish, I whip my song lyrics out of my jacket pocket. The rest
of the room follows suit, and we sing: "Just whistle while you work / For
fifteen cents an hour / Cheap labor, dear, has brought you here / And now
you work for us!" . . . And so on. We are slightly mumbly and out of sync,
like people singing hymns in church, and no one seems to be getting the
weird syncopated meter of the third and fifth verses. But this doesn't matter
all that much: there *are* nearly forty of us. We fill the space with sound like
some sort of alternate-universe Disney musical. It is weird to hear this capitalist propaganda that has been burned on to our collective unconscious
detourned into an anthem of resistance. By the time we reach the middle
of the second verse, the manager has cranked up whatever insipid Elton
Johnish dogshit they had been playing. By the third verse, an amused-
looking employee is trying to get me to stop, but the adrenaline is pumping
and barring serious injury I am going to finish this damn song. The security personnel, thinking that they now have the ringleader pegged, start to
approach me. They do not realize that I am merely a diversion.

The front doors swing open and, larger than life, in blows Reverend
Billy, arms above his head, preaching to a chorus of hoots and howls. The
employees roll their eyes. "Is this that guy you were telling me about?" says
one employee to another.

As you may have guessed Reverend Billy is not a real reverend. The Reverend is the alter ego of Bill Talen, a performance artist who has, in the process of creating a satirical evangelist character, become a sort of *de facto* religious figure for activists. He orients his church's faux-theology around issues of consumerism and development. In addition to going after Disney, he has waged war on New York University, for trying to replace the Edgar Allan Poe House with a high-rise; on sundry billboard companies, for besmirching every inert vertical surface in Manhattan; and on Starbucks, for – well, for being Starbucks.

His act grew out of a tribute to/parody of the real street preachers who once populated Times Square along with the sex shops. Most of them were garden-variety fundamentalists who had come to the heart of Sodom to earn their stripes, but many of them were as uniquely New York as the Chrysler Building: for example, the Mitzvah Tank, a Winnebago full of militant Lubavicher Hasidim seeking to reclaim secular Jews; or the Sons of David, Black Israelite Nationalists who to this day dress up like Rastafarian superheroes, pose in formation, and rant into a public address system about the coming race war. By the mid-1990s, the Giuliani administration, the Disney Company, and various other consortia had more or less successfully purged the neighborhood of crazies and other undesirables. In their place stood a new kind of preacher, one who, authenticity-wise, is to the religious nuts as Disney is to the neighborhood: Reverend Billy. By using theater, he fights Disney on Disney's terms. In a way, this development is not unlike the common phenomenon of the revolutionary using, intentionally or inadvertently, the tactics of the oppressor: Disney created an ersatz Times Square to replace the sleaze, so they end up with an ersatz street preacher to rant at them.

He began by haranguing the store from across the street, shouting into a megaphone. On occasion he would actually drop in and wreak some havoc, conducting what he calls "shopping interventions," in which his "congregation" would, at his urging, enter the store incognito and get into discussions with each other, or with imaginary people on toy cell phones, about the neurotic experience of shopping in the Times Square Disney Store. These are in part based on Invisible Theater methods developed by activists and theater artists in the 1960s and 70s, wherein actors would blend into public crowds and try to spark conversation about whatever issue they happened to be agitating over.

Reverend Billy's activist work is coupled with an actual Reverend Billy show, for which he has won an Obie award and been otherwise celebrated in national and international media. His show is run as a church service.

With an uncanny impersonation of an actual evangelist, Bill says comical, poetic, baffling things like, "We want to put the 'odd' back in God," and, "We believe in the God that people who do not believe in God believe in." I first saw the Reverend Billy show on a Sunday afternoon at Surf Reality, a performance space on the Lower East Side. There were fewer than a dozen of us in the audience, but Reverend Billy's performance was energetic and compelling enough to fill a stadium. Beneath the obvious silliness, he seemed to stir an honestly ecstatic religious impulse in that small theater.

The moment I remember most about that show is a bit wherein he holds a conversation with a giant billboard of the model Kate Moss. "She's looking at me," he fumes. "She *wants* me." He continues to flirt with the billboard and in so doing is transported back to an early adolescent romance. Suddenly, he realizes: this is my *self*. These are my *memories*. These ads are taking our memories, attaching them to products, and selling them back to us. He stops, horrified. We are completely with him. This world is fallen and so are we. He leads us in a healing ritual, a visualization wherein we see a Disney tchotchke, reach for it, then resist the temptation to buy. We are given the following directive: "*remember your name*."

It occurred to me that day how branded I am. There is a huge chunk of my memory that is someone else's property, property that someone is right now making money off of. I think about the tattoo of Bugs Bunny on my right shoulder blade. It is trademarked, licensed to the tattoo company by AOL Time Warner. In part, the gospel of the Reverend's Church of Stop Shopping is one's own life story. By lampooning the cultural figure of the right-wing televangelist, Reverend Billy seems to have hit upon a kind of liberation theology. The fallen world against which Billy and his followers struggle is the self-absorbed, amnesiac marketplace, where capital spins around us at frightful speeds, emptying our lives and our pockets as it whizzes by.

"A Call for Dramatic Disobedience," William Talen aka Reverend Billy

Sometimes I look at the service this way: We're trying to rebuild belief. "Believing in something" is such a decimated idea. Broken down by post-modern multiple viewpoints and by the cooptation of advertising. We have to blow up belief and rebuild it and reclaim it during the course of the evening. We have to do it together. Building post-ironic belief is like fighting World War Two. Everyone has to pitch in.

from "Life after Shopping: A Call for Dramatic Disobedience," www.revbilly.org (2001)

In the cosmology of the Church of Stop Shopping, shopping is the primary sin. Among other things, this is a clever comment on the relationship between capital and Puritanism. The urges of the flesh that are in most places frowned upon are instead redirected towards industrial productivity. And somewhere along the line, someone figured out that this insane level of repression could also be used to make us buy things. An extra piece of chocolate cake became sinful; buying an extra pair of shoes was deemed an act of naughtiness. The fun, dirty sins were shoehorned into magazines, ads, and websites, and sold back to us.

I confess that I do enjoy consuming. There is something in me that gets a kick out of acquisition, something that enjoys that strange little rush of power that one gets from the act of purchasing. I honestly believe that shopping, on a very primitive level, stimulates some kind of lower-brain function, some genetic memory of looking at something, wanting it, and getting it from whomever currently has it. I am often possessed by consumer fever, usually for books, CDs, or videos. I can rarely pass a bookstore without entering it, and perceptibly long for books I don't have, even though I already own dozens of books that I have not yet read. Sometimes I like to arrange and rearrange my books or CDs and just look at them, pretending to be an imaginary houseguest and admiring my discriminating taste. But I still think that shopping can be construed as an actual sin, more so than any but the most disagreeable sexual proclivities, because people suffer as a direct result of it. To paraphrase Marx's labor theory of value: when we buy a thing, we're not just buying the thing itself, we're buying the work that went into making it. And to make matters more complex, we have usually been suckered by dubious means into buying the stupid thing to begin with.

As almost everyone seems to know on some level, the idea of entertainment as social control has become remarkably well-developed. Most of us have gradually been lulled into what Reverend Billy calls "consumer narcosis," where we have been hypnotized by bright colors and marketing strategies, and those antisocial impulses that can't be policed by unspoken cues are policed by surveillance cameras, security guards, and agents of the state. In the places we go to consume, we shuffle along, watching and being watched, ingesting the show around us and deliberately or inadvertently performing it, vague, dazed, and slightly uneasy. And thanks to the work of Giuliani et al., Times Square is the quintessential example of such a place; the twenty-first century city as the Mall of America on steroids.

I remember what Times Square used to be like. I can't say I liked it, although for a time I enthusiastically frequented the neighborhood looking for pornography and amyl nitrate. I certainly don't feel any nostalgia for it. It was dangerous and apocalyptically filthy. I was robbed there more than once and harassed countless times. After the economic and social mess caused by the 1987 stock market crash, Poppy Bush's nonexistent urban policy, and Mayor David Dinkins' general incompetence, I was among the throngs of mugged liberals cheering for Giuliani to come riding in on his white horse and clean this shithole up. What can I say? I was young and from New Jersey. I didn't realize that, in New York, "neighborhood revitalization" has always had more to do with real estate profits and corporate interests (and, by extension, racism and repression) than it ever had to do with the quality of anyone's life. I had no idea what was to come. Times Square was a terrible place, sure, but it was a *place*, with people in it, people with great, weird, collective stories with which they constructed their world. Now it's a non-place, a cultural black hole where the only stories are warm, bland, and elaborately produced by committee, where anyone unpredictable, anyone who tries to invade with a story of his or her own is quickly yanked off of the stage.

Reverend Billy is at his most enormous and fearless here in the Disney Store, in this space where he is not welcome, where he is both contrasted with and actively resisting an institution that has been designed to mute contrast and prevent resistance. My arms and legs numb from excitement, I wind my way around the maze of point-of-purchase displays and lock arms with four other men who are blocking the cash register line. Billy launches into his sermon:

CHILDREN STOP SHOPPING FOR A MOMENT. LISTEN TO ME. Mickey Mouse wants to play. His bright red tongue looks like a nice ass, with the perfect little butt-crack. He reaches for us with three-fingered hands. Mickey Mouse is the Anti-Christ.

And we are in Hell now. Do you feel the burning? Do you feel the pain? It registers as a kind of minor happiness. Elton John is singing over there on the floor to ceiling monitor. All the Disney animals at the watering hole look up and smile at his sentimental junk. Winnie the Pooh and Tinkerbell are carried along on the backs of thousands of zebras. That's us.

But children, the tchotchkes in the Disney Store cause memory loss. And the question is, how many millions of us can forget our own lives and be forced here and there like water. The Disney magicians are amazed that we are still following their little smiling animals.

There is only one sin, children! Shopping. All sins are a form of shopping! That utopian jolt at the point of purchase when the product smiles at us – we are actually walking at that moment into the LAKE OF FIRE. Don't you feel the fire? Feel the pain? It's tourism!

Too many stupid minute-long vacations make our real death less interesting. I am preaching here in the Disney Store today because I am a tourist myself. Like all New Yorkers I am allowing this apocalypse to take place. I know that Manhattan in fourteen months will be entirely within the hellishly expanded Disney Store.

This is Manhattan as Suburban Mall. This is a fatal disease known as Involuntary Entertainment. This is the disease known as Continuous Shopping. This is drowning in the Sea of Identical Details.

This is the moment. We stop shopping. The revolution of no shopping. We can start trying to remember what we imagined. We can begin to recall what desire was when it was not supervised.

While Bill is ranting, the crowd, including me, are alternately shouting "hallelujah" and "praise be." The tourists, meanwhile, are continuing their purchases, simultaneously guilty and defiant, moving tensely and rapidly from the cash register, over our blockade, and out the door, their eyes fixed on the ground. I have thought about this often. In New York, it is a common reaction to demonstrations. I chalk it up to sensory overload: a person who has just avoided twenty leafleters dressed as hot dogs or video cameras is not likely to have a sudden change of heart when encountering A Cause. But I think there's something more profound happening as well.

Most anyone would be at least reluctant to enslave a child for their coffee or running shoes. The Gap's store posters, therefore, depict scrubbed young models, not Bengali children with missing fingers. ExxonMobil's cartoon mascot is a happy anthropomorphic tiger, not an oily, blackened crane. Disney does not include a bellicose, overweight riot cop in their cartoon pantheon. The act of consumption is neatly packaged in a sort of psychological version of drive-through convenience. We are encouraged to remain comfortable at all times, and there emerges no moral dissonance between buying a pair of cargo pants and hanging on to our good consciences. This is, I think, the reason for the shame and resentment we are receiving from these tourists and consumers: no matter how much spin we put on it, we are pissing on their parade. Disney wants them to relax, have fun, spend their hard-earned income on some briefly satisfying crap. We want them to think of the faceless Indonesian woman that made the crap, or of the people who were forced to leave the neighborhood to make room for it. Of course they're not going to want to listen to us. Bill talks about his actions as "complicating" the shopping experience; what Disney offers up is a life without complications.

The police have arrived and the manager has gone off to talk to them. We are sure that the Disney Company and its representatives would like nothing more than for us to quietly go away, so we are opting for arrest. As Billy demands that the sex shops be welcomed back into Times Square, we chant, "MORE BOOTY, LESS RUDY! KEEP NEW YORK SEXY," and police officers amass at the front doors. By now I am very afraid. I'm getting dizzy, and my ears are heating up. An imaginary slide-show of police brutality victims flashes behind my eyes. The cop in my head starts to tug at me, attempting to pull me up, but my limbs are too numb. The room is going blurry around the edges. I feel like I could float away were I not tethered by my arm to the line of cash register blockers. The room begins to whirl sluggishly. I want nothing more than to get up and do a running dive into a pile of stuffed animals. Instead I look over at Ron, who is chanting. Without pausing, he acknowledges me with a tiny nod and a sweet grin. For a brief moment my fear is gone and I am swept away by an overwhelming sensation of peace.

It ends soon enough. A police officer comes over and asks us if we'll get up. "Are you arresting us?" Ron asks. "I'd rather not," the cop says. "The manager just wants you out." "We won't resist arrest," Ron says, "but the only way we'll leave is if you arrest us." The cop leaves for a moment to go talk to his superior. Another cop is yelling into Reverend Billy's ear while he ignores him, continuing to preach. "Sir! If you do not stop I am going to arrest you! Sir!" He starts to take a pair of metal handcuffs off of his belt as our cop returns to us. "Okay," he says. We stand up. He cuffs us, one by one. We are marched out the store into the paddywagon, our friends chanting, cheering, and photographing.

The police are unusually nice to us. There are reasons of race, culture, class, history, and geography that can explain this, but I believe that the tone of the entire affair, right down to the demeanor of the police, has been set by the overarching unreality of the day's events. Our protest was a theatricalized version of direct action, much in the same way that Disney's Celebration, Florida is a theatricalized version of a suburb. At one point during our protest, the Disney store manager spits out at us: "All you're doing is entertaining the tourists!" She's right. We were protesting inside a place that isn't really a place under the auspices of a preacher who isn't really a preacher, represented by lawyers who are not yet lawyers (Reverend Billy arranged for our legal representation to be an NYU law school class project). It only makes sense that we were arrested by cops who seem closer to their TV counterparts than they are to themselves. When we exit the holding tank, mere hours after our arrest, a cop is performing his own monologue about something or other for the NYU students. Their professor looks on, amused.

These layers of unreality are no accident of media and culture: they are, on Disney's part at least, intended to conceal. We can't hope to overwhelm this level of late-capitalist spectacle, but we can grab it, transform it, and reverse its purpose: we can use it to reveal. This may just be the old saw about theater being "the lie that tells the truth." It may be another example of the revolutionary borrowing from the oppressor for tactical and psychological reasons; Disney's greatest weapon is its agitprop (or, more appropriately, anestheprop), so that's what we use to fight it. Perhaps it's both.

Freed, we stumble out into the chilly fall afternoon, wondering what to do with ourselves. Most of us had set the day aside, expecting to languish in jail. Now we decide to sit in a great old Hell's Kitchen dive bar, its walls festooned with black-and-white photographs of jazz musicians, and discuss the day's events over beers. In a matter of months this bar will disappear forever, another casualty of the New Times Square.

And so the question remains: What is to be done? In a few weeks the Left will surprise everyone, including ourselves, by shutting down a WTO meeting. But even if our side were to "win" what does *that* mean? The idea of utopia strikes me as an antique, like a rusted art-deco souvenir from an old World's Fair. This is probably a good thing – for most of the twentieth century, utopia turned out to be just another boondoggle, like heaven was before that, or the S&P 500 is now: a justification for the horrible things that this ridiculous society makes us do to one another.

Among other things, Disney sells itself as a kind of utopia: utopia as the regulated, managed environment, ubiquitous and frozen in time. Everything one senses and experiences has been determined in advance and it all leads up to that climactic moment of purchase. We are trained almost from birth to forget the real world, the world that we can touch and smell, that contains risk, passion, complexity and interaction. In its place we are presented with the glistening, sugary parade of consumption. By using spectacle against itself, we pulled back the curtain on a bit of fake heaven on 42nd Street and 7th Avenue, and in doing so we created a real heaven. It was fleeting, seconds even, and for all I know I may have been the only one to have experienced it, but it was real. In that moment of giddy serenity, when Ron's sweet smile gave me the resolve I needed, when I sat breaking real rules with other people who were not being paid or coerced, when all of us stood up and, just for a moment, said no to the hypnotic and formidable global corporate economy we wrote our own story. If that isn't utopia, what is?

This is the first publication of this essay.

ANDREW BOYD,
"TRUTH IS A VIRUS: MEME WARFARE AND
THE BILLIONAIRES FOR BUSH (OR GORE)"

In the following section activist Andrew Boyd explores a new and growing form of politics he calls "meme warfare." Memes are media viruses that spread throughout the population. Think of urban legends, fleeting fashions, and idiotic ad slogans that work their way into everyday conversations; these are memes. But memes can also be used as a culture of resistance. Looking at his own creation, Billionaires for Bush (or Gore), and other activist formations like Critical Mass, Earth Liberation Front, Women's Action Coalition, and Reclaim the Streets (cf. Jordan), Boyd describes a type of organization without offices or members, that is "united less by strict ideology or affiliation and more by a loose set of ideas and a certain way or style of enacting these ideas." These are political "organizations" that exist only insofar as they are an organized cultural idea; an idea that travels, virally, from group to group, is acted upon and then disappears. A supporter of meme warfare, Boyd is also a seasoned enough activist to raise questions about the efficacy of a politics that functions primarily as an ethereal cultural organism.

"Truth is a Virus." When I first saw this phrase, defiantly spray-painted on the walls of a suburban high-school, it thrilled me. So what if it was only a fantasy image in a Hollywood movie? [*Pump up the Volume*, the Christian Slater film about a pirate radio station.] It was infectious. As a political activist, it made immediate, intuitive sense; it became my mantra. I want to infect the body politic. I want to unleash a viral epidemic of truth. Eventually this desire, taking shape in fits and starts, became my calling, guiding my strange "career" in culture jamming and guerrilla media provocations. I soon came to see, however, that lies are also viruses. Lies and myth and kitsch and advertising jingles and corporate logos and mood rings and the idea that free trade is free — all of these are viruses. I came to think of the matrix of hearts and minds and media as a vast theater of viral warfare. In his book *Media Virus!*, Douglas Rushkoff describes it like this:

> Media viruses spread through the datasphere the same way biological ones spread through the body or a community. But instead of traveling along an organic circulatory system, a media virus travels through the networks of the mediascape. The "protein shell" of a media virus might be an event, invention, technology, system of thought, musical riff, visual image, scientific theory, sex scandal, clothing style, or even a pop hero – as long as it can catch our attention. Any one of these media virus shells will search out the receptive nooks and crannies in popular culture and stick on anywhere it is noticed. Once attached, the virus injects its more hidden agendas into the datastream in the form of *ideological* code – not genes but a conceptual equivalent we now call "memes." Like real genetic material, these memes infiltrate the way we do business, educate ourselves, interact with one another – even the way we perceive "reality."[1]

Rushkoff's exploration of "memes" fascinated me. But rather than viruses of clothing styles and pop heroes, I was interested in viruses of political ideas and action. For several years, as "Minister of Culture" for the social justice group United for a Fair Economy, I experimented with various media viruses, taking on issues of taxation, sweatshops, wage inequality, and corporate welfare. In the spring of 2000 we developed a very virulent strain: Billionaires for Bush (or Gore).

The Billionaires campaign was devised to educate the public about the twin evils of campaign finance corruption and economic inequality. With the pay gap between CEOs and workers at 475 to 1, both Democrats and Republicans renting themselves out to big money donors, and 97 percent of incumbents running for re-election being returned to Congress, these problems had reached crisis proportions by the 2000 presidential election. Our idea was to create a humorous, ironic media campaign that would spread like a virus via grassroots activists and the mainstream media.

In early May, I pulled together a team of talented volunteer designers, media producers, and veteran street theater activists. With support from UFE, we began to put the pieces of the campaign in place. We created a stylish logo by splicing together a donkey and elephant, and a "candidate" by digitally morphing photos of presidential candidates George W. Bush and Al Gore into a single eerie image. Riffing off of slogans like "Free the Forbes 400," "Corporations are people too," "We're paying for America's free elections so you don't have to," and "We don't care who you vote for, we've already bought them," we created bumper stickers, buttons, a series of posters, and a kick-ass website that eventually won more than a few awards (www.billionairesforbushorgore.com). We also created a set of more content-rich materials, including a political platform, a full campaign speech, a candidate product comparison chart, as well as a campaign-contribution-return-on-your-investment-analysis. We even made mock radio ads, pressed them onto CD and sent a hundred out to stations across the country. The satire was compact, funny, and politically on target. The look was slick and the message was unified across a whole range of media. It was quite a package. And we launched it all with a "Million Billionaire March" at the Republican and Democratic national conventions.

We designed the campaign to be participatory: a simple concept that was easy to execute yet allowed for rich elaboration. Through the website, activists could download all the materials they needed to do actions in their own communities. By June, wildcat chapters were springing up. In Denver a Billionaires squad barged into the Green Party convention and tried to buy off Ralph Nader, much to the delight of delegates and the media.

By the time we arrived in Philadelphia for the Republican convention in late July, we were already a minor sensation. Advance articles in *Time* magazine and major dailies, radio coverage, and Internet buzz had put us on the map. Our website was getting 100,000 hits a day (20,000 unique page views). Everybody was asking for our buttons and stickers and posters. Nearly a hundred Billionaires in full dress joined us in the streets, chanting, singing, burning money, smoking cigars. We also staged a "Vigil for Corporate Welfare" and auctioned off merchandising rights to the Liberty Bell (would it become the Taco Bell Liberty Bell or the Ma Bell Liberty Bell?) The media were all over us. FOX, MSNBC, CBS, CNN, BBC, radio, print, corporate, independent – it was a feeding-frenzy. An informal poll of photo-journalists voted us "favorite protest." We were certainly one of the more focused and cohesive. The Democratic convention in Los Angeles was more of the same. Folks there formed a very strong chapter, which included a marching band and a choir. My Billionaire character, Phil T. Rich, became a hit on the radio interview circuit and website traffic shot up to 200,000 hits per day.

As the campaign picked up, a hub-node structure arose. UFE became the organizational hub of an ad hoc network of Do-It-Yourself movement grouplets. In the weeks after the conventions, we'd get email and calls every day from people across the country, raving about the project and eager to start local Billionaires chapters. "Cheney is flying into town next week," a young student in Ashland, OR told me in a typical call. "I've gotten a bunch of folks together and we're going to meet him at the airport. The local thrift store has already donated ten tuxedos." This student had first seen the Billionaires on a late-night mainstream news program. He then went to the "Be a Billionaire" section of our website, downloaded the slogans, posters, and sample press releases. The group chose satirical names for themselves, called to give us a heads-up, and went into action. While other participants first heard about the campaign through activist email networks or via word of mouth, penetration of corporate mass media was key to the Billionaires' success.

It took ingenious "viral design" to get our message through the corporate media's editorial filters and out into the datasphere at large. We built our virus by embedding a threatening idea inside a non-threatening form. The "protein shell" of our virus: "Billionaires for Bush (or Gore)." Our meme, or hidden ideological code: Big Money owns both candidates/parties; both candidates/parties are roughly the same. Elegantly encapsulating the core ideas of the campaign into a funny five-word concept made for a sleek and potent virus. This concision also served as an "inoculation" against distortion. Even the most fragmented and de-contextualized mention in the media tended to carry our name, and thus our message. If they also got our tag line, "Because Inequality is not Growing Fast Enough," then the message deepened. If they picked up modular parts of our shtick, then it deepened further. When they invited us on the air for lengthy radio interviews, we could eventually drop character and proceed with a straight up critique. The campaign had layers of code – concentric rings of more and more elaborate messaging. Each component was modular, compact, and self-contained. It could survive in a hostile, unpredictable media environment and like a fractal, still represent the campaign as a whole.

The Billionaires used irony's double edge – its capacity to simultaneously pose both a straight literal meaning and a subversive implied meaning – to neatly flip between the virus' outer shell and its inner code. In this way we could reach our two disparate audiences – corporate media and grassroots activists – at the same time. Activists immediately picked up on the various layers of irony. While the mainstream media could be seduced to "play along" with the literal, tongue-in-cheek meaning, letting the public decode the implied and subversive meanings for themselves.

Some of the most powerful media viruses – virtual reality, smart drugs, compassionate conservatism – are actually oxymorons. Activist viruses are no exception. Groups working to rein in excessive government subsidies, hand-outs, and tax-breaks to corporations hit on the phrase "corporate welfare." By meshing two seemingly incompatible notions into a new concept, such a phrase demands thought: "Huh, corporations get welfare?" It creates its own unique conceptual slot in the minds of people who hear it. The phrase demands conscious attention, providing an opportunity for the virus to attach itself and inject its meme-code into the public mind.[2] The Billionaires virus made a similar demand: "Huh, billionaires are protesting? Huh, Bush *or* Gore?"

To be successful, a media virus need not be ironic or oxymoronic. It must, however, be mobile, easily replicable, and well suited to the particular vectors of the media ecosystem that it has to travel. The Billionaires virus was virulent partly because it was a carrier on the mega-virus of the Presidential campaign itself. It was designed to appeal to the media: it was timely, visual, funny, and accessible. It was familiar yet different: a new and provocative way to say what everybody already secretly thought. The virus attached easily to a range of physical and semantic "carriers" – logo, posters, slogans, fake radio ads, street actions, email, buzz, laughter, media story, etc. – and we introduced it into the media stream in a manner calculated to maximize its propagation. Content and humor were tightly meshed. Not only did the humor help carry the content (in the way that laughter makes it easier to bear the truth), but if the media wanted the humor (and they did), they had to take the content too. The materials were catchy and accessible and the action model was easy to DIY. Thus the meme "spread, replicated, and mutated."

Mutation was an issue, however. We, the virus designers, wanted participants to take the core idea and make it their own – to "run with it" – but we also wanted to control the degree and kinds of mutation. There was a deliberate effort to keep the core ideological code stable, while allowing wildcat chapters and interested DIYers to adapt the various code-carriers (as well as outer layers of code) to fit their own circumstances and creative inclinations.

"The task of an organizer," a movement veteran once told me, "is to set up structures so people can participate." In this sense, a meme might serve as a "virtual structure." In the Billionaires campaign, both virtual and real structures worked together to shape and steer the campaign. The hub was a meme arsenal, here we designed the core ideas and launched the call to action. Once things got rolling, several mechanisms helped us steer the campaign. One was the website. Another was the Million Billionaire March, which modeled the kinds of actions people could do in their home cities. Finally, it was the shtick and the materials themselves. Jokes were funny, content was thoroughly researched, graphic production values were high. People liked the package and were naturally drawn to stay on message.

With a strong central concept and tight message discipline across all the materials, the mutations that developed in the field generally tended to be extensions of, rather than departures from the basic framework. Most of the mutations were "tweaks," where people elaborated the main campaign by devising their own slogans, parody songs, or actions. Others were "clones." Here people came up with their own sister campaigns, such as Billionaires for Closed Debates which took on the monopolizing of the Presidential debates by the two major parties, and Billionaires for More Media Mergers which protested growing media concentration at the National Association of Broadcasters in San Francisco that fall. In most of these cases, even when the wildcat DIY actions got scrappy and somewhat tangential, the core idea came through, and the whole campaign was of a piece.

Of course, I'm not the only activist waging viral warfare. In recent years new kinds of cultural resistance and social movement formations have appeared that understand – if not consciously, then at least intuitively – that their terrain of struggle is a "viral space."[3] These formations – Woman's Action Coalition, Reclaim the Streets, Lesbian Avengers, Earth Liberation Front, Radical Cheerleaders, and Critical Mass, to name several – are often composed of loosely structured networks, don't have a single central organization with files, offices, members, etc., and often coalesce for a certain purpose or action and then dissolve. They are united less by strict ideology or affiliation and more by a loose set of ideas and a certain way or style of enacting these ideas. The cultural practices of these micro-movements spread virally, often via the Internet, but also via other media – both grassroots and corporate.

The Critical Mass bicycle rides are a good example. The format is simple, fun, and easy to replicate. On the last Friday of every month, bicycle activists and enthusiasts gather for a mass unpermitted ride through the city. With a combination of moxie and sheer numbers they take the streets. The rides are celebratory, self-organizing, and open to all. The ideological code – "bikes are traffic, deal with it" – is perfectly embodied by the action. Dubbed "organized coincidences," these rides arose in San Francisco in the late 1980s and quickly spread across the globe.

Viruses happen. Viruses are also made to happen. Some radical viruses (cultural formations such as Reclaim the Streets and Critical Mass) evolve more or less organically out of communities of resistance, while others (media campaigns such as the Billionaires) are more consciously designed and injected into the mediastream. In both cases there's an ideological code as well as a viral shell. In pop culture, we've seen how a viral shell can be made of almost anything – from an advertising jingle to a new technology.

For activist viruses, the viral shell is often a model of participatory action. For RTS the ideological code was a utopian demand to resist capital and liberate public space; the action model was a militant street carnival. It was the RTS action model that drove its viral explosion. People across the world grabbed onto the carnival, replicated it, and mutated it in their own way. As with Critical Mass, the RTS ideological code was elegantly embedded in the action itself. By doing the action, participants live the code themselves as well as deploy the code for others to reckon with. In the Billionaires campaign, the action model, though an important component, did not drive the campaign; it was more the sly and funny propaganda packaging of the ideological code.

Rushkoff speaks of a "viral syringe," an initial event that injects the virus into the datastream. For the Billionaires this was primarily accomplished through the Million Billionaire March. For the movement against sweat-shops, it was the Kathie Lee Gifford scandal – the revelation that a popular female celebrity was having her personal line of designer clothing pro-duced by young immigrant women working under sweatshop conditions. By craftily orchestrating the exposé and then riding the resulting scandal for all it was worth, activists mainlined sweatshops into the American psyche. However it is launched, a truly successful virus must eventually take on a life of its own, demonstrating self-sustaining and self-evolving proper-ties. Either it must infect the code of mainstream discourse and permanently change the habits of mainstream institutions as the Kathie Lee sweatshop scandal did or it must create alternative ongoing institutions that carry and reproduce the living meme. In this sense RTS and Critical Mass are more successful memes than the Billionaires. The Billionaire campaign was time-delimited by the presidential campaign. RTS and Critical Mass were more universal and more fostering of community – a community that has sustained and spread the meme.

Because they coalesce around an idea and/or a mode of action, rather than an organization, movements based on memes tend to be "cheap, fast, and out of control" (to borrow a phrase often used to describe the life-like behaviors of complex systems and dense information networks).[4] Cheap and fast are generally good qualities for a grass-roots movement. Out of control is a mixed blessing: on the one hand, they tend to spread quickly; on the other hand, they sometimes die just as quickly. This was the case for the Women's Action Coalition, the dynamic feminist direct action group. At its height in 1993 WAC had 300 women coming to weekly meetings (in New York alone), a furious barrage of actions and press coverage, and copy-cat chapters around the world, but by 1995 it had folded. Meme-based movements may generate passionate community and a white-hot intensity of action, but unless there's an ongoing mass ritual such as monthly Critical Mass rides or unless they develop some kind of organizational infrastructure they tend not to last.

Sometimes a meme-based movement hits upon just the right form of "non-organization" to keep itself going. This seems to be the case with the mysterious and controversial Earth Liberation Front. The ELF is an underground movement of autonomous groups who carry out economic sabotage to protect the environment. They have been linked to various acts of property destruction around the US, including $12 million in arson damage to a ski resort in Vail, Colorado, that was threatening endangered lynx habitat. A bookstore owner in Oregon (who is unconnected to any of the clandestine actions) acts as the legal spokesperson for the group. Seen through a viral lens, ELF might not be an organization at all, but more aptly described as "a meme with a press office." The various cells are turned on by the same idea, copy-cat each other's actions, and simply use the same name when they send in their communiqués. This form of meme-based "non-organization" seems to work for ELF: they are able to maintain security, encourage many separate independent actions, and still generate an influential media profile.

While ELF and other political activists have adapted viral structures to grow their resistance movements, media activists have pioneered a new form of hand-to-hand viral combat: culture jamming. Like the pranksters who creatively deface billboards, culture jammers hack into the genetic code of a corporate media virus and turn it against itself. One Uniroyal Tires ad showed a Latin American peasant under the slogan "He Knows Three English Words: Boy George, Uniroyal." With a ladder and deft use of spray paint, billboard bandits changed the three words to read "Yankee Go Home," and in so doing not only revealed the original corporate strategy but repurposed it to subversive ends.

Advertising imagery is the ultimate stealth virus. It has long been post- or pre-rational, operating by subconscious association, by veiled promise and threat, by mobilizing our longings and our dreamworld. Rational critique can't find a handle by which to challenge such a worldview. *Adbusters* magazine, the Vancouver-based anti-commercial glossy well known for its sly reworkings of corporate logos and ad campaigns, understands that culture jamming can stick where rational discourse slides off. In one of their classic "subvertisements" *Adbusters* took a Kool cigarettes logo, kept the exact color and typeface but changed the "K" to "F" and then placed it above a glossy shot of a young man half-coyly, half cluelessly smoking a cigarette. Such a pastiched image operates much like a "meme vaccine," interrupting our consumer trance and redirecting our attention. Culture jamming fights virus with virus. Over the last decade it has itself become a virulent meme, spreading far and wide and encompassing a myriad of new sub-cultural forms.[5]

If culture jamming works as a "meme vaccine," the website www.posternation.org, begun by Wesleyan art students in the mid nineties and later handed over to United for a Fair Economy, was designed as a "viral engine." The principle, "Nationwide Saturation Postering," is deceptively simple. On selected action days (Tax Day, July 4, etc.) decentralized guerrilla street-postering teams simultaneously put up a similar set of posters all across the country. The website displays the posters in easy-to-download-and-print PDF format, and facilitates the setting up of teams. A core set of themed posters are provided (the first theme was "Tax the Rich," later themes included the Billionaires) and new posters can be added by participants so long as they fit the current theme. Not only does the message spread virally, but the project does as well: every poster includes the Posternation logo and website address and thus becomes a viral advertisement for the site and campaign as a whole. Once launched and nurtured past a certain point, the project becomes largely self-organizing and almost infinitely scalable. New structures such as posternation.org, that take advantage of the Internet and new viral styles of communication, should be a spur to activists to re-imagine what is possible.

All viruses are not created equal. Some spread faster, some last longer, some mutate into more and less resistant strains, some lie dormant for years and then explode, some get injected into the media body in massive $40 million Madison Avenue dosages, some travel its hidden pathways. Some happily co-exist, some compete, while some are carriers on others. The dense complexity of networks within the infosphere cause it to operate much like an ecosystem: a huge self-organizing interpenetrating organism, a system so large and complex that it is, in a sense, wild and "out of control," or at least can't be programmed or controlled from any one point or by any one entity. Viewing the overall media body as an ecology can help activists switch focus from the hard boundaries of commercial vs. noncommercial, mainstream vs. sidestream, and top-down vs. bottom-up to a more fluid and nuanced model.[6]

Up to this point, I have emphasized the importance of memes and suggested ways to integrate an operational understanding of memes into our strategies of movement building. But a movement must also exist physically and institutionally, not just virtually. It is not an either/or thing. It is a false dichotomy to associate new/good with an ephemeral meme-based community of resistance and old/bad with a lumbering industrial-era beast of meetings and membership and ideology. There is a spectrum. Within any broad social movement – feminism, for example – there are groups that are more meme-based, such as the Women's Action Coalition and more institutionally-based such as the National Organization of Women, with its mass membership, multi-million dollar budget, and focus on policy and lobbying. Successful, long-term social movements will always include both types. These opposed tendencies are an expression of the eternal dialectic between movement building and organization building. Similar tensions existed between the go-with-the-meme-of-the-moment attitude of the loosely-affiliated Billionaires grass-roots base and United for a Fair Economy's mission which required building organizational muscle and clout in order to pursue a broad social justice agenda over the long haul. But while there was tension, there was also a great deal of synchronicity. UFE provided a campaign framework, funding, infrastructure, research capacity, media contacts, and mainstream legitimacy. The grass-roots injected energy, street smarts, and creative elaboration of the core ideas. The Billionaires campaign suggests a model for how hub and node can work together to invite open-ended DIY participation into creative actions and yet maintain artistic cohesion and a focused message.

Social movements cannot live by meme alone. Yet memes are clearly powerful – both analytically and operationally. A vital movement requires a hot and happening meme. The Declaration of Independence, the Communist Manifesto, sit-down strikes in the Thirties, campus building take-overs in the Sixties – arguably, these were all memes – no more or less, maybe, than the militant street carnival of the past decade. What is different in each case is the shape and flow of the specific media pathways these memes must travel and the culture with which they must connect. The contemporary movements profiled here and the techniques they have pioneered will hopefully be of service to those of us who believe that truth is a virus and whose aim is to subvert the corporate meme-machine with a sly guerrilla war of signs.

This is the first publication of this essay.

RICARDO DOMINGUEZ, "ELECTRONIC DISTURBANCE: AN INTERVIEW"

As more and more of our economic, political, and everyday communication moves online, electronic methods of protest are becoming more and more important. Ricardo Dominguez, co-founder of Electronic Disturbance Theater and co-creator of the popular webjamming tool FloodNet, understands this, and in the following interview elaborates on why this is so. What makes Dominguez's understanding of electronic activism so noteworthy is his insistence that EDT's activism be understood as theater. It sounds crazy but it makes sense. The web is merely the technological extension of a larger historical process: the growth of the mediated world, one of signs and symbols, meanings and understandings. This semiotic system, performed everyday, has real economic and political power — think of the stock market for instance. EDT actions function within this larger drama as a cultural counter-performance, an informational intervention: harnessing networks, clogging up websites, and generating hype (see sidebars). Dominguez's interview is a nice way to close this book, for not only does it point to the future of activism, but it reaches back to tell the life history and political education of an activist who uses culture in the service of politics in the present. And in the end there is another beginning. Dominguez finishes his story by spinning a new one: a fantastic tale to illustrate the sober truth that simple gestures and small cultural acts have the power to upset the most formidable of foes.

I was born in Las Vegas, Nevada, 1959, May 2. Las Vegas was like living in three different worlds. One was the *Happy Days* world of the Mormons, where everyone was pure and nice and no one smoked, nobody drank and nobody even had coffee. The other world was the world of the Godfather, one of cool mobsters and occasional lawyers being blown up, and everything was legal: prostitution, gambling, everything else. And then the third world was the *X-Files* world. Ninety-eight percent of Nevada is owned by the government, some of the most secretive installations in the world are in Nevada. And right across the mountain, on the other side of Las Vegas is the nuclear test site. So I grew up, every Saturday at twelve o'clock in the afternoon, hearing the sirens go off and we would get up, run to the top of the Mint Hotel, and wait for the bombs to set off and the entire earth would turn into these waves.

In a certain sense my political consciousness came not so much from an exterior politicized context but more from a popular culture context. At the same time that these nuclear bombs were going off, I was watching Saturday

Electronic Civil Disobedience, Critical Art Ensemble

At one time the control of the street was a valued item. In 19th century Paris the streets were the conduits for the mobility of power, whether it was economic or military in nature. If the streets were blocked, and key political fortresses were occupied, the state became inert, and in some cases collapsed under its own weight. This method of resistance was still useful up through the 60s, yet since the end of the 19th century it has yielded diminishing returns, and has drifted from being a radical practice to a liberal one. This strategy is grounded in the fact that capital is centralized within cities; as capital has become increasingly decentralized, breaking through national boundaries and abandoning the cities, street action has become increasingly useless. Street activism has become an anachronism now that there is no longer any geographic or physical center of economic or political power.

. . .

CAE has said it before, and we will say it again: as far as power is concerned, the streets are dead capital! Nothing of value to the power elite can be found on the streets, nor does this class need control of the streets to efficiently run and maintain state institutions. For CD to have any meaningful effect, the resisters must appropriate something of value to the state. Once they have an object of value the resisters have a platform from which they may bargain for change.

. . .

The strategy and tactics of ECD should not be a mystery to any

afternoon matinées about people with nuclear radiation turning into giant bugs or growing third eyes . . . and Blaxploitation films in North Las Vegas. Blaxploitation films were highly political: they were attacking the white man who was usually in power. For instance, I remember one of the important films for me was a film called *Three the Hard Way* with Jim Kelly, James Brown, and Fred Williamson, where they discover that there's these Nazi fascists in Florida who are developing a virus that will kill only black people. There was also science fiction films like *Soylent Green* where they discover that governments eat people, *THX1138* where the only value a human being has is the price of that individual and if you overrun that price then you are no longer of value. My political understanding of the world was both screenal and on the streets.

[Later] I heard of the work of the Living Theater. I saw Bread and Puppet Theater during the nuclear activist actions. So I began to comprehend that in film and in performance there was a way one could critique this kind of condition, that one could actually do something, and I decided to become an actor; I decided to become a classical actor. So I spent most of from 16 to 20 just traveling, doing Shakespeare around the country. All the while in the back of my head was floating Judith Malina and Julian Beck's treatise on the Living Theater.

In 1981 I decided that what I really needed to do was somehow educate myself deeper in a kind of critical theory, a discourse (of course I didn't have that language at that time). So I decided that I would go to school and get my MA in dramaturgy. And I ended up going to Tallahassee, Florida. And it was there that I started getting a deeper understanding of history and theory. I discovered that in the academic bunker there wasn't a lot of interdisciplinary or transdisciplinary process. You were a dramaturge and you studied the classics of performance theory. You didn't go to sociology and read C. Wright Mills. You didn't go to philosophy and read Wittgenstein. It was just not done.

And eventually, I was asked kindly to leave the academy since I wasn't doing what I was supposed to.

I said fine with that. I walked across the street and I got a job at Ruby Fruit books, a lesbian bookstore, the only lesbian bookstore in Tallahassee, Florida. And they were kind enough to make me their token male, if you will, and allowed me to order books. It was through this that I started finding alternative presses and some of the first Semiotext(e) Books: Virilo, Baudrillard. I was reading a lot of the radical lesbian feminists that were coming out at that time. Certainly queer theory was beginning to emerge as the high edge of a new form of embodying theory – and the theory would become not just a discourse but really play itself out.

And at that time in the 1980s there was a lot of cocaine in Florida. So you would end up going to a lot of cocaine parties. At these parties I started hearing people, "hey you should talk to so and so, 'cause they are talking in the same kind of yack that you are speaking" and you know, blah, blah, blah. And eventually through one of these cocaine parties, I ran into some of the people who would later become Critical Art Ensemble. One of them was a film maker who hated film, a poet who hated poetry, a photographer who hated photography, the first person I ever met who actually worked with a computer who hated technology, a bookmaker who hated books. I was an actor who hated acting. And we all had a fetish for cocaine and we also had a fetish for theory.

We developed this ritual where we would gather at Hope Kurtz's big glass table and she would put out lines and we would read Adorno, we would read all these great books and go "this is a great bit of critical theory; write that line down"; and then do another line of cocaine. That's all you had to do in Tallahassee. It wasn't like you had to worry about anything else happening in the world 'cause there was nothing happening, so you could read your Hegel and do lines. But what did happen was that we had a sense that something else could be created. That we could create a focus in this space

activists. They are the same as traditional CD. ECD is a nonviolent activity by its very nature, since oppositional forces never physically confront one another. As in CD, the primary tactics in ECD are trespass and blockage. Exits, entrances, conduits, and other key spaces must be occupied by the contestational force in order to bring pressure on legitimized institutions engaged in unethical or criminal actions. Blocking information conduits is analogous to blocking physical locations; however, electronic blockage can cause financial stress that physical blockage cannot, and it can be used beyond the local level. ECD is CD reinvigorated. What CD once was, ECD is now.

From *Electronic Civil Disobedience*, pamphlet, 1995, pp. 3 and 7 that we then defined as the cultural frontier. And that in the cultural frontier one could create a theoretical discourse, a practice which could be co-equal to the nexus, to New York, Chicago, LA, that could be just as vital and specific. But of course, it was very loose and not very lucid as of yet. And unfortunately, like many of these things, what did bring it into focus, what did bring it into practice, was a crisis. And the crisis that hit us was AIDS.

By 1986 and 1987, many of our good friends began to get sick. And, of course, like many at first we didn't know exactly what to do or how to play it out. But we began to hear that there were very good groups, especially Gran Fury up in New York, who had begun to initiate a directed aesthetic activist discourse and look. Gran Fury created Silence = Death, and the whole look of early ACT UP.

ACT UP really brought to the foreground the politics of the question vs. the politics of the answer. ACT UP was really calling for a single question to be answered: "Is there a cure?" It wasn't that we were saying that we were going to overthrow the state, that we were going to take over the world, or that we had answers. But we were asking the single question that was very difficult . . . to answer. Why wasn't there a cure? What was going on? What was the hold-up? So this very basic question started creating spaces.

ACT UP Tallahassee emerged as a real collective and we started working with ACT UP Miami and ACT UP Atlanta, doing coordinated actions with each other. Some of the first actions we did were what we called "butt-ins." Because Tallahassee is the Capital and of course the Governor's mansion was there, everybody was there. So we'd jump over the fence and pull down our pants. We'd have whatever comments we wanted [painted on our butts] and we'd slam our asses up against the window. Of course, these butt-ins would create these media gestures. I was an actor and a director so I created how actions would work.

One of the elements that began to occur during these street actions is things like fax jams. We would fax jam the National Institute of Health Fax, you know, What is AZT? How many people has AZT cured? So to me it predates what electronic civil disobedience could be; doing these fax jams was electronic civil disobedience. Probably one of the most important elements was what we called phone zapping. There was a large food conglomerate in the South called Publix. Probably around '90 they decided that the best way to deal with the AIDS hysteria was to stop selling condoms. How this worked in their minds, we didn't know, but we certainly knew it was wrong. So what we did with this triumvirate of ACT UP Atlanta, ACT UP Tallahassee, and ACT UP Florida was this phone tree of 24 hour action, 7 days a week where, like, I was supposed to call at 10:59,

11:59, 1:59 and say "Look, I shop in your store, I am happy to shop in your store, but I no longer want to shop in your store if I can't buy my condoms in your store." And I would call. It wasn't a kind of aggressive "we're going to take you down." It was "look, we're a shopper, we live in the community, blah blah blah." After two weeks of this they called us in, and said yes we are going to start selling condoms in the stores. We said, "Great, now we want the condoms up front because we don't want to go all the way to the back." And you know there was a kind of simple leverage of a very simple tool bringing this strong conglomerate into a more enlightened position.

But one of the things we also began to notice by 1990 was that even though our actions were more highly organized, more specific, more directed and much clearer in terms of all the information we had, they weren't getting the same kind of media that the early actions, say 1989 or 1988, were getting. And this was a turning point, at least for Critical Art Ensemble. We began to ask, what is it that we are doing wrong? Is there something we can do?

And we took to heart the William Gibson metaphor of cyberspace being a mass hallucination. And that power had now shifted into cyberspace. So we began to re-read *Neuromancer*. And in chapter three of *Neuromancer*, there is a section where Case, the hacker, and Molly Millions, the cyborg-woman, need to break into this bunker of information but they can't. They need the help of a third group that is mentioned, I think only three times, and that is the Panther Moderns. And what the Panther Moderns are is a highly self-conscious terrorist group that work in developing types of mass hallucinations. So, if you imagine that cyberspace is already a master central hallucination, they were creating other hallucinations on top of that. And what happens is that these screenal hallucinations blind power to what is actually occurring. And this allows Case and Molly Millions to enter the information bunker and get whatever it is that they were looking for. So, we began to think perhaps what needs to happen is Panther Moderns need to emerge, an activist electronic community . . . And we began to write and elucidate what later would be published in 1994 and 1995 as *The Electronic Disturbance* and *Electronic Civil Disobedience and Other Unpopular Ideas*.

But as in all things, by 1991, there was a sense of a divide in Critical Art Ensemble between theory and practice. One was that we should focus on theory; that we should continue our critique and focus now on biotechnology and nanotechnology. You could already see signs that this would be the next kind of front to be dealt with. And certainly I agreed, but I also felt that sometimes theory, because we thought of it, is now over. As

Foucault says: if it can be talked about it must now be dead. I thought that there was a need for theory to hit the ground, to hit the street. It had to be put into practice. So I decided that I should focus on placing it in action. I didn't really know how to do this, not having any training in code or computers. I had worked now for a decade in a lesbian bookstore with books, which is a good training for some things but not very good training for what I was expecting to do.

I heard that in New York City some artists had begun to build infrastructures . . . one of them was The Thing, started in 1991, by Wolfgang Staelhe, a painter and conceptual artist . . . So, I sold all the millions of books I had gathered during my ten years. I bought a little yellow Ford Fiesta for $200 that was guaranteed to get me to New York City before breaking down. I took the fifty books that I thought would be most important in developing the practice of electronic civil disobedience . . . And I drove as quickly as I could from Tallahassee, Florida. I went to where the BBS Thing.net was and I introduced myself to Wolfgang. I was only there maybe about twenty minutes. I came back out. They had broken into my car. They had taken all my clothes; they had taken all my books. So in a certain sense, I felt that New York was telling me how I needed to survive. And that is I had to become a thief.

And having been enamored of Genet, I felt that being a book thief, since that's what I knew, well that's the way I would live. And I started stealing very expensive Verso books and Lyotard's wallbook on Duchamp, $350, and I would sell them at Mercer Books. But in the mornings, I would study code at The Thing. The pedagogical method at The Thing is: There's a computer, there's books, good luck. Nobody was going to help me. It was all very do-it-yourself. And it was there that I really began to understand how these networks were created. And I would always introduce the concept of electronic civil disobedience. People would just shake their head, "Well, that's interesting Ricardo. We don't know what that is."

And again what occurred was a crisis. In 1994, one minute after midnight, the Zapatistas emerged out of the jungle. They took over the state of Chiapas, calling for autonomy for the indigenous communities there. I had come stumbling home from the Tunnel. I think I was tripping on E or something. I couldn't sleep. I checked my e-mail . . . And one of the first things I got was the Declaration of the Lacandona. To me it really began the practice and formalizing of electronic civil disobedience. And the next day as I was stumbling out, I always went to the Odessa [restaurant] to get something to eat, I saw a little post-it note at ABC No Rio [community/ cultural center] saying: "If anybody has heard anything about the Zapatistas, let's meet tonight." And that night we met in the basement of ABC No Rio. It was a cold, dank, winter basement, full of big rats in those days. And basically the New York Committee for Democracy in Mexico was born. We instantly started doing civil disobedience, like hunger strikes, over at the Mexican Consulate.

We had predicted in Critical Art Ensemble's *Electronic Civil Disobedience* that two things would be very difficult to accomplish: (1) that hackers would ever be politicized and (2) that activists would ever be technologized in terms of thinking of electronic culture as a useful leverage. And one of the things that I discovered – even though the Zapatistas became known as the avant garde of the information wars, just by using e-mail – was when we would do actions or marches or hunger strikes, it wasn't: "Let's do electronic civil disobedience." The activists would look at you and go, "That's interesting, but we don't actually know what you mean by that. We're gonna go do a march." . . . When I went to [the hacker zine] *2600*, I said, "Well, let's . . ." and they said, "Well, no. That's a stupid idea. Go away." But one of the few areas that was open, that didn't just disregard me, was the net-art community. They said, "We'll we don't know what it is but if you can do it, go ahead." So between these two blocks there was this kind of open space.

At the same time in 1994, Cecilia Rodriguez in El Paso [Texas] had been chosen as the legal representative of the Zapatistas. So we kept trying to call her. We couldn't get a hold of her because she herself wasn't prepared. She woke up one morning and found she was the legal representative. I think she didn't have a phone at the time 'cause she was too poor . . . [But] we also started to see the gleaming of this decentralized network which would later be called the International Network of Struggle and Resistance or the Intergalactic Network of Struggle and Resistance. You started seeing the blooming of hundreds of Zapatista sites all over the world. Harry Cleaver at the University of Texas, Austin, started, by 1995, the Zapatista listserv. Remember that the Zapatistas had only basically twelve days of fighting. In a certain sense the Internet radicalized them. Suddenly, they discovered they no longer had to be this kind of a modernist guerilla movement that followed, you know, "death in arms." Instead they created this kind of information guerilla movement.

Again it was through a series of crises that the electronic media really started bringing itself to the foreground. Probably the most important of these early gestures was the Chase Manhattan memo in 1996. It was an internal investment memo to be sent out only to the Chase Manhattan Investment Community but somehow it leaked out to the Zapatista community. Basically it stated that even though the Zapatistas had no direct influence on the value of the peso, they did create a certain psychological depression on the investor community. Therefore, Chase called for the elimination of the Zapatista communities with extreme prejudice. A few days later, the first major offensive by Zedillo's Mexican military since 1994 was initiated. You could see a direct connection between this memo and the offensive action.

Well because we had this memo we started doing posters of it. We did actions at Chase Manhattan. We sent it to the *New York Times*. We just spammed the entire world. Within three days the offensive stropped. And I remember Commandante Ramona [of the Zapatistas] saying that an electronic force field had been created. And this electronic force field had created not only a protective device but had actually leveraged the possibility of bringing the worldwide community to Chiapas. That forced the Mexican government by 1996 to meet the Zapatistas face to face to create the San Andreas Accords.

Basically the Zapatistas had shown that you can upload the singularity of the community and decentralize it. Chiapas globalized, it pushed itself around the world. It did end runs around the dominant media, the major media filters. We didn't need the *New York Times*. We didn't need these other spaces to allow the Zapatistas to speak to the world. And they did it without electricity; they did it without computers; they did it without all the things that we have now. To become the dominant information force was truly amazing . . . It was bare bones. Somebody writes a note. They hand it to somebody who rides a horse. The guy on the horse gives it somebody on a truck on a dirt road that takes it to San Cristobal, who then probably goes to the church or someplace, then uploads it to *La Jornada* [a left-leaning Mexican newspaper]. I mean it's a long arduous process, nobody's uploading on their wireless Palm 7. To me, these were direct signs of electronic civil disobedience. And I felt that something more could be accomplished in terms of direct action.

Through The Thing I began a pedagogical spamming of the networks that I was in contact with. I spoke to them about Zapatismo, about what was going on in Chiapas. I used these kinds of platforms to aggregate knowledge about the Zapatistas. And it was through this kind of networking, basically, I felt I was fulfilling the call that had been made through the Zapatista Encuentro to create this intercontinental network of struggle and resistance.

Encuentro means encounter. What the Zapatistas started doing as early as 1995 was inviting the world to come to Chiapas to gather. And where one would gather, they would create these tables. There's like the table of music, the table of propaganda, there was a network table, and you could join any of these tables and you would share information that you bring to that table. And there was usually one Zapatista at the table who was silent and kind of took in the information and then took it back to the command and the autonomous communities. And then there would be some response. Out of the network there was a response of: build the networks. Start gathering.

The other thing that the Zapatistas did was a very open gesture in which anyone or anything could participate in the Zapatismo in any manner they could. It could be a poem; it could be direct action on the street. There wasn't a specific Zapatista mode: you have to do this or you are not a Zapatista. So again, it was an open gesture and you use whatever tools you have at hand to create that gesture. Obviously the networks were what I had at hand. Unbeknownst to me . . . I had created the ground for what would be the direct non-violent use of the Internet, pushing it away from the paradigm of just communication and documentation. And again it happened because of a crisis. That's probably one of the most important things of all activism. It always comes from something horrible.

On December 22, 1997, the Acteal Massacre occurred in which forty-five women and children were killed by paramilitary troops trained and armed by the Mexican Military. From what we understand, the police were only about 500 feet away. A lot of rage and anger occurred in the Zapatista movement. I felt that something more needed to be done than send more e-mails and do more actions. I just wanted to shut them all down. Basically we were all so angry. So I just started spamming everybody. "It's time for direct action: on the streets and online."

After I sent out this e-mail, I received an e-mail from a group in Italy called the Anonymous Digital Coalition. They said, "Ricardo, Why don't we do this? Why don't we go to a specific URL of the Mexican Government and by taking the refresh and reload button that exists on every public browser, we just for an hour, reload over and over and over." Basically, in theory, blocking the site: creating a disturbance. I thought: "This is *fantastico*, let's go do it." I spammed everybody I knew. A few seconds later I received an e-mail from Carmin Karasic [a software engineer] up at MIT. She said, "Ricardo, I have read some of your documents on electronic monuments. What are the names of the Acteal dead? I would like to make an electronic monument." I thought that was a beautiful idea. A few beeps later, I got an e-mail from Brett Stalbaum, a net artist and teacher from San Jose, California – the Cadre Institute – who said, "Ricardo, I think what I can do is write a small Java script which will take into account how many people participate and reload for us so we don't have to hurt our little finger reloading." I said, "*Fantastico*, let's do that." But, he said, "Ricardo, I'm not a good designer. I don't want to do the skin." And I said: "Brett, let me introduce you to Carmin. Carmin, let me introduce you to Brett. Why don't you guys make an electronic monument to the Zapatistas that is active." And I let them go. At the same time Stefan Wray, then a doctoral student at New York University, wanted to do his dissertation on electronic civil disobedience theory and practice, and wanted to know if I would help him and participate in this development. At the time, I was developing a listserv for The Thing called Information Wars. So I said, "help me be co-moderator and I'll help you," and he said sure.

Stefan and I, Carmin and Brett, began to work together. The Zapatista FloodNet system emerged as a tool. And at that time we decided to become a theater. I thought it was very important to continue the performative gesture. Unbeknownst to me, I didn't know how useful a tactic it would be. We decided that we would do a performance/action twice a month – all of 1998. We would only do these actions in solidarity with the Zapatistas and we would only do them for a year. The main goal would be to spread information about the Zapatistas, secondly, to push the theory of electronic civil disobedience.

We did our first action. Some 14,800 people participated around the world. Many people said President Zedillo's website responded, "I can't fulfill your request," which to us was victory. One of the things that the Zapatista FloodNet does is it uploads the names of the dead into the server. And it also asks the server questions, this whole politics of the question, in a literal way. The Zapatista FloodNet system would ask, "Is there justice on this system?" And the system responds, "Justice is not found on this server." "Is there democracy on this server?" "Democracy is not found on this server." "Is Anna Hernandez, one of the Acteal dead, found on this server?" And this is called 404, a traditional function of the Internet that lets you know that what you are looking for doesn't exist on that server. And so by this small gesture, we create a disturbance because it takes up CPU. It takes up space. In the same way that bodies would take up space, say in real life, these kind of questions, this kind of reloading takes up the space.

The next day we were in the *New York Times*. And this started a new media level of discussion.

Then Ars Electronica in Austria – that's a big new media festival that's existed now for I guess twenty-five years – decided that their theme that year was going to be "information war" and they invited Electronic Disturbance Theater to do a presentation. We took this as an opportunity to do a really big action. We had only done virtual sit-ins against President Zedillo specifically. And we decided to do an action against the Pentagon that had just sold twenty-five Hueys [helicopters] to the Mexican army; the Frankfurt Stock Exchange, because we understood that they wanted to buy uranium rights in Chiapas (which is part of the whole NAFTA agreement, the right for companies to own land and buy land in Chiapas); and then President Zedillo's website per usual.

On September 9, 1998, the morning of the performance, I received a phone call. I was getting a lot of journalists, so I thought it was a journalist. They said, "Is this Ricardo Dominguez?" I said, "Yes." "Of the Electronic Disturbance Theater?" I said, "Yes." Then in very clear Mexican Spanish, they said, "We know who you are. We know where you are at. Do not go downstairs. We know where your family is. Do not do this performance. This is not a game. You understand." And they hung up. I said, "Wow, what a way to wake up." But I'm an addict. I need my cup of coffee. I'm gonna go downstairs. And, of course, I went downstairs. I told the cops. I told the festival. More spams . . . And that's one of the things about information war which is to out-hype the hype, which is a very important strategy . . . Instead of being, "Oh my god, the police have called"; it's "Excellent! The police have called!" Let everybody know.

The performance was supposed to start at twelve o'clock in the afternoon, Linz time, Austria. As Stefan and I were about to load up the link to the action, a group of hackers gathered around us, called Heart – Corazon – a Dutch hacker group. And they said, "Ricardo, Stefan, if you guys do this, we'll shut you down. What you are doing is wrong, pure evil, unacceptable network abuse. We will take you down." And in a sense, it was my first contact with what I call the Digitally Correct Community that believes that bandwidth is above all things, above human rights. The only thing the citizen can do is stand on the side, put up their signs, but never step out onto the superhighway. That is *Verboten*. And this is certainly something that civil rights people do in the real world: step out onto the street, so we felt we were doing much of the same sort of thing, and we said, "Well, I wish we could have had this dialog earlier . . . But the performance is going to start." So we went "Click," and the performance started.

About three hours into the action, we noticed that these Java applets were appearing in the browser. About twenty-five of them, little coffee cups going, ach! ach! ach! ach! ach! The browser would crash. We start the action again and they go, ach! ach! ach! ach! ach!, almost like a little machine gun. The browser would crash. If you can imagine the FloodNet is a little wheel, a little hamster wheel, the more people come, the faster it goes. What these applets were doing were like little sticks. And more sticks crash the browser. So we started getting e-mail from around the world,

"Virtual Sit-In at the WTO," Electrohippies

Date sent: Mon, 22 Nov 1999
11:20:20 +0000
From: ehippies@tesco.net
To: hacktivism@tao.ca
Subject: 'Virtual sit-in' to coincide with WTO Conference
Send Reply To: hacktivism@tao.ca
[:hacktivism:]

####### URGENT #######

Please forward this to everyone you know!

'VIRTUAL SIT-IN' AT A LEADING WEBSITE PLANNED TO COINCIDE WITH THE WTO'S SEATTLE CONFERENCE

For details of how to take part visit the NEW 'electrohippies' website at: http://www.gn.apc.org/pmhp.ehippies/

TARGET WILL BE REVEALED AT 00.01 GMT, 30/11/99

A new website has started up to promote 'virtual activism' in the UK and Europe. The site is all about taking action, and undertaking civil disobedience, using the core of modern society – its electronic information and communications infrastructure. Why? Because technology enables a lot of the destruction that takes places in the world, but like most technology it is not innately bad – it's just the people who are in charge of it. Technology also allows people to have anonymity because their communications and planning are kept remote from the public arena.

activists saying, "I'm joining your action and you guys have broken my browser," all this sort of stuff and we're going down. Hackers! They said they'd take us down, they've taken us down.

So we're trying to inform people. Putting stuff on web pages. Finally we get an e-mail from Wired.com, that goes, "Gentleman, I suppose you've noticed that your action is not going very well. Do you know why? We do. It's the Pentagon." Holy shit. The Pentagon. We never thought of the Pentagon. We went in view source and indeed in the pages where we were doing the sit-in were imbedded hostile Java applets. So, suddenly, of course, the hype: They've broken the Posse Comitatus law of 1878. They're attacking a civilian server in New York City, The Thing. The next day we were in the *New York Times* again.

Electronic Disturbance Theater [has always valued] transparency. We were not digitally correct, that is, we didn't use hacker methods. We were not anonymous. We didn't encrypt any of our messages. We never hid what we were going to do, when we were going to do it, how we were going to do it. So again, this made the hackers very annoyed. Because the FloodNet system is not very high level code. It's not very efficient. It doesn't crash the server. We take millions of people. It disturbs it . . . And this doesn't make hackers happy.

The reason that we use disturbance is because it's not subversion, it's not destruction. It would be very easy then for the dot.mils, the dot.govs, the dot.coms to say this is cyber terrorism, this is cyber crime. Because the way they define those paradigms is through the hacker paradigm: It has to be anonymous. It has to be very efficient. It has to be at a high level. And it actually has to work. It's very difficult to explain to the hacker that: No, we don't want it to work. We always get e-mails from these high level systems saying, "hey, I really like what you are doing, if you could just do this to the code and that, it will slam everything down." And we go, "No, we like it the way it is." It's not efficient. It doesn't function the way it should. It just blocks bandwidth. It's like a lot of people getting onto the digital highway. It's not cutting the highway or breaking it into two.

And the reason that we are looking for disturbance is because we wanted to create electronic civil disobedience that followed a non-violent direct action gesture. It was direct action because it took a great many people to create the disturbance. I couldn't do a VR-Sit In by myself, you couldn't sit by yourself with a FloodNet system and do anything. It would take a lot of people to do any sort of disturbance. And this to us was very important. And this is why we called the gesture "swarming" because it takes a swarm to actually implement a disturbance.

Many groups started asking, "Could you guys do an action for this or for that?" But we only did actions for the Zapatistas. So the other thing that we wanted to do was create [the FloodNet] in a way that would be open source, so that the code would be available . . . [later] creating what we called a Disturbance Developers Kit. We uploaded the Disturbance Developers Kit at one minute after midnight in celebration of the sixth year of the Zapatista uprising. And twenty minutes after we uploaded it here at Fakeshop.com, here in Williamsburg, Queer Nation did an action, a virtual sit-in, against GODHATESFAGS.com in Canada. A week later, the International Animal Liberation network did two actions against pharmaceuticals in Switzerland that went quite well. And then soon after that anti-arms activists in the UK did actions against arms dealer websites in the UK.

Electronic Disturbance Theater hoped that by sending out the code, other cells, other groups would begin to emerge, not necessarily following all the rules that we had set up. And sure enough we began to see cells emerge, like the Electronic Hippies who started developing the major actions against the World Trade Organization. We started connecting with other net activist groups like RTMark who helped us really create the hype. The Federation of Random Action in

What we're out to do is change all that by extending the philosophy of activism and direct action into the 'virtual' world of electronic information exchange and communications. Of course, in the scale of things we can't hope to be more effective than an annoying mosquito. But we can let them know that they can't use technology as a veil to obscure the public's concern about the future of the plant.

IN SUPPORT OF THE GLOBAL ACTION TO MARK THE WORLD TRADE ORGANISATION'S SEATTLE CONFERENCE, WE WILL BE PROVIDING AN OPPORTUNITY FOR PEOPLE TO TAKE PART IN AN ON-LINE 'VIRTUAL SIT-IN'.

At midnight, Greenwich Mean Time, on the 30th November, the 'action page' will be loaded with information on how you can register your protest against the WTO's Seattle conference. The page will operate for seven days.

We hope that during this period you will access this page as often as possible and take part in the sit-in. There will be precise details posted on November 30th. There will also be files to download in order to set up mirror-sites on your own server in order to spread the capacity of the sit-in. If you would like to receive the files direct by email on November the 30th, along with all the information on how to run the site from where ever you are in the world, then send a request to ehippies@tesco.net.

We hope that you enjoy participating in this event.

Once again, the address of the site is: http:///www.gn.apc.org/pmhp/-ehippies/

END

from the electrohippies – ehippies@tesco.net
Visit the Electronic Activism and Civil Disobedience website:
http://www.gn.apc.org/pmhp/-ehippies/
[:hacktivism:]
[:for unsubscribe instructions or list info consult the FAQ:]
[:http://hacktivism.tao.ca/:]

From an ehippies e-communiqué, November 22, 1999, www.gn.apc.org/pmhp/ehippies

France started their own cell. They're the ones who did the Oxy Oil actions in solidarity with U'wa Indians in Columbia. And because we were in the UK and all these other places traveling around, we got a chance to talk to Reclaim the Streets and the Direct Action Network.

And you started seeing in 1999 the networks, not only coagulating, but spilling out into the streets. Again, electronic civil disobedience is only a tool. It's only one level. And if you can leverage the data bodies with the real bodies on the streets, you can have this kind of aggregated direct action like the WTO in Seattle, Washington. Certainly Critical Art Ensemble, during its early writings, in a very harsh rhetorical gesture said, "The streets are dead, because information has gone elsewhere." In a certain sense, what we wanted to do was to kind of slap activists around. And so they go, what do you mean the streets are dead? But certainly the Electronic Disturbance Theater never felt this way. We always felt that it was a hybrid. Sometimes we have gotten e-mail from people who are blind, from people who are stuck at home for various reasons, people who have to work and they have to support their kids or they are too far away, they are in South Korea. They couldn't be in Seattle but in their hearts they wanted to be there. Here was the gesture that they could add to those databodies. Say that you only get 500 people at an action. Electronically, perhaps you could add another 12,000 from around the world. So all of a sudden what is considered a small local action becomes a larger global action. And that means to me that you can leverage small actions into global actions. And I think that's an important element to all of this.

And by the year 2000, there was a gathering of hackers at DefCon in Las Vegas. They actually had sessions on electronic civil disobedience and hactivism. And no longer were they snide or ironic, they were quite serious. They were listening. Here we had presentations on Thoreau's "On Civil Disobedience" and looking at 1848 as a manual for hactivism. And again, the next week members of *2600* hit the streets in Philadelphia against the Republican National Convention and ended up being in jail. So here was a very good sign of crossover.

What occurred in 1999 was not only Seattle and all these kind of hybrid actions but something else: 1999 was the year of e-commerce. Well at the end of the year, in December, E-Toys.com [an on-line toy store] decided to aggressively attack the net art group E-Toy (without an s) .com that had been around since 1994 [demanding that the art group give up their domain name]. What occurred then was basically a swarming effect: you had Fakeshop.com, RTMark, Electronic Disturbance Theater, The Thing, many networks gathering in defense. And we decided to do several different tactics all at the same time. One was a psychological operation which I think is something very useful for activists, because psychological operations have always been used *against* activists. We started infiltrating the trading boards of E-Toys.com. And letting people know, "Do you know what these guys are doing? Isn't that bad? Do you really want to support this?" And we started working on this theory that we are going to destroy E-Toys.com. Their value was at seventy-two dollars per share and we would bring it down to zero by the end of December.

And then we decided to do a Twelve Days of Christmas virtual sit-in. And of course, by now we were tactical media gurus. We had mirrors everywhere. And we started the action. On the second day, E-Toys (officially) said "No, nothing's happening" – but they decided to shut down The Thing.net, using their money and power as they had done with everything else. They called Verio, our router. You have to remember that (even though it's a bad metaphor it can still be useful) the Internet is the Wild West. If you can imagine that you and your machine are you and your horse. And your ISP is your local town with your local sheriff. You know folks there. And you got your virus scanner on your side. Once you leave your local town, you're out in the cultural frontier. There's mail tribes, banditos, but more importantly, there's railroad barons. In this case, router barons, and the router barons control everything. So what happened was E-Toys called our router and said, I don't know, "These guys are bugging us, shut 'em down." So the next morning I woke up, there was no Rdom. There was no Thing. There was no EDT, there was no RTMark, there was no Toyswars.com – cause everybody was at The Thing.

So finally we got a hold of them and they said, "Take down Rdom" – which is my site – "and we'll let The Thing back up." Of course, we were smart, we had mirrors everywhere so the action wasn't stopped. New scripts were created based on the FloodNet script, very interesting scripts, like non-linear scripts that would shop at E-Toys and then drop the shopping before they went through the order and then restart again. And of course, what did we do? We hyped it up. We were on CNN that night. And you saw the share go down, down, down, down, down. So by January 15, E-Toys.com relented. They gave E-Toy back their domain name. They paid for all the court costs.

If you disturb the Pentagon, it doesn't really disturb the power; it doesn't really stop the tanks. If you shut down the police site, it doesn't really shut down the cops 'cause they are on the streets. But if you are a virtual company that only exists online, it's an extremely powerful tool. So, if you get more companies that only exist online, electronic civil disobedience will not only be just *a* leveraging tool but *the* tool.

It's still very elitist, 98 percent of the world is not online. In a certain sense the networks themselves are this hot attracter that you create media hype with, and that's its use now. But perhaps someday, as more people go online, then maybe these actions will create a tradition, create the codes so people won't have to reinvent what to do. We've learned from Gandhi certain gestures for the street that are now ingrained in us. What do we do? We march, we sit. But we can also create other protocols that will be understood just as simply, a certain notion of electronic civil disobedience.

. . .

One day El Subcommandante and The Ocean, also known as The Sea (he has been with the Zapatistas since the beginning); and Don Dorito, the most famous beetle bug in all of Chiapas and the world were walking into a small autonomous community. And they ran into a little boy who was going around going, "beep, beep, beep, *todas a la Zapatour,* beep, beep, beep." And he bangs into Subcommandante Marcos' boots. And El Sub looked down and said, "Hey Pedrito, what are you doing there?" And he says, "Well, I'm picking up all the men and women who are going to the *consulta* on March 21." And the Old Nose looks down and says, "Well Pedrito, that's not a truck. That's a stone." And so Pedrito looks up at the Old Nose and says, "You know, that's what's wrong with you Zapatistas, you have *no* imagination." And beep, beep, beep, beep, he takes off.

And Subcommandante Marcos turns to The Ocean and to Don Dorito, the beetle and says, "Yes, that is a problem. The Zapatistas have no imagination." And Don Dorito says, "Yes, I've always told you they've had no imagination." They continue marching into the community and the elders are gathered, choosing the man and the woman who are going to go to the *consulta* the 21st. And suddenly above them a huge commander type plane, blue and yellow, from the Mexican Army Rainbow Task Force starts roaring above them. Also from the other side, a Huey from the Mexican Air Force starts making its death-like whirl and the sound is just deafening. It doesn't disturb the community. The elders just raise their voices and continue the dialogue.

But Pedrito stops in the middle of the town and looks up, very annoyed, "*Ya basta*, enough is enough. I am going to move those planes." He goes into his home. Just the speed of how fast Pedrito moves astounds El Subcommandante. Zoom, he comes back out and in his hands: a stick. And he says, "You watch now." And he lifts the stick in the air and he starts going, "Zoom, Zoom, Zoom." Suddenly, the commander type plane makes a half turn and heads back to its base. The Huey slides away to the edge of the village. The sound disappears. Pedrito, very happy with the outcome, throws down his stick, picks up his rock, I mean his truck, and, "beep, beep, beep" off he goes.

Of course, El Subcommandante, being who he is, walks over, very carefully, and picks up the stick. He gives it a thorough scientific viewing, its length, its weight, its texture, finally he turns to The Ocean and says, "It's a stick." The Ocean looks at him and says, "Yes, a stick." Subcommandante puts it in his pocket and Don Dorito and The Ocean and he continue to march out of the village. As they're at the edge of the village, they run into Commandante Tacho, who's heading the other way and he says, "Hey, Old Nose, what have you got in your pocket there." Commandante pulls out the stick.

And The Ocean turns to Commandante Tacho and says, "Mayan technology." El Commandante notices that the Huey is above him and trying to remember what Pedrito did. He lifts the stick above his head. He goes, "Zoom, zoom, zoom, zoom, zoom." Suddenly, the helicopter turns into a useless tin vulture. The sky opens. The sun is bright. And the clouds become like marzipan. End of story.

So Mayan technology, what Pedrito's stick represents, is the simple gesture, almost invisible. There was this action the Zapatistas did on January 3, 2000, where suddenly you read in the newspapers "Zapatista Air Force Attacks the Army." Now nobody even knew the Zapatistas had an air force, much less knew how to fly. But if you read the story what the Zapatista women did is they took multi-colored paper, they folded it into airplanes with messages: paper airplanes. And as the sun came up they started throwing them over the barricades and of course the soldiers are shooting at these paper airplanes. And there you have a simple gesture which to me reflects this Mayan technology.

The FloodNet repeating that little simple gesture becomes Mayan technology; that one can create a gesture that is both magical, unique, poetic, but that can change and transform the very nature of power. It can, as we speak now, melt the armies of the PRI dictatorship. Just this morning, Salazar, the new governor of Chiapas, representing a multi-party in power, declared the Zapatistas not rebels but freedom fighters, declared them to be people of honor.[1]

Ricardo Dominguez interviewed by Ben Shepard and Stephen Duncombe at the L Café in Williamsburg, Brooklyn, December 9, 2000.

NOTES

INTRODUCTION

1 For a detailed description and analysis of this and other actions of Reclaim the Streets/New York City see Stephen Duncombe, "Stepping off the Sidewalk: Reclaim the Streets/New York City," in *From ACT UP to the WTO*, Ron Hayduk and Ben Shepard (eds.), London and New York: Verso, 2002.

2 It turns out that I wasn't the only one impressed by the power of culture. As I was in the process of completing this manuscript I was forwarded a US Federal Bureau of Investigation report on the "Threat of Terrorism to the United States," dated May 10, 2001, that identified Reclaim the Streets by name as a potential terrorist threat.

3 The phrase "haven in a heartless world" is Christopher Lasch's adaptation of Marx's reference to religion as "the heart of a heartless world."

4 Marshall McLuhan, *Understanding Media: The Extensions of Man*, New York: McGraw-Hill, 1965.

5 I've also been told that "We Are Family" was used as the theme song for the perennial underdog and all-black Pittsburgh Pirates at the 1979 World Series.

I CULTURAL RESISTANCE

Christopher Hill, "Levellers and True Levellers" from *The World Turned Upside Down*

1 G.H. Sabine (ed.), *The Works of Gerrard Winstanley*, Cornell: Cornell University Press, 1941, pp. 316–17.

2 W.G. Hoskins, 'Harvest Fluctuations and English Economic History, 1620–1759', *Agricultural History Review*, XVI, pp. 15–31; cf. David Underdown, *Pride's Purge*, Oxford: Oxford University Press, 1971, pp. 90–97, 281–2.

3 *Victoria County History*, York, p. 172.

4 D.M. Wolfe (ed.), *Leveller Manifestos of the Puritan Revolution*, London: T. Nelson and Sons, 1944, pp. 71, 278.

5 [Anon.] *Salus Populi Solus Rex*, quoted by D. Brailsford, *Sport and Society*, London: Routledge & Kegan Paul, 1969, pp. 345–6.

6 [Anon.] *The Humble Representation of the Desires of the Soldiers and Officers of the Regiment of Horse for the County of Northumberland.*

7 Peter Chamberlen, *The Poore Mans Advocate*, 1649, p. 2.

8 Underdown, p. 281; Wolfe, p. 371.

9 Sabine, pp. 627–40.

10 D.W. Petegorsky, *Left-Wing Democracy in the English Civil War*, London: Victor Gollancz, 1940, p. 160.

11 E. Hockliffe (ed.), *Diary of the Rev. Ralph Josselin, 1616–1683*, London: Camden Society, 1908, p. 70.

12 Walker, *History of Independency*, Part II, pp. 152–3.

13 Petegorsky, p. 172.

14 cf. C. Hill, *Society and Puritanism in Pre-Revolutionary England*, London: Secker & Warburg, 1964, p. 213.

15 *The Kingdomes Faithfull and Impartiall Scout*, 20–27 April 1649, quoted by Petegorsky, p. 164. Thorns and briars symbolized 'the wisdom and power of selfish flesh' (Sabine, p. 237) which Winstanley's *Fire in the Bush* would consume.

16 Firth (ed.), *Clarke Papers*, London: Camden Society, 1891 and 1894, III, p. 211.

17 M.S. Harley 164 f. 96v. I owe this reference to the kindness of Professor C.M. Williams.

18 W. Blith, *The English Improver Improved* (1652), sig. C3; cf. *Victoria County History*, Surrey, III, p. 467, and Sabine, p. 260.

19 E. Arber, *An Introductory Sketch to the Martin Marprelate Controversy*, 1895, pp. 81, 95; Patrick Collinson, *The Elizabethan Puritan Movement*, Berkeley: University of California Press, 1967, p. 492. When the press was driven from Kingston the printers withdrew to Fawsley in Northamptonshire, twenty-odd miles from Wellingborough.

20 Collinson, pp. 353, 389.

21 D. Masson, *Life of John Milton*, I, London: Macmillan and Co., 1875, p. 150.

22 *Calendar of State Papers Domestic, 1635*, p. xliv.

23 H. Cary, *Memorials of the Civil War*, I, p. 120; *Portland MSS* (Historical Manuscripts Commission) I, p. 480; S. Gardiner, *Great Civil War*, London: Longmans & Co., 1891, III, p. 350; Wolfe, p. 208; W.C. Abbot, *Writings and Speeches of Oliver Cromwell*, New Haven: Yale University Press, 1937–47, I, pp. 496,561.

24 *Portland MSS*, III, p. 201; C.H. Firth, *The House of Lords in the Civil War*, London: Longmans Green, 1910, p. 233.

25 R. Barclay, *Inner Life*, London: Hodder & Stoughton, 1846, p. 343; N. Penney (ed.), *The First Publishers of Truth*, Society of Friends' Historical Society, 1907, p. 167; J. Besse, *An Abstract of the Sufferings . . . of Quakers*, 1733, I, pp. 252–4.

26 Burrough, *Works*, 1672, p. 234.

27 Sabine, p. 315.

28 *A Modest Narrative*, 29 April 1649, quoted by Abbott, II, p. 58. The journalist who reported the incident wrongly thought the Diggers had already 'left their new plantation'.

29 W. Style, *Reports*, 1658, pp. 166, 360; Sabine, pp. 20–21, 360, 432.

30 Sabine, pp. 200, 304, 356; K.V. Thomas, 'Another Digger Broadside', *Religion and the Decline of Magic*, London: Weidenfeld & Nicolson, 1971, p. 58.

31 Sabine, pp. 408, 414; Hoskins, 'Harvest Fluctuations in English Economic History, 1620–1759', *The Midland Peasant*, London: Macmillan, 1957, p. 29.

32 R. Coster, *A Mite Cast into the Common Treasury* (1649) in Sabine, p. 657.

33 Sabine, pp. 307–8, 322–3; cf. p. 420.

34 Sabine, pp. 414, 507; cf. E.G., *Wast Lands Improvement* [n.d.,?1653], pp. 1–7.

35 Sabine, pp. 190, 194, 262.

36 Thomas, p. 58; Joan Thirsk (ed.), 'Seventeenth Century Agriculture and Economic Change', *Agrarian History of England and Wales, IV (1500–1640)*, Cambridge: Cambridge University Press, 1972, p. 166.

37 E. Kerridge, *The Agricultural Revolution*, London: George Allen & Unwin, 1967, chapters VII and VIII.

38 Sabine, pp. 428, 558.

39 Sabine, pp. 433, 272–4.

40 Sabine, pp. 363, 557–8, 560.

41 H.M. Lee (ed.), 'A Vindication of Regulated Enclosure', *Diaries and Letters of Philip Henry*, London: Kegan Paul, Trench & Co., 1882, pp. 27–8.

42 Sabine, pp. 390–91, 454, 471.

43 Sabine, pp. 251–2, 269.

44 Sabine, pp. 321, 519–20, 288.

45 Sabine, pp. 303, 390. For the Norman Yoke, cf. C. Hill, *Puritanism and Revolution*, London: Panther Books, 1968, pp. 50–122.

46 Sabine, pp. 357, 381–2; cf. pp. 484–6.

47 Sabine, pp. 573–4.

48 Sabine, p. 292; cf. p. 259.

49 Sabine, pp. 316, 519–20, 595–6; cf. pp. 191–2 and epigraph to this chapter.

50 E. Dell, 'Gerrard Winstanley and the Diggers', *The Modern Quarterly*, IV, pp. 138–9.

51 Sabine, pp. 282, 512.

52 Sabine, pp. 283, 471–2, 512, 380, 197.

53 Sabine, pp. 515, 527, 535–9, 562, 571–6.

54 Sabine, pp. 539–40, 552–3, 572–3.

55 Sabine, pp. 553–4, 591–9. Rape incurred the death penalty because it takes away the freedom of the body.

56 Sabine, pp. 193, 197–8, 432.

57 Sabine, pp. 515, 552.

58 Sabine, pp. 536–42, 556–7, 599.

59 Sabine, pp. 578–9, 526; cf. the attack on town oligarchies in *Light Shining in Buckinghamshire* (Sabine, p. 620).

60 Sabine, pp. 564, 571, 580, 595.

61 Sabine, pp. 541, 548–9; cf. pp. 190–91, 194–6, 261–2, 423.

62 Walwyn also favoured a polytechnic education, W. Haller and G. Davies (eds.) *The Leveller Tracts, 1647–1653*, New York: Columbia University Press, 1944, p. 336.

63 Sabine, pp. 576–80.

64 Sabine, pp. 570–71. The point was noted by that sensitive scholar, Margaret James, in *Social Problems and Policy during the Puritan Revolution*, London: G. Routledge & Sons, 1930, p. 305.

65 Sabine, p. 473.

66 Sabine, p. 333.

67 N. Cohn, *The Pursuit of the Millennium*, London: Secker & Warburg, 1957, p. 372.

68 Sabine, pp. 262, 253–4.

69 M.W. Perkins, *Works*, 1617–18, III, p. 392; H. Clapham, *Errour on the Right Hand*, 1608, p. 46.

70 Salmon, *Anti-Christ in Man*, 1647, p. 27.

71 [Coppe] *Some Sweet Sips of Some Spirituall Wine*, 1649, pp. 10–11 and *passim*; cf. Richard Coppin, p. 71.

72 W.E., *The Mad Mans Plea*, 1653, p. 1.

73 J. Canne, *Truth with Time*, 1656, sig. B3.

74 G.F. Nuttall, *James Nayler: A Fresh Approach*, Journal of the Friends' Historical Society, Supplement 26, pp. 14–15.

75 Sabine, p. 210; cf. Walwyn, in Haller and Davies, p. 298. Belief in a world before Adam was attributed to Elizabethan Familists by John Rogers, *The Displaying of the Family of Lover* 1578, and to Thomas Hariot, Ralegh's Protégé, Thomas Nashe, *Works*, R.B. McKerrow (ed.), I, p. 171.

76 Sabine, pp. 462, 116, 128–9, 204; cf. p. 536.

77 Sabine, p. 480.

78 Sabine, pp. 113–17, 173, 215; cf. *The Saints Paradice*, pp. 21, 82–3.

79 Sabine, pp. 229–31, 234–5; cf. pp. 463, 484.

80 Sabine, pp. 184, 260.

81 Sabine, pp. 262, 161–4, 264.

82 Sabine, pp. 203, 210–18; cf. pp. 446, 457; *The Saints Paradice*, pp. 90–97, 126–34.

83 Sabine, pp. 176, 120, 457–9; cf. p. 251.

84 Sabine, pp. 480–81, 176.

85 Sabine p. 269

86 Sabine, pp. 288–9; cf. pp. 253, 256, 323, 425, 490, 673–5.

87 Thomas, p. 61.

88 Sabine, pp. 149, 173, 176–9, 569; cf. pp. 189, 206, 228, 480. Winstanley does not emphasize the point that in The Bible Jacob blackmailed his elder brother into selling his birthright for a mess of pottage.

89 *Certain Queries Presented by Many Christian People*, 1649, in A.S.P. Woodhouse, *Puritanism and Liberty*, London: J.M. Dent, 1938, p. 244.

90 Coppe, *The Fiery Flying Roll*, Part I, pp. 1–5.

91 Fox, *The Lambs Officer* (1659), p. 19.

92 Bunyan, *Works*, II, p. 445; cf. A.L. Morton, *The World of the Ranters*, London: Lawrence & Wishart, 1970, p. 139, who perceptively links Coppe and Bunyan. For Jacob and Esau see also G. Smith, *Englands Pressures, or, The Peoples Complaint*, 1645, pp. 4–5; R. Coppin, *Divine Teachings*, Part II, 1653, p. 52; W. Sprigge, *A Modest Plea for an Equal Commonwealth*, 1659, p. 54; for Cain and Abel see Sir H. Vane, *The Retired Mans Meditations*, 1655, p. 173.

93 J. Thirsk, 'Younger Sons in the Seventeenth Century', *History*, LIV, pp. 358–77.

94 D. Veall, *The Popular Movement for Law Reform in England, 1640–1660*,

Oxford: Oxford University Press, 1970, pp. 217–19; Thirsk, 'Younger Sons', pp. 369–71; Covell, *A Declaration unto the Parliament*, 1659, p. 17; [Anon.] *A Door of Hope*, 1661.

95 R.T. Vann, 'Quakerism and the Social Structure in the Interregnum', *Past and Present*, 43, p. 91.

96 Bunyan, *Works*, I, pp. 22–4, 34–5; II. pp. 442–52; cf. J. Lindsay, *John Bunyan*, 1937, chap. 9, and A.L. Morton, 'The World of Jonathan Swift', *Marxism Today*, December 1967, p. 369 – Swift on the Irish peasantry selling itself.

97 Sabine, p. 530.

98 A.L. Morton found the doctrine of the Everlasting Gospel in the writings of Crisp, Saltmarsh, Collier, and Coppe (*The Matter of Britain*, London: Lawrence & Wishart, 1966, p. 103). We may add Henry Denne (Edwards, *Gangraena*, I, p. 23); John Warr (*Administrations Civil and Spiritual*, 1648, pp. 23, 42); Major-General Harrison (C.H. Simpkinson, *Thomas Harrison*, 1905, p. 132); William Dell (*Several Sermons*, pp. 26–7); Isaac Penington (*Works*, 3rd edition, 1784, III, pp. 494–500) and George Fox (*The Lambs Officer*, 1659, p. 13). Thomas Edwards identified the Everlasting Gospel with the doctrine of universal salvation (*Gangraena*, I, p. 22); cf. Blake, *The Everlasting Gospel*.

99 Sabine, pp. 100, 105, 122, 162–3, 169, 198, 453, 458. 'Light I take to be that pure spirit in man which we call Reason, which discusseth things right and reflecteth, which we call conscience', (*Light Shining in Buckinghamshire*, in Sabine, p. 611, echoing Winstanley's *Truth Lifting up its Head*). This approaches the idea that God will ultimately abdicate (see W. Empson, *Milton's God*, London: Chatto & Windus, 1961, pp. 130–46).

100 Sabine, pp. 385, 203; cf. pp. 248, 270, 334, 383.

101 Sabine, pp. 230, 297; cf. p. 457.

102 Sabine, pp. 385, 395, 472; cf. pp. 613, 631, 636–7. See my *Antichrist in Seventeenth-Century England*, Oxford: Oxford University Press, 1971, pp. 116–18.

103 Sabine, pp. 458–9, 452; cf. pp. 454, 468, 477–8.

104 Sabine, p. 165; cf. p. 251.

105 Sabine, pp. 455, 485–6.

106 Sabine, pp. 169–70, 227, 145. My italics.

107 Firth, *Clarke Papers*, II, p. 224.

2 THE POLITICS OF CULTURE

Karl Marx and Frederick Engels, from *The German Ideology*

1 The building of houses. With savages each family has as a matter of course its own cave or hut like the separate family tent of nomads. This separate domestic economy is made only the more necessary by the further development of private property. With the agricultural peoples a communal domestic economy is just as impossible as a communal cultivation of the soil. A great advance was the building of towns. In all previous periods, however, the abolition of individual economy, which is inseparable from the abolition of private property, was impossible for the simple reason that the material conditions governing it were not present. The setting-up of a communal domestic economy presupposes the development of machinery, of the use of natural forces and many other productive forces – e.g. of water-supplies, of gas-lighting, steam-heating, etc. the removal [of the antagonism] of town and country. Without these conditions a communal economy would not in itself form a new productive force; lacking any material basis and resting on a purely theoretical foundation, it would be a mere freak and would end in nothing more than a monastic economy – What was possible can be seen in the towns brought about by the condensation and erection of communal buildings for various definite purposes (prisons, barracks, etc.). That the abolition of individual economy is inseparable from the abolition of the family is self-evident.

Antonio Gramsci, from *The Prison Notebooks*

1 Perhaps it is useful to make a "practical" distinction between philosophy and common sense in order to indicate more clearly the passage from one moment to the other. In philosophy the features of individual elaboration of thought are the most salient: in common sense on the other hand it is the diffuse, unco-ordinated features of a generic form of thought common to a particular period and a particular popular environment. But every philosophy has a tendency to become the common sense of a fairly limited environment (that of all the intellectuals). It is a matter therefore of starting with a philosophy which already enjoys, or could enjoy, a certain diffusion, because it is connected to and implicit in practical life, and elaborating it so that it becomes a renewed common sense possessing the coherence and the sinew of individual

philosophies. But this can only happen if the demands of cultural contact with the "simple" are continually felt.

2 The heretical movements of the Middle Ages were a simultaneous reaction against the politicking of the Church and against the scholastic philosophy which expressed this. They were based on social conflicts determined by the birth of the Communes, and represented a split between masses and intellectuals within the Church. This split was "stitched over" by the birth of popular religious movements subsequently reabsorbed by the Church through the formation of the mendicant orders and a new religious unity.

3 Recall the anecdote, recounted by Steed in his Memoirs, about the Cardinal who explains to the pro-Catholic English Protestant that the miracles of San Gennaro [St. Januarius] are an article of faith for the ordinary people of Naples, but not for the intellectuals, and that even the Gospels contain "exaggerations", and who answers the question "But aren't we Christians?" with the words "We are the 'prelates', that is the 'politicians' of the Church of Rome".

4 "Steeds's memoirs." *Through Thirty Years*, London, 1924, by Henry Wickham Steed, a former editor of *The Times*.

Walter Benjamin, "The Author as Producer"

1 Address at the Institute for the Study of Fascism in Paris on April 27, 1934.

2 Benjamin himself, see *Schriften*, Frankfurt/M., 1955, vol. I, p. 384.

3 In place of this sentence there was in the manuscript originally a different one that was deleted: "Or, to speak with Trotsky: 'If the enlightened pacifists attempt to abolish war by means of rationalistic argument, they simply make fools of themselves, but if the armed masses begin to use the arguments of reason against war, that means the end of war.'"

3 A POLITICS THAT DOESN'T LOOK LIKE POLITICS

1 "POLITICS – The science and art of government; the science dealing with the form, organization and administration of a state or part of one, and with the regulation of its relation with other states." *Oxford English Dictionary*, 2nd edition, Oxford: Clarendon Press, 1987.

Mikhail Bakhtin, from *Rabelais and His World*

1 See an interesting analysis of comic doublets in E.M. Meletinskii, *Proiskhozhdenie geroicheskogo eposa* (*Origin of Heroic Epics*), Moscow: 1963, pp. 55–8. The book also contains a bibliography.

2 Fevrial, or Le Feurial, was the court fool of Francis I and of Louis XII. He appears repeatedly in Rabelais under the name of Triboulet. (Translator's note)

James C. Scott, from *Weapons of the Weak*

1 For an example of such temporary gains, see the fine study by E.J. Hobsbawm and George Rudé, *Captain Swing*, New York: Pantheon, 1968, pp. 281–99.

2 Some of these issues are examined in James C. Scott, "Revolution in the Revolution: Peasants and Commissars," *Theory and Society*, 7, nos. 1–2, 1979, pp. 97–134.

3 See the fine account and analysis by Michael Adas, "From Avoidance to Confrontation: Peasant Protest in Precolonial and Colonial Southeast Asia," *Comparative Studies in Society and History* 23, no. 2, April 1981, pp. 217–47.

4 R.C. Cobb, *The Police and the People: French Popular Protest, 1789–1820*, Oxford: Clarendon Press, 1970, pp. 96–7. For a gripping account of self-mutilation to avoid conscription, see Emile Zola, *The Earth*, trans. Douglas Parmee, Harmondsworth: Penguin, 1980.

5 See the excellent study by Armstead L. Robinson, "Bitter Fruits of Bondage: Slavery's Demise and the Collapse of the Confederacy, 1861–65," chapters 5, 6, New Haven: Yale University Press, forthcoming.

6 This issue centered on the much resented "Twenty-Nigger Law," as it was known, which provided that a white man of draft age could be excused from military service if he was needed to supervise twenty or more slaves. This law, coupled with the hiring of substitutes by wealthy families, encouraged the widespread belief that this was "a rich man's war, but a poor man's fight." Robinson, chap. 5.

7 The best, most complete account of this may be found in Lim Teck Ghee, *Peasants and Their Agricultural Economy in Colonial Malaya, 1874–1941*, Kuala Lumpur: Oxford University Press, 1977. See also the persuasive argument in Donald M. Nonini, Paul Diener, and Eugene E. Robkin, "Ecology and Evolution: Population, Primitive Accumulation, and the Malay Peasantry," typescript, 1979.

8 For a careful and fascinating account of the ways in which China's production teams and brigades could, until the changes in 1978, have some influence on the definition of "surplus" grain that had to be sold to the state, see Jean C. Oi, *State and Peasant in Contemporary China: The Politics of Grain Procurement*, PhD diss., University of Michigan, 1983. Nearly all of this resistance was called "soft opposition" by those who practiced it and who made it clear that it was successful only if an "outward manifestation" of compliance was maintained. Oi, p. 238.

9 There is an interesting parallel here with some of the feminist literature on peasant society. In many, but not all, peasant societies, men are likely to dominate every formal, overt exercise of power. Women, it is occasionally argued, can exercise considerable power to the extent that they do not openly challenge the formal myth of male dominance. "Real" gains are possible, in other words, so long as the larger symbolic order is not questioned. In much the same fashion one might contend that the peasantry often finds it both tactically convenient as well as necessary to leave the formal order intact while directing its attention to political ends that may never be accorded formal recognition. For a feminist argument along those lines, see Susan Carol Rogers, "Female Forms of Power and the Myths of Male Dominance," *American Ethnologist*, 2, no. 4, November 1975, pp. 727–56.

10 Edward B. Harper, "Social Consequences of an Unsuccessful Low Caste Movement," *Social Mobility in the Caste System in India: An Interdisciplinary Symposium*, James Silverberg (ed.), supplement no. 3, *Comparative Studies in Society and History*, The Hague: Mouton, 1968, pp. 48–9, emphasis added.

11 Ann Laura Stoler, *Capitalism and Confrontation in Sumatra's Plantation Belt, 1870–1979*, New Haven: Yale University Press, 1985, p. 184.

12 See, for example, *New York Times*, August 18, 1983, p. A6, "Polish Underground Backs Call for Slowdown," in which it is noted that "The tactic of a slowdown, known in Poland as an Italian Strike, has been used in the past by workers because it reduces the risk of reprisal."

13 Peter Linebaugh, "Karl Marx, the Theft of Wood, and Working-class Composition: A Contribution to the Current Debate," *Crime and Social Justice*, Fall–Winter, 1976, p. 10. See also the brilliant analysis of piecework by the Hungarian poet-worker Miklós Haraszti, *A Worker in a Worker's State*, Michael Wright (trans.), New York: Universe, 1978.

14 Linebaugh, p. 13. In 1842, for Baden, there was one such conviction for every four inhabitants. For three centuries poaching was perhaps the most common rural crime in England and the subject of much

repressive legislation. See, for example, the selections by Douglas Hay and E.P. Thompson in Douglas Hay, Peter Linebaugh, John G. Rule, E.P. Thompson, and Cal Winslow, *Albion's Fatal Tree: Crime and Society in Eighteenth-Century England*, New York: Pantheon, 1975.

15 Apparently, the theft of wood in Germany in this period rarely touched communal forest. It goes without saying that, when a poor man survives by taking from others in the same situation, we can no longer speak of resistance. One central question to ask about any subordinate class is the extent to which internal sanctions can prevent the dog-eat-dog competition among people that can only serve the interest of appropriating classes.

16 As Hobsbawm and Rudé point out, it is not only conservative elites who have overlooked this form of resistance, but also the urban left: "The historians of social movements seem to have reacted very much like the rest of the urban left – to which most of them have traditionally belonged – i.e. they have tended to be unaware of it unless and until it appeared in sufficiently dramatic form or on a sufficiently large scale for the city newspapers to take notice."

17 But not entirely. District-level records are likely to prove rewarding in this respect, as district officials attempt to explain the shortfall in, say, tax receipts or conscription figures to their superiors in the capital. One imagines also that the informal, oral record is abundant, for example at informal cabinet or ministerial meetings called to deal with policy failures caused by rural insubordination.

Robin D.G. Kelley, "Introduction" to *Race Rebels*

1 I also worked at the McDonald's on Foothill Boulevard in East Pasadena, where my experience was quite different. The "crew" there was predominantly white and very efficient. They took the job so seriously that I was suspended for two weeks for not asking a customer (who turned out to be a manager from another store pretending to be a customer) if he wanted an apple pie. I didn't stick around to get my job back: two days later I got a job at In and Out, a drive-in hamburger stand with chain stores spread throughout California.

2 "Taylorism" refers to the system of scientific management developed by Frederick Winslow Taylor a century ago. His aim was to limit all decision-making to managers and engineers, and restructure the labor process in order to reduce unnecessary movement, lower the skill needed to perform a task, and make production more efficient. For a

thorough discussion of the Taylorizing of McDonald's, see Robin Leidner, *Fast Food, Fast Talk: Service Work and the Routinization of Everyday Life*, Berkeley: University of California Press, 1993, especially pp. 51–3, 67–9, 79–83, 129–34.

Jean Baudrillard, "The Masses: The Implosion of the Social in the Media"

1 Hans Magnus Enzensberger, "Constituents of a Theory of the Media," *New Left Review*, 64, 1970, pp. 13–36.
2 Armand Mattelart, *De l'usage des média en temps de crise*, Paris, 1979.
3 Jean Baudrillard, *A l'ombre des majorités silencieuses*, Paris, 1978.
4 Roger Caillois, *Man, Play and Games*, Meyer Barash (trans.), London, 1962, chap. 8.
5 Georg Wilhelm Friedrich Hegel, *Phänomenologie des Geistes*, Johannes Hoffmeister (ed.), M.M. (trans.), Hamburg, 1952, pp. 391–2.
6 Hegel, p. 392.

4 SUBCULTURES AND PRIMITIVE REBELS

E.J. Hobsbawm, from *Primitive Rebels*

Editor's note: Professor Hobsbawm generously agreed to the reprint of this excerpt from *Primitive Rebels* but wanted it noted that the footnotes, written in 1959, are out of date. Interested readers should read the new and extended edition of *Bandits*, London: Weidenfeld & Nicolson, 2000, Professor Hobsbawm's elaboration of the history of social bandits sketched in this earlier chapter of *Primitive Rebels*.

1 For this area I have used not only the usual printed sources, but the invaluable information of Professor Ambrogio Donini, of Rome, who has had some contact with ex-bandits, and some newspaper material.
2 J.L.H. Keep, 'Bandits and the Law in Muscovy', *Slavonic Review*, 35, 84, December 1956, pp. 201–23.
3 Ivan Olbracht's novel *The Robber Nikola Šuhaj (Nikola Šuhaj Loupežniik)*, German edition, Berlin: Ruetten & Loening, 1953, is not only, I am told, a modern Czech classic, but far and away the most moving and historically sound picture of social banditry I have come across.
4 'Angiolillo, capo di banditti', in *La Rivoluzione Napoletana del 1799*, Bari, 1912.
5 Gavin Maxwell, *God Preserve Me from My Friends*, 1956.

6 P. Bourde, *En Corse*, Paris, 1887, p. 207.

7 *Paese Sera* 6.9.1955.

8 *La Voce di Calabria* 1–2.9.1955; R. Longnone in *Unità* 8.9.1955 observes that, even when the other functions of the local secret society have lapsed, the young men still 'rapiscono la donna que amano e che poi regolarmente sposano'.

9 Velio Spano, *Il banditismo sardo e i problemi della rinascita*, Rome, Biblioteca di 'Riforma Agraria', n.d., pp. 22–4.

10 'Il banditismo sardo e la rinascita dell'isola', *Rinascita*, X, December 1953, p. 12.

11 R. Longnone in *Unità* 8.9.1955: 'When, for instance, a man commits an offence of honour in some village, and takes to the hills, the local secret society feels the duty to help him to escape, to find a refuge and to sustain him and his family, even if he is not a member.'

12 G. Alongi, *La Maffia*, Turin, 1887, p. 109. In spite of its title this book is much more useful about brigandage than about *Mafia*.

13 Bourde, pp. 218–19.

14 G. Racioppi, *Storia dei Moti di Basilicata . . . nel 1860*, Bari, 1909, p. 304. An eyewitness account by a local liberal revolutionary and official.

15 J. Pitt-Rivers, *People of the Sierra*, 1954, pp. 181–3.

16 Quoted from Pani-Rossi, *La Basilicata*, 1868, in C. Lombroso, *Uomo Delinquente*, 1896, I, p. 612.

17 E. Rontini: *I Briganti Celebri*, Florence 1898, p. 529. A sort of superior chap-book.

18 See the constant complaints of the verbose Don Julián de Zugusti, governor of Cordoba province charged with the bandit suppression, in his *El Bandolerismo*, Madrid, 1876–80, ten volumes, e.g. Introduction, vol. I, pp. 77–8, 181 and esp. 86 ff.

19 Lucarelli, *Il Brigantaggio Politico del Mezzogiorno d'Italia, 1815–1818*, Bari, 1942, p. 73; Lucarelli, *Il Brigantantaggio Politico delle Puglie dopo il 1860*, Bari, 1946, pp. 102–3, 136–6; Racioppi, p. 299. *Blunt's Dictionary of Sects and Heresies*, London, 1874, Methodists, Bryanite.

20 Pitt-Rivers, p. 183; 'Count Maffei', *Brigand Life in Italy*, 2 vols, 1865, I, pp. 9–10.

21 The main source is: B. Becker, *Actenmaessige Geschichte der Raeuberbanden an den beyden Ufern des Rheines*, Cologne, 1804.

22 Lucarelli (who provides copious references) and Racioppi provide a good introduction to the problem. Walter Pendleton, 'Peasant Struggles in Italy', *Modern Quarterly*, NS VI, 3, 1951, summarizes this research. Cf. also *Encicl. Italiana*: 'Brigantaggio.'

23 'The Lord Emperor had heard that there was this man whom no power could subdue; so he ordered him to come to Vienna to make his peace with him. But this was a ruse. When Dovbush came near, he sent his whole army against him to kill him. He himself lay in his window to watch. But the bullets glanced off him and hit the riflemen and killed them. Then the Emperor ordered the fire to cease and made his peace with Dovbush. He gave him freedom to fight wherever he wished, only not against his soldiers. He gave him a letter and seal to prove this. And for three days and three nights Dovbush was the Emperor's guest at the Emperor's court.' Olbracht, p. 102.

24 'This is how it was: he was a weakly shepherd, poor, a cripple, and a fool. For as the preachers and the interpreters of scripture say, the Lord wished to prove by his example that all of us, everyone that is frightened, humble and poor, can do great deeds, if God will have it so.' Olbracht, p. 100. Note that the leaders of the legendary bands are rarely the biggest and toughest members of them.

25 See the special Calabrian issue *Il Ponte*, 1953.

26 See M. Ganci, 'Il movimento dei Fasci nella provincia di Palermo', in *Movimento Operaio*, NS VI, 6, November–December 1954.

27 Article: 'Brigantaggio', in *Encicl. Italiana*. Even the Spanish *bandoleros* were partly the victims of Free Trade. As one of their protectors says (Zugasti, Introduction I, 94): 'Look sire, here we have many poor lads who used to go on the highways to earn a peseta by smuggling; but now there's no more of that, and the poor men don't know where their next meal is to come from.'

28 'According to another version, truly strange and fantastic, it was not Roman who fell at Vallata, but another bandit, who looked like him; for the exalted imagination of the masses considered the Sergeant, as it were, invulnerable and "immortal" owing to the Papal benediction, and Gastaldi reports that he was supposed to have been seen for many years thereafter, roaming the countryside secretly and in solitude.' Lucarelli, p. 133 n.

29 Olbracht, p. 98.

30 There is a good description of the psychological effect of the burning of the business quarter in a Spanish city in Gamel Woolsey, *Death's Other Kingdom*, 1939.

31 'Ils ont ravagé les vergers, les cultures scientifiques, coupé les arbres fruitiers. Ce n'est pas seulement par haine irraisonnée contre tout ce qui a appartenu au seigneur, c'est aussi par calcul. Il fallait égaliser le domaine, l'aplanir . . . pour rendre le partage possible et équitable . . .

(Voilà) pourquoi ces hommes qui, s'ils ignorant la valeur d'un plantation d'arbres fruitiers ou d'une exploitation perfectionnée, brisent, brûlent et saccagent le tout indistinctement.' R. Labry, *Autour du Moujik*, Paris, 1923, p. 76, on the sacking of country houses in the Chernigov *gubernia* 1905. The source is the record of interrogations of peasants.

32 Racioppi, chap XXI for all this.

33 This emerges clearly from the study of the English Labourers' Rising of 1830, of which J.L. and B. Hammond, *The Village Labourer*, is still really the only account in print.

34 Labry, reprints 'The Agrarian Troubles in the Gubernia of Chernigov in 1905' from *Istoricheski Vyestnik*, July 1913, pp. 202–26. Nine peasants and six Cossacks were killed. Labry correctly notes that this area was on the borders of the zone in which the *mir* was powerful and resistant, and that in which its break-up, and the formation of the individualist holdings, was advancing fast (p. 72 ff.).

35 Cf. Bakunin: 'The bandit is always the hero, the defender, the avenger of the people, the irreconcilable enemy of every State, social or civil régime, the fighter in life and death against the civilization of State, aristocracy, bureaucracy and clergy.' The problem is more fully discussed in F. della Peruta, 'La banda del Matese e il fallimento della teoria anarchica dell moderna "Jacquerie" in Italia', *Movimento Operaio*, NS, 1954, pp. 337–85.

36 The most dispassionate account of this movement is in W.H. Chamberlin, *The Russian Revolution*, II, p. 232 ff., from which the quotation is taken. The standard Makhnovist account is P. Arshinov's. Makhno's own memoirs . . . do not appear to go beyond 1918. The 'bandit streak' is strongly denied by anarchist, and overemphasized by Bolshevik historians, but fits in well with the remarkably pure 'primitivism' of this interesting but sadly neglected movement. It is significant, by the way, that though Makhno's activities ranged over a wide area of the Southern Ukraine, he returned time and again to his home village of Gulai-Poyle to which, like any 'primitive' peasant bandleader, he remained anchored, Chamberlin, p. 237. He lived from 1884 to 1934, after 1921 in exile. He became a convert to anarchism in his early twenties.

Robin D.G. Kelley, "OGs in Postindustrial Los Angeles"

1 Charlie Ahearn, *Wild Style* (film), 1982.

2 David Toop, *Rap Attack 2*, London: Serpent's Tail, 1991, p. 40; the Morton lyrics are quoted from the "Rockbeat" column in the *Village*

Voice, 39, no. 4, January 25 1994, p. 76; on the baaadman narratives, see John W. Roberts, *From Trickster to Badman: The Black Folk Hero in Slavery and Freedom*, Philadelphia: University of Pennsylvania Press, 1989, pp. 171–215; and on signifying, see Henry Louis Gates, Jr, *The Signifying Monkey: A Theory of African-American Literary Criticism*, New York: Oxford University Press, 1988, especially pp. 64–88; Claudia Mitchell-Kernan, "Signifying, Loud-talking, and Marking," in *Rappin and Stylin' Out: Communication in Urban Black America*, Thomas Kochman (ed.), Urbana: University of Illinois Press, 1972; Bruce Jackson, *"Get Your Ass in the Water and Swim Like Me": Narrative Poetry from Black Oral Tradition*, Cambridge, Mass.: Harvard University Press, 1974; Lawrence W. Levine, *Black Culture and Black Consciousness: Afro-American Folk Thought from Slavery to Freedom*, New York: Oxford University Press, 1977, pp. 407–20.

3 Darryl James, "Ice-T the Ex-Gangster," *Rappin'*, January 1991, p. 37; Havelock Nelson and Michael A. Gonzales, *Bring the Noise: A Guide to Rap Music and Hip Hop Culture*, New York: Harmony Books, 1991, pp. 30–31. When this book went to press, Brian Cross's incredible book on the LA hip hop scene, *It's Not about a Salary . . . Rap, Race and Resistance in Los Angeles*, London: Verso, 1993, had just come out. Unfortunately, I did not have a chance to incorporate his insights or his interviews with LA rappers into this chapter, aside from a few small corrections. It doesn't matter, however, since the material essentially reinforces my interpretation. Nevertheless, I would suggest that all serious readers and hip hop fans check out Cross's book.

4 James, "Ice-T the Ex-Gangster," p. 37; "T for Two," *Details*, July 1991, pp. 51–5; Alan Light, "Rapper Ice-T Busts a Movie," *Rolling Stone*, May 16, 1991, p. 85; David Mills, "The Gangsta Rapper," *Source*, December 1990, p. 32; Cross, *It's Not About a Salary*, p. 24; Ice-T, *Rhyme Pays*, Sire Records, 1987.

5 Mills, "The Gangsta Rapper," p. 32; Frank Owen, "Hanging Tough," *Spin*, 6, no. I, April 1990, p. 34; Nelson and Gonzales, *Bring the Noise*, pp. 80–81, 165–7; NWA, *Straight Outta Compton*, Ruthless Records, 1988.

6 Sampling refers to the practice of incorporating portions of other records, or different sounds, into a hip hop recording. Digital samplers are usually used, which enable producers to isolate specific sounds and manipulate them (change the register, the tempo, etc.).

7 Summer Jeep Slammers, *Source*, July 1993, p. 76. There are some exceptions, the most obvious being Compton's Most Wanted which is more inclined toward jazz and quiet storm tracks (see especially, CMW

Straight Check N 'Em, Orpheus Records, 1991). Nevertheless, funk dominates West Coast gangsta rap, and the introduction of reggae and jazz, unlike the East Coast, has been slow in coming.

8 The larger hip hop community has maintained an ambivalent, and occasionally critical, stance toward most gangsta rappers. See, for instance, the criticisms of Kool Moe Dee, YZ, and others in "Droppin' Science," *Spin*, 5, no. 5, August 1989, pp. 49–50; The J, "If You Don't Know Your Culture, You Don't Know Nothin'!: YZ Claims He's 'Thinking of a Master Plan' for Black Awareness," *Rap Pages*, December 1991, p. 64; "Views on Gangsta-ism," *Source*, December 1990, pp. 36, 39, 40; as well as critical perspectives in the music itself, e.g., Del tha Funkee Homosapien, "Hoodz Come in Dozens" on *I Wish My Brother George Was Here*, Priority Records, 1991; Public Enemy, "No Nigga" on *Apocalypse '91*, Def Jam, 1991; Arrested Development, "People Everyday" and "Give a Man a Fish" on *3 Years, 5 Months and 2 Days in the Life Of . . .*, Chrysalis Records, 1992; The Disposable Heroes of Hiphoprisy, especially "Famous and Dandy (Like Amos 'n' Andy)" on *Hypocrisy Is the Greatest Luxury*, Island Records, 1992; The Coup, *Kill My Landlord*, Wild Pitch Records, 1993.

9 Ice-T, *OG: Original Gangster*, Sire Records, 1991; Ice Cube, *Kill at Will*, Priority Records, 1992; Ice Cube, *The Predator*, Priority Records, 1992; Ice-T, *Power*, Warner Bros, 1988; CPO, *To Hell and Black*, Capitol Records, 1990; NWA, *100 Miles and Runnin'*, Ruthless, 1990; Dr Dre, *The Chronic*, Interscope Records, 1992; CMW *Straight Check 'n' Em*, Orpheus Records, 1991. How Ice-T's lyrics from "I'm Your Pusher" were misinterpreted was discussed on the *MacNeil-Lehrer Newshour* on a special segment on rap music.

10 Ice-T (and the Rhyme Syndicate), "My Word Is Bond" on *The Iceberg/ Freedom of Speech . . . Just Watch What You Say*, Sire Records, 1989; Ice Cube, "J.D.'s Gafflin" on *AmeriKKKa's Most Wanted*, Priority Records, 1990. West Coast rappers also create humorous countercritiques of gangsterism; the most penetrating is perhaps Del tha Funkee Homosapien's hilarious, "Hoodz Come in Dozens" on *I Wish My Brother George Was Here*, Priority Records, 1991.

11 Cube quote, David Mills, "The Gangsta Rapper: Violent Hero or Negative Role Model?" *Source*, December 1990, p. 39; see also Dan Chamas, "A Gangsta's World View," *Source*, Summer 1990, pp. 21–2; "Niggers With Attitude," *Melody Maker*, 65, no. 44, November 4 1989, p. 33; and the Geto Boys' Bushwick Bill's explanation in J. Sultan, "The Geto Boys," *Source*, December 1990, p. 33.

12 Digital Underground's "Good Thing We're Rappin" on *Sons of the P*, Tommy Boy, 1991, is nothing if not a tribute to the pimp narratives. One hears elements of classic toasts, including "The Pimp," "Dogass Pimp," "Pimping Sam," "Wicked Nell," "The Lame and the Whore," and perhaps others. Even the meter is very much in the toasting tradition. (For transcriptions of these toasts, see Bruce Jackson, *"Get Your Ass in the Water and Swim Like Me,"* pp. 106–30.) Similar examples which resemble the more comical pimp narratives include Ice Cube, "I'm Only Out for One Thing" on *AmeriKKKa's Most Wanted*, Priority, 1990, and "Sex, Sex, and more Sex" on *Son of Bazerk*, MCA, 1991.

13 See John Leland, "Rap: Can It Survive Self-Importance?" *Details*, July 1991, p. 108; Owen, "Hanging Tough," 34; James Bernard, "NWA [Interview]," *Source*, December 1990, p. 34. In fact, Ice Cube left NWA in part because they were not "political" enough. Though most accounts indicate that financial disputes between Cube and manager Jerry Heller caused the split, in at least one interview he implied that politics had something to do with it as well. As early as *Straight Outta Compton*, Cube wanted to include more songs like "F— the Police," and when the FBI sent a warning to them because of their inflammatory lyrics, Cube planned to put out a 12-minute remix in response. Of course, neither happened. It finally became clear to Cube that he could not remain in NWA after Jerry Heller kept them from appearing on Jesse Jackson's weekly TV show. Darryl James, "Ice Cube Leaves NWA to Become AmeriKKKa's Most Wanted," *Rappin'*, January 1991, p. 20.

14 Davis, *City of Quartz*, pp. 304–7; Edward Soja, *Postmodern Geographies: The Reassertion of Space in Critical Social Theory*, London: Verso, 1989, pp. 197, 201.

15 NWA, *Efil4zaggin*, Priority Records, 1991.

16 The idea that unemployed black youth turn to crime because it is more rewarding than minimum-wage, service-oriented work has been explored by a number of social scientists. See, for example, Richard B. Freeman, "The Relation of Criminal Activity to Black Youth Employment," in Margaret C. Simms and Samuel L. Myers, Jr. (eds), *The Economics of Race and Crime*, New Brunswick, NJ: Transaction Books, 1988, pp. 99–107; Llad Phillips and Harold Votey, Jr., "Rational Choice Models of Crimes by Youth," in Simms and Myers, pp. 129–87; Llad Phillips, H.L. Votey, Jr., and D. Maxwell, "Crime, Youth, and the Labor Market," *Journal of Political Economy*, 80, 1972, pp. 491–504; Philip Moss and Chris Tilly, *Why Black Men Are Doing Worse in the Labor Market: A Review of Supply-Side and Demand-Side Explanations*, New York: Social

Science Research Council Committee for Research on the Under-
class, Working Paper, 1991, pp. 90–93. For a discussion of the role of
gangs in the illicit economy, see Martin Sanchez Jankowski, *Islands in
the Street: Gangs and American Urban Society*, Berkeley and Los Angeles:
University of California Press, 1991, pp. 119–31. Despite the general
perception that dealers make an enormous amount of money, at least
one study suggests that the average crack peddler only makes about
$700 per month. See Peter Reuter, Robert MacCoun, and Patrick
Murphy, *Money from Crime: A Study of the Economics of Drug Dealing in
Washington, DC*, Santa Monica, Calif: Rand, Drug Policy Research
Center, 1990; Davis, p. 322.

17 For discussions of the ways in which the mass media depict black youth
gangs, violence, and the crack economy in inner-city neighborhoods,
see Jankowski, *Islands in the Street*, pp. 284–302; Jimmie L. Reeves and
Richard Campbell, *Cracked Coverage: Television News, The Anti-cocaine
Crusade, and The Reagan Legacy*, Durham, NC: Duke University Press,
1994; Herman Gray, "Race Relations as News: Content Analysis," *Amer-
ican Behavioral Scientist*, 30, no. 4, March–April 1987, p. 381–96; Craig
Reinarman and Harry G. Levine, "The Crack Attack: Politics and
Media in America's Latest Drug Scare," in Joel Best (ed.), *Images of
Issues: Typifying Contemporary Social Problems*, New York: Aldine de
Gruyter, 1989, pp. 115–35; Clarence Lusane, *Pipe Dream Blues: Racism
and the War on Drugs*, Boston: South End Press, 1991.

18 "Niggers With Attitude," *Melody Maker*, 65, no. 44, November 4 1989,
p. 33.

19 James, "Icc-T the Ex-Gangster," p. 38. Of course, the last part of Ice-T's
pronouncements echoes a range of conspiracy theories that continue to
float among communities under siege, and even found a voice in
Furious Styles, a lead character in John Singleton's *Boyz 'n' the Hood*.
But T's assertion cannot be dismissed so easily, since there are more
liquor stores per capita and per square mile in low-income inner-city
neighborhoods than anywhere else in the United States. See George A.
Hacker, *Marketing Booze to Blacks*, Washington, DC: Center for Science
in the Public Interest, 1987; Manning Marable, *How Capitalism Underdeveloped Black America: Problems in Race, Political Economy, and Society*,
Boston: South End Press, 1983.

20 Ice-T, *OG: Original Gangster*, Sire Records, 1991.

21 Bill Moyer's interview with Bernice Johnson Reagon, PBS; Abrahams,
Deep Down in the Jungle, pp. 58–9; Mark Zanger, "The Intelligent Forty-
year-old's Guide to Rap," *Boston Review*, December 1991, p. 34.

Stuart Cosgrove, "The Zoot-suit and Style Warfare"

1 Cited in Stuart and Elizabeth Ewen, *Channels of Desire: Mass Images and the Shaping of American Consciousness*, Minneapolis: University of Minnesota Press, 1992, p. 87.

2 Descriptions of New York's Bowery B'hoys and G'hals of the 1840s taken from Abram C. Dayton's *Last Days of Knickerbocker Life* (1882) and George C. Foster's *New York by Gas-light* (1850) respectively, both cited in Christine Stansell's *City of Women*, New York: Knopf, 1986.

3 Ralph Ellison, *Invisible Man*, New York, 1947, p. 380.

4 Ellison, p. 381.

5 'Zoot-suit Originated in Georgia', *New York Times*, June 11, 1943, p. 21.

6 For the most extensive sociological study of the zoot-suit riots of 1943 see Ralph H. Turner and Samuel J Surace, 'Zoot-suiters and Mexicans: Symbols in Crowd Behavior', *American Journal of Sociology*, 62, 1956, pp. 14–20.

7 Octavio Paz, *The Labyrinth of Solitude*, London, 1967, pp. 5–6.

8 Paz, p. 8.

9 Paz, p. 8.

10 See K.L. Nelson (ed.), *The Impact of War on American Life*, New York: Holt, Rinehart and Winston, 1971.

11 O.E. Schoeffler and W. Gale *Esquire's Encyclopedia of Twentieth-Century Men's Fashion*, New York, 1973, p. 24.

12 Paz, p. 8.

13 'Zoot-suiters Again on the Prowl as Navy Holds Back Sailors', *Washington Post,* June 9, 1943, p. 1.

14 Quoted in S Menefee, *Assignment USA*, New York, 1943, p. 189.

15 'Zoot-girls Use Knife in Attack', *Los Angeles Times*, June 11, 1943, p. 1.

16 'Zoot-suit Warfare Spreads to Pupils of Detroit Area', *Washington Star*, June 11, 1943, p. 1.

17 Although the Detroit Race Riots of 1943 were not zoot-suit riots, nor evidently about 'youth' or 'delinquency', the social context in which they took place was obviously comparable. For a lengthy study of the Detroit riots see R. Shogun and T. Craig, *The Detroit Race Riot: A Study in Violence*, Philadelphia and New York, 1964.

18 Paz, p. 9.

19 Chester Himes 'Zoot Riots are Race Riots', *The Crisis*, July 1943; reprinted in Himes, *Black on Black: Baby Sister and Selected Writings*, London, 1975.

20 El Teatro Campesino presented the first Chicano play to achieve full

commercial Broadway production. The play, written by Luis Valdez and entitled *Zoot-suit* was a drama documentary on the Sleepy Lagoon murder and the events leading to the Los Angeles riots. (The Sleepy Lagoon murder of August 1942 resulted in 24 *pachucos* being indicted for conspiracy to murder.)

21 Quoted in Larry Neal 'Ellison's Zoot-suit' in J. Hersey (ed.), *Ralph Ellison: A Collection of Critical Essays*, New Jersey, 1974, p. 67.

22 From Larry Neal's poem *Malcolm X: an Autobiography* in L. Neal, *Hoodoo Hollerin' Bebop Ghosts*, Washington DC, 1974, p. 9.

Dick Hebdige, "The Meaning of Mod"

1 A reference to the language of Tom Wolfe. See, for examples of his work: *The Kandy-Kolored Tangerine Flake Streamline Baby* (1966), *The Electric Kool-Aid Acid Test* (1969), *The Pump House Gang* (1969), *Radical Chic and Mau-Mauing the Flak-Catchers* (1971).

2 The current fashion for camp rock derives much of its creative impetus from the extreme narcissism and self-conscious urbanity of this group. Bowie and Bolan were among its more conspicuous members.

3 G. Melly, *Revolt into Style*, Penguin, 1972.

4 For a full account of the role of the media, and other elements in the 'societal reaction', in the creation of the mod/rocker dichotomy see: S. Cohen, *Folk Devils and Moral Panics*, London: Paladin, 1973.

5 D. Laing, *The Sound of Our Time*, Sheed and Ward, 1969.

6 S. Cohen, *Folk Devils and Moral Panics*.

7 I use the term to cover 'blues', 'purple hearts', 'black bombers', dexedrine, benzedrine, ephedrine, and methedrine which were easily available to the mods in the mid-60s.

8 The 'hard mods' especially emulated the negro and this emulation became explicit in the style of their direct descendants – the skinheads.

9 With the conviction of the Krays in 1969 and the introduction of new and more restrictive gambling legislation in the same year, this style took a crippling blow.

10 This is not so far fetched as it may at first appear. The mid-60s gangsterism was a game, a serious, highly dangerous and profitable game, but a game nevertheless, the rules of which had been fixed in a mythical Hollywood–Chicago years before. The effectiveness of an extortion racket depends primarily on its flair for publicity; on a consistent projection of mean psychopath (Richard Widmark-type) roles; on its convincing presentation of a real yet ultimately unspecifiable

menace. It functions through the indulgence of all those who come into contact with it in a popular fantasy and adheres rigidly to the conventions of that fantasy. It is in a word, living cinema. Overstated and oversimplified, I know, but for a detailed elaboration of this point, see my *Stenciled Paper*, no. 25, CCCS, University of Birmingham.

11 P. Barker and A. Little, 'The Margate Offenders: A Survey', *New Society*, July 30, 1964; reprinted in *Youth in New Society*, T. Raison (ed.), Hart-Davis, 1966.

12 T. Wolfe, *The Pump House Gang*, Bantam, 1969.

13 For confirmation of the centrality of speed in the mod's life-style one need look no further than to the cultural significance assigned to the scooter, the first innovative means of transport introduced by a British youth sub-culture (the motor bike was borrowed from the States). The verb 'to go' was included in both *Ready Steady Go* and *Whole Scene Going*, the two mod programmes and testifies to the importance of movement.

14 The distinction between the two styles can be best illustrated by comparing the major symbolic exhibitions of the mod's solidarity – the bank holiday gathering, with its equivalent in hippie culture – the festival. At the coast the mods were impatiently reacting *against* the passivity of the crowd; each mod was a creative subject capable of entertaining an unimaginative adult audience arrogantly displaying the badge of his identity to a nation of featureless picture-watchers. The hippies' festivals, on the other hand, deliberately avoided contact with other cultures (when contact did occur, as at Altamont, it was often disastrous) and were conducted in remote locations in a complacent atmosphere of mutual self-congratulation, and centred round the passive consumption of music produced by an elite of untouchable superstars (cf. J. Eisen (ed.), *Altamont*, Avon, 1970, for a collection of essays describing how several thousand spectators failed to do anything about a few score outlaw bikers). If this comparison seems unfair we need only look to the mods' consumption of R and B and Tamla Motown in their clubs. The mods never consumed their music statically (the hippies generally sat and watched) but would use the music as a catalyst for their own creative efforts on the dance floor, even dancing alone if need be. Perhaps the distinction can be formulated in two equations:

working class + mod + speed = action

middle class + hippie + marijuana = passivity.

15 Quoted in C. Booker, *The Neophiliacs: A Study of the Revolution in the English in the Fifties and Sixties*, Collins, 1969.

16 N. Mailer, 'The White Negro', *Advertisements for Myself*, Panther, 1968.

John Clarke, "The Skinheads and the Magical Recovery of Community"

1 S. Daniel and P. McGuire (eds.) *The Paint House*, Penguin, 1972, p. 67.
2 Daniel and McGuire, p. 68.
3 Daniel and McGuire, pp. 21–2. Our emphasis.
4 Daniel and McGuire, pp. 21, 31.
5 For fuller accounts of the changes in football during the post-war period, which had some bearing on the skinhead choice of this particular locale, see, for example I. Taylor's 'Soccer Consciousness and Soccer Hooliganism', in S. Cohen's *Images of Deviance*, Penguin, 1971, and 'Football Mad – A Speculative Sociology of Soccer Hooliganism', in E. Dunning's *The Sociology of Sport* (Cass, 1971); and C. Critchter, 'Football since the War: A Study in Social Change and Popular Culture', CCCS, *Stenciled Paper,* no. 29, University of Birmingham, 1975.

5 DISMANTLING THE MASTER'S HOUSE

1 Albert Memmi, *Colonizer and the Colonized*, New York: Beacon Press, 1965/1991.

Mahatma Gandhi, from *Hind Swaraj*

1 *Editor's note:* Manchester, England was the center of the British textile industry.

Lawrence Levine, "Slave Songs and Slave Consciousness"

1 Alan P. Merriam, "Music and the Dance," in Robert Lystad (ed.), *The African World: A Survey of Social Research*, New York: Praeger, 1965, pp. 452–68; William Bascom, "Folklore and Literature," in Lystad, pp. 469–88; R.S. Rattray, *Ashanti*, Oxford: The Clarendon Press, 1923, chap. xv; Melville Hersksovitz, "Freudian Mechanism in Primitive Negro Psychology," in E.E. Evans-Pritchard *et al.* (eds.) *Essays presented to C.G. Seligman*, London: K. Paul, Trench, Trubner & Co. Ltd, 1934, pp. 75–84; Alan P. Merriam, "African Music," in Bascom and Herskovitz, *Continuity and Change in African Cultures*, Chicago: University of Chicago Press, 1959, pp. 49–86.
2 William Francis Allen, Charles Pickard Ware, and Lucy McKim

Garrison, compilers, *Slave Songs of the United States*, New York: A. Simpson & Co., 1867, New York: Oak Publications edition, 1965, pp. 164–5.

3 Allen *et al.*, p. 43.

4 Harriet Jacobs, *Incidents in the Life of a Slave Girl*, Boston, published for the author, 1861, p. 109.

5 Lines like these could be quoted endlessly. For the specific ones cited, see the songs in the following collections: Thomas Wentworth Higginson, *Army Life in a Black Regiment*, Beacon Press edition, 1962, originally published 1869, pp. 206, 216–17; Allen *et al.*, *Slave Songs of the United States*, pp. 33–4, 44, 106–8, 131, 160–61; Thomas P. Fenner (compiler), *Religious Folk Songs of the Negro as Sung on the Plantations*, Hamptons, Virginia, 1909, originally published 1874, pp. 10–11, 48; J.B.T. Marsh, *The Story of the Jubileee Singers; With Their Songs*, Boston, 1880, pp. 136, 167, 178.

6 James Miller McKim, "Negro Songs," *Dwight's Journal of Music*, xii, August 9, 1862, p. 148; H.G. Spaulding, "Under the Palmetto," *Continental Monthly*, IV, 1863, pp. 183–203, reprinted in Jackson, *The Negro and His Folklore in Nineteenth-Century Periodicals*, p. 72; Allen, "The Negro Dialect," pp. 744–55; Higginson, *Army Life in a Black Regiment*, pp. 220–21

7 *Journal of Nicholas Cresswell, 1774–1777*, New York: The Dial Press, 1934, pp. 17–19. Quoted in Epstein, *Music Library Association Notes*, xx, Spring 1963, p. 201.

8 Jacobs, p. 180.

9 *Life and Times of Frederic Douglass*, revised edition, 1892, Collier Books Edition, 1962, pp. 146–7.

10 John Lambert, *Travels through Canada and the United States of North America in the Years, 1806–1807 and 1808*, London, 1814, pp. ii, 253–4, quoted in Dena J. Epstein, "Slave Music in the United States before 1860: A Survey of Sources (Part 2)," *Music Library Association Notes*, xx, Summer 1963, p. 377.

11 Frances Anne Kemble, *Journal of a Residence on a Georgian Plantation in 1838–1839*, New York, 1863, p. 128.

12 For versions of these songs, see Dorothy Scarborough, *On the Trail of Negro Folk-Songs*, Cambridge: Harvard University Press, 1925, pp. 194, 201–3, 223–5, and Thomas W. Talley, *Negro Folk Rhymes*, New York: Macmillan, 1922, pp. 25–6. Talley claims that the majority of the songs in his large and valuable collection "were sung by Negro fathers and mothers in the dark days of American slavery to their children who

listened with eyes as large as saucers and drank them down with mouths wide open" but offers no clue as to why he feels that songs collected for the most part in the twentieth century were slave songs.

13 Constance Rourke, *The Roots of American Culture and Other Essays*, New York: Harcourt, Brace and Company, 1942, pp. 262–74. Newman White, on the contrary, has argued that although the earliest minstrel songs were Negro derived, they soon went their own way and that less than ten percent of them were genuinely Negro. Nevertheless, these white songs "got back to the plantation, largely spurious as they were and were undoubtedly among those which the plantation-owners encouraged the Negroes to sing. They persist to-day in isolated stanzas and lines, among the songs handed down by plantation Negroes . . ." White, *American Negro Folk-songs*, pp. 7–10 and Appendix IV. There are probably valid elements in both theses. A similarly complex relationship between genuine Negro folk creations and their more commercialized partly white influenced imitations was to take place in the blues of the twentieth century.

14 McKim, "Songs of the Port Royal Contrabands," p. 255.

15 Mircea Eliade, *The Sacred and the Profane*, New York: Harper & Row, 1961, chapters 2, 4, and *passim*. For the similarity of Eliade's concept to the world view of West Africa, see W.E. Abraham, *The Mind of Africa*, London: Weidenfeld & Nicolson, 1962, chap. 2, and R.S. Rattray, *Religion and Art in Ashanti*, Oxford: The Clarendon Press, 1927.

16 Paul Radin, "Statys, Phantasy, and the Christian Dogma," in Social Science Institute, Fisk University, *God Struck Me Dead: Religious Conversion Experiences and Autobiographies of Negro Ex-slaves*, Nashville, 1945, unpublished typescript.

17 Stanley Elkins, *Slavery*, Chicago, 1959, p. 136.

18 Allen *et al.*, pp. 33–4, 105; William E. Barton, *Old Plantation Hymns: A Collection of Hitherto Unpublished Melodies of the Slave and the Freedmen*, Boston: Lamson, Wolffe & Co., 1899, p. 136.

19 Allen *et al.*, p. 47.

20 Barton, p. 19.

21 Marsh, p. 132.

22 Fenner, p. 162; A. McIlhenny, *Befo' De War Spirituals: Words and Melodies*, Boston: The Christopher Publishing House, 1933, p. 39.

23 Barton, p. 15; Howard W. Odum and Guy B. Johnson, *The Negro and His Songs*, Hatboro, Penn.: Folklore Associates, 1964, originally published 1925, pp. 33–4; for a vivid description of the "shout" see *The Nation*, May 30, 1867, pp. 432–3; see also Lydia Parrish, *Slave Songs of the Georgia*

Sea Islands, Hatboro, Penn.: Folklore Associates, 1965, originally published 1942, chap. III.

24 For examples of songs of this nature, see Fenner, pp. 8, 63–5; Marsh, pp. 240–41; Higginson, p. 205; Allen *et al.*, pp. 91, 100; Natalie Burlin, *Negro Folk-Songs*, New York: G. Schirner, 1918, pp. i, 37–42.

25 Allen *et al.*, pp. 32–3.

26 Allen *et al.*, pp. 30–31; Burlin, II, pp. 8–9; Fenner, p. 12.

27 Allen *et al.*, pp. 128–9; Fenner, 127; Barton, p. 26.

28 Allen *et al.*, pp. 70, 102–3, 147; Barton, pp. 9, 17–18, 24; Marsh, pp. 133, 167; Odum and Johnson, p. 35.

29 Allen *et al.*, pp. 102–3.

30 Mary Ellen Grissom (compiler), *The Negro Sings a New Heaven*, Chapel Hill, 1930, p. 73.

31 Marsh, pp. 179, 186; Allen *et al.*, 40–41, 44, 146; Barton, p. 30.

32 McIlhenny, p. 31.

33 *Gumbo Ya-Ya: A Collection of Louisiana Folk Tales*, compiled by Lyle Saxon, Edward Dreyer, and Robert Tallant from materials gathered by workers of the WPA, Louisiana Writers Project, Boston, 1945, p. 242.

34 For examples, see Allen *et al.*, pp. 40–41, 82, 97, 106–8; Marsh, pp. 168, 203; Burlin, II, pp. 8–9; Howard Thurman, *Deep River*, New York: Harper, 1945, pp. 19–21.

35 Thurman, pp. 16–17.

36 Higginson, pp. 202–5. Many of those northerners who came to the South to "uplift" the freedman were deeply disturbed at the Old Testament in their religion. H.G. Spaulding complained that the ex-slaves need to be introduced to "the light and warmth of the Gospel," and reported that a Union army officer told him: "Those people had enough of the Old Testament thrown in their heads under slavery. Now, give them the glorious utterances and practical teachings of the Great Master." Spaulding, "Under the Palmetto," reprinted in Jackson, p. 66.

37 Allen *et al.*, p. 148; Fenner, p. 21; Marsh, pp. 134–5; McIlhenny, pp. 248–9.

38 *Life and Times of Frederick Douglass*, revised edtion, 1892, New York: Collier Books edition, pp. 159–60; Marsh, p. 188.

39 Parrish, p. 247.

40 Higginson, p. 217.

41 "Actually, not one spiritual in its primary form reflected interest in anything other than a full life here and now." Miles Mark Fisher, *Negro Slave Songs in the United States*, New York: Citadel Press, 1963, originally published 1953, p. 137.

42 Barton, p. 25; Allen *et al.*, p. 94; McKim, "Negro Songs", p. 149.

43 Higginson, pp. 201–2, 211–12.

44 Robert Redfield, *The Primitive World and Its Transformations*, Ithaca: Cornell University Press, 1953, pp. 51–3.

45 Elkins, chap. III.

46 Elkins, chap II; Frank Tannenbaum, *Slave and Citizen*, New York: A.A. Knopf, 1946.

47 E.J. Hobsbawm, *Primitive Rebels*, New York, 1959, chap. 1.

48 C.M. Bowra, *Primitive Song*, London, 1962, pp. 285–6.

George Lipsitz, "Immigration and Assimilation: Rai, Reggae, and Bhangramuffin"

1 Sabita Benerji, "Ghazals to Bhangra in Great Britain," *Popular Music*, vol. 7, no. 2, May 1988, pp. 208, 213.

2 Philip Sweeney, *The Virgin Directory of World Music*, New York: Henry Holt, 1991, p. 17.

3 Azouz Begag, "The 'Beurs,' Children of North-African Immigrants in France: The Issue of Integration," *Journal of Ethnic Studies*, vol. 18, no. 1, pp. 2–4.

4 Sweeney, p. 9.

5 Miriam Rosen, "On Rai," *Artforum*, vol. 29, no. 1, September 1990, p. 22; David McMurray and Ted Swedenburg, "Rai Tide Rising," *Middle East Report*, March–April 1991, p. 39.

6 Rosen, p. 22; Sweeney, p. 9.

7 Banning Eyre, "A King in Exile: The Royal Rai of Cheb Khaled," *Option*, vol. 39, July–August 1991, p. 45.

8 Rosen, p. 23.

9 Sweeney, p. 12.

10 Rosen, p. 23.

11 Eyre, p. 45.

12 Rosen, p. 23; Sweeney, p. 10.

13 McMurray and Swedenburg, p. 42.

14 Sweeney, p. 10.

15 McMurray and Swedenburg, p. 42; Rosen, p. 23.

16 Begag, p. 9.

17 Anthony Marks, "Young, Gifted and Black: Afro-American and Afro-Caribbean Music in Britain 1963–88," in Paul Oliver (ed.), *Black Music in Britain: Essays on the Afro-Asian Contribution to Popular Music*, Milton Keynes and Philadelphia: Open University Press, 1990, p. 106.

18 Winston James, "Migration, Racism, and Identity: The Caribbean Experience in Britain," *New Left Review*, no. 193, May–June 1992, p. 32.

19 James, p. 28.

20 Abner Cohen, *Masquerade Politics*, Berkeley: University of California Press, 1993, p. 36.

21 Robert Hilburn, "Tracing the Caribbean Roots of the New British Pop Invasion," *Los Angeles Times*, September 24, 1989, Calendar section, p. 6.

22 James, p. 45.

23 James, pp. 34, 46.

24 Sabita Banerji and Gerd Bauman, "Bhangra 1984–8: Fusion and Professionalization in a Genre of South Asian Dance Music," in Oliver, pp. 137–8.

25 Banerji and Bauman, p. 138.

26 Banerji and Bauman, p. 146.

27 Banerji and Bauman, p. 142.

28 Thom Duffy, "Apache Indian's Asian-Indian Pop Scores UK Hit," *Billboard*, February 20, 1993, p. 82.

29 Brooke Wentz, "Apache Indian," *Vibe*, November 1993, p. 9.

30 Paul Bradshaw, "Handsworth Revolutionary," *Straight No Chaser*, no. 23, Autumn 1993, pp. 13, 26.

31 Bradshaw, p. 29.

32 Wentz, p. 86; "Apache Indian" on *No Reservations*, Mango/Island Records, 1992.

6 A WOMAN'S PLACE

Virginia Woolf, from *A Room of One's Own*

1 Cecil Grey, *A Survey of Contemporary Music*, London: Humphrey Milford, 1924, p. 246.

2 See *Cassandra*, by Florence Nightingale, printed in *The Cause*, by R. Strachey.

Radicalesbians, from *The Woman-Identified Woman*

1 Simone de Beauvoir, *The Second Sex*, H.M Parshley (ed. and trans.), New York: Vintage Books, 1952/1974, see especially her introduction.

Janice A. Radway, from *Reading the Romance*

1 See, especially, Tania Modeleski, "The Disappearing Act: A Study of Harlequin Romances," *Signs* 5, Spring 1980, pp. 444–8.
2 The italics have been added here to indicate where special emphasis was conveyed through intonation. In each case, the emphasis was meant to underscore the distance between the heroine's behavior and that usually expected of women.

John Fiske, "Shopping for Pleasure"

1 M. Schudson, *Advertising: The Uneasy Persuasion*, New York: Basic Books, 1984.
2 J. Sinclair, *Images Incorporated: Advertising as Industry and Ideology*, London: Croom Helm, 1987.
3 R. Bowlby, "Modes of Modern Shopping: Mallarmé at the Bon Marché," in N. Armstrong and L. Tennenhouse (eds.), *The Ideology of Conduct: Essays in Literature and the History of Sexuality*, New York: Methuen, 1987, pp. 185–205.
4 Bowlby, p. 189.
5 L. Ferrier, *Postmodern Tactics: The Uses of Space in Shopping Towns*, paper presented at "Moving the Boundaries" Symposium, Perth, W. Australia, November 1987.
6 Ferrier, p. 1.
7 Ferrier, p. 2.
8 R. Bowlby, *Just Looking: Consumer Culture in Dreiser, Gissing and Zola*, London: Methuen, 1985, p. 22.
9 M. de Certeau, *The Practice of Everyday Life*, Berkeley: University of California Press, 1984.

7 COMMODITIES, CO-OPTATION, AND CULTURE JAMMING

Introduction

1 Karl Marx, *Capital*, vol. 1, New York: Penguin, 1976, p. 164.

Malcolm Cowley, from *Exile's Return*

1 George Ivanovich Gurdjieff, a Russian living in France, had worked out a system of practical mysticism based largely on yoga. His chief disciple

was A.E. Orage, the editor of the *New English Weekly.* In the spring of 1924, when Orage was in New York, he gained a great many converts, chiefly among the older members of the Greenwich Village set.

Thomas Frank, "Why Johnny Can't Dissent"

1 Edward Bernays, *Biography of an Idea*, New York: Simon and Schuster, 1965, pp. 37–94.

8 MIXING POP AND POLITICS

Barbara Epstein, "The Politics of Prefigurative Community"

1 Books by Margot Adler and by Starhawk, both political activists and witches, gave prominence to anarchist/feminist Paganism and helped to spur the growth of the movement they described. Margot Adler included an attractive account of political Paganism in her study of American witchcraft, *Drawing Down the Moon: Witches, Druids, Goddess-Worshippers, and Other Pagans in America Today*, Boston: Beacon, 1979. Starhawk outlined the theory and practice of political Paganism in *The Spiral Dance: A Rebirth of the Ancient Religion of the Great Goddess*, New York: Harper and Row, 1979, and in *Dreaming the Dark: Magic, Sex, and Politics*, Boston: Beacon, 1982. Women (and some men) who were attracted to Paganism by the accounts they found in these books swelled the numbers of politically-oriented Pagans, helping to shift what had been a largely apolitical movement toward feminism and toward the Left.

2 The consensus process has been strongly criticized from within the movement. See Howard Ryan "Blocking Progress: Consensus Decision-Making in the Anti-Nuclear Movement," in *The Overthrow Cluster: Livermore Action Group*, Berkeley: Overthrow Cluster, Livermore Action Group, 1985. Ryan is an Abalone and LAG activist.

3 Noel Sturgeon, in an unpublished essay on the direct action movement, argues that anarchism has deep roots in American history, pointing to the parallels between the anarchist and the Puritan understandings of the relationship between the individual and society.

4 Margot Adler told this story at a meeting of women who have written about feminist spirituality, held at the Stonehaven Ranch in San Marcos, Texas, in March 1985.

John Jordan, from "The Art of Necessity:
The Subversive Imagination of Anti-road Protest and
Reclaim the Streets"

1 There is not space in this chapter to elaborate on the history and theory of the agitational avant-garde. One could trace a history of subversive imaginations back from DIY culture, through the Situationists, Surrealists and Dadaists. For a brief and somewhat partisan overview see Stewart Home, *The Assault on Culture: Utopian Currents from Lettrisme to Class War*, London: Aporia Press/Unpopular Books, 1988. For a view of art activism (as opposed to activist art) produced by the contemporary avant garde, see Nina Felshin (ed.), *But Is It Art? The Spirit of Art as Activism*, Seattle: Bay Press, 1995.

2 I have just stumbled upon an article in *The Times*, August 12, 1997, which presents an ironic twist to the issues in this essay. Art and life became confused when a 'mock protest' stunt to advertise an anti-road play at the Edinburgh Festival turned into a 'real protest' when 200 Edinburgh Reclaim the Streets activists turned up and blocked the road for several hours. The photo caption reads 'Anti-road campaigners who took the mock protest a little too seriously yesterday. Several were arrested.'

3 Christopher Manes, *Green Rage: Radical Environmentalism and the Unmaking of Civilization*, Boston: Little Brown, 1990.

4 When art remains a tool of representation, art *about* political issues, it fails. Applying art and creativity to real political situations is what I am talking about in this essay. German artist Joseph Beuys used the term 'social sculpture' to describe the process of creatively moulding society rather than conventional artists' materials, such as clay, wood or paint. An interesting encroachment of representative art into the DIY protest movement was the Art Bypass event, where 'art objects' created by professional artists were placed beside the route of the much contested Newbury bypass in Berkshire, southern England. Art Bypass succeeded as a publicity stunt for the media and middle England's liberal intelligentsia. It was also unique in that it was curated by an artist working for Friends of the Earth as part of its campaign strategy. But it failed as socially engaged art practice. The tree houses and numerous direct actions against the bypass were where true art and radical creativity lay.

5 Guy Debord, *The Society of the Spectacle*, 1967, p. 115, quoted in Sadie Plant, *The Most Radical Gesture: The Situationist International in a Postmodern Age*, London: Routledge, 1992, p. 16.

6 Jean Dubuffet, quoted in Andrea Juno and V. Vale (eds), *Pranks*, San Francisco: RE/Search 1987, p. 4.

7 The first wave of activists on the M11 had come from Twyford Down, where UK DIY protest was born in 1992.

8 The M11 saw several sites of resistance. First, there was the Chestnut Tree on George Green, Wanstead (evicted December 1993), which was to be the inspirational spark that ignited the whole direct action campaign against the M11 Link Road. This was followed by the first houses to be squatted and turned into the 'Independent Free Area of Wanstonia' (evicted February 1994), and a whole series of evictions in the spring and summer of 1994, including Leytonstonia, an area of woodland, 'Euphoria', and then the final house left on the route (July 1995). Claremont Road was by far the largest and the most significant site for the final months of the campaign.

9 Dolly became ill after the first attack of the DoT on Claremont Road (August 2, 1994) and was moved to a nearby residential home. Mrs Leighton (aged 78) was less lucky – the state provided 11 bailiffs, 40 security guards and 160 policemen to move her from her house around the corner from Claremont Road, and she died a few months later – homesick and heart-broken.

10 *Détournement*: a French term which literally means a diversion or a rerouting. It was developed as a Situationist concept and is defined by Greil Marcus, in *Lipstick Traces*, as 'theft of the aesthetic artifacts from their contexts and their diversion into contexts of one's own devise', *Lipstick Traces: A Secret History of the Twentieth Century*, London: Secker & Warburg, 1989, p. 168.

11 Claremont Road was a prime example of what Hakim Bey terms a Temporary Autonomous Zone. For more on this concept see Bey, *TAZ: The Temporary Autonomous Zone, Ontological Anarchy, Poetic Terrorism*, Brooklyn, NY: Autonomedia, 1991.

12 Tyres proved to be both practically and symbolically a perfect barricading material. They fill space efficiently and are easy to move by hand, but difficult for the bulldozer buckets to shift because they bounce! At the end of the eviction the Department of Transport was left with the burden of disposing of some of the unsustainable waste product of its own car culture.

13 The conflict between art and political action was repeated here when some campaigners decided to close the art house down and turn it into a barricade for defensive reasons. The 'artists' argued that it should be left as it was so that when the bailiffs arrived they were confronted with

the prospect of destroying something beautiful. Perhaps a naïve belief: why should they see art as more beautiful and valuable than a 300-year-old yew tree, that they cut down without blinking a few months before?

14 The tower was inspired by a French children's book, *The House that Beebo Built*, London: Paul Hamlyn, 1969, which tells the story of Beebo and his friend whose fantasy self-built house is to be demolished by developers. It ends with him escaping from bailiffs up an enormous wooden tower on the top of his house.

15 This was a direct act of defiance, as the Criminal Justice Act had been passed weeks before, and it had made a point of singling out rave music.

16 Many activists left London and went on to become key participants at other road protest camps that were starting up, including Pollok Free State in Glasgow, Fairmile in Devon, and Newbury in Berkshire.

17 'Reclaim the Streets was originally formed in London in autumn 1991, around the dawn of the anti-roads movement . . . Their work was small-scale but effective and even back then it had elements of the cheeky, surprise tactics which have moulded RTS's more recent activities . . . However the onset of the No M11 Link Road Campaign presented the group with a specific local focus, and RTS was absorbed temporarily into the No M11 campaign in East London', Del Bailie, 'Reclaim the Streets', *Do or Die*, no. 6, 1997, p. 1. This issue has several articles about Reclaim the Streets, as has no. 5, all written by activists.

18 Del Bailie, RTS *Agitprop*, no. 1, July 1996.

19 Del Bailie, *Agitprop*. Reclaim the Streets agit-props present a multi-faceted collage of texts that attempt to describe the group. Some of the texts are written by individual activists, others are stolen or paraphrased from outside sources. The DIY direct action movement defines itself more by deed and strategy than by theory – not what are we *about* but what do we *do*.

20 These alliances were conscious strategies of Reclaim the Streets, intended to highlight the common social forces against which radical ecologists and social justice campaigners are fighting. 'We're saying that the power that attacks those who work, through union legislation and casualization, is the same power that is attacking the planet with over-production and consumption of resources; the power that produces cars by 4 million a year is the same power that decides to attack workers through the disempowerment of the unions, reducing work to slavery' Ian Fillingham, 'Why Reclaim the Streets and the Liverpool Dockers?', *Do or Die*, no. 6, 1997, p. 9.

21 Del Bailie, *Agitprop*.

22 Jean-Jaques Lebel, 'Notes on political street theatre 1968–69', *Drunken Boat*, no. 1, 1994.

23 Phil McLeish, activist on M11 and RTS, *Agitprop*, no. 1, July 1996.

24 Quoted in Del Bailie, 'Reclaim the Streets', p. 5.

25 Paraphrased from Del Bailie, *Agitprop*, no. 1, July 1996.

26 Lautréamont (Isidore Ducasse), *Poésies*, London and New York: Allison & Busby, 1980, p. 75.

27 Reclaim the Streets does not just put on street parties. Two road blockades using tripods have taken place, at Greenwich and Streatham in South London – and various small-scale actions, including hanging an enormous 'MURDERERS' banner outside the Shell AGM, locking on to the entrance of the Nigerian High Commission, numerous acts of subvertising (creatively changing car billboards) and a procession and banner hang during the Earls Court Motor Show. For the sake of this essay I am concentrating on the street party form.

28 Wooden tripods had been used before by antilogging campaigners in Australia. Reclaim the Streets were the first to substitute metal scaffolding poles. The idea of a tripod is that it can block a road and the police cannot pull it down without risking serious injury to whomever is suspended from the top of the tripod 20 feet above ground. See Road Alert!, *Road Raging: Top Tips for Wrecking Roadbuilding*, 1997 (available from Road Alert! PO Box 5544, Newbury, Berkshire, RG14 5FB, UK for £3) for details of making and erecting tripods.

29 A reference to the Paris '68 graffito 'Beneath the cobblestones – the beach.'

30 Exactly a year after the Reclaim the Street party, Islington Council held an *official* street party in Upper Street as part of the Islington festival. Recuperation or inspiration?

31 Richard Schechner, *The Future of Ritual: Writings on Culture and Performance*, London: Routledge, 1993, p. 84.

32 Author's conversation with Del Bailie, July 1997.

33 An ecological *détournement* of 'Beneath the cobblestones – the beach' – 'Beneath the tarmac – the forest'.

34 Schechner, p. 83.

Andrew Boyd, "Truth Is a Virus: Meme Warfare and the Billionaires for Bush (or Gore)"

1 Douglas Rushkoff, *Media Virus! Hidden Agendas in Popular Culture*, New York: Ballantine Books, 1994, pp. 9–10.

2 Rushkoff, pp. 11–12.

3 Is anything really new here? The terms meme and media virus might be new, but the phenomena they describe – fads and social movement explosions – have been with us for a long time. Originally coined by evolutionary biologist Richard Dawkins, in his late-1980s book *The Selfish Gene*, memes have become a hot concept among cognitive scientists, media theorists, digital hipsters, and cultural activists. *Wired* magazine has a regular "meme watch" section, which tracks the spread of new concepts and trends. In the best-selling *Consciousness Explained*, philosopher Daniel Dennett goes so far as to argue that human consciousness is itself a huge complex of memes. Even the concept of a meme is a meme – and you, oh reader, have been infected. Given the hype and indiscriminate use, I sometimes wonder if memes are just fancy new metaphorical dressing for age-old happenings. Then again, what is good social theory if not a robust and serviceable metaphor? Richard Dawkins, *The Selfish Gene*, Oxford: Oxford University Press, 1990; Daniel Dennett, *Consciousness Explained*, Boston: Little, Brown and Company, 1991.

4 Kevin Kelly, *Out of Control: The Rise of Neo-biological Civilization*, New York: Addison-Wesley, 1995.

5 Mark Dery, *Culture Jamming: Hacking, Slashing and Sniping in the Empire of Signs*, Westfield, NJ: Open Magazine Pamphlet Series, 1993; Guerrilla Media, Vancouver, BC, www.guerrillamedia.org

6 Garreth Branwyn, *Jamming the Media: A Citizen's Guide to Reclaiming the Tools of Communication*, San Francisco: Chronicle Books, 1997.

Ricardo Dominguez, "Electronic Disturbance: An Interview"

1 In his inaugural address on December 8, 2000, Pablo Salazar Mendiguchia, the newly elected opposition Governor of the southern Mexican State of Chiapas, recognized the grievances of the Zapatistas as legitimate and called for an end to the government-waged war against them. Ginger Thompson, "New Governor of Chiapas Promises, 'No More Bloodshed'," *New York Times*, December 9, 2000, p. 4.

CONTRIBUTORS

Theodor W. Adorno (1903–69) Probably the best known scholar of the Frankfurt School, Adorno wasn't always recognized for his brilliance; his first thesis on aesthetic theory was rejected. His second thesis, *Kierkegaard: The Construction of the Aesthetic*, was accepted in 1933 and published on the day of Hitler's rise to power. Adorno later left Germany to escape the Nazis, eventually settling in Los Angeles (which, predictably, he despised). Nevertheless he wrote several of his most important works in America, including *The Dialectic of Enlightenment*, published with Max Horkheimer in 1947. After the war, Adorno returned to the Frankfurt Institute to become its director. Adorno was also an amateur composer of atonal music.

Matthew Arnold (1822–88) Arnold penned essays on topics ranging from the translation of Homer, to investigations of education in France and democracy in the United States, to, of course, culture and politics in the United Kingdom. He was equally well known for his poetry, publishing his famous "Dover Beach" in 1869. Arnold was elected Professor of Poetry at Oxford University and was appointed national Inspector of Schools for England.

Mikhail Bakhtin (1895–1975) Relatively unknown in both the West as well as his mother Russia for much of his life, Bakhtin is now recognized as one of the greatest Soviet literary critics. His work *Rabelais and His World* was written in the 1930s but, because of official hostility (Bakhtin was once arrested for "unreliability") and later neglect, it was not published in the USSR until 1965. It was then translated into English in 1968. In addition to his work on Rabelais, Bakhtin also published a study of Dostoevsky in 1929.

Jean Baudrillard Baudrillard is one of the most prolific and provocative, and certainly the most popular, of the French postmodernists. Famous for exploring and developing the idea of a society of simulacra, Baudrillard began his intellectual life as a Marxist and concern with capitalism continues to mark his writing. His most important works include *Forget Foucault* (1977), *Simulacra and Simulations* (1981), *America* (1986), and *Cool Memories* (1987).

Walter Benjamin (1892–1940) Another member of the Frankfurt School, Benjamin is best known for his essay "Art in the Age of Mechanical Reproduction." Benjamin was always an intellectual outsider: from the time of his youth and his involvement with the most radical and idealistically intellectual wing of the youth movement in Berlin, to his fascination with the French Surrealists and shopping arcades during his exile in Paris. His friend and admirer Hannah Arendt called Benjamin "probably the most peculiar Marxist ever." After he committed suicide while trying to flee the Nazis, his colleague Theodor Adorno took it upon himself to publish a collection of Benjamin's works so that his scholarship would be recognized and appreciated after his death.

Hakim Bey Bey, aka Peter Lamborn Wilson, is the elusive author of numerous essays, musings, and rants on the subject of ontological anarchy. A Sanskrit scholar, he spent much of the 1970s travelling eastward then disappeared further into his own imaginary pirate kingdom, emerging to publish *TAZ* (1991). Bey has been alternately referred to as "the goofy Sufi" and "The Marco Polo of the SubUnderground," and his works can be found on websites with titles such as "A Molotov Cocktail for the Soul."

Bertolt Brecht (1898–1956) Inventor of the "epic theater" or "theater of alienation," Brecht is the author and adapter of such plays as *Bael* (1922), *Threepenny Opera* with Kurt Weil (1927), *Mother Courage* (1939) and *Caucasian Chalk Circle* (1943). He fled Nazi Germany during the war and worked in exile in Los Angeles, where he wrote a series of anti-Nazi plays. Forced to testify before the House Un-American Activities Committee after the war, Brecht left the US and returned to East Berlin. Back in Germany, he founded and directed the famous Berliner Ensemble until his death.

Andrew Boyd Boyd is a professional activist and writer. He has worked as an organizer with United for a Fair Economy, Reclaim the Streets, and

Billionaires for Bush (or Gore). In addition to *The Activist's Handbook* (1997) Boyd's writing has appeared in the *Village Voice* and in a number of odd little books with odd titles like *Life's Little Deconstruction Book: Self-Help for the Post-hip* (1998) and *Daily Afflictions: The Agony of Being Connected to Everything in the Universe* (2002).

John Clarke From his early work on subcultures with the Centre for Contemporary Cultural Studies at the University of Birmingham (CCCS), Clarke has gone on write a number of works on state and welfare policy, including *The Managerial State* (1997) and *Rethinking Social Policy* (2000). He has also published a polemic decrying the depoliticization of cultural studies: *New Times and Old Enemies* (1991). Clarke is Professor of Social Policy at the Open University.

Stuart Cosgrove In addition to his work on "The Zoot-suit and Style Warfare" (1984), Cosgrove has written a number of articles about theater and politics and is co-editor of *Theatres of the Left, 1880–1935* (1985). He has long since left the academy for the world of media, currently working in Scotland as Channel 4's head of programs.

Malcolm Cowley (1898–1989) Launching his literary career with the publication of a collection of poetry, *Blue Juniata* (1929), Cowley went on to become a celebrated editor of *The New Republic* from 1929 to 1944. He also wrote and edited numerous books of literary criticism, essays, and poems, including his memoir of bohemian life in Greenwich Village, *Exile's Return* (1934). He is credited with being among the first to recognize the brilliance of the "lost generation" of writers in the 1920s and of rescuing William Faulkner from obscurity by editing *The Portable Faulkner* in 1945.

Ricardo Dominguez A founding member of the Critical Art Ensemble and the Electronic Disturbance Theater, Dominguez is a co-editor of *Hacktivism* (2001) and co-author of *Digital Resistance* (2001). In addition to being a cyber-activist, Dominguez works on terra firma as a solidarity organizer with the Zapatistas.

Elaine Goodale Eastman (1863–1953) Raised in genteel surroundings, Elaine Goodale left New England in 1886 for the Dakota Territories to become a school teacher on the Great Sioux Reservation. There she witnessed the eradication of Indian life which she wrote about in a collection of articles later brought together in her memoir *Sister to the Sioux*. In 1891 she married the Sioux doctor and writer Charles A. Eastman and, in collaboration with him and on her own, published over fifteen books on Indian life.

Barbara Epstein An activist who was once on the editorial collective of the journal *Socialist Revolution* (now *Socialist Review*), Epstein is currently a Professor of History of Consciousness and teaches in the Jewish Studies program at the University of California at Santa Cruz. Her publications include *Politics of Domesticity: Women, Evangelism and Temperance in Nineteenth Century America* (1981) and *Political Protest and Cultural Revolution* (1991). She is the co-editor of *Cultural Politics and Social Movements* (1995).

John Fiske Fiske is Professor Emeritus of Communication Arts at the University of Wisconsin in Madison and the general editor of the journal *Cultural Studies*. He is also the author of a number of books including *Understanding Popular Culture* (1989), *Reading the Popular* (1989), *Media Matters* (1994), and co-author of *Reading Television* (1978).

Thomas Frank Frank is the founding editor of *The Baffler* and pioneered its signature style of two-fisted cultural criticism. He is the author of *Conquest of Cool* (1997) and *One Market Under God: Extreme Capitalism, Market Populism and the End of Economic Democracy* (2000), and co-editor of a selection of writings from *The Baffler* entitled *Commodify Your Dissent* (1997).

M.K. Gandhi (1869–1948) Born into a political family, Gandhi was trained for law in London which he then practiced in South Africa. It was there that he began his career as a non-violent political activist, leading the Indian community in a mass refusal to carry required ID cards. Upon returning to India at the age of 45, Gandhi joined the long and eventually victorious non-cooperation movement against British rule. India won its independence in 1947, but Gandhi continued protesting the divisions between Hindus and Muslims. For this he was assassinated in 1948 by a Hindu extremist.

Antonio Gramsci (1891–1937) Leader of the first Italian Communist Party, Gramsci was a journalist and later editor of Socialist party papers, writing on subjects from war to strikes to political policy to theater. Soon after becoming general secretary of the PCI and a member of the Italian Parliament he was arrested by the Fascists and thrown into prison, where he wrote the 2,848 pages that were smuggled out of prison and posthumously edited into the *Prison Notebooks* (1971). His health broken by his stay in prison, Gramsci died six days after his sentence was over.

Jason Grote Grote is an activist with the Lower East Side Collective and Reclaim the Streets, both based in New York City. He is also a playwright whose works include *Pipe Bomb Sonata*, a drama about the Thompkins Square Riots, and he writes on culture and politics for a variety of publications.

Stuart Hall One of the founders of British cultural studies, Hall directed the Centre for Contemporary Cultural Studies from 1972 to 1979. He was an editor of the *New Left Review* in the late 1950s, and is the author and/or editor of more than twenty-five books, including *The Popular Arts* (1964), *Resistance through Rituals* (1976), and *Policing the Crisis* (1978), *Politics and Ideology* (1986) and *Visual Culture* (1999). Until 1998, he was a Professor of Sociology at the Open University.

Kathleen Hanna Hanna was lead singer for the punk band Bikini Kill, editor of *Bikini Kill* zine, and one of the founding mothers of Riot Grrrl. She has also organized numerous DIY music and culture festivals.

Dick Hebdige Emerging from the Birmingham School, Hebdige has written extensively on contemporary art, design, music, the media, and critical theory. He is best known for his seminal work on punk rock, *Subculture: The Meaning of Style* (1979), but has also written books such as *Cut 'n' Mix* (1987) and *Hiding in the Light* (1988). He is currently Dean of the School of Critical Studies at the California Institute of the Arts.

Christopher Hill One of the eminent social historians of England, Hill was Master of Balliol College, Oxford University, and a visiting professor at the Open University. He is the author of more than thirty books on religion, literature and history, including *The English Revolution* (1940), *Milton and the English Revolution* (1978), and *The World Turned Upside Down* (1972). Professor Hill published his latest book, *Origins of the English Revolution* (1997), at the age of eighty-five.

E.J. Hobsbawm Best known for his magisterial four-volume treatise on modern European history, *Age of Revolution* (1962), *Age of Capital* (1975), *Age of Empire* (1987), and *Age of Extremes* (1994), Hobsbawm is also the author of more off-beat socio-political works such as *Primitive Rebels*

(1959), *The Jazz Scene* (1959), and, with George Rudé, *Captain Swing* (1969). Hobsbawm was a Professor of Economic and Social History at the University of London and a visiting professor at the New School for Social Research in New York City.

Abbie Hoffman (1936–89) Hoffman was one of the founders and leaders of the Youth International Party, better known as Yippie, in 1968. The author of *Steal this Book* (1971) and *Revolution for the Hell of It* (1968), Hoffman went underground in 1973, set up by the police on a drug rap. While living incognito he continued his activism working as an organizer in local campaigns in rural upstate New York. Hoffman returned to New York City and his own name in 1980. He killed himself in 1989.

Richard Hoggart The founding director of the CCCS, Hoggart was a pioneer of British cultural studies. Hoggart was also a defense witness in the trial of the book *Lady Chatterley's Lover* and later served as Assistant Director General of UNESCO. In addition to his seminal work in cultural studies, *The Uses of Literacy* (1957), Hoggart is the author of thirty volumes on literature, pedagogy, mass-media, and cultural policy, including no fewer than *three* autobiographies.

C.L.R. James (1901–89) Writer, historian, newspaper editor, political activist, and cricket fanatic, James was the author of *The Black Jacobins* (1938) and *Beyond a Boundary* (1963) and sometimes cricket correspondent for the *Manchester Guardian*. In addition to history and cricket, James also wrote on literature, Marxist theory, Hegelian philosophy, and African politics. Born and raised in Trinidad, James was active in democracy and pan-African struggles in the West Indies, Britain, and the United States – from which he was deported in the 1950s for his Marxist politics.

John Jordan A former organizer with Reclaim the Streets in London, Jordan is also a multi-media artist who performs and exhibits throughout Western Europe. Jordan has lectured in departments of fine arts, critical studies, architecture, theater, and biology and integrates his broad interests into the environmental, political, and visual themes of his work. He is currently a visiting lecturer of fine art in the School of Cultural Studies at Sheffield Hallam University.

Robin D.G. Kelley Kelley is a Professor of History and Africana Studies at New York University. In addition to *Race Rebels* (1994), he is the author of *Hammer and Hoe* (1990), *Yo' Mamma's Disfunktional!* (1997) and co-editor of *To Make Our World Anew: A History of African Americans* (2000). Kelley is currently working on a book on pianist/composer Thelonious Monk.

Lawrence Levine A past president of the Organization of American Historians and MacArthur Prize recipient, Levine is the Margaret Byrne Professor of History at the University of California at Berkeley. In addition to the collection of essays bound together in *The Unpredictable Past* (1993) Levine is the author of *Black Culture and Black Consciousness* (1977), *Highbrow/Lowbrow: The Emergence of Cultural Hierarchy in America* (1988) and *The Opening of the American Mind* (1996).

George Lipsitz A Professor of Ethnic Studies at the University of California at San Diego, Lipsitz has authored numerous books on culture, politics, and ethnicity, including *Time Passages: Collective Memory and American Popular Culture* (1990), *Rainbow at Midnight: Labor and Culture in the 1940s* (1994), *The Possessive Investment in Whiteness: How White People Profit from Identity Politics* (1998), as well as *Dangerous Crossings* (1994).

Karl Marx (1818–83) and **Frederick Engels** (1820–95) Radical theorists who collaborated most famously on *The Communist Manifesto* (1848) as well as *The German Ideology* (1846), Marx and Engels also wrote independently: Marx writing, among other works, the three volumes of *Capital* (1867, 1885, 1894) and Engels penning *Condition of the English Working Class* (1845) and *Origin of the Family, Private Property and the State* (1884).

Radicalesbians The Radicalesbians (beginning as Lavender Menace) arose out of the Second Congress to Unite Women, held in New York City in May 1970. Their position paper "The Woman-Identified Woman" first came out in the underground newspapers *Rat* and *Come Out!*, and later appeared in a pamphlet produced by Gay Flames, a group made up of members of New York's Gay Liberation Front.

Janice Radway Francis Fox Professor of Literature at Duke University, Radway is passionate about books and reading, authoring *Reading the Romance: Women, Patriarchy and Popular Literature* (1984) and *A Feeling for Books: The Book-of-the Month-Club, Literary Taste, and Middle-class Desire* (1997). She is the outgoing president of the American Studies Association.

Jean Railla Railla is the founder and editor of *Get Crafty*, a craft site for women at www.getcrafty.com. Railla also shot and directed a documentary video on the Los Angeles alternative music scene and produced a zine entitled *Work*. Railla currently works as a freelance writer and web producer for public radio in New York City.

Adolph Reed Jr. A political scientist at the New School University, Reed is the author of *Class Notes* (2000), *The Jesse Jackson Phenomenon* (1986), and *Without Justice for All* (1999), and the editor of *Race Politics and Culture* (1996). As a journalist his writings have appeared in publications such as *The Nation* and *Village Voice*. Reed also works organizing the Labor Party in the United States.

Simon Reynolds Reynolds is the author of four books on culture and popular music, including *Blissed Out: The Raptures of Rock* (1990), *Sex Revolts: Gender, Rebellion and Rock 'n' Roll* (1995), and *Generation Ecstasy* (1998). Reynolds was a senior editor at *Spin* magazine and has written for *Rolling Stone*, *Artforum*, and *The New York Times*.

Riot Grrrl A loose network of post-punk women, linked by music and zines, Riot Grrrl was "founded" in Olympia, Washington, in the early 1990s and soon spread across the country. Riot Grrrl's heyday was in the mid- to late 1990s but still continues in the form of websites, zines, and Grrrl-centered DIY music shows today.

Jerry Rubin Along with Abbie Hoffman, Rubin was one of the founders of the Yippies and a co-defendant in the Chicago conspiracy trials. Rubin has written four books, including *Do It!: Scenarios of the Revolution* (1970) and *Growing up at Thirty-Seven* (1976). Unlike Hoffman, Rubin turned in his Yippie credentials in the 1980s (in fact, it is said that the term "Yuppie" was originally coined in an article about Jerry), and became a successful capitalist and multi-level marketer in the 1990s.

James C. Scott Sterling Professor of Political Science and Anthropology and Director of Agrarian Studies at Yale University, Scott researches politics in rural peasant societies and non-State resistance. Scott's works include *The Moral Economy of the Peasant* (1976), *Weapons of the Weak* (1985), *Domination and the Arts of Resistance* (1990), and, most recently, *Seeing Like a State: How Certain Schemes to Improve the Human Condition Have Failed* (1998). Scott also serves on the board of Asia Watch.

Raymond Williams (1922–88) Author of *Culture and Society* (1958), *The Long Revolution* (1961), and *Keywords* (1976), Williams was central in creating the field of British Cultural Studies. Like Hoggart, his working-class background and experiences in teaching adult education classes influenced his focus on class struggle. He was a Fellow of Jesus College at Cambridge University.

Virginia Woolf (1882–1941) Woolf is one of the most renowned authors of the twentieth century. A novelist whose works include *Mrs Dalloway* (1925), *To the Lighthouse* (1928), and *Orlando* (1928), she also wrote essays including *A Room of One's Own* (1929). Ending a life-long battle with depression, Woolf killed herself in 1941.

PERMISSIONS

Theodor W. Adorno: "On the Fetish-Character in Music and the Regression of Listening" from *The Essential Frankfurt School Reader*, Andrew Arato and Eike Gebhardt (eds.), copyright 1982 by The Continuum Publishing Company. Reprinted by permission of the publisher.

Mikhail Bakhtin: from *Rabelais and His World* by Mikhail Bakhtin. Copyright 1968 by the Massachusetts Institute of Technology. Used by permission of The MIT Press.

Jean Baudrillard: "The Masses: The Implosion of the Social in the Media" by Jean Baudrillard, *New Literary History*, 1985, 16, 3, pp. 577–89. Copyright The University of Virginia. Reprinted by permission of the Johns Hopkins University Press.

Walter Benjamin: from *Reflections* by Walter Benjamin, Peter Demetz (ed.), Edmund Jephcott (trans.), copyright 1978 by Harcourt Brace Jovanovich, Inc. Used by permission of Harcourt, Inc.

Hakim Bey: from *TAZ: The Temporary Autonomous Zone* by Hakim Bey, published by Autonomedia. Anti-copyright, 1985, 1991.

Sheena Bizarre: "Train Parties" by Sheena Bizarre, 2001, in an unpublished manuscript by Azoteas. Used by permission of Azoteas.

Andrew Boyd: "Truth Is a Virus: Meme Warfare and the Billionaires for Bush (or Gore)" by Andrew Boyd. Used by permission of the author.

Bertolt Brecht: "Emphasis on Sport" from *Brecht on Theatre*, John Willett (ed. and trans.). Translation copyright 1964, renewed 1992 by John Willett.

Jason Grote: "The God that People Who Do Not Believe in God Believe In: Taking a Bust with Reverend Billy" by Jason Grote. Used by permission of the author.

Stuart Hall: from "Notes on Deconstructing 'the Popular'" by Stuart Hall, *People's History and Socialist Theory*, Raphael Samuel (ed.). Copyright: 1981 History Workshop Journal. Used by permission of Oxford University Press.

Kathleen Hanna: from *Punk Planet*, interviewed by Daniel Sinker, 1998. Used by permission of Punk Planet.

Dick Hebdige: "The Meaning of Mod" by Dick Hebdige, originally printed in *Working Papers in Cultural Studies*, no. 7/8. Copyright 1976, The Centre for Contemporary Cultural Studies, University of Birmingham. Used by permission of The Centre for Contemporary Cultural Studies.

Christopher Hill: from *The World Turned Upside Down* by Christopher Hill, copyright 1972 by Christopher Hill. Used by permission of Viking Penguin, a division of Penguin Putnam Inc.

E.J. Hobsbawm: from *Primitive Rebels* by E.J. Hobsbawm, copyright 1959 by E.J Hobsbawm. Reproduced with permission of the author and Greenwood Publishing Group, Inc., Westport, CT.

Richard Hoggart: from *The Uses of Literacy* by Richard Hoggart, published by Chatto & Windus. Used by permission of the Random House Group Limited.

Ice-T: "Squeeze the Trigger" words and music by Ice-T and Afrika Islam. Copyright 1988 Colgems-EMI Music, Inc. and Rhyme Syndicate Music. All rights reserved. International copyright secured. Used by permission.

C.L.R. James: from *Beyond a Boundary* by C.L.R. James, published by Hutchinson. Used by permission of The Random House Group Limited.

John Jordan: from "The Art of Necessity" by John Jordan in *DIY Culture*, George McKay (ed.), published by Verso Books. Copyright 1998 by John Jordan. Used by permission of Verso Books.

Robin D.G. Kelley: reprinted and abridged with the permission of The Free Press, a Division of Simon & Schuster, Inc. from *Race Rebels: Culture, Politics and the Black Working Class* by Robin D.G. Kelley. Copyright 1994 by Robin D.G. Kelley.

Starhawk: from "Spirals: How to Conjure Justice" by Starhawk. Used by permission of the author.

Raymond Williams: from *Keywords*, revised edition, by Raymond Williams, copyright 1976, 1983 by Raymond Williams. Used by permission of Oxford University Press, Inc. and HarperCollins Publishers Ltd.

Reverend Billy: from "Life after Shopping: A Call for Dramatic Disobedience" by William Talen. Used by permission of the author.

Virginia Woolf: from *A Room of One's Own* by Virginia Woolf, copyright 1929 by Harcourt Brace & Company. Used by permission of Harcourt, Inc.

"Huge Mob Tortures Negro . . .": from *100 Years of Lynching*, Ralph Ginzburg (ed.), published by Black Classic Press, copyright 1962. Used by permission of Black Classic Press.

For coherence and ease of reading, the essays in this book have been standardized in either US *or* UK format, depending on their country of origin.

The editor has made every effort to obtain the proper permissions for all the essays reprinted in this anthology. If I have inadvertently overlooked any I will be pleased to make full acknowledgement in subsequent editions of this book of any rights not acknowledged here.